THE INTEREST
GROUP CONNECTION

THE INTEREST GROUP CONNECTION

Electioneering, Lobbying, and
Policymaking in Washington

Second Edition

✧ ✧ ✧

Edited by

PAUL S. HERRNSON
University of Maryland

RONALD G. SHAIKO
Dartmouth College

CLYDE WILCOX
Georgetown University

CQ PRESS

A Division of Congressional Quarterly Inc.
Washington, D.C.

CQ Press
1255 22nd Street, N.W., Suite 400
Washington, D.C. 20037

202-729-1900; toll-free, 1-866-4CQ-PRESS (1-866-427-7737)

www.cqpress.com

∞ The paper used in this publication exceeds the requirements of the American National Standard for Information Sciences–Permanence of Paper for Printed Library Materials, ANSI Z39.48-1992.

Printed and bound in the United States of America

08 07 06 05 04   5 4 3 2 1

Cover design by Brian Barth

Library of Congress Cataloging-in-Publication Data

The interest group connection : electioneering, lobbying, and policymaking in Washington / edited by Paul S. Herrnson, Ronald G. Shaiko, Clyde Wilcox. -- 2nd ed.
    p. cm.
    Includes bibliographical references and index.
    ISBN 1-56802-922-5 (alk. paper).
    1. Pressure groups--United States. 2. Political campaigns--United States. 3. Lobbying--United States. 4. United States--Politics and government--20th century. 5. United States--Politics and government--2001- I. Herrnson, Paul S., 1958- II. Shaiko, Ronald G., 1959- III. Wilcox, Clyde, 1953-. IV. Title

JK1118.I563 2005
324.4'0973--dc22   2004025622

In memory of Edward Artinian

Contents

✧ ✧ ✧

Tables, Figures, and Boxes

✧ ✧ ✧

Tables

Figures

Boxes

Preface

✧ ✧ ✧

Organized interest groups—sometimes called "special interests" or "factions"—have always played important roles in U.S. politics. Factions weighed heavily on the minds of the framers of the Constitution, and, later, they were a major concern of populist and progressive reformers at the turn of the twentieth century. At the dawn of the twenty-first century, individuals and groups claiming to be proponents of honest, clean government continued to label organized interest groups as the villains of American politics. Reformers succeeded in passing the Bipartisan Campaign Reform Act of 2002 (BCRA) to help stem the flow of interest group money to political parties, but, as the 2004 elections soon demonstrated, interest group money has continued to wend its way into federal election campaigns.

Notwithstanding the often well-reasoned, occasionally illogical, and frequently inflammatory debates surrounding the issue of campaign finance reform, it is important to recognize that interest groups play a valuable role in the political arena. They organize constituencies that are affected by what government does—protecting their rights, defending their interests, and giving them a say in the political process. Without organized interests, many workers, business leaders, and issue advocates living in places across the United States and abroad would feel that they had no influence on the political process. These groups help to connect Americans to their government.

Interest groups pervade American political life. They spend money and mobilize voters in elections, lobby Congress and the White House, and attempt to influence the courts. The fortunes of individual interest groups may rise and fall with political trends and events—election outcomes, legislative initiatives, executive orders, and judicial decisions—but interest groups as a whole maintain their presence in each of these arenas. They are, however, subject to the reforms specifically targeted at the labor, business, trade association, and nonprofit group lobbyists who frequent the hallways of Capitol Hill. Those reforms can have a profound impact on the connection between American citizens and their government.

This second edition of *The Interest Group Connection*, like the first, examines interest group activities during a time of partisan polarization and political uncertainty in the nation's capital. The goal of the first edition of this book, published in 1998, was to look closely at interest group activities after two catalytic events: the election of Bill Clinton as president in 1992 and the Republican

Contributors

Robert Biersack is acting press officer at the Federal Election Commission. While at the Commission he has been responsible for electronic filing of campaign finance reports and dissemination of campaign finance data. A graduate of Marquette University and the University of Wisconsin–Milwaukee, he has written extensively on campaign finance, political parties, and interest groups, and is coeditor of *After the Revolution: PACs, Lobbies, and the Republican Congress* (1999) and *Risky Business? PAC Decisionmaking in Congressional Elections* (1994).

Nathan S. Bigelow is a PhD candidate at the University of Maryland–College Park, where he works as a graduate research assistant with the Center for American Politics and Citizenship. His research interests include political parties, interest group politics, political campaigning, and campaign finance at both the state and national level. His dissertation will address political representation in the state legislatures.

Paul R. Brewer is assistant professor of journalism and mass communication at the University of Wisconsin–Milwaukee. His research has appeared in such journals as the *American Journal of Political Science, Journal of Politics, Public Opinion Quarterly,* and *Social Science Quarterly.* One of his current projects is a study of trust in government, trust in people, and trust in other nations that has been funded by the National Science Foundation and the Russell Sage Foundation.

Cynthia L. Cates is associate professor of political science at Towson University. She is the author with Wayne McIntosh of *Law and the Web of Society* (2001) and *Judicial Entrepreneurship* (1997). Their latest book, *The Politics of Litigation,* is due to be published in 2005. Prior to coming to Towson, Cates was a senior policy analyst with the U.S. Advisory Commission on Intergovernmental Relations.

Christopher J. Deering is professor and chair of political science at the George Washington University. He is the coauthor of *Committees in Congress,* 3rd edition (1997), and has written a number of articles and chapters on committees, leadership, and Congress's role in foreign and national security policymaking. He is a former American Political Science Association Congressional Fellow and Brookings Research Fellow.

Linda L. Fowler is the Frank Reagan Chair in Policy Studies at Dartmouth College. She has written books on congressional elections and numerous articles on American politics. As director of the Nelson A. Rockefeller Center from 1995

Although civil liberties groups raised questions about the powers being granted to the executive branch in the new war on terrorism, support for this initiative was widespread in both parties. Democrats who questioned the reach granted to the Justice Department were mollified by a sunset provision that would end several of the more intrusive investigative powers of the executive branch after four years. Only through reauthorization by Congress would these agencies continue to have such powers.

As the homeland security policy network began to take shape with the creation of the Department of Homeland Security and the Select Committees on Homeland Security in the House and Senate, organized interests began to reorganize and respond to the policy vacuum. New positions of vice president for homeland security were created within the corporate structures of the major defense contractors. With the reconfiguration of more than 150,000 federal jobs as well as scores of bureaucratic entities under the new Department of Homeland Security, along with the creation of new federal agencies (for example, the Transportation Security Administration), organized interest groups scrambled to make sense of the new chain of command and lines of jurisdiction in Congress, in the new Department of Homeland Security, and in preexisting government agencies and departments. In a similar fashion, the Supreme Court, prodded by organized interests, began to fulfill its role as the ultimate arbiter of the constitutionality of the USA PATRIOT Act and other related actions taken by the executive branch in the war on terrorism.

Today, all three branches of government are fully engaged in the war on terrorism, as are hundreds of corporations, associations, public interest groups, unions, and state and local governments. Although the policy domain is far from stable, in a relatively short period of time the federal government and organized interest groups of all political and economic stripes have begun to forge connections that will likely endure for decades to come.

In the electoral context of Washington politics, a less cataclysmic political vacuum was created by passage of the Bipartisan Campaign Reform Act of 2002 (BCRA). Prior to its passage, "soft money"—large contributions to political parties unregulated by the Federal Election Commission (FEC)—was becoming an increasingly dominant form of political fund-raising for political parties. In the 1999–2000 election cycle, soft money expenditures reached $500 million, almost double the amount raised in the 1995–1996 election cycle by the two major parties and five times more than that raised by the Democratic and Republican Parties for the 1992 elections.

By contrast, "hard money" contributions to national parties, federal candidates, and political action committees (PACs) were (and still are) subject to disclosure, as well as limitations on the amounts and sources of contributions under FEC guidelines. Direct, hard money contributions to federal candidates are limited by the FEC, while independent expenditures—hard money expenditures by PACs that are independent of federal candidate campaign organizations—must be disclosed to the FEC, but are not limited. As a result, unlimited soft money contributions filled the coffers of each of the major political parties as well as those of a growing number of "527" political committees— that is, those organizations that use a loophole in the Internal Revenue Code, Section 527, to spend money on political communications that technically are not focused on elections, and that therefore report their unlimited expenditures on political communications to the Internal Revenue Service (IRS) rather than the FEC. For the 2000 elections, the Republican Party raised $250 million in soft money, fully 35 percent of the funds it collected; the Democratic Party collected $245 million in soft money, which represented 47 percent of its total funds. More than a thousand organizations, corporations, unions, and wealthy individuals made soft money contributions of $100,000 or more in the 1999–2000 cycle.[1]

At the top of the soft money contributions list were labor unions and major corporations. The top five soft money donors included four unions—American Federation of State, County, and Municipal Employees (AFSCME), Service Employees International Union (SEIU), the Carpenters and Joiners Union, and the Communications Workers of America. Collectively, these unions gave $15 million to the Democratic Party and $30,000 to the Republican Party. AT&T was the remaining donor in the top five; it gave $3.8 million in soft money contributions—$1.4 million to Democrats and $2.4 million to Republicans. The top five corporate soft money donors (AT&T, Freddie Mac, Philip Morris, Microsoft, and Global Crossing) collectively gave $13 million in soft money contributions—$5 million to Democrats and $8 million to Republicans.

Yet another reason for the unique character of the 1999–2000 election cycle was the unprecedented use of issue advocacy advertisements. Many were funded by organized interests, but because they did not expressly advocate the election or defeat of a particular candidate they were not regulated by the FEC. As a result, unlimited funds were used to disseminate these messages to the public. Some of these ads appeared to be grassroots lobbying efforts, for they singled out specific policymakers and urged viewers to contact them to ask that they vote in a particular way on an upcoming bill. But most issue ads were really electoral ads in disguise.

By the 2003–2004 election cycle, the relationships among organized interests, political parties, and the federal election process were altered significantly. The presidential and congressional elections took place under new rules handed down by Congress through the Bipartisan Campaign Reform Act. The act appears to have altered the balance of power between political parties and organized interests in the federal electoral process. Justices John Paul Stevens and Sandra Day O'Connor, writing for the majority of the Court in *McConnell v. FEC* (540 U.S. ___ [2003]), directly addressed this relationship in upholding the power of Congress to treat parties and interest groups differently:

> Congress is fully entitled to consider the real-world differences between political parties and interest groups when crafting a system of campaign

finance regulation. . . . Interest groups do not select slates of candidates for elections. Interest groups do not determine who will serve on legislative committees, elect congressional leadership, or organize legislative caucuses. Political parties have influence and power in the legislature that vastly exceeds that of any interest group. As a result, it is hardly surprising that party affiliation is the primary way by which voters identify candidates, or that parties in turn have special access to and relationships with federal officeholders. Congress' efforts at campaign finance regulation may account for these salient differences.

The opinion of the Court may be a bit simplistic, and perhaps even politically naïve, for organized interests are often intimately linked with candidate selection, committee leadership, and legislative caucuses more than the justices would have us believe. But the impact of the ruling upholding the BCRA is to place disproportionate constraints on political parties and the party campaign committees at the federal level. Neither the Democratic National Committee (DNC) nor the Republican National Committee (RNC), nor any of their federal congressional campaign committees, may raise and spend soft money. But no such limitation is placed on organized interests, apart from spending those funds on issue advocacy advertisements thirty days prior to primary elections and sixty days prior to the general election at the federal level. As a result of this distinction, the roughly $500 million in soft money raised by the major political parties in the 1999–2000 election cycle could not be raised by the parties in 2003–2004.

Interest groups, largely in the form of 527 political committees, have been quick to fill the political vacuum by seeking large soft money donations. During the 2003–2004 campaign season, organizations allied with the Democratic Party took an early lead in raising and spending soft money donations on issue advocacy campaigns targeted at defeating President George W. Bush. By the spring of 2004, nine of the top ten 527 organizations were liberal/Democratic-leaning groups. America Coming Together and the Media Fund led the group; they raised in excess of $19 million and $15 million, respectively. The only conservative/Republican-leaning group was the Club for Growth, which raised $2.6 million.

After the FEC hearings on 527s in April 2004, no action was taken to rein in 527s before the conclusion of the 2003–2004 election cycle. It is likely, therefore, that Congress will have to amend the BCRA in order to close the latest loophole in campaign financing that tilts the electoral process in favor of organized interests and away from political parties.

On another front, the relationships between interest groups and their lobbyists and officials in the executive branch faced the constitutional scrutiny of the U.S. Supreme Court in 2004. In the early days of the Bush administration, Vice President Richard B. Cheney conducted a series of closed-door meetings with representatives of various stakeholders in the U.S. energy sector—corporations and interest groups—aimed at formulating federal energy policy for the administration. Executive branch officials may conduct private meetings as long as they are attended only by government employees. Lawyers for the Bush administration argued before the Supreme Court in *Cheney v. U.S. District Court for the District of Columbia* (2004) that presidential administrations must have the ability to consult with external interests to receive their input in a confidential manner prior to formulating federal policies to be proposed to Congress. In June 2004, the Supreme Court returned the case to the District Court, ensuring that the dispute would be drawn out for at least another year.

Interest groups must be constantly attentive to the changing political and regulatory landscapes in Washington. Some organized interests are more conservative than others in their responses to changing federal laws and regulations and tend to maintain their organizational structures and methods of operation. Cutting-edge interest groups tend to respond to changes in the political and legal rules of the game by adapting their organizational structures and methods of influence to the ever-changing political realities in order to make their connections to the federal electoral and policymaking processes as firm and lasting as possible. In their attempts to achieve these connections, organized interests may select one or more organizational forms to make their voices heard in the halls of government.

Forms of Political Representation in Washington

Interest groups differ greatly in their mix of funding for electioneering and lobbying. Some political organizations—nonconnected political action committees and 527 political committees, for example—spend no money on lobbying. Other organizations expend significant resources on lobbying, yet spend no money on political campaigning. In fact, most nonprofit organizations are barred from any electioneering activities by their 501(c)(3) nonprofit, tax-exempt status from the IRS. Such organizations include universities, philanthropic organizations, and a majority of public interest, social welfare organizations.

Today, in addition to the representation of individual interests by citizens themselves in petitioning their government for a redress of grievances and in voting, two basic forms of political representation are found in American politics: direct organizational representation and surrogate representation through lobbying firms. Direct organizational representation takes three forms: that exercised through (1) the Washington offices of American and international corporations; (2) associations and unions; and (3) special-interest or "public interest" organizations.

In each of the three forms, there may or may not be an electoral representational element, depending on the existing laws prohibiting such activities or the wishes of organizational leaders to engage or not engage in electoral politics. For example, 501(c)(3) groups are barred from electioneering activities, but they can conduct research, education, and outreach that has various degrees of partisan implications. Corporations, associations, unions, and eligible public interest often choose to create a PAC to raise hard money (that is, funds limited and regulated by the FEC) or to create a 527 political committee to raise unlimited funds, unregulated by the FEC, for issue advocacy purposes. Such entities are registered with the IRS and may not engage in "express advocacy" (that is, directly supporting or opposing the election of a federal official); they may, however, raise unlimited funds from individual donors for issue advocacy—soft money. Some organizations maintain several groups to influence federal elections and politics more generally.

For those organized interests that are unable or unwilling to maintain a permanent physical presence in Washington or for those interests already established in Washington that wish to garner the assistance of additional representatives, there are three forms of surrogate representation: (1) multiple-client "boutique" lobbying firms; (2) major Washington law firms; and (3) megafirms that provide one-stop shopping for all public relations and government relations needs. Organizations providing these forms of surrogate representation also may maintain PACs or other organizations to provide additional electoral representation. In fact, political contributions from law firms, lobbying firms, and megafirms, as well as from lawyers and lobbyists, are significant in each election cycle. For example, from 1997 to 2004 more than thirteen hundred registered lobbyists gave more than $1.5 million to Republican George W. Bush, while he served as governor of Texas and president. During the same period, more than four hundred lobbyists gave more than $500,000 to Democratic senator John Kerry, Bush's opponent for the presidency in 2004 (Birnbaum 2004, A8).

Direct Representation: Interest Group Lobbying and Electioneering

The most effective organized interests in American politics are the permanent interests—those entities with the financial wherewithal to maintain full-time offices in Washington, D.C. Whether corporate or membership-based, such organizations are distinctly advantaged by having a permanent presence on the front lines of federal policymaking.

Direct Corporate Representation

Before 1920, only one corporation, U.S. Steel, had a permanent office in Washington. By 1968, more than 175 corporations had established corporate offices in the nation's capital (Epstein 1969, 90–91). Today, more than 600 corporations maintain full-time Washington offices and employ corporate representatives who hold titles such as vice president for governmental relations or vice president for federal affairs. The latest wave of direct corporate representation includes many of the high-tech, new-economy firms. Although many fledgling dot-com corporations never made it to Washington, a significant number of computer firms and software companies are now permanent fixtures in D.C. politics, although the trek to Washington from corporate headquarters was made slowly and sometimes grudgingly. There is no better example of the dramatic increase in corporate representation in Washington than the efforts of Microsoft Corporation. With barely a presence in Washington less than a decade ago, Microsoft has climbed into the upper echelon of corporate lobbying as well as in American electoral politics.

In 1997 Microsoft spent $1.9 million on lobbying in Washington. Its lobbying expenditures then climbed to $3.7 million in 1998 and to $6 million by 2000. By 2003 Microsoft had surpassed the $10 million plateau in lobbying expenditures. Today, Microsoft ranks in the top twenty-five top lobbying spenders. Even more telling of Microsoft's heightened engagement in politics is the dramatic increase in campaign expenditures over the last two election cycles. In the 1997–1998 election cycle, Microsoft contributed $1.35 million to candidates and political parties (35 percent to Democrats and 65 percent to Republicans). About $750,000 of those contributions took the form of soft money (20 percent to Democrats and 80 percent to Republicans). But these campaign contributions did not place Microsoft in the top twenty-five contributors in the cycle. By the 1999–2000 election cycle, Microsoft was fully engaged in electoral politics, ending the cycle as the fifth largest contributor in the country, with $4.6 million in total contributions (47 percent to Democrats and 53 percent to Republicans). Over $2.3 million of these contributions were in the form of soft money (43 percent to Democrats and 57 percent to Republicans).

These increases did not occur in a political vacuum. In both its lobbying and electioneering activities, Microsoft was strategically seeking a better outcome than it faced with the Clinton administration's Justice Department. Lawyers in that department sought heavy penalties against Microsoft for what they believed were monopolistic marketing practices in violation of U.S. antitrust statutes. In the 1998 election cycle, the giving pattern of Microsoft was indicative of its displeasure with the treatment being administered by the Clinton administration in its antitrust case against the software giant. By the 2000 cycle, however, it was pursuing a more pragmatic approach to electioneering and lobbying. Corporate leaders at Microsoft were sure of one thing — President Clinton would be out of office in January 2001. Either a Gore or a Bush Justice Department might have a different view of the Microsoft litigation, so political bets were hedged. Microsoft recognized that a Bush Justice Department was likelier to have a more favorable response to its antitrust case, but it did not want to risk totally alienating the Democratic Party should Gore win the election. One thing has been certain, however; Microsoft's greater engagement in political representation has served the corporation well. Today, Microsoft is represented by a team of sixteen full-time lobbyists, as well as by a host of associations and surrogate representatives (see Box 1-1).

Association/Union Representation

Political representation through associations and unions predates the representation of corporations in Washington. Associations provide cost-effective representation and other political and economic services to their members,

Box 1-1   Political Representation in Washington: Mighty Microsoft

In Washington, D.C., Microsoft Corporation is now a significant force. In addition to its corporate Washington office, Microsoft is represented by the following lobbying firms, law firms, and public relations firms:

Arthur Andersen
BSMG Worldwide
Barbour, Griffith and Rogers
Clark and Weinstock
Creative Response Concepts
Dittus Communications
Covington and Burling
Downey McGrath Group
Edelman PR Worldwide
Fontheim International
Groom Law Group
Hooper, Owen and Winburn
Lackman and Associates
McSlarrow Consulting
PodestaMattoon
Powell Tate
Quinn Gillespie and Associates
Preston, Gates et al.
Swidler, Berlin et al.
Vander Stoep, Remund et al.
Verner, Lipfert et al.
Washington Council Ernst and Young
Washington Group

Microsoft also belongs to the following associations:

Association for Competitive Technology
Business Software Alliance
Chamber of Commerce of the United States
Information Technology Association of America
Information Technology Industry Council
Interactive Digital Software Association
National Association of Manufacturers
U.S. Internet Service Providers

Finally, Microsoft has its own political action committee, Microsoft Corp-PAC.

Sources: Eileen McGoldrick, *Government Affairs Yellow Book* Summer (New York: Leadership Directories, 2001), 169–170; Valerie Sheridan, ed., *Washington Representatives, 2001* (Washington, D.C.: Columbia Books), 522–523; Microsoft Corp. Federal Government Affairs.

whether their memberships are made up of individual citizens, such as workers, or individual economic interests, such as business, professional, educational, industrial, or trade groups. The number of associations is growing steadily in the United States, at a rate of about a thousand new associations each year. In 1955 there were about 5,000 national associations; two decades later, there were 13,000. Today, more than 147,000 associations are active in the United States, including more than 20,000 national associations; the over 125,000 state, regional, and local associations; and the more than 2,000 international associations that have their headquarters in the United States (ASAE 2004).

The breadth and diversity of association representation in Washington is dramatic. In addition to the better-known associations such as the American Medical Association, American Bar Association, Chamber of Commerce of the United States, National Association of Manufacturers, American Association of Retired Persons (now called simply AARP), and the American Automobile Association are the thousands of lobbying organizations that represent an immensely broad array of political interests. Their names begin with American or National, Association, Society, Federation, Institute, or Academy. In the District of Columbia telephone directory, just those with names beginning with "American" and "National" occupy more than fifteen pages of listings, with more than 2,500 entries.

The most recent trend in the expansion of associational representation is the representation of political minorities within businesses, trades, and professions. For example, there are trade and professional associations for women (National Association of Women Accountants), African Americans (National Society of Black Engineers), Hispanics (National Association of Hispanic Journalists), gays and lesbians (National Gay Pilots Association), and for people with disabilities (American Blind Lawyers Association) (Shaiko 1997, 137). Beyond such associations are those that cater to other narrow segments. For example, the lobbying profession itself has associations that provide political representation, including the American League of Lobbyists, National Association of Registered Lobbyists, Women in Government Relations, and the American Society of Association Executives.

Union representation in Washington is similar to association representation, because these economic organizations are also organized by craft, trade, profession, and industry. Moreover, there is a layering of representation, from individual locals to national and international unions to umbrella organizations such as the AFL-CIO. Today, labor unions represent more than 12 percent of the American workforce. The AFL-CIO provides broad political representation in Washington for more than eighty national and international unions, many of which have their own lobbying and electioneering capabilities. Recent leadership changes in the AFL-CIO and in labor unions more generally have resulted in the reinvigoration of the labor movement in Washington and around the country.

Like corporations, many associations and unions, in addition to lobbying on public policy issues, are active in electoral politics. Associations are registered as nonprofit organizations with the Internal Revenue Service, but are given a different status than universities or philanthropic organizations. Most associations are designated as 501(c)(6) "business associations" and, as such, may engage in electoral politics by creating a PAC or 527 organization (or both) and endorsing or working against candidates. Roughly one-third of associations seek 501(c)(3) tax-exempt nonprofit status (Shaiko 1997, 125). This status prohibits these organizations from engaging in electoral politics of any kind. Unions receive 501(c)(5) tax status, which carries with it allowances similar to those extended to "business associations." Unions are therefore eligible to conduct issue advocacy campaigns and provide campaign contributions and in-kind electoral assistance to candidates and parties through PACs and 527s.

Special-Interest, Public Interest, and Governmental Representation

Beyond seeking direct representation through joining an association, union, or some other economic organization, individuals may join membership organizations to advance their noneconomic goals in a collective fashion. Millions of people belong to groups that advocate a clean environment, consumer protection, animal rights, family values, gun control, abortion rights, tax reform, religious values, and scores of other causes. Many ideological perspectives are often represented in policy debates, though not always equally.

Public interest groups are often not as well heeled as their corporate or association counterparts—their collective strength lies in their ability to mobilize and activate the hundreds of thousands, or perhaps millions, of citizens who support their goals. For example, the collective wealth of the entire national environmental movement in the United States is about $2 billion (Wal-Mart has annual revenues of $258 billion). Nonetheless, the United States is not without some rather wealthy public interest groups. For example, the Nature Conservancy, with revenues and property holdings of $972 million, accounts for about half of the wealth of the environmental movement. AARP, the largest nonreligious organization in the United States, with more than 33 million members, posts annual revenues of more than $520 million. More commonly, however, public interest groups have national memberships of under 500,000 and annual budgets of under $5 million.

Over the past several decades, a variety of social movements have grown and matured, but the gay and lesbian rights movement and its affiliated organizations at the national level have grown more rapidly than any other political movement in the United States. Although national gay rights organizations are still a fledgling group from a financial perspective, their sheer growth in numbers, along with their significant budgetary growth, is noteworthy. Today, more than twenty-five national organizations are representing gays and lesbians, including the Human Rights Campaign and the Lambda Defense Fund. The collective wealth of these groups has surpassed $50 million.

Compared with the collective wealth of all national environmental organizations of about $2 billion, the financial state of the gay rights movement is about where the environmental movement was on Earth Day 1970 (Shaiko 1999, 24). Nonetheless, it is likely that the gay rights movement will reach the $1 billion mark far more quickly than the environmental movement. In just the past five years, the collective organizational wealth of the movement has doubled (Fox 2002).

Many of the national gay rights groups are well funded and professionally managed and directed. In 2000 gay rights organizations registered as lobbying entities reported $1.6 million in lobbying expenditures. Campaign contributions in the 2000 elections totaled roughly $2.5 million, with the vast majority of contributions going to Democrats. Led by the Human Rights Campaign PAC, which has raised and spent more than $1 million in each of the last three election cycles and more than $1.5 million in the 2003–2004 election cycle, gay and lesbian rights groups, including partisan organizations such as the Stonewall Democrats and the Log Cabin Republicans, are energized by the national debate over gay marriage and are politically activated at the state and locals levels as well as at the federal level.

Like past American social movements, the gay rights movement is the beneficiary of significant foundation support. Whereas the Ford Foundation and other well-known foundations were instrumental in the creation of third wave environmental organizations in the 1960s and 1970s, contemporary national, state, and local gay rights organizations are benefiting from the philanthropy of the Gill Foundation, founded in 1994 (see Box 1-2).

Three additional factors bode well for the future of the gay rights movement. First, gay rights activists have been very successful in telemarketing for initial contributions from people who have signed petitions at rallies and marches. Few other social movements have had similar success in initial fundraising efforts (Shaiko 1999). Second, the Internet will prove to be a very useful means of organizing, raising funds from, and mobilizing gay and lesbian advocates. Third, the heightened attention nationwide to the issue of gay marriage and civil unions has energized gay and lesbian rights groups and their members. These three factors, along with the foundation support provided by the Gill Foundation's Tim Gill and others, will result in the rapid growth of this social movement over the next decade.

In addition to the gay and lesbian rights organizations active in American politics, more than two thousand national public interest nonprofit organizations are representing a myriad of political and ideological interests. This sector also includes government entities such as state governments, city and county governments, and even small towns, public utilities, and regional authorities. Virtually every state has a government relations office in Washington; in fact, many of the state offices are found in the same building, The Hall of the States, strategically located just off Capitol Hill. The Commonwealth of Pennsylvania recently contracted out its political representation to a lobbying firm headed by a former member of Congress from Philadelphia, Robert Borski.

Public interest nonprofit organizations are granted special status by the federal government. They are exempt from corporate taxation; they benefit from

---

Box 1-2   The Gill Foundation

The second largest gay and lesbian rights contributor in the 1999–2000 election cycle was Quark Inc., a desktop publishing software company in Denver, Colorado. Tim Gill, the founder of Quark, was motivated to act politically when a statewide referendum in Colorado in 1992 "effectively stripped homosexuals of anti-discrimination protections" (Gray 2000). In the 2000 elections, Gill and his corporate PAC contributed over $400,000 to candidates advocating gay rights across the United States (all Democrats). Within days of the 2000 election, Gill sold his remaining stake in Quark and turned his attention to funding some of the more than eight hundred gay rights organizations that the Gill Foundation had identified. As of mid-2004, the Gill Foundation had invested more than $54 million through grants and assistance in organizations promoting gay and lesbian rights as well as in HIV/AIDS service providers. It has a $225 million endowment (Gill Foundation 2004).

Gill, a multimillionaire with sufficient personal wealth to warrant inclusion in *Forbes* magazine's list of the wealthiest Americans, is not the only wealthy benefactor of the gay rights movement. Gill created a network of wealthy gays and lesbians, OutGiving, to facilitate the growth and financial stability of the movement (Gray 2000).

---

subsidized postal rates; and citizen contributions to 501(c)(3) nonprofit organizations are tax-deductible. These government subsidies are provided to all eligible organizations, regardless of political orientation. During the last thirty years, the political influence of public interest organizations of all political and ideological stripes has grown dramatically.

Related to the efforts of some social movements is one final means of direct representation in the political process. Most often, organizations providing campaign contributions are linked to some larger economic interest or political organization. However, citizens may seek direct electoral representation through entities whose sole purpose is to influence electoral outcomes. These so-called nonconnected political action committees provide no political representation in the policymaking process. Rather, these PACs raise funds and organize fund-raisers in order to "bundle" contributions to candidates warranting support. For the most part, these PACs are single-issue oriented, often with a strong ideological bent.

Surrogate Representation: Guns for Hire

Corporations and a wide variety of political organizations that are unwilling or unable to invest in direct representation through a permanent, physical presence in Washington, or that wish to supplement their existing direct representation efforts, often choose to "contract out" their lobbying services. These political interests may choose from a host of multiple-client lobbying firms, law firms, and large public affairs firms. The wealthiest political interests will seek the services of all three types of surrogate political representation.

Multiple-Client Lobbying Firms

A growing number of multiple-client lobbying operations in Washington are serving the needs of a broad array of social, political, economic, and nonprofit interests. Some lobbying firms are organized around substantive policy expertise to serve a homogeneous client base, such as telecommunications companies, health care providers, or oil and energy companies. Other firms serve the needs of a distinct client base, regardless of the policy focus. Examples are state and local governments seeking appropriations funding for a variety of local projects, or colleges and universities that may have interest in funding basic research through the National Institutes of Health, but also interest in competing for research funds or contracts through the Departments of Energy, Defense, and Interior or through the U.S. Agency for International Development. Still other firms provide lobbying services for special interests on a variety of issues; the clients of these firms tend to be attracted by a particular lobbyist in the firm. This attraction is especially prevalent when former members of Congress and high-ranking administration officials join the ranks of lobbyists. Although they are prohibited from lobbying for one year after their departure from Congress, former members remain sought-after commodities in the lobbying industry. Even with similar postemployment restrictions on executive branch employees, former administration officials are still attractive hires for many multiple-client lobbying firms.

Today, more than 150 former members of Congress are registered as lobbyists. A majority are employed by multiple-client lobbying firms or have founded such firms. The remaining former members took senior positions with major Washington law firms (Ota 2002). Because few multiple-client firms are able to cater to the entire spectrum of political interests, these firms have focused their lobbying efforts on specialized sets of policy or client interests; as such, they are known as "boutiques" or specialty shops.

A recent trend in the lobbying industry is the acquisition of boutique firms by large public relations firms. The top ten multiple-client lobbying firms include Cassidy and Associates, the perennial revenue leader among multiple-client lobbying firms; it earned $28.6 million in 2003. The firm, which represents more than a dozen universities, is quite successful in securing federal government grants, contracts, and research funds for its clients, including $10.3 million for the University of Hawaii-Manoa in 2001.

Some multiple-client firms specialize in representing foreign governments. To represent such entities, lobbyists must register with the U.S. Department of Justice as "foreign agents" under the Foreign Agents Registration Act of 1938. Filing as a foreign agent is more onerous than filing as a lobbyist under the Lobbying Disclosure Act of 1995 (discussed later in this chapter). Despite the lengthy quarterly filings, some firms seek out such clients and regularly generate significant substantial revenues from representing foreign governments. During the first six months of 2003, 152 foreign governments spent more than $150 million for political representation by lobbying firms; 30 governments spent more than $1 million each for political representation in Washington during the six-month period (Gettlin and Veida 2004). Table 1-1 lists the top ten countries in spending for political representation during the first half of 2003. Canada, Great Britain, Japan, and Mexico are major trading partners with the United States. The Republic of Korea, Liberia, and some other countries depend on the United States for foreign aid and defense.

The Lawyer-Lobbyists

Rather than seek surrogate representation from lobbying firms, some organized interests find greater comfort in the hands of Washington law firms. Top law firms such as Patton Boggs; Akin, Gump, Strauss, Hauer and Feld; and Piper Rudnick also attract the top echelon of corporate America for lobbying as well as legal counsel. Major corporations and associations look to these law firms not only for their representation before Congress and relevant executive agencies, but also for legal advice and expertise in managing their corporate business affairs. In addition to these powerful downtown law firms representing corporate economic interests, public interest law firms provide legal representation for traditionally underrepresented interests in the judicial arena. In 2003 the top ten lobbying law firms in Washington, including those just mentioned, collected revenues ranging from $19 million to $59.4 million (Goldman 2004).

Table 1-1   Lobbying Expenditures of Top Ten Foreign Governments, January 1–June 30, 2003

Country	Expenditures (millions of U.S. dollars)
1. Japan	$21.42
2. Republic of Korea	11.87
3. Liberia	10.58
4. Bermuda	8.90
5. Hong Kong (China)	8.62
6. Great Britain	7.06
7. Ethiopia	6.30
8. Canada	5.83
9. Mexico	5.10
10. Australia	5.03

Source: Robert Gettlin and Bora Veida, "FARA Tab: $157 Million in Early '03," *National Journal* (February 28, 2004), 648.

There is also a surrogate electoral connection among lobbyists and lawyer-lobbyists. Although client fees may not be directly funneled into electoral campaigns, lobbyists are expected to contribute significant amounts of money to political parties and federal candidates. Often viewed as "the price of doing business," it is difficult for lobbyists to reject a request for campaign support from a member of Congress with whom the lobbyist must work. It is therefore not uncommon for lobbyists or lawyer-lobbyists to give $10,000 or more in hard and soft money to candidates and parties in an election cycle. Before passage of the BCRA, the largest donors from the lobbyist ranks gave more than $100,000 per cycle. Collectively, lobbyists and their firms contributed $16.33 million in the 1999–2000 election cycle; of that, $13 million was contributed by individual lobbyists. Cassidy and Associates and its lobbyists were the top donors, with more than $750,000 in contributions.

Megafirms: Public Relations and Government Relations Services

A growing trend in Washington surrogate representation among multiple-client firms is the expansion beyond traditional government relations (GR) services to include public relations (PR) services. In a similar fashion, large international public relations firms are acquiring smaller boutique lobbying firms to add to their arsenal of client services. Public relations work involves a broad range of services, including advertising, media relations, marketing, and convention management. These services often have little to do with government relations. Nonetheless, a growing number of Washington public relations firms are attracting new clients by offering one-stop service for all the public relations and government relations needs of corporations, associations, and other organized interest groups.

The traditional PR giants, Hill and Knowlton and Burson-Marstellar, remain among the top firms in Washington; they earned $32.3 million and $46.4 million, respectively, in 2000. However, a new agency, Weber Shandwick Worldwide, is now at the top of the megafirm list, reporting $68.3 million in annual revenues in 2000. It reached its new position by purchasing some of the most powerful lobbying shops in Washington, including Cassidy and Associates, the top multiple-client lobbying firm; Powell Tate, a public affairs firm; and six related affiliates (Ackley 2001, 1–2).

Through one or more of these direct and surrogate forms, organized interests receive political representation in the federal policymaking and electoral processes. Microsoft Corporation, discussed earlier in the chapter, well represents the multilayered approach to lobbying in Washington (see Box 1-1). In addition to its own permanent lobbying team, the software giant contracts with more than twenty multiple-client lobbying firms, law firms, and megafirms in Washington and belongs to various associations that serve its economic interests. It also operates a political action committee that contributed the fifth largest amount of money to candidates and parties during

the 1999–2000 election cycle. Beyond these forms of representation, corporations, associations, public interest groups, and citizens often expand their
political representation by joining forces with organizations with similar interests in the policy debate. Furthermore, such organizations may seek to mobilize their memberships, employees, customers, and attentive citizens at the
grassroots level. Coalition building and grassroots lobbying are vital components of the interest group arsenal in the twenty-first century.

The Changing Rules of the Game: Campaign Finance Reform and Lobbying Disclosure

Interest groups, corporations, associations, and the vast array of organized
interests in Washington, along with their attendant lobbyists, PAC directors, and
supporters, operate under a variety of federal statutes and regulations. These rules
of the game encompass virtually all activities associated with influencing the federal policymaking process, including electioneering and campaign financing, legislative branch lobbying, executive branch lobbying, and the interactions between
lobbyists and government officials.

Federal Campaign Finance Provisions

The events of the 1999–2000 election cycle, with its attendant soft money
spending spree and increased issue advocacy campaigning, coupled with the collapse of the Enron Corporation in December 2001 and a variety of other corporate scandals, served as catalysts for campaign finance reformers, both inside
Congress and among the pro-reform public interest sector, to make significant
changes in existing campaign finance laws. For years, campaign finance reform
measures were proposed, yet they consistently lacked the majority support needed to move them through the legislative process. The 2000 elections were conducted under rules passed by Congress and signed into law in 1971—the Federal Election Campaign Act (FECA). This act, amended by Congress in 1974 and
refined by a series of U.S. Supreme Court rulings, has served as the framework
for the conduct of federal elections for more than twenty-five years. FECA
established limits on hard money campaign contributions by individuals, corporations, and other organizations; it also codified the activities and limitations of
political action committees.

Over the past twenty-five years, creative political entrepreneurs have weakened FECA by searching out loopholes and winning cases in federal courts about
the constitutionality of the regulations. After the 2000 elections, the pressure for
a comprehensive overhaul of federal campaign finance regulations began to build.
Two legislative vehicles emerged to provide form and substance to the reform
debate—the bill introduced by Christopher Shays, R-CT, and Martin Meehan,
D-MA, in the U.S. House of Representatives and the bill introduced by John
McCain, R-AZ, and Russell Feingold, D-WI, in the U.S. Senate. After some

highly charged debates in both chambers, the bills were finally passed and signed into law in 2002 as the Bipartisan Campaign Reform Act. The new law, by clearly changing some of the rules of the game for campaign financing, will have significant impacts on political parties, federal candidates, organized interests, and individual citizens. The BCRA eliminates soft money contributions from corporate or union treasuries to federal political parties. Prior to the BCRA, about half of the funds raised by the Democratic Party took the form of soft money, and a little more than a third of the funds raised by the GOP fell in that category. The law doubles the individual contribution limits to federal candidates, from $1,000 per candidate per election to $2,000. The maximum aggregate amount that can be given by an individual to parties and candidates rises from $25,000 per year to $95,000 per two-year cycle.

In addition to banning soft money, the BCRA bans the use of issue ads within thirty days of a primary election and sixty days of a general election. This provision is particularly constraining on the efforts of organized interests to have a more direct effect on electoral outcomes under the guise of issue advocacy that does not expressly call for the election or defeat of a candidate for federal office. Some of the most powerful interests in American politics have not operated PACs or provided campaign finance support to any candidates, including the AARP, the Christian Coalition, and the National Association of Manufacturers. Yet in recent election cycles such organizations have engaged in significant issue advocacy campaigns.

In 1996, for example, the Christian Coalition, National Association of Manufacturers, and U.S. Chamber of Commerce joined forces with several other interest groups aligned with the Republican Party (they called themselves the Coalition) to wage a multimillion-dollar issue advocacy campaign to counter a similar $35 million campaign waged by the AFL-CIO in support of the Democratic Party. In the 2000 elections, Planned Parenthood spent an estimated $12 million through its PAC, 501(c)(4) organization, and 527 political committee, including $7 million in advertising in ten states (Malbin et al. 2002, 24). The funding of issue advocacy campaigns through 527 political committees was pioneered by the Sierra Club, but was quickly adopted by organized interests across the political spectrum.

These two major provisions of the BCRA will surely have a significant impact on how elections are conducted in the future. Since the ruling by the U.S. Supreme Court in *McConnell v. FEC* that upholds the two provisions, political parties, interest groups, PACs, and 527 organizations find themselves playing under a set of new complex rules that are likely to require further tinkering by Congress down the road.

Federal Lobbying Disclosure Provisions

Organized interests must abide by disclosure rules established by Congress. Until the mid-1990s, the lobbying industry was regulated by a comparatively toothless law passed in 1946. Under those rules, virtually no one needed to register as a lobbyist, because the definition of lobbying was so restrictive. After a series of failed attempts to reform the rules on disclosure, Congress passed the Lobbying Disclosure Act of 1995 (LDA). After the law went into effect in 1996, Congress, through the Lobbying Disclosure Technical Amendments Act of 1998 (TAA), passed several technical amendments to it to clarify ambiguities that existed in the original statute.

Under these laws, organized interests and their representatives must disclose to Congress their lobbying activities and the expenditures on such activities on a biannual basis. The LDA and TAA statutes provide broad definitions of lobbying. A lobbyist is defined as any person employed or retained by a client or organization for financial or other compensation and whose lobbying activities constitute more than 20 percent of his or her activities over a six-month period. One is exempted from registering as a lobbyist and filing biannual lobbying reports of activities if total income from lobbying for a particular client is less than $5,500 over a six-month period. Similarly, an organization that employs its own lobbyists and spends less than $22,500 on lobbying activities need not register. Contacts with members of Congress and their staffs and with high-level executive branch officials are included as lobbying activities (Offices of the Clerk of the House and Secretary of the Senate 2001).[2]

A significant change made by these new laws, beyond the broader definition of lobbying, is the identical treatment of foreign and domestic economic interests. A French or German company and its representatives register and file lobbying reports in a fashion identical to that of American corporations. Before passage of the LDA, lobbying representatives of a foreign corporation had to register as foreign agents with the Department of Justice under the Foreign Agents Registration Act of 1938 (FARA). Today, under the new laws, only representatives of foreign governments and foreign political parties must register as foreign agents.

By the arrival of the first six-month deadline for registration and reporting in 1996, more than 10,000 lobbyists had registered, with reported expenditures of more than $400 million (Drinkard 1996). Total expenditures reported for the first year were roughly $1 billion. Five years later, according to the Office of the Secretary of the Senate, 18,894 lobbyists from 5,160 firms and organizations reported representing 15,941 clients for the first six months of 2001. During that reporting period, lobbying expenditures totaled $790 million, a 5 percent decrease from the previous reporting period. For the twelve-month period July 2000–July 2001, $1.62 billion in lobbying expenditures were reported (Political Money Line 2002). By 2003, $1.8 billion in lobbying expenditures were filed under LDA, and by the end of 2004 annual lobbying expenditures reached the $2 billion mark for the first time. The most recent lobbying reports for 2004 include 24,872 lobbyists from 6,005 registering entities (corporations, unions, multiple-client firms, law firms) representing 15,317 clients (Office of the Secretary of the Senate 2004).

The LDA and TAA statutes are significant improvements over their predecessors. Today, citizens, journalists, and academics know far more than ever before about the activities of organized interests in Washington. Nonetheless, glaring weaknesses in the current laws remain. First, grassroots lobbying, which has emerged as a central component of political engagement, is not mentioned. Issue advocacy campaigns constitute grassroots lobbying, yet Congress had decided not to seek disclosure of the tens of millions of dollars expended on such campaigns each year. Some of the wealthiest grassroots lobbying firms in Washington go undetected by the LDA.

In the electoral context, Congress has viewed such issue advocacy campaigning to be so pernicious that it warrants being banned within thirty days of a primary election and sixty days of a general election. Yet Congress will not pass legislation to disclose activity such as grassroots lobbying under the Lobbying Disclosure Act—one of the many unexplained paradoxes in Congress today.

In a similar vein, the statutory language crafted to identify coalitions in Washington is too vague to capture the variety of ways in which coalitions operate. Many of the activities undertaken by lobbyists are directed at grassroots mobilization and broad issue advocacy media campaigns. Neither of these activities constitutes lobbying under LDA. Therefore, multimillion-dollar coalitions can avoid registering as lobbying entities so long as each of the coalition members provides less than $10,000 biannually for lobbying purposes, as defined by LDA.

One additional change in the relationships between policymakers and organized interests occurred in the mid-1990s. The common practice in which interest groups provided members of Congress and their staffs with gifts, free meals, and free travel was severely curtailed in both houses of Congress. Groups may give members and their staffs only meals and gifts of nominal value. The irony of the gift and meal restrictions, supported in large part by nonprofit organizations seeking to take money out of politics, is that, instead of reducing the importance of money in the day-to-day operations of Congress, they have made contacts with members and staff more difficult for organizations prohibited from electioneering. Monied interests are able to wine and dine members and staff after business hours as long as it is in the context of a campaign fund-raiser.

Creating the Connection: Organized Interests in Elections, Congress, the Executive Branch, and the Courts

Divided into five parts, the chapters that follow describe in detail the connections between interest groups and the electoral process and between those groups and the policymaking processes in Congress, the executive branch, and the federal courts. The lead chapters of each part provide a broad overview of the institutional context within which organized interests seek to influence electoral and policy outcomes.

Part I, on the electoral connection, reveals that members of Congress and, to a lesser degree, candidates for president rely on interest groups and their associated PACs not only for financial support, but also for strategic assistance in orchestrating

Interest group involvement in the executive branch (Part III) is rather different from lobbying Congress. In Chapter 13, Kathryn Tenpas provides an overview of lobbying the executive branch and executive branch lobbying. First, the relations between executive agencies and departments and organized interests are more codified. Dealing with the White House may be closer to the legislative model, with access at a much higher premium, because there is a reelection element present, at least during the first term of a president. Second, the process of attempting to influence executive branch policymaking is more structured than in Congress. For the most part, lobbyists are responding to actions taken or possibly to be taken as a result of a legislative mandate passed by Congress and signed by the president. Arguments made to convince members of Congress to pass enabling legislation may fall on deaf ears in the implementing executive agency or department. Third, knowledge of the agency rulemaking processes is crucial to any lobbyist seeking to sustain the actions of Congress through sound implementation of policy by the executive branch. If, from the lobbyist's perspective, Congress erred in its passage of legislation, the rulemaking process may be the best place to derail the implementation of the perceived inadequate or unjust policy. In either instance, it is vital that interest groups and their representatives understand the rulemaking process and the policymaking calculus undertaken by the bureaucrats responsible for implementing policies.

In Chapter 14, Suzanne J. Piotrowski and David H. Rosenbloom present a comprehensive assessment of the legal and institutional norms and structured procedures surrounding lobbying the executive agencies and departments. Scott R. Furlong then provides in Chapter 15 an empirical analysis of the patterns of interest group mobilization and influence in the federal rulemaking processes. In Chapter 16, Paul J. Quirk and Bruce F. Nesmith conclude the analysis of the executive connection with an assessment of the policy interplay between Congress, the White House, and organized interests in the policy domains of public lands, tax expenditures, farm subsidies, and pollution control.

Part IV explores the judicial connections between interest groups and the federal judiciary. Far from being what Alexander Hamilton labeled "the least dangerous branch," the federal judiciary today is a key player in public policymaking. Each term, the Supreme Court of the United States, in reviewing legislative acts as well as executive branch implementation efforts, serves as the final arbiter in the policymaking process. And, in the absence of congressional will to make national policy, the federal courts address state-level issues on constitutional grounds, resulting in de facto federal policies. Ultimately, the Supreme Court sits in judgment of the abilities of Congress and the executive branch to craft legislation that is clear and concise and able to be faithfully executed. To the extent that organized interests of all political and ideological stripes have a collective interest in not arriving at such clarity of legislation and such faithful execution of laws, then the federal courts will remain busy places for organized interests to make their best case.

In Chapter 17, Karen O'Connor leads the exploration into the relationships between organized interests and the federal judiciary. She offers an overview of the policy actors in the judicial arena and the roles of attentive interest groups in setting the stage for policy influence by lobbying the judicial nomination process, as well as the strategies and tactics employed by the litigation arms of organized interests in their attempts to influence the outcomes of federal court cases. In Chapter 18, Wayne V. McIntosh and Cynthia L. Cates look at two of the more explosive issues in the federal courts fought by organized interests and their corporate combatants in recent years—guns and smoking. Hans J. Hacker concludes the judicial exploration with an assessment in Chapter 19 of conservative Christian litigation.

In Part V, devoted solely to the conclusions, volume editors Herrnson, Shaiko, and Wilcox, in Chapter 20, look at the bigger picture as interest group politics moves into the twenty-first century.

While delving into the chapters that follow, readers are asked to keep in mind two truisms about lobbying in Washington. First, there are "no permanent friends, no permanent enemies, only permanent interests" in D.C. lobbying. Although some groups may be closely aligned with one party or the other, on a fundamental level the interests of the organization are paramount. It is rare, indeed, when the interests of either political party will override the interests of a particular organization, no matter how close the political ties. Second, for most organized interests in Washington, having nothing happen is a winning proposition. Most organized interests are in Washington to protect the status quo. Granted, every interest group, corporation, union, and association has a wish list or agenda at the beginning of every new Congress or new administration. Nonetheless, most organizations in Washington are risk averse. Any prospect of loss far outweighs the prospect of potential gain. The legislative process itself reflects this mindset. A bill must leap many hurdles before it clears one house of Congress. The legislative process is chock full of opportunities for organized interests to mobilize a relatively small group of members or staff to kill a piece of legislation. The deck is stacked severely against those interests who wish to change public policy in Washington.

Notes

1. Unless otherwise noted, all campaign contribution and lobbying expenditure data presented in this chapter are derived from the databases of the Center for Responsive Politics (http://www.opensecrets.org).
2. The original LDA set thresholds at $5,000 per client and overall revenues at $20,000 over each six-month period. In 2001 the thresholds were adjusted to reflect economic changes over the first five years of the act.

References

Ackley, Kate. 2001. "Branching Out Gets Results on K Street." *Influence: The Business of Lobbying*, May 16, 1–2.

often secondary to that of political parties, which traditionally have played a more central role in candidate recruitment.

As for organizational contributions, labor unions, ethnic clubs, and business concerns provided campaign volunteers, sponsored rallies, endorsed candidates, and helped the candidates disseminate their messages. One of the groups' most important contributions to the campaign was to deliver the votes of their members on election day. Groups that had a large concentrated base strongly identified with and committed to the group's political causes were highly influential in elections. Some groups, particularly labor unions, had enough members and political clout to provide a candidate with the support needed to secure a party nomination and win the general election.

Corporations, trade associations, unions, and other groups historically have helped to finance election campaigns. For much of U.S. political history, many groups gave contributions directly from their own treasuries or organized fund-raising committees and events (Alexander 1992, chap. 2).

Interest groups continue to participate in these aspects of federal elections, but they have adapted their activities to meet the opportunities and constraints that exist in the current legal, technological, and political environments. The modern political action committee (PAC), for example, emerged during the 1970s as a specialized form of organization that contributes money and other kinds of campaign support directly to federal candidates. A PAC can be most easily understood as the election arm of an interest group. In most cases, a business, union, trade association, or some other "parent" group is responsible for establishing a PAC. Most "ideological" or "nonconnected" PACs, however, are self-created.

The 1974 amendments to the Federal Election Campaign Act (FECA) and the Federal Election Commission's (FEC) SunPAC decision are primarily responsible for the rise of PACs as a major force in federal elections. FECA, whose provisions governing PACs were left intact after passage of the Bipartisan Campaign Reform Act of 2002 (BCRA), prohibits corporations, unions, trade associations, and most other groups from making campaign contributions to federal candidates, but it allows these organizations to set up PACs to collect donations from individuals and distribute them as campaign contributions to federal candidates. These funds, which are raised and spent within the confines of FECA, are often referred to as federal or "hard" money. PACs are allowed to accept contributions of up to $5,000 per year from an individual or another PAC in hard money. To qualify as a PAC, an organization must raise money from at least fifty donors and spend it on five or more federal candidates.

The law allows PACs to contribute a maximum of $5,000 per congressional candidate during each phase of an election cycle (primary, general election, and runoff).[1] A PAC can also contribute up to $5,000 to a candidate for the presidential nomination and give another $5,000 to any candidate in the general election who opts not to receive federal funds. Nevertheless, the rules governing campaign finance have been cast in two ways that have discouraged the participation of PACs in presidential elections. First, the public funding provisions for presidential nomination contests provide matching funds for individual but not PAC contributions, thereby encouraging most candidates to pursue individual rather than PAC contributions. And, second, the public funding provisions for the general election ban presidential candidates who accept federal funds from taking contributions from any sources, including PACs. The fact that every major-party general election candidate for the presidency accepted public funding until the 2000 elections, when it was rejected by Republican nomination candidate George W. Bush, encouraged most PACs to direct their efforts toward congressional rather than presidential elections.[2] PACs continued to focus on congressional campaigns in ensuing elections, despite the rejection of matching funds by Bush and the top two Democratic nomination candidates in the 2004 election, Massachusetts senator John Kerry and former Vermont governor Howard Dean. Indeed, none of these candidates raised more than two percent of his funds from PACs during the 2004 nomination contest.

PACs, as well as corporations, unions, and other groups also participate in some other important aspects of federal elections. One is the financing of party committees and their campaign activities. PACs are allowed to contribute up to $15,000 a year to the federal accounts of national party committees. The parties can redistribute these funds as campaign contributions and expenditures that are made in direct coordination with federal campaigns or, as the result of a 1996 Supreme Court ruling, as independent expenditures made without the knowledge or consent of individual candidates.[3]

Before passage of the BCRA in 2002, PACs, individuals, and other organized groups could make unlimited contributions to the national, state, and local parties' "soft money" or nonfederal accounts. These funds were channeled outside the confines of FECA regulations. The BCRA bans soft money contributions to national party organizations and greatly limits the amounts of soft money that can be contributed to other party committees. Over the course of the 2000 elections, interest groups, including organizations and individuals associated with various political causes, contributed roughly $495.1 million in soft money to the Democratic and Republican National Committees. The Democratic National Committee (DNC) raised more than $136.5 million, and the party's congressional and senatorial campaign committees raised an additional $120.4 million. Their GOP counterparts raised $166.2 million and $92.0 million, respectively.

Corporations, such as AT&T, and labor unions, such as the Association of Federal, State, County, and Municipal Employees (AFSCME), were among the top soft money contributors in the 2000 elections. AT&T and its affiliated companies and employees donated more than $2.3 million in soft money to Republican Party committees. And for safe measure, the group contributed $1.4 million to Democratic Party organizations. Many other top corporate donors also favored the GOP, but contributed to both parties. AFSCME and the other top labor donors, by contrast, had no qualms about pursuing a fully larger role in shaping the pool of potential candidates and waging campaigns for the nomination.

Some contemporary interest groups work to encourage politicians who are sympathetic to their causes to run for Congress. Among them are EMILY's List, which recruits pro-choice Democratic women (Burrell 1994; Nelson 1994; Day and Hadley 2004); the Clean Water Action Vote Environment PAC (CWAVE PAC), which recruits environmentalist candidates of both parties (Hicks 1994, 177–178); and the Club for Growth, which supports pro-growth Republicans who favor free-market principles. These groups promise campaign contributions and other forms of support to those who ultimately decide to run for Congress. A few labor and professional association PACs, such as the Committee on Political Education (COPE) of the American Federation of Labor–Congress of Industrial Organizations (AFL-CIO) and the American Medical Association's AMPAC, take polls to encourage politicians who support their group's positions to run for office. These PACs combine favorable polling numbers with brief sketches of possible campaign strategies in order to entice their preferred candidates into the race (Fowler and McClure 1989, 205–207). Prior to the 1996 election, Save American Free Enterprise Trust, the PAC of the National Federation of Independent Businesses, went so far as to host a campaign training school for prospective candidates who supported the group's pro-business agenda. PAC activities can be important in helping an individual decide to run for Congress, but interest groups are less influential in candidate recruitment than are parties. Moreover, both groups and parties pale in influence when compared with a potential candidate's family and friends (Herrnson 1988, 85–88; 2004, 47–48).

Campaign Activities

PACs play an important role in the financing of congressional elections. Over 4,600 PACs were registered with the FEC during the 2002 election cycle, and just over 3,000 of these PACs contributed to the nearly $266.2 million in PAC dollars that were raised by primary and general election candidates for the House and the Senate. The biggest spenders were corporate PACs, which contributed roughly $91.6 million. These were followed by trade association PACs, which contributed $71.5 million; labor PACs, $52.2 million; and nonconnected PACs, $44.6 million. PACs sponsored by corporations without stock and cooperatives contributed another $4.0 million and $2.5 million, respectively. The scales of PAC giving are clearly tipped in favor of business over labor interests.

PAC contributions are fairly concentrated among a relatively small number of groups. Six hundred and thirty-three PACs, 14 percent of all registered committees, distributed roughly $232.4 million in contributions, or 82 percent of the total distributed, in the 2002 election cycle. Just 258 PACs (slightly less than 6 percent of all PACs) accounted for $175.4 million in contributions (62 percent of the total). Few elements of American society are represented in the top 6 percent of PACs, and most are not represented in the top 14 percent. The figures for 2004 indicate a similar concentration of PAC activity. Many groups, such as the poor and homeless, have no representation in the PAC community. Although PAC goals and strategies vary, and PAC contributions may offset each other under some circumstances, figures on PAC formation and PAC spending serve to dispel pluralist notions that all societal interests are equally represented in the PAC community and have a comparable impact on the financing of congressional elections.

The distribution of PAC contributions to congressional candidates further demonstrates that other systematic biases are found in interest group election activities. PACs contributed $60.3 million in major party–contested House elections in 2002.[5] The lion's share of this money—roughly 76 percent—went to incumbents. Contestants for open seats received 18 percent, and challengers received a mere 4 percent. The patterns for Senate elections were similar. Of the nearly $52 million that PACs spent in the contested Senate elections, 58 percent went to incumbents, 18 percent went to challengers, and 24 percent went to open-seat candidates. The pro-incumbent bias in PAC activity in 2002 is consistent with previous elections, and preliminary data suggest this pattern will persist beyond 2004.

The incumbent orientation of most interest group activity largely stems from the contributions of business-oriented committees, including most corporate and trade association PACs. Most of these committees focus on narrow issues that could affect their profits or those of their members. Their contributions are directed toward ensuring that their lobbyists have access to important policymakers (Sabato 1984, 78; Langbein 1986; Grenzke 1989; Wright 1990, 1996, chap. 5; Sorauf 1992, 64–65). Backing likely winners is one of their first decision rules. As a result, most of their money goes to incumbents, who enjoy reelection rates of well over 90 percent in the House and almost 90 percent in the Senate. Corporate PACs made 87 percent of their House contributions and 64 percent of their Senate contributions to incumbents during the 2002 elections. Trade association PACs distributed their funds in a similar pattern. A second decision rule is to back individuals who could influence legislation of importance to the PAC and its parent organizations. Access-oriented PACs give a great deal of their money to party leaders and the chairs, ranking members, and members of committees and subcommittees that legislate in areas of concern to their sponsors. These patterns have been in evidence for over two decades and are likely to continue into the future.

A second set of interest groups is more concerned with influencing the composition of Congress than with seeking economic gain or maintaining access to the legislature's current membership. Nonconnected PACs, often called ideological committees, contribute to candidates who share their views on one or more highly charged issues. EMILY's List, CWAVE PAC, and the Club for Growth fall into this category. Ideological PACs contribute a greater portion of their funds to congressional challengers and open-seat contestants than do most other

House elections and just under $7 million in Senate contests. Similar amounts were spent in the 2002 midterm elections. Most of these expenditures were associated with contests in which the outcomes were unpredictable.

Parallel campaigns are similar to independent campaigns in that they are designed to influence competitive contests, require substantial organization and planning, and depend mostly on communications that flow directly from an interest group to voters. They differ in a variety of ways, however. First, most of the parallel campaigns run by interest groups are financed with money raised outside the limits imposed by federal law. Second, although they may state the name or present the likeness of a specific candidate, such campaigns do *not expressly* advocate a candidate's election or defeat. Instead, they typically present a candidate's record, experience, or issue positions in an unflattering light, either through direct criticism or an unflattering comparison. Third, until passage of the BCRA, these campaigns were not subject to federal disclosure laws, making it impossible to determine exactly how much interest groups spent on them.

Coordinated campaigns embrace traditional grassroots campaigning, enhanced by innovations in voter targeting, database management, communications, and mobilization. Working with candidates and party committees, interest groups register supportive voters and communicate with them by handing out leaflets and voter guides, canvassing door to door, making telephone calls, or arranging various public forums and private meetings. During the 2002 elections, a few groups began to experiment with using the Internet as an organizing and fundraising tool for their coordinated campaigns.

Although interest group expenditures on parallel and coordinated campaigns were not fully disclosed before enactment of the BCRA, the evidence suggests that recent elections benefited from significant spending. Soft money expenditures on issue advocacy ads, for example, dwarfed independent expenditures during the 2000 elections. Interest groups spent in excess of $115 million in connection with issue ads during the 2000 congressional elections.[7] Most of these ads were financed by a small number of groups. The AFL-CIO was responsible for 28 percent of the ads aired in House contests. Citizens for Better Medicare (representing the pharmaceutical industry), the U.S. Chamber of Commerce, and the Business Roundtable accounted for 27 percent, 14 percent, and 9 percent, respectively. Another twenty-four groups financed the remaining 22 percent. A somewhat larger number of groups financed issue ads in Senate contests. However, a mere five groups aired 59 percent of all of these ads, with another twenty-four groups accounting for the remainder. An overwhelming number of these ads were aired in elections decided by 10 percent of the votes or less (Herrnson 2002).

Interest group parallel and coordinated campaigns also had a substantial impact on the 2002 congressional elections, particularly in a select group of competitive races. During those campaigns, interest groups spent about $20 million, accounting for roughly 6 percent of the total spent by candidates, political parties, and groups on television advertising. The United Seniors Association, funded mainly by the largest U.S. pharmaceutical companies, spent more than any other interest group: about $7.5 million on almost 14,000 ads aired in connection with twenty House and three Senate races. The AFL-CIO spent the second largest amount: an estimated $5.6 million on more than 5,600 advertisements aired in four House and seven Senate contests. Most of this spending occurred in competitive elections. Republican House and Democratic Senate candidates were the greatest beneficiaries of interest group spending on TV advertising in 2002 (Goldstein and Rivlin 2003). The efforts of groups such as the Media Fund and America Coming Together (discussed later in this chapter) suggest that most interest group electronic media issue advocacy ads aired in 2004 were intended to help the Democrats. Indeed, Democratic presidential candidate John Kerry appears to have been the biggest beneficiary of issue advertisements during that election.

Nevertheless, candidates of both parties have routinely benefited from interest group efforts to mobilize voters. Labor unions have a long history of carrying out grassroots voter mobilization drives in support of Democratic candidates. The National Rifle Association, National Association for the Advancement of Colored People, and groups representing other large memberships have recently become active in this area. A variety were very active in the 2000 and 2002 elections (see, for example, Chapter 3 in this volume by Biersack and Viray), and interest group participation continued to flourish in 2004. A combination of heightened electoral competition, the availability of new database and targeting technology, and the BCRA's prohibitions against soft money–financed televised and radio interest group advertising during the period immediately preceding a primary or the general election encouraged several existing groups and a number of new ones to focus on voter registration and turnout.

Some candidates find interest group assistance to be extremely helpful. For a few facing very close elections, it may even have been critical to their success. As a group, PACs are the second largest source of campaign contributions in congressional elections, surpassed only by individuals. During the 2002 elections, PAC funds accounted for one-third of the money collected by all House primary and general election candidates and 18 percent of that collected by all Senate ones. Incumbents were the greatest beneficiaries of most of this funding. Congressional candidates and their campaign aides consider PACs and other interest groups to be a major source of assistance in fund-raising (see, for example, Herrnson 2004, 154–155).

Congressional campaigners also consider interest groups helpful in other aspects of campaigning requiring technical expertise, in-depth research, political connections, and grassroots efforts. During the 1994 congressional elections, interest groups such as the National Association of Home Builders, Chamber of Commerce, National Federation of Independent Business, and the Christian Coalition helped to finance the research and advertising that went into the House Republicans' "Contract with America" and the nationalized election campaign that accompanied it. Nevertheless, most candidates appraise the assistance they receive from interest groups to be somewhat less important than that they receive from party committees (Herrnson 1988, 88–111; 2004, 154–158).

The Road to the White House

The formal process by which a candidate secures a major-party nomination lasts roughly a year, but aspirants for the White House spend years laying the groundwork for their campaigns. Interest groups often play important roles in this process by inviting candidates to address their members and donating funds to the PACs, tax-exempt organizations, and nonprofit foundations that the candidates use to finance these preliminary presidential forays (Corrado 1992).

As noted earlier, individual contributions are much more important than PAC contributions to the financing of presidential nomination campaigns. Although PACs have had only a negligible role in the financing of modern presidential primary campaigns, interest groups have been influential in these contests. These groups have and continue to influence the financing of presidential nomination campaigns by organizing fundraising events, sharing their mailing lists, and coordinating the contributions of their members (Brown, Powell, and Wilcox 1995, chaps. 4–7). Barred from contributing directly to candidates during the general election, groups assist candidates indirectly by contributing funds to their political party. Prior to enactment of the BCRA, groups could contribute unlimited amounts of soft money to party committees to influence presidential campaigns. In the 2000 election cycle, groups contributed nearly $500 million in soft money to Democratic and Republican Party organizations. Thirteen groups each gave at least $1 million to help the parties finance their national conventions, including three groups—General Motors, Microsoft, and AT&T—that gave $1 million apiece to both parties' convention committees (Center for Responsive Politics 2001c).

After the election, groups contributed over $10 million more to help finance the efforts of both presidential candidates to settle the contested Florida vote count (Corrado 2002). As noted earlier, the BCRA bans soft money contributions to national party organizations and greatly limits the amounts of soft money that can be contributed to other party committees.

In addition to fundraising assistance, interest groups also conduct many of the same activities in presidential primaries and general elections that they use to influence congressional elections. Interest groups conducted substantial independent, parallel, and coordinated campaigns in 2000. They spent almost $7 million on internal communications to inform group members of their preferred choices and another $6.1 million in independent expenditures to make sure their views were known by the general public. Organized groups also undertook considerable efforts to mobilize voters.

As they do in congressional contests, interest groups also underwrite the broadcast of issue advocacy ads designed to influence presidential elections without expressly calling for a candidate's election or defeat. In 2000, groups spent millions of dollars to advance the causes of their preferred candidates. Some of these ads were aired a full year ahead of the general election. Perhaps the most controversial ads were televised by Republicans for Clean Air, a front organization made up of two wealthy Texans—brothers Sam and Charles Wyly—that attacked Sen. John McCain of Arizona in order to advance George W. Bush's candidacy for the Republican nomination (Center for Public Integrity 2000).

Issue ads thoroughly permeated the 2000 presidential general election. Led by Planned Parenthood and the AFL-CIO, groups that supported the Gore-Lieberman ticket spent $12.4 million, accounting for 14 percent of all of the political spots intended to help the Democrats' standard-bearers. Groups played a significantly smaller role in the efforts to elect the Bush-Cheney ticket; they contributed less than $2.6 million, or 4 percent of the total spent on spots aired to help the two Republicans. Most of these ads were broadcast in media markets covering battleground states.[8]

A Continuous Journey

To remain influential in elections, and in politics more generally, interest groups must adapt to changes in the political environment. Shifts in the partisan control of political institutions or alterations in the legal framework in which interest groups operate may require groups to alter existing patterns of behavior and adjust their relationships with candidates, political parties, and other groups. What were considered standard practices at one time sometimes need to be replaced by new courses of action.

Turnovers in partisan control of the White House and Congress have led to a significant change in the pattern of interest group contributions to congressional campaigns. The 1992 presidential and 1994 congressional elections ushered in a reversal of the then-standard pattern of divided government: Republican control of the presidency gave way in 1992 to Democrat Bill Clinton's occupancy of the White House, and forty years of uninterrupted Democratic control of the House and dominance over the Senate was replaced in 1994 by GOP control of both chambers. The Republicans were able to maintain their slim majorities in the legislature, and the Democrats held on to the White House until the 2000 election. Then, Republican George W. Bush won the presidential election, and the Senate became equally divided—at least until Republican senator James M. Jeffords of Vermont declared himself an independent. After the 2002 midterm elections, the Republican Party found itself in control of the White House, Senate, and House. Most of the interest group activity in elections that occurred before 1994 was conditioned by the Democrats' control of Congress. Not surprisingly, congressional Democrats were the primary beneficiaries of most interest group activity prior to the Republican takeover.

The 1994 elections ushered in a new era on Capitol Hill. The Republican-controlled Congress created a new set of realities and possibilities for interest groups, and many responded to the new environment. The contribution patterns for the House are particularly striking. The Republican takeover had a profound

impact on the partisan distribution of PAC money. Corporate and trade association PACs dramatically reversed their contribution patterns from moderately
favoring Democratic candidates to strongly favoring Republicans. From the 1994
to 1996 election cycles, the percentages switched from 57 percent to 43 percent
in favor of the Democrats to 70 percent to 30 percent in favor of the Republicans
(Figure 2-1). Both sets of PACs continued to favor the GOP through the 2002
elections, and preliminary figures suggest they will continue to do so through the
2004 contests. These groups' support of the GOP's pro-business agenda and
their desire to gain access to Republican committee and subcommittee chairs and
congressional party leaders are principally responsible for the initial switch in
contributions. Groups' determination to maintain access to powerful members of
both parties is an important factor in both the PACs' switch to the Republicans
and their continued contributions to incumbent Democrats. The closeness of
partisan control over Congress, the possibility of a Democratic victory in the
2004 presidential election, and the need to build bipartisan coalitions in support
of some of the groups' legislative priorities also discouraged some PACs from
completely abandoning the Democrats in favor of the GOP.

Nonconnected ideological PACs also were influenced by the 1994 Republican takeover of Congress. They were able to galvanize their members, collecting
and spending substantial sums. Their post-1994 contributions suggest that conservative PACs mobilized their members in order to help the GOP maintain
control of the House. These PACs contributed three times more money to House
Republicans during the 1996 elections than they did in 1994. Their contributions
rose in terms of raw dollars and as a proportion of all nonconnected PAC contributions. Meanwhile, the contributions of liberal PACs to Democratic House
candidates fell slightly.

Labor PACs, which traditionally have been among the staunchest supporters of Democratic candidates, were the least affected by the shift in power. A few
labor PACs increased their support for Republican candidates after the GOP
takeover, and labor's support of Republicans rose from 3 percent of their total
House contributions to between 7 and 8 percent. The Seafarers International
Union PAC is an example of a group that became more generous to Republicans
after their takeover of the House, and then withdrew some of its support when a
Democratic majority became increasingly likely in 2000. The PAC gave only
$51,100, or 10 percent of its House contributions, to fourteen House Republi-
cans prior to the 1994 election cycle. During the 1996 elections, after the Republican takeover of Congress, it gave $132,000, or 23 percent of its House contri-
butions, to thirty-five GOP House members. Similarly, during the 1998 election
it gave $110,000, or 23 percent of its House donations, to thirty-six Republicans.
During the 2000 elections, when the seat margin was the narrowest it had been
since the Republican takeover of Congress, the union gave GOP candidates only
$53,400, or 12 percent of its total House contributions. The Republican Party's
capture of the White House in 2000 and its greatly enhanced control of the
levers of government led the Seafarers union to once again increase its support

Figure 2-1   The Distribution of PAC Contributions in
House Elections, 1994–2000

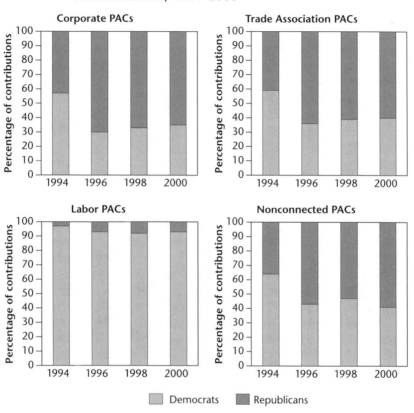

Source: Figures compiled from Federal Election Commission data.

for GOP candidates. During the 2002 elections, its PAC contributed $72,500, 22 percent of its House contributions, to Republican candidates.

It is more difficult to assess the impact of the Republican takeover of the Senate on PAC activities, because different Senate seats are up for election every two years, and the idiosyncrasies of the states and candidates involved can have a major impact on campaign finance patterns. Nevertheless, the evidence suggests that many PACs, especially corporate committees, adjusted their giving in Senate races in response to the GOP takeover of the upper chamber. Corporate PACs gave 58 percent of their Senate contributions to Republicans and 42 percent to Democrats during the 1994 elections (see Figure 2-2). In 1996 these numbers changed radically; corporate committees gave 81 percent of their money to Republicans and 19 percent to Democrats. Trade association PACs also responded to the GOP's 1994 success. The Senate contributions of these groups

Figure 2-2   Distribution of PAC Contributions in Senate
                 Elections, 1994–2000

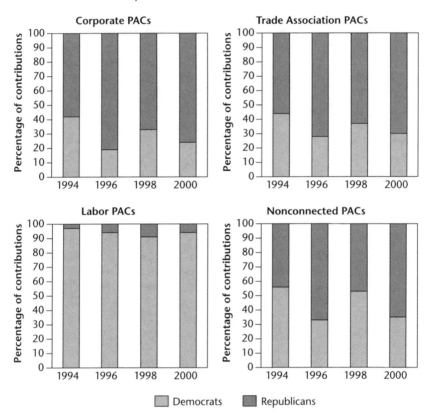

Source: Figures compiled from Federal Election Commission data.

slightly favored Republicans in 1994, but the groups donated more than four-fifths of their dollars to GOP Senate candidates in 1996. Like their donations to House candidates, both sets of PACs continued to favor Republican Senate candidates after the 1996 elections. Their continued contributions to Democratic candidates were probably inspired by the recognition that the GOP was unlikely to secure enough seats to put together a filibuster-proof majority and their understanding that procedures in the upper chamber almost always require groups to attract the support of members of both parties in order to achieve legislative success.

The 1994 GOP takeover of the Senate also influenced the partisan distribution of contributions by ideological and labor PACs. Republicans collected 44 percent of the ideological PAC money distributed to Senate candidates during the 1994 elections. The mobilization of conservative PAC dollars enabled GOP candidates to gather two-thirds of the PAC money ideological PACs distributed in the 1996 contests and to continue to raise nearly as much if not more money than their Democratic counterparts. Republican Senate candidates also made small inroads into the labor community, increasing their share of labor funds from 3 percent in the 1994 election to between 6 and 9 percent in the ensuing contests. Although the patterns of PAC activity in congressional elections have changed, candidates—primarily incumbents—of both parties continue to raise substantial sums in PAC dollars (see, for example, Herrnson 2004, 145–149). Rather than fully abandoning the Democratic Party, many PACs, including those representing corporations and trade associations, have responded cautiously to the new order on Capitol Hill. They are more supportive of Republicans because the GOP has become the majority party in both chambers and is more inclined to enact pro-business legislation, but most PACs continue to give substantial amounts to powerful incumbents on both sides of the aisle.

The changes in the flow of PAC dollars since the 1994 elections are informed by a sense of caution and a set of strategic considerations that emphasize supporting incumbents. PAC contributions are influenced by the party that controls Congress at a given time, the uncertainty surrounding the question of which party will control Congress in the future, and a strategic premise shared by most corporate, trade association, and other business-oriented PACs that emphasizes maintaining access to powerful congressional leaders of both parties. To some degree, the distribution of PAC money also reflects control of the executive branch. An ability to set the political agenda and direct the implementation of federal programs gives the occupant of the White House tremendous fund-raising clout and an ability to influence the flow of PAC dollars to congressional candidates. When party control of legislative chambers or the executive branch changes, or the partisan ratios of House or Senate seats are altered again, PACs will continue to adjust their contribution strategies.

Interest groups also will continue to adjust their other campaign efforts in response to changes in the environment governing campaign finance and the shifting fortunes of political parties. In Chapter 3, Biersack and Viray discuss the impact that FECA has had on the evolution of the interest group community. They show that the law's enactment paved the way for the formation of thousands of new PACs and led most interest groups to initially channel the vast majority of their election-oriented activity through these organizations. As a result of the efforts of party leaders, interest group officials, and politicians, as well as rulings by the courts and the FEC, FECA eroded over time. Biersack and Viray demonstrate that this erosion has resulted in some interest groups carrying out a substantial portion of their electioneering using issue advocacy ads, internal communications, and other voter mobilization efforts. They report that business groups and other organizations that lack a large membership base concentrate on candidate contributions and issue advocacy ads, whereas unions and other large membership groups find internal communications and voter mobilization drives to be among their most potent forms of electioneering.

In Chapter 4, Richard J. Semiatin and Mark Rozell further explore the theme of interest group adaptation to environmental change. They show that some groups began to use "top-to-bottom" communications strategies during the 2000 and 2002 elections. By airing issue advocacy ads and carrying out voter mobilization efforts in areas of the country to influence competitive elections for several offices, groups were able to ensure that their messages permeated elections at all levels in these localities. They also were able to have a major impact on the politics of particular regions.

Unlike in congressional elections, most of the interest group activity associated with presidential elections held in the latter half of the twentieth century occurred while a Republican was president or favored to be elected. Bill Clinton's victory in 1992 represented a reversal of fortunes for the GOP, which had held the White House for the previous twelve years. Assessing the impact of Clinton's 1992 and 1996 victories and Bush's 2000 victory on interest group activity in elections is more difficult than untangling the impact of a change in partisan control of the House or the Senate contests because presidential candidates rely mainly on money collected from individual citizens and the federal government to finance their campaigns. PAC dollars do not play a big role in their campaigns.

As noted earlier, however, interest group money, advertising, and grassroots campaign efforts do make their way into presidential nomination and general election campaigns. The case study of the New Hampshire primary in Chapter 5 by Linda L. Fowler, Constantine J. Spiliotes, and Lynn Vavreck demonstrates that groups become involved in presidential nomination campaigns for two main reasons: to influence the election outcome or affect the campaign discourse. Those trying to influence the outcome of the election seek to help their favored candidate win their state's convention delegates and their party's nomination. Those hoping to affect the campaign discourse often seek to raise the salience of their priority issues among party activists and the media or to frame the issues in a particular way. Moreover, they work to force the candidates to address their priority issues. Chapter 5 also reveals that the political context influences the efficacy of the different campaign activities undertaken by interest groups. Because New Hampshire holds the nation's first primary, with all its symbolic value, candidates spend a disproportionate share of their funds to air television ads in the state, and the media devote an exceptional amount of its primary coverage to the state. As such, most interest groups do not invest heavily in broadcasting their message in New Hampshire, and those that did in 2000 had little impact on the race. A few organizations, however, particularly the AFL-CIO, carried out massive grassroots organizing and voter mobilization activities in the state. The unions' efforts are credited with having a major impact on the outcome of the state's 2000 Democratic presidential primary, which was won by Vice President Al Gore.

Unions, corporations, and other groups are extremely active in the presidential general election, despite the fact that the PACs they sponsor do not become very involved in them. As Stephen J. Wayne explains in Chapter 6, interest groups become involved in the pre-candidacy stage of presidential elections by contributing to the leadership PACs, tax-exempt foundations, and other nonprofit organizations that help to finance research, travel, and the other expenses of undeclared candidates who hope to be competitive once they declare their candidacies and formally begin campaigning. Their members also help candidates to raise money during the nomination stage of the election, frequently by soliciting contributions or bundling checks. Interest groups are prohibited from directly contributing funds to presidential nominees who accept public funds. However, many groups have assisted their preferred candidate by contributing soft money to political parties that the parties then use to improve the candidate's prospects. Some groups also have spent and continue to spend money directly as independent expenditures or as issue advocacy advertisements. As Wayne reveals, like in congressional elections, interest groups learned to work both within and outside the confines of FECA to influence who is elected president.

Taken together, the chapters on the electoral connection show that interest groups can further a candidate's progress on the road to the White House or to Capitol Hill, or they can stand as obstacles blocking the candidate's way. The chapters also demonstrate that whereas candidates have clear-cut destinations and routes, interest groups often do not. They must respond to the changing fortunes of candidates and political parties.

Blazing New Paths of Influence

When political reform shuts down some paths of influence, interest groups that wish to remain important players in electoral politics must blaze new ones. Just as passage of the 1974 amendments to FECA required interest groups to learn how to participate in a political environment governed by a new set of rules, enactment of the BCRA in 2002 meant groups had to learn a new set of lessons to maximize their impact on federal elections. Most of the reform's influence on interest groups will stem from its provisions banning soft money. These are designed to limit the abilities of interest groups to use soft money to influence elections, gain access to public officials, or otherwise seek to affect the policymaking process.

The BCRA directly limits interest group activity in federal elections by prohibiting corporations, unions, and trade associations from airing soft money–financed issue advocacy advertisements referring to a clearly identified federal candidate on broadcast, cable, or satellite television, or radio within thirty days of a primary or sixty days of a general election. In the months leading up to this "blackout" period, interest groups can carry out these activities. However, once the blackout period has commenced, hard money–financed independent expenditures by PACs become the only interest group spending permissible on television and radio advertising.

The BCRA indirectly limits interest group influence in federal elections through regulations governing the soft money contributions corporations,

Notes

1. The regulations and contribution limits discussed in this chapter and this section of the book were in effect during the elections held between 1976 and 2002. While a variety of changes were made in federal campaign financing as a result of the passage of the Bipartisan Campaign Reform Act of 2002 and the subsequent Supreme Court ruling in *McConnell v. FEC* (2003), regulations regarding PACs remained unchanged.
2. Candidate-sponsored PACs are the exception to the rule. These committees are frequently used to pay for some of the activities that politicians undertake prior to declaring their candidacies for the nomination (see Corrado 1992, chaps. 4–7).
3. See *Colorado Republican Federal Campaign Committee v. Federal Election Commission* (518 U.S. 604 [1996]).
4. Soft money was raised and spent largely outside of the federal law, but was and continues to be subject to limits imposed by state laws (Drew 1983; Sorauf 1992,147–151; Corrado et al. 1997).
5. These figures are for general election candidates only.
6. These races were decided by margins of 20 percent or less.
7. A small portion of this spending was on televised independent expenditure ads. This figure underestimates the parties' and groups' actual expenditures, because it only includes media buys (not production costs), only includes spending in the nation's seventy-five largest media markets (excluding 135 smaller markets), and is based on television stations' published rates rather than the actual charges levied by the stations, which were inflated as the election date approached. The figure was compiled from data collected by the Campaign Media Analysis Group (CMAG)—see Herrnson (2002).
8. Dollar figures compiled from CMAG data and percentages taken from Goldstein and Freedman (2002).
9. Contributions to 501(c)(3) organizations are tax deductible; 501(c)(4) organizations are exempt from federal taxes; and 501(c)(6) organizations may accept unlimited donations without disclosing their donors (see, for example, Herrnson 2004, 135–136, 295).

References

Alexander, Herbert E. 1992. *Financing Politics: Money, Elections, and Political Reform.* Washington, DC: CQ Press.

American Federation of Labor–Congress of Industrial Organizations (AFL-CIO). 2000. "People-Powered Politics: Working Families Vote." AFL-CIO, Washington, DC. http://www.aflcio.org./labor2000/election.htm.

———. n.d. "The Union Difference Political Program for Working Families." http://www.aflcio.org/issuespolitics/politics/fs_0202.cfm.

Brown, Clifford W., Jr., Lynda W. Powell, and Clyde Wilcox. 1995. *Serious Money: Fundraising and Contributing in Presidential Nomination Campaigns.* London: Cambridge University Press.

Burrell, Barbara C. 1994. *A Woman's Place Is in the House: Campaigning for Congress in the Feminist Era.* Ann Arbor: University of Michigan Press.

Carney, Eliza Newlin, Peter H. Stone, and James A. Barnes. 2003. "New Rules of the Game." *National Journal,* December 20.

Center for Public Integrity. 2000. "The 'Black Hole' Groups," *The Public I: An Investigative Report of the Center for Public Integrity.* http://www.public-i.org/adwatch_02_033000.htm.

Center for Responsive Politics. 2001a. "Democratic Party: Top Contributors." http://www.opensecrets.org/parties/contrib.asp?Cmte=DPC.

————. 2001b. "Republican Party: Top Contributors." http://www.opensecrets.org/parties/contrib.asp?cmte=RPC.

————. 2001c. "$100,000+ Donors to the Democratic National Convention and Soft Money, PAC & Individual Contributions, 1999–00." http://www.opensecrets.org/alerts/v5/alertv5_51b.asp.

Corrado, Anthony. 1992. *Creative Campaigning: PACs and the Presidential Selection Process.* Boulder, CO: Westview Press.

Corrado, Anthony, Thomas E. Mann, Daniel R. Ortiz, Trevor Potter, and Frank J. Sorauf. 1997. *Campaign Finance Reform: A Sourcebook.* Washington, DC: Brookings.

————. 2002. "Financing the 2000 Presidential General Election." In *Financing the 2000 Election,* edited by David B. Magleby. Washington, DC: Brookings.

Day, Christine L., and Charles D. Hadley. 2004. *Women's PACs: Abortion and Elections.* Saddle River, NJ: Prentice Hall.

Drew, Elizabeth. 1983. *Politics and Money: The New Road to Corruption.* New York: Macmillan.

Edsall, Thomas B. 2000. "Unions in High-Tech Fight for their Fortune." *Washington Post,* October 31.

Fowler, Linda L., and Robert D. McClure. 1989. *Political Ambition: Who Decides to Run for Congress.* New Haven, CT: Yale University Press.

Francia, Peter F., John C. Green, Paul S. Herrnson, Lynda Powell, and Clyde Wilcox. 2003. *The Financiers of Congressional Elections: Investors, Ideologues, and Intimates.* New York: Columbia University Press.

Goldstein, Ken, and Paul Freeman. 2002. "Lessons Learned: Campaign Advertising in the 2000 Elections." *Political Communication* 19:5–28.

Goldstein, Ken, and Joel Rivlin. 2003. "Advertising in the 2000 Election." Unpublished manuscript, University of Wisconsin-Madison.

Grenzke, Janet M. 1989. "PACs and the Congressional Supermarket: The Currency is Complex." *American Journal of Political Science* 33:2–24.

Hardesty, Rex. 1976. "The Computer's Role in Getting Out the Vote." In *Labor in American Politics,* edited by C. Rehmus, D. McLaughlin, and F. Nesbitt. Ann Arbor: University of Michigan Press.

Herrnson, Paul S. 1988. *Party Campaigning in the 1980s.* Cambridge, MA: Harvard University Press.

————. 1994. "The National Committee for an Effective Congress: Liberalism, Partisanship, and Electoral Innovation." In *Risky Business? PAC Decisionmaking in Congressional Elections,* edited by Robert Biersack, Paul S. Herrnson, and Clyde Wilcox. New York: M. E. Sharpe.

————. 2002. "Political Party and Interest Group Advertising in the 2000 Congressional Elections." In *Television Advertising in American Elections,* edited by Kenneth M. Goldstein. Upper Saddle River, NJ: Prentice Hall.

————. 2004. *Congressional Elections: Campaigning at Home and in Washington,* 4th ed. Washington, DC: CQ Press.

Herrnson, Paul S., and Diana Dwyre. 1999. "Party Issue Advocacy in Congressional Elections." In *The State of the Parties,* 3d ed., edited by John C. Green and Daniel M. Shea. Lanham, MD: Rowman and Littlefield.

Hicks, Robyn. 1994. "Grassroots Organizations in Defense of Mother Nature: The Clean Water Action Vote Environment PAC." In *Risky Business? PAC Decisionmaking in Congressional Elections,* edited by Robert Biersack, Paul Herrnson, and Clyde Wilcox. Armonk, NY: M. E. Sharpe.

Langbein, Laura I. 1986. "Money and Access: Some Empirical Evidence." *Journal of Politics* 48:1052–1062.

Magleby, David B. 2001. "Election Advocacy: Soft Money and Issue Advocacy in the 2000 Congressional Elections." Center for the Study of Elections and Democracy, Brigham

Young University, Provo, UT. http://www.byu.edu/outsidemoney/2000general/ contents.htm.

Martelle, Scott. 2000. "Campaign 2000: On the Razor's Edge in Michigan." *Los Angeles Times*, August 2.

Nelson, Candice J. 1994. "Women's PACs in the Year of the Woman." In *The Year of the Woman: Myths and Realities*, edited by Elizabeth Adell Cook, Sue Thomas, and Clyde Wilcox. Boulder, CO: Westview Press.

Nelson, Candice J., and Robert Biersack. 1999. "BIPAC: Working to Keep A Pro-Business Congress." In *After the Revolution: PACS, Lobbies, and the Republican Congress*, edited by Robert Biersack, Paul S. Herrnson, and Clyde Wilcox. Boston: Allyn and Bacon.

Rimmerman, Craig A. 1994. "New Kids on the Block: The WISH List and the Gay and Lesbian Victory Fund." In *Risky Business? PAC Decisionmaking in Congressional Elections*, edited by Robert Biersack, Paul S. Herrnson, and Clyde Wilcox. New York: M. E. Sharpe.

Sabato, Larry J. 1984. *PAC Power: Inside the World of Political Action Committees*. New York: Norton.

Sorauf, Frank J. 1992. *Inside Campaign Finance: Myths and Realities*. New Haven, CT: Yale University Press.

Warlick, Drew. 2004. "Rocking the Vote: Music for America Uses the Music Scene to Register Voters." Center for Responsive Politics. http://www.capitaleye.org/inside.asp?ID=133.

Wilcox, Clyde. 1994. "Coping with Increasing Business Influence: The AFL-CIO's Committee on Political Education." In *Risky Business? PAC Decisionmaking in Congressional Elections*, edited by Robert Biersack, Paul S. Herrnson, and Clyde Wilcox. New York: M. E. Sharpe.

Witham, Larry. 2002. "Religious Vote Credited in GOP Wins." *Washington Times*, November 7.

Wright, John R. 1990. "Contributions, Lobbying, and Committee Voting in the U.S. House of Representatives." *American Political Science Review* 84:417–438.

———. 1996. *Interest Groups and Congress: Lobbying, Contributions and Influence*. Boston: Allyn and Bacon.

3. Interest Groups and Federal Campaign Finance: The Beginning of a New Era

Robert Biersack and Marianne H. Viray

During most of the 1980s, campaign finance reform advocates bemoaned the pernicious influence of political action committees (PACs). They made much of the fact that the number of PACs had increased rapidly and that they provided half of the money raised by House incumbents. The cumulative effect of so many PACs giving so much money appeared to be a serious problem for American democracy. So much so that the battle cry of Common Cause, the perennial campaign finance reform organization, was "People Against PACs." In *Still the Best Congress Money Can Buy,* reform advocate Phil Stern wrote: "PACs do have an ax to grind. They do expect something in return for the support they give candidates—namely, influence, or at least preferred access to the powerful. . . . [PAC favoritism] crushes the American ideal that political office should be open to all citizens, regardless of their wealth or station in society" (Stern 1992, 37, 38).

Politicians also were critical of PACs' influence. In the words of Senate Majority Leader Robert J. Dole, R-KS: "When these political action committees give money, they expect something in return other than good government. It is making it difficult to legislate. We may reach a point where everybody is buying something with PAC money. We cannot get anything done" (quoted in Sabato 1984, xiv). Not surprisingly, then, most reform proposals in the 1980s centered on banning PACs altogether, or at least reducing the size of their contributions in an effort to reduce their influence.

Less than a generation later, the financing of federal campaigns has changed so much that PACs, at some point, were considered by some as quaint artifacts of an old regulatory system, drowned out by the effects of soft money campaigning by parties and interest groups. We argue that this perception of PACs has been challenged by the Bipartisan Campaign Reform Act of 2002 (BCRA), which bans soft money contributions to political parties, so that hard money from all sources, including PACs, is once again vital. PACs are seen today as responsible political entities, giving relatively small amounts that are fully disclosed—especially when compared with the other ways in which interest groups are involved in campaign finance.

Interest groups have many resources that might be utilized to affect the outcome of elections. They have members who can volunteer, and they have communications channels to reach those members with endorsements or other appeals. They have money in their treasuries, and their members have money to contribute as well. They have arguments to make to voters and expertise to bring to bear in making those arguments. Campaign finance regulations limit the resources that groups can use in election campaigns and the way that they can use them (Wilcox et al. 2001). In the past, many groups made large, unregulated soft money donations to political parties, and some spent large sums on "issue advocacy" that were at best only partially disclosed. Unlike PAC activity, these transactions were beyond the limits and prohibitions of the original campaign finance regulatory regime created during the 1970s. In the spring of 2002, Congress took steps to rectify this situation. The BCRA banned soft money contributions and regulated and disclosed issue advocacy spending, while leaving PAC activity virtually unchanged.

The Federal Election Campaign Act (FECA), as amended, requires that groups seeking to participate in federal campaigns form PACs funded primarily by voluntary contributions from group members. Treasury funds generated by corporate profits or group membership dues cannot be given directly to candidates through PACs, but they can be used to pay the overhead expenses of the PAC. PAC funds can be contributed directly to federal candidates, to party committees, or to other PACs, but the size of these contributions is limited. PACs can also spend unlimited amounts to advocate the election or defeat of a candidate, but that spending cannot be coordinated with the candidate. All individual contributions over $200 to PACs, and all contributions by PACs to candidates, parties, and other PACs, must be fully disclosed to the Federal Election Commission (FEC).

As noted, the PAC regime limited campaign contributions by groups to the funds they could raise in voluntary contributions from their members. Groups with a few very wealthy members could not channel that money to candidates, and groups with sizable treasuries from dues or profits could not use those funds to finance federal electoral activity.

Increasingly, however, groups are active in ways that fall outside of the FECA regulatory framework and in ways that allow them to use these additional resources. Groups can spend unlimited amounts to communicate with their members. They can endorse candidates, or they can create voter guides that make it clear to their members which candidates are most likely to support the group's policy goals.

Groups also can spend money to advocate issue positions, and they can use mailings, telephone calls, newspaper advertising, or the Internet to discuss these issues, even mentioning candidates and officeholders without restrictions. The BCRA limits only the *sources* of funds (no corporations or unions) that can be used for broadcast issue ads that identify candidates just before elections. Issue advocacy campaigns allow groups to define the issues of a campaign, because the group controls the content of the communication.

These new campaign tools provide groups with alternatives to simple PAC contributions. Many organizations maintain a PAC, but also mount issue advocacy campaigns from other segments of the organization. Do these new tools alter interest group electoral strategies? In this chapter, we first explore the evolution of regulated PAC activity, and then we examine the growth of soft money and issue advocacy. Next, we assess the role of PACs in the new regulatory regime under the Bipartisan Campaign Reform Act, and show how groups are changing their tactics in response to new opportunities and regulations. We conclude with a close look at the activities of four organizations in recent election cycles: the American Federation of Labor–Congress of Industrial Organizations (AFL - CIO), the National Rifle Association (NRA), Americans for Job Security, and the National Association for the Advancement of Colored People (NAACP).

Federal PACs

Unions and a few other groups, most notably the American Medical Association, already had political action committees prior to the passage in 1974 of comprehensive amendments to the 1971 Federal Election Campaign Act. FECA codified PACs, allowing all kinds of groups to form separate voluntary organizations to pool contributions from their members and to contribute those funds to federal campaigns, to parties, or to other PACs. More specifically, the act sanctioned the creation of PACs by corporations, trade associations, and membership groups (Corrado 1997). The contributions from members to these PACs, and contributions from PACs to other campaign committees, were limited by law. Individuals could give up to $5,000 a year to a PAC, and PACs could give up to $5,000 to any federal candidate in any election (primary, general, or runoff). Unlike other limits, these were not changed with passage of the BCRA in 2002.

The formal codification of PACs as the vehicle for interest group participation in federal campaign finance unleashed a period of significant growth in the number of PACs and their financial activity. At a time when candidate - centered campaigning had become the norm, members of Congress and congressional candidates were finding a new source of financial support critical to their electoral prospects (Herrnson 2000). The number of PACs grew considerably from the 1970s through the mid - 1980s, with particularly strong growth for corporate and nonconnected (generally ideological or single - issue groups) PACs (see Figure 3 - 1). By the late 1980s, the number of PACs had stabilized, and the growth in the magnitude of their financial activity had slowed. Figure 3 - 1 reveals that the number of corporate PACs has actually declined since 1986, and other types of PACs have seen little change. Contributions by PACs leveled off in the mid - 1980s, but increased again after the 1994 election brought a new majority and tight margins to Congress (see Figure 3 - 2). During the 1980s, direct contributions by PACs were the primary ways in which interest groups participated in federal elections.

Not All PACs Are Created Equal

The aggregate stability in the numbers and activity of PACs masks considerable turnover as new PACs are created and others go out of business (Sorauf 1992). More important, the aggregate statistics about PACs mask the diversity of these groups in size, partisanship, and overall contribution strategy.

Figure 3-1   Number of PACs by Type, 1978–2002

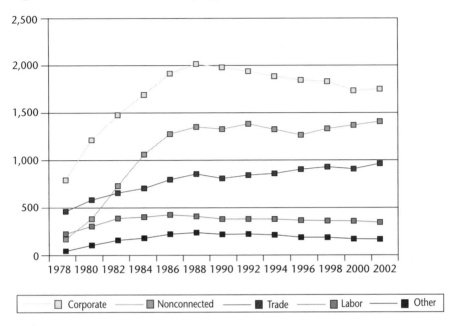

Source: Federal Election Commission financial reports and databases.

Although more than four thousand PACs have registered with the FEC in each election cycle since the mid-1980s, most PAC contributions and expenditures are made by a small number of committees with large revenues. In 2002 the 210 largest PACs made about 62 percent of all PAC contributions to candidates. Studies have shown that larger PACs are more likely to have institutionalized rules for contributing (Biersack, Herrnson, and Wilcox 1994), with the result that the contributions by these PACs are more predictable (Wilcox 1989). Research has also suggested that the larger PACs make contribution decisions that differ somewhat from those of other PACs; they direct more of their money to challengers and open-seat candidates (Eismeier and Pollock 1984; Wilcox 1989).

How did large PACs differ in their contributions from smaller PACs in 2002? A simple comparison of the contributions of the largest PACs (those that made contributions of at least $500,000) with those of smaller committees seems to indicate that large PACs are significantly more likely to back Democratic candidates (see Table 3-1). Yet this finding stems entirely from the fact that many labor PACs are found among the largest PACs, and labor committees have consistently been strongly Democratic. If only nonlabor PACs are compared, there

Figure 3-2 PAC Contributions, 1980–2002 (in millions of 2000 dollars)

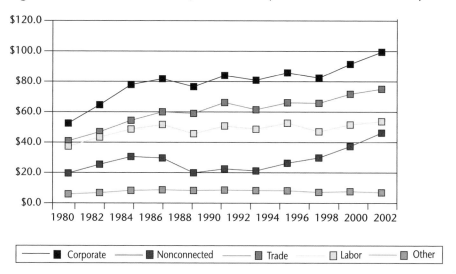

Source: Federal Election Commission financial reports and databases.

appears to be little difference in the contributions of large and small PACs in 2002, either in partisanship or in support for nonincumbents.

Small and large PACs alike gave more than 60 percent of their money to Republican candidates in 2002. This finding agrees with the common notion that interest groups use their PACs primarily to seek access to policymakers (Republicans controlled Congress in 2002), but that they also give to legislators of both parties in an effort to maintain cordial relations. Although this notion does fit some PACs, many other PACs support primarily or exclusively the candidates of one party. This is true not only of nonconnected, ideological PACs and labor committees, but also of corporate PACs and those associated with trade associations.

Table 3-2 includes only those committees that gave at least $20,000 in 2002 to congressional candidates, thereby eliminating small committees that may give only to state house or senate candidates. In 2002, 144 corporate PACs contributed at least 80 percent of their funds to candidates of only one party, and these PACs gave 14 percent of all corporate PAC contributions. The 216 nonconnected committees and 88 trade association PACs were equally partisan. Nearly 72 percent of nonconnected giving comes from partisans, along with nearly 23 percent of trade PAC giving. Finally, 75 labor PACs were partisan, and they represented more than 82 percent of all labor PAC giving. Partisan giving, then, is more common among union and nonconnected PACs. Although some corporate and trade PACs are partisan as well, they give to candidates of both parties, suggesting that their goal is access to legislators. All of the "partisan"

Table 3-1   Contributions by Large and Small PACs, by Type of Candidate and
by Political Party (percentage)

	All PACS		
	Incumbents	Challengers	Open seats
Large PACs	74	10	16
Small PACs	78	10	12
	Democratic	Republican	
Large PACs	55	45	
Small PACs	39	61	

	All PACs minus labor PACs		
	Incumbents	Challengers	Open seats
Large PACs	75	9	16
Small PACs	78	10	12
	Democratic	Republican	
Large PACs	40	60	
Small PACs	37	63	

Source: Federal Election Commission data.

Note: Large PACs are defined as those spending at least $500,000 during the 2001–2002 election cycle.

labor PAC contributions were directed at the Democrats, making these PACs a
far more predictable and reliable source of funds than any category of PAC has
been for Republicans.

Two of the organizations featured in case studies later in this chapter have
PACs. The AFL-CIO's PAC, the Committee on Political Education (COPE),
can trace its roots to the early twentieth century when John Lewis formed labor's
Nonpartisan League. A large PAC, COPE is the lead PAC among labor committees, and its contributions serve as important cues for other PACs (Wilcox
1994). COPE gives most of its money to Democrats. It acts as a "strategic politician" by supporting vulnerable incumbents in good Republican years and switching to back promising nonincumbents in good Democratic years. The Republican takeover of Congress in 1994 was a major setback for the AFL-CIO, which
was immediately denied access to policymakers and lost its offices on the Hill
(Gerber 1999). As a consequence, the AFL-CIO increased its spending on issue
advocacy in the late 1990s (Francia 2000).

The National Rifle Association's Institute for Legislative Action was founded in 1975, and the NRA's Political Victory Fund is one of the largest PACs

Table 3-2 "Partisan" PAC Contributions, 2002

	Number of PACs	Contributions to dominant party	Percentage of all contributions by PAC category
Republican PACs			
Corporate	133	$13,201,673	13.26
Labor	0	0	0.00
Nonconnected	120	18,602,507	40.12
Trade/member/health	72	11,354,479	15.11
Other	9	584,026	8.28
Democratic PACs			
Corporate	11	$903,133	0.91
Labor	75	44,493,478	82.55
Nonconnected	96	14,585,550	31.46
Trade/member/health	16	6,024,199	8.02
Other	1	20,750	0.29

Source: Federal Election Commission data.

Note: Partisan PACs gave at least 80 percent of their contributions to members of one party and contributed $20,000 or more to congressional candidates.

associated with a membership organization. The NRA supports candidates based on their records on gun-related issues. In the early 1980s, the NRA supported some Democrats (especially in the South and in rural districts), but throughout the 1990s the PAC channeled increasing portions of its funds to Republican candidates (Patterson 1999). The NRA also makes significant independent expenditures to oppose or support candidates.

Soft Money Contributions

From the mid-1980s through 2002, groups and individuals were asked to help finance elections by contributing "soft" money in addition to the "hard" money. This kind of giving traditionally took the form of contributions to national and state party organizations that were used for a variety of election-related functions not specifically devoted to federal campaigns. Soft money was spent on party-building activities and on generic electoral activity that was not directly linked to specific federal candidates. No limits were placed on the amounts of soft money contributions, and sources that normally could not be tapped, such as corporate treasury funds and union dues, were allowed to contribute. Many groups found it easier to give soft money than hard money, because soft money was taken from an organization's treasury and often required no approval by a PAC board. Party committees moved aggressively during this period to solicit soft money contributions in settings that offered intimate interactions between policymakers and donors (Rozell and Wilcox 1999).

Soft money grew rapidly as a portion of party receipts. In 1984 each party raised an estimated $20–$25 million in soft money donations; in 2002 each party raised roughly $250 million in soft money. Some groups, such as the AFL-CIO, provided soft money to national, state, and local party committees for many years (Wilcox 1994), and often used that money as leverage to induce state and local party committees to create electoral plans. Other organizations, such as the NRA, only recently began to give soft money in response to solicitations from party leaders.

Soft money was not generally directed to particular races, although when major donors asked that party officials support particular candidates, their wishes were often honored (Jackson 1988). The parties that raised soft money also created devices that associated soft money funds with particular federal candidates, even though the money could not be used specifically for campaigning in those races. Senate campaigns, for example, typically included "joint fundraising" committees with names that identified individual campaigns. Some of the funds raised at committee-sponsored events (hard money) went to the candidates, while the soft money went to party committees for uses that presumably benefited these campaigns. Soft money was therefore most useful in gaining access to congressional policymakers and powerful party leaders. Yet unions have long been a major source of Democratic soft money, primarily because they believe that their fortunes are furthered when Democrats are in the majority. Soft money, then, became the loophole of choice for many contributors and party committees—so much so that its elimination for national parties was a primary element of the new Bipartisan Campaign Reform Act of 2002.

The rise of soft money provided interest groups with two distinct tools in the electoral arena. But did groups adopt similar strategies for their soft money and hard money? In 1991 the FEC began to require that parties systematically disclose the sources of their soft money, but, because soft money was not channeled through PACs, it was sometimes difficult to identify the sources of the money, particularly when it came from individuals. Nevertheless, the Center for Responsive Politics, a nonpartisan nonprofit research organization, has classified soft money contributors between the 1992 and 2002 elections. The center examined the flow of soft money from organizations and the individuals associated with those organizations—mainly corporations, their employees, and families.[1] It suggests that private economic interests contributed much more soft money to national parties than did ideological or labor organizations (see Table 3-3). Economic groups, which sponsor the most pragmatic incumbent-oriented PACs, gave most of the soft money contributions to the national parties. Indeed, the extent of corporate and trade association dominance in the soft money arena is evidenced by the fact that corporations and trade associations gave more soft money to Democratic national, congressional, and senatorial campaign committees than labor unions. Although interest group soft money donations increased

Table 3-3   Campaign Contributions by Economic Sector, 2002

	Total contributions	Contributions from individuals	Contributions from PACs	Soft money contributions
Agribusiness	$54,386,759	$17,228,667	$17,593,355	$19,564,737
Communications/ electronics	114,859,801	25,462,701	17,464,154	71,932,946
Construction	45,466,754	27,306,917	9,645,860	8,513,977
Defense	15,962,586	2,434,909	8,995,922	4,531,755
Energy/natural resources	57,778,378	14,341,857	20,442,732	22,993,789
Finance/insurance/ real estate	230,482,871	91,873,647	47,019,482	91,589,742
Health	95,105,057	38,213,062	27,391,216	29,500,779
Lawyers/lobbyists	112,193,564	77,744,752	10,759,067	23,689,745
Transportation	46,294,165	13,636,897	17,456,888	15,200,380
Misc. business	140,039,843	62,315,763	26,887,437	50,836,643
Labor	96,584,777	438,805	60,277,966	35,868,006
Ideology/single issue	135,718,967	24,356,821	87,516,331	23,845,815
Other	108,132,416	94,372,468	925,603	12,834,345
Total	1,253,005,938	489,727,266	352,376,013	410,902,659
Percentage		39.08	28.12	32.79

Source: Center for Responsive Politics, www.opensecrets.org/bigpicture/
sectors.asp?Cycle=2002&Blkdn=Source&Sortby=Sector.

fourfold over the last decade, the overall relative distribution of contributions by types of group has remained stable.

Issue Advocacy

In the late 1990s, the courts created a new avenue for interest group activity in elections. Earlier, in 1976, the Supreme Court, in *Buckley v. Valeo* (424 U.S. 1), sought to balance the importance of free speech during elections with the importance of a government free of corruption and the appearance of corruption. In decisions in the 1990s, the federal courts often found that communications that do not *expressly* advocate the election or defeat of clearly identified candidates are not campaign spending and therefore are not subject to regulation under the FECA (Potter 1997). Companies, unions, and citizen groups were thus free to develop advertising campaigns that supported or challenged issue positions held by elected officials or candidates. These campaigns were sometimes directed at policy decisions before Congress or the administration. They also addressed issues that occupied a place on the agenda in upcoming elections.

The issue advocacy model proved very effective in defeating President Bill Clinton's health care reform package in 1994. A coalition of groups opposing the plan aired issue advocacy ads that attacked the plan for its potential to drastically increase the role of the federal bureaucracy in health care and circumscribe citizens' health care provider options. Perhaps the most memorable ads were the "Harry and

Louise" commercials sponsored by the Health Insurance Association of America. The ads featured what appeared to be a middle-class couple sitting at their kitchen table voicing their fears about the Clinton health plan. Other groups have used issue ads to attack public policy issues before Congress. Most issue advocacy ads are negative and end with an exhortation for voters to contact congressman X or candidate Y to voice their concerns about the politicians' policy views.

Campaign strategists immediately recognized the potential electoral payoffs of issue advocacy. Issue ads could be paid for by interest group treasuries, or by one or more wealthy group members. Because it was not considered electoral activity, issue advocacy was disclosed only in a limited way to the Internal Revenue Service (IRS) until the BCRA was enacted in March 2002. Under the new law, any broadcast ad that refers to a federal candidate in the days just preceding an election and is targeted to the electorate must be disclosed to the FEC, and may only be purchased by contributions from individuals.

The AFL-CIO mounted a huge issue advocacy campaign in the 1996 election in an effort to return the House of Representatives to Democratic control. Labor focused its efforts on congressional districts where they believed new Republican House members were vulnerable. Their ads featured exhortations, such as "call Congressman X and tell her to stop tampering with Social Security." In campaigns undertaken since, the airwaves and mailboxes have been filled with calls for voters to telephone, write, or otherwise contact elected officials about a variety of issues. Most of the ads have appeared in competitive campaigns where the ad's sponsor believed the message might make a difference in the outcome of the election (for examples, see Herrnson 2000, 2001). Ultimately, most of the Republicans targeted by labor won reelection, although there is some evidence that their reelection margin was narrowed by the spending (Jacobson 1999).

The other prominent example of issue advocacy during the 1996 campaign was more successful. Shortly after the 1994 midterm elections switched control of both houses of Congress to the Republicans, the conventional wisdom in Washington was that President Clinton could not possibly win reelection. During the summer of 1995, however, a series of issue ads began appearing around the nation. Purchased with Democratic National Committee (DNC) soft money, the ads touted the accomplishments of the administration and focused on issues that would be important and helpful to the Clinton reelection effort. These ads are widely credited with changing the electoral environment in ways that could not have been achieved under the hard money contribution and expenditure limits that exist in the presidential public funding program.

These two tactical innovations—using labor ads to attack candidates and using political party ads to support the administration without "express advocacy"—caused a fundamental shift in thinking about how soft money could be used in federal elections. The BCRA eliminated party soft money, corporate and union financing, and candidate soft money fund-raising as elements in this process, but the new law did not prohibit the kinds of messages being conveyed with these new techniques. It does require disclosure of individual and group ad campaigns just prior to elections when the most egregious manipulation of the process was seen in past campaigns. Under the BCRA, corporations and unions may not use treasury funds to run political campaign advertisements thirty days prior to a primary election or sixty days prior to a general election if the ads mention a federal candidate in the advertisement and target voters in that election. These organizations must rely on hard dollars raised by their PACs in limited and reported amounts.

Scholarly efforts to monitor issue advocacy campaigns by interest groups suggest they grew from between $54 and $69 million in 1996 (Beck et al. 1997) to $347.8 million in the 2002 campaign (Slass et al. 2001), although these estimates include spending by party committees. Scholars also have found that most issue ads are similar to candidate ads in that both omit *express* advocacy (Krasno and Seltz 2000). They differ, however, in that issue ads tend to be more negative or comparative in tone (Herrnson and Dwyre 1997; Herrnson 2001).

Interest Group Strategies in Recent Elections — and Beyond

Interest groups now have a variety of tactics available to them. They can raise money for a PAC and give that money to candidates, parties, or other PACs. They can spend money from the PAC to advocate the election or defeat of a candidate. They also can still give soft money contributions to some state and local party committees, financed through their group's treasury, to be used for state and local elections. And they can spend money on election-related advertisements targeting a large audience, and still have the ability to communicate with their members, hoping to activate their membership in behalf of candidates. How did groups use these strategies in 2000 and 2002? And how will they use them in future elections? We have chosen four cases for detailed examination. Two of these — the AFL-CIO and the NRA — have been active in elections for many years and have large, institutionalized PACs. One, Americans for Job Security (AJS), is an organization created by the insurance industry and various corporations as a way to mount advertising campaigns without damaging the reputation of the sponsoring companies. Finally, the NAACP is a well-established civil rights organization that in 2000 decided to form electoral units.

AFL-CIO

The AFL-CIO is one of the most active groups in electoral politics, using a variety of resources and tactics (Francia 2000; Wilcox et al. 2001). In 1996 the AFL-CIO spent $35 million on television advertisements in more than thirty congressional districts nationwide (Magleby 2000).

The AFL-CIO "Labor 2000" Campaign. In the 2000 presidential election, labor spent $40 million; however, less than one-quarter of that money was spent on broadcast advertising. Why did labor reduce its reliance on political advertising, and what new strategy did it adopt between 1996 and 2000? Labor learned in 1998 that the greatest way to affect the election outcome and get its 13 million members to vote was not through broadcast communications, but through grassroots, person-to-person contact. Grover Norquist, head of antiunion Americans for Tax Reform, noted this change of strategy: "Unions have learned that they activate their opponents when they use TV/radio. By using grassroots and mail, they mobilize their folks and not opponents" (Magleby 2000).

Labor 2000, as union leaders dubbed their 2000 election cycle effort, was the most comprehensive and expensive election effort labor has ever conducted. More impressive than the financial investment was the investment of human capital—thousands of volunteers and paid staffers conducted extensive grass-roots efforts to register voters and campaign for a Democratic ticket. Labor targeted more than seventy congressional districts in twenty-five states as well as the presidential race.

The AFL-CIO trained and deployed more than a thousand field coordinators and trained thousands of local volunteers. The number of field coordinators was more than double that of the 1998 election and five times greater in 2000 than in 1996. Labor also utilized a National Labor Political Training Center to train many of the nine hundred union members that ran for office. The number of union members running for office was 30 percent greater in 2000 than in 1998 (AFL-CIO 2000b).

According to a labor press release, through labor's efforts union members increased the voter rolls by 2.3 million. In the final weeks of the campaign, Labor 2000 embarked on a "people-powered" bus tour in which more than twenty union leaders boarded buses that rolled through twenty-five cities in Pennsylvania, Kentucky, Ohio, Michigan, Washington, West Virginia, and Oregon. Labor also created a "Texas Truth Squad." Four Texans—a prison guard, a food service worker, a teacher, and a sheet metal worker—went on tour to address other union members on the impact Gov. George W. Bush had had on union families in Texas. The Truth Squad made more than twenty stops nationwide (AFL-CIO 2000b).

Labor campaigned on five principal issues: affordable health care, better public education, safer workplaces, a strong Social Security program, and trade policies. These issues were the cornerstones of labor's campaign, starting with the presidential primary season in a videotaped endorsement of Democratic presidential candidate, Vice President Al Gore, by AFL-CIO President John Sweeney. The videotaped endorsement was disseminated to 25,000 union households in Iowa and New Hampshire. According to David Magleby's research on interest group activity in the presidential primaries, the AFL-CIO was more active than any other group during the primary season; he called it the "most important interest group involved in electioneering on the Democratic side" (Magleby 2000, 11).

Labor conducted a well-orchestrated and diverse campaign in the general election, utilizing all the latest campaign technologies—pollsters, consultants,

phone banks, direct mail, the Internet, and the like. Phone banks were more popular than ever this election cycle—even candidates conducted phone banks and
disguised the recording so that it would sound like one from an interest group.[2]
During the 2000 election cycle, labor made eight million phone calls, 31 percent
more than in 1998. In Washington State alone, 400,000 calls and 600,000 pieces
of mail were sent out before election day (Galvin 2000). Pennsylvania was ring-
ing with 20,000 labor phone calls a day the week prior to the election (AFL-
CIO 2000b). Labor also sent out fourteen million mailers—not including those
disseminated by some of labor's sixty-eight local union affiliates or federations.
And it created more than 750 different types of mailers or leaflets, one-third
more than it did in 1998. Nearly half of all union members nationwide received
at least three forms of communication from their union.

The Internet proved to be an exciting new tool for candidates and interest
groups alike—connecting and mobilizing volunteers for action nationwide. Sixty
thousand e-cards were sent out to friends and union members' families urging
them to vote. Two and a half million flyers were downloaded and distributed to
neighborhoods and worksites (AFL-CIO 2000d).

Overall, labor opted to run its own campaign and spend a large part of its
financial resources on tactics and messages uncoordinated with national parties
or candidates. However, it did contribute, in long-standing fashion, to local,
state, and national political parties and many Democratic candidates. Related
labor groups that file with the IRS were responsible for $2 million in expendi-
tures throughout the election cycle, with $1.3 million, or 66 percent, of those
funds going to state and national Democratic parties (IRS 2000). These expenditures were in addition to the FEC-regulated and FEC-disclosed $78.4 mil-
lion that labor unions contributed to Democratic parties and candidates.

Although labor spent less on television and radio broadcasts and much more
on person-to-person contacts, direct mail, and phone banks, a few issues and
some candidates received broadcast advertising attention. According to the
Campaign Media Analysis Group's television tracking data, the AFL-CIO
spent $3.1 million on advertisements in support of Al Gore and $5.1 million on
advertisements in support of Democratic House candidates during the 2000
election cycle (Brennan Center for Justice 2000).

Labor unions were also vocal about some pieces of legislation that came to
the floor of Congress for a vote during the election cycle. Bills dealing with the
U.S. trade status with China and health care were two examples. Labor unions
strongly disagreed with normalizing trade relations with China, and they ran a
$2 million television campaign urging representatives to vote against it because
it was bad for American and Chinese workers. One prominent sixty-second ad
featured Wei Jingsheng, a Chinese dissident: "I voiced my opinion that China
ought to protect workers' rights, people ought to have human rights. For that, I
spent 18 years in prison and was very nearly executed" (*Star Tribune* 2000). The
AFL-CIO also ran $1 million in ads supporting the Patient's Bill of Rights in
1999 (Slass et al. 2001).

What did labor determine its effect was on the 2000 election cycle? According to Sweeney (2000), "America's working families and their unions played a critical role in this election." Union members constituted 26 percent of all voters, up from the two previous cycles when union members represented 23 percent of the voting population (AFL-CIO 2000a). An AFL-CIO poll found that union members voted overwhelmingly for Al Gore by nearly a two-to-one vote (63 percent to 32 percent). Union members also voted Democratic 70 percent of the time in congressional races (AFL-CIO 2000c). Meanwhile, unions successfully defeated "paycheck protection" ballot initiatives in Oregon and two voucher initiatives in Michigan and California by a two-to-one margin.

AFL-CIO 2002 People-Powered Politics. In the 2002 midterm election cycle, the AFL-CIO continued to develop its grassroots networking and activism. Labor spent $33 million in 2002, slightly less than it did in 2000, but its ground efforts were closely matched (Associated Press 2002). According to a union press release, four thousand local coordinators mobilized, and tens of thousands of union volunteers distributed seventeen million flyers at worksites, called five million union homes, conducted more than half a million person-to-person door contacts, and sent fifteen million mail pieces to union homes (AFL-CIO n.d.). Labor also reported sending out 750 staff from the AFL-CIO and affiliate unions to work with field coordinators and union volunteers in spreading the union message (AFL-CIO 2002).

Labor's focus was on the ground war, but it did not ignore the airwaves—it just ran its advertisements early, pre-Labor Day, typically when the heat of the fall campaign kicks in, in order to influence which issues would be discussed and how those issues would be shaped. Labor spent $3.6 million on 5,616 ads in close to fifteen separate media markets (Wisconsin Advertising Project 2002). Two-thirds of the ads ran before Labor Day and one-third after. Labor focused on Social Security, education, corporate corruption, and the economy. The AFL-CIO's PAC, Committee for Political Education, contributed $1,223,625 to federal candidates in the 2002 cycle and 94 percent of that went to Democratic candidates (FEC data, http://www.opensecrets.org/pacs/lookup2.asp).

The AFL-CIO also continued to train union members to work in public service. By 2000, 2,141 union members already held or were running for public office, and labor's goal was to have 5,000 members in public service in 2002. To this end, labor created a separate PAC—When Workers Run, Workers Win—to help educate, train, and support union candidates for public service. Also in 2002 the AFL-CIO created the National Political Leadership Institute to teach union members campaign management and candidate skills (AFL-CIO n.d.).

Looking Ahead: The AFL-CIO in 2004. AFL-CIO press statements in 2003 indicated that the organization anticipated conducting the largest and earliest voter mobilization and voter education effort to date in 2004 and planned to spend $33 million to do so (Knowles 2003). The AFL-CIO intended to "dedicate more staff and mobilize more political activity than in any previous election" to promoting its core issues and defeating President Bush. It would use many of the same tactics it had employed successfully in past election cycles—person-to-person contacts, phone calls, door knockers, volunteer networks, coordinators, trainers, and online political and organizational toolkits (AFL-CIO n.d.).

Although these efforts are consistent with the AFL-CIO and labor's activities in previous election cycles, the labor movement made a strategic decision in late 2002 to create political organizations that would operate outside the federal regulatory structure and conduct separate independent campaigns. One such organization, Partnership for America's Families, was founded in 2003 by former AFL-CIO political director Steve Rosenthal. The Partnership is a Section 527[3] organization that presents labor's views on political issues. The goal of the Partnership is to augment labor's efforts with its own members and to mobilize the rest of the Democratic base—in particular, the millions of African Americans, Hispanics, and working women who are not union members (AFL-CIO 2003). It was expected that Partnership would receive millions of dollars in contributions from unions—contributions that, under the former regulatory system, used to be given to the Democratic Party as soft money but are now illegal under the BCRA.

In May 2003, Gerald McEntee, president of the American Federation of State, County, and Municipal Employees (AFSCME), and other Partnership board members resigned over disagreements about the organization's mandate and level of minority outreach expected for the 2004 election cycle (Greenhouse 2003). After McEntee resigned, he formed Voices for Working Families, a separate Section 527 political organization with the mandate of mobilizing African American, Hispanic, and women voters in more than fifteen battleground states and throughout the South (Dart 2003). Voices hopes to raise $20–$25 million for voter mobilization efforts. As McEntee described it, the objective of Voices is to "reach households in the targeted communities with at least 10 personal contacts, including door-to-door visits, telephone calls, mail and e-mail" (Gutsche 2003).

According to filings made with the IRS, the Partnership raised $1.2 million from labor groups during the period April–September 2003. Cillizza (2003) reported that most of the Partnership's activities and fund-raising were to be merged into America Coming Together, a separate political organization also led by Steve Rosenthal and EMILY's List President and CEO Ellen Malcolm. By the end of 2003, Voices for Working Families had reported receipts of $780,000 to the IRS.

Labor is making substantial use of Section 527 organizations. According to the Center for Public Integrity, two 527 organizations operated by AFSCME have spent a total of nearly $38 million since 2000, or $7 million more than AFSCME has contributed to its PACs, federal candidates, and the national political parties over the past fourteen years (Willis and Pilhofer 2003).

National Rifle Association

The National Rifle Association is one of the nation's largest single-issue associations. Its PAC, the NRA Political Victory Fund, has millions of donors and is consistently involved in endorsing candidates to its members and supporting or opposing select candidates in congressional and presidential elections. The NRA is also involved in many state legislative races, through state-level PACs.

The 2000 and 2002 Election Cycles. The National Rifle Association approached the 2000 election cycle with great enthusiasm and large expectations — Republicans were trying to hold onto their majorities in the House and Senate as well as capture the White House. The NRA spent more money campaigning for Republicans in 2000 than it spent in the two previous cycles combined — a reported $20 million. It also contributed more than four times as much to political parties in 2000 as it did in 1998 ($1,489,222 in 2000 compared with $350,000 in 1998) and $1.5 million directly to candidates (less than it had contributed to candidates in the previous election cycle). The NRA's political action committee spent $14 million throughout the election cycle, including $1.5 million on direct communications with its members via the NRA Institute for Legislative Action, a related political organization, and $5 million on reported independent expenditures. It also mounted a large grassroots mobilization effort, spending a big portion of its funds on voter mobilization (Bailey 2000).

In 2000 the NRA was one of a handful of interest groups that chose to run independent expenditure campaigns, which allowed the group the luxury of directly supporting or opposing candidates with purely political language. In exchange for the right to use language such as "vote for," "elect," and "support," the NRA had to finance its campaigns only through the voluntary contributions below the $5,000 a year limit from individuals, report these activities to the FEC, and always identify itself clearly in its advertising. In 2000 the NRA was active in 11 primary races, 404 general House races (93 percent of all House races), 35 Senate races, and both the presidential primaries and general election. This massive campaign, entitled "Vote Freedom First," encouraged Americans to vote solely on the issue of gun control. According to NRA Acting Director of Federal Affairs Chuck Cunningham, the NRA mailed tens of thousands of flyers and telephoned every recipient of mail (Baker and Magleby 2002). The NRA also ran ads criticizing members of Congress as part of the "Vote Freedom First" campaign. It spent nearly $2 million on six senatorial bids through television commercials, flyers, billboards, and NRA President Charlton Heston's sixteen-city tour in the six states conducting the U.S. Senate elections. Dave Dieball, district coordinator for the NRA in Michigan, where it waged fights in multiple congressional districts, as well as the senatorial race, learned that "the grassroots efforts were far more valuable than any money spent on ads and campaigns" (Freedman and Carter 2001, 201). This single-issue strategy differs from the multiple-issue strategies of other interest groups such as labor unions (see Chapter 11) or the Christian Coalition (see Chapter 10).

Often, interest groups collide in the face of the same constituency. Gun ownership and NRA membership are high in states such as West Virginia, Pennsylvania, Michigan, and Washington. And many NRA members work for unions but support gun rights. In Hershey, Pennsylvania, Charlton Heston attracted a large crowd of five thousand such members. At one rally in Michigan, Heston said, "Find every gun owner and union member and get them out to the polls on November 7. We will elect leaders who uphold our rights with Bush" (McClellan 2000). The NRA's efforts challenged the unity of the AFL-CIO's union members, and labor countered the NRA's "Defend your guns, defeat Al Gore" message with a message of its own: "Al Gore doesn't want to take your gun away, but George Bush wants to take away your union" (Eilperin and Edsall 2000). Steve Rosenthal, the AFL-CIO's political director, later observed that "in the guns vs. unions fight, we won overwhelmingly. There was no struggle over these members. From the reports we've heard, this election wasn't about the NRA. It was about issues like health care and Social Security" (Macpherson 2000). Gun control interest group leaders would tend to agree with Rosenthal, pointing to Al Gore's victories in Pennsylvania and Michigan, as well as the defeat of four of the six NRA-backed senatorial candidates: Spencer Abraham (Michigan), John Ashcroft (Missouri), Bill McCullom (Florida), and Rod Gramms (Minnesota).

In the 2002 midterm election, the NRA tried to focus more on the person-to-person efforts and less on advertising campaigns. It kicked off its efforts with a grassroots workshop in conjunction with its annual meeting in early 2002. It also conducted more than sixty grassroots election workshops in more than thirty different states, training five thousand NRA members to conduct election-related activities in their communities (NRA 2002b). During the 2002 election cycle, the NRA had election volunteer coordinators in over three hundred congressional districts, working with local pro-gun organizations in handing out literature, making phone calls, and conducting get-out-the-vote drives (NRA 2002a).

According to an NRA press release, the NRA-endorsed candidates won almost 94 percent of the 270 federal races in which a candidate was endorsed, for a net gain of thirteen pro-gun U.S. representatives and two senators. NRA's efforts were not just felt at the federal level, but also in state and local elections; in the nearly 2,300 election races in which it participated, the NRA enjoyed an 85 percent success rate (NRA 2002c).

In 2002, the NRA's PAC, the Political Victory Fund, spent $1.3 million on independent expenditure advertisements on television and radio stations in targeted markets. The PAC also contributed $1.2 million to federal candidates — 18 percent to Democrats and 88 percent to Republicans (FEC data, as of December 8, 2003). Targeted campaigns like the one conducted in the Arkansas senatorial race included radio and television advertisements, phone banks, a public rally with NRA President Charlton Heston, and four mailings targeting sixty thousand people on a list developed by the Republican Party from a hunting and fishing licensee listing (Barth and Parry 2003).

The 2004 Election. For the 2004 election, the NRA set up a news operation, NRANews.com, with a $1 million investment geared at providing the NRA with a platform for discussing political candidates and issues throughout the election cycle. Operating an online and satellite radio news service is the NRA's way around portions of the BCRA. The news programming includes "updates on national political races, Grassroots Elections Workshops, and other grass-roots-related activities" (NRA-ILA 2004). By August 1, 2004, the NRA had raised almost $8 million in hard money for its PAC, but it contributed only about $600,000 to federal candidates, the clear majority of whom were Republican. The NRA has $7.1 million on hand as it enters the heat of the election season that it can use for hard money advertisements, get-out-the-vote efforts, and other election-related activities.

Americans for Job Security

Americans for Job Security has been involved in politics in an obscure way since 1998. It does not have a Web site, and it does not discuss its donors or members. Because it does not file as a political committee, it is able to avoid public scrutiny. Its purpose is to conduct large-scale broadcast advertising campaigns in support of targeted candidates.

The 2000 and 2002 Election Cycles. The 2000 election cycle was a watershed year for a certain segment of interest groups that behave like political action committees but have one crucial advantage over these groups: they act in secret. Trade associations are not required to file disclosure reports with the FEC, because they do not make direct contributions to political parties and candidates—actions that would require them to disclose their donors and register as a PAC. These groups also are not required to file disclosure reports with the IRS, because they are formed under provisions of the tax code that are outside the reach of current disclosure laws for 527 political organizations. Americans for Job Security is such a group, and it is likely that there will be more of them in the future.

The Americans for Job Security trade organization was created in 1997, after a larger coalition of Republican business groups and trade associations, the "Coalition," disbanded. The "Coalition" fought against organized labor in the 1996 campaign, and Americans for Job Security promised to be active in future elections with issue advocacy campaigns. Investigative journalists have been able to discover that the AJS received $1 million in seed money from the American Insurance Association (AIA) and was founded by AIA President Robert Vagley. The AJS later received additional funds from the AIA, the American Forest and Paper Association, and Microsoft—but a comprehensive list of additional donors is not public record.

AJS President Michael Dubke has said, "We don't discuss our members. The reason is we find that in other groups that have attempted to do what we're doing, that their membership becomes the issue rather than the issue they're trying to advocate. We find that sticking to a strict mantra of not discussing our members allows our issue to come to the forefront" (Kotok and Thompson 2000, 31). But its refusal to discuss membership has not served to deflect questions about the sources of AJS funding. The group reportedly spent between $8 and $10 million in 2000, and at least $1.5 million in 2002, but it did not make its plans public, maintain a Web site, issue press releases, or adopt any other tool that would help people understand what the group stood for and why it was targeting certain candidates in either election cycle. For example, the group targeted a sitting judge on a state supreme court, three U.S. Senate incumbents, and a presidential candidate in 2000, and a handful of state legislative offices scattered nationwide in both the 2000 and 2002 elections. The only commonality in each of the advertising campaigns was that all the ads were designed to help the Republican candidate.

The target of the 2000 campaign against a sitting state supreme court judge was Alice Robie Resnick, a twelve-year veteran of the Ohio Supreme Court. In recent years, Resnick had made a series of decisions stinging business interests. The radio ad that the AJS ran read, "I thought Ohio was on the leading edge of reining in outrageous lawsuits . . . until Alice Resnick fixed it for the trial lawyers and overturned real reforms proposed by the governor and the legislature" (Hunt 2000). The advertisement, only one of many run against Resnick, got her attention: "My opponent is insignificant," Judge Resnick told a reporter. "It's the special-interest groups I'm running against" (Hunt 2000).

The greatest headlines in 2000 were made in Michigan, where the AJS ran a series of advertisements defending vulnerable first-term Republican senatorial incumbent Spencer Abraham. An anti-immigration group called FAIR—Federation for American Immigration Reform—heavily targeted Abraham. FAIR, like the AJS, is a stealth group that does not reveal its donors and conducts primarily issue advertising campaigns. One advertisement in FAIR's $700,000 campaign against Abraham suggested that he was " 'trying to make it easy' for 'terrorists' to enter the country" and pictured Abraham next to Osama bin Laden, the terrorist responsible for the worst acts of terrorism in history (Isikoff 2000). The AJS responded to FAIR's strike on Abraham. According to the *Washington Post*, Sen. Trent Lott, R-MS, "pressured" high-tech companies such as Microsoft, Intel, and Motorola to fund AJS's defense of Abraham, and Lott even gave the companies AJS's contact information for ready donations (Allen 2000). Abraham's own campaign asked companies to refrain from donating directly to his campaign coffers and to act independently in his defense (Isikoff 2000). Often, certain campaign messages—such as the hard-hitting response to FAIR—are better done by an interest group than by a candidate.

According to Campaign Media Analysis Group, Americans for Job Security spent $2,475,393 in 2000 on television advertisements supporting presidential candidate George W. Bush and multiple Republicans in hotly contested U.S. Senate races such as those in Michigan and Washington. Among all interest groups, the AJS ranked third in spending on the presidential race and fifth on its Senate advertising budget (Brennan Center for Justice 2000).

In 2002 the AJS spent at least $1.5 million on issue advertisements targeting candidates during the election cycle—the third highest expenditure of any interest group in the country (Wisconsin Advertising Project 2002). One such candidate, Democratic senator Mary L. Landrieu of Louisiana, who was running to protect her seat, was targeted with an advertising campaign in the final week before her runoff election against Republican Suzanne H. Terrell (Alpert 2002).

Apparently, Americans for Job Security did not conduct get-out-the-vote efforts, phone banks, or extensive voter mobilization efforts in either the 2000 or 2002 election cycles. Its campaigns were primarily broadcast ones, targeting candidates at all levels—judicial, state legislative, congressional, and presidential. It is difficult to gauge the impact of Americans for Job Security on any given issue, primarily because it did not direct its efforts toward any single issue. It ran advertisements on river dams, education, gas prices, drug plans, term limits, and taxes. No other group addressed such an array of topics—without much congruence between message content from race to race. Each message uniquely targeted a particular candidate's record or agenda.

If any of the companies that have funded Americans for Job Security had run many of these advertisements in their own names, public reaction to the negative advertising might have hurt their corporate image. In fact, according to AJS President Dubke in 2002, the American Insurance Association stopped funding the AJS so that the organization could not be labeled an insurance industry front group (Alpert 2002).

The 2004 Election. The media have begun to scrutinize trade associations such as the AJS and other types of nonprofit organizations that do not disclose their activities to the IRS or FEC. Opponents of the Bipartisan Campaign Reform Act argue that the existence of these types of organizations is a failing of the current regulatory structure. Proponents of the laws argue that the BCRA was not intended to address these types of political groups, but was intended to break the nexus between politicians and deep-pocketed special interests. Proponents also believe that trade associations and other nondisclosing politically active groups are the next frontier for reform.

In the 2004 presidential primaries, Americans for Job Security targeted one of the Democratic presidential candidates, Sen. John Edwards. Breaking with tradition, AJS ran a newspaper advertisement in Edwards's home state of North Carolina targeting him for his expensive Washington, D.C., home. The AJS also ran a broadcast advertisement with the same message (Associated Press 2003). In late August 2004, the AJS began running advertisements supporting Republican candidates in Alaska, Colorado, Oklahoma, North Carolina, and South Carolina. News reports indicate that the AJS has already spent more than $600,000 in North Carolina and $700,000 in South Carolina alone. This group is choosing to run its advertisements right up to the sixty-day pre-general election window—that is, before any ad run in support of federal candidates must be funded by limited and disclosed donations (Christensen 2004; Robertson 2004).

National Association for the Advancement of Colored People

Established in 1910, the NAACP is a civil rights group that encourages political, social, economic, and educational equality for minorities. It is a vast network of more than 2,200 state and local affiliates, with a membership of 500,000 nationwide. In August 2000, just three months before the election, the NAACP created two separate advocacy organizations to carry the NAACP into the twenty-first century of partisan campaign and election activity. The National Voter Fund, an advocacy organization, and the Americans for Equality, a soft money segregated fund of the National Voter Fund, were created to, for the first time, run issue advocacy campaigns and support candidates on behalf of the NAACP, as well as to ramp up the NAACP's voter mobilization and registration efforts (NAACP 2000). NAACP Chairman Julian Bond defended the NAACP's choice to become more politically active in election-related activities: "We're in an atmosphere where other groups, including some hostile to justice and equality, use these tools. We want to put our oar in the water" (Mintz 2000).

Heather Booth, director of the National Voter Fund, reported that the two new wings of the NAACP spent $11 million in the 2000 election cycle to boost black voter registration and to mobilize voters to vote on election day (Booth 2000). The NAACP was very precise with its targeting, selecting those areas where the minority vote would have the greatest electoral impact. The National Voter Fund attempted to contact repeatedly particular African American voters in these key battleground regions and gave special attention to infrequent voters. Eighty field organizers were placed in Arkansas, Florida, Georgia, Illinois, Kentucky, Michigan, Missouri, New Jersey, New York, Ohio, Pennsylvania, Wisconsin, and Virginia. More than eight thousand volunteers knocked on an average of forty thousand doors in each city within these thirteen states. Canvassing and literature drops were conducted in targeted states at a cost of $2 million. Seven million flyers and 400,000 posters or banners were provided, as well as seven separate mailers on topics such as hate crimes, education, racial profiling, and voting. Scholars who have examined different approaches to voter mobilization have found that personal contact is far more effective in bringing voters to the polls than other communication techniques (Gerber, Green, and Nickerson 2001).

A political data-entry firm, Voter Datalink Systems, amassed a registry of 3.8 million African Americans in thirteen states, including major cities in forty congressional districts, whom the National Voter Fund intended to contact personally between July and election day. The fund eventually made seven separate phone calls to over one million minority households at a cost of an additional $2 million.

All of this activity was promoted by multiple organizations and subsidized by individual donors promoting civil rights. Donors such as the AFL-CIO, AFSCME, music producer Quincy Jones, the Congressional Black Caucus, and actress Jane Fonda's new political organization, Pro-Choice Vote, all contributed to Americans for Equality, according to IRS records. In the end, reported contributions to Americans for Equality totaled $263,221 (IRS 2000). The National Voter Fund's $11 million primarily came from a single donor, whose name was not made public.

According to Booth, a million more African Americans voted in 2000 than in 1996, in part because of the NAACP's efforts. The NAACP also touted an additional 207,129 newly registered minority voters. Booth pointed out that the NAACP's efforts in targeted states tipped the scales in California, Michigan, Missouri, New Jersey, and New York at the House, Senate, and presidential levels. In New York, for example, the 2000 African American turnout was 22 percent higher than the 1996 turnout; Florida's turnout increased by 50 percent; and Missouri's increased by an astounding 140 percent (Booth 2000).

In 2002 the NAACP continued to focus on voter turnout among minority populations. Forty-two full-time staffers worked in twenty-one states to add nearly a half-million new voters to the registration rolls (NAACP 2002). According to IRS records, the Americans for Equality did not spend or raise any money in 2002 and raised very little in the first portion of 2003.

Conclusion

Interest groups approach federal elections with different goals and different resources. Groups choose their strategies and tactics based on these goals and resources, and on federal regulations that limit or ban the use of some of those resources. The FECA channeled most interest group electoral activity through PACs. Over time, however, new avenues for group involvement opened, including soft money and issue advocacy. As a result, interest groups in 2000 were less constrained in the use of their resources than ever before, and many chose multiple tactics to try to maximize their impact on election outcomes. The result was a greater diversity in group involvement and strategies in congressional and presidential elections.

The case studies in this chapter demonstrate this diversity. Three of the groups possess large, loyal national memberships. The AFL-CIO is typical of most unions in that its members align themselves with these organizations because of economic motives, primarily the quest for higher pay and decent working conditions. The NRA and NAACP are typical of most ideological and identity groups in that their memberships' loyalties derive from specific identities, issues, and broad-based beliefs about the role of government in society. These three groups have focused much of their electoral efforts on voter mobilization and communications targeting their large memberships. Although each spent money on mass communications directed to the general public, the groups described their membership mobilization and communications efforts as their most important contribution to the 2000 elections. This finding agrees with political science research that suggests that personal contact is the best way to stimulate turnout (Gerber and Green 2000).

Americans for Job Security is typical of an organization created and financed by business interests in that it had no broad-based membership it could mobilize in recent elections. As a result, it focused most of its efforts on mass communications, aiming to demobilize portions of the electorate and to change the vote of those who did turn out. AJS is a group, but it is also a tool of the business community. Companies have PACs and in the past have given parties soft money, but they also can fund groups that air primarily negative issue advertising. In this way, companies receive the benefits of the advertising without having to suffer any backlash that affects their corporate image.

With the passage of the Bipartisan Campaign Reform Act, it is likely that groups will focus even more on grassroots mobilization in future elections. But issue ads will still air—and they may air earlier to avoid the disclosure required by the BCRA for ads run thirty days prior to primaries and sixty days prior to the general election. The 2004 election will therefore be an interesting one to study and note the ways in which groups change their strategies in elections as they continue to learn, target segments of the population, and act in accordance with new laws.

Notes

1. The implicit assumption underlying the data is that the motives of individual contributors are indistinguishable from the motives underlying contributions given by organizations under the individuals' control. In many cases, this is a reasonable assumption because organizations try to maximize their impact on the political landscape. In other cases, however, the political interests of organizations and the individuals associated with them differ significantly—that is, individual contributions probably better express the donor's partisan or ideological beliefs, whereas organizational donations better reflect another set of institutional goals.
2. Presidential candidate John McCain paid for a "Catholic Voter Alert" recorded phone message in Michigan. The message led listeners to believe that a Catholic network had concerns about Republican presidential candidate George W. Bush's ties with anti-Catholics. Nowhere in the message did it state that McCain's campaign paid for the call. Senator McCain later admitted that he should not have allowed his campaign to conduct the misleading phone campaign under the guise of the "Catholic Voter Alert."
3. A Section 527 organization is a political organization that files with the Internal Revenue Service but does not register with the Federal Election Commission as a PAC. Therefore, it does not have to abide by the contribution limitations of PACs and can receive unlimited donations from corporate and labor sources, as well as individuals. It cannot, however, donate these funds to federal candidates or national parties and must disclose these funds and how they are spent to the IRS.

References

Allen, Mike. 2000. "The Secret Money Chase." *Newsweek,* June 5, 23.

Alpert, Bruce. 2002. "Latest Ads Criticize Landrieu on Taxes, Unions; Groups Won't Say Who's Footing the Bill." *Times-Picayune,* December 4.

American Federation of Labor–Congress of Industrial Organizations (AFL-CIO). 2000a. "In the 'Cliffhanger' Presidential Election, Massive Mobilization and High Turnout by Union Members Made the Difference in Key States." Press release, November 8.

———. 2000b. "Labor 2000: Unprecedented Grassroots Power." Press release, November 8.

———. 2000c. "Union Members' Presidential and U.S. House Votes." Post election survey, November 8.

———. 2000d. "Unions Reached Their Members." Post election survey, November 8.

———. 2002. "The 2002 Union Vote, Survey by Peter D. Hart Research for the AFL-CIO Among 1,020 Voting Union Members, conducted November 5, 2002." Press release, November 6. http://www.aflcio.org/mediacenter/prsptm/pr1106a2002.cfm.

———. 2003. "Forging a Greater Political Voice for Working Families." Press release, February 25. http://www.aflcio.org/aboutaflcio/ecouncil/ec02252003.cfm.

———. n.d. "The Union Difference: Political Program for Working Families." Press release. http://www.aflcio.org/issuespolitics/politics/fs_0202.cfm.

Associated Press. 2002. "Groups Involved in 2002 Elections." August 31.

———. 2003. "GOP Group Launches Anti-Edwards Campaign." May 14.

Bailey, Eric. 2000. "Foot Soldiers Fight to Boost Turnout." *Los Angeles Times,* October 29, 1.

Baker, Anna Nibley, and David B. Magleby. 2002. "Interest Groups in the 2000 Congressional Elections." In *The Other Campaign: Soft Money and Issue Advocacy in the 2000 Congressional Elections,* edited by David B. Magleby. Lanham, MD: Rowman and Littlefield.

Barth, Jay, and Jeanine Parry. 2003. *The Last Hurrah? Soft Money and Issue Advocacy in the 2002 Congressional Elections,* edited by David B. Magleby and J. Quin Monson. Provo, UT: Center for the Study of Elections and Democracy, Brigham Young University.

Beck, Deborah, Paul Taylor, Jeffrey Stanger, and Douglas Rivlin. 1997. "Issue Advocacy Advertising during the 1996 Campaign." Annenberg Public Policy Center of the University of Pennsylvania. http://www.appcpenn.org/issueads/index.html.

Biersack, Robert, Paul S. Herrnson, and Clyde Wilcox , eds. 1994. *Risky Business? PAC Decisionmaking in Congressional Elections.* Armonk, NY: M. E. Sharpe.

Booth, Heather. 2000. "Seminar V—Financing Nonprofit Advocacy." Nonprofit Advocacy and the Policy Process Series, Urban Institute, December 8. http://www.urban.org/advocacyresearch/heather%20booth.html.

Brennan Center for Justice. 2000. "2000 Presidential Race First in Modern History Where Political Parties Spend More on TV Ads than Candidates." Press release, December 11.

Christensen, Rob. 2004. "Bowles Says GOP Planning Ad Blitz." *News Observer* (Raleigh, NC), August 19.

Cillizza, Chris. 2003. "Soros, Labor Pooling Efforts." *Roll Call,* September 18.

Corrado, Anthony. 1997. "Money and Politics: A History of Federal Campaign Finance Law." In *Campaign Finance Reform: A Sourcebook,* edited by Anthony Corrado, Thomas E. Mann, Daniel R. Ortiz, Trevor Potter, and Frank J. Sorauf. Washington, DC: Brookings.

Dart, Bob. 2003. "Anti-Bush Forces Scope Out Battlefields." *Toronto Star,* October 7.

Eilperin, Juliet, and Thomas B. Edsall. 2000. "For Democrats, Gun Issue Is Losing Its Fire." *Washington Post,* October 20, A1.

Eismeier, Theodore J., and Philip H. Pollock III. 1984. "Political Action Committees: Varieties of Organization and Strategy." In *Money and Politics in the United States,* edited by Michael J. Malbin. Chatham, NJ: Chatham House Publishers.

Francia, Peter L. 2000. "Awakening the Sleeping Giant: The Renaissance of Organized Labor in American Politics." Ph.D. diss., Department of Government and Politics, University of Maryland, College Park.

Freedman, Eric, and Sue Carter. 2001. "The 2000 Michigan Eighth Congressional District Race." In *Election Advocacy: Soft Money and Issue Advocacy in the 2000 Congressional Elections*, edited by David B. Magleby. Provo, UT: Center for the Study of Elections and Democracy, Brigham Young University Press.

Galvin, Kevin. 2000. "Political Ground War: Close Up." *Seattle Times*, October 24, A3.

Gerber, Alan S., and Donald P. Green. 2000. "The Effects of Personal Canvassing, Telephone Calls, and Direct Mail on Voter Turnout: A Field Experiment." *American Political Science Review* 94: 653–676.

Gerber, Alan S., Donald P. Green, and David Nickerson. 2001. "Testing for Publication Bias in Political Science." *Political Analysis* 9:385–392.

Gerber, Robin. 1999. "Building to Win, Building to Last: AFL-CIO Takes on the Republican Congress." In *After the Revolution: PACs, Lobbies, and the Republican Congress*, edited by Robert Biersack, Paul S. Herrnson, and Clyde Wilcox. New York: Allyn and Bacon.

Greenhouse, Steven. 2003. "Labor Group on 2004 Vote Suffers Split." *New York Times*, May 24.

Gutsche, Robert, Jr. 2003. "Dean's Efforts Click with the Internet Generation." *South Florida Sun-Sentinel*, October 7.

Herrnson, Paul S. 2000. *Congressional Elections: Campaigning at Home and in Washington*. Washington, DC: CQ Press.

———. 2001. *Playing Hardball: Campaigning for the U.S. Congress*. Upper Saddle River, NJ: Prentice Hall.

Herrnson, Paul S., and Diana Dwyre. 1997. "Party Issue Advocacy Campaigns: Setting the Table and Forcing It Down Their Throats." Paper presented at Conference on Party Leadership and Grassroots Politics, Ray C. Bliss Institute of Politics, University of Akron, Akron OH, September 10–11.

Hunt, Spencer. 2000. "Business, GOP Work to Book Resnick." *Columbus Enquirer*, June 25. http://enquirer.com/editions/2000/06/25/loc_business_gop_work_to.html.

Internal Revenue Service (IRS). 2000. "Data from the Third Quarter, Pre-election and Post Election 8872 Reports for the Americans for Equality." http://eforms.irs.gov.

Isikoff, Michael. 2000. "The Secret Money Chase." *Newsweek*, June 5, 23.

Jackson, Brooks. 1988. *Honest Graft: Money and the American Political Process*. New York: Knopf.

Jacobson, Gary C. 1999. "The Effect of the AFL-CIO's 'Voter Education' Campaign on the 1996 House Elections." *Journal of Politics* 61:185–194 (February 1999).

Knowles, Francine. 2003. "AFL-CIO Planning Big Effort to Increase Voter Turnout." *Chicago Sun-Times*, August 6.

Kotok, C. David, and Jake Thompson. 2000. "Political Ad's Donors Are Kept Secret." *Omaha World-Herald*, October 27, 31.

Krasno, Jonathan, and Daniel Seltz. 2000. "Buying Time." Brennan Center for Justice, New York.

Macpherson, Karen. 2000. "NRA's Election Spending Has Mixed Results." *Pittsburgh Post-Gazette*, November 10, A13.

Magleby, David, ed. 2000. *Election Advocacy: Soft Money and Issue Advocacy in the 2000 Congressional Elections*. Provo, UT: Brigham Young University.

McClellan. Theresa D. 2000. "Heston Declares War on Gore." Chronicle News Service, October 18. http://www.muy.mlive.com/news/index.ssf?/news/stories/20001018 mheston090.frm.

Mintz, John. 2000. "NAACP Affiliate's Ads Attack GOP Hopefuls." *Washington Post*, September 22, A16.

National Association for the Advancement of Colored People (NAACP). 2000. "NAACP National Voter Fund Launches Unprecedented Voter Education Initiative." Press release, September 21.

————. 2002. "NAACP Voter Empowerment Program 2002 Year End Report." http://www.naacp.org/work/voter/annualreport1-131.pdf.

National Rifle Association (NRA). 2000a. "Election Day 2002—Less than Two Weeks Away." Press release, October 29.

————. 2002b. "Make Plans to Attend NRA-ILA Grassroots Workshop in Reno." Press release, March 15.

————. 2002c. "You Did It! NRA and Gun Owners Enjoy Tremendous Success at Polls." Press release, November 10.

National Rifle Association–Institute for Legislative Action (NRA-ILA). 2004. "National Rifle Association Launches Live News Web Site," April 17. www.nraila.org/currentlegislation/read.aspx?ID=1084.

Patterson, Kelly D. 1999. "Political Firepower: The National Rifle Association." In *After the Revolution: PACs, Lobbies, and the Republican Congress,* edited by Robert Biersack, Paul S. Herrnson, and Clyde Wilcox. Needham Heights, MA: Allyn and Bacon.

Potter, Trevor. 1997. "Issue Advocacy and Express Advocacy." In *Campaign Finance Reform: A Sourcebook,* edited by Anthony Corrado, Thomas E. Mann, Daniel R. Ortiz, Trevor Potter, and Frank J. Sorauf. Washington, DC: Brookings.

Robertson, Gary D. 2004. "National GOP Group Plans Ads, Bowles Seeks Third-Party Deal Again." Associated Press, August 18.

Rozell, Mark J., and Clyde Wilcox. 1999. *Interest Groups in American Campaigns: The New Face of Electioneering.* Washington, DC: CQ Press.

Sabato, Larry J. 1984. *PAC Power: Inside the World of Political Action Committees.* New York: Norton.

Slass, Lorie, Erika Falk, Natalie Gridina, and Nicole D. Porter. 2001. "Issue Advertising in the 1999–2000 Election Cycle." Annenberg Public Policy Center of the University of Pennsylvania. http://www.appcpenn.org/issueads/index.html.

Sorauf, Frank J. 1992. *Inside Campaign Finance: Myths and Realities.* New Haven, CT: Yale University Press.

Star Tribune (Minneapolis). 2000, "Airwaves Buzzing as the Vote on China Trade Still too Close to Call." May 22, A1.

Stern, Philip. 1992. *Still the Best Congress Money Can Buy.* New York: Pantheon.

Sweeney, John. 2000. AFL-CIO Press Briefing, November 8.

Wilcox, Clyde. 1989. "Organizational Variables and the Contribution Behavior of Large PACs: A Longitudinal Analysis." *Political Behavior* 11:157–173.

————. 1994. "Coping with Increasing Business Influence: The AFL-CIO's Committee on Political Education." In *Risky Business? PAC Decisionmaking in Congressional Elections,* edited by Robert Biersack, Paul S. Herrnson, and Clyde Wilcox. New York: M. E. Sharpe.

Wilcox, Clyde, Mark J. Rozell, Michael J. Malbin, and Richard Skinner. 2001. "Interest Group Campaign Adaptations in the Elections of 2000." Paper presented at the annual meeting of the Southern Political Science Association, Atlanta.

Willis, Derek, and Aron Pilhofer. 2003. "Silent Partners: How Political Non-profits Work the System." Center for Public Integrity, September 25. http://www.publicintegrity.org/527/report.aspx?aid=7.

Wisconsin Advertising Project. 2002. "One Billion Dollars Spent on Political Television Advertising in 2002 Midterm Election." Press release, December 5.

4. Interest Groups in Congressional Elections

Richard J. Semiatin and Mark J. Rozell

From the mid-1990s to 2002, issue advocacy played a critical role in the outcomes of competitive congressional elections. These efforts allowed groups to define campaign issues and to frame the debates in close races (see Rozell and Wilcox 1999; Magleby 2001). But with passage of the Bipartisan Campaign Reform Act of 2002 (BCRA) and the Supreme Court's decision in *McConnell v. FEC* (540 U.S. ___ [2003]) which upholds it, the activities of candidates, parties, and interest groups are being significantly altered. The combined effect of the BCRA and the Court ruling is that interest groups can no longer spend unlimited sums of unregulated money in campaigns.

Interest groups nevertheless remain important players in many congressional races. They pursue electoral strategies aimed at persuading their members and other voters to support (or not to support) a particular candidate. In doing so, they may spend money to communicate an endorsement to their members, or they may advertise on television or the radio. Or they may distribute voters' guides in churches or outside welfare offices, or mail voters' guides to their members along with a letter urging them to distribute the guides.

Such efforts are far more complicated than simply giving money to the candidate or a political party. A political action committee (PAC) contribution to a campaign usually consists of writing a check and attending a breakfast or a fundraising dinner. In the 2002 election cycle, PAC contributions accounted for about one-third of the funds raised by House incumbents and one-fifth of the money raised by their Senate counterparts.

By contrast, communicating with members and other voters requires planning, production, and careful research. Before the 2004 election cycle, interest groups spent unprecedented amounts of unregulated—sometimes referred to as "soft" or "outside" money—on get-out-the-vote (GOTV) activities and issue advocacy ads. They also made large soft money contributions to political parties (Herrnson 2004). After enactment of the BCRA in 2002, interest groups could no longer make soft money contributions to the political parties' national organizations. Moreover, as noted in Chapter 2, the new law prohibits interest groups from using soft money to finance issue advocacy ads during the thirty-day blackout period that precedes primaries and the sixty-day blackout period that precedes general elections. Instead, groups wishing to air television or radio ads during the closing days of these contests must make independent expenditures. There is no limit on the amount a group can spend on independent expenditure ads. However, these ads must be financed solely with hard money (federally regulated campaign contributions). Unlike issue advocacy ads, independent expenditures can expressly advocate the election or defeat of a candidate for federal office.

This chapter describes and analyzes the various strategies and tactics of interest groups in congressional elections. We pay special attention to recent developments in interest group activities, particularly during the 2000 and 2002 election cycles. Our research concludes with an examination of the implications of the BCRA for the 2004 elections.

Interest Group Goals

Interest groups, like political parties, set goals they wish to achieve in both the policymaking arena and in their campaign strategy. For example, during the 2000 congressional elections the National Abortion and Reproductive Rights Action League (NARAL) focused on states where pro-choice women were running for the Senate. In the state of Washington, former Democratic House member Maria Cantwell, a Democrat, was challenging the incumbent senator, Republican Slade Gorton. To implement its pro-choice strategy in the campaign, NARAL used tactics that included contacting 132,000 pro-choice voters by means of about three phone calls and three pieces of mail that described Gorton's anti-choice voting record. Interest groups can, then, play a crucial role in targeting key supporters and ultimately may be able to affect the outcome of a closely contested race. Indeed, Cantwell won this Senate race by slightly more than 2,000 votes out of the 2.4 million cast, demonstrating that large and small efforts alike by interest groups can make a difference in victory or defeat. Nevertheless, interest group victories in one election may be followed by failures in another. NARAL lost most of the congressional elections it targeted in 2002.

Campaign Communications

Interest groups implemented more aggressive media strategies in the last several election cycles — to the point that many advocacy commercials were hard to distinguish from those launched by the candidates' campaigns themselves. Interest groups have become a powerful third voice in election campaigns, directing voters to their issues, though not necessarily to the ones the candidates want to accentuate.

One example in 2000 was the race for the Sixth Congressional District in northern Kentucky. Health care interest groups dominated the agenda in the contest between former House member Scotty Baesler, a Democrat, and his Republican opponent, freshman representative Ernest Fletcher, a physician. Outside groups outspent the candidates in what became the state's most expensive House race. Sounding like a bystander, Baesler observed that "the independent groups are having it out right here . . . and, no question, the No.1 fight is the insurance companies versus the doctors" (Clines 2000).

The issue, better known as the Patients' Bill of Rights, was whether patients should be restricted in the right to sue their health maintenance organizations (HMOs). Republicans favored such a restriction; Democrats and trial attorneys were against it. Baesler estimated that at least half of the ads that ran against him were about health care. Most of those ads were run by physicians' groups such as the PAC of the American Medical Association. Meanwhile, the ads had a ripple effect on candidates, who then had to advertise more on the airwaves to manage their own messages. In this district, where past congressional races had cost less than $1 million, campaign expenditures ran about $6 million in 2000, including candidate, party, and interest group spending (Clines 2000).

Issue Advocacy Communications

Before the BCRA went into effect for the 2004 election cycle, interest groups found it more time- and cost-effective to raise soft money to engage in issue advocacy instead of raising the hard money required for independent expenditures. In issue advocacy, a group had only to avoid overtly endorsing a candidate with the words "vote for" or "vote against." Thus the inability to explicitly endorse a candidate was only a minor hindrance. As noted in Chapter 2, the BCRA prohibits naming or presenting the likeness of a federal candidate in an interest group–financed electronic media ad aired within thirty days of a primary or sixty days of a general election unless the ad is paid for by regulated or "hard money" expenditures. A result of the Supreme Court's decision in *McConnell v. FEC* to uphold the BCRA's provisions limiting issue advocacy prior to a primary or general election will be curtailment of the communications activities of groups such as NARAL, the Sierra Club, the Chamber of Commerce of the United States, and the National Rifle Association (NRA) during the closing days of these campaigns.

The 2000 senatorial race in Michigan between Democratic House member Debbie Stabenow and the Republican incumbent, Spencer Abraham, is an example of the intensity of issue advocacy. Late in the campaign season, for every Stabenow issue advocacy advertisement by groups such as the American Federation of Labor–Congress of Industrial Organizations (AFL-CIO) and League of Conservation Voters, multiple ads urged constituents to "write Debbie Stabenow" or to "tell Debbie Stabenow" how they felt about her vote in Congress on some issue (Broder 2000). Issue advocacy campaigns were the attractive alternative, because groups could use treasury funds and raise money in very large contributions from their members and from nonmembers to finance the efforts. Now, post-BCRA, candidate-focused interest group communications during the blackout period must be paid for by hard or regulated money, which is raised in increments of a maximum of $5,000 per year from individual donors.

The power of issue advocacy is heightened where dollars can be targeted to the most competitive races. Planned Parenthood, for example, does not have to spend a lot of money in congressional races in noncompetitive districts in Manhattan where the electorate is liberal and Democratic. Thus interest groups make strategic decisions as to where they can maximize the impact of their issues advocacy ads, particularly in an election year in which only a few seats will make the difference between whether Democrats or Republicans have control of the House and Senate. For example, in the 2000 race for the open seat in the Eighth Congressional District of Michigan (vacated by Stabenow), a plethora of interest groups ran issue advocacy campaigns. The two candidates, state senators Dianne Byrum, a Democrat, and Mike Rogers, a Republican, found that their campaign messages were often obscured by the massive labor and antilabor issue advocacy efforts in the presidential and senatorial races in Michigan (including the Stabenow-Abraham race). The following interest groups allied with the Democrats bought ad time in the eighth district: the AFL-CIO, Michigan Democrats (not the state party), EMILY's List, Planned Parenthood, Coalition for the Future of the American Worker, Sierra Club, League of Conservation Voters, Handgun Control, and the National Voter Fund of the National Association for the Advancement of Colored People (NAACP). The total advertising buy was $2,899,185, whereas Byrum spent $561,555 and political parties in the district spent $1,498,200 (Freedman and Carter 2001, 204). Interest groups allied with the GOP— including the Chamber of Commerce of the United States, Business Roundtable, Michigan Chamber of Commerce, Citizens for Better Medicare (CBM), Alliance for Quality Nursing Home Care, Americans for Job Security, and the Committee for Good Common Sense—bought $2,147,115 in advertising time, compared with $294,400 by the candidate and $1,991,735 by the political parties in the district (Freedman and Carter 2001, 204). Although it is not possible to disaggregate the spending aimed at senatorial or presidential races in the district, it is clear that interest groups outspent the candidates and parties combined in the district.

In the 2000 and 2002 elections, when there was no limit on what could be spent independently in any campaign to educate voters, soft money spending exceeded PAC contributions. As noted in Chapter 2, PACs are limited to contributing a maximum of $5,000 in each phase of an election. In the 2002 elections, the national party congressional campaign committees raised over $496 million in soft money contributions (Center for Responsive Politics 2002). These contributions and dollars spent on issue advocacy translated into significant influence in congressional campaigns.

In the 2000 Washington State U.S. Senate race described earlier, the First American Education Project, a coalition comprised of western state Indian tribes, spent over $1 million on advertisements that cast Gorton as a foe of the environment. The ads specifically criticized him for pushing legislation in behalf of a controversial gold mine near a Native American reservation in Okanagan County (Pierce 2000, 2249; http://opensecrets.org/2000elect). Environmental groups, Native Americans, the American Medical Association, and prescription drug manufacturers all worked against Gorton in his reelection bid. This coalition of environmental and medical groups was very effective in maximizing Cantwell's vote total in the Seattle-Tacoma metropolitan area, appealing to socially liberal and economically moderate swing voters.

Endorsements and Internal Communications

Endorsements are another means by which groups seek to influence elections. Most organizations have a formal process for deciding which candidate to endorse. Groups consider the voting records of incumbents, and, for nonincumbents, any voting record in state or local government, answers to the group's questionnaires, and information provided by local activists. Many groups also assess the viability of the candidate, and they withhold their endorsement from candidates who have no chance of winning. For example, EMILY's List, a group that endorses pro-choice Democratic women, will not endorse a candidate who cannot make a viable bid for election—that is, the candidate must either have or be able to raise a substantial amount of money. (Non-endorsement decisions often create hard feelings in candidates who support a group's agenda but cannot get a formal nod of approval because of the perception that they are not electorally viable.) Other groups, such as the AFL-CIO or the NRA, will endorse candidates regardless of their viability, although they will shy away from actually devoting resources to some races. Organizations such as the pro-environment Sierra Club will project an image of bipartisanship by prominently endorsing both Republicans and Democrats. For example, during her reelection bid in 2002 the Sierra Club ran a television advertisement endorsing Sen. Susan Collins, R-ME, for her efforts to prevent drilling in the Arctic National Wildlife Refuge (Ambinder 2002). Nevertheless, because more Democrats than Republicans are environmentalists, most of the group's endorsements go to Democratic candidates.

Until recently, the effectiveness of interest group endorsements and internal communications was probably underestimated. Business groups such as the U.S. Chamber of Commerce have now expanded their internal communications efforts, largely in response to organized labor activities. Using Web sites, e-mail, and faxes, large membership organizations such as the Chamber of Commerce, Sierra Club, and NRA can send their members on a daily or even hourly basis the information members or local chapters need to coordinate political activities at the local level. The NRA's Institute for Legislative Affairs (NRA-ILA), for example, sends out the "NRA-ILA Fax Alert" to its coordinators and grassroots volunteers and also posts the alert on its Web site (http://www.nraila.org). Such tactics help to keep the NRA's national organization in touch with its four million members on a regular basis.

Citizens who belong to multiple groups may receive communications with different campaign messages, and feel conflicting loyalties. For example, in states such as Michigan, Missouri, Pennsylvania, and West Virginia many gun owners are also members of labor unions. The NRA's "Vote Freedom First" campaign has attempted to persuade these potentially conflicted voters to put their loyalty to gun owners' rights over their union interests.

Endorsements may matter most among groups where membership is voluntary, especially when group members share a common position on issues, consider those issues central to their politics, and trust the organizational leadership to evaluate candidates. Ideological organizations are the most likely to meet these criteria—organizations such as the Christian Coalition, the NRA, NARAL, the Sierra Club, and the NAACP. Yet union membership, which is not voluntary in most states, also provides a rational motivation—economic self-interest in this case—to vote for the group's preferred candidate.

Who Were the Big Spenders in 2000 and 2002?

The 2000 and 2002 elections demonstrated the power of interest groups, whose spending had grown substantially since the 1996 national and 1998 midterm elections. The big spenders in the 2000 national races for Republican candidates were the Citizens for Better Medicare ($65 million), NRA ($25 million), U.S. Chamber of Commerce ($15 million), and Business Roundtable ($6 million), yielding a total of $111 million in soft and hard money spending. The big spenders in national races on the Democratic side were the AFL-CIO ($45 million), EMILY's List ($20 million), Planned Parenthood ($14 million), NAACP Voter Fund ($11 million), Sierra Club ($9.5 million), National Education Association (estimated at over $9 million), NARAL ($8 million), Handgun Control ($5 million), and League of Conservation Voters ($4 million), yielding a total of $125.5 million in soft and hard money expenditures (Magleby 2001, 26–27). Thus the biggest spending interest groups weighed in more on the side of Democrats than Republicans. However, the data do not include expenditure figures from the Christian Coalition, a social conservative group that distributed millions of voter guides before the election (Magleby 2001, 26–27).

In the 2002 elections, the United Seniors Association (a pro-privatization group for retirement benefits) led all interest groups in broadcast advertising spending ($9 million), nearly triple that expended by the second-place AFL-CIO ($3.5 million—see Goldstein 2002). From the 2000 to the 2002 elections, issue advocacy spending declined substantially because there was no presidential election in 2002, and because redistricting led to fewer competitive congressional races. According to political scientist Paul S. Herrnson, only 24 percent of the major-party House candidates involved in contested elections won by margins of 20 percentage points or fewer, as opposed to 28 percent in 2000, 35 percent in 1998, and 41 percent in 1992—the last post-redistricting election (Herrnson 2004, 31).

The spending totals for 2000 and 2002 are not disaggregated by presidential, congressional, and state-level races, because much of the money was spent as a coordinated effort to influence voter choices in all federal elections. Some commercials by groups such as Citizens for Better Medicare asked viewers to call "the President and Congress" to advocate a particular point of view. In this way, groups could be more cost-effective in their advertising strategies. Nevertheless, one study reports that groups spent approximately $364 million in the 2000 congressional races alone on issue advocacy, independent expenditures, and internal communications (Magleby 2001, 47). Most of this spending was concentrated in a relatively small number of congressional districts with competitive races. According to Section 527 of the Internal Revenue Code, political organizations that collect and spend money exclusively for issue advocacy purposes do not have to report contributions under $200. Contributions of $200 and more do have to be reported to the Internal Revenue Service (IRS) on a monthly basis by virtue of legislation passed by Congress in July 2000. Some organizations such as the NAACP and Sierra Club that conduct voter registration and GOTV efforts have established "527" groups (Magleby 2001, 7).

The Republican Majority Issues Committee (RMIC), an independent expenditure group formed under the tutelage of House Majority Whip Tom DeLay, R-TX, was one of the first major players as a 527 group. Established as a counterweight to organized labor, the RMIC focused on competitive House races in the Northeast in the 2000 elections. By filing under Section 527, the RMIC was able to refuse to disclose its donors, except those who contributed after July 2000. The RMIC was active in the Eighth Congressional District race in Michigan, which was won by Republican Mike Rogers, and also in the primary defeat of Democrat Michael Forbes of Long Island, a former Republican. Although the RMIC did not raise the anticipated $25 million for the election (it raised less than $10 million), it was able to target twelve to fifteen races in jurisdictions where mostly Republican incumbents were facing close reelection campaigns (Eilperin 2000).

One of the emerging stories from the BCRA decision is whether 527 groups (called stealth PACs by some) are the new interest group players in campaigns for federal offices. Even many of the people who oppose campaign finance reform do support the principle of full disclosure of campaign contributions. For example, in 2002 Republican representative John Doolittle of California introduced such legislation, even though he otherwise opposed contribution limits.

Only in mid-2000 did Congress begin to require 527 groups to disclose their contributions and election spending. In the 2002 election cycle, 527 groups raised $175.4 million for congressional campaigns, or about one-fourth of all soft money raised. Among the major spenders were AFSCME ($17.5 million), IMPAC 2000 ($6.6 million), EMILY'S List ($5.6 million), New American Optimists ($4.3 million), and the Club for Growth ($4.0 million). More than two dozen groups raised at least $1 million each in 2002 (http://opensecrets.org).

Voter Mobilization

One lesson that Republicans learned from Democrats in the 1998 midterm elections was that they had to pay more attention to voter mobilization. In those elections, members of interest groups associated with Democrats—such as labor and minority voters—voted in higher percentages than they had during the midterm election of 1994 when Republicans swept Congress and gained control of the House and Senate for the first time in forty years. Democrats owed their wins in the governor's races in Alabama, Georgia, and South Carolina in 1998 to the large turnout of minorities.

In the 2000 congressional elections, the turnout of minorities, labor, environmentalists, and pro-choice voters was central to the Democratic Party's efforts to win Senate races in states such as Michigan, Missouri, New York, and Washington. Republicans directed their efforts toward Senate races in states where Christian conservatives and pro-life and pro-gun voters could ensure a Republican victory. In particular, they sought to take over two seats held by Democrats in Nevada and Virginia and retain control of the Republican seat held by Rod Gramms of Minnesota.

In the 2002 elections, conservative groups did indeed improve their voter mobilization, and numerous close races favored the GOP in a year in which the party controlled the White House. Social conservative groups, particularly in key races in Georgia, were crucial to the surprisingly favorable results for GOP candidates.

Voter mobilization efforts usually take the form of voter registration drives, direct mail and commercial advertising, phone banks, and transportation to the polls on election day. Traditional Democratic groups, such as labor unions, have focused on voter mobilization longer than Republicans and, in doing so, have learned that internal communications are important. According to an influential conservative group coalition builder, Grover Norquist, "Unions have learned they activate their opponents when they use TV/radio. By using grass roots and mail they mobilize their folks and not their opponents" (Magleby 2001, 46). This approach represents a complete change in strategy from the 1996 election, when unions spent over $30 million on television advertising in key congressional districts, hoping to take back the House for the Democrats (Rozell and Wilcox 1999). That bitter lesson translated into grassroots operations for the 1998, 2000, and 2002 congressional elections. By 2002 total interest group spending on direct advertising in elections amounted to only $20 million, or less than 3 percent of all soft money spending in that cycle (http://opensecrets.org).

Minority Interest Group Efforts

The NAACP National Voter Fund has played an important role in registering and mobilizing African American voters. It has directed much of its effort toward direct voter contact, as well as radio and TV spots, and a 1-800 hotline for voter registration. And it has especially tried to reach occasional voters in the African American community—that is, those registered voters who have voted two or fewer times in the past four election cycles. The group has sponsored a voter registration drive through the nationally popular Tom Joyner morning radio show. It also has employed radio messages from celebrities such as Bill Cosby, Spike Lee, and Michael J. Fox on stations popular with black listeners to enhance turnout in cities such as Chicago, Detroit, and Philadelphia (Dao 2000).

In 2000 the NAACP National Voter Fund was integral to Senate races in New York and Missouri. In New York, preelection polls in the Senate race showed that Democrat and former first lady Hillary Rodham Clinton had a five-to seven-point lead in the days leading up to the election over her opponent, Republican representative Rick Lazio. On election day, Clinton's margin in New York City was huge, which contributed to her 55–43 percent victory, particularly in heavily African American neighborhoods.

The National Voter Fund also conducted a massive GOTV effort in the 2000 Missouri Senate race between the incumbent, Republican John Ashcroft, and his challenger, Democratic governor Mel Carnahan. When Carnahan died in a plane crash in mid-October, his wife, Jean Carnahan, agreed to serve in his place if he was elected posthumously. The fund purchased radio and newspaper advertising, including in African American newspapers, and conducted a door-to-door campaign. Other civil rights organizations joining in those efforts included the Black Caucus PAC and the A. Philip Randolph Institute (Kropf et al. 2001, 83). The African American vote as a percentage of the electorate in the state more than doubled from the 1996 cycle to 2000 (Voter News Service exit polls). In the very close election outcome, the African American vote proved decisive in sending Mrs. Carnahan to the Senate.

The NAACP, in a very innovative tactic, also registers prison inmates to vote—primarily in the South—even though the number is not substantial enough to change any outcomes of congressional or other national races. In Florida, Mississippi, North Carolina, and Tennessee alone, the NAACP has registered about 11,400 prisoners. Overall, the NAACP has attempted jailhouse voter registration in twenty-two states, including those outside the South (Dao 2000).

Labor, Gun Control, and Other Interest Group Efforts

Among interest groups in the United States, the AFL-CIO and its subsidiary organizations are the architects of get-out-the-vote operations. Labor's efforts to organize workers to exercise the franchise are more than a century old. In 2000 the AFL-CIO's GOTV apparatus was so formidable that the Democratic National Committee scaled back its own voter mobilization efforts. Just prior to the 2000 elections, the chairman of the AFL-CIO political committee predicted that unions would have 100,000 campaign workers on the streets on election day to drive retirees to the polls, make phone calls, and distribute leaflets (Dao 2000). These efforts were aimed at getting union members to vote for the Democratic presidential and, often, congressional candidates.

In 2002 the AFL-CIO's massive GOTV effort was especially visible in Iowa, the site of a competitive Senate race and several competitive House races. The AFL-CIO, in coordination with the Iowa Federation of Labor, distributed leaflets that were customized for each congressional candidate (all Democrats) endorsed by labor to most of the state's 135,000 union members. The leaflets were distributed in four of Iowa's five congressional districts where substantial labor support existed. Other member contacts included videos, phone banks, labor meetings for GOTV, and actual GOTV operations. The Iowa Federation spent $250,000 and the national AFL-CIO another $200,000 on these efforts, which helped to reelect Democratic senator Thomas R. Harkin, reelect Democratic House member Leonard Boswell, and almost defeat Republican congressman James Leach (Redlawsk and Sanders 2003).

The multimillion-dollar effort by the NRA's Institute of Legislative Affairs to get voters to the polls was somewhat different than the personal door-to-door or on-site approaches used by the AFL-CIO. The NRA grassroots efforts focused primarily on advertising, direct mail, and phone banks to encourage voters to go to the polls. The NRA, similar to the AFL-CIO, runs its voter mobilization programs in conjunction with its state branches. This approach enables the national, state, and even local chapters to coordinate a voter mobilization strategy that incorporates every major election from the national to the local level.

The battle royale between pro-gun and anti-gun rights activists occurred in 2000 in Kentucky's Sixth Congressional District, where both the NRA and Handgun Control (the largest opponent of the gun rights lobby) met toe-to-toe. The NRA backed the GOP incumbent, Ernest Fletcher, with radio ads featuring NRA President Charlton Heston, television ads, billboards, phone banks, and mailings. Handgun Control, which named Fletcher one of the "Dangerous Dozen," because the group viewed him as an extremist on supporting gun owners' rights, contributed $3,000 in hard money to his Democratic opponent, Scotty Baesler, and also reported independent expenditures of $170,154. Despite the large-scale efforts by Handgun Control to counter the NRA, Fletcher won an overwhelming victory by a margin of eighteen percentage points (Miller and Gross 2001, 187). The magnitude of the victory demonstrated that Fletcher's incumbency and Baesler's own unpopular run for the U.S. Senate in 1998 may have transcended any effort by either interest group.

The issue of health care seemed to permeate the 2000 race for Pennsylvania's Tenth Congressional District in the northeastern corner of the state. Anchored by Scranton and formerly one of the busiest mining areas in the country, the tenth district has one of the nation's largest populations of seniors. Thus issues such as environmental pollution, prescription drugs for seniors, and health maintenance organization (HMO) reform resonated throughout the district. The two candidates, incumbent Republican Don Sherwood and his challenger, Democrat Pat Casey (son of a former governor), had already met in 1998, with Sherwood winning a narrow victory. With its closely contested House race, the tenth district became a prime target for major interest groups in the 2000 election. Both the U.S. Chamber of Commerce and Citizens for Better Medicare weighed in on the side of Don Sherwood, while the AFL-CIO and the Sierra Club supported Pat Casey.

Voter mobilization through ad wars was prominent in the district. An AFL-CIO ad featured a pharmacist who said about seniors, "I know they're skipping medication so they can pay for food." The ad concluded by blaming Sherwood for not supporting a prescription drug benefit for all seniors. By contrast, Citizens for Better Medicare produced an ad that showed an elderly woman named Edith, who said, "I paint, I write and I have my family. And I'm pretty stable with my cancer. I would be struggling very hard if it weren't for medicines." The ad went on to say that Don Sherwood was doing everything he possibly could to bring the cost of medicine down for seniors. The U.S. Chamber of Commerce produced a similar type of ad on prescription drugs (Clymer 2000).

The Sierra Club took another tack, emphasizing in its advertising that "streams and woods" were being polluted; Pat Casey would work to save them, the ad said, but Don Sherwood was against such efforts. The Sierra Club, however, used only cable television for these ads, probably aiming at the higher-income baby boomers living in the district. The Sierra Club employed a similar minimalist strategy in Pennsylvania's Thirteenth Congressional District, using only one issue ad called "strip malls" to point to the spread of urban growth in the district (Kolodny, Suarez, and Kreider 2001, 255). Despite the large-scale efforts of interest groups and political party functionaries and visits from Environmental Protection Agency Director Carol Browner, Pat Casey lost in his second bid to Don Sherwood by a 53–47 percent margin.

The Pennsylvania race showcased one of the more noteworthy developments in interest group politics: the creation of political "front" groups by industries that seek to disguise their electoral activities. The most prominent such group was Citizens for Better Medicare, created in 1999 by the Pharmaceutical Research and Manufacturers of America. CBM was the brainchild of Apco Associates, a public relations firm that understood that running advertisements with the line "paid for by Citizens for Better Medicare" sounded much better than effectively saying "paid for by the big drug companies." A coalition of business and health groups supported CBM, among them the National Association of Manufacturers, U.S. Chamber of Commerce, and Healthcare Leadership Council. The watchdog group Public Citizen reported that some CBM members received significant funding from the pharmaceutical industry (Public Citizen 2000). Ultimately, CBM was a large player in the 2000 elections, spending $50 million on television advertising and more money on House of Representatives races than any other interest group (Brennan Center for Justice 2000; Miller and Miller 2000).

Effects of the BCRA on Interest Group Politics in Congressional Campaigns

The Supreme Court decision *McConnell v. FEC* (2003) that upheld the major provisions of the BCRA will have major implications for organized interest group strength as a third force in congressional elections. The Court's decision to validate the ban on issue advocacy advertising that names a candidate thirty days prior to a primary and sixty days before the general election will affect powerful organized interest groups such as the Sierra Club, National Rifle

Association, and Christian Coalition. These organizations will have to use their PACs, once again, as their primary source for their electronic media advertising efforts during the closing days of the campaign. Because PACs raise money in much smaller increments than in the 1996–2002 era of issue advocacy, it is likely that groups will need to be more strategic, targeting fewer resources in a far less permissive and stronger regulatory environment.

New 527 groups are springing up all over the post-BCRA political landscape. These groups are political organizations that, as defined under the Internal Revenue Code, "operate primarily for the purpose of directly or indirectly accepting contributions or making expenditures . . . to influence the selection, nomination, election or appointment of an individual" (IRS n.d.). Unlike groups such as the Sierra Club or National Rifle Association, 527 political organizations do not lobby, but simply exist to influence the outcomes of elections.

Liberal or progressive 527 groups associated with Democrats have been the most aggressive in raising money. Because Republicans hold a vast edge in raising hard money over Democrats ($402 million to $220 million in 2002), newly formed 527 interest groups are trying to fill the void that leaves Democrats at a distinct disadvantage (Federal Election Commission 2002). Groups such as the Partnership for Working Families, Voices for Working Families, and America Coming Together represent various labor and progressive interests, and they are the new players in the electoral game. According to the nonpartisan Center for Public Integrity, 527 groups associated with the political parties spent nearly $268 million in the 2001–2002 election cycle, with at least $185 million of that money going to Democrats (see Willis and Pilhofer 2004). Noted liberal activist and actress Jane Fonda has given nearly six times more money than any other contributor to 527 groups ($13 million) since August 2000, when these data began to be tracked (Center for Public Integrity 2004). More recently, billionaire George Soros gave the largest single contribution ever to a 527 group—$10 million to America Coming Together in late 2003 (York 2003).

The new interest group system arising from the BCRA involves relatively few donors who can donate millions of dollars. It is hard to differentiate in advance whether that money is spent jointly or separately on congressional and presidential races. However, the growing power of the new and largely exclusive 527 groups means that interest group influence on elections has mutated into a new and effective form.

Conclusion

The 2000 and 2002 congressional elections continued a trend of interest groups employing strategies and tactics that had been used in the past primarily by both political parties and candidates. Interest groups, through issue advocacy, operated much like political parties in that they helped to set the campaign agendas, communicated internally with members, and communicated externally with masses of voters. The BCRA and the Supreme Court decision upholding that law will have a profound effect on the role of groups in the 2004 elections and beyond. Although still very important in elections, interest groups can never attain the same level of electoral influence as the major political parties, which have broader ideological bases of support. The one fundamental difference that will always separate groups from parties is that only parties can nominate and elect candidates to public office. However, interest groups such as the AFL-CIO or the National Federation of Independent Businesses can provide surrogate support to the political parties and candidates by mobilizing large numbers of supporters. They can mobilize voters driven by a single issue (for example, abortion, guns, or the environment), or they can mobilize a demographic group to go to the polls (such as women, African Americans, or conservative Christians).

Interest group communications are now largely the province of smaller and more exclusive 527 interest groups. The characteristics of 527 groups are fewer donors contributing larger sums of money. The effect could be a greater specialization of interests in federal elections, an unintended consequence of the Bipartisan Campaign Reform Act of 2002.

References

Ambinder, Marc J. 2002. "Environmental Politics Are Local," June 24. http://abcnews.com.

Brennan Center for Justice. 2000. "2000 Presidential Race First in Modern History Where Political Parties Spend More on TV Ads than Candidates." Press release, December 11.

Broder, David S. 2000. "In Michigan Ad Campaigns a 'Frightening Finale.'" *Washington Post,* October 23, A12.

Center for Public Integrity. 2004. "Major Individual Donors to 527 Committees." http://publicintegrity.org.

Center for Responsive Politics. 2002. "Where the Money Came From." http://www.opensecrets.org/bigpicture/wherefrom.asp?cycle=2002>.

Clines, Francis X. 2000. "The 2000 Campaign: A Kentucky Race." *New York Times,* October 12, A20.

Clymer, Adam. 2000. "Special-Interests' Ads Saturate a District." *New York Times,* October 21, A8.

Dao, James. 2000. "The 2000 Campaign: The Voters." *New York Times,* November 7, A22.

Eilperin, Juliet. 2000. "Conservatives Take a Page from Labor." *Washington Post,* October 12, A7.

Federal Election Commission. 2002. "Party Fundraising Reaches $1.1 Billion in 2002 Election Cycle." Press release, December 18.

Freedman, Eric, and Sue Carter. 2001. "The 2000 Michigan Eighth Congressional District Race." In *Election Advocacy: Soft Money and Issue Advocacy in the 2000 Congressional Elections,* edited by David B. Magleby. Provo, UT: Center for the Study of Elections and Democracy, Brigham Young University Press. http://www.byu.edu/outside-money/2000general/contents.htm.

Goldstein, Kenneth M. 2002. "Final Report on the 2002 Election by the Wisconsin Advertising Project." December 5.

Herrnson, Paul S. 2004. *Congressional Elections: Campaigning at Home and in Washington.* 4th ed. Washington, DC: CQ Press.

Internal Revenue Service (IRS). n.d. "Tax Information for Political Organizations—Exemption Requirements. http://www.irs.gov/charities/political/article/0,,id=96350,00.html>.

Kolodny, Robin, Sandra Suarez, and Kyle Kreider. 2001. "The 2000 Pennsylvania Thirteenth Congressional District Race." In *Election Advocacy: Soft Money and Issue Advocacy in the 2000 Congressional Elections*, edited by David B. Magleby. Provo, UT: Center for the Study of Elections and Democracy, Brigham Young University. http://www.byu.edu/outsidemoney/2000general/contents.htm.

Kropf, Martha E., Anthony Simones, E. Terrence Jones, Dale Neumann, Allison Hayes, and Maureen Gilbride Mears. 2001. "The 2000 Missouri Senate Race." In *Election Advocacy: Soft Money and Issue Advocacy in the 2000 Congressional Elections*, edited by David B. Magleby. Provo, UT: Center for the Study of Elections and Democracy, Brigham Young University. http://www.byu.edu/outsidemoney/2000general/contents.htm.

Magleby, David B., ed. 2001. "Election Advocacy: Soft Money and Issue Advocacy in the 2000 Congressional Elections." Provo, UT: Center for the Study of Elections and Democracy, Brigham Young University. http://www.byu.edu/outsidemoney/2000general/contents.htm.

Miller, Alan C., and T. Christian Miller. 2000. "Election Was Decisive in Arena of Spending." *Los Angeles Times*, December 8, 8.

Miller, Penny M., and Donald A. Gross. 2001. "The 2000 Kentucky Sixth District Race." In *Election Advocacy: Soft Money and Issue Advocacy in the 2000 Congressional Elections*, edited by David B. Magleby. Provo, UT: Center for the Study of Elections and Democracy, Brigham Young University. http://www.byu.edu/outsidemoney/2000general/contents.htm.

Pierce, Emily. 2000. "Gorton Besieged by Outside Groups." *CQ Weekly*, September 30, 2249.

Public Citizen. 2000. "Citizens for Better Medicare: The Truth behind the Drug Industry's Deception of America's Seniors." June.

Redlawsk, David, and Arthur Sanders. 2003. "The 2002 Iowa House and Senate Elections: The More Things Change . . ." PSonline symposium, July. http://apsanet.org.

Rozell, Mark J., and Clyde Wilcox. 1999. *Interest Groups in American Campaigns: The New Face of Electioneering*. Washington, DC: CQ Press.

Willis, Derek, and Aron Pilhofer. 2004. "Silent Partners: How Political Non-profits Work the System." Center for Public Integrity. http://publicintegrity.org.

York, Byron. 2003. "Democrats Throw the Spirit of Reform out the Window." *The Hill*, November 5.

5. Group Advocacy in the New Hampshire Presidential Primary

Linda L. Fowler, Constantine J. Spiliotes, and Lynn Vavreck

Until recently, interest groups were behind-the-scenes players in election campaigns. Once content to make donations to parties and candidates, groups now intervene directly in the day-to-day operation of campaigns (Rozell and Wilcox 1999; West and Loomis 1999). Through issue ads, groups endeavor to influence campaign agendas and define candidates' images. Through mobilization of their members, groups attempt to shift turnout in a tight race to their favored office seeker. These tactics can raise the price tag of today's election contests, and even drown out the candidates' own messages. More troubling, perhaps, groups' electoral advocacy is exempt from many of the regulations that govern parties and individual candidates, and so they are able to raise and spend unlimited sums with limited disclosure. Thus interest group advocacy undoubtedly plays a role in creating the expensive, negative, and unaccountable election campaigns that American voters find so distasteful.

The Bipartisan Campaign Reform Act of 2002 (BCRA) sought to limit the influence of issue advocacy groups by restricting the ability of these groups to advertise thirty days before a primary election and sixty days before the general election and by subjecting them to more stringent disclosure requirements and contribution limits.[1]

Regulation is not the only means of constraining advocacy groups, however. Equally important are the incentives that motivate their entry into electoral campaigns. Groups spend resources on candidate advocacy when they expect a high rate of return from their investment. Practically speaking, such payoffs occur in *closely fought races with low information and low turnout* when campaign expenditures may change the minds of enough undecided voters to make the difference between a candidate's victory and defeat.

For this reason, issue advocacy groups have become highly visible players in U.S. House and Senate elections where the marginal gains are high. Their efforts in presidential races, however, have tended to be less important because of the higher saliency of such contests to voters and the media, although the activities of groups such as Americans Coming Together and Swift Boat Veterans for Truth during the summer of 2004 may signal a change. The subordination of advocacy groups was particularly evident in the New Hampshire presidential primary. In 2000 groups were active in the Granite State, but very much in the shadow of the candidates' campaigns and the national press coverage; in 2004 they were hardly present at all. Thus the importance of group advocacy appears highly contingent on the political context of a particular election.

The 2000 general elections saw an explosion of interest group activities at all levels of government, from statewide referenda and judicial contests to races for Congress and the presidency. Of the over half-billion dollars devoted to issue advocacy in federal elections on radio and television, fully 68 percent came from groups and the remainder from the political parties.[2] The party money, too, drew largely from groups and wealthy individuals in the form of "soft money" donations, which at that point were not subject to contribution limits. Citizens for Better Medicare, a righteous-sounding group that actually represented the pharmaceutical industry, spent over $65 million on issue ads, followed by two corporate lobbies, the Coalition to Protect America's Health Care with $30 million and the Chamber of Commerce of the United States with $25.5 million (Annenberg Public Policy Center 2001, 4). The American Federation of Labor–Congress of Industrial Organizations (AFL-CIO) weighed in with $21.1 million, and other high-spending groups included the National Rifle Association (NRA), the Business Roundtable, U.S. Term Limits, Planned Parenthood, and the League of Conservation Voters (Annenberg Public Policy Center 2001, 7). Among the most competitive races for the House and Senate in that election cycle, seventeen involved issue advocacy spending by parties and groups that exceeded the candidates' expenditures by a ratio of two to one (Campaign Insider 2001, 2).

In addition to injecting large sums of money into the 2000 election, some groups also helped to set a negative tone for the campaign. During the Republican presidential primary fights in South Carolina and Michigan, for example, the Christian Coalition and other evangelical groups accused George W. Bush's chief rival, Arizona senator John McCain, a POW during the Vietnam War, of neglecting the concerns of veterans. They also funded telephone banks that attacked McCain's commitment to the pro-life agenda and accused him of fathering a black child—a crude distortion of the fact that McCain and his wife had adopted a little girl from India. Citizens for Clean Air ran ads in the California primary challenging McCain's environmental record. Initially anonymous, the group was later identified as two millionaire brothers from Texas named Wyly who actively supported Bush. Another mysterious group, Hands Across New Jersey, charged former Democratic senator Bill Bradley with hypocrisy on campaign finance reform during the New Hampshire primary (see Box 5-1). Although both Bush and Gore benefited from the group attacks on their opponents, they did not have to take responsibility for the ads' distorted content. Moreover, in both cases citizens had no way of identifying the sources of these criticisms and evaluating their validity.

As such ads became widespread, they exerted a substantial effect on the debate over campaign finance reform. Many congressional candidates who supported reform, for example, backed away from spending caps because they saw limits as a kind of unilateral disarmament that would leave them vulnerable to outside groups that might decide to spend millions of dollars attacking them. Other politicians, however, saw the increasingly costly and aggressive participa-

---

Box 5-1 Hands Across New Jersey Television Ad Attacking Democratic
Candidate Bill Bradley in 2000

MAN NO. 1: We need real campaign finance reform, not lip service.

MAN NO. 2: Yeah, Bill Bradley says he's for reforms, yet he's raised millions
from special interests.

WOMAN: Yeah, and even he had to return illegal contributions to a big insurance
company.

*(On screen: Bradley had to return illegal contributions. Source: Federal Election
Commission.)*

MAN NO.1: Bradley even got caught intervening with the Commerce Department
for one of his big-money contributors.

(On screen, newspaper headline: Bradley downplays letter written to help Jersey firm.)

MAN NO.2: Bill Clinton makes the Lincoln bedroom available to contributors,
and Bradley does favors for his big-money friends.

WOMAN: It's all the same, and it's got to stop.

(On screen: Call Bill Bradley, 973-731-2100. Paid for by Hands Across New Jersey)

MAN NO.1: We need to urge people to call Bill Bradley and tell him to support
real campaign finance reform.

Source: "Ad Spotlight," *National Journal,* February 1, 2000. http://nationaljournal.com/
members/adspotlight/2000. Copyright 2004 by National Journal Group Inc. All rights
reserved. Reprinted by permission.

---

tion of groups as an incentive to support campaign finance reform. Sen. Thad
Cochran, R-MS, a longtime opponent of the Senate campaign finance reform
bill, named for its sponsors, Sen. John McCain and Sen. Russell Feingold, D-
WI, eventually embraced it and its modest attempts to regulate issue advocacy
and independent expenditures (Steel and Posner 2001; Willis 2001). After
observing the frenzy of group activity around the country in 2000, Cochran
observed, "We're defenseless against the juggernaut of huge, unregulated, undis-
closed expenditures by groups" (Willis 2001, 217).

Although the trend toward increased group advocacy in elections raises
troubling issues about the legitimacy of the electoral process in the United States,
it has not yet inspired much systematic research. Some scholars have focused on
political action committees (PACs) and their contributions to individual candidates (Herrnson 1997), while others have concentrated on group lobbying tactics
in Washington (Scholzman and Tierney 1986; Walker 1991; Baumgartner and
Leech 1998; Kollman 1998). Campaign specialists have only recently begun to
study the impact of issue advocacy and have focused primarily on congressional
elections (Herrnson 2000; Magleby 2000, 2003).

This scholarly neglect is partly a function of the relative newness of the issue advocacy phenomenon, but the most important reason for the dearth of research is the lack of systematic data about groups' behavior. Before passage of the BCRA, interest groups engaging in issue advocacy did not have to identify their funding sources or report their expenditures, unless they explicitly endorsed a particular candidate (O'Brien 1995; Wayne 1998).[3] Production costs for ads, field staff, mass mailings, and get-out-the-vote drives aimed at group members counted as internal operations and also were exempted from reporting. Complicating matters further was the fact that radio and television stations did not have to report group expenditures on issue advocacy, although they did have to make a list of groups that bought broadcast time available to the public. Since the passage of campaign reform, the reporting and monitoring of groups are still relatively loose; restrictions are aimed primarily at the timing of advocacy ads.

Until Congress closed it in the summer of 2000, a loophole in the Internal Revenue Service (IRS) regulations (Section 527) governing nonprofit organizations provided another way in which groups could raise and spend money without disclosure.[4] The Federal Election Commission (FEC) recently issued an advisory that appears to give 527 committees the ability to engage in a variety of communications activities, including candidate-specific ads, but it does require them to file semiannual reports.[5] For all these reasons, then, the true dimensions of group involvement in issue advocacy have proved elusive, except for a few case studies of a particular group (Drew 1997) or a handful of individual congressional races (Magleby 2000, 2003).

Is interest group advocacy a widespread threat to democratic elections? Or is it simply another vehicle whereby citizens exercise their First Amendment right to petition the government? We offer a partial answer to this question based on a detailed case study of the 2000 New Hampshire presidential primary and some observations of the 2004 primary. We examine the primary in New Hampshire because it provides a useful laboratory for analyzing the strategic possibilities and limitations of issue advocacy in a high-stakes, high-visibility race. Historically, the New Hampshire primary has been a place for individual candidates to test their messages and organizational skills rather than an arena for group competition. The 2000 contest, however, sparked a substantial increase in group activity over that of previous years, and by election day, February 1, roughly forty-five groups were active in New Hampshire with advertisements, direct mail, telephone banks, and get-out-the vote drives.

Using ad buy data, interviews, and a convenience sample of volunteers who monitored contacts from candidates and groups, we demonstrate that the context in New Hampshire, with its high primary voter turnout, intensive campaigning by the candidates, and pervasive media coverage, reduced the impact of group advocacy in a campaign.[6] At the same time, the outcome of the primary race underscores the value of group mobilization in encouraging voter participation.

Despite their intense activity, the candidates drowned out the interest groups, dominating the airwaves and print media. By contrast, the AFL-CIO and the National Education Association (NEA) pursued a less visible strategy of mobilizing their members to turn out for Vice President Al Gore. In the end, these were the only groups that had any effect on the outcome, and not all observers agreed on the magnitude of their contribution to Gore's victory.

In the 2004 primary, fewer groups came into the state. The amount they spent on ads was minimal, and few engaged in member-to-member mobilization. Thus New Hampshire provides examples of two very different patterns of electoral advocacy by interest groups. On the one hand, both primary battles demonstrate how the electoral context and efforts of candidates reduce the impact of group advocacy in a campaign. On the other hand, the 2000 case underscores the dependence of some candidates on the capacity of their parties' affiliated groups to get members to the polls.

Opportunities and Obstacles for Issue Advocacy

Interest groups have several options when it comes to affecting public policy—insider lobbying, grassroots mobilization, litigation, campaign contributions, and issue advocacy. By issue advocacy, we mean the efforts of groups to influence elections through issue ads, as well as personal contacts with prospective voters through mass mailings, telephone banks, and get-out-the-vote drives. Many groups avoid issue advocacy altogether, and those that do participate in election politics pick their battles strategically in order to maximize the payoffs from their efforts (Kollman 1998).[7] Groups must decide which offices matter most to the achievement of their political goals and whether they have sufficient resources to accomplish their objectives. Then, they must determine whether they want to influence the *campaign discourse* among political activists and the media by raising the salience of their issues or framing them in a particular way. Or they must choose whether to affect the *election outcome* directly by mobilizing their members to turn out or by shaping the images of the candidates through advertisements. Thus group involvement in electoral politics is extremely sensitive to the political context and dynamics of a particular race.

Like candidates, groups confront several constraints on their ability to shape either the discourse or the outcome of an election. Voters' attention to campaigns is limited, and their choices about candidates are dependent on long-standing political dispositions, such as party identification (Miller 1991; Zaller 1992; Bartels 2000). In addition, the impact of political advertising is uncertain: in some cases it appears to elicit a response in voters; in others its effects are negligible (Ansolabehere and Iyengar 1995; Finkel and Geer 1998; Freedman and Goldstein 1999; Lau et al. 1999; Vavreck 2000). Therefore, when groups decide to engage in issue advocacy, they cannot count on getting a good return on their investment.

The New Hampshire presidential primary offers an interesting venue in which to study the range of strategic calculations confronting groups that engage in electoral issue advocacy. Presidential primaries present challenges that are different from those in congressional races (Magleby 2000), because they are usually shorter and attract more national attention. A group can mount a brief, intense effort in the full glare of the national spotlight and then turn its attention to other priorities. At the same time, groups with narrow, specialized issues face tough competition for space on the campaign agenda from those that advocate broader concerns. The unique status of New Hampshire's first-in-the-nation primary adds additional strategic complications. The race typically attracts a disproportionate share of all presidential primary coverage, and so it becomes a prime location for candidates to establish momentum (Bartels 1988). Thus interest groups have an opportunity in New Hampshire to establish their clout before a national audience and to earn the gratitude of a favored candidate at a critical time in the campaign.

The very characteristics of the race that make it so attractive to groups also impose limits on their potential influence. Because of the salience of the primary to New Hampshire residents, turnout is high compared with that of other states, and groups have to get large numbers of members to the polls to affect the outcome at the margins. In 2000, for example, 50.4 percent of registered New Hampshire voters turned out when both parties had a primary, while turnout exceeded 40 percent for both 1996 and 2004 when only one party contested the primary.[8] By contrast, South Carolina's 2000 primary, which took place three weeks later but involved only Republican candidates, sparked turnout of just 27.3 percent.[9] In addition, the amount of attention that candidates and the press lavish on New Hampshire ensures that voters have ample information and therefore have less need of cues from interest groups. Finally, the primary election is part of a sequence that extends over several months, which makes the timing of a group's intervention a potential complication.

The calendar for the 2000 primary elections gave groups a special incentive to come into the state, because the races that followed New Hampshire's were extremely close together. Key groups in both parties understood that New Hampshire could either encourage the challenges by McCain and Bradley to their respective political establishments, or bring their insurgencies to a halt. Both men were counting on their ability to attract the state's sizable pool of independent voters, who could participate in either party primary, so McCain had put all his effort into New Hampshire, and Bradley, too, courted the state's voters strenuously. With the length and intensity of the entire primary contest at stake, groups such as High Technology Leaders for Bush spent several days stumping the state using a series of panels on e-business to attract entrepreneurs and technical workers to their candidate's flagging campaign. Similarly, the AFL-CIO was determined to avoid embarrassment over its early endorsement of Gore by mobilizing its members to turn out for the vice president.

In 2004 an equally truncated primary schedule depressed the inclination of organized labor to play a role in New Hampshire. In part, the union movement was divided, and it had concentrated all of its efforts in Iowa on a losing battle between Missouri House member Richard A. Gephardt and former Vermont governor Howard Dean. In addition, the candidates themselves, particularly Dean whose campaign used the Internet in an innovative fashion, took on the role of voter mobilization that interest groups had undertaken in the previous election cycle.

The Players

Many groups arrived in New Hampshire in 2000 to take advantage of the media spotlight that shown so brightly on the state. They wanted to get the candidates talking about their concerns by inducing the press to ask questions about a particular issue. Relatively obscure groups, especially, hoped that the insatiable appetite of the press for stories in New Hampshire would give them exposure they would not otherwise receive (see Table 5-1). For example, very few people could have seen the ads sponsored by People for the Ethical Treatment of Animals (PETA), because they were placed at stations with small audiences, but many people probably read about them subsequently in several different newspaper articles. Still other groups attempted to draw attention to the president's discretion to manage the nation's regulatory programs or to appoint judges. The Sierra Club, for example, was eager to retain a Democratic administration in Washington as a bulwark against the attempts by Republicans in Congress to roll back environmental protections. Both the National Abortion and Reproductive Rights Action League (NARAL) and the National Right to Life Committee came to New Hampshire because they were intensely interested in the president's responsibility to nominate judges to the Supreme Court.

Nevertheless, many powerful groups that play a major role in congressional elections were missing from the 2000 New Hampshire presidential primary scene. The National Rifle Association, which is often active in the state, was largely silent throughout the primary. With the major Republican contenders solidly in its corner, it could afford to wait for the general election before becoming involved. Similarly, the Chamber of Commerce of the United States, the Association of Trial Lawyers of America, the National Association of Realtors, and many other prominent organizations were conspicuously absent, while the American Medical Association confined itself to a few mailings. Such major unions as the Teamsters and United Auto Workers did not come into the state at all.

Equally interesting was the tendency of some groups to wait and see how New Hampshire turned out before becoming involved in later primaries. Most notable for their modest efforts were the groups that make up the Christian Right, which contrasted sharply with their subsequent involvement in South Carolina and Michigan. In addition, some organizations such as the American Association of Retired Persons (now called simply the AARP) confined their efforts to urging their members to vote. Mainstream groups such as the Business Roundtable were present in the state, but their presence was not extensive enough to have an impact. Indeed, one of the most striking features of races in New Hampshire is the comparative obscurity of many of the groups that engage in electoral advocacy.

What factors influenced groups to stay out of New Hampshire or to mute their efforts not only in 2000, but also in 2004? The most important were the

Table 5-1   Interest Groups Active in the 2000 New Hampshire Presidential Primary

Group	Ad buy data	Citizen reports
AARP	X	X
AFL-CIO		X
Alliance for Quality Nursing Home Care	X	
American Association of Health Plans	X	
American Federation of Teachers		X
American Cancer Society	X	X
American Medical Association		X
Americans for Democratic Action		X
Americans for Tax Reform	X	X
Amherst Democratic Committee		X
Bob Dole		X
Business Leaders for Sensible Priorities	X	X
Business Roundtable	X	
Citizens Against Government Waste		X
Citizens for Better Medicare	X	X
Citizens for Life	X	X
Coalition for Long-Term Care	X	
Committee for Good Common Sense	X	
Common Cause		X
Friends of the Earth		X
Granite State Independents		X
Hands Across New Jersey (anti-Bradley)	X	X
High Technology Leaders for Bush		X
Human Rights Campaign	X	X
Interfaith Alliance		X
League of Conservation Voters		X
Log Cabin Republicans	X	
Nami New Hampshire		X
NARAL	X	X
National Council of Senior Citizens		X
National Education Association		X
National Right to Life Committee	X	X
National Tax Limitation Committee		X
NH Citizens Alliance for Action		X
NH Democratic Committee		X
NH Democratic Party		X
NH Peace Action		X
People for the Ethical Treatment of Animals	X	X
Public Citizen Health Research Group		X
Republican Leadership Council	X	X
Republican National Committee	X	X
Sierra Club		X
STAR-PAC		X
Taxpayers for Accountability		X
United for a Fair Economy		X

Sources: Data compiled by authors from media outlets and volunteer reports. Ad buy data from major television and radio stations in the NH media market. "Citizen reports" are based on a convenience sample of 196 households that reported 2,416 instances of group and candidate contact.

Table 5-2   Distribution of Television and Radio Ad Buys by Groups and Candidates in 2000 New Hampshire Primary (percentage)

Organization	Radio	Television	Total
Candidate	85.0	77.8	80.6
Independent groups	14.8	18.4	17.0
Party	0.00	3.8	2.4
Total	100 (161)	100 (261)	100 (423)

Source: Data collected by authors from the public files of television and radio stations in the New Hampshire media market (New Hampshire, Vermont, and Massachusetts).

Note: Pearson chi-square = 7.6382, p < 0.022.

intensive campaign efforts of the candidates and the overwhelming presence of the news media. In such an environment, groups would have a difficult time competing for voters' attention. In addition, they would have to contend with the media's obsessive coverage of the "horse race" aspects of the campaign in tight races.

In terms of sheer volume of communication, the candidates dominated the airwaves in New Hampshire's 2000 primary. Candidates accounted for 80 percent of the political ad buys during the entire primary season, and this result held for both television and radio (see Table 5-2). With eight major candidates personally campaigning in New Hampshire and spending almost $7 million on advertising, groups recognized that they had formidable rivals for citizens' attention. This prompted one highly respected GOP activist to comment, "When groups called me to talk about getting involved in the New Hampshire primary, I always told them not to waste their money because their voices would be drowned out by the candidates and the media." [10]

Because there was a state-by-state spending cap, the campaign spending data for New Hampshire significantly underestimate the expenditures that were actually aimed at New Hampshire voters. Ad buy data in 2000, for example, indicate that Bradley, Gore, and McCain each spent a million dollars or more on ads, even though they reported total state spending in accordance with the legal cap for the state of $675,600 (see Table 5-3). [11] Federal law allowed candidates to charge many expenses to surrounding states, which prompted one Bush operative to observe that McCain had credited 70 percent of his ads to neighboring Massachusetts, where there was no campaign, so that he could stay below the legal ceiling. [12] The ad buy data reveal that spending by Republican candidates Bush and Steve Forbes, a wealthy businessman, was probably substantial, but those data were not verifiable through federal campaign finance records because neither candidate was accepting public funds. Neither had to report expenditures or observe state spending limits, although Bush did file with the FEC during the primary.

Table 5-3   Candidate Spending in 2000 New Hampshire Primary

Candidate	Total N.H. spending	TV/radio spending	Number of ad buys
Gary Bauer (R)	$93,666	$725	1
Bill Bradley (D)	657,647	1,456,049	49
George W. Bush (R)	1,860,000	1,636,615	90
Steve Forbes (R)	—	1,234,903	91
Al Gore (D)	588, 414	1,368,867	53
Alan Keyes (R)	249,086	9,776	9
John McCain (R)	599,179	941,207	42
Total	$4,047,992	$6,648,142	335

Sources: Federal Election Commission; data compiled by authors from the public files of television and radio stations in the New Hampshire media market (New Hampshire, Vermont, and Massachusetts) and estimates based on interviews.

— = Not available because candidate did not accept public funding.

We had even more difficulty calculating a total 2000 spending figure for groups because stations did not have a legal obligation to report the dollar value of issue advocacy buys. The figures that are available, however, suggest relatively modest spending levels for groups (Table 5-4).[13] Two patterns emerge from Table 5-4. First, groups ran relatively few ads compared with the candidates— only three groups made ten or more ad buys. The cost of the ads varied with the time slot and the number of times per day an ad ran. Second, it appears that several groups followed PETA's lead and bought minimal amounts of time in the hope of attracting media attention.

The same holds for the contacts that volunteers reported from groups and candidates' campaigns. In Table 5-5, several differences emerge from the volunteer reports about the amount of contact by candidates and groups in 2000. The table shows that all of the candidate organizations relied heavily on mail, phone, and television to reach potential primary voters. The volunteers also reported that the front-runners were generally able to have some personal contact with voters, although our group of contact monitors did not report any individual meetings with McCain, despite his 110 town meetings in the state. Although these data are very imprecise, they do capture the candidates' greater intensity of voter contact. All of the major candidates used five or more types of contact to reach voters. Among groups, only the AFL-CIO and National Education Association appear to have made at least three different types of contacts.

Because of the dominance of the candidates and the exceptionally high turnout in New Hampshire's primary, only highly organized groups were able to affect the outcome. Indeed, our data suggest that only the unions were mobilized sufficiently to make a difference in 2000, but, four years later, even the unions were overshadowed by the candidates' volunteer organizations. Apparently, the unions, which were split in their support of Democratic candidates Gephardt and Dean, were not as active in the state as they had been in the previous election. Veterans groups were a

Table 5-4   Selected Ad Buys in 2000 New Hampshire Primary by Groups Active in the N.H. Media Market before Primary

Group	Number of ad buys	Average cost
AARP	1	$3,536
AFL-CIO	1	—
Alliance for Quality Nursing	3	9,660
American Association of Health Plans	3	—
American Cancer Society	1	—
Americans for Tax Reform	1	—
Business Leaders for Sensible Priorities	10	4,953
Business Roundtable	1	2,775
Citizens for Better Medicare	14	1,162
Citizens for Efficient Regional Transportation	1	—
Citizens for Life	3	1,487
Coalition for Long Term Care	4	4,230
Committee for Sensible School Funding	3	2,336
Committee for Good Common Sense	1	—
Handgun Control	3	3,700
Hands Across New Jersey	1	—
Human Rights Campaign	1	—
Log Cabin Republicans	1	—
Massachusetts Teachers Association	1	—
Massachusetts Voters for Clean Elections	1	—
Merit Construction Alliance	1	—
NARAL	5	1,490
PETA	2	—
Republican Leadership Council	7	—
Republican National Committee	2	—
Sierra Club	10	3,942
Total	72	$3,457.03

Source: Data collected by authors from the public files of television and radio stations in the New Hampshire media market (New Hampshire, Vermont, and Massachusetts).

— = Not available.

Note: By law, stations do not have to disclose ad buy data on independent group buys; they merely have to make the list of groups that bought time available to the public.

significant factor in the get-out-the-vote effort in New Hampshire, however, particularly for Massachusetts senator John Kerry and to a lesser extent for retired general Wesley Clark. Firefighter organizations also helped the Kerry campaign on the ground. Thus highly energized campaigns operating in the full glare of the news media appear to constrain the efficacy of advocacy groups significantly.

Campaign Tactics: Ground Wars and Air Wars

Interest groups depend primarily on issue ads to influence the outcome of an election, but they also use a variety of grassroots mobilization techniques such as mass mailings, phone banks, and even push polling. In New Hampshire,

Table 5-5 Citizen Contact Reports by Candidates and Groups in 2000 New Hampshire Primary

Candidate	Mail	TV	Paper	E-mail	Fax	Phone	Video	Visit
Bill Bradley (D)	X	X		X	X	X		X
George W. Bush (R)	X	X	X			X		X
Steve Forbes (R)	X	X	X		X	X	X	X
Al Gore (D)	X	X			X	X		X
Alan Keyes (R)	X	X				X		
John McCain (R)	X	X		X		X		
Group								
AARP		X				X		
AFL-CIO	X					X	X	
Americans for Tax Reform		X						
Business Leaders for Sensible Priorities		X						
NARAL	X							
National Education Association	X	X	X					
National Right to Life Committee	X	X						
Republican Leadership Council		X						
Sierra Club	X	X						

Source: Data collected by authors using a convenience sample of 196 New Hampshire households. Respondents tracked all campaign contacts (N = 2,416) with their household during the primary. Republican candidates Gary Bauer and Orrin Hatch were not included, because no contacts for either campaign were reported.

groups appeared to specialize in one technique or the other. Ground wars seemed to be the tactic most suitable for affecting voters' choices, but air wars were the vehicle for influencing campaign agendas. Interestingly, in 2000 very few Democratic-affiliated groups opted for the airwaves, while most groups supportive of the Republican Party chose this strategy.

Influencing Vote Choice

During the 2000 primary, organized labor in New Hampshire relied on grass-roots mobilization, which has a long history in the union movement. This tactic was perfected during the 2000 Iowa caucuses and in congressional races in 1998 under the leadership of AFL-CIO president John Sweeney (Fackler et al. 2000). The NEA followed a similar strategy, albeit on a smaller scale. Both groups relied on intensive personal contact with their members to build a favorable image of Gore and ensure that his supporters went to the polls. The advantage of this tactic is that it qualifies under the law as "internal communication" and therefore is unregulated.

AFL - CIO officials aimed to have their members make up 18 percent of the total Democratic vote, and on election day they exceeded their expectations with 23 percent of the vote.[14] They accomplished this objective by means of a grass-roots effort that generated seven contacts for each union household, with a heavy emphasis on personal visits from union volunteers, as well as mail and telephone contacts. The mailings included a videotaped endorsement of Gore by AFL-CIO President John Sweeney, followed by pro-labor remarks from Gore. The same 25,000 labor families also received mailings contrasting Gore and Bradley and urging support for Gore.

In the final days of the 2000 campaign, union families received multiple telephone calls urging a Gore vote, which were backed up with a get-out-the-vote effort on election day. The AFL-CIO's professional staff coordinated the mobilization effort, and on weekends labor leaders from surrounding states walked key precincts for Gore.[15] In addition, the union made phone banks available for Gore's campaign, charging it per call, and the paid labor staff working the state volunteered their after-hours time to the Gore campaign.[16]

The NEA did not commit its staff resources to the Gore candidacy, relying instead on its member volunteers within the state. The group had made a conscious decision not to engage in independent expenditures for advertising because the airwaves were already so saturated. Besides, NEA polls indicated that it could make a difference just by focusing on its own members. Despite the more modest field operation, which cost an estimated $28,000, primarily for mailings, the NEA still met its target of having teachers make up 5 percent of the electorate in the Democratic primary.[17]

How important was the labor effort in 2000? Not surprisingly, Steve Rosenthal, political director of the AFL-CIO, described labor's activity in New Hampshire as having an "enormous impact."[18] One local NEA representative noted that its 5 percent of Democratic voters was similar in size to Gore's four percentage point margin over Bradley. Campaign staff for Gore, Bradley, and the AFL-CIO all agreed it mattered. Anita Dunn, deputy campaign manager in the Bradley campaign, recalled that "labor was significant" in the outcomes of the New Hampshire primary and Iowa caucuses.[19] Donny Fowler, national field director of the Gore campaign, said the AFL-CIO and its unions were "very good partners with Al Gore." He went on to say that the unions made a "big effort in communicating with members by telephone, through the mail, at the workplace, and door-to-door."[20]

Labor's claims of influence in Gore's victory were predictable, and they were confirmed by the Gore and Bradley campaigns for political reasons. Moreover, exit polls by the Voter News Service (VNS) tend to support the candidates' interpretations. Bradley won among nonunion voters by 51 percent to Gore's 47 percent, but he lost among union households with only 38 percent to Gore's 60 percent.[21] Others point out that 23 percent of Democratic voters were union members and that Gore's margin among these voters more than exceeded his four-point victory margin. Even the pollster for the Bush campaign, Jan Van

Lohuizen, pointed out that "the only reason Bradley lost [New Hampshire] was the unions." [22]

The unions had some assistance from a television ad campaign by the anti-tax group Hands Across New Jersey described earlier. This innocuous sounding group had come into existence during the 1993 Florio-Whitman gubernatorial campaign in New Jersey, but it reappeared in 2000 to run ads critical of Bill Bradley on campaign finance reform. Its identity and total spending are impossible to trace under current regulations. When asked if the group made any difference, Bradley's deputy campaign manager, Anita Dunn, responded that "in an election decided by 5,000 votes, it was likely a factor." [23]

Even without this obscure group's involvement, it would be a mistake to attribute Gore's victory solely to organized labor. One seasoned Democratic campaigner who backed Gore commented after the election that "the influence of labor was overblown. There is no labor voting bloc in New Hampshire to speak of." [24] A senior staff member in Bradley's New Hampshire organization held a similar view and observed that "both Democratic candidates dwarfed the spending by the national groups." [25] In short, the national politicos and the locals had a slightly different take on what really happened in New Hampshire.

Interest groups commonly engage in the hyperbole of claiming that their votes spelled the difference between victory and defeat. But every vote has equal weight in producing a winning total, which means that many factors had to fall into place for labor's effort to matter. Gore had many things going for him besides labor's grassroots effort. First, he had the backing of the governor and the majority of local party activists. Second, he created a formidable grassroots effort on his own, supplemented with out-of-state volunteers recruited by his organization. Third, Gore's aggressive advertisements attacking Bradley took their toll, aided by Bradley's refusal to respond to them and the lull in his New Hampshire campaign while he made a futile gesture in the Iowa caucuses. Finally, and most important, substantial numbers of independent voters, who liked both Bradley and Republican John McCain, decided at the last minute not to vote in the Democratic primary and supported McCain in the Republican contest instead.

In such a tight race, small shifts in strategy and turnout would have been enough to stem the labor tide. But in their absence, labor could claim credit for delivering a key state to Gore in 2000. No such claims from labor were heard in the Granite State in 2004, however.

Influencing the Campaign Discourse

Some groups sought to influence individual voters in the 2000 Republican primary as well, although most were intent on affecting the campaign discourse. Most notable were Americans for Tax Reform and the National Right to Life Committee PAC, which tried to derail John McCain's insurgency by attacking his proposals for campaign finance reform as harmful to their efforts to represent

---

Box 5-2 Citizens for Life and National Right to Life Radio Ad Attacking Republican Candidate John McCain in 2000 New Hampshire Primary

This radio script for "Emperor McCain" criticizes the provision in McCain's campaign finance reform bill that would increase regulation of issue advocacy. The ad cites a 1997 interview with NBC moderator Tim Russert in which McCain joked, when asked if he was interested in becoming president, "I prefer to be emperor."

MAN: Honey, I see here in the morning paper that John McCain would like to ban all negative ads about politicians as a type of campaign reform.

WOMAN: I think that's an outrageous idea. A politician wants to pass a law that says you can say only positive things about him?

MAN: McCain says that negative ads don't contribute to "healthy" political debate.

WOMAN: I say, let people say what they want, and then let us decide. Politicians should not have the power to decide which messages are "positive" or "healthy." What does McCain think this is, a monarchy?

MAN: Well, (laughs), it's funny you say that. I read that in 1997, Tim Russert of NBC asked McCain if he wanted to be president, and guess what McCain said?

WOMAN: What?

MAN: He said, "I prefer to be emperor."

WOMAN: "I prefer to be emperor"?

MAN: Yeah. I'm sure he was joking . . . don't you think?

NARRATOR: In the February 1st primary, let John McCain know that freedom of speech about politicians is no joke. Vote for somebody else.

This positive and healthy message is paid for by Citizens for Life PAC, a New Hampshire pro-life group, and National Right to Life PAC. Not authorized by any candidate.

Source: "Ad Spotlight," *National Journal,* January 20, 2000. http://nationaljournal.com/ members/adspotlight/2000. Copyright 2004 by the National Journal Group Inc. All rights reserved. Reprinted by permission.

---

their members' views (see Box 5-2). Eventually, McCain's campaign staff members felt that these attacks actually reinforced their campaign message. When Grover Norquist of Americans for Tax Reform visited New Hampshire, for example, McCain identified him as a registered lobbyist for foreign interests and labeled him a Washington insider.[26] Thus McCain reinforced his outsider image by highlighting the attacks on him by a highly paid Washington lobbyist and several Beltway groups. Such stories delighted political junkies, although it is doubtful that voters paid much attention to this kind of "inside baseball," especially when they had so much other information available.

The relatively low profile of various groups affiliated with the Christian Right in the 2000 Republican primary in New Hampshire contrasted dramatically with their intense activities in South Carolina and some other states, in part because there are fewer religious conservatives in New Hampshire, where only 16 percent of Republican primary voters described themselves as members of the religious right.[27] Citizens for Life ran several ads and sent out several mailings, and the National Right to Life PAC report to the FEC noted total spending in New Hampshire to oppose John McCain of $45,000. The same primary exit polls showed that McCain received a slightly higher percentage of the religious right vote in New Hampshire (26 percent) than in South Carolina (24 percent). Also in New Hampshire, just over a majority of GOP primary voters (52 percent) favored abortion rights in most or all cases.[28]

McCain was not the only Republican target of issue advocacy. The Republican Leadership Council (RLC), a group founded by GOP business leaders, used advertising to shape the discourse of the campaign by publicly urging Steve Forbes to avoid the negative attacks on his fellow Republicans that had been the hallmark of his 1996 primary campaign. The RLC also used negative phone calls to attack Forbes and then asked if the listener would like to speak to the Forbes campaign. The infuriated citizen would be patched through to the Forbes campaign, which then had to explain that the group forwarding the call was a pro-choice Republican organization.[29]

George W. Bush, too, contended with group attempts to define his candidacy in 2000. Both the Sierra Club and NARAL, for example, ran early ads in the fall of 1999 calling attention to Bush's record on the environment and abortion, respectively (see Box 5-3). Their messages that Bush was neither as moderate nor as compassionate as he presented himself were attempts to encourage the press to challenge Bush on those issues. Neither group is a stranger to hardball electoral politics, but during the primaries they saw no gain from backing a particular candidate in either party in New Hampshire. At the time, as a NARAL official explained, there was not much difference between Gore and Bradley, so the group decided not to get involved in the New Hampshire Democratic primary.[30] Later, NARAL endorsed Gore after Bradley began portraying him as deficient in his support of abortion rights. NARAL wanted to ensure that abortion rights would be on the agenda, even though the group did not expect it to be a defining electoral issue until the fall 2000 campaign. The group was attracted to the spotlight on New Hampshire and wanted people to start thinking about Supreme Court appointments. More important, the group's political strategists thought that the press had given Bush a free ride on the reproductive choice issue, and they wanted to motivate reporters to ask questions about where Bush really stood.

Finally, some groups avoided the candidates altogether in 2000 and concentrated instead on getting their issues in front of the public. They sought to change the discourse in the campaign by educating citizens about their particu-

---

Box 5-3   NARAL Television Ad Attacking George W. Bush, 2000

(Photos of George W. Bush and Pat Buchanan on screen)

FEMALE ANNOUNCER: Which Republican presidential hopeful said, "I will do everything in my power to restrict abortion"?

(Buchanan photo zooms forward)

Nope. George W. Bush did.

(Photos of George W. Bush and Dan Quayle on screen)

And which presidential hopeful said he would write a constitutional amendment to outlaw almost all abortions?

(Quayle photo zooms forward)

Again, it's George Bush.

(Photos of George W. Bush and Steve Forbes)

So, which presidential hopeful said, "I think the Republican Party ought to maintain its pro-life tenor"?

George W. Bush did.

Get the picture? George W. Bush

Source: "Ad Spotlight," *National Journal,* September 1, 1999. http://nationaljournal.com/ members/adspotlight/1999. Copyright 2004 by National Journal Group Inc. All rights reserved. Reprinted by permission.

---

lar issue. For example, Business Leaders for Sensible Priorities, founded by Ben Cohen of Ben and Jerry's Ice Cream, a Vermont company known for its progressive business philosophy, deliberately avoided overt electioneering because of its status as a nonprofit, educational 501(c)(3) organization. The group's ads and activities were expressly designed to call attention to the trade-offs on defense and education investments, with the intent of raising the profile of such issues. Citizens for Better Medicare, an organization funded by the pharmaceutical industry, endeavored to get Medicare financing on the campaign docket.

In the end, the swell of support among independents for McCain was so great that the impact of group efforts against him were negligible, and Bush lost by eighteen percentage points. "New Hampshire voters are hard to mobilize on a group basis," a Republican activist noted, "because we simply don't have large enough concentrations of people with similar interests to make group-based organizing worthwhile." [31]

In 2004 many fewer groups endeavored to affect the discourse of the campaign. Both NARAL and the Sierra Club, relatively active in the previous election, made cameo appearances, spending only $10,000 each on ads in the state targeting President Bush.[32] The conservative-leaning Club for Growth issued a small sally against Howard Dean, and a newly formed 527 committee called Americans for Progressive Values also attacked Dean. Two groups did take advantage of the national spotlight on New Hampshire to call attention to their concerns in what can only be described as "pure issue advocacy." The American Federation of Government Employees, for example, drew attention to the outsourcing of veterans' care,[33] and the Nuclear Threat Initiative—brainchild of former U.S. senators Sam Nunn, D-GA, and Warren Rudman, R-NH—warned of the dangers of inadequate security measures against "suitcase bombs" and other nuclear threats from terrorists.[34] In comparison with the high campaign expenditures by the candidates, which some observers estimate to be at least three times greater than those in the 2000 campaign, the interest group totals were trivial.[35] Indeed, political scientist Mark Wrighton, who studied the participation of advocacy groups in the 2002 Senate race, observed: "When you look at the Senate and House races in 2002, you saw a blizzard of ads and mail, as well as extensive on-the-ground activity. By comparison, the 2004 presidential primary was just a small spritz of snow." [36]

Conclusion

Interest groups may have been important to the outcome of the 2000 New Hampshire Democratic presidential primary, but they made little difference in the Republican outcome. The ability of the AFL-CIO and teachers to turn out their members in substantial numbers for Vice President Al Gore demonstrated that in close contests what interest groups do for candidates on the ground can be important. The magnitude of the 2000 victory by John McCain in the Republican primary indicates that the interest group attacks on him had little impact. McCain's accessibility to voters, his frequent visits to the state, and the intense press coverage of his maverick style all appealed to New Hampshire's large number of independent voters. The saturation effects of the campaign constrained groups' ability to attract the voters' attention, and the unique electoral environment of the state limited the scope of what groups could accomplish by criticizing McCain.

In 2004 Democratic candidate John Kerry won the primary by a twelve-point margin, and the presence of groups was barely noticeable. In fact, none of the organizations that were active in the state had an impact on the outcome. The extensive effort at voter mobilization evident in the state was driven primarily by the candidates, particularly former Vermont governor Howard Dean. In the end, the tradition of retail politics in New Hampshire was too strong for groups to overcome in 2000, and in 2004 they did not even try.

Interest group advocacy in the New Hampshire primary also proved difficult to measure. Despite extensive fieldwork and the assistance of hundreds of volunteers who monitored contacts from candidates and groups during the 2000 campaign, we have an incomplete picture of what actually occurred.[37] In some instances, we were able to approach groups that helped us to understand what happened, but much of our uncertainty stems from the lack of public information on how much groups spend on advertising. For example, although most radio and television stations were eager to assist with this research, the major TV station in the state declined to provide more than the legal minimum of names and dates for the groups that placed ads. Similarly, many group activities involved operating expenses for voter mobilization and ad production, the costs of which were not reported because they can be considered internal communications. Often, the difficulty of gathering data was heightened by groups' practice of splitting costs between the national and state affiliates. Although the passage of the BCRA introduces more reporting requirements for advocacy groups, many of these obstacles to uncovering the scope of group activity remain. Moreover, the consequence of the trend toward 527 groups for regulating group participation in campaigns remains unclear.

In 2000, groups appear to have had different objectives for their involvement in the New Hampshire primary that, in turn, shaped their choice of strategies. Thus groups that were engaged in agenda setting (for example, Citizens for a Sound Economy, Business Leaders for Sensible Priorities) or framing discussion about particular candidates (for example, Republican Leadership Council, Sierra Club, Americans for Tax Reform) were visible through their use of television ads, but they encountered enormous competition from the candidates. Other groups that had a lower public profile because they relied on targeted mobilization of their own members (for example, the AFL-CIO and NEA) had a substantial impact, at least in 2000.

It is tempting to speculate that the new rules in 2004 restricting group advertising thirty days before the primary were responsible for the dearth of group advocacy. The contrast with 2000 suggests a more complicated interpretation, however. In a presidential primary, candidates exert a prodigious effort toward retaining control of their message and sidestepping attempts by groups to define the candidates' image or their agenda during the campaign. In both electoral contests, the candidates were remarkably successful in this effort, because the press was focused almost entirely on the rival participants. With so much competition to be heard, the returns from group advertising were simply not worth the investment.

In addition, a crowded primary field makes it difficult for groups to target a particular favorite or to claim credit for that candidate's success. The 2000 primary was essentially a two-person race in each party, which meant that a group's efforts would not benefit a third party. In the 2004 caucuses in Iowa, however, negative attacks by rival unions aimed at Democrats Gephardt and Dean ended up making both candidates look bad and drove supporters into the hands of Kerry and Edwards. Finally, groups do not have unlimited resources, and they have to determine which races provide the greatest payoff. For some groups in 2000, ensuring the candidacy of Gore and Bush seemed worth the effort, but in 2004 those same organizations seemed to be husbanding their resources for an intensely competitive general election campaign.

In summary, the political context of presidential primaries sharply constrains their attractiveness to groups. As campaign reformers debate the efficacy of the new rules under the BCRA, they should remember that regulation is only part of the solution. Competitive, well-financed candidates, a mobilized electorate, and an attentive press are also part of the equation in restraining undue influence by advocacy groups.

Notes

1. The BCRA bans the contribution of unregulated "soft money" to the parties, with the limited exception of money used for state and local party-building activities. It also prohibits the issue ads that could be run by corporations and unions thirty days before the primary and sixty days before the general election and requires groups that run issue ads to disclose individual contributions of $1,000 or more. Although it does not regulate independent expenditures by groups that do not coordinate with the candidates or parties, it imposes reporting requirements on groups that spend more than $1,000 within twenty days of the election and more than $10,000 within twenty-one or more days of the election (Willis 2001; Steel and Posner 2001).

2. This figure is more than double the spending on issue advocacy in the 1996 election cycle and does not include any candidate spending. It significantly underestimates the amount of money involved, because it does not include media production costs, internal expenditures by groups on get-out-the-vote drives and staff, and explicit endorsements of candidates (Annenberg Public Policy Center 2001, 3–4). Moreover, it does not include independent expenditures by groups or activities funded through nonprofit groups formed through a loophole in the Internal Revenue Service regulations known as Section 527.

3. The U.S. Supreme Court held in *Buckley v. Valeo* (424 U.S. 1 [1976]) that Congress could regulate *express advocacy*, which entailed communications containing the words: "vote for, elect, cast your ballot for, Smith for Congress, Vote against, defeat, reject." But it exempted *issue advocacy*, which does not employ such phrases, from federal rules (see *Buckley v. Valeo* in O'Brien 1995; Wayne 1998). In 2003 the Supreme Court upheld the time restrictions on groups' ability to engage in issue advocacy.

4. Some groups have now organized as 501(c)(4) organizations, which enables them to continue to circumvent disclosure to the IRS as provided in the new statute.

5. Such groups are expected to provide an escape hatch for the prohibitions in the BCRA against soft money contributions to the political parties, which turned out to be especially true for the Democrats (Justice 2004).

6. Our analysis relies on several different types of data. First, we compiled information on all of the ad buys in the state and in neighboring Massachusetts in order to assess the relative frequency of candidate and group spending. Second, we recruited volunteers from among Dartmouth alumni, members of Common Cause, and the League of Women Voters to monitor all contact from candidates and groups during the January campaign. Third, we sent out over 3,800 letters inviting participation in our study and ended up with a convenience sample of 196 households that monitored direct mail, telephone calls, and other types of contact from candidates and groups. Finally, we conducted interviews with political activists, campaign strategists, and interest group officials around the state and drew on interviews with national organizations conducted by David Magleby and Jason Beal, as well as our own telephone conversations with such officials.

7. Kollman (1998) makes a similar argument about groups' decisions to engage in grass-roots lobbying.

8. Data from the New Hampshire Secretary of State Web site (http://www.sos.nh.gov/ presprim2000/index.htm) and communication from the office of the New Hampshire Secretary of State.

9. Calculated by the authors from data in Scammon, McGillivray, and Cook (2001, 1015) and the South Carolina Election Commission, http://www.state.sc.us/cgi-bin/ scsec/vhist?election=vhrep00&countykey=ALL&regvot=REG&demo=ALL.

10. Telephone interview by Linda L. Fowler, June 15, 2000.

11. Because McCain himself campaigned extensively in the state, he must have spent more on in-state travel and related expenses.

12. Telephone interview by Linda L. Fowler, June 15, 2000.

13. Table 5-4, for example, lists all of the groups that bought ads during the primary, although the dollar figures came mostly from the stations with smaller audiences. The most significant omission from the list of ads are those placed with WMUR, which is the state's largest and most prominent television station, as well as some of the major Boston television outlets. These stations declined to make the specifics of the ad buys available because they were not obligated under the law to do so.

14. Telephone interviews with various local union officials by Linda L. Fowler, June 13–15, 2000.

15. Steve Rosenthal, AFL-CIO political director, telephone interview by David B. Magleby and Jason Beal, June 30, 2000. Rosenthal could not specify the number of paid staff who worked in New Hampshire for Gore, but Magleby interviewed a national staff member of the American Federation of State, County, and Municipal Employees (AFSCME) in Manchester, who reported that eleven paid staff from the AFL-CIO affiliate were in the state mobilizing union families for Gore. Information on union walks from interview with Rosenthal.

16. Donny Fowler, Gore campaign national field director, telephone interview by David B. Magleby and Jason Beal, June 23, 2000.

17. Local NEA officials, telephone interview by Linda L. Fowler, June 13–15, 2000.

18. Steven Rosenthal, telephone interview by David Magleby and Jason Beal, June 30, 2000.

19. Anita Dunn, deputy manager, Bradley campaign, telephone interview by David B. Magleby and Jason Beal, May 15, 2000.

20. Donny Fowler, national field director, Gore campaign, telephone interview by Linda L. Fowler, June 13, 2000.

21. Voter News Service exit polls; CNN, http://www.cnn.com/ELECTION/2000/.

22. Jan Van Lohuizen, Voter Consumer Research president, telephone interview by David B. Magleby and Jason Beal, June 21, 2000.

23. Anita Dunn, telephone interview. The actual vote margin was 6,395 votes.

24. Telephone interview by Linda L. Fowler, June 10, 2000.

25. Telephone interview by Constantine J. Spiliotes, May 4, 2000.

26. Rick Davis, McCain campaign manager, telephone interview by David B. Magleby and Jason Beal, June 14, 2000.

27. This is not to underestimate the energetic opposition to abortion by then Republican senator Bob Smith of New Hampshire.

28. Voter News Service poll.

29. Bill Dal Col, Forbes campaign manager, telephone interview by David B. Magleby and Jason Beal, March 2, 2000.

30. Local and national NARAL representatives, telephone interview by Linda L. Fowler, June 26, 2000.

31. Interview by Linda L. Fowler, June 22, 2000.

32. Prof. L. Patrick Devlin, Department of Communications, University of Rhode Island, interview, Feburary 18, 2004.

33. Prof. Mark Wrighton, Department of Political Science, University of New Hampshire, interview, February 17, 2004.
34. Devlin interview.
35. Devlin estimated the total candidate spending on ads for 2000 at over $3 million and suggested that it could go as high as $12 million when he finished compiling all of the data (February 18, 2004).
36. Interview with Wrighton.
37. Citizen reports of group activity were also highly variable. For the most part, our volunteers were fairly sophisticated and interested observers of the political scene, but what they noticed and remembered did not necessarily correspond with what the groups were doing. We believe they were quite accurate about mail and phone contacts, but had difficulty in reporting radio and television ads, particularly sponsors.

References

Annenberg Public Policy Center. 2001. "Issue Advertising in the 1999–2000 Election Cycle." Philadelphia: University of Pennsylvania.

Ansolabehere, Stephen, and Shanto Iyengar. 1995. *Going Negative: How Political Advertisements Shrink and Polarize the Electorate.* New York: Free Press.

Bartels, Larry M. 1988. *Presidential Primaries and the Dynamics of Public Choice.* Princeton, NJ: Princeton University Press.

———. 2000. "Partisanship and Voting Behavior, 1952–1996." *American Journal of Political Science* 44:35–50.

Baumgartner, Frank R., and Beth L. Leech. 1998. *Basic Interests: The Importance of Groups in Politics and in Political Science.* Princeton, NJ: Princeton University Press.

Campaign Insider. 2001. "Inside Report." *Campaigns and Elections* 6, no. 2. http://campaignline.com.

Drew, Elizabeth. 1997. *Whatever It Takes: The Real Struggle for Power in America.* New York: Penguin Books.

Fackler, Tim, Nathalie Frensley, Eric Herzik, Ted G. Jelen, Tod Kunioka, and Michael Bowers. 2000. "The 1998 Nevada Senate Race." In *Outside Money: Soft Money and Issue Advocacy in the 1998 Congressional Elections,* edited by David B. Magleby. Lanham, MD: Rowman and Littlefield.

Finkel, S. E., and John G. Geer. 1998. "A Spot Check: Casting Doubt on the Demobilizing Effect of Attack Advertising." *American Journal of Political Science* 42:573–595.

Freedman, Paul, and Kenneth M. Goldstein. 1999. "Measuring Media Exposure and the Effects of Negative Campaign Ads." *American Journal of Political Science* 43:1189–1208.

Herrnson, Paul S. 1997. "Money and Motives: Spending in House Elections." In *Congress Reconsidered,* 8th ed., edited by Lawrence C. Dodd and Bruce J. Oppenheimer. Washington, DC: CQ Press.

———. 2000. *Congressional Elections: Campaigning at Home and in Washington,* 3d ed. Washington, DC: CQ Press.

Justice, Glenn. 2004. "Advocacy Groups Allowed to Raise Unlimited Funds." *New York Times,* March 11, A1.

Kollman, Ken. 1998. *Outside Lobbying: Public Opinion and Interest Group Mobilization.* Princeton, NJ: Princeton University Press.

Lau, R. R., Lee Sigelman, C. Heldman, and P. Babbitt. 1999. "The Effects of Negative Political Advertising: A Meta-Analytic Assessment." *American Political Science Review* 93:851–875.

Magleby, David B., ed. 2000. *Outside Money: Soft Money and Issue Advocacy in the 1998 Congressional Elections*. Lanham, MD : Rowman and Littlefield.

———. 2003. *The Other Campaign: Soft Money and Issue Advocacy in the 2000 Congressional Elections*. Lanham, MD: Rowman and Littlefield.

Miller, Warren E. 1991. "Party Identification, Realignment, and Party Voting: Back to the Basics." *American Political Science Review* 85:557–568.

O'Brien, David M. 1995. *Constitutional Law and Politics*, 2d ed. Vol.1. New York: Norton.

Rozell, Mark J., and Clyde Wilcox. 1999. *Interest Groups in American Campaigns: The New Face of Electioneering*. Washington, DC: CQ Press.

Scammon, Richard M., Alice V. McGillivray, and Rhodes Cook. 2001. *America at the Polls, 1960–2000*. Washington, DC.: CQ Press.

Schlozman, Kay Lehman, and John T. Tierney. 1986. "More of the Same: Washington Pressure Group Activity in a Decade of Change." *Journal of Politics* 45:351–377.

Steel, Michael, and Michael Posner. 2001. "Campaign 2000 Lends Urgency to Reform Bills." *National Journal*. January 20, 188–189.

Vavreck, Lynn. 2000. "How Does it All Turnout? Exposure to Attack Advertising, Campaign Interest, and Participation in American Presidential Elections." In *Campaign Reform: Insights and Evidence*, edited by Larry M. Bartels and Lynn Vavreck. Ann Arbor: University of Michigan Press.

Walker, Jack L. 1991. *Mobilizing Interest Groups in America: Patrons, Professions, and Social Movements*. Ann Arbor: University of Michigan Press.

Wayne, Stephen J. 1998. "Interest Groups and the Road to the White House." In *The Interest Group Connection: Electioneering, Lobbying, and Policymaking in Washington*, edited by Paul S. Herrnson, Ronald G. Shaiko, and Clyde Wilcox. Chatham, NJ: Chatham House Publishers.

West, Darrell M., and Burdett A. Loomis. 1999. *The Sound of Money: How Political Interests Get What They Want*. New York: Norton.

Willis, Derek. 2001. "Campaign Finance Kickoff." *CQ Weekly*. January 27, 215–217.

Zaller, John. 1992. *The Nature and Origins of Mass Opinion*. Cambridge: Cambridge University Press.

6. Presidential Elections: Traveling the Hard and Soft Roads to the White House

Stephen J. Wayne

The road to Congress may be paved with contributions from political action committees (PACs), but the road to the White House is not. However, that road is cluttered with the election activities of the candidates' parties, their sympathizers, and nonparty groups, which have a noticeable effect on the presidential contest.

Some of these electoral activities provide direct support for the presidential candidates; they fund appeals that expressly ask voters to elect or defeat the candidates. Others lend indirect support; they fund candidate-centered or party-centered issue advocacy ads in which not-so-subtle appeals are made for or against particular candidates and their policy positions. In the vast majority of cases, the ads are so slick that voters cannot tell the difference between direct and indirect advocacy. In short, the difference makes no difference.

Why are these supplemental campaigns permitted if the intent of the federal law is to limit the contributions and expenditures of the major party presidential candidates? One reason is to invigorate the electorate—get more people involved and get them out to vote. The 1979 amendments to the Federal Election Campaign Act (FECA) permitted parties to raise and spend unlimited amounts of money on party building and get-out-the-vote efforts. The so-called "soft money" provision had the effect of opening up a giant loophole in the law that encouraged parties to solicit large contributions to supplement the hard money—money that was subject to contribution limits.

Although the soft money loophole has existed from 1980, the breach was widened and the FECA regulations were circumvented by the actions of the Clinton administration during the 1995–1996 election cycle. Here is what happened.

When the Democrats lost control of Congress in the 1994 midterm elections and President Bill Clinton's approval rating dropped significantly, the president's reelection looked doubtful. To reverse his downward spiral, Clinton turned to a former political adviser and campaign strategist, Dick Morris, who recommended that the president change his policy course and adopt more centrist policy positions. This strategy of "triangulation" had Clinton focus on policy issues previously associated with the Republican Party, take moderate but popular positions on these issues, and use his bully pulpit to paint the Republicans as extremists.

The strategy worked well, so well, in fact, that Morris proposed spending $2.5 million in the summer and fall of 1995 on an advertising campaign to reinforce Clinton's new posture and contrast it with the congressional Republicans' Contract with America, the conservative agenda they articulated in the 1994 midterm election cycle.

But where would they get the money? Harold Ickes, deputy chief of staff with political responsibilities, came up with the solution. They would let the Democratic Party pay for the advertising with soft money. Because the ads were policy-oriented, they could be considered issue advocacy so long as they did not directly advise people to vote for Clinton. After the Democratic Party's lawyers gave their approval, claiming that the plan did not violate the election law, the money race began, and it has not stopped.

The Republicans followed the Democrats' lead. They, too, raised millions of dollars in soft money to support a generic advertising campaign for Sen. Robert J. Dole after he won the GOP primaries. In fact, the Republicans raised even more than the Democrats in 1996. Four years later, the race resulted in contributions of almost $500 million to both parties. Table 6-1 reveals the growth of soft money as a source of revenue in the decade of the 1990s.

In response to these huge sums of money that the candidates and their parties were soliciting and spending, demands for campaign finance reform began to be heard. Legislation was introduced in Congress to ban soft money. Although it was enacted in the House, the bill died in the Senate, the victim of a Republican filibuster.

The debate over campaign finance reform, however, continued into the 2000 presidential election. Republican senator John McCain of Arizona and former Democratic senator Bill Bradley of New Jersey raised serious questions about the adequacy of the campaign finance system and its impact on a democratic electoral process. They pointed out that the money did not come from a diversified cross section of the American polity. Relatively few individuals and groups contributed. The fact that wealthy individuals and groups gave disproportionately to the parties fueled the perception of special-interest politics.

McCain and Bradley's criticism of the campaign finance system hit a responsive chord. Although neither candidate defeated his rival for the nomination, each generated support for reforming campaign finance to reduce or eliminate the influence that wealthy individuals and groups have on electoral politics.

When the 107th Congress convened after the 2000 election, Senator McCain, along with two Democratic colleagues, Russell Feingold of Wisconsin

Table 6-1   Soft Money Revenues: Major Parties, 1992–2002 (millions)

	Democrats	Republicans
1992	$36.3	$49.8
1994	49.1	52.5
1996	123.9	138.2
1998	92.8	131.6
2000	245.2	249.9
2002	246.1	250.0

Source: Federal Election Commission, "Party Committees Raise More than $1 Billion in 2000–2002," March 20, 2003. http://www.fec.gov/press/press2003/20030320party/ 20030103party.html.

and Ernest Hollings of South Carolina, sponsored legislation that banned the national parties from soliciting and spending soft money and limited issue advertising by nonparty groups that mention candidates by name thirty days or less before a primary and sixty days or less before the general election.

With the atmosphere in Congress more amenable to reform legislation, in part because of the alleged corruption of business executives and the failures of industry giants Enron and WorldCom, the Bipartisan Campaign Reform Act (BCRA), or the McCain-Feingold bill as it came to be called, was enacted into law in 2002. Opponents immediately challenged the constitutionality of the law, primarily on the grounds of the free speech protections of the First Amendment. A bare majority of the Supreme Court, however, rejected that argument and upheld the major provisions of the law. The loophole had been closed; soft money was finally out at the national level—or was it?

This chapter will answer that question. It will describe patterns of individual and group contributions and expenditures in recent presidential campaigns from precandidacy through the general election. It will also point to some of the tangible and intangible benefits that seem to accrue to those who give or spend a lot of money. In this way, the chapter will confront what many regard as a major democratic issue: Are U.S. presidential elections the best money can buy?

Precandidacy

Political action committees, notably leadership PACs, play a large role in the precandidacy stage of presidential campaigns. The law permits candidates to form their own PACs, and many do so in anticipation of their forthcoming presidential quest. These leadership PACs are used primarily by prospective candidates to fund and promote their activities before they declare their official candidacy and create their campaign committees.

One of the earliest and most successful leadership PACs was Citizens for the Republic. Created in 1977 with $1.6 million left over from Ronald Reagan's 1976 presidential campaign, this organization had within a year raised $2.5 million and spent $1.9 million on operations. Total expenditures were more than $6 million (Alexander and Corrado 1995). Most of this money was used for fund-raising, travel, and other expenses for the PAC's principal speaker, Ronald Reagan. In the process of raising money, the organization developed a list of more than 300,000 contributors, which was sold to the Reagan campaign committee for a nominal fee. The Reagan PAC became the prototype for other presidential candidates, Republican and Democratic.

Since the success of Reagan's precandidacy PAC, candidates of both major political parties have regularly established their own leadership and issue-oriented PACs prior to launching their official nomination campaigns. The latter PACs focus on particular policy areas with which the candidate is identified. The 2000 and 2004 elections are no exception. In both elections, most of the presidential candidates had leadership PACs that supported their precandidacy activities, helped them to develop donor lists, and provided them with money to contribute to other candidates for federal office.

To skirt the soft money prohibition that took effect in November 2002, some of the leadership PACs created soft money conduits called 527s (named for the section of the Internal Revenue Code that permits tax-exempt organizations to engage in political activities). So long as they carry out their activities alone and not in conjunction with the parties or their candidates' campaigns, 527s are not subject to the soft money restrictions. In other words, they can solicit large contributions from wealthy individuals and groups. Initially, they did not even have to disclose their donors, but in 2003 Congress enacted legislation that now requires them to do so.

Even before passage of the Bipartisan Campaign Reform Act, however, 527s played an important role in presidential elections. Most notably in the 2000 Florida vote controversy, both Al Gore and George W. Bush relied on them to raise money for their legal, staffing, and other costs (Knott and Armendariz 2003). In the period leading up to the 2004 nomination process, candidate 527s on the Democratic side—such as North Carolina senator John Edwards's New American Optimists, Massachusetts senator John Kerry's Citizen Soldier Fund, and Missouri senator Richard A. Gephardt's Effective Government Committee—raised, spent, and transferred money to their respective leadership PACs. Of these groups, Edwards's was the most successful, raising $4.6 million through February 2004 (Federal Election Commission, 2004). Democratic candidates Howard Dean, former governor of Vermont, and Joe Lieberman, U.S. senator from Connecticut, did not create 527s, and both criticized their opponents for doing so.

Prenomination: The Contested Stage

Once individuals declare their candidacy, all of their campaign expenditures must be paid by their official election committee. At this point, leadership PACs become less important, but contributions and activities by nonparty groups such as corporations, labor unions, and trade associations, as well as nonconnected groups that stand alone and do not have corporate, labor, trade, or other affiliations, become more valuable.

Although election law prohibits corporations and labor unions from making direct contributions to political campaigns, it does allow their employees, stockholders, or members to form political action committees and fund them through "voluntary" contributions. These groups can directly affect the presidential selection process in four ways: by endorsing a candidate, by giving up to $5,000 to a single candidate, by spending an unlimited amount of money independently for or against a candidate, and by communicating to their members and the general public about "their" issues and then using their organization to turn out voters.

Direct donations are probably the least important of these ways because of the limitations placed on the size of contributions. PAC contributions to presidential campaigns usually make up a very small percentage of the total amount raised by the candidates. In 1992 these contributions were under $1 million, or less than 1 percent of the total revenues the candidates collected; in 1996 they were $2.5 million, 1 percent of the total; in 2000, they were $2.9 million, but still less than 1 percent of all revenues. Even for the candidates who received the most money from PACs, Dole in 1996 and George W. Bush in 2000 and 2004, the amount represented only a tiny percentage of all the income they received, about 2 percent in 2000 and 1 percent in 2004.

Although PAC contributions to the candidates represent a relatively small percentage of candidates' total revenues, expenditures by PACs and other nonparty groups on election activities designed to benefit particular candidates are another story. Issue ads, grassroots organizing efforts, and mail and phone campaigns have been waged with increasing frequency and at increasing cost. Some examples follow.

During the 2000 presidential primaries, a Republican-oriented PAC, Republicans for Clean Air, sponsored $2.5 million of commercials in New York that viciously attacked Republican John McCain's environmental record (Oppel and Perez-Pena 2000, A1, 12). This PAC was really a front (that operated out of a post office box in Virginia) for two wealthy Texans, friends of George W. Bush.

In addition to being lambasted on the airwaves, McCain also suffered at the grassroots level as the Christian Coalition and pro-life, gun, and tobacco groups mounted extensive telephone and direct-mail campaigns against him in the early primary states. McCain's organization was unable to overcome this organized grassroots activity in South Carolina and Virginia, halting the momentum he had gained from his New Hampshire and, later, Michigan victories.

On the Democratic side, the AFL-CIO endorsed Gore and worked hard for his nomination. Labor's organized efforts in Iowa and New Hampshire helped Gore to defeat Bradley in both states. In Iowa, labor unions and the State Education Association turned out Gore supporters en masse for the caucuses. In New Hampshire, labor activists contacted every household with a union member not once but seven times to ensure a strong Gore vote (see Chapter 5).

In 2004 the labor unions did not initially coalesce around a single candidate. Gephardt and Dean each received early endorsements from different unions, but not from the umbrella organization, the AFL-CIO. The battle in Iowa, and to a lesser extent in New Hampshire, was fought at the grass roots between organizers and workers from affiliated AFL-CIO unions, the National Education Association, the Communication Workers of America, and the American Federation of State, County and Municipal Employees (AFSCME). Once John Kerry emerged as the leading Democratic candidate, he received the endorsements of all the major unions and their promise to work for his election.

In addition to their PAC contributions and activities, businesses, labor unions, and other nonparty organizations solicit individual campaign contributions from their executives, members, supporters, and their families, bundle them together, and send them to the appropriate candidates. The Center for Responsive Politics, a public interest group concerned with the relationship between money, campaigns, and governance, reported that during the 2000 nominating process "presidential candidates . . . received thirty-eight bundles of contributions of $50,000 or more from executives and families connected with thirty-three different organizations. All but two came from business groups" (Center for Responsive Politics 2001). The process of bundling continued into 2004.

Bundling has the effect of raising the proportion of giving in the top categories. In 2000 more than 75 percent of Bush's, Bradley's, and Gore's funds and 42 percent of McCain's came from donors who gave the maximum amount, which was $1,000 in that election. The same trends were evident for most of the candidates in the 2003–2004 election cycle. With the exceptions of Howard Dean and Dennis Kucinich, candidates received much of their money from large donors particularly at the beginning of the nomination process (see Table 6-2).

Where does the money come from? The Bush campaign received the most money in both election cycles from those in the financial and real estate sectors, followed by lawyers, lobbyists, and those in the health care professions. For the Democratic candidates, the order was lawyers and lobbyists, the investment community, and the dot-coms (Center for Responsive Politics 2001, 2004).

Table 6-2 Candidates' Fund-Raising from Individual Contributions, 2004 Election (through August 31, 2004)

Candidate	Total	$2,000 %	$1000+ %	$200–999 %	Less than $200 %
Democrats					
Wesley Clark	$29,514,554	31	49	20	31
Howard Dean	52,925,731	8	19	22	60
John Edwards	33,526,925	48	70	16	14
Richard Gephardt	21,576,664	45	71	16	13
Bob Graham	5,062,439	49	72	19	9
John Kerry	248,021,185	24	44	20	37
Dennis Kucinich	12,450,051	5	11	19	70
Joe Lieberman	19,006,993	44	74	17	9
Carol Mosley Braun	616,492	26	49	26	25
Al Sharpton	676,602	44	63	24	14
Total	$423,377,635	25	44	20	36
Republican					
George W. Bush	$260,565,424	44	57	12	31

Source: Campaign Finance Institute, October 4, 2004, http://www.lists@CFinst.org.

Note: All $2,000 contributors are also included in the $1,000+ category.

Prenomination: The Uncontested Stage

Once the successful candidates emerge, there is usually a three- to four-month period in which the preordained nominees consolidate their base by reaching out to their vanquished opponents, repair any damage to their image from a divisive primary process, and lay the foundations for their general election campaign. All of these activities require money, lots of it.

Unopposed candidates, such as Clinton in 1996 and Bush in 2004, create their war chests primarily for use during this period as well as to discourage anyone from challenging them. Thus Clinton had $37 million to use against his Republican rival, Robert Dole, and Bush had close to $200 million to spend from March through August 2004 against John Kerry. These presidents' strong financial positions, their ability to use their bully pulpits to reach the public, and the fact that practically everything they did was newsworthy placed their opponents at a significant financial disadvantage. Dole's war chest was almost empty. Because he had accepted federal funds in the form of matching grants, he could not exceed the spending limits, which he had almost reached by the middle of March 1996. In that election, the Republican Party came to his rescue with a generic advertising campaign that cost about $20 million, much of which consisted of soft money the party had raised. Similarly, in 2000 Gore, who had accepted matching funds, had almost reached his limit when he became the effective winner of the Democratic nomination process, while Bush, who had not accepted government funds, had no limit. Thus Bush continued to raise and spend money. However, with soft money still permitted in 2000, the Democratic National Committee came to Gore's rescue much as the Republican National Committee had come to Dole's.

Fast forward to 2004. An unopposed president with an initial fundraising goal of $175 million—he actually raised more than $250 million—seemed to have an overwhelming advantage over any Democratic challenger. The Bush strategy was to maximize this advantage. The campaign planned to spend the bulk of its war chest from the middle of March until the Republican convention at the end of August. Bush's strategists anticipated that a Democrat would emerge from the pack battered and broke. But they were wrong. John Kerry did become the preordained nominee by early March, but he was not battered and he would not be broke. Because Kerry had not accepted federal funds, he could raise unlimited amounts of hard money, and he quickly set out to do so. His goal of $80 million was soon raised to $100 million and then raised once again. By the end of August, Kerry had raised more than $248 million (see Table 6-2). Thus when the Bush campaign ran its first series of ads critical of Kerry in the key battleground states, Kerry's campaign retaliated with ads of its own that were critical of the president. The 2004 presidential campaign therefore got off to a fast, expensive, and early start, with Bush spending $6 million and Kerry $1.8 million in the opening week of attacks, almost eight months before the election was to be held (Rutenberg 2004a).

But that is not all. The Democrats anticipated that their candidate would need additional funds and that the party would not be able to raise a sufficient amount of hard money to close the financial gap. So, party supporters coordinated a stealth campaign to promote Democratic candidates. They created a series of 527 groups to raise money, not subject to the federal restrictions, and use it for electioneering in behalf of Democrats during the four-and-a-half-month period after the Democratic nomination had been effectively decided and before the Democratic National Convention and after the conventions.

The groups included America Coming Together (ACT), an organization composed of Emily's List, which raises money for pro-choice women candidates, primarily Democrats, and the American Federation of Labor-Congress of Industrial Organizations (AFL-CIO), the largest labor organization in the country. Directed at grassroots organizing, ACT sought to create a massive database of potential Democratic voters in the key battleground states and then reach them over the course of the campaign by mail, telephone, and house-to-house contacts. Its goal, to raise $95 million for this activity, was aided by donations from billionaire financier George Soros, Peter Lewis, and labor unions (Edsall 2003a, 2003b). ACT raised $51 million through September 2004 (Willis 2004).

A second group, the Media Fund, headed by Harold Ickes, former deputy chief of staff in the Clinton administration, raised money—$46 million through September 2004—for advertising campaigns in the key battleground states, positive ads that promoted Senator Kerry, confrontational ads that criticized the president, and ads that responded quickly to any negative Republican allegations about the Democratic nominees (Willis 2004). The New Democratic Network, another media group, was set up to appeal to the Latino community and sponsor ads in Spanish in areas with large Hispanic populations such as New Mexico, Arizona, and Nevada. Yet another media group, MoveOn.org Voter Fund, also solicited money for anti-Bush television and Internet advertising. All three groups coordinated their activities with one another, although they could not do so with the Democratic National Committee (Rutenberg 2004b).

In addition, a network of liberal groups formed a 527 group, America Votes, to coordinate the environmental, abortion, and civil rights interests on behalf of the Democrats (Edsall 2003c). Table 6-3 lists the Democratic advocacy groups active during the 2003–2004 election cycle.

Naturally, Republicans were concerned about the creation of these groups. They believed the groups violated the letter and the spirit of the McCain-Feingold law—a law Democrats had supported but many Republicans had opposed. To raise the legal issue and to be prepared in case that issue was not resolved favorably, Republicans formed their own 527 group, Americans for a Better Country. This group immediately asked the Federal Election Commission (FEC) for an advisory opinion on the legality of raising and spending soft money for electoral activities.

The FEC considered the issue in May 2004, after the Democratic primaries were effectively concluded but well before the general election campaign.

Table 6-3 Pro-Democratic Advocacy Groups, 2004 Presidential Election

Group	Function	Financial goal
Alliance for Economic Justice	Promote job and trade issues	Undetermined
America Coming Together	Mount major voter mobilization campaign	$95 million
America Votes	Coordinate other advocacy groups to avoid overlap in their efforts	$2.5 million
Environment 2004	Promote sound environmental policies	$5 million
Grassroots Democrats	Supplement Democratic campaign activity at the state level	$12 million
Media Fund	Design and air radio and television advertising in key battleground states	$95 million
MoveOn.org Voter Fund	Run anti-Bush television and Internet ads	$10 million
New Democratic Network	Media group, sponsoring Spanish-language ads in areas with large Hispanic populations, primarily in the Southwest	Undetermined
Partnership for America's Families	Labor-based, grassroots activities	$10–12 million
Voices for Working Families	Labor-based, grassroots activities	$20 million

Sources: Thomas B. Edsall, "Money, Votes Pursued for Democrats," *Washington Post,* December 8, 2003, A8, and "Preparing for Battle," *Washington Post,* December 7, A8.

The Republicans argued that groups that solicited both hard and soft money had to pay for ads that mentioned federal candidates with hard money only. By contrast, the Democrats contended that the soft money restriction only applied to the national parties, not nonparty groups and state parties. In the end, the FEC decided not to get involved during the 2003–2004 election cycle. Although it rejected a proposal that would have subjected these groups to federal limits, several commissioners suggested that they would revisit the issue after the election.

In the summer of 2004, the Bush-Cheney reelection committee and the Republican National Committee again challenged the rights of these groups, urging the judiciary to force the FEC to prohibit such activities.

The Republican appeal stemmed from a controversial series of ads sponsored by a pro-Bush group, Swift Boat Veterans for Truth, which challenged Kerry's Vietnam War record and his protest activities after he left military service. The ads, to which the Kerry campaign did not immediately respond, seemed to be having an impact on public perceptions of the Democratic candidate, particularly among veterans. They also became a news item, prompting several investigative reports by leading newspapers. The news reports criticized the veracity of the claims in the ads; they also revealed the connection between the ads' sponsors and the Bush-Cheney campaign. As a consequence, pressure was put on the president by prominent veterans such as Sen. John McCain and former senator Max Cleland of Georgia to repudiate the group's advertisements and ask them to withdraw the ads. Instead, Bush responded by denouncing all 527 groups and urging that their soft money solicitation and expenditure be banned—thus the legal action.

Convention Activities

The support of nonparty groups does not end with the winning of the nomination. Good will, expressed in dollars and in-kind contributions, continues to flow to the parties and indirectly to their nominees at the national conventions. Despite the fact that these conventions are party affairs and are funded in part by a government grant ($14.6 million in 2004) and by the states and cities that host them, corporations, labor unions, and trade associations continue to "help out" and provide "good will" to the tune of $103.5 million (Campaign Finance Institute 2004).

At recent Democratic and Republican National Conventions, corporate giants such as Anheuser-Busch, AT&T, Bank of America, and Philip Morris/Kraft, RJR/Nabisco were major sponsors, giving substantial sums to each of the parties to help defray their convention costs (Willis 2000).[1] In 2004, 110 individual and group donors gave $100,000 or more to the Democrats, who spent about $42 million on their convention. The Republicans spent more on their convention, an estimated $64 million, much of it from private donors (Campaign Finance Institute 2004). These corporate contributions were in addition to their PAC contributions to the candidates and their soft money contributions to the parties.

"Indirect," in-kind benefits supplement the direct money gifts. Corporations host elaborate receptions to which the delegates are invited and wined and dined. Telecommunications companies provide pages, phones, and high-speed Internet connections. Major automobile manufacturers provide cars.

The parties also reward their major donors and most active fund-raisers with VIP treatment at their convention, private dinners with party leaders, and deluxe hotel accommodations. The Republicans held a special cruise on a private yacht on the Delaware River for their biggest donors in 2000 and even invited some to go on a fishing trip with House Speaker Dennis Hastert (Broder and Van Natta 2000).

In addition to funding events, groups try to influence the party's platform positions. The Christian Coalition and the National Rifle Association (NRA) have exercised considerable influence at recent Republican conventions, the Christian Coalition on platform positions on social issues such as abortion and the NRA on the right to bear arms. Organized labor regularly exerts its muscle at Democratic conventions, as does the National Education Association and several of the gender, racial, and ethnic groups that make up the Democrats' electoral coalition.

The benefits for ideological and issue groups are obvious — acceptable platform language, visibility for their spokespeople at the conventions, and, it is hoped, commitments by the candidates to the groups' priorities and positions. But what do the economic groups, such as the corporate and labor ones, and those donors who sympathize with them get for their money?

Most business, labor, and individual donors view their contributions as sound political investments. Doors open to large contributors. They have the access to make their cases and the resources to support their positions. They can hire the best lobbyists and public relations firms, and they do.

There are personal benefits as well. In addition to the VIP treatment and invitations to receptions, briefings, and trips with elected party leaders, ambassadorships to desirable countries also serve as a reward for generous donors. Table 6-4 lists George W. Bush's choice of European ambassadors, along with their contributions to the Republican Party.

Table 6-4 Ambassador–Contributor Connection, George W. Bush Administration, 2001–2005

Country	Nominee	Contribution to Republican Party
Austria	W. L. Lyons Brown	$136,450
Belgium	Stephen Brauer	413,830
Czech Republic	Craig Stapleton	61,500
Denmark	Stuart Bernstein	182,600
Finland	Bonnie McElveen-Hunter	107,750
France	Howard Leach	399,359
Germany	Dan Coats[a]	3,500
Hungary	Nancy Brinker	125,000
Ireland	Richard J. Egan	480,100
Italy	Melvin Sembler	127,600
Luxembourg	Denis Coleman	105,000
Netherlands	Clifford Sobel	299,700
Norway	John Ong	181,735
Portugal	John Palmer	166,850
Slovak Republic	Robert Weiser	45,250
Spain	George Argyros	134,000
Sweden	Charles Heimbold	365,200
Switzerland	Mercer Reynolds	456,173
United Kingdom	William S. Farish	142,875

Source: Center for Responsive Politics, "2000 Presidential Race" and "Embassy Row," http://www.opensecrets.org/2000elect.

[a] Coats was a former U.S. senator (R-IN) who was interviewed for defense secretary but did not get that position. Germany was his consolation prize.

The General Election

Although PAC contributions to the major-party presidential candidates in the general election are not permitted if the candidates accepted federal funds, they are allowed for third and independent party candidates. In 1992, however, third-party candidate H. Ross Perot did not solicit such money and only a small amount of PAC contributions filtered in to the other minor-party candidates. Similarly, in 1996 and 2000 minor-party candidates, with the exception of the Reform Party, which was eligible for federal funding, received only a trickle of outside financial support, forcing them to depend on free media for making their policy appeals. The exclusion of third-party candidates from the presidential debates further relegated them to the shadows of the 2000 election, with only Ralph Nader able to gain visibility by virtue of his own notoriety, his modest fundraising efforts, and his potential for siphoning enough votes from Gore in several key states such as Florida, Wisconsin, Iowa, and Oregon that he would toss the election to Bush.

Soft Money and Issue Advocacy

The bulk of the soft money that finds its way into presidential campaigns is spent on issue advocacy. The Annenberg Public Policy Center at the University of Pennsylvania has estimated that, for the entire 1995–1996 election cycle, the two major parties spent $150 million on issue advocacy and party-building activities (Falk 2000). In that election cycle, the number of nonparty groups that advocated their issue positions through this type of electoral activity was small. Both party and nonparty involvement in issue advocacy increased during the 1997–1998 midterm election cycle and mushroomed by the 2000 election.

According to the Annenberg study, $509 million was spent in this manner to influence the 2000 election. Of this amount, the major parties raised and spent about one-third of it, $162 million. They sponsored about two-thirds of the issue advocacy television and radio advertising in the principal media markets (Slass 2001). For the first time, the national parties spent more on advertising that benefited their presidential candidates, directly or indirectly, than did the candidates themselves (Brennan Center for Justice 2000).

After examining the seventy-five top media markets, the researchers at Annenberg found that almost $250 million was expended on ads. Eighty-seven percent of the issue ads were candidate-centered. As the election approached, this percentage increased to 94. Of the candidate-centered ads, the presidential candidates appeared in 42 percent of them. Most of the ads contained attack and contrast components (Brennan Center for Justice 2000).[2] And as noted earlier, the public could not differentiate these ads from those sponsored by the candidates.

The advertising pace accelerated in 2004. In the first five months, the candidates spent a combined total of $66.3 million (Nielsen News Releases 2004).

Although Bush outspent Kerry during this period, nonparty advocacy groups, such as MoveOn.org and the Media Fund, which supported the Democratic candidate, made up much of the difference. The advertising focused on the major battleground states and aired during local news, morning news, syndicated talk shows, even game shows (University of Wisconsin Advertising Project 2004).

In addition to issue advocacy advertising, party and nonparty groups have also used soft money to operate telephone banks, print and distribute campaign literature, and recruit field organizers and other political operatives. The presidential candidates depend on the state parties for these activities as well as to pay for the candidates' public relations and grassroots staffers who are based in the states.

Nonparty Groups and Issue Advocacy

Nonparty groups have also become more directly involved in the electoral process in general and issue advocacy in particular. During the 1995–1996 election process, the participation of outside groups was limited. The AFL-CIO raised $35 million in a special assessment and spent it in the key battleground states to educate the public and help to secure a Democratic Congress. The Coalition, a group of large business organizations, tried to counter labor's campaign by spending $4 million, mostly in behalf of Republican candidates.

By 2000 the expenditures of outside groups had greatly increased, with much of this money spent on issue advocacy. Table 6-5 indicates the amount spent by parties and nonparty groups on issue advocacy advertising in 1999–2000.

The six groups listed in Table 6-5 accounted for one-third of the issue advocacy spending in 2000; the major parties accounted for another third. References to the candidate dominated both party and nonparty advocacy commercials.

Table 6-5 Spending on Issue Ads, 1999–2000 Election Cycle

	Amount (millions)
Political parties	
Democratic	$78.4
Republican	83.5
Interest groups	
Citizens for Better Medicare	65.0
Coalition to Protect America's Health Care	30.0
U.S. Chamber of Commerce	25.5
AFL-CIO	21.1
National Rifle Association	20.0
U.S. Term Limits	20.0
Others	166.2
Total	$509.0

Source: Lorie Slass, "Spending on Issue Advocacy in the 2000 Cycle," in *Issue Advocacy Advertising in the 1999–2000 Election Cycle,* ed. Kathleen Hall Jamieson (Philadelphia: Annenberg Public Policy Center at the University of Pennsylvania, 2001).

Issue advocacy is not the only device used by groups to communicate with the electorate. Like parties, they also use telephone and direct-mail campaigns. The National Association for the Advancement of Colored People (NAACP) spent an estimated $10.5 million to target and turn out African American voters in thirteen battleground states in 2000. The campaign included recorded telephone messages from Bill Clinton and Jesse Jackson. The NAACP also ran ads criticizing George W. Bush for vetoing a hate crime bill when he was governor of Texas (Malbin 2001).

Independent Expenditures

In addition to the expenditures on issue advocacy and get-out-the-vote activities, individuals and groups may also spend money independently in support or opposition to particular candidates, but they cannot do so in collusion with the parties. Independent spending has usually favored Republican presidential candidates more than their Democratic opponents. Ronald Reagan in 1980 and in 1984 and George Bush in 1988 both had more spent for them and more spent against their opponents. Even when enthusiasm waned for George Bush in 1992, he still received 75 percent of the independent expenditures spent for a candidate; Clinton was the target of 70 percent of expenditures spent against a candidate (Alexander and Corrado 1995).

The election of 2000 saw $10.6 million spent independently by both parties. More was spent for Bush than for Gore, but also more was spent against Bush than Gore. Table 6-6 lists these expenditures.

Two wealthy businessmen and three organizations accounted for the bulk of independent spending in 2000. Stephen Adams spent $1 million in behalf of Bush, and Steven T. Kirsch spent almost $1.1 million against him. The National Rifle Association and National Right to Life Committee expended $2 and 1.8 million, respectively, to elect Bush. The National Abortion and Reproductive Rights Action League (NARAL) was Gore's biggest independent spender at $3.5 million. The League of Conservation Voters, a Republican-oriented group created for the 2000 campaign, and the National Rifle Association spent the most against Gore.

Table 6-6   Independent Expenses, 2000 Presidential Election

Candidate	For	Against	Total
George W. Bush	$4,938,309	$1,172,226	$6,110,535
Al Gore	3,953,782	571,046	4,524,828
Total	$8,892,091	$1,743,272	$10,635,363

Source: Calculated on the basis of data provided by the Federal Election Commission.

Conclusion

Presidential campaign organizations are not the only groups active on the road to the White House. The major political parties and nonparty groups supplement the presidential selection process to the point where the presidential candidates now depend on their activities. They depend on PACs and individual contributions for the competitive stage of the nomination process; on parties and, increasingly, on 527 groups during the noncompetitive stage in the months prior to the nominating conventions; and on the parties and nonparty groups for issue advocacy and grassroots organizing for the general election. In fact, three presidential campaigns are run every four years: one by the candidates and their organizations, one by the national parties and their local affiliates, and one by allied but not coordinated nonparty groups.

Presidential candidates used to look to their parties for soft money, but now they must rely on friendly, nonparty groups to raise it and spend it in their behalf. Although the presidential candidates and their parties are prohibited by law from coordinating the electoral participation of nonparty groups, they can, at the very least, adjust their campaigns to this expected activity. In fact, they often benefit when their nonparty supporters take the low road by making flagrant allegations against their opponents as the Swift Boat Veterans for Truth did against John Kerry and MoveOn.org did against George W. Bush in 2004. The candidates and the parties can distance themselves from these remarks, while profiting from the fallout that the accusations may produce.

Although the supplemental campaigns of the parties and nonparty groups have extended the range of presidential campaigns, and raised their costs substantially, these campaigns also have reduced the control that the presidential candidates and their organizations can exercise directly over the campaign. Moreover, these additional efforts to elect or defeat the major-party nominees have effectively circumvented the goals and spirit of the Federal Election Campaign Act (1974 and 1976) and the Bipartisan Campaign Reform Act (2002) to limit the influence of wealthy donors, to reduce the dependency of the parties and the candidates on indirect funding, and to eliminate the time and effort that presidential nominees spend raising money.

Not only have these supplemental campaigns undercut the campaign finance system, but they also have contributed to the public perception that special-interest politics dominates elections and influences government decision making. The connection between big bucks, open doors, personal benefits, and prestigious appointments has been a salient one for the last two decades, and promises to be one for the current decade as well.

Although the presidential campaign is not the principal conduit through which outside money travels and on which it is spent, that campaign still benefits from the financial involvement of party and nonparty groups. In this sense, the fellow travelers on the road to the White House are part of the problem, because they contribute to the perception that the presidential election is the best money can buy.

Notes

1. The Democrats refused to take money from tobacco companies and gun manufacturers in 2000.
2. Total expenditures from all political advertising during the 2000 election campaign were between $771 million and $1 billion, according to a joint study by the Alliance for Better Campaigns and the Norman Lear Center at the University of California (Alliance for Better Campaigns 2001).

References

Alexander, Herbert E., and Anthony Corrado. 1995. *Financing the 1992 Election.* Armonk, NY: M. E. Sharpe.
Alliance for Better Campaigns. 2001. *Gouging Democracy: How The Television Industry Profiteered on Campaign 2000.* Washington, DC: Alliance for Better Campaigns. http://www.bettercampaigns.org/Doldisc/gougesumm.htm.
Brennan Center for Justice. 2000. "2000 Presidential Race First in Modern History Where Political Parties Spend More on TV Ads than Candidates." Press release, December 11. http://www.brennancenter.org.
Broder, John M., and Don Van Natta Jr. 2000. "Perks for Biggest Donors, and Please for More Cash." *New York Times,* July 30, A1.
Campaign Finance Institute. 2004. "New Disclosures Show Former Soft Money Donors to Republican Party Fuel New York Republican Convention," August 23.
———. 2004. "The $100 Million Exemption," July 7. http://www.cfinst.org/pr/070704.
Center for Responsive Politics. 2001. "2000 Presidential Race" and "Embassy Row." http://www.opensecrets.org/2000elect.
———. 2004. "Election Overview: Who Gives?" http://www.opensecrets.org/2004election.
Edsall, Thomas B. 2003a. "Groups Join Forces, Funds to Oppose Bush in 2004." *Denver Post,* August 8, A14.
———. 2003b. "Money, Votes Pursued for Democrats," *Washington Post,* December 8, A8.
———. 2003c. "Preparing for Battle." *Washington Post,* December 7, A8.
Falk, Erika. 2000. "Issue Advocacy Advertising through the Presidential Primary 1999–2000 Election Cycle." Annenberg Public Policy Center at the University of Pennsylvania, Philadelphia. http://www.appepenn.org/issueads/2000issuead.htm.
Federal Election Commission. 2003. "Party Committees Raise More than $1 Billion in 2000–2002," March 20. http://www.fec.gov/press/press2003/20030320party/20030103party.html.
———. 2004. "FEC Approves Matching Funds for 2004 Presidential Candidates," March 31. http://www.fec.gov/press2004/20040331/20040331matching.html.
Knott, Alex, and Agustin Armendariz. 2003. "Politician 527s Committees Tied to Lawmakers Adjust to New Regulations." Center for Public Integrity, Washington, DC. http://www.publicintegrity.org/527/report.
Malbin, Michael J., ed. 2001. "Issue Ads: Recommendations for a New Approach." Campaign Finance Institute, George Washington University. http://www.cfinst.org/disclosure/report1/toc.htm.
Nielsen News Releases. 2004. "John Kerry Local Political Ad Spending on the Rise—George Bush Scaling Back," June 17.
Oppel, Richard A., Jr., and Richard Perez-Pena. 2000. "The Power Broker: Role in Ads Puts Focus on Bush Friend." *New York Times,* December 6, A1, A22.
Rutenberg, Jim. 2004a. "Kerry, Focus of Attack Ad, Reacts with One of His Own." *New York Times,* March 13, A11.

————. 2004b. "Political Groups Taking on Bush in New Ad Campaign." *New York Times*, March 10, A16.

Slass, Lorie. 2001. "Spending on Issue Advocacy in the 2000 Cycle." In *Issue Advocacy Advertising in the 1999–2000 Election Cycle*, edited by Kathleen Hall Jamieson. Philadelphia: Annenberg Public Policy Center at the University of Pennsylvania. http://www.appepenn.org/issueads/2000issuead.htm.

University of Wisconsin Advertising Project. 2004. "High Volume of Presidential Campaign TV Advertising in Battleground States, Yet 60 percent of Americans Live in Areas Where No Ads Have Aired," July.

Willis, Derek. 2000. "Putting on a Convention Takes Money—and Cars, Phones, Internet Connections . . ." *CQ Weekly*, July 29, 66.

————. 2004. "527 Fundraising Nets a Record Haul," Center for Public Integrity, October 19. http://www.centerforpublicintegrity.org/527/report.

Part II
Congressional Connection

7. Continuity and Change
in the Congressional Connection

Clyde Wilcox and Dong-Young Kim

If political scientists were charged to design a national legislature to maximize interest group influence, they would be hard-pressed to improve on the U.S. Congress. Because any member can introduce legislation, groups can often find someone to write their pet policy into a bill and drop it in the hopper. Because members can vote the way they choose, groups can bargain with and persuade individual members of both parties instead of dealing with the kind of central party leadership found in a parliamentary system. Because policy is rewritten in subcommittees and committees of both the House and Senate and in conference, and is sometimes amended during floor debates, groups have many opportunities to insert special provisions that benefit their members. Because legislation is increasingly altered in conference committees that bargain out differences between the House and Senate version of legislation, groups have an ample opportunity to insert still more provisions. Finally, because majorities must be assembled at many points during the legislative process, groups that favor the status quo have many chances to convince enough legislators to kill a bill. Clearly, then, groups have many points of access to Congress.

Members of Congress also have incentives to listen to interest groups. First, members must frequently make decisions on several very large, highly technical pieces of legislation in a single day, especially at the end of the legislative session. Because any single vote can become an issue in the next campaign, members are often quite interested in obtaining information from groups about the policy and political implications of legislation. Second, members must assemble their own electoral coalitions, sometimes without a great deal of help from their party. Groups have important resources to help candidates reach voters, including infrastructure, communication channels, and volunteers. Moreover, candidates must raise the money to finance their campaigns, and so, faced with the skyrocketing cost of modern campaigns, they find the financial contributions and spending of interest groups quite attractive.

For all of these reasons, Congress is quite open to interest group influence. The institution has been permeable to groups throughout its history, but changes in institutional arrangements, in the interest group universe, and in technology have affected the extent and the manner of group influence, as well as the kinds of groups that are influential. For as long as political scientists have been studying congressional lobbying by interest groups, however, two main types of tactics have been used by these groups in lobbying Congress: an "inside" strategy and an "outside" strategy.

Inside Strategies

Inside strategies generally involve quietly persuading a member of Congress, in a meeting with interest group lobbyists, to act or vote in a particular way. Lobbyists usually present information in these meetings—probably some combination of technical information about the likely impact of legislation and political information about the constellation of actors who might support and oppose a bill. The arguments and information that the lobbyists present do not always carry the day. But they do so often enough to spur many groups to use in-house and outside lobbyists to try to influence the content of legislation and its odds of passage.

How Do Groups Use Inside Strategies?

Inside strategies work only for groups that are able to gain access to members and key congressional staffers. Of the variety of strategies used to gain access, one of the most common is to contribute to a legislator's campaign, usually through a political action committee (PAC), but occasionally through coordinated giving by several interest groups.

The evidence that campaign contributions do help groups gain access to members of Congress is considerable (see, for example, Langbein and Lotwis 1990). Indeed, members organize fundraising events that guarantee group lobbyists access. Moreover, they frequently hold such events the evening before a critical markup session when changes to legislation are made. Many committee chairs host "PAC breakfasts," so that selected interest group representatives can sit down and talk directly with the member. In Chapter 8, Paul R. Brewer and Christopher J. Deering report on another way that groups can give money to gain access—by supporting the efforts of members to win the chairmanship of committees or a party leadership post. Groups can give money to the leadership candidate's campaign committee or to his or her PAC or foundation. Some groups even contribute to the campaigns of other members and candidates at the request of prospective leaders (Wilcox 1990).

Groups do not merely give money to candidates, they also mobilize volunteers, try to get out the vote, and often run advertisements that seek to define the debate both in the election and on Capitol Hill. This electoral support may be at least as valuable as cash and therefore establish a connection between legislators and interest groups. In Chapter 11, Peter L. Francia shows how the American Federation of Labor–Congress of Industrial Organizations (AFL-CIO) has used a variety of electoral tools to parlay this electoral activity into impacts on public policy.

Giving money and offering other electoral support are not the only ways to gain access to a member of Congress. Interest groups with sizable numbers of members in a given state or district can often gain the ear of their senator or representative simply because they represent many voters (Wright 1996). Grassroots organizations may have access because of their ability to mount voter mobilization campaigns, or because of their ability to communicate with their members. In Chapter 10, John C. Green and Nathan S. Bigelow show how the Christian Coalition has used its electoral strengths to gain access to GOP policymakers. Organizations that possess important technical information can often find a member or key staff aide to pay attention to their data. Groups with large budgets may hire professional lobbyists who have access to certain key legislators or committees.

Sometimes, interest groups seek to connect only with congressional committee staffers, because these staffers often play a major role in drafting technical legislation and they meet frequently with lobbyists who have information to convey. Lobbyists also seek out meetings with members' office staffs, who often are involved in meetings in which members are deciding key votes or discussing possible legislative initiatives. Before passage of the congressional gift bans, free tickets to hockey games were frequently the carrot that led to staff discussions. Today, staffers may join lobbyists at hockey games or other sporting or entertainment events, but they must pay for their own tickets.

All this said, most groups do not get direct access to every member. Republicans with strong ties to polluting industries may not take the time to meet with lobbyists from the Sierra Club, for example, and Democrats from socially liberal constituencies may not meet directly with lobbyists from the Christian Coalition. Generally, groups with sizable memberships can at least meet with office staff, but in some cases even these meetings cannot be arranged.

Many groups seek not only to gain access to members, but also to enlist some of them to champion their cause. In Chapter 9, Joseph White describes how groups recruit champions—or "horses" as some lobbyists call them (Walker 1997)—for the appropriations process. When a group succeeds in forming a close relationship with some legislators, it may give them useful political information, short speeches to deliver on the floor, and longer speeches to deliver elsewhere. The staff of the interest group may even take on some of the functions of congressional staffers. The member, in turn, may introduce legislation, offer amendments, or try to change legislation during committee markup. Such functions have become especially important to groups now that the standard policymaking process has broken down in Congress, allowing for unconventional policymaking (Sinclair 2000).

In the House, interest groups especially try to gain access to members of substantive committees, the Appropriation Committees, and the Rules Committee, because legislation that comes out of committee usually passes on the floor, often under restrictive rules that limit amendments. In Chapter 9, White describes how and why groups try to influence the appropriations subcommittees in the House. In the Senate, however, any member can "hold" a bill until his or her substantive issues are addressed—a practice that allows interest groups to cultivate any member for any issue. In that body, policy negotiations are often more informal, including senators from the substantive committee and others with an interest in the legislation (see, for example, Cohen 1992).

Once a group has gained access to a member of Congress, its lobbyists must persuade the member to support its position. At this point, information is generally critical—both technical information on the merits of the case and political intelligence about the constellation of actors supporting or opposing a bill.

Does Inside Lobbying Matter?

It is often argued that campaign contributions not only buy access but also political support for legislation, but to date political science research has uncovered only a weak link between PAC contributions and roll call voting—far weaker, in fact, than the effect of constituency opinion or strong persuasion by the president or party leaders (see, for example, Chappell 1981; Wright 1985; Grenzke 1989). The conclusion of this research is that you can buy some of the votes some of the time, but that you cannot buy all of the votes all of the time.

Yet many political actors charge that money has a very strong influence on congressional policymaking. Retiring members frequently complain that their colleagues (but not themselves) have been bought by special interests, although few admit that money influenced their own votes. Many journalists who cover campaign finance believe that contributions have a profound influence on legislation, and they can supply numerous anecdotes to support their claims (see, for example, Drew 1983; Jackson 1988). Some PAC directors will even admit to having influenced votes by contributions, though never on the record.

How, then, can one reconcile the finding of political scientists that contributions have only a modest impact on roll call voting with the widespread view that Congress is for sale? There are several possibilities. First, it may be that the widespread cynicism about Congress that generates the conventional wisdom is simply wrong, and that sound scientific research has dispelled a common myth.

Second, it may be that political scientists have measured campaign contributions too narrowly. Most studies do not include bundled contributions from individual members of groups, or soft money contributions (when they were legal), issue advocacy support, or noncash electoral support. When these are added to PAC contributions, a relationship between money and policymaking might emerge.

Third, perhaps political scientists and insiders are looking at different questions and both claims are true. On any given roll call vote, most votes can be determined by ideology, partisanship, and elite cues, but those votes that are swayed by contributions may be sufficiently numerous to affect the outcome. Indeed, some recent research suggests that money may be especially influential on the votes that determine the outcome of legislation, especially in committee (Gordon 2001). Political scientists might therefore conclude that contributions influenced few votes, and journalists might report that the bill passed or was defeated because of political money.

Fourth, it may be that roll call votes are not the main way that money influences the legislative process. Major legislation frequently contains many paragraphs, sentences, or even clauses that can greatly affect groups, and it may well be in the formal and informal negotiations and bargaining that decides the final wording of legislation that the impact of money is most important.

Finally, the linkage of roll call voting to campaign contributions also ignores the fact that much of the relationship between interest groups and their lobbyists and members of Congress, as it relates to money and politics, revolves around ensuring that a roll call vote never happens (see Bachrach and Baratz 1963 for a discussion of this type of political power). This absence of legislative activity is a much more perplexing measure of interest group influence. Political scientists are only starting to wrestle with this aspect of the interest group connection in Congress.

Whatever the impact of campaign contributions on voting or nonvoting, it is clear that the information provided by interest groups does influence legislation. Groups seek access using whatever resources they can muster, and then try to use that access to persuade members to back their policy proposals. Inside lobbying is most successful when it is not noticed—when a group quietly succeeds in getting its proposals through Congress or in blocking legislation that it finds objectionable. Many of the lobbyists for the Christian Right groups discussed in Chapter 10 by Green and Bigelow claim that their greatest successes have been in preventing liberal social legislation from becoming law.

Changing Inside Strategies

Although inside strategies have long been part of Congress, the problems and opportunities that confront groups that use these strategies have changed over time. Three factors stand out. First, changes in the levels of centralization in congressional decision making affect groups' ability to target lawmakers. Second, changes in the control of Congress and in the unity and margin of the majority party have an impact. Finally, changes in congressional budgetary policies and norms have affected the way in which groups seek to practice insider lobbying.

A Shift in Levels of Centralization. After the revolt against Speaker Joseph G. Cannon, R-IL, early in the twentieth century, Congress was ruled by a few powerful men who chaired influential committees. Interest groups could have an effect on legislation by cutting deals with a few committee chairs and party leaders, confident that these men could control the committees and the floor debate (see Davidson 1981). The corporate and labor interests that dominated the interest group environment of the time formed stable and cozy relationships with committee chairs and other leaders.

The 1974 election, however, saw many new liberal Democratic members voted into Congress, and they immediately sought to change the institutional norms and power arrangements. The norm of deference of younger members to committee chairs and party leaders was seriously eroded by this eager class of reformers, who helped to increase the power of subcommittees and create mechanisms to remove committee chairs who abused their power. They were aided in this task by a series of scandals that beset powerful committee chairs. For example, House Ways and Means Committee chair Wilbur Mills, D-AR, was caught cavorting in Washington's Tidal Basin with stripper Fannie Foxe — an escapade that ended his reign as one of the most powerful men in the nation's capital.

Decentralization presented interest groups with new opportunities and new problems. As subcommittees proliferated, important legislation was often referred to several committees and subcommittees. Where once a powerful interest group could block a bill by approaching a single committee chair, now many committee and subcommittee chairs were involved, and none of them could guarantee the votes of other committee members. The opportunities to insert special provisions into legislation multiplied, but so did the opportunities for other groups to insert provisions that would be harmful to the group's interests.

Because they found it so difficult to gain access to so many members, a surprising number of whom were relatively new to Congress, groups began to rely much more frequently on coalitions. Some of these coalitions are formal and enduring; others are ephemeral and informal. Some are predictable, such as when environmental groups worked together on Clean Air legislation in 1990; others are surprising, such as when the Christian Coalition and the American Civil Liberties Union (ACLU) joined forces in 1995 to oppose elements of lobby reform legislation. In Chapter 12, Kevin W. Hula describes one surprising coalition — between environmentalists and social conservatives in opposition to new genetic technologies such as cloning. Coalitions play a vital role in the modern Congress as groups combine their various resources and their lists of friendly members to lobby more effectively. By working together in coalitions, groups are able to have some degree of contact with far more key members of Congress.

Meanwhile, in response to the institutional reforms in Congress professional lobbying firms began to offer a brokering service; they would assemble a coalition of actors who would support or oppose specific legislation on an ad hoc basis. For example, in the 1993 debate surrounding the North American Free Trade Agreement (NAFTA), the Wexler Group, a Washington-based lobbying firm that specializes in coalition building, managed the pro-NAFTA forces. Some of these coalitions adopt names and couch their appeals in terms of the public interest, but in fact are financed by one or a few economic interests. For example, the National Wetlands Coalition is a group of oil drillers, land developers, and major gas companies; the Consumer Foundation is dominated by Sears, Woolworth, and Walgreen; and the Coalition for Health Care Choices is primarily financed by the Health Insurance Association of America (HIAA), the organization that aired the "Harry and Louise" commercials during the national debate on health care in 1994 (Shaiko 1995, 168). Yet some coalitions are genuine cooperative efforts. During consideration of the Clean Air bill in 1990, the major environmental groups met regularly and coordinated their efforts under the name of Clean Air Coalition, while industry groups worked together under the name of the Clean Air Working Group.

Changes in Congressional Party Leadership. The new Republican majority in the House in 1994 sought to increase the power of the party leaders over the committee chairs. It limited the terms of the chairs and gave the Speaker more influence in choosing chairs. As the traditional legislative process has become stymied, increasingly party leaders have emerged as important actors in shaping legislation. Although this new centralization is far from that exercised by Cannon, it does represent a change from the subcommittee government of the late 1970s.

Once in office, the new Republican leadership lobbied its members to deny access to some interest groups and to open their doors to others. Environmental groups and labor unions lost their easy access to the majority, but the National Rifle Association (NRA) and the Christian Coalition increased their influence. The NRA-organized hearings on the 1992 Ruby Ridge, Idaho, shootings are an example of the close ties between interest groups and the Republican leadership, which approved of the hearings.

More important, the actual implementing legislation for the Contract with America (the campaign manifesto devised by Republicans during the 1994 midterm elections) was written in part by a group of lobbyists who made large donations to the Republican Party and who agreed to support the entire package of proposals that came out of the process. Thus the American Petroleum Institute helped to draft legislation that would reduce liabilities from toxic wastes. And lobbyists for corporations wrote the legislation on regulatory relief that limited the ability of the bureaucracy to enforce existing environmental and worker safety rules (Greider 1992; Judis 1995).

That interest groups draft legislation is not new: Democrats often allowed their allies to help craft bills. But they balanced a constituency of labor, environmentalists, women, and minorities with business interests, while the new Republican House majority essentially excluded liberal groups from the formulation process. The result was legislation that often included lobbyists' wildest dreams, but that failed to pass the more moderate Senate and led to very unfavorable public evaluations of Gingrich and Congress.

By the end of the 1990s, interest groups began to face a new reality. The two political parties were increasingly different in their policy preferences as a result of both the steady gains by conservatives in GOP primaries and the defeat of moderate southern Democrats in the 1994 elections. In addition, the two parties were almost deadlocked for control of Congress: the election of 2000 produced a tie in the U.S. Senate (soon changed by the defection of one Republican senator) and a very narrow margin in the House.

This new polarized politics combined with narrow margins made it more difficult for groups to seek access to policymakers of both parties. Whereas business groups had traditionally supported many Democrats and liberal social groups had supported some moderate Republicans, such support became problematic when any given seat might decide who the next Speaker of the House or Senate majority leader would be. Electoral politics became more polarized (Malbin et al. 2002), and lobbying began to change with it. Moreover, both parties began to give greater authority to their leaders as part of a "conditional party government" (Aldrich and Rhode 2000).

Changes in Congressional Budgetary Policies. Changes in budgetary rules and norms have altered the nature of interest group lobbying as well. In the 1970s, agricultural groups lobbied together for price supports for all crops, and defense contractors for additional military spending. But changes in the budget rules in the late 1980s and early 1990s forced Congress to think of the budget in zero-sum terms: additional funds for one group meant fewer funds for another. In the late 1990s, budgetary constraints seemed less important as economists forecast budget surpluses for as far as the eye could see. But by 2002, after a large tax cut and large increase in spending for military and domestic security, the country again faced deficits and conflicts among groups for scarce resources.

The Popularity of Inside Strategies

Overall, the use of inside strategies has increased somewhat over time. The number of PACs peaked in the late 1980s at more than four thousand, but many groups have expanded their campaign finance activity in an effort to gain greater access to members. Schlozman and Tierney (1984) found that substantial majorities of the interest groups they surveyed in the 1980s reported engaging more often in a variety of inside strategies: seeking direct contact with policymakers, testifying at hearings, presenting research results or technical information, engaging in informal contacts with policymakers, helping to draft legislation, and making financial contributions to campaigns. Such trends continued in the1990s.

Outside Strategies

If the inside strategy is the carrot, the outside strategy is the stick. Grassroots lobbying involves using interest group members (or the general public) to pressure congressional lawmakers to support the group's agenda. Generally, such lobbying brings with it an implicit or explicit threat that group members will work to defeat the targeted member of Congress if she or he refuses to support the group's policies. Yet the threat is sometimes coupled with the promise of electoral support if the member agrees to promote the group's goals. Grassroots strategies are the principal tools of the Christian Right (see Chapter 10).

Outside strategies involve contact between a group's members and the offices of legislators. The oldest and still most common means of grassroots pressure is the letter-writing campaign. In the 1960s, only a few groups such as the NRA, with its network of gun clubs and frequent newsletters, could mount coordinated mail campaigns. With the advent of powerful desktop computers and word processing programs, however, nearly any group can now contact its members, provide them with information, and urge them to sign a postcard or form letter, or to draft a letter in their own words. Moreover, improvements in computer technology have allowed groups, using mailings, to mobilize only special segments of their constituency—for example, members from particular districts or states, or members who have shown a special interest in a key issue (Fowler and Shaiko 1987). And groups can contact their members and activists by e-mail, urging them to e-mail or write to their representatives.

Congressional offices are routinely barraged with postcards and form letters, and most of them simply count these mass-produced communications but do not reply to them. More effective are hand-written letters by individual constituents. The NRA often instructs their members to write a letter in their own hand and in their own words, expressing their view on a bill. Although the letters may miss some of the details of the legislation under consideration, they nonetheless reflect constituent intensity in a way that mass-produced mail does not.

Because legislative offices receive an enormous volume of mail daily, some groups have adopted novel tactics to get a member's attention. One group representing the elderly instructed its members to include two pennies with each letter to "get in your two cents' worth." The National Association of Home Builders, together with timber interests, once coordinated a campaign of notes written on short pieces of 2 X 4 lumber. Such campaigns are more likely to be noticed by the legislator, although there is little evidence that they represent more effective lobbying.

Grassroots pressure also comes in the form of coordinated calls, which can tie up the phones on Capitol Hill for days. In one such effort by the Christian Right in response to a bill that would have reversed some recent Supreme Court decisions on civil rights, conservative pastors called to complain that the bill would "force churches to hire known, practicing homosexuals as youth pastors," although no such language was contained in the bill.

Perhaps the most effective form of grassroots lobbying is a face-to-face meeting between group members and a legislator or the legislator's staff. After major pro-choice and pro-life demonstrations in Washington, delegations from each House district seek to meet with their representative and then band together to meet with the senators from their state. Some groups such as the Sierra Club have a membership lobbying corps that comes to Washington when key bills are under consideration to lobby members and their staffs. In another approach, various professional and trade associations hold their national conventions in Washington and then schedule a "lobby day," when their members contact their representatives and senators.

Groups need not have ready access to a member to pursue an outside strategy; indeed, many organizations use the tactic only when dealing with members who are on the fence on an issue. Pressuring legislative allies is not usually good politics, and the Moral Majority was the subject of much ridicule when it was disclosed that it had flooded the offices of Republican senator Orrin Hatch of Utah with mail and phone calls in the early 1980s, a process that succeeded primarily in irritating one of their strongest supporters in the Senate. The Christian Coalition was much more sophisticated in targeting its lobbying efforts (see Chapter 10).

Many groups do not use grassroots strategies in dealing with members who strongly oppose their policy preferences, because it would be at best a waste of effort and at worst it might actually motivate the member to work harder against them. Many highly ideological groups do, however, urge their members to bury their opponents in letters and postcards, but the rationale for this behavior has more to do with the dynamics of fund-raising than with lobbying strategies. Members of conservative groups may find it satisfying to send a strongly worded postcard or letter to Democratic senator Edward M. Kennedy of Massachusetts, a longtime spokesman for liberal causes, and therefore will be more likely to contribute to their group.

Groups with a large and ideologically cohesive membership are best suited to using grassroots strategies. Organizations such as the National Rifle Association, Christian Coalition, National Abortion and Reproductive Rights Action League (NARAL), and Common Cause are able to mobilize their large and geographically diverse memberships into political action. This is not to say, however, that organizations with fewer members but whose members possess significant resources cannot also use grassroots strategies. The Business Roundtable has on occasion mobilized its members—primarily CEOs of major corporations—to make direct contact with key members of Congress.

Whereas once only a few highly organized groups such as the NRA could generate grassroots pressure, technological change has made it much easier for all groups to use this tactic. In response, legislators, whose congressional offices have become buried in piles of mail and burdened by the demands of coordinated phone campaigns, find themselves trying to distinguish more and more between genuine grassroots passion and coordinated efforts that require little initiative from group members. Most congressional offices have boxes of postcards that the staff will not answer and complicated computer routines to handle the growing avalanche of mail.

Some companies now specialize in generating grassroots campaigns even when there is little interest among group members for an issue. These firms can print many versions of letters to create the appearance that the letters are drafted by a constituent, and a few have gone so far as to print signatures of group members on the letters. The Competitive Long Distance Coalition, later organized as the Unity Coalition, representing MCI, Sprint, and AT&T, reportedly called individuals who used their long-distance services, asked them a question, and then sent multiple letters to members of Congress on behalf of those whose answers conformed to the coalition's positions. These "astroturf" campaigns, as some call them, are designed to create the appearance of strong opinion in a district or state. As for Congress itself, a growing number of members now have Web pages and e-mail addresses, which only facilitate grassroots contacts. And beyond Congress, hundreds of political organizations have Web sites that attract millions of contacts every day. Indeed, some grassroots campaigns have begun in cyberspace, with groups e-mailing their members and urging them to send e-mails to members of Congress (Browning 1996).

Interest Groups, Lobbying, and Congress: An Evaluation

Interest groups serve several vital functions in Congress. By aggregating individual preferences and relaying them to the legislature, they are a conduit for public opinion to influence public policy. By presenting technical information to key committee members and their staffs, they help to inform the legislative process. And by providing financial and other aid to members during their reelection campaigns, interest groups help to organize the electoral process and help candidates to communicate their policy positions to voters.

Yet these benefits come with costs. Although the flourishing of public interest and citizens' groups in the 1960s and 1970s served to increase diversity in the interest group community, not all groups are represented. As Sen. Robert J. Dole, R-KS, often noted, there is no food stamps PAC, and it is clear that lobbyists for corporate interests occupy a dominant position on Capitol Hill. Moreover, often differences in interest group resources may produce public policy that is clearly opposed by the public.

The balance between the positive and negative aspects of interest group lobbying in Congress is influenced by lobbying and campaign finance regulations, which provide the rules of the game and limit the excesses of resource-rich, interested groups. The concluding chapter of this volume will consider some proposed reforms that would affect the ways in which groups press their case to government.

References

Aldrich, John H., and David W. Rhode. 2000. "The Consequences of Party Organization in the House: The Role of the Majority and Minority Parties in Conditional Party Government." In *Polarized Politics,* edited by Jon R. Bond and Richard Fleisher. Washington, DC: CQ Press..

Bachrach, Peter, and Morton S. Baratz. 1963. "The Two Faces of Power." *American Political Science Review* 56:947–952.

Browning, Graeme. 1996. *Electronic Democracy: Using the Internet in American Politics.* Wilton, CT: Online Inc.; Pemberton Press.

Chappell, Henry. 1981. "Campaign Contributions and Voting on the Cargo Preferences Bill: A Comparison of Simultaneous Equation Models." *Public Choice* 36:301–312.

Cohen, Richard E. 1992. *Washington at Work: Back Rooms and Clean Air.* New York: Macmillan.

Davidson, Roger H. 1981. "Subcommittee Government: New Channels for Policy Making." In *The New Congress,* edited by Thomas Mann and Norman Ornstein. Washington, DC: American Enterprise Institute.

Drew, Elizabeth. 1983. *Politics and Money: The New Road to Corruption.* New York: Macmillan.

Fowler, Linda L., and Ronald G. Shaiko. 1987. "The Grassroots Connection: Environmental Activists and Senate Roll Calls." *American Journal of Political Science* 31:484–510.

Gordon, Stacy B. 2001. "All Votes Are Not Created Equal: Campaign Contributions and Critical Votes." *Journal of Politics* 63:249–269.

Greider, William. 1992. *Who Will Tell the People: The Betrayal of American Democracy.* New York: Touchstone Books.

Grenzke, Janet M. 1989. "PACs and the Congressional Supermarket: The Currency Is Complex." *American Journal of Political Science* 33:2–24.

Jackson, Brooks. 1988. *Honest Graft: Money and the American Political Process.* New York: Knopf.

Judis, John. 1995. "The Contract with K Street." *New Republic* 4:18–25.

Langbein, Laura I., and Mark A. Lotwis. 1990. "The Political Efficacy of Lobbying and Money: Gun Control in the U.S. House, 1986." *Legislative Studies Quarterly* 15:413–440.

Malbin, Michael J., Clyde Wilcox, Mark J. Rozell, and Richard Skinner. 2002. *New Interest Group Strategies—A Preview of Post McCain-Feingold Politics.* Washington, DC: Campaign Finance Institute.

Schlozman, Kay Lehman, and John Tierney. 1984. *Organized Interests and American Democracy.* New York: Addison Wesley.

Shaiko, Ronald G. 1995. "Lobby Reform: Curing the Mischiefs of Faction?" In *Remaking Congress: Stability and Change in the 1990s,* edited by James A. Thurber and Roger H. Davidson. Washington, DC: CQ Press.

Sinclair, Barbara. 2000. *Unorthodox Lawmaking: New Legislative Processes in the U.S. Congress.* Washington, DC: CQ Press

Walker, Charles E. 1997. "A Four Decade Perspective on Lobbying in Washington." In *The Interest Group Connection,* edited by Paul S. Herrnson, Ronald G. Shaiko, and Clyde Wilcox. Chatham, NJ: Chatham House Publishers.

Wilcox, Clyde. 1990. "Member to Member Giving." In *Money, Elections, and Democracy,* edited by M. Nugent and J. Johannes. New York: Westview Press.

Wright, John R. 1985. "PACs, Contributions, and Roll Calls: An Organizational Perspective." *American Political Science Review* 79:400–414.

———.1996. *Interest Groups and Congress: Lobbying, Contributions and Influence.* Boston: Allyn and Bacon.

8. Musical Chairs: Interest Groups, Campaign Fund-Raising, and Selection of House Committee Chairs

Paul R. Brewer and Christopher J. Deering

In the House of Representatives, committee chairs, arguably among the most powerful positions in American politics, were doled out for most of the twentieth century almost strictly according to seniority—that is, with few exceptions they went to the member of the committee who had served longest on that particular panel.[1] In the early 1970s, House Democrats weakened the seniority rule within their own party caucus and even went so far as to deprive three senior committee chairs of reappointment to their positions of power. But with those exceptions and virtually no others, seniority continued to be the determining factor for advancement.[2]

Now that situation has changed, at least for House Republicans. On gaining control of the House in 1995, Republicans, led by Newt Gingrich of Georgia, decided that they, too, would diminish the influence of seniority on the selection of committee chairs. They went an important step further, however, by limiting chairs to no more than three consecutive Congresses at the helm of any given standing committee. This rule ensured that someone other than the most senior committee member would have to be elevated to the head of each of the nineteen House standing committees. Furthermore, Republicans invested their party leader, the Speaker, with unusually great influence in the process of naming these chairs—power not seen since the days of Speaker Joseph G. Cannon, R-IL, who served in the House from 1873 to 1923, with the exception of two terms.

For six years, relative calm ensued. Speaker Gingrich did violate seniority in naming a handful of chairs at the outset of the 104th Congress, but none of these violations was truly dramatic, and none of consequence followed. So there the rule sat—a "Newt time bomb," as columnist Cragg Hines (2001) called it. In subsequent Congresses, Republicans continued to hold their majorities. Finally, in 2000 the bomb was triggered, as the first set of committee chair term limits expired.

A free-for-all rush for positions ensued—a game of "musical chairs," to borrow a metaphor from *New York Times* reporter Lizette Alvarez (2000) and others. As the would-be chairs scrambled, they tried to divine what "tune" would dictate the outcome of this new game. Contenders hitched their hopes to many credentials: seniority, expertise, legislative skills, popularity with colleagues, ideological purity, or skeleton-free closets. More than a few, however, thought money would call the tune. And for good reason—at least one disappointed contender reportedly heard Majority Leader Dick Armey, R-TX, say that it would take a million dollars of fund-raising "just to be considered." Not surprisingly, then, chair candidates, with and without seniority, began touting their money-raising prowess as a trait worthy of consideration.

Interest groups, for their part, gave heavily to some of the would-be chairs. Such groups have traditionally used campaign giving as a means to many ends: winning access to committee members, cementing relationships with them, influencing their agendas (if not their votes per se), encouraging their participation (or lack thereof) on certain issues, and assisting their reelection efforts (Wright 1990; Hall and Wayman 1990). By contributing to the fundraising drives of would-be committee *chairs*, groups stood to win the friendship, attention, and involvement of members whose powers would far outstrip those of ordinary backbenchers. As one corporate media relations director noted, "The chairman of the committee sets the agenda and there is no more powerful tool than the decision whether or not to take up an issue" (Alvarez 2000). And so interest groups donated money not only to the campaign committees of the wannabes, but also to their leadership political action committees (PACs), organized by party and committee leaders to funnel money to fellow candidates.

This chapter examines the role that campaign fund-raising played in the selection of House committee chairs for the 107th Congress (2001–2003) and the role that interest groups played in funding the would-be chairs. It begins by looking at the behavior of interest groups. Who exactly was funding this game of musical chairs? And why did they give more to some hopefuls than others? Next, it looks at what the contenders did. Which would-be chairs gave the most money to their party or to their fellow members? And what did they say about their fundraising efforts to colleagues, particularly to the Steering Committee that held the reins of power? Finally, this chapter looks at how the game turned out. When the music is over, does money matter?

The Rules of the Game for 'Musical Chairs'

First, though, a brief look at the rules of the game is in order. In 1995 House Republicans wrote term limits into the House rules.[3] The limitation read: "No member may serve as the chairman of the same standing committee, or as the chairman of the same subcommittee thereof, for more than three consecutive Congresses, beginning with the 104th Congress (disregarding for this purpose any service for less than a full session in any Congress)" (Rule X, 6[b]).[4] In addition, Republican Conference rules limit members to a single committee or subcommittee chair (as do Democratic Caucus rules) and prohibit the top six party leaders from serving as chairs (Rule 2).[5]

Chairs are selected in a three-step process. In the first step, the Republican Steering Committee makes recommendations to the Republican Conference. The Steering Committee is made up of twenty-six members: fifteen designated members and the representatives of eleven geographical regions.[6] The Speaker has five votes on the Steering Committee and the majority leader has two. All others have one vote. In the second step, the Steering Committee's nominations are forwarded to the full Republican Conference. Under Republican rules, the nominee "need not be the Member with the longest consecutive service on the committee" (Rule 14). Although secret-ballot Conference Committee votes are prescribed for each nominee, a motion from the floor led Republicans to approve their chairs as a slate for the 107th Congress. In the third and final step, chairs are approved, along with other committee members, by a resolution of the full House. Here it is important to note that House rules clearly provide that the respective *parties* are responsible for nominating their members for each committee (Rule X, 5[a][1]).

As the first round of forced turnover approached, nervous critics emerged (Palmer 1997). Don Young, R-AK, who would vacate the chair of the Resources Committee, said the rule was "a stupid idea to begin with" (Gugliotta 1998). W. J. "Billy" Tauzin, R-LA, spearheaded a move to alter or abolish the House rotation rule. Late in 1997, Tauzin met with Speaker Gingrich to make his case, but these and subsequent pleadings fell on unsympathetic ears. Proponents of congressional term limits linked the two issues closely. And most back-bench Republicans opposed any relaxation, much less abolition, of the rule.

In mid-June 1999, the Republican leadership announced that sitting chairs would not be prohibited from moving from one leadership position to another. The issue arose because some members were uncertain about how strictly to read the language of the rule itself, which provides only that a member may not chair the *same* committee for more than three consecutive Congresses. By a narrow margin, Republicans retained their majority in the House on November 7, 2000. Within the week, the Speaker and other members of the Republican Steering Committee began to receive entreaties from would-be chairs. Not that everyone waited. Indeed, some chair candidates complained that a few "sooners" had jumped the gun in pushing for their slots, even though Speaker Dennis Hastert, R-IL, had asked them to wait until after the election. As one hopeful put it early in November, "While some of our colleagues did not heed the Speaker's wishes (and were asking you for support all during the summer and fall), I hope you understand why I waited to begin my campaign for chairman . . . until after we renewed our majority." [7]

The newly reelected leadership announced that candidates for the various chairs would have to appear before the Steering committee early in December and interview for the positions. On December 5, 6, and 7, a parade of twenty-nine chair wannabes appeared before the twenty-three Steering Committee members to tout their qualifications (three designated members of the committee — the chairs of Appropriations, Rules, and Ways and Means — did not participate, because they had not yet been selected and therefore were not formally part of the Steering Committee). The morning session of the first day was devoted to four candidates for the Budget Committee. The other three sessions had no particular theme. Most of the candidates sat at a circle of tables in the spare, white Capitol meeting room. Some, like Budget candidate Jim Nussle, R-IA, stood in the middle to make a presentation and field questions. Several candidate presentations were quite elaborate. Curt Weldon, R-PA, advertised his Armed Services Committee candidacy with a glossy thirty-six-page brochure (Kammer 2000). Nussle and Peter Hoekstra, R-MI, made PowerPoint presentations (Hines 2001). Some candidates brought tokens as not-so-subtle remembrances: for example, Saxby Chambliss, R-GA, gave the Steering Committee members peanuts from his home state; Ways and Means Committee hopeful William M. Thomas, R-CA, brought California pistachios (Foerstel 2000). Most of the candidates followed up their appearances with thank-you notes to the members of the Steering Committee. And a handful attempted to mend damage they felt might have been done during the interviews.

The 107th Congress convened on January 3, 2001. New members were sworn in, Hastert's reelection as Speaker was formalized, and the House readopted its formal rules. Those rules, unveiled the previous day by leaders, included a substantial shift in two committees' jurisdictions by moving insurance and securities issues from the Commerce Committee to the renamed Financial Services Committee (formerly Banking and Financial Services).[8]

The import of this move was immediately clear. Speculation was rife that if Billy Tauzin gained the chair of the Commerce Committee, his principal opponent Michael Oxley, R-OH, might be awarded the gavel of the new Financial Services Committee or at very least a substantially upgraded subcommittee post (Bowman 2000; Eilperin 2001a). In this scenario, Marge Roukema, R-NJ, the ranking Republican on the former Banking and Financial Services Committee and one of only two women given a chance to gain a chair, would be pushed aside. Roukema herself perceived the import: "I'm in favor of expanded jurisdiction, but it shouldn't be done for the purpose of buying a chairmanship" (Eilperin 2001a). Tauzin and Oxley ranked first and third among all chair candidates in giving to the 2000 Republican campaign effort.

The next day, January 4, the Steering Committee met in a room on the West Front of the Capitol to cast their nominating ballots. The twenty-three members cast secret ballots serially for each of the positions, but the results were not revealed until after all the ballots had been counted. The Speaker's office refused to divulge information about the balloting process. However, press reports and occasional comments from legislative staff have filled in some of the details. Later, members of the Conference Committee were presented with the Steering Committee's slate, and challenges were then in order to any of the nominations. None were mounted, however, and the Conference Committee endorsed a motion from the floor to accept the slate as presented.

Questions and Evidence

So what happened? Who won and why? The rest of this chapter focuses on the twenty-nine candidates actually interviewed by the Steering Committee. Rumor had it, however, that several other members put themselves forward for consideration. Table 8-1 lists these twenty-nine contenders for the thirteen

Table 8-1 Contributions Made to Congressional Candidates and the National Republican Congressional Committee (NRCC) by U.S. House Committee Chair Contenders, 2000 Election Cycle

Committee	Contenders[a]	Campaign to NRCC	Campaign to candidates	Leadership PAC to candidates	Total
Armed Services	*Bob Stump (AZ)*	$40,000	$11,000	$0	$51,000
	Duncan Hunter (CA)	5,000	20,827	0	25,827
	Curt Weldon (PA)	0	26,000	49,800	75,800
Banking	*Marge Roukema (NJ)*	40,000	0	0	40,000
	Richard H. Baker (LA)	150,000	42,000	0	192,000
Budget	*Saxby Chambliss (GA)*	12,000	1,000	70,000	83,000
	Jim Nussle (IA)	100,000	3,505	7,500	111,005
	Nick Smith (MI)	15,000	4,999	0	19,999
	John E. Sununu (NH)	15,000	1,000	0	16,000
Education and the Workforce	*Tom Petri (WI)*	0	3,500	115,317	118,817
	John A. Boehner (OH)	1,812	1,996	447,407	451,215
	Peter Hoekstra (MI)	15,000	12,150	0	27,150
Energy and Commerce	*"Billy" Tauzin (LA)*	270,000	27,060	293,204	590,264
	Michael Oxley (OH)[b]	170,000	59,100	193,000	422,100
International Relations	*James A. Leach (IA)*	0	0	0	0
	Henry J. Hyde (IL)	105,000	2,100	0	107,100
	Douglas K. Bereuter (NE)	57,500	3,500	0	61,000
Judiciary	*James Sensenbrenner (WI)*	84,000	0	0	84,000
	George W. Gekas (Pa.)	25,000	22,000	0	47,000
Resources	*James V. Hansen (UT)*	10,000	27,600	0	37,600
Science	*Sherwood Boehlert (NY)*	65,000	22,500	18,500	106,000
Small Business	**Donald Manzullo (IL)**	15,000	16,100	0	31,100
	Sue W. Kelly (NY)	65,000	5,000	0	70,000
Transportation	*Don Young (AK)*	25,000	0	45,390	70,390
Veterans' Affairs	*Christopher Smith (NJ)*[b]	50,000	3,000	0	53,000
	Michael Bilirakis	82,750	25,000	0	107,750
Ways and Means	*Philip M. Crane (IL)*	80,000	56,000	132,000	268,000
	Bill Thomas (CA)	252,000	43,000	133,000	428,000
	E. Clay Shaw Jr. (FL)	100,000	0	22,000	122,000

Sources: Federal Election Commission and Center for Responsive Politics.

[a] New chairs appear in boldface; senior members appear in italics.

[b] Oxley interviewed for the Commerce chair but was named head of the Financial Services Committee, a somewhat expanded version of the former Banking Committee. Smith was interviewed for International Relations, but was the ranking member on Veterans' Affairs, where he was given a chair.

chairs vacated by term limits. The winners are highlighted in bold, and the names of the most senior committee members appear in italics.

As noted at the outset, throughout the twentieth century seniority was the sole criterion for advancement on committees (Polsby, Gallaher, and Rundquist 1969; Hinckley 1971). And so long as that was the case, career advancement was largely an issue of how long the lines might be and whether some moved more rapidly than others (Shepsle 1978; Hibbing 1991; Deering 1996). But even a quick look at Table 8-1 reveals ample evidence that seniority was not the sole criterion for advancement this time around. Of the thirteen committees requiring change, six new chairs advanced without being the most senior member (counting Donald Manzullo, R-IL, who faced competition but not from the more senior Joel Hefley, R-CO). In three of the seven cases in which the senior member did advance, no competition emerged. Thus seniority was violated in six of the ten competitive situations. This is not to say that mere neophytes earned gavels on the House panels. The winners were still among the most senior party members in terms of service. The least experienced of the new chairs, Small Business's Manzullo, had been in the House for eight years at the time of these elections.

What else made a difference then? The new chairs were a geographically diverse lot. With perhaps two exceptions — Sherwood Boehlert, R-NY, of the Science Committee and Christopher Smith, R-NJ, of Veterans' Affairs — they were a pretty conservative group and sported healthy party support scores. Boehlert's party unity score (the percentage of the time he voted with fellow Republicans against Democrats when the parties disagreed) was 68 in the 106th Congress. Smith's score was 73. Their competitors were not significantly different in this regard. So geography, ideology, and voting loyalty seemed to offer little. Could fund-raising, emblazoned in the press, be the answer? Perhaps Steering Committee members were swayed by the fundraising prowess demonstrated by chair candidates in behalf of the party and its members. And if that was the case, who provided the funds, and which contributors got the chairs they wanted?

The first question is easily answered: money clearly mattered. In seven of the thirteen cases, seniority prevailed.[9] In five of the six cases where it did not, the leading fund-raiser prevailed. And in seven of the ten competitive cases, money prevailed. The other two issues are more difficult to address. According to one press report, Paul Weyrich of the conservative Free Congress Foundation was quite open in his support of Weldon for Armed Services, Henry Hyde, R-IL, for International Relations, and Thomas for Ways and Means (Bolton 2000). For the most part, however, interest groups avoided the risk of offending one potential chair by openly endorsing another. Such a move would be, in the word of one lobbyist, "suicidal" (Alvarez 2000). But it was not that they did nothing. They could contribute, and, it is said, some made their wishes known privately to Steering Committee members with whom they had access.

Similarly, Steering Committee members did not see fit to explain the reasons behind their specific choices — reasons that might have included not only fund-raising, but also seniority, expertise, and party loyalty. Two years earlier, according to Steering Committee member Sonny Callahan, R-AL, fundraising ability was suggested to the committee as a selection criterion for the first time; in 2000, however, members were not quick to elaborate on just how much weight this criterion carried (Bolton 2000).

That leaves the circumstantial evidence—namely, the money trail from interest groups to would-be chairs to the party and individual members. The following account draws on clues about this trail provided by data compiled by the Federal Election Commission and the Center for Responsive Politics, a campaign finance watchdog organization. We begin by examining a set of particularly prominent and revealing contests in some detail. For each of these contests, the campaign contributions that interest groups made to would-be chairs are analyzed to find clues about those groups' preferences. Then we assess the candidates' use of that money in the 2000 election cycle. We conclude by looking at who won each of the chairs and how decisive fund-raising seemed to be in determining the victor.

The Battle at Ways and Means

Of the chairs at stake, Ways and Means was the most powerful. The committee's turf is vast, encompassing both taxation and federal entitlement spending. All told, it oversees the disbursement of 45 percent of the federal budget (Tyson 2000). Whoever won the chair was sure to be a major player in shaping federal policy on a host of agenda-topping issues, including tax cuts, Medicare prescription drug benefits, and Social Security reform.

Three members sought to succeed William R. Archer Jr., R-TX, the retiring chair: William M. Thomas, R-CA; Philip M. Crane, R-IL; and E. Clay Shaw Jr., R-FL. Under the rule of seniority, Crane would have won the post. The seventy-year-old was a sixteen-year veteran of the committee, chair of its trade subcommittee, and a thirty-year veteran of the House. Crane's colleagues lauded him for his good-natured personality. Yet some also "praised" him for his 1999 decision to seek treatment for alcohol dependency (Simon 2001) and criticized him for not doing enough committee work.

Like Crane, Thomas had assets and liabilities. On the plus side, he chaired his own Ways and Means subcommittee on health and was widely reputed to be both a hard worker and a skilled coalition builder on thorny issues such as Medicare. He also had good working ties with the health care industry. On the minus side were concerns about his temper. People who drew Thomas's ire soon learned of it; Republican National Chair Jim Nicholson, for example, had once received a sarcastic letter from Thomas that read, "Thank you very much for your mucho carboned C.Y.A. [cover your ass] letter" (Alvarez 2001). Thomas had a skeleton in his own closet, too: a "personal relationship" with health care lobbyist Deborah Steelman. Thomas responded to both concerns with characteristic directness: he said that he had "never traded a public responsibility for a personal one" (Simon 2001) and that he "unleashed [his temper] mostly on the deserving" (Alvarez 2001). At the same time, he made clear to the Steering Committee that he was prepared to change: "I realize that to be chairman of the committee I can't be the Bill Thomas you're used to seeing on the committee" (Eilperin 2001c).

And what of Shaw? He touted his business experience and presented himself as a compromise choice. House watchers, however, labeled him a long shot (Simon 2001).

Who Gave the Money?

Though few of them would have admitted it, many health care industry lobbyists were undoubtedly pleased by the prospect of Thomas as chair of the Ways and Means Committee. First, there was his unquestioned expertise on the industry. "After Mr. Thomas wound up on the Ways and Means Health Subcommittee," one source noted, "he immersed himself in Medicare minutiae for two years, rising at 4 a.m. to crack the books" (Alvarez 2001). Moreover, those in the industry knew that major health care policy initiatives loomed on the horizon, including a prescription drug plan for Medicare recipients. Thomas had designed such a plan for the Republicans in the previous Congress (Simon 2001).

With these concerns presumably in mind, health care industry donors put their money on Thomas. Reporter James T. Tyson (2000) described the dance between contributor and recipient thusly: "The chardonnay is flowing, strings of golden light twinkle from columns wrapped in white chiffon, and a six-piece band in black ties plays 'You Send Me' as [Thomas] glides among campaign donors in Philadelphia at an exclusive wine tasting paid for by the American Hospital Association."

There were many such moments for Thomas and the health care industry over the course of the 2000 election cycle. Table 8-2 lists the top contributors to the campaign committees of Thomas and his two rivals by industry. The health care industry was easily the number-one source of funds for Thomas. The table reveals that contributors in the pharmaceutical and health products industry gave his campaign committee a total of $402,440, making Thomas the leading House recipient of funds from the health care industry. Doctors and health care organizations also gave heavily to the Congressional Majority Committee, a leadership PAC organized by Thomas.

Although Crane had his own deep-pocketed friends, the contributors to his campaign committee were not concentrated in any one industry (see Table 8-2). He certainly won the favor of the trade community, however. Jon Kent, legislative representative for the National Customs Brokers and Forwarders Association of America, openly endorsed Crane as the industry's "best bet" (JoC Online 2000). In particular, free traders appreciated Crane's past efforts to promote trade relations with China and Africa (Tyson 2000). Not coincidentally, perhaps, the name of Crane's leadership PAC was the Fund for a Free Market America.

Table 8-2 Contributions to the Campaign Committees of the Contenders for Leadership of the House Ways and Means Committee, 2000, by Industry (Top Six Listed)

Contributions to William M. Thomas (Calif.)

1. Pharmaceuticals/health products	$156,833
2. Insurance	132,650
3. Health professionals	126,335
4. Crop production and basic processing	65,280
5. Hospitals/nursing homes	63,922
6. Health services/HMOs	55,350

Contributions to Philip M. Crane (Ill.)

1. Insurance	$95,872
2. Health professionals	73,379
3. Securities and investment	56,250
4. Lawyers/law firms	41,320
5. Retail sales	39,000
6. Pharmaceuticals/health products	38,000

Contributions to E. Clay Shaw (Fla.)

1. Health professionals	$134,614
2. Insurance	128,900
3. Lawyers/law firms	128,864
4. Retired	107,725
5. Leadership PACs	88,018
6. Real estate	86,396

Source: Center for Responsive Politics.

Note: Figures are based on contributions from political action committees and individual donors giving more than $200 for the 1999–2000 election cycle, as reported to the Federal Election Commission. Based on data released electronically on February 1, 2001.

Shaw's campaign committee, like Crane's, was not dominated by any one sector (see Table 8-2). Perhaps the most interesting feature of his list is that leadership PACs came in fifth place. According to figures from the Center for Responsive Politics, Shaw's own leadership PAC, the Sunshine PAC, did not receive any contributions of $200 or more from individual donors over the course of the 2000 election cycle. These were not good signs for Shaw.

Where Did the Money Go?

To state an obvious but crucial point: to win a committee chair, a member must first win reelection. For Shaw, reelection in itself proved to be a difficult task. Faced with a strong general election challenger, he was forced to devote his campaign committee funds to eking out a 50.1 percent to 49.9 percent victory. He therefore had nothing left over to distribute to his fellow Republican House members. Nor did he give any money over the course of the 1999–2000 election cycle to the National Republican Congressional Committee (NRCC), the organization formed by House Republicans to aid the campaign efforts of party members. Shaw's Sunshine PAC did distribute $22,000 to Republican candidates for federal office, but, as noted earlier, its efforts came to a halt during the course of the 1999–2000 election cycle. Simply put, Shaw's tough reelection fight left him with very little opportunity to demonstrate fundraising prowess in behalf of the party.

Thomas and Crane, by contrast, had the luxury of safe districts. Thomas won his district with 72 percent of the vote; Crane won his with 61 percent. Thus each had plenty of time and energy to focus on raising money that could be funneled to colleagues and to the NRCC. Indeed, both Thomas and Crane collected well-nigh staggering sums of money to do just that.

Through his campaign committee, Thomas donated $43,000 to individual candidates for federal office and $252,000 to the NRCC. In addition, his leadership PAC distributed $133,000 to federal candidates, for a total of $428,000. Though smaller, Crane's totals in the same categories also were impressive. His own campaign committee gave $56,000 to candidates for federal office and $80,000 to the NRCC, while his leadership PAC gave another $132,000 to federal candidates. Crane's contributions totaled $268,000.

Even those numbers, however, do not capture the full extent of the fund-raising that the two rivals performed in behalf of their party and its members. Each also contributed to the GOP's coffers through less direct means—hosting fund-raisers and finding donors, for example. Crane bragged that he had raised a grand sum of $2.5 million for House candidates and an additional $816,000 for Battleground 2000, Speaker Hastert's own House campaign fund (Bresnahan 2000). Included in the $2.5 million was a $500,000 check that he secured from software company founder Tom Siebel. Thomas, for his part, claimed to have donated $1.6 million to his Republican House colleagues since 1994. He reportedly raised $150,000 for Battleground 2000 (Bolton 2000).

Who Got the Gavel?

Having demonstrated their fundraising skills, Thomas and Crane attempted to capitalize on them in their campaigns for the Ways and Means chair. As the battle heated up, reporters took note of the rivals' strategies: "[Crane] pledges to aggressively raise more money as chairman with the aim of increasing the GOP's narrow majority in the House. Thomas has countered that he contributed more money to colleagues over a longer period. During a recent appearance at [the Steering Committee meeting], he brought a list detailing . . . donations that he had made to 70 fellow Republicans over the last three election cycles. 'If you want to look at future behavior, sometimes looking at prior behavior when it wasn't under the spotlight . . . is useful,' he said" (Simon 2001). Crane, in fact, had questioned party requests for campaign donations in the past, a point that may have played in Thomas's favor (Eilperin 2000).

Still, the Steering Committee had other considerations to ponder. There was Crane's seniority, but there was also his drinking problem. There was Thomas's expertise, but there was also his relationship with Steelman. And then there was Thomas's temper, which Crane alluded to while touting his own candidacy: "Never in my entire tenure in Congress have I allowed my temper to insult, berate, or offend a colleague" (Simon 2001). To counter concerns about his personality, Thomas promised the Steering Committee that he would "contain his temper and adopt a slightly more accommodating manner when presiding over the panel" (Eilperin 2001b). In a development that further complicated the Steering Committee's decision, House Republican whip Tom DeLay, R-TX, endorsed Crane, whereas most Republicans on the Ways and Means Committee signed a letter to Speaker Hastert that endorsed Thomas.

The Steering Committee chose Thomas. Given the wide range of criteria at play in this contest and the ambiguity over whether Thomas or Crane was truly the best fund-raiser, the outcome cannot be read as a clear triumph for fundraising prowess. But Thomas clearly demonstrated such prowess, a fact that he happily and frequently pointed out to his colleagues. Indeed, he argued that it was only common sense for the Steering Committee to consider it as a criterion: "If these are your key committees and you aren't making legally the kind of money you could make, then why would you put somebody in as chairman who wouldn't maximize the return?" (Tyson 2000). Judging by the money trail, the Steering Committee's selection did not represent a victory for Thomas alone; it was also a victory for the health care industry that had contributed so much money to its preferred would-be chair.

The Clash of Titans Spills Over

Meanwhile, another high-profile contest was under way between Billy Tauzin and Michael Oxley, the two contenders for the chair of the Energy and Commerce Committee. The clash between these fundraising titans led to an unusual outcome—one that offers perhaps the strongest clues that campaign fund-raising did play a crucial role in the House chair selection process.

Although Tauzin had once opposed term limits, he was now trying to win the chair of the term-limited Thomas J. Bliley Jr. of Virginia. But Tauzin, an eleven-term House veteran and ten-term Energy and Commerce veteran, faced a potential stumbling block: he was a relatively recent convert to the Republican Party. In 1995 the former "Blue Dog" (conservative) Democrat had switched to the GOP. Speaker Gingrich promised Tauzin that his tenure as a Democrat on the committee would count toward his seniority in the chair selection process (Alpert 2001). Speaker Hastert later affirmed that decision, thereby giving Tauzin a seniority edge over his rival, Oxley. Tauzin's allies argued that a decision not to give him the chair would discourage future party switching toward the GOP. As Tauzin spokesman Ken Johnson put it, "If Billy is denied the chairmanship . . . the 'Not Welcome' sign would be on the front door" (Eilperin 2000).

Oxley had served ten terms in the House and nine on the Energy and Commerce Committee; he was also chair of its finance subcommittee. Although he was formally competing with Tauzin for that committee's chair, he also had a backup plan—to make a deal with the Steering Committee in which he would cede Energy and Commerce to Tauzin in return for the chair of a reconfigured Banking Committee. However, two members of that committee—of which Oxley was not a member—were campaigning aggressively for chair: Richard H. Baker, R-LA, and Marge Roukema, whose seniority on Banking outranked not only Baker's seniority on that committee but also Oxley's seniority at Energy and Commerce.

Who Gave the Money?

Table 8-3 lists the top eight sources of contributions to Tauzin's and Oxley's campaign committees, by industry. As a representative of a state heavily dependent on its oil and gas industries, Tauzin was an old ally of oil, gas, and electric utility companies (Morgan and Eilperin 2001). And he had a history of delivering on their concerns: he had worked to repeal a ban on natural gas burning by utility companies and to block a bill to limit retail fuel prices, for example (Ota 2001). Over the course of the 1999–2000 election cycle, the oil and gas industries were Tauzin's second highest donors, and contributors associated with electric utilities nearly matched the industries' total.

Not content merely to maintain ties with his old allies, Tauzin also used his leadership of the Energy and Commerce subcommittee on telecommunications, trade, and consumer protection to establish himself as a key player in telecommunications policymaking. For example, he sided with the "Baby Bell" telephone companies in their fight against federal regulations that restricted them from offering long-distance service and thus Internet access (Ota 2001). Tauzin also opposed "open access" requirements forcing cable companies to allow others to transmit data across their lines. Interests in the telecommunications sector—donors associated with television, movies, and music; telephone utilities; and telecommunications services and equipment providers— responded by giving heavily to Tauzin's campaign committee (Table 8-3). Tauzin was the top House recipient of contributions from commercial TV and radio stations and from cable and satellite TV production and distribution. He was the number-two recipient of donations from telecommunications services and equipment providers, the number-four recipient of donations from the television, movie, and music industry, and the number-eight recipient of dona-

Table 8-3　Contributions to the Campaign Committees of the Contenders for Leadership of the House Energy and Commerce Committee, 2000, by Industry (Top Eight Listed)

Contributions to W. J. "Billy" Tauzin (La.)	
1. TV/movies/music	$73,776
2. Oil and gas	73,274
3. Electric utilities	72,214
4. Securities and investment	63,950
5. Telephone utilities	55,200
6. Insurance	46,460
7. Accountants	41,424
8. Telecom services and equipment	38,768

Contributions to Michael Oxley (Ohio)	
1. Securities and investment	$69,900
2. Electric utilities	62,522
3. Telephone utilities	60,305
4. TV/movies/music	53,699
5. Insurance	50,900
6. Oil and gas	42,382
7. Accountants	42,000
8. Pharmaceuticals/health products	40,250

Source: Center for Responsive Politics.

Note: Figures are based on contributions from political action committees and individual donors giving more than $200 for the 1999–2000 election cycle, as reported to the Federal Election Commission. Figures are based on data released electronically on February 1, 2001.

tions from telephone utilities. "I wouldn't say he's close to the business community," explained Tauzin spokesman Johnson. "I would say the business community's close to him because of his fervent, pro-market deregulatory beliefs" (Morgan and Eilperin 2001).

Telephone utilities also occupied a prominent spot on Oxley's donor list: number three, to be exact. Indeed, he was the number-three House recipient of that industry's campaign giving. Unlike Tauzin, Oxley's allies were the long-distance carriers, not the Baby Bells (Alvarez 2000). These companies, not wanting new competitors, favored the regulations that Tauzin and the Baby Bells opposed (Ota 2001).

The top source of contributions to Oxley's campaign committee, however, was the financial services sector. Oxley had already demonstrated his expertise and involvement in issues that influenced Wall Street. As chair of the finance subcommittee, for example, he had brokered a compromise between major accounting firms and the Securities and Exchange Commission over conflict of interest rules (Morgan and Eilpeirn 2001). One of the accounting companies affected by that decision, Deloitte and Touche, gave the maximum $10,000 to Oxley's campaign committee (Morgan and Eilperin 2001). All told, his committee received not only the donations shown in Table 8-3 from securities and investment interests, insurance companies, and accountants, but also $25,900 from commercial banks.

Where Did the Money Go?

In 2000 Tauzin ran in a very safe district, which he won with 78 percent of the vote. Thus he was able to funnel much of his campaign money to his party and its members. Over the course of the 1999–2000 election cycle, Tauzin's campaign committee gave $270,000 to the NRCC and $27,060 to individual candidates for federal office. The true engine of his fundraising efforts, however, was his leadership PAC, the Bayou Leader PAC, which raised money from the same industries that gave to his campaign committee. Tauzin had a reputation for throwing entertaining fund-raisers: "A typical appearance featured a feast of jambalaya and other Louisiana delicacies—sometimes prepared by his cousin Jimmy Gravois from recipes in the campaign cookbook—and a raconteur's turn by Tauzin, who revels in telling tall tales and jokes involving 'Boudreaux,' a fictional Cajun bon vivant" (Ota 2001).

The Bayou Leader PAC gave $293,204 to candidates for federal office, pushing Tauzin's total to $590,264. Tauzin also assisted the party's fundraising efforts through other means: by entertaining at the Republican National Convention and the Louisiana Jazz Festival; by hosting a Florida fishing trip on behalf of the NRCC; and even by imitating Gen. George S. Patton in a party fundraising video (Morgan and Eilperin 2001; Ota 2001).

Oxley's fundraising efforts on behalf of the GOP almost matched Tauzin's. He, too, held a safe seat, which he won in 2000 with 67 percent of the vote. His campaign committee distributed $170,000 to the NRCC and $59,100 to candidates for federal office. He also raised another $193,000 for his colleagues through his leadership PAC, the Leadership PAC 2000, bringing his total up to $422,100. Oxley, like Tauzin, knew how to show potential contributors a good time. His leadership PAC sponsored one fundraising event at a ski resort in Vail, Colorado: "This year's event, which kicked off last night with a reception at the Vail Ski Museum, features ski packages with special discounts for the 50 to 60 guests. There will also be a 'mini-fund-raiser' for four House Republicans; a gondola and snowcat ride to a mountaintop restaurant; two cocktail parties and dinner at the $1.7 million home of Catherine P. Bennett, Pfizer Inc.'s vice president for federal tax and trade policy" (Morgan and Eilperin 2001). Among the guests were representatives of numerous telecommunications and financial services interests, including Microsoft Corporation, Independent Insurance Agents of America, and United States Telecom Association (Morgan and Eilperin 2001).

Who Got the Gavel?

Both Tauzin and Oxley interviewed for the Energy and Commerce chair. Both came before the Steering Committee with sterling fundraising credentials, and, in a surprise ending, both came away with chairs. The Steering Committee awarded Tauzin the Energy and Commerce chair, but it also gave the chair of the new Financial Services Committee to Oxley. That decision left the two contenders for the Banking chair, Baker and Roukema, standing when the music ended.

Ironically, Baker had relied on his own campaign fundraising efforts to bolster his bid against the more senior Roukema. Although he did not have a leadership PAC, he donated $150,000 to the NRCC and $42,000 to individual federal candidates through his campaign committee. He also engaged in other fundraising activities in behalf of the party; in a seven-page letter to the Steering Committee, he claimed to have raised $1.6 million for the GOP over the 1999–2000 election cycle (Eilperin 2000).

Unlike Baker, Roukema gave relatively little to the NRCC ($40,000) and nothing to individual Republican candidates for federal office. Nor did she have a leadership PAC. She pointed out to the Steering Committee that a costly primary battle had limited her opportunities to raise funds in behalf of the party (Eilperin 2000). But she also argued against using fundraising ability as a criterion for chair selection: "I don't think our Republican Party wants to be known as a party where you can buy a chairmanship," she said (Eilperin 2000). Perhaps not, but Roukema claimed in early January that someone in the Republican leadership pointed out to her that she had raised only a modest sum for the party (*Bergen Record* 2001).

Did their fundraising prowess win Tauzin and Oxley their chairs? The *Bergen Record* in Roukema's home state of New Jersey certainly thought so. "Sold to the Highest Bidder," it opined in a January 8 editorial. Even Roukema's Democratic opponent complained that Republican Party bosses had substituted money for seniority in choosing committee leaders. She wrote in an op-ed piece for the *Record*, "Raise money, your party notices." Raise the most money, you get elected. Raise even more money, give it back to your party, you chair a committee" (Mercurio 2001).

Again, factors other than money may have influenced the outcome. In particular, Roukema may have been too moderate to suit the Steering Committee's tastes (Alvarez 2000). Her 82 percent party-support score ranked her fifth from the bottom among the candidates interviewed by the Steering Committee and a full standard deviation below the party's average score of 90. Tauzin, a former Democrat, came in at 90, while Oxley sported a 96 percent rating (one point higher than the party median). Still, two colleagues with lower scores than Roukema's were awarded gavels, albeit on committees of lesser importance to the leadership.

It is therefore difficult to conclude that fund-raising did not matter in this case. The Steering Committee awarded one chair to the contender who distributed more money through leadership PACs and campaign committee expenditures than any other chair hopeful: Tauzin. It awarded the second chair to another candidate who raised almost as much money as Tauzin: Oxley. And it chose to bypass a poor fund-raiser and a moderate, Roukema, even though she had the edge in seniority and would have been the first Republican woman to lead a major House commit-tee—not a minor political consideration (Alvarez 2000).[10]

Following the money trail back to the interest groups reveals that the inter-ests that gave the most money to Tauzin and Oxley also got what they wanted. The oil, gas, and electric utility industries got an old friend as a new chair: Tauzin. The telecommunications industry got a new friend as a new chair: again, Tauzin. And interests in the financial services sector got a chair whom they had supported, too, thanks to the Steering Committee's decision to move Oxley and a key jurisdiction to another chair slot.

The Bigger Picture

Now it is time to look beyond the selection of three particular chairs and at the bigger picture. Table 8-1 summarizes the fund-raising performed by each of the contenders for House committee chairs in 2000 in behalf of the Republican Party and its members. The first column lists the amount the contender's cam-paign committee gave to the NRCC; the second, the amount the contender's campaign committee gave to individual candidates for federal office; and the third, the amount that the contender's leadership PAC gave individual candidates for federal office (for contenders who had leadership PACs).

Beyond the contests just described, several others deserve notice. In three additional contests, the most senior committee member contending for the chair was beaten by another member. And each was the leading fund-raiser:

- Tom Petri, R-WI, who distributed $116,137 to colleagues (almost entire-ly through his leadership PAC), lost the Education and the Workforce chair to John A. Boehner, R-OH, who distributed almost half a million dollars through his leadership PAC. Insurance companies, manufacturers, and financial service providers gave heavily to Boehner's campaign com-mittee and leadership PAC.
- Saxby Chambliss raised $70,000 for fellow Republican candidates through his leadership PAC, the Common Sense Leadership Fund, but lost the Budget chair to Nussle, whose campaign committee gave $100,000 to the NRCC. Nussle raised much of this money from insur-ance companies and health professionals.
- James A. Leach, R-IA, who gave nothing to his colleagues or his party, lost out at International Relations to Henry J. Hyde, R-IL, who gave $105,000 to the NRCC. The chair Hyde won was actually his second choice; he had unsuccessfully appealed for a term-limit waiver to keep his Judiciary chair. Hyde's donor list was topped, not by a corporate sector, but by retirees, who gave his campaign committee $139,025.

In each instance, the victor put more money on the table for colleagues and the NRCC than the more senior loser. If money did not speak, it at least shaded the outcomes of these important contests.

It is also worth noting that these candidates trumpeted their fund-raising in behalf of the party and fellow Republicans. We were able to obtain forty-seven letters or memos written by twenty-four of the twenty-nine candidates to members of the Steering Committee. Fully one-third of them mentioned their fundraising efforts in their entreaties to the committee. Campaign appearances, total sums, and a variety of in-kind contributions were mentioned. "Who has done more to help our House Republican team?" wrote one. "In addition, I will commit to helping Members of the Committee—particularly vulnerable members—reach their fundraising goals," asserted another. And "I am committed to aggressively raising money as the Chairman . . . and to increasing our majority in the future," wrote a third. Battleground 2000 (the Speaker's fundraising effort to maintain control of the House), party building, and the Republican team effort all appeared as leitmotifs in this stream of letters. No doubt, as the press reported, their personal presentations to the Steering Committee's members were the same.

Although a fundraising edge always accompanied a departure from the rule of seniority, such an edge did not guarantee a victory over a more senior rival. A case in point was the triumph of Bob Stump, R-AZ, over Curt Weldon, R-PA, in the battle for the chair of the Armed Services Committee. Weldon campaigned for the chair on his fundraising record: in addition to distributing money through his own campaign committee and leadership PAC (much of it raised from the defense industry), he played host to colleagues at the Republican National Convention in Philadelphia and paid five aides to work on other candidates' campaigns (Eilperin 2000). Stump, for his part, argued that Weldon should not be awarded the chair because of his fund-raising: "'I think if that's what we're raising chairmanships on, that's the wrong approach. Certainly we're not in the business of selling chairmanships'" (Kammer 2000). Stump managed to win his without "buying" it.[11]

But how do the committees look from a cost perspective? Based on the sums in Table 8-1, Commerce was clearly the most "expensive" committee; Ways and Means was a fairly close second; and Education and the Workforce was third. How does this rating stack up against the overall importance of committees? To use one broad measure of attractiveness constructed by Groseclose and Stewart (1998), it does reasonably well. They judge committee attractiveness by examining intercommittee transfers. Simply put, members transfer from less important committees to more important ones. That pattern yields a hierarchy of committees and attendant attractiveness coefficients. And the correlation between those "scores" and the amount of money raised by candidates for chairs is a modest but significant 0.59. Thus if the chair competition is not a case of "getting what you pay for," it certainly is a case of "paying for what you get."

The Implications of Musical Chairs

So who won this game of musical chairs? Back in the twentieth century a good doctor, a favorable ancestral gene pool, and a supportive electorate would do the trick. Today, House committee chairs, like doctors, appear to cost more money. Just after the Steering Committee made its decisions, Speaker Hastert declared: "The American people and the American voters know that this Congress needs new faces . . . (and) new input. We did our best to put the best people in each slot. We had to make some tough decisions (but) I'm very happy with the decisions we made" (quoted in Lipman 2001).

New faces? Well, five of these "new faces" had gavels in the previous Congress, albeit on different committees. All, or nearly all, of the rest had chaired a subcommittee. And they all were white, male, and conservative. The new set of chairs was virtually indistinguishable from the old set in terms of party support, for example, with a party support mean of 90.85 versus 91.15. Thus our first conclusion is that seniority is not precisely dead. The most senior members garnered chairs in a majority of the cases. Therefore, the Steering Committee had a difficult time saying no to the "old bulls."

At least two Republican women worked hard to gain chairs, Marge Roukema and Sue W. Kelly of New York. And both were interviewed. But Roukema and Kelly were near the bottom of the group seeking chairs in terms of their party support scores—at 82 and 73 percent, respectively. And, perhaps worse, of the twenty-nine interviewees, their "party-building" activities amounted to $40,000 for Roukema and $70,000 for Kelly. That figure put Roukema, who had a fairly tough reelection fight on her hands, eighth from the bottom. It put Kelly just about in the middle of the pack at sixteenth overall. And although not overwhelming, a modest positive correlation exists between the party unity scores of those interviewed and the amount of money they provided the party and its candidates (correlation coefficient 0.3). Thus our second conclusion is that money did indeed matter. In those contests in which seniority failed, money prevailed.

Not surprisingly, watchdog groups and citizens organizations were quick to join Roukema in the ranks of the displeased and disappointed. Gary Ruskin, head of the watchdog Congressional Accountability Project, observed, for example, that "those who win the chairmanships are in hock up to their necks to special interests. The system means the [business] PACs win. What we have is fake term limits and not the real thing" (Morgan and Eilperin 2001). So, although the intention of reformers was to weaken the connection between long-standing chairs and the interests over whom they wield authority, it may have had the reverse affect. If money is the next most important criterion for advancement, then the chairs may owe their positions to these well-heeled supporters—at least for the duration of their tenures.

But many Republicans share Hastert's enthusiasm. Robert Walker, former GOP stalwart from Pennsylvania, erstwhile reformer, and now a Washington lobbyist, opined: "I think it's worked pretty well. There are all kinds of folks downtown who are scrambling to figure out how they develop relationships to [new chairmen] they never had relationships with before" (Morgan and Eilperin 2001). Now it may well be that 2001 was an unusual year, with retirements, the odd defeat, and so forth roughly evening out the number of chairs forced to turn over in any future Congress, but the bar has been set pretty high. With fewer chairs at stake in any given year (only four in the 108th Congress), the financial pressure might actually escalate, at least on a per committee basis.[12] For that, one can only wait and see as succeeding Congresses unfold.

As for Roukema, she was publicly displeased: "Average people are saying why wouldn't they in this day and age have a qualified woman as a chair? I worry about it, but what can we do?" (Eilperin 2001b). As early as December 2000, rumors in Washington had Roukema headed for an appointment to be U.S. treasurer, or perhaps to head the Government National Mortgage Association (Ginnie Mae), as a consolation prize (Arnold 2001; Bresnahan 2001; Espo 2001). The offer of U.S. treasurer is notable, and an insult, inasmuch as the position is largely honorific, typically held by a woman, and publicized only as the "other" and lesser signature on U.S. currency opposite that of the secretary of the Treasury. Roukema preemptively declined the position, vowing to soldier on for the party: "I will be gracious and a good sport as a member of the Republican team" (Lipman 2001). At seventy-one years of age, Roukema apparently said she would take nothing less than an undersecretary position at the Department of Health and Human Services (Bresnahan 2001). In the end, however, she did not get that nomination. She retired at the end of the 107th Congress.

Our third conclusion, therefore, is that term limits on House committee chairs have altered the "structure of opportunities" within the House, to use a notion developed by Loomis (1988). In other words, musical chairs introduces disruptions into a process traditionally consisting of long queues of patient partisans waiting for their turn at chair. Long-term, relatively stable relationships now have become short-term propositions, or investments. Interest groups, for their part, must scramble to acquaint themselves with a new group of committee and subcommittee chairs. To the extent that money is part of the process, ambitious chair candidates will be laying the tab on their favorite, and perhaps not so favorite, funding sources. A few examples of altered career decisions will make this clear.

In 1996 Charles Patrick "Pat" Roberts, R-KS, abandoned the chair of the House Agriculture Committee after only two years to seek and win one of two open Kansas Senate seats. Roberts was the first sitting chair to run for a Senate seat in sixty years. Absent term limits might he have stayed? In 2000 Rep. James M. Talent, R-MO, abandoned his gavel on the Small Business Committee to pursue his state's governorship. He lost. And Archer, Bliley, William F. Goodling and E. G. "Bud" Shuster of Pennsylvania, and John R. Kasich of Ohio all simply retired when their chairmanships expired. "After being quarterback of a Super Bowl championship team, I have no desire to play back-up," said Shuster in announcing his retirement (Macpherson 2001).

Although the net effect likely is to shorten House careers, a result dear to the hearts of term limiters, it is not entirely one-sided. Robert L. Livingston, R-LA, decided to extend his stay in the House when it became known to him that Speaker Gingrich would step down (not because of a scandal at that time but to pursue a bid for the presidency).[13] In 1997 Billy Tauzin, who then stood second on Resources and on Commerce, announced that he would remain in the House rather than run for a Louisiana Senate seat. Although he did not say so publicly, his decision was presumed to have been based, in part, on the prospect of chairing the Commerce Committee. Douglas K. Bereuter, R-NE, was explicit in declaring that he would pass up a run for governor in the hope of succeeding Gilman as chair of the International Relations Committee. But Bereuter ranked fifth on the committee behind four other members, all of whom were full committee chairs. Any one of them might stake a claim to the position and be in a good position to gain it. Hyde and Leach did, and Hyde won. If the Tauzin and Bereuter cases are indicative, term limits will actually prolong some House careers.

Although we will try to avoid some of the florid headlines that have appeared in the daily and specialized press, it seems safe to conclude that House committee chair term limits have indeed had a significant impact on the House. Certainly, we do not yet know the full impact of the rule—the Democrats could regain their majority and, as they claim they will do, abolish it (Foerstel 2000). Yet based on circumstantial evidence presented here, the results are pretty dramatic: a half-dozen members retiring before "their time," a half-dozen violations of seniority in a single Congress, and unprecedented sums of money raised, at least in part, because of a slew of open chairs. When the music is over, in this case at least, do not turn out the lights.

Notes

1. The authors wish to thank Robert Biersack of the Federal Election Commission for providing the data used in the preparation of this chapter. Neither Biersack nor the commission bear any responsibility for the interpretations and use of that data as presented here.
2. The additional exceptions all involved capacity. Democrats Jamie Whitten of Mississippi, Glenn Anderson of California, Melvin Price of Illinois, and Frank Annunzio of Pennsylvania were displaced largely for reasons related to their age and health. For details on these violations and several by the Republicans, see Deering and Smith (1997).
3. Limits are not unprecedented. House rules already required turnover in the leadership of the Budget, Intelligence, and Standards of Official Conduct Committees.
4. A recodification of the House rules was adopted at the outset of the 106th Congress. The clause on term limits, slightly reworded but substantively unchanged, now can be found at Rule X, 5(c)(2).
5. These are the Speaker, floor leader, and whip, together with the chairs of the Conference, the Policy Committee, and the Campaign Committee.
6. To be precise, there could be either ten or eleven geographic representatives under rules that prevailed at the time of these events. The procedures included a "small-state option" that is triggered if each of the ten regionally elected representatives

comes from a state with three or more Republican members. In that event (the norm, as it turns out), all of the states with one or two Republicans would become an at-large region and elect an eleventh committee member. For the 107th Congress, the small-state category comprised fourteen states, ranging geographically from New Hampshire to Nevada and from Alaska to Mississippi. Don Young of Alaska was the small-state representative during these deliberations.

7. Quoted from a copy of private communication obtained by the authors on condition of anonymity.

8. This was not the only jurisdictional switch contemplated or advocated. Some also toyed with the idea of breaking Education and the Workforce into two distinct panels. And at least one chair candidate supported the idea.

9. Again, in three of the seven cases (Resources, Science, and Transportation) no competition emerged, so those three "winners" were, by definition, the leading fund-raisers. In the remaining four cases, the leading fund-raiser won twice (Energy and Commerce and Judiciary) and lost twice (Armed Services and Veterans' Affairs).

10. Mae Ella Nolan, R-CA, was the first woman to chair a congressional committee—the House Committee on Expenditures in the Post Office Department. Nolan served in the House from 1923 to 1925. Since the consolidation of the House committee system pursuant to the Legislative Reorganization Act of 1946, only a handful of women have chaired House full committees. Mary Norton, D-NJ, who had previously chaired the District Committee and the Labor Committee (prior to its merger with Education), acceded to the chair of the House Administration Committee; Edith Nourse Rogers, R-MA, chaired the Veterans' Committee; Lenor K. Sullivan, D-MO, had the gavel of the Merchant Marine and Fisheries Committee; and Jan Meyers, R-KS, led the Small Business Committee for a short time after Republicans gained the House in 1995.

11. It is worth noting that Weldon suffered the same fate again at the outset of the 108th Congress. Stump retired after just two years at the helm of Armed Services. When Duncan Hunter, R-CA, the senior Republican on the committee, made a strong move to claim the chair, Weldon withdrew from the contest.

12. And only one of these House committees, Government Reform, would open because of term limits—Agriculture, Armed Services, and Resources featured retirement-induced openings. But two of the four, Government Reform and Resources, involved seniority violations. Tom Davis of Virginia, a top Republican fund-raiser as former head of the National Republican Congressional Committee, received the nod over Christopher Shays of Connecticut. Davis contributed $525,000 to the Retain Our Majority Program headed by Majority Leader Tom DeLay. Shays contributed "only" $50,000 and spearheaded a campaign finance reform effort unpopular among his fellow Republicans. On the Resources Committee, Richard Pombo, R-CA, jumped past five more senior committee members to gain the top slot. Seeing the writing on the wall, and DeLay's strong support for Pombo, several of the senior members did not even bother to declare themselves candidates.

13. Livingston quickly reversed his decision because his own personal scandal—an extramarital affair—became public knowledge. Thus Hastert became Speaker.

References

Alpert, Bruce. 2001. "La. Stands To Gain Clout in Congress." *New Orleans Times-Picayune*, January 1, 1.

Alvarez, Lizette. 2000. "House Republicans Play Musical Chairs for a Chance to Lead." *New York Times*, December 6, A24.

————. 2001. "Blustery, Independent Panel Chief to Hold Sway on Bush Economic Agenda." *New York Times*, January 31, A18.

Arnold, Laurence. 2001. "Spurned N.J. Rep. Rejects Offer to Be U.S. Treasurer." Associated Press. January 4.

Bergen Record. 2001. "Sold to the Highest Bidder," January 8, L2.

Bolton, Alexander. 2000. "House Chairmanship Candidates Cite Funds." *The Hill*, December 6.

Bowman, Tom. 2000. "House Faces Free-for-All for Committee Chairmanships." *Baltimore Sun*, December 6, 16A.

Bresnahan, John. 2000. "DeLay Boosts Crane?" *Roll Call*, October 23.

————. 2001. "Roukema May Get Bush Administration Position After All." *Roll Call*, January 15.

Deering, Christopher J. 1996. "Career Advancement and Subcommittee Chairs in the U.S. House of Representatives: 86th to 103rd Congresses." *American Politics Quarterly* 24 (January): 3–23.

Deering, Christopher J., and Steven S. Smith. 1997. *Committees in Congress.* Washington, DC: CQ Press.

Eilperin, Juliet. 2000. "House GOP's Chair Shuffle Begins." *Washington Post*, November 14, A4.

————. 2001a. "GOP's New Rules Bolster House Banking Committee." *Washington Post*, January 3, A4.

————. 2001b. "House GOP Revamps Panels' Leadership." *Washington Post*, January 5, A1.

————. 2001c. "The Undoubting Thomas." *Washington Post*, March 9, A25.

Espo, David. 2001. "New Jersey Congresswoman Put Forward for Post in New Administration." Associated Press. January 3.

Foerstel, Karen. 2000. "Choosing Chairmen: Tradition's Role Fades." *CQ Weekly*, December 9, 2796–2801.

Groseclose, Timothy, and Charles Stewart III. 1998. "The Value of Committee Seats in the House, 1947-91." *American Journal of Political Science* 42 (April): 453–474.

Gugliotta, Guy. 1998. "Term Limit Prompts House Chairmen to Hunt New Perches." *Washington Post*, March 23, A17.

Hall, Richard L., and Frank W. Wayman. 1990. "Buying Time: Moneyed Interests and the Mobilization of Bias in Congressional Committees." *American Political Science Review* 84 (September): 797–820.

Hibbing, John R. 1991. *Congressional Careers: Contours of Life in the U.S. House of Representatives.* Chapel Hill: University of North Carolina.

Hinckley, Barbara. 1971. *The Seniority System in Congress.* Bloomington: Indiana University Press.

Hines, Cragg. 2001. "A Newt Time Bomb Finally Explodes." *Houston Chronicle*, January 7, 2, Outlook.

JoC Online. 2000. "Election Results to Bring Trade Community Changes." November 9, http://www.joc.com.

Kammer, Jerry. 2000. "Stump Has Rival for Post in House." *Arizona Republic*, December 7, A1.

Lipman, Larry. 2001. "House Plays Musical Chairmen; New Heads Chosen for 13 Committees." *Atlanta Journal and Constitution*, January 5, 3A.

Loomis, Burdett. 1988. *The New American Politician.* New York: Basic Books.

Macpherson, Karen. 2001. "Shuster Quits After Losing Powerful Job." *Pittsburgh Post-Gazette*, January 5, A1.

Mercurio, Linda. 2001. "Shame on Congress for Denying Roukema a Leadership Post." *Bergen Record*, January 11, L9.

Morgan, Dan, and Juliet Eilperin. 2001. "A House GOP Reform Boomerangs." *Washington Post*, January 12, A1.

Ota, Alan K. 2001. "Chairman Tauzin Charts a Bold Course for Commerce." *CQ Weekly*, February 3, 258–266.

Palmer, Elizabeth A. 1997. "Republicans Hope to Change Term Limits for Panel Leaders." *Milwaukee Journal Sentinel*, September 19, 26.

Polsby, Nelson W., Miriam Gallaher, and Barry Spencer Rundquist. 1969. "The Growth of the Seniority System in the U.S. House of Representatives." *American Political Science Review* 63 (September): 787–807.

Shepsle, Kenneth J. 1978. *The Giant Jigsaw Puzzle: Democratic Committee Assignments in the House of Representatives*. Chicago: University of Chicago Press.

Simon, Richard. 2001. "Californian Thomas Gets House Ways and Means Chairmanship." *Los Angeles Times*, January 5, A15.

Tyson, James T. 2000. "Cash Talks in Power Play." *Chicago Sun-Times*, October 1, 41.

Wright, John R. 1990. "Contributions, Lobbying, and Committee Voting in the U.S. House of Representatives." *American Political Science Review* 84 (June): 417–438.

9. Making Connections to the Appropriations Process

Joseph White

The influence that interest groups have on congressional decision making depends on characteristics of the groups, the decision makers, and the decisions themselves. Within Congress, the most basic distinction among decisions is between those that authorize programs and those that appropriate the funds for their operation. The funds for most programs are provided in bills written by the House and Senate Appropriations Committees rather than by the committees, such as House Armed Services or Senate Energy and Natural Resources, that wrote the underlying authorization. Although the boundary between appropriations and other legislation is continually a subject of conflict, the appropriations process has its own distinct dynamic.[1]

Characteristics of the Appropriations Process

Appropriations provide what congressional budget process rules call "discretionary" funding for the federal government. The fiscal year (FY) 2005 appropriations bills fund agencies for the twelve-month period from October 1, 2004, to September 30, 2005.[2] If such funds are not provided in legislation at the beginning of a fiscal year, an agency (subject to various exceptions) is not able to operate. If funding for a significant portion of federal agencies is allowed to lapse, a government shutdown commences, which, as the conflict between President Bill Clinton and Congress in 1995 and 1996 showed, can be highly unpleasant both for the public and for whoever is blamed for the conflict (Maraniss and Weiskopf 1996; Killian 1998).

As a result, the appropriations process, far more than anything else in Congress, is organized to pass bills. The Senate and House Appropriations Committees divide their jurisdiction identically into thirteen subcommittees each (though some names differ), and each subcommittee drafts one "general appropriations bill" per year. Because each bill is very similar in structure to the previous year's, writing the bills is a routine process. With rare exceptions, such as some of the freshman Republicans appointed to the House Appropriations Committee in the 104th Congress (1995–1996), committee members are oriented toward passing legislation, even as they also are selected from party loyalists. The orientation has been even stronger among committee staff in both chambers (White 1989). Partisan divides can be very deep, but even highly ideological members appear to recognize that they will have to compromise in the end.

Because each side of any dispute knows the bills must pass, brinksmanship may emerge, with each side assuming that the other will give in. Appropriations bills attract many objections, and in spite of rules against changing the underlying law (authorizations) on appropriations bills, they also attract riders—attempts to change policy that go beyond simple funding of agencies. As a result, in some years the passage of certain bills on the House or Senate floor has been stymied. In 1995 many agencies received temporary, continuing funding for more than half the year before the FY 1996 bills were settled. In 2002 House appropriators believed they could not pass eight of their bills on the House floor if they conformed to spending targets set by President George W. Bush and House Republican leaders. Eventually, eleven of the thirteen appropriations for FY 2003 were packaged in an omnibus law that was not enacted until January 2003, and most of its contents never reached the House floor until the up or down vote on the omnibus bill's conference report (Schatz 2003; Taylor 2003a). Whether in separate bills or otherwise, however, each year each of the thirteen appropriations bills somehow shows up in a conference report. When other members of the House or Senate are not allowed to vote on individual provisions, the influence exercised by members of the House or Senate Appropriations Committees only increases.

This dynamic creates a situation for interest groups that is unlike those faced in other legislative struggles. If Congress enacts an appropriation into law, settled interpretation keeps the agency in business even if the underlying authorization has lapsed. For example, if the reauthorization for the Department of Justice is hung up by disputes about issues such as busing, school prayer, or abortion, no disaster is forthcoming as long as the appropriations are made. In the authorizations arena, then, groups have an incentive to bring up controversial issues that mobilize their constituents; when a bill is deadlocked, they can say they blocked legislation that their members would have disliked. In the appropriations arena, the committees, and ultimately legislative leaders, cannot afford to let such disputes prevent passage of a bill. When such issues are raised in the appropriations process, there is a strong bias in favor of dropping them at the end of the process. There is no such thing as a "killer amendment." There are only awkward provisions that must eventually be dropped in conference, whenever conference is somehow reached. Nor can members of Congress or the president "strategically disagree" to settle the bills themselves (Gilmour 1995). Appropriators can, however, promise disappointed parties that they will fix something in the next round—which may or may not be credible, but is much more plausible than for regular legislation, where there may not be a "next round" for years.[3]

In addition to being must-pass legislation, most appropriations bills are quite varied packages. For example, the Departments of Labor, Health and Human Services (HHS), and Education are all included in one bill known as Labor-HHS. Another large conglomeration, known as VA-HUD, includes the Department of Veterans Affairs (VA), Department of Housing and Urban Development (HUD), Environmental Protection Agency (EPA), National Science Foundation (NSF), and National Aeronautics and Space Administration (NASA), plus a host of smaller agencies. Even a bill that basically finances one department, such as those for Interior or Defense, may in fact include very different, and rival, agencies. Because hardly anyone other than the staff and senior members of a given appropriations subcommittee knows much about the range of agencies in a given bill, it is hard for anyone else to make either political or policy judgments about trade-offs in the bill. Yet trade-offs are normally necessary, because congressional budget rules, or the mood of the time, set some standard for the total size of the bill, forcing anyone who seeks to add money for one purpose to usually "offset" it with a cut in other accounts.[4]

In a classic interest group battle such as those over telecommunications or financial services deregulation, the opposing forces attack each other's arguments. The "Baby Bells" can claim to know something about long-distance service, or AT&T about local service. In the appropriations process, many opportunities exist for direct conflicts among interest groups—say, between environmentalists and mining or timber interests within the Department of the Interior appropriations bill. But the most basic conflicts are less direct. NASA, the EPA, and the VA compete for funds within the VA-HUD bill, but nobody imagines that advocates for NASA know anything about how much money the VA should get. Thus, rather than fight rivals, most groups just cultivate their own support from Congress and the administration.

Because the basic task of appropriators is to finance agencies, those agencies figure in the process in a way that is not true of all legislation. To budget for agencies, the appropriations subcommittees must delve into the details of agency activities, for it is those details that add up to spending. In funding agency activities, the appropriations subcommittees are the most important players in traditional distributive politics.[5] Appropriations are the home of the classic "pork barrel" politics of rivers and harbors, and the new-wave pork barrel of academic earmarks, which are described later in this chapter (Savage 1999).

Even if a program is not designed to fund projects on a geographic basis, it can raise major distributional concerns. As a senior committee aide explained in 1990, "If you make a decision on a weapon, compounded with other decisions, it can destroy that manufacturer, those workers, that industrial base, and it can be that that's all there is in that district. . . . Hughes Aircraft makes Phoenix, Maverick, Sidewinder and Amraam missiles, all in Phoenix. The plant overhead is spread over all those programs. So if you kill one, the cost of the others goes up, which makes them more vulnerable . . . [and] pretty soon the defense industry in Arizona is rolling up the sidewalks."

As Mark A. Peterson (1995) has argued, both members of Congress and voters understand distributional information better than "policy analytic" information. Appropriations Committees certainly pay attention to both. Thus any discussion of the role played by interest groups in the appropriations process must address how groups compete for distributive benefits. Because members of the Appropriations Committees are minorities of the House and Senate, they must tread carefully to avoid backlash from the majority of legislators, who may feel treated unfairly. And they face strong challenges in certain areas, such as the ability of the transportation authorizing committees to direct funds in the occasional highway bills, or especially the Armed Services Committees' annual authorizations for the Department of Defense. Yet appropriators have a far greater reach than that of any other committee: they have the final word on whether money is available for a given purpose, and they have lots of ways to enforce their preferences upon agency administrators.[6]

Types of Decisions on Appropriations

Most members of Congress neither know nor care about most of the decisions made as part of legislation most of the time. Committees and their members have a louder voice in those aspects of legislation that do not attract broad interest. Interest groups engage in the legislative process in different ways, depending on their ability to make an issue salient to many or few members of Congress. The decisions in appropriations bills can be very roughly sorted into five types, each with its own dynamic of participation: total spending, spending on each bill, programs, projects, and riders.

Total spending on the appropriations bills conditions all other decisions, but is essentially imposed on the process from the outside. It depends on the partisan makeup of the government and broad budgetary conditions, such as the level of deficit or surplus. Groups can try to affect these conditions, especially with electoral support for the party that favors their programs. Yet that process is very different from lobbying the appropriations process per se.

Total *spending for each bill* means the relative funding for each bill. These decisions are shaped by the strength of the parties, the president's influence, and the public's mood, During the initial consideration of legislation, however, the formal decision on the distribution of funds across subcommittees — that is, what portion of the total can be spent on each bill — is entirely within the authority of the Appropriations Committees. In practice, the committee chairs set the figures (see White 1989). The committees receive a total allocation from the budget process, which they are then required to subdivide into 302(b) allocations to the thirteen subcommittees (302[b] refers to a section of the Congressional Budget Act in one of its iterations). Bills and amendments that exceed these allocations are out of order on the House and Senate floor.[7]

When the 302(b) process was created at the end of 1985, groups recognized that it would be in the interest of all the claimants for spending within a given bill to join forces to increase that bill's allocation. But lobbyists "lack leverage" (Munson 1993, 25). Supporters of programs in one bill can claim no knowledge about why programs in other bills should get less, or how they could get less. It is also hard to change a decision by the full committee chair, because increasing the allocation for any one bill requires cutting another. Any subcommittee chair that wants more will be opposed by both supporters of the bill from which any "offsets" would come and the full committee chair, just for starters.

The subcommittee allocations are made with knowledge that distributions may change at the end of the process, after bargaining with the White House when the bill goes to the House-Senate conference committee. In this context, even building up political support for the spending in a given bill may not help with the allocation. As one committee aide interviewed for this study put it, "The allocation can be used in reverse." When appropriators believe their total allowance from the budget resolution is unreasonably low, they often allocate less to the bill that is the most popular and hold it to the end, thereby forcing conservative legislators or a recalcitrant president to explicitly oppose that bill's programs if they want to maintain the cap on total spending. Lobbying that makes those programs more popular does help to achieve more spending, but only at the end of the process, rather than raise the 302(b) allocation. Staff and members of the committees agree that forming coalitions to influence allocations is not worthwhile.

Program priorities are set within each bill. Each appropriations subcommittee establishes levels of funding for each agency and major program or unit within the agency, and then seeks to defend that funding level in subsequent stages of the process. At times, voter sentiment shapes program choices with little mediation from interest groups. Occasionally, one party may set itself up to get rolled by public opinion. In 1995 the Clinton administration attacked congressional Republicans for slashing the Safe and Drug Free Schools program. "Separate and apart from whether the program works," an administration official recalled, "killing a program with that name to it was stupid in and of itself. I must say, people like me did not have a very hard job after that, the talking points write themselves." When a program is very popular, both parties may even compete for credit for increasing spending, regardless of the merits. For many years, appropriations staffers with links to both parties watched with dismay as the political system poured resources into the "drug war" and other attacks on crime. "It's not as if this is an award-winning Department of Justice we've got here," two senior aides moaned in 1996. Routine funding for agencies also may not attract much group lobbying. There is no powerful Department of Justice, or even Federal Bureau of Investigation, lobby group.

Most often, programs have supporters but no mobilized, constituency-based opponents. For example, the National Institutes of Health (NIH) have wide support and hardly any opposition. Categorical grants for special education garner narrow but intense support and hardly any opposition. In some cases, as with NASA's space station, spending may be opposed by a set of groups, but, because they have little to gain directly from a cutback in spending, they do not campaign hard on the issue (Munson 1993). Only a subset of programs—such as the B-1 or B-2 bombers, roads within national forests, enforcement by the Occupational Safety and Health Administration (OSHA), or funding for the National Endowment for the Arts—involves interest groups working both for and against spending.

When there is little opposition, advocates still have to fight for their share of a limited pie. Producer interests—private firms, public bureaucracies, or nonprofit organizations that provide a good or service—are the most reliable program advocates because of their direct financial stake. That financial stake may give them both the ability and a reason to use campaign contributions in their advocacy. In general, however, producers are few and consumers—or beneficiaries—more numerous. Therefore, advocates will try to rally consumers—for example, passengers who ride the northeast corridor trains for Amtrak, or farmers who use extension services—to convince politicians that votes are more directly at stake.

The "vaunted health lobby," according to a former White House science adviser, "is the model everyone wants to emulate." As *Science* magazine reported, "What sets the NIH coalition apart from other science lobbying efforts is its longtime alliance with dozens of grassroots patient groups, pushing for cures to everything from cancer to rare genetic disorders" (Malakoff 2001, 832). By way of contrast, research universities, which can be major economic engines within congressional districts, also have a strong producer interest in funding for the physical sciences, but there is no comparable set of citizen claimants to help win congressional support for that funding.

Project decisions are the most detailed level of appropriations. They are often described as "earmarks," meaning that some of an agency's funds are earmarked for a specific project with language in the appropriations bill or accompanying report. Occasionally, a project or purchase can be so large that it turns into a policy and priority issue. Supersonic transport (SST) in the 1970s, the Tennessee-Tombigbee Canal in the 1980s, and the Clinch River breeder reactor also in the 1980s are examples. But even very large projects, such as the Central Arizona Project to distribute water from the Colorado River, can remain below the radar of debate about government priorities.

Only an extremely small proportion of the many thousands of projects in each year's appropriations can be invested with the symbolic value that allows conflict to be brought to the House or Senate floor in spite of the fact that a given project is of direct interest to only one or a few members. Project allocation is therefore an inside game. The vast majority of decisions are made by subcommittee leadership, but members of subcommittees have some voice in those choices. Other members of Congress lobby subcommittee leaders and other subcommittee members, and those who have a stake in a project lobby anybody they can reach.

From the subcommittee leadership's perspective, the challenge is how to sort through the funding requests and approve a package that maximizes support for the appropriations bill. Because a bill must be approved first in subcommittee, later in full committee, and only then on the floor, subcommittee chairs and staff first want to ensure that their own members are satisfied. Then they worry about legislators who could make particular trouble for the bill on the floor, such as the chairs of authorizing committees (who might rally their own members to support a challenge) or party leaders. There is therefore a natural hierarchy of who will get the most from the distributive process on a given bill. From an interest group's perspective, then, it is best to start as far up the totem pole as possible. Projects in the districts of subcommittee chairs and members certainly have an advantage over projects that do not (Savage 1999).[8]

Interests cannot confine distributive politics to the people at the top of the hierarchy because there are too few appropriators, in too few districts, relative to the demands. Most legislators seem to understand, though, that the central brokers in any legislative bargain will take some extra for themselves as a fee, and appropriators are no different from, say, members of tax-writing committees when "transition rules" are being drafted. But it is possible to be too greedy. In the House especially, appropriators also need to attend to the concerns of party leaders. Leaders seek projects both for themselves and for vulnerable incumbents who need to claim some credit with their voters.

Because appropriators cannot come close to meeting the demand for projects, they create rationales for saying no: "We don't earmark in this program." "That amount would be too large a share of the account in question." "We need a sign-off from the authorizing committee." "The committee has already given you more than your share in other projects." And so on. Lobbyists for a given project thus have to know how to fit it within the guidelines in effect at the time (and which keep changing).

Personal relationships (it helps to be a former Appropriations Committee staff member) can be used to lobby subcommittee staff for particular projects. But the norm is to lobby the committee through members—that is, to find a "champion." Here again, the volume of potential claims becomes a factor. A representative or senator will be asked to support far more projects than he or she can possibly get approved. The legislator's challenge, then, includes how to assign priority to requests, how to get the best package possible in policy or political terms, and how to avoid blame from those lobbyists or constituents who do not get what they want. The lobbyist's or interest group's challenge is to move its particular project up the legislator's informal priority list, so the legislator does not give it up to get something else.

Meanwhile, there must be some kind of "electoral connection." After all, it is hard to imagine legislators pursuing projects if it would hurt them. Yet researchers have never discerned strong relationships between district funding and electoral margins. One reason is that the average voter is likely to have a vague notion at best of his or her representative's relative success at distributing federal government largesse, and many factors other than representatives' own efforts affect the distribution of federal funds among districts. But the statistical results (or nonresults) also might reflect the fact that demand varies across districts. Distributive politics is more predominant in some states and districts than in others.[9] In such high-demand constituencies, a high response is simply expected; the legislator gets no special credit because he or she is compared not with the national norm but with his or her predecessor or neighbor.

Demand also varies over time. Although earmarking has increased dramatically in recent years, at times members of Congress, or challengers, have found it more advantageous in some districts to criticize distributive politics. The value of academic earmarks declined substantially in decisions made during 1993, 1994, and especially 1995, and then recovered slowly before zooming upward in

1998.[10] One appropriator interviewed in 1996 noted that "politically there is always an ebb and flow to this. I remember when spending was associated with inflation, in the Carter era." By 1998 the deficit had gone away, so it was hard to blame members for pork barrel spending that created deficits.

In short, "pork" is a taste preference for legislators. One House subcommittee chair explained his own taste as "a sense of accomplishment on the part of a member who is approached by constituents—generally it is local government types, the town council, the school board, the airport authority—who have a problem and they think federal money will help. . . . [I]f you do an $800,000 innovative housing project, it won't change the face of that town. But it tells the town, 'We think what you're doing has merit, it might be seen as a model,' . . . [and] so the member and the community both feel pretty good." Because legislators have such views, stalemate in other areas will divert legislators to projects in search of discrete, or literally concrete, accomplishments. A second former subcommittee chair remarked that, in a diverse district, projects for one part might elicit criticism from another part: "The suburbs object to agriculture support, and the country to HUD." The constituency for projects is not ordinary voters, but, "the educated elites and economic interests in the district. . . . It's not campaign contributions, but an acceptance by the establishment. . . . The consequences of spending don't show up immediately. If there is no flood in 10 years on the Santa Ana River due to current spending on flood control projects, that won't help the current members from Orange County now. And probably won't be noticed then. But it is noticed by local influentials."

These comments indicate that, although in situations such as major weapons contracts the operative definition of "constituency pressure" may be ordinary voters whose jobs are at stake, in many other situations legislators are trying to impress the "local influentials" or simply to feel that they have done some good. Passion can thus be a relevant resource for interest groups: the intensity of demand can affect the legislator's sense that meeting a demand is doing good. Part of the challenge for an interest group, then, is to make sure that its project is something the member will feel good about pursuing—or bad about not pursuing. And that is true about some program priorities as well as projects. The most powerful example of the importance of emotional factors such as passion and sympathy, the desire to do good or prevent harm, is the success of the AIDS activists (Kondracke 2001, 212–213).

Riders, the last category of decisions in appropriations bills, are provisions that specify that money cannot be spent for some activity (a "limitation amendment" which is in order as an appropriation), or authorizing legislation that is tacked onto a bill despite rules against doing so. Riders are "a popular way to try to change policy when it is otherwise impossible to amend the underlying authorization law" (Taylor 2003c, 1893). The politics of riders depends on their salience and visibility; some are of interest to only one member, while others, such as restrictions on abortion or provisions that ended U.S. military involvement in Vietnam, have been extremely controversial. Low-salience riders occur

when the administration requests a small change in a law, or when a local difficulty does not quite meet the standards for federal help under existing law but is
close enough that a change in the authorization will not excite much controversy. In these situations, "people look to the process to fix problems that don't fit
one program or another." "On very narrowly focused legislative issues," observed
a senator who had chaired both an authorizing committee and an appropriations
subcommittee, the Appropriations Committee "has more ability to act than the
authorizing committees." One Senate aide called Appropriations "the fix-it
committee." When it comes to such "fix-it" riders, the role of interest groups
resembles its role in distributive politics—to seek help within a large group of
other claimants, if the issue engages groups at all.

In other situations, the rider is major, but the appropriations bill to which it
is attached is being used simply as a convenient vehicle. The appropriators do not
care how it turns out, so long as the authorizers and administration settle the dispute. In 1984 an omnibus crime bill was tacked onto the continuing resolution
that would fund most of the federal government.[11] Appropriations staff left the
authorizers to "work out this crime control [stuff]." The appropriations staff
recalls that when they returned to find the Republicans "eating Chinese food in
one room, the Democrats pizza in another," they threatened to just choose
whichever versions had fewer pages! As one close observer of the process put it,
the appropriators sometimes view a rider as an issue that "they want no part of,"
especially if it involves substantial conflict, and they try to get others to settle the
dispute—if they can.

In some instances, however, the appropriators cannot or do not want to steer
clear of a conflict. Abortion, termination of the Vietnam War, and the Istook
amendment of 1995 (an attempt to "defund the left") are examples of extremely
controversial issues that were fought out at the appropriations level and not
passed on to authorizing committees for negotiation. When interests bring these
kinds of issues into the appropriations arena, the outcome will depend not only
on their own efforts but also on the specific policy context of that conference
negotiation in that particular year.

Advocates of riders must seek to show that their supporters are so fervent
that they might even reject an appropriations conference report rather than
accept defeat, and that is a high standard. Whoever benefits from the status quo
will have the advantage in such a conflict, but probably not as great as in normal
legislative battles, because the option of simply preventing all action does not
exist. Yet no matter how salient the rider, lots of other stakes will enter into any
conference negotiation. The major players (House versus Senate, party factions,
administration) that lose on such an issue will expect to win on something else.
Thus it will be easier to deep-six a controversial rider that has strong support if
another such rider has support largely from the other side of the political spectrum. A paradigmatic case of that dynamic arose when some (mostly liberal and
eastern moderate) legislators attempted to raise grazing fees, while others (mostly conservatives) sought to punish the National Endowment for the Arts (NEA)

for its support of "obscene" art, such as the photography of Robert Mapple-thorpe—both in the same Department of the Interior appropriations bill. Both riders were dumped in what was known, inexactly, as the "corn for porn" trade. Truly brilliant strategic players might be able to invent extra issues that allow such trades, but in general one has to suspect that advocates for the arts, for example, are not likely to invent an effort to raise grazing fees. The combination of issues, and thus to some extent the result, is, from the perspective of interest groups, relatively random.

How Groups Contribute to the Appropriations Process

Interest groups may make a positive contribution to policymaking by improving the information available, or a negative one by distorting the facts and substituting raw power for the public interest. Their influence may be based on money, substantive expertise, process expertise, or political connections. Group input into policymaking may fit a pluralist model, in which interests mobilize along many shifting fault lines, or a partisan model, in which social forces line up with Democrats or Republicans and are mobilized by the parties on individual issues. Which of these various descriptions applies best to groups within the appropriations process?

Information

Appropriators get much of their information from agencies, and agency budget officers in particular (White 1990). Even in the traditional pork barrel process, the subcommittees look to the agencies for information about requests to ensure that a project is feasible and will not generate any embarrassment. The agencies' role limits the abilities of groups to "distort" the process. Appropriators do not worry too much that they will get only one viewpoint of a project—and if they do, they may worry as much about getting only the administration's view. "Interest groups get a bum rap," one veteran commented. "One of the things I always thought as a staff guy was that the administration would submit its pro-posals, and people would line up for or against it—[Ralph] Nader, [Joan] Clay-brook, etc.—and it would put the staff person in a position as an observer. . . . [Y]ou knew their biases, but like a referee you could stand in the middle, see their volleys back and forth, and hopefully, if you were a good listener and read the material, you could cut through the b.s. and learn more about the subject."

During the Ronald Reagan and George H. W. Bush administrations, appropriators had to worry that agencies were under pressure from the Office of Management and Budget (OMB) not to provide information. The subcommit-tees usually got it anyway, but in this situation interest groups were viewed as a positive alternative source. An OMB official, when asked about the ability of agency officials to keep information from the subcommittees, remarked that "most of the [issues] in education [the appropriators] . . . could extrapolate for themselves. Or get it from the groups, if not the department." In the foreign aid arena, a subcommittee clerk commented that "there are a huge number of groups, they spend their whole day tracking issues, and they are very responsive to us. Often they have information faster than the State Department." Contractors, such as those involved in defense and NASA issues, not only offer information, but also tend to generate communities of the trade, with publications and newsletters, and those media provide further information.

Members of Congress are far more likely than staff to get one-sided information, and interest groups able to offer interesting junkets or campaign contributions will have an advantage in getting legislators' attention. So will groups that can invite members to visit facilities in their districts. Manufacturers build support for major defense purchases by seeding subcontracts all around the country, in as many districts as possible. They then use those venues to pitch the merits of whatever they manufacture, with those merits being more or less transparently a rationale for local jobs. One should not, however, see such tactics as simply "interest groups" shaping policy. In fact, in many cases the groups are working hand in hand with the bureaucracy or political executive who is proposing the program, as happened in the 1991 fight over preserving NASA's space station (Munson 1993).

Contributions versus Constituents

The most controversial interest group resource, campaign contributions, does influence appropriations decisions. But many of the affected interests—local governments, foreign governments, universities, poor people—either have little money to give or are not allowed to give it directly. A lobbyist and former appropriations aide noted that the groups with "large commercial interests involved have always played that game. Everybody else is playing it a little bit more, but not a lot. Because to be a real player you have to pay a lot of money."

During the last two decades, an entire industry of appropriations lobbying has emerged, and the lobbyists in that business can play a significant role in fund raising. "I raise money and I give money," the leader of one firm reported (the order of his statement reflects the effect of campaign finance rules). A lobbyist can do more by assembling others to give than by giving directly himself. Some firms explicitly impose levels of campaign giving on their professional staff and put more emphasis than other firms on helping members with fund-raising.

In the words of one lobbyist, who, both by his own account and that of others, has been a particularly active fund-raiser,

> like it or not, the rules of the system dictate that you have to be involved
> with fund-raising. That provides visibility, it provides access, to some extent
> it provides some credibility. . . . That said, there are very good ways to access
> the Hill, get involved, make your points without doing fund-raising.
> It's important for nonprofits to understand that. I never gave to PACs

[political action committees], I never told clients to start a PAC, and this may sound like I'm arguing with myself, but if people do it right, they don't have to play the money game. But it takes a lot of organization, a lot of fol-low-up.

Even lobbyists who do not want to get drawn into contributions get hit up for cash in the current fundraising frenzy. Some manage not to take calls that they do not want to take, but, especially if the call is from someone with more authority in the appropriations process, "it's tough saying no to somebody who's about to give you a candy bar." Lobbyists take refuge behind the individual con-tribution limits in the campaign finance laws. "That's a great excuse, let me tell you, I've done it often, 'I'd like to help you but I can't, I've maxed.' " But that will not end the pressure to put together a fund-raiser.

It is difficult to trace the effects of contributions through an Appropriations Committee perspective because the subcommittee staff, who draft the bills and reports, do not see the contributions. As one veteran put it, "The money buys access far more strongly in personal offices than in committees. The personal office hierarchy is more aware of where the money is coming from." Money might affect how a member ranks projects on his or her priority list, but either many of those projects are too small to justify significant contributions or those benefiting from the projects are not likely to be donors (for example, local librar-ians are unlikely to donate for local library grants). Contributions will be more pertinent if a group does not have a strong constituency hook to a member but believes that member is a potential champion for other reasons, or if a member knows a group has money and so expects some. Because most lobbyists have been in the business for a long time and develop relationships, they also will contribute on their own to those members they consider friends and allies.

Under normal circumstances, money has its greatest influence on "smaller, low-profile issues that [mean] a lot to the company or industry involved" (Kil-lian 1998, 323). When it comes to the details in regulatory legislation, which tend to fly below the radar of media attention, the access that money buys to authorizing committee members may be primary. But in the appropriations arena, where the stakes are more often district-specific projects, it is constituen-cies, more than contributions, that fly below the radar. All observers and partic-ipants who were interviewed argued that legislators in the appropriations process care more about constituents than contributions. Thus they described personal and constituency relationships as paramount in finding a champion—even on program issues. For example, when the National Association of Broadcasters had a problem with federal funding of TV Marti, an anti-Castro station based in South Florida that could interfere with commercial broadcasts, it went looking for a member with a constituency incentive to make nice with Cuba. They found William V. Alexander Jr., D-AR, a member of the appropriate subcommittee in the House, who represented rice growers with an interest in exporting to Cuba and who would therefore not be criticized at home for failing to be tough enough on Fidel Castro. Although at times a producer interest will find it worthwhile to seek a champion through contributions to members without a constituency stake, the role of contributions is relatively secondary in pork barrel politics, more a way to "grease the skids" than the engine of influence.

Skill

Why does skill matter at all if constituency is primary? Lobbying involves skills of persuasion, a willingness to be insistent, an understanding of the targets, and an understanding of budget accounts, all of which specialists possess to a far greater extent than do their clients and even some members of Congress.

Professionals better understand the game of finding a champion. Convincing a politician to seem friendly and supportive to one's interest may be easy, but convincing him or her to actually do something can be hard. "The private sector hears a senator or congressman saying, 'I support you,'" one specialist in the defense area commented, "and they think the deal is done." But that is not true; the supportive member may do little. "I've had people write a letter saying, 'Please support this,' and get back something that is wishy-washy. And I make them write back and say, 'Is that a yes or a no, and what will you do specifically?'" One committee staffer described a well-known lobbying firm's tactics. When that firm gets a client, he reported, "they go to the member that represents the client and say this is in your district, you need to help us get this done. They tell the people from the institution that this guy has this kind of access, and they work the system more on the basis of people's obligation to represent their constituents than with money." As another lobbyist explained, to push legislators and subcommittee staff "it's not two times that you have to do things, it's eight times, in combination with having your timing right and knowing when things will happen on the Hill." When he was asked how he avoided being seen as obnoxious, he replied, "You don't. That's the key. If someone says, 'Oh God, he's here again, he wants to talk about cancer research,' that means your message has gotten through."

Once a champion is found, the request must still be maneuvered through the appropriations process. Lobbyists will point out the various pots of money available. All agree that, when dealing with busy appropriations staff, lobbyists must know what they want and not just ask for help. "If we hand them a problem and say, 'Here's what it is,' they say goodbye. If we say, 'Here are three possible solutions,' then they'll talk." Specialists know how to draft a provision in "the language the committee speaks." Requests will have better prospects if skillful lobbyists work the agency to line up support, or at least neutrality from the affected agency. In that way, the agency will not claim the request could cause embarrassment or screw up how a program works.

Lobbyists experienced within the appropriations process have access based on personal relations and knowledge, such as how the chair of a subcommittee is likely to react to various potential champions. They also see themselves as interpreters, especially when the issue is more programmatic. They translate clientspeak for the "uninitiated," while explaining politicians' concerns to clients: "[Our client] can have something that goes bang and kills people, and the Congress says no, we want something that kills people when we want it to kill people, but doesn't get left on the battlefield and go bang and kill kids. And that's not always first on the mind of the defense industrial complex that wants to build widgets at least cost."

These skill factors help to explain why there has been dramatic growth in the specialized profession of lobbying the Appropriations Committees, with a large role played by former appropriations staff and members.[12]

Partisanship

Interest group politics becomes more clearly partisan as groups become more tightly linked in coalitions with one party or another, especially supporting one or the other party in electoral politics (Herrnson, Shaiko, and Wilcox 1998). The appropriations process is affected by both partisan and nonpartisan patterns, but the trend is clearly toward greater partisanship.

Partisan cleavages have always been a major factor in battles about program-level funding and riders (Fenno 1966). In the partisan battles between President Clinton and congressional Republicans, education, environmental, and labor groups were particularly likely to align with the Democrats, and sometimes worked largely through the administration and the Democrats, seeking more to strengthen the administration's resolve than to cut a deal with the Republicans. As one OMB source reported, "If the administration was trying to prove its bona fides on these two areas to the public at large, it needed the groups to be satisfied with the funding levels that it was pursuing and to say nice things about the president and the administration in general."

Appropriations battles during this period, like all other legislative conflict, were more partisan in the House than the Senate. Some House Republican appropriators saw "lost opportunities" for friendlier relations with lobbyists (such as those in higher education), because much of the Republican rank and file insisted on adhering to tight budget caps. Sometimes, agencies and even the administration and groups were more willing to compromise than House Democrats, led by Minority Leader Richard A. Gephardt, D-MO, and ranking Appropriations member David Obey, D-WI, who "would be saying we might lose, but by keeping the issue we might show the right wing for what they are and maybe pick up seats." Thus interest group politics in areas that could be expected to be partisan became extremely so.

Yet even in some largely partisan areas, groups would work both sides. Interviewed sources emphasized that House Republicans had thirty to forty members who would resist outright attacks on labor interests, and a similar number who could be rallied to oppose eliminating support for the National Endowments for the Arts and Humanities. Partisan effects were muted in Defense, where a large segment of the Democrats, particularly appropriators, joined with Republicans in favoring more spending on particular weapons systems. The greatest interest group success, the massive increases in spending for the National Institutes of Health, was led by Republicans because they were the subcommittee leaders, but members of both parties tend to like the NIH, and the research and disease-specific lobbies worked to build support from all legislators.

Most recently, united Republican control of the government gave President George W. Bush a very strong hand. Party leaders essentially sided with the president, and the combination shaped decisions even when majorities on the floors of both the House and Senate expressed different preferences. In 2003 in some battles over both programs and riders, majorities or large factions in Congress opposed the administration's positions. Among these issues were spending on VA medical care, the use of vouchers for public education in the District of Columbia, efforts to eliminate restrictions on travel to Cuba, efforts to block Labor Department regulations that stripped some white-collar workers of their right to overtime pay, an attempt to block a ruling by the Federal Communications Commission (FCC) that allowed large media corporations to own stations in more markets, and an Agriculture Department decision to delay a requirement that food labels include the country of origin. In some of these cases, the House and Senate even adopted identical language, but party leaders ensured that the conference agreement eliminated that language and adopted the administration's position (Taylor 2003b; Byrd 2004; Schatz 2004). Riders will be more significant when Congress and the presidency are controlled by different parties.

Since the election of 1994, partisanship has become more important in distributive politics, though the process has been complex. Many participants reported shock when Speaker Newt Gingrich, R-GA, made a point of instructing House appropriations subcommittee leaders to pay special attention to whether there were "any Republican members who could be severely hurt by the bill or who need a specific district item in the bill?" [13] A committee insider reports that in the early years of the House Republican majority "it was a constant conflict; the leadership wanted to help members with projects at home, and the committee wanted to make sure it was evenly distributed, because if it wasn't evenly distributed that made it difficult to pass the bill." Committee leaders assumed that they had to have some Democratic support to pass a bill, because some Republicans would vote against virtually anything, and eventually a Democratic president, Bill Clinton, would have to sign the bill. Thus, as committee members and staff reported, the allocation of projects remained essentially acceptable to both partisan sides—which does not mean that the Democrats got exactly their proportional share, but they did not feel they were getting shafted.

One reason that the politics of distribution did not immediately become a matter of partisan disgruntlement is that after 1996 the volume of earmarked projects ballooned. In 1990 the Labor-HHS bill had hardly any earmarks; in 2000 Congress put over 1,100 in the bill and report for FY 2001. Within this context, after 1996 whatever the Republican leadership pushed to give vulnerable Republicans was just a splash in the bucket. Even if the minority got less than the majority, it was getting more than it got before. Until the late 1990s, the process of distribution in House subcommittees worked as follows. Members would submit their project requests to the subcommittee staff, chair, or other subcommittee members, in a variety of ways. Most projects for members of both parties were vetted by the subcommittee staff and approved by the chair. The chair would consult the ranking minority member for some matters. He or she also would give the ranking minority member a small amount extra for that member's projects and perhaps a few more. The explosion of earmarking created a management challenge, with the chair and subcommittee staff feeling overwhelmed by the volume of demands. Subcommittees responded by creating more formal application processes (standard forms appear on some of their Web sites), and some created a partisan division of labor. The largest domestic spending subcommittees, Labor-HHS and VA-HUD, developed processes in which the chairs allocated projects only to Republicans, while the ranking minority members were simply given pots of money to allocate to Democrats.

In 2003 this partisan division of labor amid relative peace was upset by conflict over priorities and spending on the Labor-HHS and VA-HUD bills, which left participants and observers wondering if the process would be much more partisan in the future. The central question for interest groups was how much sense it would make in the future to go to members of the minority party for help with projects.

When the Labor-HHS appropriations bill was brought to the floor of the House in July 2003, House Democrats had planned "to use the bill as their venue for a larger debate about the priorities of the federal government, especially whether a consequence of recently enacted tax cuts should be a limiting of federal spending on schools, community health programs and enforcement of labor laws" (Swindell 2003a). In addition to offering amendments to highlight differences, House Democrats, strongly urged by party leaders, voted unanimously (198–0) against final passage of the bill. But the bill passed because Republicans supported it overwhelmingly, 215–9. Although partisan division on bills is not new, a veteran aide recalls that "all the Democrats voting against the bill was almost unique [and] the whipping of the bill to force all Democrats to vote no was unusual." At the time, *CQ Weekly Report* suggested that "one of the reasons the Labor-HHS bill attracted so little Democratic support in the House is that there was nothing to be lost politically by opposing it. The bill is traditionally kept clean of member earmarks when it advances through the House, and they are typically added later in conference" (Taylor and Schatz 2003, 1739),

Such calculations, if made, were wrong. On October 29, the chair of the Labor-HHS subcommittee, Ralph Regula, R-OH, sent a letter to David Obey, ranking Democrat on both the full Appropriations Committee and the subcommittee, saying that the final bill would deny district projects to any member who opposed the measure in July's floor vote. Regula said money that would have gone to those projects would instead go to some of the programs Democrats had claimed were their priorities. House Democrats reportedly asked for a total of $3 billion in such earmarks, and a total of $1 billion (for all members of the House and Senate) was expected to come out of conference (Swindell 2003c, 2838).

Because Regula had never been known to be highly partisan, his move was particularly unexpected. One explanation may be that Democrats, who had been blasted as pork barrelers by Republicans when they were in the minority, had begun to use the same argument to highlight Republican hypocrisy as levels of earmarking reached levels unimagined when the Democrats controlled the House. Democrats escalated the rhetoric after Regula's letter (see, for example, Minority Staff of the House Appropriations Committee 2003). Regula also had to worry that his reputation for moderation might prevent him from being reselected as subcommittee chair, or ascending to full committee chair, in the next Congress. In any event, as a close observer put it, "When Mr. Regula said to his caucus that he was not going to give projects to people who voted against the bill, including Republicans; and when Mr. Obey wrote a declaration of war letter saying 135 million Americans would not get any projects . . . I didn't think anyone would back down. And they didn't."

During House consideration of the VA-HUD bill, members could not so easily imagine that there would be no consequences to opposing the bill. Democratic Party leaders were trying to embarrass Republicans on spending for medical care for veterans, but "Democratic members reported threats from their appropriations colleagues that special projects in their districts would be dropped from the bill if they voted against it" (Schuler and Sorrels 2003, 1910). Although most Democrats (and Republicans) did support the bill, VA-HUD chair James T. Walsh, R-NY, asked ranking member Alan Mollohan, D-WV, to remove projects in some categories of the bill for Democrats who voted nay. Mollohan mostly complied, reportedly reasoning that if he did not do so his power to approve projects would be taken away. He did make exceptions for vulnerable Democrats who might be most vulnerable in the 2004 election and so had the most need to claim credit for projects.

Both bills were finally enacted as part of an omnibus appropriations act. Out of that bill, Appropriations ranking minority member Obey got $20 million for what one respondent called "ash and trash" for the Democrats. He gave $16 million to vulnerable Democrats from Labor-HHS and passed $4 million to Rep. Mollohan to distribute in VA-HUD. But Democrats received much less in total than might have been expected—without the "punishment" they could have received $180 million in projects on Labor-HHS alone (Nichols 2003).

These events could be interpreted as nonpartisan: it just happened that Democrats were more likely to vote against the bills, so they were most likely not to get rewards. And there had always been some expectation that members who got special favors (say, on the Energy and Water bill, which has always been project-oriented) would support the bills (White 1989). But events in 2003 were different in two ways. First, earmarks had become so extensive that they became the norm. As one respondent commented, whereas projects once were clearly rewards, now they were expected, and to deny projects was to deny some districts what other districts got as a matter of course.[14] Second, overall appropriations politics had become so partisan that the consequence of project denial was much more likely to be partisan. In the past, both Democrats and Republicans might have requested a water or highway project and then voted against the Energy and Water or Transportation appropriation as a way of posturing (as appropriators saw it) in favor of economy. But when there are huge substantive differences from the outset, linking projects to support of the bills must be expected to greatly favor one party over the other. Thus the events of 2003 could be viewed as a major escalation of congressional partisanship.

From the standpoint of interest groups, this situation certainly suggested that Democratic champions might become of much less use. If Democrats had to vote for whatever bills Republicans wrote in order to get projects, they might become less willing to ask. Moreover, because Republicans received much the larger share of funding in 2003 in a couple of bills and there were no consequences, they might decide to do the same on other bills. One observer speculated that, even though Democrats would always have a share of projects, it might go down from roughly 40 percent to 30, 20, or even 10 percent if Republicans in the House became really hard-nosed. The Senate seemed likely to remain a different story because of the power of the filibuster, but that would help neither House Democrats nor the interests represented by them.

Even in the Senate partisanship is increasing. Referring to both chambers, the director of a clearly nonpartisan group commented that, with Republicans in the majority, "I think we as an interest group over the last several years have realized where the power is, and put forth our Republican members with more prominence than before. Before we thought, I guess, let's make sure that we have a Democrat and a Republican; now it's let's have a Democrat and two Republicans, and make sure one Republican is not a moderate." It also becomes more important that a lobbying firm have a strong Republican tinge.

Conclusion: Looking to the Future

Appropriations bills require a vast array of specific decisions that must be packaged and approved in some form. In most cases, interest groups compete for approval of projects from the subcommittees rather than directly oppose each other. Even in a highly partisan era, nonpartisanship does have a place, with subcommittee leaders especially playing a strong role as brokers.

The funding increases for the NIH, mentioned earlier in this chapter and which were pursued as a commitment to double the NIH budget over five years, revealed both the relevance of interest group efforts and the importance of factors such as overall budgetary conditions and the committee leadership's discretion (on the lobbying, see Kondracke 2001 and Malakoff 2001). Many participants in the NIH effort have argued that the increases were possible only because "Newt Gingrich decided that was a necessary priority and [Labor-HHS subcommittee chair] John Porter [R-IL] agreed with him." Porter's own commitment to the NIH was such that "he pushed it to the exclusion of a lot of other programs," something other subcommittee chairs would not do even with their top priorities. But others emphasize how leaders of the most prominent groups went with Porter to meet with Speaker Gingrich and won him over. Big increases for even a popular agency, at a time of constraint, risked a backlash from the rest of Congress. It helped that interest groups "really generated a groundswell on the outside that the members who were interested could say demonstrated support from the public at large." It also helped that members came to committee leaders and said such things as "I just had 13 people from the juvenile diabetes chapter in my office, saying we ought to double spending for biomedical research." And even that support might not have been sustained if the budget had not moved into massive surplus, which meant that, in the end, big NIH increases could be funded without squeezing everything else in the Labor-HHS bill. After the political commitment to doubling NIH funding ended and deficits burgeoned again, the NIH was in line for much smaller increases for FY 2003 (Swindell 2003b).

Although the effect of group influence on individual decisions varies, the visibility of group attempts to influence the appropriations process has increased greatly. The visible signs are the proliferation of lobbying firms and the huge increase, especially since 1996, in both the number of specific requests to the appropriators and the number of earmarked projects in the bills and reports. For example, one source observed that there is now "much more congressional interest in the details of the budget, in the numbers of specific units of equipment being acquired. It's not just six F-18s versus seven, but whether you're buying 300 or 400 sensor-fuse weapons canisters." Earmarking burgeoned further during the George W. Bush administration. A close observer commented that "the academic earmarks have become so huge in numbers that [higher education organizations opposed to earmarks] have stopped calculating them; it's over $2 billion per year now." An antispending group counted 7,931 earmarks totaling $10.7 billion in the omnibus that combined seven bills and passed in early 2004 (also see Minority Staff of the House Appropriations Committee 2003; Taylor 2004). Overall, the bills passed for FY 2004 are informally estimated to have contained nearly 10,000 earmarks, with the House receiving nearly 40,000 requests.

These figures raise the question of "hyperpluralism"—that is, whether there has been a proliferation of interest group activity that threatens gridlock, "demosclerosis" (Rauch 1994), or simply decisions that favor powerful special interests at the expense of the public interest. It does seem that the pursuit of particular interests is generating ever greater pursuit of those interests. As the role of government diversifies and society itself grows, more groups make demands of the appropriations bills. Programs create demand for projects. "If there were no Land and Water Conservation Fund," a subcommittee chair once remarked, "there would be no appropriations; and if there were no appropriations, I would get no requests. These things grow up."

Government policies also generate not just constituents but side effects. For example, anti-Castro TV Marti was created to meet the demands of Cuban exile groups, but then, in the classic stimulus/response process described in pluralist theory, it attracted the interest of the National Association of Broadcasters (Truman 1951). Subinterests develop within a wider interest: "You take an institute that was studying, say, arthritis. There was always an arthritis foundation, but now there's juvenile arthritis. The outside world has organized around smaller and smaller issues, and they have money, and they come to town and hire people like us." Some foundations, technically not allowed to lobby, have put resources into creating lobbying organizations for causes they favor (Malakoff 2001, 832). In essence, private sector sources of funds have discovered that they can leverage their money by using it—not in direct grants to the causes they favor, but in efforts to get the government to give much larger amounts to those causes.

The professional lobbying community, seeking new business, searches for new programs in which to promote projects. And, as interests and organizations see the government supporting others, they begin to believe it is their duty to get some for themselves. One appropriations aide reported that his sister was a city planner, who several years ago took a VA bill to the City Council and said, "We are losing out; if you're not getting your earmark you're not getting your share." Government relations staff for universities have noted that faculty are now going directly to the Hill—perhaps on their own or perhaps with encouragement from the lobbying firms that are bypassing university hierarchies in their search for clients.

All this said, readers should not conclude that an era of congressional interference has displaced an era of bureaucratic neutral competence. Veterans of the process emphasize that until the Reagan years congressional influence was largely exercised in back channels, directly through the agencies; conflict between Congress and the Reagan administration led to increased (bipartisan!) earmarking because quiet deals were no longer as possible. And that situation has persisted. As one current interviewee put it, there is now inherent distrust, not of "the administration, but an administration." Even in the area where earmarks were most famously discouraged—the NIH in the years of House Labor-HHS chair William H. Natcher, D-KY—"there were under-the-table tables."

Nor should they imagine that Congress has nothing to offer to policymaking. Even in biomedical research, an area in which Congress issues far fewer directions than usual, it is important to remember that the public funds the NIH to develop ways to treat diseases, and there is no reason scientists should be able to decide what diseases should have priority. Nor are the science establishment's notions of how to pursue cures infallible.[15] In other areas, distributional concerns may seem to drive out policy and operational issues, but they actually are hard to separate. Maintaining the defense industrial base—that is, the plant and personnel that manufacture the weapons needed by the nation's military—may be as much a part of readiness as training troops.

Still, the proliferation of visible earmarking means the competition for projects has become a larger part of congressional activity. The danger from this proliferation is not so much politicized decisions or even gridlock. (The appropriations process, in spite of dramatic delays, is not subject to gridlock.) However, the limited resources of the appropriations process in recent years have tended to be diverted to processing project requests at the expense of gathering more programmatic or management information to inform decisions. Computers help (it would have been impossible to keep track of the current level of requests twenty years ago), but the increased workload in the past few years has far exceeded the staff's ability to keep up. Routinization of the application process has made it easier to process requests, but such a process also may encourage more requests. Forms allow some sorting out of "things that on their face seem inappropriate or unauthorized in the particular pool," but serious comparison of merit is impossible. These problems only become greater when project politics expands into some domains, such as the economic development initiatives in the VA-HUD bill, where there is no history of standards and the agencies have little capacity to help vet the projects.

From the perspective of interest groups, this inability of appropriators to assess merit just makes getting fervent champions even more important. Decisions are likely to be based on raw political power (in terms of which members get most), on conforming to a small set of rules (legality, traditions in particular accounts), and then on the intensity of requests. Further proliferation of earmarks seems likely only to intensify the pattern.

A further concern is how the greater expectation of earmarks will affect other decisions. If members are virtually addicted to projects, appropriators or party leaders may be more able to coerce colleagues on program or priority decisions. On February 12, 2004, the chair of the House Appropriations Subcommittee on Transportation, Treasury and Independent Agencies, Ernest J. Istook, R-OK, sent a letter that illustrated the potential trend.[16] He wrote to all House members who, in 2003, had signed a "Dear Colleague" letter advocating that his subcommittee's appropriations bill include $1.8 billion to subsidize Amtrak, the national rail passenger corporation. President Bush had requested only $900 million; the Consolidated Appropriations Act of 2004 provided $1.217 billion, and Istook preferred both the president's number and his demand for significant changes in how Amtrak operates. Therefore in his letter, Istook explained that extra funding for Amtrak could only reduce spending for other parts of the bill such as "funding for airport and highway projects in Members' districts." "Before you consider endorsing Amtrak's latest request," he asked, "please consider the impact on other transportation needs, both nationally and in your own state and district." And, just in case anyone missed the point, he reminded members that shortly they would be submitting their lists of transportation priorities for their districts for possible inclusion in the 2005 bill. "As you submit these important priorities for your district," he urged, "please bear in mind that any request for Amtrak funding, even if submitted in a separate document, must and will be weighed against your other requests, and I will consider it as a project request for your district."

At one level, one could suppose that many supporters of Amtrak do have a district interest in its services, and so Istook was simply calling for consistency—

that Amtrak be in the same pot as other projects. At another level, Amtrak is an ongoing activity of the government that has sparked substantial partisan and policy dispute and therefore differs significantly from the average small highway project. The source who gave this author the Istook letter is involved in a group that normally would lobby for Amtrak. When asked what his organization would do about the Istook letter given its intimidating effect on possible Amtrak advocates, the source commented that his group might not ask its usual House champions to get involved and might focus its energies instead on the Senate.

One has to wonder what other linkages between more programmatic and more distributive concerns might be made and how those linkages will influence both the legislative and lobbying processes. Will the dynamic in which the proliferation of interests feeds on itself, through imitation, fragmentation, the stimulus/response dynamic, and pursuit of profit, reverse or otherwise be altered significantly? Readers should remember that ebbs and flows have characterized earmarking over the years. Even as projects have proliferated in recent years, a contrary norm was put in place on the new Homeland Security appropriations subcommittees, which in 2003 did not do earmarks. Perhaps some combination of a revived conservative antipork campaign, deficits that become more politically important because of high inflation or interest rates, or even presidential leadership could cause a reversal. Yet it is hard to imagine that the new system in which the Appropriations Committees process tens of thousands of grant applications by individual members of Congress is going to fade very easily.

Partisan factors are a wildcard for any prediction about the future of interest group relations in the appropriations process. The system could conceivably become so partisan that groups need majority party connections to even get projects. Then the minority party would have no stake at all in comity and would feel free to launch an all-out attack on the process. The more right-wing anti–pork barrel groups would find themselves in an unintentional alliance with the Democrats (assuming they remain in the minority). Whether that would lead to either more bipartisanship or fewer projects is impossible to say; nor is it easy to predict what would happen if the Democrats regained control of the House in particular, save that the cleavages in society and processes of group mobilization that have pushed interest groups into alliance with one party or the other are likely to remain.

Notes

1. This chapter is based on hundreds of interviews with various participants in the appropriations process between 1983 and 1996, supplemented by seventeen reinterviews of former respondents, specifically on interest groups, in 2001 and three in 2004. Although I cannot thank sources by name, this is as much their work as it is mine (not that all of them would agree with my analysis!). Special thanks goes to James D. Savage for his work and counsel.
2. Major exceptions do not change the analysis in this article. For example, the bills provide funds for certain "mandatory" spending, or "appropriated entitlements," such as food stamps.

3. Recent examples include promises made to Sen. Tom Harkin, D-IA, after funds for a land and water conservation fund he strongly supported were slashed in final negotiations for the FY 2003 omnibus bill (Taylor 2003a), and promises made about country of origin labels on food, after the first case of mad cow disease in the United States threatened to upset the conference agreement that packaged the final appropriations in January 2004 (Jalonick 2004).

4. The need for offsets is enforced by supermajority rules if Congress passes a budget resolution that then is the basis for the 302(b) allocation, discussed later in this chapter. Usually (2002 being one exception) a resolution is passed. The president's budget proposal for a given bill also may be relevant because of veto threats.

5. But see Lee and Oppenheimer (1999) for an excellent discussion of programs in which authorizations allocate a pot of money by formula, such as highway funds.

6. If administrators ignore an instruction in report language, appropriators might write the original instruction into law. They also might decide to punish the agency with a cut in an area selected because it would mean far more to the administrators than to anyone else in Congress—such as the administrator's personal office expenses.

7. There are exceptions, however, such as designation as an "emergency," or simply a vote by a majority in the House or sixty members of the Senate to waive the point of order.

8. As Savage (1999) discusses, some political scientists doubt the effect of position within Congress on the distribution of benefits. Yet the interviews have been very explicit and consistent as to the decision rules of the subcommittees. Favoritism by position is limited by the characteristics of programs—that is, a member with no large rivers cannot get large dams. Subcommittee biases should matter most if a program has many possible recipients. Academic earmarking, especially to the extent that it is a Senate process, meets these criteria: every state has some universities, and there are few standards as to which should get the money.

9. Pennsylvania has been cited as such a state in interviews. Western states certainly expect assistance with public lands and water issues.

10. The figures, provided by James D. Savage in a personal communication, were $728 million for the appropriations, made in 1992 for FY 1993; $586 million in 1993; $529 million in 1994; $328 million in 1995; $440 million in 1996; $528 million in 1997; $797 million in 1998; and $1,044 million in 1999.

11. A continuing resolution is supposed to provide temporary funding before other bills are passed, but occasionally it becomes the vehicle to settle many bills at once.

12. Changes within the appropriations process, especially partisan turnover making jobs less permanent, are another factor.

13. The quote is from a memo, "Proposed Principles for Analyzing Each Appropriations Bill," dated May 29, 1996, in author's possession.

14. Arguably, earmarks had always been the norm for the Energy and Water and Military Construction bills. The difference is that those bills involved few broad policy disputes beyond distributional politics, so there was not the same likelihood that members could be punished on the project side for their votes on policy choices that represented a much larger portion of the bill's content.

15. Some critics argue that the National Cancer Institute wasted years pursuing an approach that emphasized the role of viruses in causing cancers, and others argue that the quest to understand basic science before developing a vaccine for AIDS is contrary to the history of the development of virtually all other vaccines, beginning with the work of Louis Pasteur.

16. The author obtained a copy of this letter, which is in his possession.

References

Byrd, Robert C. 2004. "Terrible Precedents in the Omnibus Conference Report." Press release, U.S. Senate Committee on Appropriations Democratic staff, January 21. http://appropriations.senate.gov/demoinfo/record.cfm?id=217276.

Fenno, Richard F., Jr. 1966. *The Power of the Purse: Appropriations Politics in Congress.* Boston: Little, Brown.

Gilmour, John B. 1995. *Strategic Disagreement: Stalemate in American Politics.* Pittsburgh: University of Pittsburgh Press.

Herrnson, Paul S., Ronald G. Shaiko, and Clyde Wilcox, eds. 1998. *The Interest Group Connection: Electioneering, Lobbying, and Policymaking in Washington.* Chatham, NJ: Chatham House.

Jalonick, Mary Clare. 2004. "Mad Cow Case in Washington State Pushes Labeling Issue to Fore." *CQ Weekly Report,* January 24, 210.

Killian, Linda. 1998. *The Freshmen: What Happened to the Republican Revolution?* Boulder, CO: Westview Press.

Kondracke, Morton. 2001. *Saving Milly: Love, Politics, and Parkinson's Disease.* New York: Public Affairs.

Lee, Frances E., and Bruce I. Oppenheimer. 1999. *Sizing Up the Senate: The Unequal Consequences of Equal Representation.* Chicago: University of Chicago Press.

Malakoff, David. 2001. "Perfecting the Art of the Science Deal." *Science,* May 4, 830–835.

Maraniss, David, and Michael Weisskopf. 1996. *"Tell Newt to Shut Up!"* New York: Simon and Schuster.

Minority Staff of the House Appropriations Committee. 2003. "Grand Old Porkers." Draft, November 17. http://www.house.gov/appropriations_democrats/PorkReport.pdf.

Munson, Richard. 1993. *The Cardinals of Capitol Hill: The Men and Women Who Control Government Spending.* New York: Grove Press.

Nichols, Hans. 2003. "GOP Punishes Foes, Strips More Earmarks." *The Hill,* December 3. http://www.hillnews.com/news/120303/earmarks.aspx.

Peterson, Mark A. 1995. "How Health Policy Information Is Used in Congress." In *Intensive Care: How Congress Shapes Health Policy,* edited by Thomas E. Mann and Norman J. Ornstein. Washington, DC: American Enterprise Institute and Brookings.

Rauch, Jonathan. 1994. *Demosclerosis: The Silent Killer of American Government.* New York: Times Books.

Savage, James D. 1999. *Funding Science in America: Congress, Universities, and the Politics of the Academic Pork Barrel.* New York: Cambridge University Press.

Schatz, Joseph J. 2003. "Appropriators Try to Ease Pain in Overdue Spending Bills." *CQ Weekly Report,* January 4, 29–30.

———. 2004. "Contentious Fiscal '05 Looms over Signing of $820 Billion Omnibus." *CQ Weekly Report,* January 24, 209–212.

Schuler, Kate, and Niels C. Sorrels. 2003. "Arm-Twisting House Leaders Push VA-HUD Bill to Passage over Veterans' Strong Opposition." *CQ Weekly Report,* July 26, 1910–1911.

Swindell, Bill. 2003a. "Both Chambers Ready to Tackle Contentious Labor-HHS Bill." *CQ Weekly Report,* June 28, 1620–1621.

———. 2003b. "Labor-HHS Conferees Wrangle Over Size of NIH Increase." *CQ Weekly Report,* October 18, 2562–2563.

———. 2003c. "Regula to Labor-HHS Naysayers: Don't Tug on Superman's Cape." *CQ Weekly Report,* November 15, 2838–2839.

Taylor, Andrew. 2003a. "Fiscal 2003 Omnibus Completed, But More Budget Chores Loom." *CQ Weekly Report,* February 15, 385–388.
———. 2003b. "Pace Intensifies for Wrapping Up Unfinished Bills Into Omnibus." *CQ Weekly Report,* November 15, 2836–2839.
———. 2003c. "Will Republicans Push the President to Wield Veto against His Own Party?" *CQ Weekly Report,* July 26, 1890–1893.
———. 2004. "Pet Projects Prevail." *CQ Weekly Report,* January 24, 212.
Taylor, Andrew, and Joseph J. Schatz. 2003. "House Appropriations Stay 'On Track,' While Senate Will Test Spending Caps." *CQ Weekly Report,* July 12, 1738–1739.
Truman, David B. 1951. *The Governmental Process.* New York: Knopf
White, Joseph. 1989. "The Functions and Power of the House Appropriations Committee." Ph.D. diss., University of California, Berkeley.
———. 1990. "The Two-Faced Profession." *Public Budgeting and Finance* 10:92–102.

10. The Christian Right Goes to Washington: Social Movement Resources and the Legislative Process

John C. Green and Nathan S. Bigelow

The Christian Right, a social movement based among evangelical Protestants and dedicated to returning "traditional values" to public policy, has been a staple of American politics since the late 1970s (Hertzke 1988; Wilcox 1992, 1996). Under various guises, this movement has achieved some electoral success: it has mobilized voters, influenced Republican Party organizations, and helped to nominate and elect candidates, including members of Congress (Wilcox 1996, 73–83). In these areas, the movement has generally met its expectations, despite numerous disappointments along the way. The Christian Right has experienced much less success, however, in changing public policy, especially in Congress. By and large, federal law has not returned to "traditional values," and the modest exceptions have fallen far short of the movement's expectations (Wilcox 1996, 111–127). Like the protagonist in Frank Capra's classic movie *Mr. Smith Goes to Washington* (1939), an idealistic Christian Right went to the nation's capital, only to experience the frustrations of the political process.

What explains this disjunction between electoral success, on the one hand, and a lack of legislative success, on the other? Two answers come readily to mind, each arising from the fundamental nature of social movements. First, the political ineffectiveness of the Christian Right in Congress may reflect its lack of resources and lobbying experience. Such ineffectiveness is common among social movements. After all, if their adherents were already capable of influencing the government, there would be little call for such movements. To achieve political success, a movement typically must learn to operate within political institutions such as Congress.

Second, the Christian Right may have had an unpopular agenda, one that would have been difficult to advance under any circumstances. Unpopular goals are also common in social movements: if a movement's agenda were widely accepted, there would be few incentives for a movement in the first place. Political success frequently involves moderating the movement's original agenda, but the political reality is that changing government policy is difficult within the U.S. system of separated powers—something that movement adherents often find difficult to accept.

In this chapter, we review the involvement of the Christian Right in congressional politics over two decades. In this review, we find some support for both of these explanations. The movement has struggled to become an effective force in congressional politics, but it has been slow in developing the resources and skills needed for lobbying, in large part because of its organizational instability. When movement leaders make concessions in the name of political expediency and reality, the loyalty of the movement's passionate grassroots corps is jeopardized. In this

sense, the challenges confronting the Christian Right are emblematic of those facing many social movements.

Strategies for Influencing Congress

Influencing Congress was a central goal of the Christian Right from its
inception in the late 1970s. It sought that goal using three kinds of strategies:
organizational strategies aimed at building new groups with the resources and
skills needed to influence Congress; *outsider* strategies directed at altering the
makeup and agenda of Congress; and *insider* strategies directed at influencing the
writing and passage of legislation. Although often closely related in practice, each
kind of strategy is conceptually distinct (Wilcox 1998).

Organizational Strategies

Most accounts of group influence in Congress properly assume the existence
of political organizations. After all, it is just such entities—lobbies, interest
groups, and political action committees (PACs)—that do the influencing. However, one of the first tasks of a new social movement is to create new organizations to achieve its purposes. At its core, movement politics is the mobilization
of new people to challenge existing institutions in behalf of passionately felt
grievances (Salisbury 1989). In this sense, movements typically begin as "disor-
ganized politics" and develop new organizations to embody their special challenge to the "establishment." In fact, one measure of the success of a movement
is the extent to which new interest groups are created, thereby giving movement
adherents entree to the political process (Lowi 1971). The line between a "social
movement organization" and an "interest group" is often a fine one, but, conceptually, the former challenges political institutions and the latter animates them.

The difficulties encountered in building and maintaining political organizations are well documented in the literature (see Baumgartner and Leech 1998,
chap. 4). Even well-established interest groups must overcome the problems of
collective action to secure the necessary support. Social movements have a special advantage—and a serious disadvantage—in dealing with such problems.
On the plus side, the grievances that motivate movement politics can induce
individuals to provide the money, time, and talents needed to build organizations
to do the movement's work.[1] Thus movements run on passion. On the minus
side, there are limits to the uses of passion in maintaining organizations. As passions cool, the support for and therefore the effectiveness of the new organizations can decline sharply. To survive, such organizations must move beyond just
passion and find other kinds of incentives to secure support—in a word, they
must "institutionalize" (McAdam 1982; Green 1999).

The Christian Right is a textbook example of the use of passion to build
organizations. Religious conservatives, especially evangelical Protestants, are
deeply aggrieved by the decline of traditional morality in American society.

Legalized abortion, the spread of gay rights, and the removal of religion (such as prayer) from public schools are just some of the items at the top of their list of grievances. By voicing their complaints about this situation, movement leaders were able to secure enough support to build new organizations, of which the Moral Majority and the Christian Coalition are the best-known examples (Green et al. 1996).

However, these new organizations have been unstable: the Moral Majority lasted for just a decade (1979–1989), and the Christian Coalition appears to be in serious decline after enjoying prominence from 1991 to 2001 (Rozell and Wilcox 1996). Such instability makes it difficult for a movement to maintain the resources and expertise necessary to influence Congress.

Outsider Strategies

At their inception, social movements tend to be self-conscious "outsiders," and one purpose of movement organizations is to bring such outsider pressure to bear on political institutions such as Congress. Two broad strategies are important here: participating in elections (see Rozell and Wilcox 1999) and grass-roots lobbying (Goldstein 1999). Christian Right organizations have been able to deploy their resources using both of these strategies with some success.

Participating in elections is, of course, one of the basic means by which citizens are able to connect to Congress, and an array of special institutions have been established to foster this connection, including candidate campaign committees, political parties, and PACs (Herrnson 1998). The Christian Right has been very active in elections, emulating and infiltrating these institutions. In doing so, the movement's main resource has been an extensive network of grass-roots activists, which can be deployed to mobilize the votes of religious conservatives. This voting bloc is potentially large, making up roughly 15 percent of the electorate nationwide, a figure larger in parts of the South and Midwest, though rarely an outright majority (see Green 2000a). By mobilizing religious voters, the movement's activist corps has been able to help nominate and elect senators and representatives who are sympathetic to the movement's goals. These activists have also become influential within the Republican Party, where they have occupied positions in local, state, and national organizations (see Rozell and Wilcox 1995, 1997; Green, Rozell, and Wilcox 2000).

Such influence has not come easily, however. The activist networks have been difficult to develop and maintain, and their impact has not always been positive. "Amateur" candidates recruited from within the movement itself have rarely won nomination or election, and movement supporters have frequently warred with "professional" party leaders. In addition, too close an association with the movement has often hurt mainstream candidates at the polls (Wilcox, Green, and Rozell 2001). Indeed, the Christian Right has been most successful when it has operated as part of a broader conservative coalition (Green, Guth, and Hill 1993).

This reality has often presented movement leaders with a dilemma: whether to back candidates who can win and risk alienating the movement's passionate activist corps, or to back candidates who share the movement's passions and risk defeat at the polls. This dilemma has been most easily resolved at the district level, such as in races for the U.S. House of Representatives, and it has been most difficult to resolve at the state and national levels, especially in senatorial and presidential contests.

The movement also has employed a variety of other electoral techniques, such as forming PACs to provide candidates with campaign funds and running its own issue advocacy advertising and telephone and direct-mail campaigns. But its most famous technique has been calling on its activist network to distribute "voter guides" in evangelical churches (see Rozell and Wilcox 1999). The reason is straightforward: the Christian Right's activist corps largely overlaps with the passionate supporters who built and maintained the movement organizations. Indeed, once in place, the activist networks are tailor-made for "grassroots lobbying," in which they stimulate the movement's constituency to contact members of Congress. The result has been a large volume of mail, telephone calls, e-mails, and personal contacts with lawmakers (Gimpel 1998).

Insider Strategies

An important goal of social movements is to gain entree to political institutions and thus be able to use the traditional "insider" strategies to influence legislation. Two such strategies are particularly important: lobbying members of Congress and their staff and participating in legislative coalitions with other interest groups. These strategies require access to lawmakers, political and policy expertise, and connections with other groups (Wolpe 1990; Hula 1995; Shaiko 1998). The Christian Right lacked these things at its inception and has struggled to acquire them ever since.

In large part because of its outsider strategies, the movement has slowly gained access to members of Congress, especially Republican members of the House. Such access has been greatest when the Republicans have controlled one or both chambers of Congress, such as the Senate between 1981 and 1986 and both houses from 1995 to 2000. The Christian Right also gained some leverage during the Reagan and both Bush administrations. However, eras of GOP control of government have not been kind to the movement's strength. Instead, the Christian Right has prospered in opposition, growing during the Carter and Clinton administrations and when the Democrats controlled at least one congressional chamber (Green 2000b).

Despite its access, the movement organizations have had considerable difficulty developing the specialized resources necessary to exploit and expand such access effectively (Bruce 1988; Hertzke 1988; Hofrenning 1995). One reason is that the Christian Right's key resource, passionate people, does not translate easily into successful politics inside the Washington Beltway. Moreover, movement organizations have often lacked the level and consistency of funding needed to hire lobbyists and pay for adequate Washington offices. Such instability has limited the Christian Right's capacity to carry out basic activities such as tracking bills and keeping in touch with congressional allies.

Consequently, Christian Right lobbyists have not been able to consistently provide members of Congress and their staffs with the kinds of political information that is critical to successful lobbying (Moen 1989; Hofrenning 2001). They have also frequently fallen short in another area: policy expertise. The chief motivation for the Christian Right's agenda is passionately held religious values, and to many movement leaders and activists these values are the warrant for their policy goals. Movement organizations have therefore been slow to develop reputable knowledge on social policy, including practical information on the impact of existing or proposed policies (Moen 1992). This kind of information is critical to drafting and amending legislation, as well as to securing the support of members of Congress.

The role of policy expertise points to another problem: tension between the pragmatic tendencies of the movement's lobbyists and the passions of its activist corps (see Reed 1996, chap. 7; Watson 1999). Typically, movement lobbyists have pushed for narrower, short-term objectives, justified by facts and appeals to general benefits. By this means, they have sought to modify the least popular elements of the movement's agenda. By contrast, movement activists have typically demanded broader, longer-term objectives, justified by appeals to the movement's special religious values. This approach arouses determined opposition, but stokes the passions of the movement's activist base.[2]

These tensions have often hampered the ability of the Christian Right to participate in coalitions with other interests. The movement organizations have a history of feuding with one another and other conservative interest groups, and they have been slow to form broader coalitions (Moen 1992). However, the movement's modest legislative successes appear to have occurred when they were part of a broader conservative coalition. Like elections, the legislative process has often presented movement leaders with a dilemma: how to achieve tangible results and also maintain the support of the passionate activist corps. But unlike elections, this dilemma is difficult to resolve in national lawmaking.

Washington Resources Circa 2000

By the beginning of the twenty-first century, the Christian Right had developed a presence in Washington, D.C., including seven major groups that were reporting substantial resources: the Christian Coalition; two groups each associated with Focus on the Family and the Moral Majority networks of activists; and two more specialized organizations. These resources reflected the harnessing of the movement's passions and revealed a capacity to engage in the legislative process. But by 2004, many insiders believed the Washington offices of these groups were undergoing a significant retrenchment,[3] a pattern that certainly fits with the movement's instability over time. One reason for this retrenchment was the Republicans' victories in the 2000 and 2002 elections: with George W. Bush in the White House and the GOP in charge of Congress, it became difficult to keep the movement mobilized.

The Christian Coalition

Founded out of the remnants of the Reverend Pat Robertson's 1988 campaign for the Republican presidential nomination, the Christian Coalition became the chief symbol of the Christian Right in the 1990s (Watson 1999). It operated at arm's length from Robertson's extensive television ministry, the Christian Broadcasting Network, a multimillion-dollar enterprise with a reputation for political messages. Under its founding executive director, Ralph Reed, the Coalition specialized in grassroots electoral activities, but also in lobbying, with an overall budget rumored to have been $26 million.

These efforts earned the Christian Coalition a ranking of sixty-fifth out of the top one hundred Washington lobbies in a survey conducted by *Forbes* magazine in 2001 (Birnbaum 2001). But because this reputational study involved Washington insiders, the results must be viewed with some caution. It may be, for example, that the Coalition was a stand-in for all the Christian Right groups and perhaps the entire range of social issue conservatives (no other such groups were on the list). However, this ranking represents a sharp decline from a 1999 *Forbes* survey, where the Christian Coalition ranked thirty-fifth.

The Coalition has declined in other respects as well, such as the level of funds devoted to lobbying. For example, in 1994 it claimed to have spent $1.4 million against President Bill Clinton's health care plan—more than its total reported lobbying expenses in 2000—and in 1995 it reported lobbying expenses of $9 million. In 2000 and 2002, the Coalition reported the most extensive lobbying resources of any of the movement groups: it claimed spending of $1 million and seven lobbyists.[4]

The pattern of decline corresponds with other evidence of the Coalition's organizational problems since 1996, when Reed left to form his own political consulting firm whose services include lobbying (Stephens 2002). Pat Robertson's resignation as its president in 2001 may have contributed to further organizational decline (O'Keefe 2001). In 2000 its overall funding was rumored to have declined to $3 million. But as of 2004 the Christian Coalition continued to maintain a modest presence on Capitol Hill.

The Focus on the Family Network

In the 1990s, a chief rival of Pat Robertson for leadership in the Christian Right was James Dobson, a psychologist and founder of Focus on the Family, a ministry dedicated to the preservation of the traditional family. Dobson is best known for his radio programs and books on parenting. As with Robertson's televangelism, Dobson's multimillion-dollar ministry operated at arm's length from several associated political groups.

The most prominent of these groups was the Family Research Council (FRC), founded in 1983. In part, the FRC serves as a think tank for the Christian Right, developing and disseminating policy expertise on "pro-family" issues. The FRC sponsors a lobbying affiliate that was originally named American Renewal but was renamed FRC Action in 2003. In 2000 American Renewal had a budget of more than $400,000 and a half-dozen lobbyists, and it reported $60,000 in lobbying expenses.

The FRC has experienced some recent retrenchment as well. In 1997 it reported revenues of almost $15 million; after 2000, revenues were estimated at about $10 million. The turmoil at the top has been considerable: longtime president Gary Bauer left to run for the 2000 Republican presidential nomination. Bauer has established a political action committee, the Campaign for Working Families, which filed no lobby disclosure report in 2000, but provides extensive information on congressional politics to its supporters. President Ken Connor left in 2003 and was replaced by Tony Perkins amid continued rumors of tight finances.

The Moral Majority Network

Although the Moral Majority was disbanded in 1989, its founder, the Reverend Jerry Falwell, has sought to recover some of his past political prominence. One example of this effort is the Liberty Alliance, which he founded in 1992. In 1998 it reported a total budget of more than $2 million, and in 2000 it reported $350,000 in lobbying expenses and one lobbyist. By 2002 reported lobbying expenditures had declined to $100,000. A related organization is the Christian Action Network (CAN), which was founded in 1990 with the support of former Moral Majority activists. In 1998 CAN claimed a budget of $2.8 million, and in 2000 it reported $240,000 in lobbying expenses and two lobbyists.

In many respects, the trajectory of the Moral Majority is illustrative of instability in many movement organizations. It burst onto the political scene in 1980, and although it never had the financial resources, popular following, or grassroots organization of the Christian Coalition, in its heyday it had some impact on elections and was active in the legislative process (Bruce 1988). Its collapse in the late 1980s was as swift as its rise to prominence. The remnants of its activist network persist and can be organized in new ways under favorable circumstances. The Christian Coalition and other movement organizations may follow a similar path.

Specialized Groups

During the 1990s, the third most prominent movement group was Concerned Women for America (CWA). The CWA is an evangelical women's group that was founded in 1979 by Beverly LaHaye, the wife of the Reverend Tim LaHaye, the longtime movement operative author of the best-selling "Left Behind" series of novels. Like the FRC, it also sponsors a lobbying affiliate, the Concerned Women for America Legislative Action Committee (CWALAC). In 1998 the CWA reported a budget of some $10 million, and CWALAC reported spending of almost $2 million. In 2000 CWALAC reported three lobbyists but no lobbying expenses; in 2002 it reported $164,000 in lobbying expenses. The CWA has also experienced some retrenchment in recent years, reflecting the retirement of Beverly LaHaye and her replacement with Sandy Rios.

One movement organization that experienced some growth in the late 1990s was the Traditional Values Coalition (TVC). Founded in 1980 by the Reverend Lou Sheldon, the TVC claims a membership base of 43,000 churches, mostly located in California and other western states; the organization is best known for its opposition to gay rights. In 2000 the TVC's total budget was reported to be much larger than in previous years, more than $13 million or roughly five times larger than in the previous election cycle. The TVC also sponsors a lobbying affiliate. In 1997 it claimed a budget of about $200,000. In 2000 it reported $180,000 in lobbying expenditures and four lobbyists, and in 2002, $300,000 in expenses and two lobbyists. Other groups associated with the Christian Right filed no lobby disclosure information in 2000.[5]

The resources described in this section are not trivial, but their significance and impact are far from clear. A useful way to put the Christian Right's lobbying resources in context is to compare them with those of gun owner organizations. In 2000 the top six gun owner groups reported $2.5 million in lobbying expenses and a dozen lobbyists—figures comparable with those of the Christian Right. However, two of the gun owner groups were listed in the *Forbes* top one hundred lobbies: the National Rifle Association (number one) and the Gun Owners of America (number seventy-one). It may be that some Christian Right groups have overstated their resources, or that their resources are used to much less effect than those of the gun owner groups.

Outsider Pressure, 1998–2002

Despite organizational instability, the Christian Right was able to exert considerable outsider pressure on Congress in the late 1990s through electoral activities and grassroots lobbying. In 1998 and 2000 the movement was active in various congressional races, and it reported generating a substantial volume of grassroots communication with Congress. These activities are the most direct results of harnessing the passions of grassroots activists, but they also reveal the development of resources and expertise. Here, too, there is some evidence of retrenchment after 2000.

Electoral Activities

In 2000 the Christian Right played a significant role in over one hundred House races, or in just under one-quarter of all House districts (Ostling 2000).

Nearly all of the candidates backed were Republicans, and the vast majority of them won the general election. The major factor behind such success was the power of incumbency. Many of these candidates probably would have won anyway, and it is unclear how much help the movement activists actually provided. However, many of these candidates were first elected with movement backing, and its assistance may well have mattered in the closest races. Meanwhile, the Christian Right fared less well in open-seat races, and the challengers it backed did poorly.

The movement was involved in an even larger number of House races (138) in 1998, a year in which the Republican Party, and thus the Christian Right, was much less successful (Green 2001). One difference between 1998 and 2000 was the larger number of divisive primaries in 1998. The best known was a special election held in the Twenty-second Congressional District in California, where the movement strongly backed a pro-life conservative against a more moderate candidate recruited by the GOP establishment (Soper and Fetzer 2000). The movement-backed candidate won the bitter encounter and then narrowly lost the general election. The Christian Right has been involved in many such battles since 1980, with the number varying from election to election.

Despite rumors to the contrary (Rozell 2003), the Christian Right was quite active in the 2002 congressional elections, where it contributed to the Republican success. Surely the best example was in Georgia, where it helped to defeat Democratic senator Max Cleland and Democratic governor Roy Barnes. Christian Right mobilization was critical to this success (Green 2003). Overall in 2002, the movement was involved in at least fifty congressional races, and the candidates backed succeeded a little less than two-thirds of the time.

The movement's involvement in House campaigns has increased over time. In the 1970s and 1980s, the Christian Right was typically involved in between eighty and ninety campaigns (Guth and Green 1993). The low points were in 1978 (thirty races), just before the founding of the Moral Majority, and in 1990 (thirty-eight races), just before the rise of the Christian Coalition. Although the level of 2000 activity was down a bit from the mid-1990s, the movement probably helped Republicans to retain control of the House in 2000 and in 2002, confirming the movement's small but significant contribution to the Republican takeover of Congress in 1994 (Green et al. 1995).

The Christian Right fared less well in the Senate during this period. Although the movement contributed to the GOP takeover of the upper chamber in 1994, its impact was smaller than in the House. After 1994, Republicans lost ground in the Senate. In 1998, for example, the defeat of several high-profile, movement-backed Senate candidates such as Lauch Faircloth in North Carolina presaged the debacle of 2000, when the GOP lost six Senate seats and won two, for a net loss of four seats and a 50–50 split—that is, until Sen. James M. Jeffords of Vermont left the Republican column to become an independent and give the Democrats a one-seat margin of control in 2001 (Green et al. 1998; Guth et al. 2001a). In 2002 movement efforts helped the GOP to regain control of the Senate by a single seat. The involvement of the Christian Right in Senate campaigns appears to have been fairly constant since 1980.

These differences between the House and the Senate are instructive: the Christian Right has done best in the smaller scale congressional races where concentrations of religious voters are more important. The movement's resources are simply not as potent in the more diverse state-level Senate constituencies across the country.

With its main organizations in decline, how did the Christian Right maintain its electoral activity in 1998–2002? Three factors are important. First, the Christian Coalition and other groups decayed slowly, and many activists remained involved. Electoral activities appeared to be down a bit in 2000 but still significant, especially in close races (Guth et al. 2002).

Second, other organizations stepped in to fill the gaps. In 1998 Gary Bauer's PAC, the Campaign for Working Families, raised and spent $7 million. In 2000 these resources were largely directed toward Bauer's quest for the GOP presidential nomination, but the CWF was active in congressional races and mounted a twelve-state get-out-the-vote drive. In 2002 the CWF spent nearly $800,000 on electoral activities. Elsewhere, in 2000 Jerry Falwell operated a voter registration forum called "People of Faith 2000," and former Christian Coalition operatives did similar work with "Vision America." Also in 2000 the Traditional Values Coalition was especially prominent, running a grassroots program and fielding a PAC. Finally, several new PACs were active in 2000 and 2002: the Madison Project Fund, which was associated with home-schooling groups; the Susan B. Anthony PAC, which supported conservative women candidates; and the "Government Is Not God PAC," which was founded by William Murray, the son of the late atheist Madeline Murray O'Hare and a convert to Christianity (People for the American Way 2000). Together, these PACs spent over $500,000 in each of the 2000 and 2002 campaigns.

Third, twenty years of movement participation in elections had built a strong political base. For example, some former movement activists became Republican Party operatives and leaders, such as Ralph Reed, formerly of the Christian Coalition, who served as the Republican state chairman in Georgia during the 2002 victory. Although the movement presence in Republican organizations decreased a bit in 2000, it was still significant.[6] In addition, the religious constituency of the Christian Right had become, on balance, Republican, and it voted heavily for GOP candidates favored by the movement, even without extensive contacts (Guth et al. 2001b). There is some evidence, however, that the turnout of this voting bloc declined overall in 2000. This decline may stem from a contraction of Christian Right activity, but it also could reflect the lack of competitive races in 2000.

Grassroots Lobbying

The level of grassroots lobbying by Christian Right organizations is more difficult to assess than the movement's involvement in campaigns. However, observers believe that contacts by conservative Christians are now commonplace in congressional politics (Gimpel 1998, 101). One insider interviewed described the situation this way: "You must distinguish between the everyday activities of interested citizens, some of whom just happen to be conservative Christians, and the special efforts of [movement] groups. The former are a constant; the latter are rare; and both can be effective at getting lawmakers' attention." Certainly, the movement organizations reported stimulating both kinds of contacts. One operative described his organization's efforts this way: "We are constantly putting out information to our members, educating them on issues, and urging them to contact their congressmen and senators. You never know what issue may spark some interest. We see all these efforts as 'money in the bank.'" He then added: "Many of our people are relentless letter writers, real gadflies; it doesn't take much to motivate them." Another leader remarked, "We are most interested in training our people to be their own lobbyists."

Survey evidence suggests that contacting government officials, including members of Congress, is a common activity among movement activists. For example, in a 2000 public opinion survey 46 percent of self-identified members of Christian conservative or pro-family groups reported contacting a public official during the previous four years, and 27 percent claimed a contact in 2000. Surveys of movement activists in the late 1990s found almost 40 percent reported making such contacts in a given year, and surveys of clergy in evangelical denominations found roughly the same results in 2000. These numbers appear to be comparable with those of contacts by other kinds of political activists.[7]

The number of Christian Right activists is difficult to access with any accuracy. An estimate of 100,000 for 2000 is reasonable (Green 2000a, 2000b), although this number varies, depending on the definition of activist used. A movement lobbyist interviewed offered the following estimates: "Well, if you count anyone who has expressed any kind of interest or give us any form of support in some way, it could be 400,000: our main publication reaches 270,000 homes on average in a month; we get about 80,000 hits on our Web site each week; some 27,000 people get our policy publications; and about 4,000 receive regular faxes."

Movement insiders agree that the number of "hard-core contactors" is between 8,000 and 15,000 per organization. If one assumes a 50 percent overlap between these organizations, then a minimum estimate of the number of contactors for the six major movement organizations would be about 24,000. When asked how these numbers compared with those of other groups, one movement lobbyist admitted, "It is probably a good bit smaller than major groups, like the gun owners, labor or the corporate sector, and a little smaller than the environmental or feminist groups."

Movement insiders stressed the importance of technology, especially the Internet, in generating contacts. "Our Web site is worth a thousands calls, faxes or pieces of mail," claimed one lobbyist. The Web sites of the movement organizations contain a vast amount of information useful for making contacts. Besides the organization's positions and priorities, they often list the names and postal and e-mail addresses of members of Congress and key staff members, as well as detailed instructions on how to make contact. E-mails, telephone banks, faxes, regular mailings, and other publications all play a critical role in stimulating contacts—and serve as potent conduits back to members of Congress. All the interviewees also stressed the importance of a presence in the news media that can serve as an "outsider lobby." As one lobbyist put it, "The more our issues are in the news, the more our people respond." Not surprisingly, media and public relations were consistently regarded as prime activities by the Christian Right organizations.

Many of the lobbyists noted that personal visits to Capitol Hill are also effective. "We do very well after pro-life rallies," noted one insider, "because many of the participants from beyond the Beltway visit [congressional] offices." Others stressed personal contacts back home: "It can be pretty effective when a member is button-holed after church services in the district." There is a consensus that contacts are more effective in the House than in the Senate. "Senate offices are big enterprises and it is harder to get through," reported one insider.

"When it comes to generating useful contacts," one lobbyist noted, "timing is everything," and another commented that "targeting the message is as important as the volume of messages." Generating numerous contacts with key legislators at a strategic moment in the legislative process is regarded as critical but difficult to achieve. For one thing, it requires a fairly long lead time and careful preparation. The best-documented grassroots lobbying campaign by the movement occurred in 1993 over the issue of gays in the military. The *Washington Post* documented a "gospel grapevine" that aroused congressional opinion against President Clinton's initiative.[8] Informants reported similar campaigns on the Defense of Marriage Act, a school prayer constitutional amendment, the impeachment of President Clinton, and stem cell research funding. Since 2002, other informants have noted a similar level of contacts aimed at a ban on partial-birth abortion and President Bush's judicial appointments.

Is this grassroots lobbying effective? One movement insider claimed it "can be devastating," but then noted, "it can also backfire." Another remarked that "it helps to have muscle with a group of people (the larger the better). I'm not sure how important any group would be without a [grassroots] constituency." Still another claimed that "these campaigns usually just fizzle out," and that "the big problem is that our folks are not always very persuasive. They send angry letters to liberals, which go right into the circular file under 'right-wing nut.' It makes the writer feel better, but it doesn't help much." In keeping with the literature (Goldstein 1999), one movement insider reported that "those phony post-card campaigns almost never work," while "nothing beats a well-written personal letter from a constituent."

Other observers, some sympathetic to the Christian Right, cast some doubt on the reported volume and effectiveness of the movement's grassroots communication in 2000. As one observer put it, "If this is really going on, then it is either ineffective or directed to the wrong places." Another noted: "The potential is probably large, but the reality rarely lives up to the potential."

Insider Activities, Late 1990s to Early 2000s

The Christian Right's outsider activities have generated greater access for the movement to members of Congress (Wilcox 1996, 86–87). One crude measure of such access is the number of members who are sympathetic to the movement's basic agenda, as assessed by movement organizations themselves.[9] By this measure, 145 House members were movement supporters after the 2000 elections and probably slightly more after the 2002 ones. Nearly all of these members were Republicans, and they accounted for roughly two-thirds of House Republicans. For comparison, after the 1978 election, when the movement was just getting its legs, eighty-four House members were movement supporters, and they made up about half of the GOP membership.

By this rough measure, the movement enjoyed less support in the Senate— just twenty-five members after 2000 (or about half of the GOP membership), and this figure probably increased a bit after the 2002 election. In any event, this figure has increased since 1978, when there were just nine (less than a quarter of the GOP membership). In addition, the number of both evangelical Protestants and religious conservatives in the GOP memberships of both chambers increased during this period (Guth and Kellstedt 2001).

This crude measure must, however, be viewed with considerable caution: the movement's agenda has changed considerably since the late 1970s, and, given the strong links between the movement and the GOP, movement leaders have strong incentives to approve of the behavior of Republican legislators. But the congressional parties have become sharply polarized since the 1980s, and votes on social issues have been part of the polarization (Poole and Rosenthal 1997; Layman 2000). Converting this basic sympathy, reflecting the movement's passions, into actual votes on controversial legislation remains a daunting task and one that requires resources and their skillful use.

Yet Christian Right lobbyists certainly have a larger number of strong supporters with whom to work in pursuing insider strategies. For example, a larger number of members of Congress are pushing elements of the movement's agenda than in the past such as those in the Family Caucus and Pro-Life Caucus. The most important of these groups is the Values Action Team (VAT), a caucus of thirty-six members organized by House Republican whip Tom DeLay and headed by Republican representative Joe Pitts of Pennsylvania.[10] VAT is also formally associated with forty-two interest groups, including the Christian Coalition, FRC, CWA, TVC, and CAN. VAT holds weekly meetings to discuss pending legislation and consult with House leaders. Indeed, movement advocates include high-ranking Republican leaders such as Tom DeLay in the House and James M. Inhofe of Oklahoma in the Senate (Guth and Kellstedt 2001).

Lobbying Activities

Christian Right organizations report lobbying activity on a wide variety of issues. For example, in 2000 the Christian Coalition claimed to have lobbied members on eighty-six bills in thirteen areas; the Family Research Council fifty-four bills in six areas; the Christian Action Network twenty-seven bills in six areas; the Concerned Women for America twenty-four bills in eight areas; and the Traditional Values Coalition twenty-six bills in eighteen areas. The Liberty Alliance was the least active, claiming to have worked on six bills in a single area.[11] Overall, the level of activity appears to have declined somewhat by 2002. As might be expected, family issues, abortion, and education were the top areas of concern. The lobbyists interviewed claimed that they meet regularly with a large number of members, but especially VAT members, committee chairs, and party leaders. "More doors are open," said a movement insider, "and we have more 'horses' to carry the load."

Although access is important, movement lobbyists report that there is no substitute for persistent attention to the legislative process. One argued that regular contact was "very important—[members] can tell you what's really happening—feasibility, obstacles, inside information, issue development. We work closely with members who have the same priorities, for short- and long-term objectives." Another argued the most important thing is "relationships—about ideas—good ideas do carry the day. Specifically, we try to develop relationships with those who control gates to the members (staff, etc.)."

The effectiveness of these efforts is doubted by the lobbyists themselves. One claimed that Christian conservatives spend too much time with "their friends" and not enough with "persuadables"—that is, members who can be persuaded to support a particular issue. Another noted that the movement organizations "spread their resources too thin. There is no way they can effectively lobby on dozens of bills at once. This is 'once over lightly' lobbying." Other observers were critical of the absence of this kind of regular work by Christian Right activists: "There has been a lack of attention to the nuts and bolts of the legislative process—partly because [we] don't have the experienced people and resources, and partly because some [people] would rather talk about the process than work the process." Another observer remarked, "I don't see a lot of people around at meetings and hearings and so forth anymore." And yet another said, "These folks want to hold meetings, write manifestos, and engage in arcane arguments over details." The high turnover among movement lobbyists was reported as a big problem. One lobbyist had an ironic lament: young Christian women learn the legislative ropes and then leave politics to have children.

Pragmatism and Politics

The Christian Right lobbyists we interviewed are strongly pragmatic. When asked to describe what constituted a good lobbying effort, one insider said, "You need to have something passable; good coalitions; real connection with the grass roots; communication from constituents; good staff work by outsider organizations; and persuasive materials to bring over the winnables, and not just the standard members who always agree with us." A colleague responded to the same question by remarking, "Doing what is possible and leaving the dreams for the future." This pragmatism did not characterize the Washington activities of the movement in the 1980s (Moen 1989) nor the passions of many of the grass-roots activists.

Some lobbyists disagree sharply about the role of policy expertise in successful lobbying. For example, one lobbyist argued it was "crucially important; the truth is mighty and will prevail. We are conscious of having something substantive to say. Policy expertise is our engine and much more important than lobbying." But another lobbyist was less sure: "It helps, but you can always get answers elsewhere; the important thing is knowing where to go [to get information]." A longtime observer concluded: "Christian conservatives are better advocates of policy than in the past, but they don't have the reputation of other think-tanks, like Heritage or Cato."

The Christian Right lobbyists interviewed were strong advocates of coalition building. When asked about the importance of coalitions, one lobbyist remarked, "Very important—you absolutely need them." He then went on to describe how he builds coalitions: "My process is to start with groups that think like we do, these are the constant partners. Second, I look to other organizations on the right (tax groups, etc.). Third, I consider groups that are specific to the issue, but not constant partners (trade associations, veterans groups). Finally, I look at the issues and search for groups that might not agree with me (left groups) but would come on board in this instance. For example, the sex trafficking issue involved a strange coalition." Another insider added: "Coalitions arise naturally when one finds common ground on policy objectives; they are often made up of diverse characters—like the bar room scene in *Star Wars*." This emphasis is also a far cry from the Christian Right in the 1980s—when this famous movie scene was used by moderate Republicans to dismiss Christian conservatives.[12]

None other than House GOP whip Tom DeLay described the need for such coalitions (and for VAT): "We cannot get the National Association of Manufacturers to work together to save the unborn. We can't get the right-to-life organizations to work to cut taxes. We can't get the Christian Coalition to work on environmental policy. We can't get regulatory reform groups to work on the marriage penalty. That's a huge disadvantage in this town" (Jones 1998). Other observers stress the difficulty of organizing such coalitions. One noted that "a coalition of the religious right is an oxymoron." Others reported that the internecine feuding that has characterized the movement is still a problem.

The Christian Right did, however, participate in some broad-based coalitions after the Republicans took control of Congress in 1994, including those supporting the Defense of Marriage Act and Religious Freedom Restoration Act and opposition to trade with China and religious persecution abroad (Campbell and Davidson 1998). Perhaps the most interesting example is the fragile coalition that formed in the early days of the Bush administration between Christian conservatives and environmentalists on the issues surrounding cloning and stem cell research.

The Perils of Pragmatism

This pragmatism produced some modest successes for items on the Christian Right's agenda in the 1990s. For example, both houses of Congress passed bans on partial-birth abortion (which President Clinton vetoed). And in 2003, a majority of the House of Representatives voted for a constitutional amendment allowing school prayer (but fell short of the two-thirds necessary for passage).[13] In addition, some modest restrictions on abortion and actions against pornography and popular culture also passed (Carney 1997). But, without a doubt, the single biggest victory was the passage by both houses of a $500-per-child tax credit in 1997, which President Clinton signed into law. The business community strongly opposed such a tax provision, and pressure from the Christian Right was critical in gaining support from the GOP leadership (Chandler 1997).

Yet these modest gains produced passionate criticism from within the movement itself. Columnist Cal Thomas, who once worked for the Moral Majority, captured this dismay: "When Christian activists emerged from their churches into the political arena, they targeted pornography, offensive television, drugs, the gay-rights movement and crumbling families. Pornography is worse than ever, television continues to stink, drugs remain a problem, the gay-rights agenda (despite a few setbacks) advances and the divorce rate remains the same. The Christian Coalition takes credit for the $500-per-child tax credit in the budget bill, heretofore unrevealed as a Christian doctrine" (Thomas 1997). Many movement insiders admit that many of the broader goals of the movement have not yet been achieved. The $500-per-child tax credit is one of the few elements in the "Contract with the American Family," offered by the Christian Coalition in 1995, that has been enacted (Wilcox 1996, 87).

Surely the biggest disappointment, however, revolved around the impeachment of President Clinton in 1998 (Weyrich 1999). Many Christian Right activists pushed hard for articles of impeachment, which passed on a narrow, party-line vote, and then worked for a conviction of Clinton in the Republican-controlled Senate, where it failed—with the blessing of none other than Pat Robertson. This turn of events, combined with the strong public opposition to removing Clinton from office, was deeply discouraging to the movement activists. Many Christian conservatives concluded that the nation as a whole did not share many of their values, and, worse yet, many soon discovered that public opinion on key issues, such as abortion and gay rights, had not moved in their direction since 1980. Indeed, in some important instances it had moved in a more liberal direction (Wilcox 1996, 134–138). Some movement leaders reacted to this disappointment by arguing that conservative Christians should become less active in politics and reemphasize the religious pursuits to "change the culture" that underlies politics (Thomas and Dobson 1999). This argument amounted to a redirection of the passions that undergird the movement itself.

During the George W. Bush administration, the Christian Right strongly supported a few of the president's initiatives, such as reduction of the "marriage penalty" in the tax code. Many movement leaders appreciated the style and ethos of the Bush administration and the Republican congressional leadership, and welcomed some administration actions, such as the appointment of Attorney General John Ashcroft, the nomination of conservative judges, and the executive orders issued on abortion and stem cell research. However, many members of the Christian Right feared that such actions are largely symbolic and were aimed more at co-opting the movement than at advancing its agenda.[14] Indeed, some key movement demands, such as abolishing the Department of Education and the National Endowments for the Arts and Humanities, were dropped by the Republican leadership, and more controversial goals, such as support for school vouchers and restrictions on abortion, were put on the back burner.

As a consequence, there has been only lukewarm support for many of the Bush administration's initiatives. A good example was the Christian Right's approach to Bush's "faith-based initiative" extending charitable choice to more social services (Edsall and Milbank 2001). To begin with, the initiative was never among the top legislative priorities of the movement, and it was of interest only because it elevated the public role of religion. Members of the Christian Right were deeply disturbed by the compromises required to gain passage, such as prohibiting discrimination in hiring and extending the program to all religious groups. As one observer put it, "President Bush's faith-based initiative is in deep trouble because it lacks a constituency committed to its success, and because every move the administration makes to appease the idea's opponents weakens support from likely allies" (Dionne 2001).

The movement did little to assist passage of the House version of the bill in 2001 and had virtually no impact on the Senate version in 2002. Indeed, movement lobbyists were largely impediments to the bill's passage.[15] A similar situation may be developing on the topic of same-sex marriage, which was suddenly placed on the political agenda in 2003 by a decision of the Massachusetts Supreme Court. Both President Bush and the Republican congressional leadership were initially reluctant to advance a constitutional amendment defining marriage in the traditional fashion, preferring a less controversial response. As of mid-2004, the administration's lack of decisiveness on the issue is deeply troubling to Christian conservatives. Sandy Rios of the CWA said, "[President Bush] can't possibly guarantee a large turnout of evangelical Christian voters if he does not do what is morally right and take leadership on this issue as he did on the [Iraq] war. . . . The strength of this president is in his convictions, but our people do not admire his indecision and lack of leadership on an issue so basic as the sanctity of marriage" (Hallow 2004).

Not surprisingly, the Christian Right is often stridently critical of the Bush administration and GOP congressional leaders. Such rhetoric is partly an attempt to maintain some pressure on the party, but it also is directed at stoking the passions of the movement's core supporters, many of whom are less than inspired by the GOP agenda. Indeed, movement lobbyists disagree on the value of the Republican control of Congress and the White House. One insider said, "Yes! It is always better when the GOP controls Congress; when Democrats are in control our role becomes one of blockage, which is easier but less rewarding." But another informant was not so sure: "Sure, some Republicans strongly support us, but as a whole, the party will sell us out if they need to. For them it is about power, for us it is about values." Yet another remarked, "I'm pleased George W. Bush is president because I like a lot of his policies. But he and [Speaker J. Dennis] Hastert are sucking the air out of conservative politics. Thank goodness for [Senate Democratic leader] Tom Daschle—it is good to have someone to rally against." And still another said, "The GOP must remain pro-life and pro-marriage; these are the nonnegotiable issues."

Despite these frustrations, the movement has had some tangible successes during the period of unified Republican control of government. For example, in 2003 the House and the Senate both passed a ban on partial-birth abortions, which President Bush signed into law. Congress also approved an experiment with school vouchers in Washington, D.C., public schools. And there have been some smaller victories as well, including exempting homeschoolers from mandated testing and obtaining an increase in funding for "character education" in public schools. These gains have taken the edge off the movement's criticism of the GOP at the beginning of the 2004 campaign.

Overall, there is little evidence that Christian conservatives are executing an immediate, wholesale withdrawal from politics. However, the passion of movement activists appears to have waned compared with that of the mid-1990s. This decline may help to account for the movement's retrenchment after 1998.[16] One insider remarked, "In a sense, we are in danger of being victimized by our own, limited successes." Whether this situation represents a temporary pause in the movement similar to the one in 1990 or the beginning of a permanent decline remains to be seen. Indeed, the debate over same-sex marriage could well revive the movement in 2004.

Conclusion

Like in the classic film *Mr. Smith Goes to Washington*, the Christian Right entered congressional politics with fervor and idealism, only to be frustrated by political reality. Some activists were horrified by what they perceived to be corruption, while others developed a taste for the struggle. After some two decades, the movement has slowly developed the resources and skills to influence Congress. The Christian Right has been most effective in its pursuit of outsider activities, including involvement in elections and grassroots lobbying. It has been somewhat less effective in its organizational activities, which have been plagued by instability. Partly because of such instability, the Christian Right has been least effective in its insider activities. And where there have been gains in this area, the associated pragmatism and moderation have threatened to undermine the basis of the movement itself: the passionate demands of conservative Christians to restore traditional values to public policy.

At the outset of this chapter we asked: why is there a disjunction between the electoral success of the Christian Right, on the one hand, and its failure to change public policy, on the other? We can now offer two more definitive answers to that question. First, the movement has been slow to develop the skills needed to operate effectively inside congressional politics. Second, it has often been unwilling or unable to compromise on its unpopular agenda. Underlying these answers is the important role played by passion in social movements. In this sense, the Christian Right is an excellent example of the strengths and weaknesses of social movements in the legislative process.

Notes

1. Christian Right leaders also secured some support from religious institutions, such as evangelical churches, religious broadcasters, and missionary groups, but these organizations rely by and large on passionate individual contributors as well.
2. Christian conservatives have faced a similar situation in pursuing litigation: the movement has slowly developed effective legal resources, and these efforts have often provoked disputes between pragmatic and purist lawsuits (see Brown 2001).
3. This chapter is based in part on interviews with approximately a dozen current and former Christian Right lobbyists, movement leaders, activists, and observers conducted in the summer and fall of 2001. The interviews were carried out with a promise of confidentiality. Unless otherwise noted, comments and quotes come from these interviews.
4. The information on lobbying resources comes from interviews with movement insiders, from Derk Wilcox (2000), and from lobbying reports filed under the Lobbying Disclosure Act of 1995 (see http://sopr.senate.gov).
5. Such groups include the Eagle Forum, an antifeminist organization founded in 1972 by Phyllis Schlafly, and the American Family Association, founded by the Reverend Donald Wildmon in 1977 as a watchdog of the mass media. In 1999 House Republican whip Tom DeLay of Texas founded the U.S. Family Network, a tax-exempt "527" committee. However, after Congress in the summer of 2000 required the Internal Revenue Service (IRS) to disclose the financial activities of 527 committees, the U.S. Family Network's activities declined precipitously.
6. A survey conducted by John Jackson found that supporters of the Christian Right made up 25 percent of the delegates to the Republican National Convention in 2000, down from 39 percent in 1996, but the number of Christian Right sympathizers was 32 percent, up from 26 percent in 1996. A study of state Republican organizations found the movement to be strong in eighteen states — about the same as in 1994, but with considerable flux among the states (Conger and Green 2002).
7. These data come from surveys of the mass public, clergy, and evangelical elites conducted by the authors in 2000.

8. See Weisskopf (1993). This report was a source of controversy because it identified Christian conservatives as "largely poor, uneducated and easy to command." This description aroused considerable passion in the Christian Right and helped to spur movement organizing.

9. This rough estimate is based on an average voting score of greater than 90 percent for movement-supported initiatives or evidence of strong movement electoral support. Guth and Kellstedt (2001) found that the "Christian Right" faction among House Republicans accounted for about 53 percent of the House's GOP membership and a "Traditional Conservative" faction accounted for another 40 percent. All of the supporters of the movement's agenda identified here fell into these two factions, and most in the former.

10. See http://www.house.gov/burton/RSC/vat.htm for information on VAT.

11. These figures came from lobbying reports filed under the Lobbying Disclosure Act of 1995 (see http://sopr.senate.gov).

12. The most famous use of this comparison came in 1987 as the Robertson forces prepared to contest the 1988 Republican presidential nomination campaign in Michigan; see Hertzke (1993) on the animosity among GOP regulars toward the movement.

13. Of course, some members of Congress may have voted for these measures because the measures had little chance of actually becoming law.

14. For an account of the slow progress on the Christian Right's agenda as seen by VAT, consult its 2001 annual report found at http://www.house.gov/burton/RSC/vat.htm. But also see the 2002 and 2003 reports, which show some additional gains.

15. The authors are indebted to Douglas Koopman and Amy Black for their insights on this process.

16. See Kohut et al. (2000). A 2000 survey of evangelical elites by the authors found no support for the claim that Christian conservatives are withdrawing from politics, despite considerable disappointment with the political process. There was, however, considerable skepticism about the Christian Right and movement politics.

References

Baumgartner, Frank R., and Beth L. Leech. 1998. *Basic Interests.* Princeton, NJ: Princeton University Press.

Birnbaum, Jeffrey H. 2001. "The Power 25." *Forbes,* May 17.

Brown, Steven P. 2001. *Trumping Religion: The New Christian Right, the Free Speech Clause, and the Courts.* Auburn University, unpublished manuscript.

Bruce, Steve. 1988. *The Rise and Fall of the New Christian Right.* Oxford: Clarendon Press.

Campbell, Colton C., and Roger H. Davidson. 1998. "Coalition Building in Congress: The Consequences of Partisan Change." In *The Interest Group Connection,* edited by Paul S. Herrnson, Ronald G. Shaiko, and Clyde Wilcox, 116–136. Chatham, NJ: Chatham House.

Carney, Dan. 1997. "Conservatives Repackage Agenda on Social Issues. *Congressional Quarterly Weekly Report,* September 20, 2225–2228.

Chandler, Clay. 1997. "Child Tax Credit Plan Creates Unusual Alliance." *Washington Post,* May 31.

Conger, Kimberly H., and John C. Green. 2002. "Spreading Out and Digging In: Christian Conservatives and State Republican Parties." *Campaigns and Elections* 23:58–60, 64–65.

Dionne, E. J. 2001. "The Dwindling 'Armies of Compassion.'" *Washington Post,* July 13.

Edsall, Thomas B., and Dana Milbank. 2001. "Blunt Defense of 'Faith-Based Aid': Bush Aide Rebukes Evangelical Critics of Administration Plan." *Washington Post,* March 8.

Gimpel, James G. 1998. "Grassroots Organization and Equilibrium Cycles in Group Mobilization and Access." In *The Interest Group Connection*, edited by Paul S. Herrnson, Ronald G. Shaiko, and Clyde Wilcox, 100–115. Chatham, NJ: Chatham House.

Goldstein, Kenneth M. 1999. *Interest Groups, Lobbying, and Participation in America.* Cambridge: Cambridge University Press.

Green, John C. 1999. "The Spirit Willing: Collective Identity and the Development of the Christian Right." In *Waves of Protest: Social Movements Since the Sixties*, edited by Jo Freeman and Victoria Johnson, 153–168. Lanham, MD: Rowman and Littlefield.

———. 2000a. "The Christian Right and the 1998 Elections: An Overview." In *Prayers in the Precincts: The Christian Right in the 1998 Elections*, edited by John C. Green, Mark J. Rozell, and Clyde Wilcox, 1–20. Washington, DC: Georgetown University Press.

———. 2000b. *The Christian Right at the Millennium.* New York: American Jewish Committee.

———. 2001. "Elections and Amateurs: The Christian Right in the 1998 Congressional Campaigns." In *Congressional Primaries and the Politics of Representation*, edited by Peter F. Galderisi, Marni Ezra, and Michael Lyons, 77–91. Lanham, MD: Rowman and Littlefield.

———. 2003. "The Undetected Tide." *Religion in the News* 6(1).

Green, John C., James L. Guth, and Kevin Hill. 1993. "Faith and Election: The Christian Right in Congressional Campaigns, 1978–1988." *Journal of Politics* 55:80-91.

Green, John C., James L. Guth, Lyman A. Kellstedt, and Corwin E. Smidt. 1995. "Evangelical Realignment: The Political Power of the Christian Right." *Christian Century*, July 5.

———. 1998. "The Religious Right and the 1998 Election: A Defeat, Not a Debacle." *Christian Century*, December 23–30, 1238–1245.

Green, John C., James L. Guth, Corwin E. Smidt, and Lyman A. Kellstedt. 1996. *Religion and the Culture Wars.* Lanham, MD: Rowman and Littlefield.

Green, John C., Mark J. Rozell, and Clyde Wilcox, eds. 2000. *Prayers in the Precincts: The Christian Right in the 1998 Elections.* Washington, DC: Georgetown University Press.

Guth, James L., and John C. Green. 1993. "Politics in the Promised Land: The Christian Right at the Grassroots." In *Research in the Social Science Study of Religion*, edited by Monty L. Lynn and David O. Moberg, 5:219–234. Greenwich, CT: JAI Press.

Guth, James L., and Lyman A. Kellstedt. 2001. "Religion and Congress. " In *In God We Trust?* edited by Corwin E. Smidt, 213–233. Grand Rapids, MI: Baker Press.

Guth, James L., John C. Green, Corwin E. Smidt, and Lyman E. Kellstedt. 2001a. "Partisan Religion." *Christian Century*, March 21.

Guth, James L., Lyman A. Kellstedt, John C. Green, and Corwin E. Smidt. 2001b. "America Fifty/Fifty." *First Things*, October.

———. 2002. "A Distant Thunder? Religious Mobilization in the 2000 Elections." In *Interest Group Politics*, 6th ed., edited by Allan J. Cigler and Burdett A. Loomis. Washington, DC: CQ Press.

Hallow, Ralph Z. 2004. "Evangelicals Frustrated by Bush." *Washington Times*, February 20.

Herrnson, Paul S. 1998. "Interest Groups, PACs and Campaigns." In *The Interest Group Connection*, edited by Paul S. Herrnson, Ronald G. Shaiko, and Clyde Wilcox. Chatham, NJ: Chatham House.

Hertzke, Allen D. 1988. *Representing God in Washington.* Knoxville: University of Tennessee Press.

———. 1993. *Echoes of Discontent.* Washington, DC: CQ Press.

Hofrenning, Daniel J. B. 1995. *In Washington But Not of It.* Philadelphia: Temple University Press.

———. 2001. "Religious Lobbying and American Politics: Religious Faith Meets the Real World of Politics." In *In God We Trust?* edited by Corwin E. Smidt, 118–141. Grand Rapids, MI: Baker Press.

Hula, Kevin. 1995. "Rounding up the Usual Suspects: Forging Interest Group Coalitions in Washington." In *Interest Group Politics*, 5th ed., edited by Allan J. Cigler and Burdett Loomis. Washington, DC: CQ Press.

Jones, Bob, IV. 1998. "Cracking the Whip." *World*, July 18.

Kohut, Andrew, John C. Green, Scott Keeter, and Robert Toth. 2000. *The Diminishing Divide: Religion's Changing Role in American Politics*. Washington, DC: Brookings Institution.

Layman, Geoffrey. 2000. *The Great Divide*. New York: Columbia University Press.

Lowi, Theodore. 1971. *The Politics of Disorder*. New York: Basic Books.

McAdam, Doug. 1982. *Political Process and the Development of Black Insurgency, 1930–1970*. Chicago: University of Chicago Press.

Moen, Matthew C. 1989. *The Christian Right and Congress*. Tuscaloosa: University of Alabama Press.

———. 1992. *The Transformation of the Christian Right*. Tuscaloosa: University of Alabama Press.

O'Keefe, Mark. 2001. "The Paradox of the Christian Right." *Newhouse News Service*, December 11.

Ostling, Richard N. 2000. "Religious Right Far from Dead." Associated Press, November 18.

People for the American Way. 2000. "Election Countdown: How the Religious Right Mobilizes Their Voters," December 7. http://www.pfaw.org/issues/right.

Poole, Keith L., and Howard Rosenthal. 1997. *A Political-Economic History of Roll-Call Voting*. New York: Oxford University Press.

Reed, Ralph. 1996. *Active Faith*. New York: Free Press.

Rozell, Mark J. 2003. "What Christian Right?" *Religion in the News* 6(1).

Rozell, Mark J., and Clyde Wilcox. 1996. *Second Coming*. Baltimore: Johns Hopkins University Press

———. 1999. *Interest Groups in American Campaigns*. Washington, DC: CQ Press.

Rozell, Mark J., and Clyde Wilcox, eds. 1995. *God at the Grassroots*. Lanham, MD: Rowman and Littlefield.

———. 1997. *God at the Grassroots 1996*. Lanham, MD: Rowman and Littlefield.

Salisbury, Robert H. 1989. "Political Movements in American Politics: An Essay on Concept and Analysis." *National Journal of Political Science* 1:15–30.

Shaiko, Ronald D. 1998. "Lobbying in Washington: A Contemporary Perspective." In *The Interest Group Connection*, edited by Paul S. Herrnson, Ronald G. Shaiko, and Clyde Wilcox, 3–18. Chatham, NJ: Chatham House.

Soper, J. Christopher, and Joel Fetzer. 2000. "The Christian Right and the Republican Party in California: Necessarily Yoked." In *Prayers in the Precincts*, edited by John C. Green, Mark J. Rozell, and Clyde Wilcox. Washington, DC: Georgetown University Press.

Stephens, Joe. 2002. "Reed Offered Clout to Help Enron." *Washington Post*, February 17.

Thomas, Cal. 1997. "Onward Political Soldiers." *Tampa Tribune*, September 21.

Thomas, Cal, and Ed Dobson. 1999. *Blinded by Might*. Grand Rapids, MI: Zondervan.

Watson, Justin.1999.*The Christian Coalition*. New York: St. Martin's Griffin.

Weisskopf, Michael. 1993. "Energized by Pulpit or Passion, The Public Is Calling." *Washington Post*, February 1.

Weyrich, Paul. 1999. "The Moral Minority." *Christianity Today*. September 6.

Wilcox, Clyde. 1992. *God's Warriors*. Baltimore: Johns Hopkins University Press.

———. 1996. *Onward Christian Soldiers*. Boulder, CO: Westview Press.

————. 1998. "The Dynamics of Lobbying on the Hill." In *The Interest Group Connection*, edited by Paul S. Herrnson, Ronald G. Shaiko, and Clyde Wilcox, 89–99. Chatham, NJ: Chatham House.

Wilcox, Clyde, John C. Green, and Mark J. Rozell. 2001. "Social Movements and Party Politics: The Case of the Christian Right." *Journal for the Scientific Study of Religion* 40 (3): 413–426.

Wilcox, Derk A. 2000. *The Right Guide.* Ann Arbor, MI: Economics American Inc.

Wolpe, Bruce C. 1990. *Lobbying Congress.* Washington, DC: CQ Press.

11. Protecting America's Workers in Hostile Territory: Unions and the Republican Congress

Peter L. Francia

Organized labor has a long history of involvement in American politics, dating back as early as the 1830s when the Workingmen's Party fought to win policies and laws beneficial to the interests of the working class. In these early years of the twenty-first century, the lead voice of the labor movement is the American Federation of Labor-Congress of Industrial Organizations (AFL-CIO). It represents more than thirteen million workers and is one of the most influential political organizations in the United States.

The strength of the AFL-CIO and the labor movement in American politics has waxed and waned over the last several decades. The 1980s and first half of the 1990s were particularly difficult times for labor. Union membership dropped precipitously as a percentage of the U.S. workforce; workers' wages stagnated while CEO salaries skyrocketed; and labor found itself trapped in an antiunion political climate fostered by the presidencies of Republicans Ronald Reagan and George Bush. The landslide victory for congressional Republicans in the 1994 midterm elections was one of labor's most devastating political setbacks, transforming labor from an "insider" to an "outsider" group with limited access to the new congressional majority (Gimpel 1998, 112; Gerber 1999, 79).

The AFL-CIO moved swiftly to reverse labor's rapid decline by electing John J. Sweeney of the Service Employees International Union (SEIU) its new president in 1995. Sweeney and the new AFL-CIO leadership have intensified labor's political action, investing heavily in advertising campaigns and grass-roots activities, such as get-out-the-vote drives and political education for union members. Also since Sweeney's election, organized labor has worked to defeat some antiunion Republican members of Congress, and it has succeeded in a few close races. However, unions have been unable to elect Democratic majorities to the House or Senate since 1994, and have had to contend with the antiunion policies of Republican president George W. Bush since 2000, severely limiting labor's policy prospects.

Organized labor has, nevertheless, fought aggressively to block various Republican-led policy proposals. This chapter discusses organized labor's legislative successes and failures on Capitol Hill since Sweeney's election. It begins by describing how labor uses its resources to shape legislative policies in Congress, and then addresses recent changes in union political activities and their effects on congressional policymaking. It concludes by weighing labor's future policy prospects in the event of continued Republican control of Congress.

Union Resources and Public Policy

Unions influence congressional policy by relying on their economic and political resources. *Economic resources* refers to the methods available to labor for affecting economic events and production, such as collective bargaining, strikes, and slowdowns (Dark 1999, 36). Unions' economic resources allow them to gain access to policymakers eager to avoid disruptions in the economy.

Political resources refers to those resources that allow labor to influence elections directly, such as campaign contributions and expenditures, political advertising, and grassroots activities designed to mobilize union members to participate in the political process. Unions, through campaign contributions and services, seek to shape the ideological composition of Congress by electing candidates who espouse pro-labor positions. Unions also offer campaign assistance to members of Congress who serve on powerful committees. This support allows unions to gain access to the influential members of Congress who shape labor policies (Eismeier and Pollock 1988; Sorauf 1992). In recent years, unions have struggled to win legislative battles on high-visibility issues (Freeman and Medoff 1984, 192; Neustadtl 1990). However, some research suggests that union contributions and other union services may affect congressional voting behavior on at least some roll call votes (Kau and Rubin 1981; Kau, Keenan, and Rubin 1982; Saltzman 1987; Wilhite 1988; Burns, Francia, and Herrnson 2000).

Political resources also include those that relate directly to the legislative process. The AFL-CIO relies on several of its departments to assist in these efforts. Its legislative department holds issue forums and town meetings to listen to members' concerns and to pursue specific policy platforms. Its political department provides union members with information on pressing political issues and on candidates' positions on those issues. The public policy department develops labor's specific social, economic, and trade policies. And then there are the legislative action committees (LACs) that help organized labor to apply grassroots pressure to members of Congress. Through its LACs, the AFL-CIO stations labor activists in swing congressional districts. These activists meet with congressional incumbents to discuss pending labor legislation (Heberlig 1999, 169).

Labor engages in a variety of lobbying methods as well. One of its most common techniques is grassroots lobbying, in which unions mobilize their members to put pressure on legislators, often through massive letter and postcard campaigns. Labor also uses radio and television advertising campaigns to generate public support on a particular issue. A successful advertising campaign is a valuable lobbying tool when it convinces citizens that a group's position is the correct one, and then the citizens, in turn, convey the group's message to Congress (Loomis and Sexton 1995; Browne 1998; West 2000).

To compensate for its weakening economic resources, labor has had to rely increasingly on political resources to influence political policies. Union membership as a percentage of the U.S. workforce has declined consistently over the last half-century (see Figure 11-1). In the 1980s, the overall number

Figure 11-1   Union Membership as a Proportion
of the Labor Force, 1948–2002

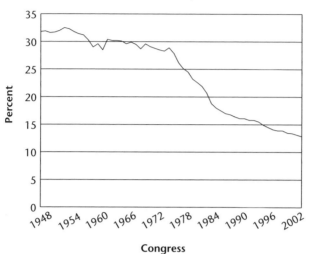

Source: Labor Research Association, http://www.laborresearch.org/
charts.php?id=29.

of union workers actually dropped for the first time since the 1920s (Masters 1997, 1). Indeed, union membership is at its lowest percentage of the overall workforce since the Great Depression. Only one in seven workers now belongs to a labor union compared with three in ten workers represented by unions in the mid-1950s.

The leadership of the AFL-CIO has attempted to deal with the problem of declining union membership by devoting a substantial portion of its operating budget to organizing activities. One of Sweeney's first actions was the creation of a new organizing department, which assists unions in their organizing efforts. It also oversees the Organizing Institute, which trains new organizers and activists so that they can help workers organize campaigns. The AFL-CIO executive council has provided strong financial backing for its organizing department by significantly increasing its organizing fund (Cooper 1996, 2).

Organizing efforts, however, remain a difficult challenge. Right-to-work laws, which prohibit union membership as a condition of employment, exist in twenty-one states (National Right to Work Committee, http://www.nrtwc.org). Employers also are waging more intensive antiunion campaigns, using tactics that include dismissing workers for engaging in organizing activities, holding one-on-one supervisor meetings with employees, and distributing antiunion letters and leaflets (Bronfenbrenner and Juravich 1998, 28). Certification success rates in National Labor Relations Board (NLRB) elections are still less than 50 percent (Bronfenbrenner and Juravich 1998, 20). Rebuilding union membership will then be a difficult process, and it reflects a long-term political strategy. For the more immediate future, the AFL-CIO continues to invest heavily in its political resources to influence government and public policies. This investment has included aggressive mass media advertising campaigns and grassroots activities to mobilize union members, whose political participation dipped to just 14 percent of the electorate in the 1994 elections (Galvin 1998). One objective of labor's advertising and grassroots campaign has been to put pressure on members of Congress to implement pro-union policies. As Sweeney explained, "The AFL-CIO will work to make government more accountable to working people by mobilizing in greater and greater numbers" (AFL-CIO 1999). Similarly, its advertising campaign is designed to set a pro-labor agenda and to hold members of Congress accountable on labor issues. According to Deborah Dion, a spokeswoman for the AFL-CIO, labor's ad campaign helps to "hold voting records under a microscope and shine a light on them" (Wolfson 1996, 40).

The Air War

The AFL-CIO spent $25 million on paid media in 1996 (Beck et al. 1997). The media campaigns were financed by the $1.80 taken from each union member's annual dues (Swoboda and Edsall 1996, A6). The AFL-CIO ran issue ads on the minimum wage, Medicare, Social Security, education, and other important labor issues in carefully targeted districts where members of Congress faced serious competition in the upcoming election. Steven Rosenthal, the political director of the AFL-CIO, explained that "running an issue ad in a district . . . where a member of Congress was elected with 53 percent of the vote is a very, very valuable tool in our legislative program" (Magleby 2000, 41–42). The AFL-CIO directed its major advertising efforts against forty-four Republican incumbents in the 1996 elections (Beck et al. 1997, 12).

Many of the advertisements brought attention to members' voting records on labor issues. In New Jersey's Eighth Congressional District, the AFL-CIO targeted Republican incumbent Bill Martini in its ad campaign. The ads, which criticized Martini for supporting $10 billion in student loan cuts and tax breaks for the wealthy (*The Record* 1996, L2), damaged Martini and helped his opponent, Democratic state assemblyman and Paterson mayor Bill Pascrell, a strong union supporter, win a close election in 1996 by a 51–48 percent margin (Barone and Ujifusa 1997, 929).

The AFL-CIO scaled back its issue advertising campaign in the 1998 midterm election (Stranger and Rivlin 1999). Its less expensive ad campaign focused on education, health care, Social Security, and other labor-related issues. In April 1997, for example, the AFL-CIO spent roughly $700,000 on ads supporting additional funding for public schools. Although the AFL-CIO mainly targeted Republican incumbents in its issue ad spots, in a few instances it also ran ads critical of Democrats (Stranger and Rivlin 1999).

The AFL-CIO's health care ads highlighted legislation known as the "patients' bill of rights," which allowed patients to sue their health maintenance organizations (HMOs) for malpractice. The ads aired in fourteen states at a cost of $2 million. The AFL-CIO ran several other issue ads in October 1998 that attacked congressional Republicans' attempts to use $80 billion from the federal budget surplus for tax cuts instead of strengthening Social Security. The ads urged viewers to call their members and tell them to "put Social Security first" (AFL-CIO 1998). Although Congress ultimately failed to pass the patients' bill of rights in 1998, organized labor played a role in stopping the Republican tax cuts.

In 2000 the AFL-CIO spent $21.1 million on its issue ad campaign (Jamieson 2001), although many of the ads were designed to help the Democratic presidential candidate, Al Gore. During the final two months of the 2000 election, the AFL-CIO spent more than $1 million a week running ads in the "battleground" states of Ohio, Michigan, Missouri, and Pennsylvania that were critical of the record of the Republican presidential candidate, George W. Bush, as governor of Texas. In the Philadelphia media market alone, the AFL-CIO spent almost $300,000 in one week on advertisements (Meckler 2000).

Labor again invested heavily in issue ads in 2002.[1] In a sample of some of the most competitive races, the AFL-CIO spent $5.6 million on advertisements, a figure that ranked behind only that of the United Seniors Association among interest groups (Magleby and Monson 2003, 26). These ads focused on issues related to health care, pension reform, and free trade. Many of the ads carefully targeted competitive congressional districts. For example, in contests in which a Democratic incumbent was running for reelection in 2002, 61 percent of the AFL-CIO's issue advertisements targeted competitive races compared with 39 percent that targeted uncompetitive races (a competitive race is defined as a contest decided by twenty points or less).

Union members were supportive of the issues covered in the AFL-CIO advertising campaign. During the 1998 and 2000 elections, Social Security was the issue most frequently mentioned by union members (see Table 11-1). In 2000 the AFL-CIO spread its message on Social Security through ads that attacked Republican presidential candidate George Bush. The ads, which ran in Michigan, Missouri, Ohio, and Pennsylvania, alleged that Bush's tax cuts would lead to benefit cuts and an increase in the retirement age (see Box 11-1).

As the economy went into a down cycle in 2002, the AFL-CIO directed many of its advertisements toward the economy and jobs. Its most frequently run issue advertisement was on fast-track trade authority and its impact on American manufacturing jobs (see Box 11-2). The ads ran in Arkansas, Connecticut, Illinois, Maine, Missouri, Mississippi, North Carolina, and Pennsylvania. Perhaps not surprisingly, union members resoundingly cited the economy and jobs as one the most important issues in the 2002 congressional elections.

The AFL-CIO's issue advertising campaign, however, is only one facet of its overall efforts to influence the issue agenda, elections, and policy. The AFL-CIO has also sought to mobilize union members themselves to influence elections and

Table 11-1   Most Important Issues in Congressional Elections among Union Members: 1998, 2000, and 2002 (percentage)

	Election		
Issue	1998	2000	2002
Economy and jobs	28	33	44
Health care and prescription drugs	23	33	34
Social Security	34	37	25
Education	33	25	—
Terrorism and national security	—	—	24
Taxes	17	17	17
Moral values	13	17	14
Gun issues	—	13	12
Crime and drugs	14	—	—

Source: Peter D. Hart Research Associates, AFL-CIO Election Night Surveys (1998–2002).

Notes: — Less than 1 percent. Numbers do not add to 100 because respondents could select more than one issue.

policy battles important to organized labor. Indeed, labor's "ground war" has become one of its most significant weapons since Sweeney's election.

The Ground War

The AFL-CIO's 1996 ground war included 100 permanent union grass-roots activists in each congressional district and the recruitment of an additional 2,500 union activists and staff for the final six weeks of the election for get-out-the-vote efforts. Sweeney stepped up the AFL-CIO's grassroots efforts by establishing the National Labor Political Training Center. The center recruited more than 750 union volunteers for get-out-the-vote activities and political education efforts in competitive congressional districts (AFL-CIO 1999). To mobilize union members to participate in elections and vote for union-endorsed candidates, the AFL-CIO sent out 9 million pieces of direct mail in the general election and distributed flyers in 114 congressional districts. Local unions and central labor councils mailed an additional 2.5 million voter guides (Gerber 1999, 84). Unions also worked in concert with Democratic Party committees, exchanging strategic campaign information and sponsoring voter contact drives (Rozell and Wilcox 1999, 25).

Box 11-1   AFL-CIO Issue Advocacy Advertisement on Social Security

JENNINGS: "I didn't expect to get rich when I went into teaching but I did expect to have a decent retirement fund. When George W. Bush first ran he promised not to cut our retirement fund. Then, he went and raided it because he wanted to pay for other things."

ANNOUNCER: "Now, George W. Bush says he'll protect Social Security while pushing a massive tax cut. But, studies show Bush's plan would lead to benefit cuts and an increase in the retirement age or both."

JENNINGS: "George W. Bush broke his promise to the people of Texas."

Source: Campaign Media Analysis Group.

The 1998 ground campaign included 300 full-time paid activists (Bernstein and Dunham 1998, 53). In the final week of the 1998 election alone, the AFL-CIO sent 7 million pieces of mail to union members urging them to vote. Union workers and volunteers made 14.5 million phone calls for the AFL-CIO and local unions combined (Lawrence and Drinkard 1998, 6A).

Overall, labor's grassroots campaign in 1998 was effective in reaching union members. Exit polling from Hart Research Associates found that 70 percent of union members reported that their unions had contacted them about the 1998 elections. Some 84 percent of union workers reported that the information sent

---

Box 11-2   AFL-CIO Issue Advocacy Advertisement on Jobs

WOMAN: "They have taken all of our jobs over there and they're paying them slave wages. And, we're out of luck."

MAN 1: "Telling my wife that I was out of work was probably the hardest thing I've ever had to do."

MAN 2: "I've worked there for twenty years. I don't know what I'm going to do. My job is gone."

ANNOUNCER: "Unfair trade laws have already cost Mississippi thousands of jobs. Now Chip Pickering has put more of our jobs at risk by siding with the big corporations and voting to fast track future trade deals. Call Congressman Pickering and tell him his job-killing vote hurt Mississippi."

Source: Campaign Media Analysis Group.

to them by their union was at least somewhat informative (Hart Research Associates 1998). These efforts helped to mobilize workers in behalf of the AFL-CIO legislative agenda and contributed to a union household turnout of 23 percent of the electorate in 1998—a 9 percent increase from 1994 (Galvin 1998). Labor's successful grassroots campaign caught the attention of several members of Congress. Rep. John Linder of Georgia, chair of the National Republican Congressional Committee (NRCC), recognized that labor "had a huge turnout with phone banks in regions across the country, and I've got to congratulate them" (Greenhouse 1998, A28).

In 2000 the AFL-CIO spent more than $40 million in seventy-one competitive congressional districts, and 1,600 workers coordinated voter education programs in thirty-five states (Swoboda 2000, A14). Unions registered 2.3 million new union household voters, made 8 million phone calls to union households, and handed out more than 14 million flyers and leaflets at union work sites. The national AFL-CIO alone sent more than 12 million pieces of direct mail to union households (AFL-CIO 2000c). Meanwhile, the AFL-CIO continued to stress member-to-member contact. "We want to break it down to one-to-one, because talking about issues and candidates really works better on the shop floor when people hear it from someone they know," explained Duane McConville, president of the Steelworkers Local 19806 (AFL-CIO 2000a). Organized labor's efforts even extended beyond union members. The AFL-CIO and the American Federation of State, County, and Municipal Employees (AFSCME) spent a combined $6 million on grassroots activities to mobilize African American and Latino voters. In some instances, labor sent trucks into minority neighborhoods trumpeting political messages (Hoffman 2000, A14). Union households made up 26 percent of the national electorate in 2000 (AFL-CIO 2000c).

During the 2002 midterm election, the campaign efforts of organized labor once again centered on grassroots activities. Under the AFL-CIO, 750 paid union officials and more than 4,000 local union coordinators worked around the country on targeted campaigns. These coordinators and volunteers distributed more than 17 million work site flyers, sent 15 million pieces of mail to union households, and made more than 5 million telephone calls. The AFL-CIO and its affiliates were active in forty-seven congressional races and sixteen Senate contests (AFL-CIO 2002).

In waging its grassroots efforts from 1996 to 2002, labor targeted its resources more efficiently than in past years. According to reports filed by union political action committees (PACs) with the Federal Election Commission (FEC), during that period more than 80 percent of labor's grassroots expenditures (internal communications in behalf of or against House candidates undertaken by union PACs) targeted congressional districts with competitive elections—that is, races decided by twenty points or less. By comparison, in the four previous elections the AFL-CIO, under the leadership of Lane Kirkland, directed only 54 percent of its grassroots expenditures toward competitive congressional districts. Organized labor's improved ability to target its efforts in competitive races has made it a stronger force in congressional elections (Jacobson 1999; Francia 2000). However, whether this stronger influence has translated into policy success is still open to question.

Congressional Support for Union Policies

The AFL-CIO monitors congressional support for labor legislation by compiling a record of each representative's and senator's roll call votes on union-supported policies. These voting records, known as "COPE scores" for the AFL-CIO's Committee on Political Education, range from a high score of 100 to a low of 0, indicating the percentage of the time that a member of Congress supported union-favored policies. The scores cover a broad range of issues, and they are generally good indicators of bills that organized labor wishes to influence.

An analysis of these COPE scores indicates that from the 100th Congress (1987–1988) to the 107th Congress (2001–2002), House Democrats consistently supported organized labor policies more than 80 percent of the time (see Figure 11-2). In some Congresses, Democratic support for union policies averaged more than 90 percent. Indeed, unions have long depended on their close relationship with Democratic members of Congress to stave off antiunion proposals from business groups and their allies (Dark 1999). House Republicans, by contrast, have grown increasingly less supportive of pro-labor policies. House Republicans' COPE scores averaged 30 percent during the 100th Congress, but fell to less than 15 percent by the 104th Congress (1995–1996) when Republicans gained majority status in the House. These results suggest that labor's relationship has remained strong with congressional Democrats, but that the increasing conservatism of congressional Republicans has made it more difficult for unions to win pro-labor policies since the GOP takeover of Congress.

These broad trends in labor support highlight the difficult political environment that labor encounters in a Republican-controlled Congress. However, labor has succeeded in some instances since the Republican takeover of Congress. In 1996 unions played an instrumental role in passing an increase in the federal minimum wage. In 1997 and 1998 organized labor also succeeded in blocking fast-track trade authority.

Winning a Minimum Wage Increase

In May 1996, the AFL-CIO ran issue advertisements supporting a minimum wage increase from $4.25 an hour to $5.15 in carefully targeted congressional districts. The ads focused on the rise of corporate executive salaries and the hypocrisy of congressional members, who voted themselves a 30 percent pay raise but refused to support an increase in the minimum wage—something that had not been done in five years (AFL-CIO 1996b). The AFL-CIO targeted twenty-nine House Republicans who had previously opposed a minimum wage increase. The ad campaign included radio spots urging several freshmen Repub-

Figure 11-2 Average COPE Scores for House Incumbents

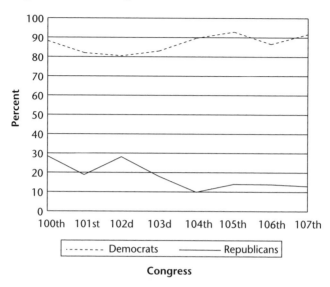

Source: J. Michael Sharpe, *Directory of Congressional Voting Scores and Interest Group Ratings,* 3d ed. (Washington, DC: CQ Press, 2000).

Note: Cases include incumbents running for reelection.

licans in the 104th Congress, such as Representatives Peter Blute and Peter Tork-ildsen of Massachusetts, to support the increase (Astell 1996, A1). The AFL-CIO also sponsored television ads that criticized House members, such as Andrea Seastrand of California, who, an ad claimed, had voted four times to block the minimum wage while supporting a "big tax break to the rich" (Bennet 1996, B7; also see Box 11-3).

The AFL-CIO organized an effective grassroots campaign as well in support of the minimum wage increase, with union members staging several demonstrations across the nation. In Seastrand's district, union workers held a press conference in front of a local supermarket and featured a shopping cart filled with $40 of food—the equivalent of what a worker could purchase with the wage increase.

The ads and grassroots campaign divided the conservative leadership of the House against the more moderate members in the Northeast and Midwest. One GOP House leader, Majority Leader Dick Armey of Texas, vowed to fight a wage increase "with every fiber of my being" (Clymer 1996, A1). Republican House member Peter King of New York countered that his own party's leaders were "knee-jerk Neanderthals" on labor issues (Greenhouse 1996, A9).

In the end, the AFL-CIO's relentless ad and grassroots campaigns put pressure on Republican members in competitive districts and helped to force a

---

**Box 11-3   AFL-CIO Issue Advocacy Advertisement on the Minimum
Wage, 1996**

ANNOUNCER: "In 1991, the minimum wage was just $4.25 an hour. Since
then, corporate profits and executive salaries have soared. And Congress gave
itself a 30 percent pay raise. But our Congresswoman voted four times to block a
minimum wage increase. And that's after she voted to cut Medicare and college
loans, all to give a big tax break to the rich."

UNION WORKER: "That's just wrong. Our Congresswoman should stop playing political games and start voting for working families for a change."

ANNOUNCER: "Tell Congresswoman Seastrand: Raise the minimum wage."

Source: Quoted in James Bennet, "The Ad Campaign: Labor Takes on Its Congressional
Foes," *New York Times*, May 24, 1996, B7.

---

vote on the House floor. Despite the strong objections of the House Republican
leadership, a federal minimum wage increase passed the House by a 281–144
vote. The bill won support from 187 Democrats and 93 Republicans. Nearly half
of the twenty-nine Republicans targeted by the AFL-CIO ad campaign ultimately voted in favor of the minimum wage increase. Sweeney noted, "We
[labor] were a major factor in the recent passage of the minimum wage increase.
We ran extensive ads, and in the end, half the members of Congress we named
in the ads voted for the increase" (AFL-CIO 1996a). Sweeney also credited
labor's grassroots campaign, proclaiming that the minimum wage increase
stemmed from "the tremendous efforts of our members in congressional district
after district who wrote letters, made phone calls, and participated in events to
insist their elected representatives vote for an increase" (Hall 1996).

Blocking Fast-Track Trade Authority in the 105th Congress

In the 105th Congress (1997–1998), "fast track" was the major free trade
roll call vote. In granting the power of fast track to the president, Congress allows
the president to negotiate trade pacts with foreign nations with the assurance
that Congress cannot later alter the terms of the agreement. In other words,
Congress can vote to approve or not approve the agreement, but it cannot amend
it. Organized labor opposed fast-track trade authority because the bill did not
contain sufficient language requiring future trade agreements to include labor
and environmental protections for U.S. trading partners. Absent these protections, labor leaders argued, U.S. manufacturers could produce their products at a
cheaper cost in other nations, resulting in factory relocations to foreign countries
and lost jobs for American workers.

With a vote scheduled in Congress for late 1997, Sweeney and organized labor announced plans to spend $1 million on media efforts against fast track, and pledged to send more than a million pieces of mail to union households across the nation (Swoboda 1997). Many labor leaders also threatened fast track supporters, saying that unions would "hold their feet to the fire" (Baker 1997, A16).

In the end, roughly three-fourths of congressional Democrats and several Republicans opposed the legislation, forcing the bill's withdrawal in 1997. One year later, Republican congressional leaders attempted to revive fast track. Unions responded with a massive grassroots response, holding hundreds of rallies, making roughly 800,000 phone calls, and sending out more than 750,000 postcards in opposition to fast track (AFL-CIO 2000b). When the vote was finally taken, the House defeated fast track by 243–180. Labor won 171 of 200 Democratic votes and 71 of 222 Republican votes. Republican House whip Tom DeLay of Texas credited the union efforts for making a difference: "The labor unions got off the dime a lot quicker. [Unions] work[ed] this issue for months, spending a lot of money" (Yang 1997, A6).

Shifting Fortunes

Despite several legislative victories early in Sweeney's tenure, unions have suffered several policy setbacks. In 2000 organized labor invested heavily in the campaigns of congressional Democrats and Vice President Al Gore's run for the presidency, but failed to prevent Republicans from winning the executive and legislative branches of the federal government. Not surprisingly, the early days of the Bush administration were difficult for organized labor. Bush suspended regulations implemented under the Clinton administration that prohibited federal contracts from being awarded to companies that violated labor laws. The Senate also reversed ergonomic standards proposed by the Occupational Safety and Health Administration (OSHA) that were designed to protect workers from repetitive motion injuries.

The AFL-CIO staunchly opposed a $1.6 trillion tax cut offered by the Bush administration in 2001, calling the proposal "morally wrong," "unwise," and "unfair" because the largest beneficiaries would be the wealthiest Americans (Swoboda 2001, E16). Labor leaders argued that the Bush tax plan would further jeopardize important policy priorities, including a prescription drug benefit for Medicare and efforts to shore up the Social Security trust fund. Labor was unable, however, to stop Congress from enacting the Bush tax cuts.

Organized labor also lost a significant free trade vote in 2002 when Congress approved fast-track trade promotion authority for President Bush. The Republican-led House passed the bill by a narrow 215–212 vote that included support from 190 Republicans and 25 Democrats. The opposition included 183 Democrats, 27 Republicans, and 2 independents (Bernard Sanders of Vermont and Virgil Goode Jr. of Virginia). A month later, the Senate passed fast-track trade promotion authority for President Bush by a 64–34 margin with the support of 43 Republicans, 20 Democrats, and 1 independent.

Organized labor did win a significant battle for steelworkers in 2002 when President Bush and Congress agreed to tariffs on foreign steel. The United Steelworkers of America and American steel industry executives argued that foreign nations were subsidizing their steel industries and unfairly undercutting competition by allowing their steel producers to sell steel for less than the cost of production—a practice known as "dumping." The United Steelworkers of America began a five-year, $5 million campaign that called for legislation to impose a 40 percent tariff on foreign steel to level the playing field.

Several House Republicans opposed the tariff, arguing that it would create job losses in other sectors of the economy. Republican Phil Crane, chairman of the House Ways and Means subcommittee on trade, remarked, "Tariffs mean higher prices and a transfer of jobs out of the country. The benefits will go to a select few at the expense of the many" (Marx 2002). Even some union officials echoed similar concerns. Jack McCann, president of the International Longshoremen's District Council in the Philadelphia area, predicted that the tariffs would lead to the loss of two thousand jobs at Philadelphia's port on the Delaware River (Marx 2002).

Still, the aggressive campaign waged by the United Steelworkers of America was enough to convince President Bush to enact tariffs ranging from 8 to 30 percent on foreign steel. The increases were hailed by most American steel unions and industry executives as a major legislative victory. As United Steelworkers of America president Leo Gerard remarked, "It's not as comprehensive as we had hoped, but it certainly is the first time we've seem some light at the end of a long, dark tunnel" (Strope 2002).

This victory, however, was short-lived. In December 2003, the Bush administration opted to remove the tariffs on foreign steel. In a statement to the press, President Bush announced that the tariffs "have now achieved their purpose, and as a result of changed economic circumstances it is time to lift them" (White House 2003).

The Bush administration was also intent on rewriting labor laws governing overtime pay for workers. The Bush proposal put forward in 2003 reclassified many workers as executive, administrative, or professional employees, denying them the overtime pay benefits specified in the Fair Labor Standards Act. The AFL-CIO intensely lobbied to block the Bush proposal, arguing that more than eight million workers, including police officers, nurses, and store supervisors, and even military veterans, could lose their overtime pay protections.

The AFL-CIO ran advertisements against the proposals and mobilized workers against the proposal with letter and e-mail blitzes to members of Congress (see Box 11-4). Although Congress can pass legislation to modify the Bush classifications, the new regulations do not require congressional approval. The

---

Box 11-4   AFL - CIO Mobilization E- mail on Overtime Pay

"Overtime Extra Innings/Job Crisis on Deck"

The fight to block President Bush's overtime pay take - away is going into extra innings. A select group of senators and representatives is meeting behind closed doors to hammer out differences between the U.S. Senate and House versions of legislation that includes a measure to protect overtime pay.

But President Bush is so determined that he is still threatening to veto the legislation if it blocks his overtime pay cut — when he really should be withdrawing his take - away. Please take one minute to send a protest to the White House by clicking on the link below to tell the Bush administration to WITHDRAW the overtime pay cut now. We'll keep you posted on developments in the fight to protect overtime pay.

http://www.unionvoice.org/campaign/bushcutsot/338aaejbt

President Bush's attack on overtime pay is just one way the administration is driving America's job crisis home. Instead of giving employers an incentive to create jobs, President Bush's proposed overtime pay cut will make it easier for employers to force workers to work longer hours for less pay. Why hire more people?

At the AFL - CIO, we're deeply concerned about America's growing jobs crisis — and the refusal of the administration and congressional allies to address it. In the coming weeks and months, we'll be asking you to get involved in the fight for good jobs.

Together, we're going to fight for a fundamental CHANGE IN AMERICA that improves job quality and security for all and puts jobless people back to work.

Look for future e - mail action alerts when your voice is needed on important jobs issues such as overtime pay, job creation, outsourcing, trade, help for the unemployed and more.

Tell President Bush: Withdraw your overtime pay take - away.

http://www.unionvoice.org/campaign/bushcutsot/338aaejbt

Thanks for all you do.

Source: AFL - CIO, "Overtime extra innings/Jobs crisis on deck," E- mail from peoplepower @aflcio.org, October 15, 2003.

Senate successfully acted to prohibit the curtailment of overtime coverage on several occasions. However, the House leadership opted against taking a vote on the measure, marking another significant defeat for organized labor in the Bush era and increasing labor's stake in the outcome of the 2004 presidential election and Bush's try for a second term in office.

Notes

1. Thanks are extended to Prof. Kenneth Goldstein for sharing advertising data from the Campaign Media Analysis Group (CMAG) for the 2002 election.

References

AFL-CIO. 1996a. "AFL-CIO Releases New TV and Radio Ads Aimed at Members of Congress Who Voted to Slash Medicare." AFL-CIO press release, August 28. http://www.aflcio.org/mediacenter/prsptm/pr08281996a.cfm (accessed October 28, 2004).
———. 1996b. "Stop Voting to Block a Minimum Wage Increase, AFL-CIO Ads Tell Congress This Week." AFL-CIO press release, May 20. http://www.aflcio.org/mediacenter/prsptm/pr05201996.ctm (accessed October 28, 2004).
———. 1998. "AFL-CIO Launches Grassroots Push on Social Security." AFL-CIO press release, October 2. http://www.aflcio.org/mediacenter/prsptm/pr10021998.cfm (accessed October 28, 2004).
———. 1999. "Building to Win, Building to Last," http://www.aflcio.org/convention99/sr15_building.htm (accessed January 5, 2000).
———. 2000a. "Member-to-Member Mobilization," http://www.aflcio.org/labor2000/news_mobilization.htm (accessed December 14, 2000).
———. 2000b. "New Television Ads Tell Members of Congress, 'Keep China on Probation.'" AFL-CIO press release, February 23. http://www.aflcio.org/mediacenter/prsptm/pr02232000.cfm (accessed October 28, 2004).
———. 2000c. "People-Powered Politics: Working Families Vote," http://www.aflcio.org/labor2000/election.htm (accessed January 3, 2001).
———. 2002. "The Union Difference Political Program for Working Families," http://www.aflcio.org/issuespolitics/politics /fs_0202.cfm.
Astell, Emilie. 1996. "Republicans Break Rank on the Minimum Wage." *Telegram and Gazette,* April 19, A1.
Baker, Peter. 1997. "Don't Punish Democrats Over Trade, Clinton Urges." *Washington Post,* September 25, A16.
Barone, Michael, and Grant Ujifusa. 1997. *Almanac of American Politics.* Washington, DC: National Journal Group.
Beck, Deborah, Paul Taylor, Jeffrey Stranger, and Douglas Rivlin. 1997. "Issue Advocacy Advertising during the 1996 Campaign." Annenberg Public Policy Center, University of Pennsylvania.
Bennet, James. 1996. "The Ad Campaign: Labor Takes on Its Congressional Foes." *New York Times,* May 24, B7.
Bernstein, Aaron, and Richard S. Dunham. 1998. "Unions: Laboring Mightily to Avert a Nightmare in November." *Business Week,* October 19, 53.
Bronfenbrenner, Kate, and Tom Juravich. 1998. "It Takes More than House Calls: Organizing to Win with a Comprehensive Union-Building Strategy." In *Organizing to Win,* edited by Kate Bronfenbrenner, Sheldon Friedman, Richard W. Hurd, Rudolph A. Oswald, and Ronald L. Seeber, 19–36. Ithaca, NY: ILR Press.
Browne, William P. 1998. "Lobbying the Public: All-Directional Advocacy." In *Interest Group Politics,* edited by Allan J. Cigler and Burdett Loomis, 343–363. Washington, DC: CQ Press.
Burns, Peter F., Peter L. Francia, and Paul S. Herrnson. 2000. "Labor at Work: Union Campaign Activities and Legislative Payoffs in the U.S. House of Representatives." *Social Science Quarterly* 81: 507–522.
Clymer, Adam. 1996. "House Approves Increase to $5.15 in Minimum Wage." *New York Times,* May 24, A1.

Cooper, Muriel H. 1996. "Organizing Program Seeks Innovation." *AFL-CIO News*, March 8, 2.

Dark, Taylor E. 1999. *The Unions and the Democrats: An Enduring Alliance.* Ithaca, NY: ILR Press.

Eismeier, Theodore J., and Philip H. Pollock III. 1988. *Business, Money, and the Rise of Corporate PACs in American Elections.* New York: Quorum Books.

Francia, Peter L. 2000. "Onward Union Soldiers: Labor's Grassroots Campaign Activities and the Renaissance of Organized Labor in American Politics." Paper presented at annual meeting of the American Political Science Association, Washington, DC, August 31–September 3.

Freeman, Richard B., and James L. Medoff. 1984. *What Do Unions Do?* New York: Basic Books.

Galvin, Kevin. 1998. "Labor Claims Victory in Elections." Associated Press, November 4.

Gerber, Robin. 1999. "Building to Win, Building to Last: AFL-CIO COPE Takes on the Republican Congress." In *After the Revolution: PACs, Lobbies, and the Republican Congress,* edited by Robert Biersack, Paul S. Herrnson, and Clyde Wilcox, 77–93. Boston: Allyn and Bacon.

Gimpel, James G. 1998. "Grassroots Organizations and Equilibrium Cycles in Group Mobilization and Access." In *The Interest Group Connection,* edited by Paul S. Herrnson, Ronald G. Shaiko, and Clyde Wilcox, 100–115. Chatham, NJ: Chatham House.

Greenhouse, Steven. 1996. "Some Republicans Condemn House Leadership's Attacks on Labor as Divisive." *New York Times,* May 11, A9.

————. 1998. "Republicans Credit Labor for Success by Democrats." *New York Times,* November 6, A28.

Hall, Mike. 1996. "Campaign Boosts Minimum Wage, House Hears Workers; Senate Now Must Act." *AFL-CIO News,* June 7. http://www.aflcio.org (accessed April 5, 2001).

Hart Research Associates. 1998. "AFL-CIO Election Night Study #5341." Hart Research Associates, November 3.

Heberlig, Eric S. 1999. "Coordinating Issues and Elections: Organized Labor in the Republican Era." *American Review of Politics* 20:163–180.

Hoffman, Kathy Barks. 2000. "Unions, Blacks Helped Democrats Gain in the Senate." *The Record,* December 3, A14.

Jacobson, Gary C. 1999. "The Effects of the AFL-CIO's 'Voter Education' Campaigns on the 1996 House Elections." *Journal of Politics* 61:185–194.

Jamieson, Kathleen Hall. 2001. "Issue Advertising in the 1999–2000 Election Cycle," http://www.appcpenn.org/ISSUEADS/02_01_2001_1999-2000issueadvocacy.pdf.

Kau, James, and Paul H. Rubin. 1981. "The Impact of Labor Unions on the Passage of Economic Legislation." *Journal of Labor Research* 2:133–145.

Kau, James, Donald Keenan, and Paul H. Rubin. 1982. "A General Equilibrium Model of Congressional Voting." *Quarterly Journal of Economics* 97:271–293.

Lawrence, Jill, and Jim Drinkard. 1998. "Getting Out the Vote." *USA Today,* October 29, 6A.

Loomis, Burdett A., and Eric Sexton. 1995. "Choosing to Advertise: How Groups Decide." In *Interest Group Politics,* edited by Allan J. Cigler and Burdett Loomis, 193–214. Washington, DC: CQ Press.

Magleby, David B. 2000. "Interest-Group Election Ads." In *Outside Money: Soft Money and Issue Advocacy in the 1998 Congressional Elections,* edited by David B. Magleby, 41–61. Lanham, MD: Rowman and Littlefield.

Magleby, David B., and J. Quinn Monson. 2003. "The Last Hurrah? Soft Money and Issue Advocacy in the 2002 Congressional Elections." In *The Last Hurrah? Soft Money and Issue Advocacy in the 2002 Congressional Elections.* Provo, UT: Center for the Study of Elections and Democracy.

Marx, Claude R. 2002. "Top GOP House Member on Trade Urges No New Steel Tariffs." *Associated Press State and Local Wire,* February 28.

Masters, Marrick F. 1997. *Unions at the Crossroads: Strategic Membership, Financial, and Political Perspective.* Westport, CT: Quorum Books.

Meckler, Laura. 2000. "AFL-CIO Spending Heavily to Criticize Bush." *Associated Press State and Local Wire,* September 26.

Neustadtl, Alan. 1990. "Interest-Group PACsmanship: An Analysis of Campaign Contributions, Issue Visibility, and Legislative Impact." *Social Forces* 69:549−564.

Rozell, Mark J., and Clyde Wilcox. 1999. *Interest Groups in American Campaigns: The New Face of Electioneering.* Washington, DC: CQ Press.

Saltzman, Gregory. 1987. "Congressional Voting on Labor Issues: The Role of PACs." *Industrial and Labor Relations Review* 40:163−179.

Sharpe, J. Michael. 2000. *Directory of Congressional Voting Scores and Interest Group Ratings.* 3d ed. Washington, DC: CQ Press.

Sorauf, Frank J. 1992. "Political Parties and Political Action Committees: Two Life Cycles." *Arizona Law Review* 22:445−463.

Stranger, Jeffrey D., and Douglas G. Rivlin. 1999. "American Federation of Labor and Congress of Industrial Organizations (AFL-CIO)." Annenberg Public Policy Center, University of Pennsylvania, http://appcpenn.org/issueads/profiles/aflcio.htm.

Strope, Leigh. 2002. "Steelworkers Call Bush Steel Decision First Step in Getting Workers Back on the Job." *Associated Press State and Local Wire,* March 5.

Swoboda, Frank. 1997. "Labor Plans Ads, Lobbying on Trade Pact." *Washington Post,* September 17, A6.

———. 2000. "Labor Targets 71 House Districts in 'Watershed Year.' " *Washington Post,* February 16, A14.

———. 2001. "Labor Offers Own Tax Plan." *Washington Post,* February 15, E16.

Swoboda , Frank, and Thomas B. Edsall. 1996. "AFL-CIO Endorses Clinton, Approves $35 Million Political Program." *Washington Post,* March 26, A6.

The Record. 1996. "GOP Claims AFL-CIO Is Illegally Targeting Martini." October 8, L2.

West, Darrell. 2000. "How Issue Ads Have Reshaped American Politics." In *Crowded Airwaves,* edited by James A. Thurber, Candice J. Nelson, and David A. Dulio, 149−169. Washington, DC: Brookings Institution.

White House. 2003. "President's Statement on Steel." Office of the Press Secretary press release, December 4. http://www.whitehouse.gov/news/releases/2003/12/20031204-5.html.

Wilhite, Allen. 1988. "Union PAC Contributions and Legislative Voting." *Journal of Labor Research* 9:79−90.

Wolfson, Bernard J. 1996. "Labor Declares Election Victory." *Boston Herald,* November 7, O40.

Yang, John E. 1997. "Trade Vote Reflects Variety of Economic, Political Efforts." *Washington Post,* November 10, A6.

12. Dolly Goes to Washington: Coalitions, Cloning, and Trust

Kevin W. Hula

Although human cloning has been discussed in the realm of science fiction for decades, the potential for the successful application of cloning technologies to human beings took a giant leap forward in 1997 when scientists in Scotland announced that they had successfully cloned an adult mammal. The announcement was destined to generate waves of intense political debate over the possible uses and abuses of the technology and give rise to an attempt to broker an intriguing coalition of traditional adversaries.[1]

Despite the adage that politics makes strange bedfellows, scholars have noted for over a decade that organized interests tend to work primarily with groups similar to them. This chapter examines coalition building efforts by organizations opposed to human cloning and embryonic stem cell research, and it reveals the effects that trust issues and reputation-related concerns have on these attempts to build sturdy alliances. Despite general agreement on an issue position, membership organizations that have defined themselves with their constituencies in ideological or expressive terms face high barriers to forging coalitions across traditional lines. Repeated cooperative interaction between groups (both inside and outside the public policy arena) and shared cultural assumptions simplify the coalition broker's ability to forge coalitions.

Cloning and Stem Cells: Technology Sets the Agenda

When Dolly the sheep was introduced to the world in 1997, she stirred up considerably more controversy than the average farm animal. Unlike lambs on other farms throughout Scotland and the rest of the world, Dolly was a clone. Scientists had been cloning DNA (deoxyribonucleic acid) and other biological material for years, but the cloning of an adult mammal that would actually lead to live birth and survival was purely the stuff of science fiction—until Dolly. Dolly not only survived birth, but also grew into a reasonably healthy adult.

Dolly was cloned from DNA taken from the udder of an adult sheep; the DNA was used to replace the nucleus of an unfertilized egg cell from a second sheep. The egg cell and a mammary gland cell with its DNA were fused with an electric current, cultured, and implanted into the uterus of a third sheep (Wilmut et al. 1997). Dolly was then, in essence, an identical twin of the female sheep that supplied the udder cell with her DNA, albeit a much younger "twin." Notably absent from the reproductive process was any contribution by a male sheep: the egg donor, the DNA donor, and the surrogate mother were all females. Cloning is, by definition, a strictly asexual form of reproduction.

Reactions were swift, if sharply divided. Some public voices expressed praise for the Scottish scientists who had accomplished the herculean task. Alongside the awe, however, came questions and concerns about the implications of the event. The cloning generated both excitement and fear, because it indicated that the cloning of human beings was not only technologically feasible, but perhaps imminent. Bioethicist Leon R. Kass, appointed in 2001 by President George W. Bush to chair the President's Council on Bioethics, testified before the National Bioethics Advisory Commission one month after Dolly's introduction, arguing that the repugnance many felt toward human cloning should be viewed as "the emotional bearer of deep wisdom, beyond reason's power fully to articulate it" (Kass 1997).

In the years since Dolly's arrival, scientists around the world have cloned other mammals, including pigs and monkeys, and in 2001 members of a scientific team in the United States announced their plan to clone a human being in a procedure leading to a live birth (Morell 1999; Cooper 2001, C01; Weiss 2001, A02). Aside from unsubstantiated claims by the Raelians (an organization promoting belief in extraterrestrial visitors) that a different team in their employ had achieved a live human birth from a cloned embryo, there is no evidence that this scientific breakthrough has actually taken place (Kurtz 2003).

Human cloning is only one of several controversial issues related to recent developments in biotechnology and genetic research. The isolation of human stem cells in 1998 led to another controversial new field of research. Stem cells are self-renewing, unspecialized cells that can develop into a wide range of specialized cells performing different functions throughout the body (National Institutes of Health 2001, i). As a human embryo develops from a fertilized egg (one cell), it divides repeatedly into stem cells, which then begin to take on the special characteristics and functions that differentiate, for example, a bone cell from a brain cell from a blood cell from a kidney cell. One set of stem cells might develop into an eye, while another set might develop into a pancreas. In this flexibility lies the potential of stem cells for therapeutic use in the future. For example, some believe that it may be possible for individuals suffering from debilitating conditions such as Parkinson's disease to experience a halt or even reversal in deterioration through the implantation of specialized cells.

Stem cells are found in adults as well as in embryos, and this fact has raised several ethical and scientific debates that have made their way into the political arena. Research on adult stem cells is currently more advanced than research on embryonic stem cells. As such, some observers argue that adult stem cells research is closer to providing actual therapies. A representative of Concerned Women for America (CWA) explained, "We're in support of adult stem cells, which is much more advanced and it's already providing treatment" (Wendy Wright, director of communication, CWA, interview by author, Washington, D.C., August 13, 2001). Others argue that embryonic stem cells are more flexible and capable of a wider range of specialization than adult stem cells and so may have greater therapeutic utility over the long run. An advocate for embryonic stem cell research wrote: "The prevailing view of expert scientific opinion is that it is far too early to know if adult stem cells have the same potential as embryonic stem cells. It is important to convey to the public the limitations and preliminary nature of much of the research on adult stem cells. It is likely to take years to discover whether adult stem cells will be effective in treating many diseases that may be treatable sooner with embryonic or fetal stem cells" (Good et al. 2001).

If the debates were limited to the question of short-term and long-term utility, they would undoubtedly be carried out between the covers of refereed journals. But another factor involved has brought stem cell research to the forefront of national debate: to harvest embryonic stem cells, scientists must destroy the embryo (a fertilized human egg). For many people who might benefit from the results of the research, this is a small price to pay. For many pro-lifers, this act is tantamount to intentionally taking one life in the hope of helping another.

Cloning and other new developments in biotechnology such as stem cell research raise fundamental questions about the appropriate role of technology in human society. Although scientists have produced incredible medical breakthroughs that have improved the lives of millions, many people are uncomfortable with some uses of these emerging technologies. Organizations representing institutions and individuals with conflicting views about the new biotechnologies have called on members of Congress and the executive branch to enact new laws, rules, and regulations to enable or curtail this research. And therein lies the fundamental political debate: Should government fund research into human cloning and related fields? Should it ban the research altogether? Or should it take a wait-and-see attitude, allowing research to proceed with private funding but not encouraging it?

Soon after his inauguration in January 2001, President Bush directed Secretary of Health and Human Services Tommy Thompson to review federal policy on stem cell funding, and several bills were introduced in the House and Senate in the spring of 2001 to either stop or regulate cloning. With the biotechnology issues front and center in the media and on the legislative agenda, organized interests moved into high gear in an effort to sway the public, mobilize the grass roots, and convince decision makers to adopt their positions on cloning and embryonic stem cell research. One of the key strategies employed by concerned organizations was the development of lobbying coalitions.

Coalition Basics

Leaders of organized interests often find it beneficial to work together as they pursue their policy goals. Why? The size and complexity of government, the number of legislators and executive branch officials in decision-making roles, and the number of competing voices in the public arena have made it progressively more difficult to pass legislation alone (Loomis 1986; Browne 1988).

What Is a Coalition?

These obstacles create incentives for groups to join coalitions. Coalitions are "purposive groups of organizations united behind a symbiotic set of legislative or regulatory goals" (Hula 1999, 22). Membership in a coalition allows organizations to gather information efficiently about developments in the public policy process and gives them an opportunity to have a voice in framing debates or shaping a compromise position on an issue (Berry 1977, 254–55; Salisbury 1990, 219; Hula 1995). Coalition membership also allows group leaders to combine their resources and divide the workload. As a Washington representative for an organization that lobbies on issues in higher education explained,

> Ultimately, I think coalition building is a response to the diffuse nature of how things are done now in the federal government and on the Hill. There are just too many places where too much is going on. You don't have the ability of targeting one or two places and saying, "This is all I need to do to watch out for my membership." And since you can't be everywhere at once, you rely on coalitions to help you gather information, share information, share ideas about what's going on, and try to figure out, "Well, what can we do about it?" or "How do we promote certain kinds of things?"

Despite the advantages provided by working in a coalition, coalitions do not arise by themselves; they are brokered (Loomis 1986). The role of the brokers is to identify organizations with symbiotic interests, to draw them together, and to forge a coalition through developing a mutually satisfactory exchange of incentives (Hula 1999, 22–38). It is quite possible that no two groups join a coalition for exactly the same reason. Some core members are attracted by the prospect of enhancing the likelihood of strategic legislative victory, but more peripheral members of the coalition may join for symbolic reasons such as self-promotion (Hula 1995, 239–258; 1999, 22–50). Although coalitions are a type of collective action, they do not necessarily pursue collective goods—that is, goods that, if produced, would be enjoyed by a broad set of political actors (even the general public) whether the individual actors expended resources to pursue the benefit through collective action or not. According to economist Mancur Olson, the pursuit of collective goods creates an incentive for rational actors to free-ride if they are part of a large group, unless selective benefits are available or coercion is present.

The goods pursued by coalitions are not, however, always collective goods. As an entity, a coalition seeks what are called here composite goods—that is, a set of goods composed of policy items that have been linked through the process of forging the coalition itself. Some of the benefits sought by individual coalition members, such as information or symbolic benefits, are strictly selective. Other benefits, such as the ability to participate in framing the debate, refining the terms, or piggybacking a pet project onto the coalition's position, are also outside the proper definition of a collective good.

Group leaders are more likely to accept a broker's deal and join a coalition when they have broad interest in an issue, when they perceive strong opposition to their goals, and when they believe that groups pivotal to their success will participate in the coalition (Hojnacki 1997). When a group leader's interest in an issue is narrow, or when the leader is primarily concerned with developing a policy niche or a stand-alone reputation, then he or she has an incentive to work alone (Berry 1977, 261; Browne 1990; Browne 1998).

Strange and Familiar Bedfellows

As noted frequently, politics does make strange bedfellows. Organizations that have clashed in the past often bury the hatchet temporarily to work on the same side in a legislative battle (Browne 1998, 146). The proverb of cooperation between enemies has been repeated so often that it may seem axiomatic, but in fact these events are more the exception in day-to-day lobbying than the rule. While politics may make strange bedfellows, groups go home to familiar partners more often than not. Indeed, large-scale surveys of interest group leaders indicate that most groups tend to find their allies within their own organizational category or issue community—for example, farm commodity groups tend to identify other farm commodity groups as their allies (Schlozman and Tierney 1986, 285–287; Salisbury et al. 1987, 1225). Repeated interaction between groups within an issue domain or long-term institutional links between organizations can foster communications and grease the wheels for forming coalitions. "Rounding up the usual suspects" to build a coalition is not only a popular strategy, but an effective one as well (Hula 1999, 75).

Although a wide range of organizations had voiced their opposition to human cloning even before Dolly was introduced in 1997, the expanded coverage of biotechnology in the media in the late 1990s led to broad public discussion about a wide range of loosely related issues. Human stem cells were isolated in 1998, and the media covered extensively their potential for use in medical treatments. Because much scientific research is funded through government grants, the ethical debates found a political target in September 1999 in a funding provision for stem cell research in the appropriation bill for the Departments of Health and Human Services and Education (Bettelheim 2000, 357). Organized interests moved promptly to develop coalitions to address these issues.

Forging a Coalition against Cloning

The remainder of this chapter examines a set of related attempts to form a coalition of strange bedfellows to oppose human cloning and funding for embryonic stem cell research. This examination will illustrate the role of trust in a situation in which similar policy goals may not be enough to pull a coalition together.

234 Kevin W. Hula

Core Members and the Usual Suspects

By early March 2001, a core group of people representing organizations such as the Family Research Council, the Southern Baptist Convention, the Wilberforce Forum (an arm of Prison Fellowship addressing cultural and public policy issues), and the Conference of Catholic Bishops had founded an ad hoc coalition to address the emerging biotechnology issues. The core group sought to expand the ad hoc coalition by integrating a handful of the "usual suspects"—in this case, representatives from organizations that generally would be categorized as conservative and pro-life such as the Christian Medical Association and the Catholic Medical Association.

Sometimes, though, rounding up the usual suspects is not enough, and coalition brokers need to expand a coalition or develop new alliances. But this can be tricky business, especially if there is no history of cooperation or interpersonal links between organizations to smooth the path (Hula 1999, 51–77). Brokers forge coalitions out of interests and incentives and temper them with trust. William Browne has identified four characteristics of the forging process that highlight the development of a symbiotic set of policy goals as well as the exchange of incentives between groups. According to Browne (1998, 151), brokering a coalition involves "targeting a single piece of legislation, encouraging each participating interest to find or incorporate something it wants in the proposed bill, asking all allies to stick to the agreement, and minimizing the problems of different organized interests with different voices." Although much of traditional coalition building involves establishing *common interests,* that term may be too exclusive. Expanding a coalition or developing new alliances involves identifying *compatible interests* and developing the incentives and trust to pursue these interests together.

With six or seven group representatives in the expanded core, the ad hoc coalition on biotechnology issues developed a two-prong strategy of integrating similar groups into the coalition directly, while quietly exploring the possibility of future alliances with select groups on the left. Meeting as needed throughout the spring and summer of 2001, generally weekly or biweekly, members of the coalition core shared information about their respective resources and tactics. Of the biotechnology issues on the table, the cloning issue was the clearest cut and most compelling for immediate action. One coalition member used the expression "very obvious" to explain their approach to the cloning issue. "What we had to do was clear, and that was, we notify and energize our base and communicate with the members of Congress with whom we have some clout." Another member explained: "Frankly, the momentum on the cloning debate is a momentum of its own. You don't have to do as much on that; [opposition to human cloning] seems clearer to me than stem cells for the most part."

Members of the coalition each brought their own individual resources to bear in support of a bill that would outlaw the cloning of human embryos. The bill was introduced in the House in April 2001 by Florida Republican Dave Weldon and in the Senate by Kansas Republican Sam Brownback. Coalition members contacted members of Congress and their staffs to urge hearings on the legislation, provided expert testimony on cloning and its implications, and turned to the White House for additional help in moving the bills. A key participant in the anticloning effort explained their efforts to stimulate action within the White House:

> We wanted to get the White House involved, and we had a number of private conversations with people in the White House, contacts of ours from things that we've done over the years, as well as a letter that we organized from a variety of the groups to the White House in June asking the President to take a public stand in favor of the Brownback-Weldon bill, which he did do shortly after the letter was received. The letter was signed by people ranging from Jim Dobson and Chuck Colson to Ken Connor, Bill Kristol, Bill Bennett . . . so it was kind of a wide-ranging conservative letter to the President.

Expanding Outside the Comfort Zone

Conservatives were not the only ones concerned about cloning. Green and environmental groups on the left had been discussing biotechnology for many years. Indeed, in Europe the Greens had long been at the forefront of the anticloning movement, and their concerns about genetic manipulation and genetically modified food had few parallels among conservatives in the United States. Small but intellectually sophisticated organizations on the left such as the Exploratory Initiative in the New Human Genetic Technologies (now called the Center for Genetics and Society) and the Council for Responsible Genetics had expertise and connections in the broader green and environmental communities. These characteristics made them attractive to the ad hoc coalition as potential allies.

Some people on the left looked to a European model of cooperation on biotechnology issues; in 2000 the European Parliament passed a resolution voicing concern about Great Britain's decision to allow therapeutic cloning (also called "cloning for biomedical research"). One American observer noted the significance of this action:

> [The resolution said] that's contrary to human dignity, and so the other countries of Europe are going to work against all forms of human cloning, even for research. And that was certainly supported by the pro-life members of the European Parliament, but the resolution was offered by the Green Party! That's the kind of thing that could possibly happen if people set aside their past distrust and decided that for their somewhat distinctive reasons they agreed on this move. But this is in the early stages, so you've got a new political realignment before our eyes that is in formation.

The idea of expanding the coalition into a pan-ideological alliance presented both an opportunity and a challenge for the young coalition. The *challenge* lay in the ideological gulf between the right and the left. Because many of the groups in the core held pro-life views and the environmental and green communities were largely pro-choice, this gulf was felt most acutely in the realm of abortion. The *opportunity* to move outside the usual suspects and broker a broader coalition that crossed the ideological spectrum was attractive because long-term success with only the usual suspects was unlikely. According to one Washington representative active in the coalition, crossing the ideological divide was a long-term strategic imperative: "If we don't come together, even with those who are pro-choice on the life issues but who are with us on stuff like this embryonic stem cell stuff and cloning, we'll lose, because the libertarians on the left and on the right will come together and say, 'technology is technology and we ought to just let it run its course.'"

The adage that politics makes strange bedfellows, while often true, does not address the difficulty coalition brokers face in trying to bridge the chasm between ideologically motivated groups that regularly disagree in the strongest terms on their most fundamental issues. Several participants in these conversations pointed to past hostilities as a central difficulty in connecting across the pro-life/pro-choice divide: "The rhetoric has been so strong, and frankly because we believe the stakes are high. But the rhetoric has been so strong on both sides, I think there's a sense that we want to be careful that neither one of us are co-opted, that the partnership is genuine and there's parity, without having to compromise on our position." At its heart, building a coalition beyond the usual suspects is an exercise in building trust.

Trust

Sociologist Pietr Sztompka defines trust as "a bet about the future contingent actions of others" (Sztompka 1999, 25). This conception of trust has two related components: first, holding a set of beliefs about the actions others will take, and second, acting on those beliefs in a manner akin to placing a bet. As group leaders evaluate whether to join a coalition or pursue their interests alone, they evaluate each other's trustworthiness. As they evaluate both the professional reputation of their potential allies and the potential ramifications of working with them, they themselves are evaluated. An education lobbyist ticked off a checklist of typical concerns: "For us, when we think about coalitions, we ask, 'Is it to our political advantage to be in with these groups? Do they have more clout? Can they help us? Is it going to be good for us to get in bed with them? What can they bring to the table?'" These questions are crucial, because a reputation is a form of political capital that affects one's ability to participate in coalitions. Another education lobbyist concurred: "I think that whether the coalitions are easy to form depends upon what kind of a person you are as a member, as a coalition member. What is your reputation? How viable are you? Are you somebody one wants to be in a coalition with or not?"

Bases for Trust

Sztompka (1999, 71–81) identifies three bases on which people assess the trustworthiness of others: *reputation, performance,* and *appearance.* It is easier for interest group leaders to observe and evaluate these attributes when they have worked together in the past or when they are in a position to observe each other's activities. "Closeness, intimacy, [and] familiarity open access to relevant information, and also diminish the chances of manipulation and deceit" (Sztompka 1999, 81). Experience allows lobbyists to evaluate a potential ally's trustworthiness. More than that, though, repeated interaction can actually create incentives for future cooperation by enhancing one's reputation for trustworthiness. "The longer one spends building a reputation, the less likely one is to risk it by taking one quick gain. Reputation builds to greater and greater levels as one consistently forgoes greater opportunities for rewards from cheating. As a consequence, each increase in reputation also creates greater opportunity costs for shirking, as the future value of one's reputation grows. The relationship is self-reinforcing in this sense" (Ensminger 2001, 199). Conversely, parties that rarely interact have fewer incentives to do so honestly. As Adam Smith (1997, 17) pointed out in 1766, "Where people seldom deal with one another, we find that they are somewhat disposed to cheat, because they can gain more by a smart trick than they can lose by the injury which it does their character."

Violations of trust in a coalition do not go unnoticed. One longtime Washington representative related her frustration with leaders of a coalition (not related to cloning) that she was ready to exit: "It's [a case of] one association being viewed as trying to pull the wool over the eyes of the other associations. That's not quite the right phrasing. Ultimately it's gonna stand for the same thing: pull a fast one on the rest of us. . . . In this particular case, they have enabled their [written] agenda to become the [de facto] agenda of the broader group even though it is truly not the agenda of the broader group. But what they have also done is they've put everybody else on notice that they're not to be trusted."

Levels of Trust

Interpersonal trust is crucial in coalition building, because coalitions are not built out of thousands of group members marching lockstep, arm in arm. Rather, coalitions are built out of groups' officers, staff members, lobbyists, or executives. Because groups are not monolithic entities, evaluation of trust in coalition building can occur at three levels. The first level of trust, discussed earlier, is between the actual coalition participants, the organizational leaders and professional staff. When an organization has no members or traditional allies, or when these members and traditional allies are unaware of coalition activities, this level is, for all practical purposes, the only one at which trust is evaluated. A second level of trust is associated with "embedded interactions" (Raub and Weesie 1990). To the degree that an organization's members or traditional allies are aware of the organization's participation in a coalition, those individuals can make their own evaluation of the trustworthiness of the organization's coalition partners. This second-level evaluation gives rise, in turn, to a third evaluation, in which group members or allies potentially modify their views about their own group's leadership because of the coalitions those leaders have joined. Some groups become quite concerned that a coalition partner's bad reputation could rub off on them, although this attitude is reportedly less prevalent among public interest group leaders than among business groups (Hall 1969; Berry 1977).

Thus it is possible for two Washington representatives to have a mutual trust for each other, but for cooperation between the groups to be awkward (if not impossible) because the *members or traditional allies* of those two organizations are suspicious of each other or of their own leaders. The opinions of leaders and group members may differ significantly if leaders have different information or have devoted more thought to an issue (Govier 1997, 206).

Organizational focus and attention to information determine when the second- and third-level evaluations of trust are relevant, and, conversely, when interest group leaders have a free hand in pursuing coalition partnerships with nontraditional allies. Of these, organizational focus is the more easily identified.

Organizational Focus. Some groups pursue primarily ideological or social cause–driven goals related to a commitment to principles. These groups are often called "expressive" or "purposive" groups because they attract members by providing an opportunity for people to express their heart-felt convictions or to participate in a political quest to achieve a noble purpose. Other organizations pursue more materialistic goals, such as promoting their members' monetary self-interest. Robert H. Salisbury has suggested that many of the expressive citizens groups lobbying in Washington are actually not good candidates for membership in coalitions in which compromise would be required. In contrast to the pragmatism of more self-interested organizations, many expressive groups display an "emotional intensity and resistance to compromise" that impedes their ability to compromise and broker agreements (Salisbury 1990, 210).

Statistical evidence supports this claim. Organizational representatives from purposive groups are much more likely to display consistency (or even constraint) in their issue positions than leaders of economically self-interested groups, who are uniformly more flexible in addressing secondary issues (Jenkins-Smith, St. Clair, and Woods 1991). This does not mean that pragmatic groups are more likely to form coalitions than expressive (or purposive) groups; groups with members drawn by expressive or purposive membership benefits are, in fact, more likely than occupational or corporate interests to join coalitions (Hojnacki 1997). The real issue is whether these expressive groups are likely to join a coalition with their traditional enemies.

Even if group leaders generally agree on an issue position, membership groups that have organizational identities defined in ideological or expressive terms face high barriers to forging coalitions with traditional adversaries. Members of an economically self-interested organization (for example, the stockholders of a corporation) might see eye to eye with their lobbyist's decision to ally with an economic competitor if it would help their own organization's bottom line. From their perspective, a coalition is a strategic alliance, joint venture, or temporary cooperation with a competitor (Child and Faulkner 1998; Faulkner and de Rond 2000). One implication of Salisbury's argument, however, is that the leaders of expressive groups would find such a decision to cooperate much more difficult to sell to group members. Ideologically motivated members are more likely to make their own evaluation of the potential ally, and a negative evaluation of the coalition partner may raise questions in their minds about the judgment of their own lobbyist or officer. In these terms, the same coalition may appear to members of expressive groups as collaboration with the enemy.

Information. Just how a group's members or traditional allies learn about its coalition activities is a separate question. Generally, members rely on group leaders to be their primary source of information about their group's activities. Robert Michels (1962) takes this tendency to the logical extreme, arguing in 1915 that an organization's leaders will impute their own agenda to the organization itself and will evolve into the sole source of information about the organization's activities. As members become entirely dependent on the staff for information, the staff members become entrenched and able to pursue their own goals with relative impunity.

This asymmetry of information between members and staff creates a principal–agent problem. This problem arises when an individual or set of individuals (the principal) entrusts a responsibility to another individual or set of individuals (the agent), often based on the agent's expertise (Ross 1973). The principal is then dependent on the agent for information about the agent's activities. The old adage "when the cat's away, the mice will play" indicates the problem created by such a situation. Because officers at corporate headquarters, members of a trade association, or individual members of an interest group are dependent on the government relations staff for information on how their dues are being spent in Washington, there is at least the potential for withholding information or even outright malfeasance.

One traditional means of overcoming the problems associated with agency is to monitor the activities of the agent. If monitoring reveals misbehavior by the government relations staff in a corporate setting, the corporation might replace the vice president for government affairs. In an organizational setting, members could withhold their dues or transfer their membership to another organization (Hirschman 1970). Although careful monitoring of agents is often difficult, and members of most associations probably do not think in those terms or with those suspicions, traditional organizational allies may be in a better position to monitor the behavior of a group. However, even if both the organization and its ally are based in Washington, both operate in the same policy subsystem, and both interact frequently, there are always opportunities to keep secrets.

When the relevant issues have high visibility in the media, an organization's members and its allies will find it easier to get supplemental information about their organization's activities if they are attentive. News coverage lowers the costs of monitoring. A news story describing a coalition's lobbying strategy on a bill may include details about which groups are going to the legislative hoedown together, and the bedfellows are then out of the closet.

For most coalitions composed of traditional allies, that kind of news coverage is not a problem — it is a success. The benefits of coalition strategies are often dependent on creating the impression of broad support behind a particular legislative agenda. But in the early stages of brokering a coalition between traditional adversaries, the relationships are much more sensitive, the views of the membership are much less predictable, and the compatibility of the interests are much more fragile. Untimely information presented to an unprepared membership can raise the unwelcome evaluations that group leaders prefer to avoid, particularly in expressive groups.

Brokers as Bridge Builders

Coalition brokers are in the business of building bridges (Loomis 1986). The deeper the divide and the further apart the parties, the more difficult it is to bridge the gap. Not everyone can be a bridge builder, because the tasks of successfully building bridges and brokering coalitions require the implicit trust of all the parties concerned. Speaking solely for his own organization, one conservative director of legislative affairs concluded, "[We] can reach across organizational boundaries and ideological lines and so forth on some issues, but on other issues we're just not in a position to do that, given the profile that we have and so forth. Anybody that we'd try to reach out towards would not trust us."

Within the ad hoc coalition against human cloning and embryonic stem cell research, four people emerged as the principal bridge builders to groups across the ideological divide: Nigel Cameron and Mariam Bell of the Wilberforce Forum, Richard Doerflinger of the Catholic Conference, and Mary Cannon of the Bioethics Project. Many of the group representatives with whom they spoke individually agreed about the dangers posed by the unbridled development of the new biotechnologies, particularly those related to reproductive cloning (cloning to produce children) and germ line engineering. But policy agreement is only a necessary prerequisite for membership in a coalition, not a sufficient reason to join.

The Pursuit of Trustworthiness

The challenge faced by the coalition bridge builders has been summed up well by a lobbyist who is not involved in biotechnology issues or this coalition effort, but who has a long history of working with environmental groups: "Environmental groups are very leery of just hopping into bed or joining with someone who they might regret down the road. There's a longer term focus. It's like,

'Am I going to regret having done this a year from now, two years from now, three years from now?' There's always a longer term 'what's this going to do to my reputation?' type of focus." Formed around principles in pursuit of collective goods, environmental groups are archetypical of the expressive groups discussed earlier, and they demonstrate the constraints on compromise faced by this kind of organization. Even when there is common ground, concerns about a group's long-term reputation raise complicated trust issues. This was a challenge for the bridge builders in the biotechnology coalition.

Distrust greatly hampers efforts to negotiate a compromise (Govier 1997, 200). On the issue of cloning, the difficulty of working together was acknowledged on both sides of the ideological chasm. As one key bridge builder lamented, "It's a little difficult to find a way to have an official coalition with . . . people on the left signing on with groups that they have anathema for in some ways on other issues."

Reputation, Appearance, and Performance

Reputation, appearance, and performance—the three bases identified by Sztompka (1999, 71–81) on which individuals can assess the trustworthiness of others—each played a role in the attempts to broker a pan-ideological coalition on biotechnology. Reputation is based on past performance or, when past performance is unknown, on credentials (Sztompka 1999, 72). As noted earlier, the longtime pro-life stance held by the core groups in the coalition was a stumbling block for the left. However, organizational and individual reputation is tempered by current appearance and performance.

Appearance is the least rigorous tool for evaluating trustworthiness, because it is based on demeanor and subjective assessments of whether one seems suspicious or credible (Sztompka 1999, 79–80). Although the organizations in the ad hoc coalition had reputations for supporting a pro-life position, the core members recognized that it was critical not to appear to be a *strictly* pro-life coalition. Indeed, the coalition did not even take a name, in part because of the fear of being pigeonholed or of unintentionally creating additional barriers to broader participation in a pan-ideological alliance. According to an early participant in the ad hoc coalition,

> One of the things we have tried to do in the early stages of this is to make sure that we are not just seen as strictly a pro-life coalition, because if we are, we do not have hope of reaching out across those barriers to those who are not pro-life to try to have this left-right kind of connection. So the core group was a group that was comfortable with the fact that we were willing to work with those who were adamantly pro-choice if they agreed with us on the core principles we were talking about here. So that core group, for instance, did not include the groups that were strictly right-to-life kind of groups. We very deliberately did not include them, did not

include those known to be [single-issue] life groups. And that was a delib-
erate choice; we were trying to have a core group that had a very high comfort level with reaching across the barrier, and that did not in any way see
that as a selling out in a sense, but that saw that as moving towards a goal.

For this reason, some of the individuals who emerged as bridge builders
from the coalition were not typical of the broader circle of usual suspects.
Nigel Cameron, for example, had served as executive director of the Center for
Bioethics and Human Dignity before becoming dean of the Wilberforce
Forum. He had already published widely in the field of bioethics and was not
a new name in commentary on biotechnology issues. Another key participant
pointed out a helpful characteristic of bridge builder Mary Cannon of the
Bioethics Project: "Some [on the left] feel more comfortable working with a
group . . . that has a little bit more of an intellectual approach and is not
already affiliated with one religious faith or an agenda that goes beyond the
bioethics realm."

The third basis for evaluating trustworthiness is performance—that is,
how one behaves in the present. The past may be "bracketed," so that the eval-
uator looks at "actual deeds, present conduct, and currently obtained results"
(Sztompka 1999, 77). How organizational leaders and coalition brokers handle
themselves in their current negotiations is important to potential allies. Sharing
information with potential allies, focusing on groups' common ground and compatible ground rather than differences, and respecting requests for confidentiality with information from potential allies all contribute to enhanced evaluations
of trustworthiness.

Second-Level Trust Issues

The members and potential allies of the ad hoc coalition were generally
expressive groups, which complicated the coalition building process just as Salisbury (1990, 210) predicted. A participant noted, "The groups that have been
most interested in this issue over time [are not like] labor getting together with
National Federation of Independent Business to work on some regulation.
They're much more emotional. . . . There are just more fundamental questions
that are being focused on by these groups, and so . . . I do think that makes it
more difficult." Expressive groups, as noted earlier in this chapter, face particular
challenges in coalition building because of the constraints on the leadership in
developing compromise positions.

Even though many of the bridge builders were able to develop loose relationships with organizational leaders on the left, moving beyond the common
ground of abstract disapproval of cloning "designer babies" to joining together
in a formal coalition faced high hurdles. Coalition brokers need to build personal trust between group leaders, and they may need to address other relationships as well. Even though a potential ally may trust the broker, members of the

potential ally's organization may not. Similarly, the potential ally's traditional coalition partners might distrust the broker. In either of these cases, distrust for the broker by other parties may lead to distrust of the potential ally within their traditional circles. Consorting with perceived enemies reflects badly on third-party evaluations of the potential ally's appearance, performance, and (if it develops into a pattern) long-term reputation. According to one of the bridge builders, "The groups on the left that realize the need for making common cause are concerned about groups in their traditional coalition who would be offended by that, about making common cause with the right. And they're very ginger about that. And they don't want to go ahead of their own [members] making holy alliances with the religious right. . . . [T]hat's a major reason right now for the fact you don't already have such coalitions in existence." These fears are not merely theoretical. One coalition participant lamented, "People on the left who have been supportive of the [Weldon] bill, supporting of the cloning ban, have encountered some people giving them a hard time about getting involved with these right-to-lifers."

Such responses brought home the need for the groups on the left to maintain a public face consistent with their organizational identity—that is, the "central, distinctive and enduring aspects" of their groups (Albert and Whetten 1985, 292). Organizational identity is significant not only for consistency when political organizations stake out their turf in the political arena with policymakers, but for recruiting and maintaining members as well: "Organizational identity provides a cognitive and emotional foundation on which organizational members build attachments and with which they create meaningful relationships with their organization" (Hatch and Schultz 2000, 16). Although coalitions require common or compatible ground, one coalition participant argued, "Among our constituencies, we will have to be able to maintain our traditional rhetoric on the matters that concern us, and yet, on these targeted, nuanced, and discrete issues, we're going to have to come up with common language that we can use, so that we speak univocally."

Pulling Prospects toward Participation

Solomon and Flores (2001, 47) point out eloquently that "building trust requires talking and thinking about trust." To move the discussion among coalition members, bridge builders, and some of the green and environmental groups to a new level, during the summer of 2001 the bridge builders quietly took steps to bring together many of the actors involved for a face-to-face meeting. One participant indicated that the guest list was limited, but it included "not only various academics and policy strategists on the traditional pro-life side, but also a group that represents the traditionally pro-choice, green, environmentalist side, and maybe some in between those two poles." The goal was to get a broad circle of potential allies with common and compatible interests around the table for an explicit discussion of future collaboration. According to another coalition member, the questions that needed to be addressed and the interests involved were generally straightforward:

> Where in terms of principle are we? Where are we going to have to agree to disagree? But what are our mutual enemies in a sense? We feel, the enemy of my enemy is my friend. And we're really in a whole new area. . . . We are hopeful that this is the beginning of a whole new coalition of people who do have a mutual enemy, and it is that technology is not God, and it seems like there are those who really believe that. There are those who believe that if it *can* be done, it *should* be done. And we say . . . , "We should control technology. It should not control us."

Bringing traditionally antagonistic group leaders together was in itself something of a coup, and organizers were cautiously optimistic about what could emerge. One predicted at the time, "My suspicion is that there will be very targeted coalitions, that we will kind of rally around various but very discrete topics, and for the first time in a long time, people who have only met one another in battle so to speak will not only converse but will sort of gel around these issues that we think we have common cause in, even though our common cause might be for different reasons."

Holding such a meeting, though, was not without risk. A premature meeting that devolved into disagreement over past disputes could damage trust and poison the atmosphere by resurrecting negative reputations among the circle of participants. Such an outcome could foster suspicions that the current appearance and performance of brokers was disingenuous. Beyond the immediate effects of a failed meeting within the circle of participants, reports of its failure could give new vitality to opposing coalitions and tactical guidance on how to keep the potential alliance from gelling in the future. Furthermore, misinformation about the goals or the results of the meeting could filter out to the participating groups' members and traditional allies and create second-level trust issues. Members who were unaware of the actions group leaders were taking on their behalf could be offended, particularly if they disapproved of the potential coalition partners.

One way to contain second-level trust issues in the short term is to exploit the principal–agent problem by limiting the flow of information or diverting attention away from the coalition partners. The parallel challenges of developing trust between the groups involved and postponing second-level trust issues are illustrated by the meeting's venue and the level of secrecy surrounding it. Rather than meeting in a Washington office, participants gathered at a secret location away from the battles of the past. The elaborate conditions for the meeting were reminiscent of summits between the superpowers during the cold war. Prior to the meeting, one person involved in its planning explained the thinking that went into it: "We wanted to pick a neutral site. We didn't want to be in the Beltway; we didn't want it to have [the pressure] of the Potomac on it. So it's going to be in a neutral site. Actually, semi-neutral. It will be hosted by someone who represents the more left-leaning side of the discussion. It will be hosted by them, but jointly chaired . . . by a left and right person if I can use those terms." The meeting took place at the end of August 2001, and afterward participants and organizers applied the same secrecy that surrounded the planning of the meeting to the results. One simply said, "I was involved in trying to pull it together, and I think it was successful, you know, I mean it's going to take a lot of these things over a period of time for people to become comfortable with one another and for people to refine the issues that we want to work on together, what our priorities are."

In 2004 a participant in the bridge building efforts looked back with evident disappointment at the insurmountable challenges to formalizing a coalition between the left and the right on biotechnology issues.

> There was some substance, but I don't think it's born fruit to the degree that we'd hoped it would. It did have a positive impact in some ways, but it was really limited. We didn't really have an opportunity to break through with the bigger groups on the left with the broadest constituencies. . . . We hoped that it might open a door to a broader coalition, but the groups we worked with were never quite able to bring along the others. It was never a formal coalition, it was all ad hoc. But as I say, it has born some fruit and continues to bear some fruit. There's still a biotech listserv with people on the left and the right who stay in touch.

Perhaps the best advice for the bridge builders as they try to foster trust and broker stronger relationships between current and prospective coalition members was given by Solomon and Flores (2001, 87): "Understanding trust means understanding what must be and what must not be said, avoiding those cataclysmic comments that provoke fear and suspicion. It consists of assurances, in deed as well as in word, and both the continual making and keeping of promises (trustworthiness) and the encouragement of others to make and keep their promises (trust)."

The Ongoing Challenge of Biotechnology

On July 31, 2001, the House of Representatives passed a bill by a vote of 251–176 that would have outlawed the creation of cloned human embryos (Weiss and Eilperin 2001). Although the vote was initially seen as a broad victory for opponents of cloning, the Senate was slow to take action on the bill. After the House vote, the ad hoc coalition turned its attention to lobbying the Bush White House to oppose federal funding for embryonic stem cell research. President Bush announced a compromise position on August 9 that authorized funding for research on sixty stem cell lines that the government had already identified, but banned expenditure on stem cells derived from newly destroyed embryos.

The terrorist attacks on the United States on September 11, 2001, radically shifted the president's attention and Congress's agenda away from biotechnology to national security. Even had this not been the case, it is unclear whether the anticloning bill would have been brought up for a vote in the Senate—a similar bill had been killed there in 1998. But despite the abrupt shift in focus, the story of coalition building on cloning, stem cell research, and other biotechnology-related issues is just beginning. In July 2002, the President's Council on Bioethics proposed "a congressionally enacted ban on all attempts at cloning-to-produce-children and a four-year national moratorium (a temporary ban) on human cloning-for-biomedical-research" (President's Council on Bioethics 2002). In 2003 the House passed another bill to ban human cloning. The 2003 legislation, like the 2001 bill, stalled in the Senate (Fagan 2004, A07).

In the meantime, the venue for debates over embryonic stem cell research and cloning for biomedical research is beginning to shift to the states. In 2004 New Jersey became the tenth state to pass a law pertaining to human cloning. Despite a late flurry of lobbying by the anticloning interests, the New Jersey legislation promotes embryonic stem cell research and explicitly permits the cloning of human cells. The legislation bans the cloning of a "human being," but intriguingly defines "human being" for the purposes of the ban as a clone that progresses "through the egg, embryo, fetal, and newborn stages into a human individual," leading some to ask how far short of the newborn stage clones may legally be cultivated in New Jersey (Fagan 2004, A07). One thing is certain: as long as these issues are debated on ethical, moral, and scientific grounds, coalition brokers and bridge builders will be looking for bedfellows.

Notes

1. This author thanks the Washington representatives, group leaders and staff members, and other involved parties who agreed to participate in interviews about the coalition building efforts discussed in this chapter. Because of the sensitivity of the ongoing political debate and these coalition building efforts, the quotations taken from interviews are not attributed. Respondents identified as education lobbyists in the chapter were interviewed during research for another project and are not involved in the coalition discussed here. I am grateful for their contribution to my understanding of coalitions as well.

References

Albert, S., and D. A. Whetten. 1985. "Organizational Identity." In *Research in Organizational Behavior*, vol. 7, edited by L. L. Cummings and M. M. Staw. Greenwich, CT: JAI Press.

Berry, Jeffrey M. 1977. *Lobbying for the People: The Political Behavior of Public Interest Groups.* Princeton, NJ: Princeton University Press.

Bettelheim, Adriel. 2000. "Senate Argues Promise and Peril of Human Stem Cell Research." *CQ Weekly.* February 19.

Browne, William P. 1988. *Private Interests, Public Policy, and American Agriculture.* Lawrence: University Press of Kansas.

———. 1990. "Organized Interests and Their Issue Niches: A Search for Pluralism in a Policy Domain." *Journal of Politics* 52:477–509.

———. 1998. *Groups, Interests, and U.S. Public Policy.* Washington, DC: Georgetown University Press.

Child, John, and David Faulkner, eds. 1998. *Strategies of Cooperation: Managing Alliances, Networks, and Joint Ventures.* Oxford: Oxford University Press.

Cooper, Glenda. 2001. "The Double Vision of 'Dr. Miracle.' " *Washington Post,* August 8.

Ensminger, Jean. 2001. "Reputations, Trust, and the Principal Agent Problem." In *Trust in Society,* edited by Karen S. Cook. Russell Sage Foundation Series on Trust, vol. 2. New York: Russell Sage Foundation.

Fagan, Amy. 2004. "Critics Say N.J. Law Encourages Cloning: Supporters Dismiss 'Scare Tactic.' " *Washington Times,* January 7.

Faulkner, David O., and Mark de Rond, eds. 2000. *Cooperative Strategy: Economic, Business, and Organizational Interests.* Oxford: Oxford University Press.

Good, Mary L., Chair, American Academy for the Advancement of Science Board of Directors, et al. 2001. Letter to President George W. Bush, March 6. Coalition for the Advancement of Medical Research, http://www.stemcellfunding.org/fastaction/letters.asp?id=13.

Govier, Trudy. 1997. *Social Trust and Human Communities.* Montreal: McGill-Queen's University Press.

Hall, Donald. 1969. *Cooperative Lobbying—The Power of Pressure.* Tucson: University of Arizona Press.

Hatch, Mary Jo, and Majken Schultz. 2000. "Scaling the Tower of Babel: Relational Differences between Identity, Image and Culture in Organizations." In *The Expressive Organization: Linking Identity, Reputation, and the Corporate Brand,* edited by Majken Schultz, Mary Jo Hatch, and Mogens Holten Larsen. Oxford: Oxford University Press.

Hirschman, Albert O. 1970. *Exit, Voice, and Loyalty: Responses to Decline in Firms, Organizations, and States.* Cambridge, MA: Harvard University Press.

Hojnacki, Marie. 1997. "Interest Groups' Decisions to Join Alliances or Work Alone." *American Journal of Political Science* 41:61–87.

Hula, Kevin W. 1995. "Rounding up the Usual Suspects: Forging Interest Group Coalitions in Washington." In *Interest Group Politics,* 4th ed., edited by Allan J. Cigler and Burdett A. Loomis. Washington, DC: CQ Press.

———. 1999. *Lobbying Together: Interest Group Coalitions in Legislative Politics.* Washington, DC: Georgetown University Press.

Jenkins-Smith, Hank C., Gilbert K. St. Clair, and Brian Woods. 1991. "Explaining Change in Policy Subsystems: Analysis of Coalition Stability and Defection over Time." *American Journal of Political Science* 35:851–880.

Kass, Leon R. 1997. Testimony before the National Bioethics Advisory Commission, Washington, DC, March 14. http://bioethics.gov/transcripts.

Kurtz, Howard. 2003. "Clonaid, Generating at Least One Kind of Copy." *Washington Post,* January 6.

Loomis, Burdett A. 1986. "Coalitions of Interests: Building Bridges in the Balkanized State." In *Interest Group Politics,* 2d ed., edited by Allan J. Cigler and Burdett A. Loomis. Washington, DC: CQ Press.

Michels, Robert. [1915] 1962. *Political Parties,* translated by Eden and Cedar Paul, with an introduction by Seymour Martin Lipset. New York: Free Press.

Morell, Virginia. 1999. "Cloning Offers New Hope for the Childless." In *Cloning: For and Against,* edited by M. L. Rantala and Arthur J. Milgram. Chicago: Open Court.

National Institutes of Health. 2001. *Stem Cells: Scientific Progress and Future Research Directions.* Washington, DC: National Institutes of Health.

President's Council on Bioethics. 2002. *Human Cloning and Human Dignity: An Ethical Inquiry.* Washington, DC: President's Council on Bioethics.

Raub, Werner, and Jeroen Weesie. 1990. "Reputation and Efficiency in Social Interactions: An Example of Network Effects." *American Journal of Sociology* 96:626–654.

Ross, Stephen A. 1973. "The Economic Theory of Agency: The Principal's Problem." *American Economic Review* 63 (May): 134–139.

Salisbury, Robert H. 1990. "The Paradox of Interest Groups in Washington—More Groups, Less Clout." In *The New American Political System*, 2d ed., edited by Anthony King. Washington, DC: American Enterprise Institute.

Salisbury, Robert H., John P. Heinz, Edward O. Laumann, and Robert L. Nelson. 1987. "Who Works with Whom? Interest Group Alliances and Opposition." *American Political Science Review* 81:1217–1234.

Schlozman, Kay Lehman, and John T. Tierney. 1986. *Organized Interests and American Democracy.* New York: Harper and Row.

Smith, Adam. [1766] 1997. "Lecture on the Influence of Commerce on Manners." In *Reputation: Studies in the Voluntary Elicitation of Good Conduct*, edited by Daniel B. Klein. Ann Arbor: University of Michigan Press.

Solomon, Robert C., and Fernando Flores. 2001. *Building Trust in Business, Politics, Relationships, and Life.* Oxford: Oxford University Press.

Sztompka, Pietr. 1999. *Trust: A Sociological Theory.* Cambridge, UK: Cambridge University Press.

Weiss, Rick. 2001. "Scientists Declare Progress on Human Cloning," *Washington Post*, August 8.

Weiss, Rick, and Juliet Eilperin. 2001. "House Votes Broad Ban on Cloning." *Washington Post*, August 1.

Wilmut, I., A. E. Schnieke, J. McWhir, A. J. Kind, and K. H. S. Campbell. 1997. "Viable Offspring Derived from Fetal and Adult Mammalian Cells." *Nature* 385 (February): 810–813.

Part III
The Executive Connection

13. Lobbying the Executive Branch:
Outside-In and Inside-Out

Kathryn Dunn Tenpas

It is vain to say that enlightened statesmen will be able to adjust these clashing interests, and render them all subservient to the public good. Enlightened statesmen will not always be at the helm.

—*James Madison, Federalist No. 10*

The prescient words of James Madison endure. Enlightened or not, elected officials simply cannot channel the will of powerful interest groups to respond to the "public good." By definition, interest group leaders are self-interested actors, many of whom have become pivotal players in the national policymaking arena. While presidents and members of Congress come and go, interest group leaders remain, often bolstering their strength by hiring former legislative and executive branch officials to fine-tune their efforts to influence the policy process.

The unitary power of the executive, combined with a national election that selects the president, creates a perception that the executive branch of government is the representative of the *nation's* interest, not special interests, but the pluralistic nature of American politics negates any possibility that presidential policies will have beneficial consequences for all citizens. Presidential policymaking is bound to favor some interests over others. Recognizing this reality, interest groups are eager to influence the process where possible, whether during the early stages of drafting legislation or during the implementation phase.

Although interest group participation is certainly a legitimate component of representative democracy, the degree of influence exerted by certain groups raises suspicions about the ties between public officials and interest group leaders. Since President George W. Bush's inauguration in January 2001, the media has frequently reported on the administration's strong ties to various interest groups. They have pointed to the role of the energy industries in Vice President Richard B. Cheney's energy task force, the fall of energy giant Enron and the personal relationship of Enron executive Kenneth Lay to President Bush, the reform of

Medicare and the perceived benefits for the pharmaceutical industry, and the awarding of contracts in postwar Iraq to the Halliburton Corporation (Vice President Cheney's previous employer). As these examples reveal, the role of interest groups in policymaking spans the issue spectrum—foreign affairs, domestic affairs, fiscal policy, and even the relatively recent addition of homeland security. The sky is the limit, and as the government enlarges its sphere of influence, interest groups respond in kind, seeking to enhance their role in the policy process.

The history of presidential involvement with powerful interests is a sordid one. In 1908 Arthur Bentley wrote that interest groups only sought the president's assistance "when they found other pathways blocked" (quoted in Pika 1987, 648), but much has changed since then. Interest groups now have multiple incentives and opportunities to influence the executive: "The nationalization of American industry, the necessity of curbing monopolistic practices resulting from this development, the conservation movement of the first Roosevelt, the rise and consolidation of the labor movement, the altered outlook on the proper scope of governmental function that the Great Depression produced, and finally two great wars and their aftermath have all conspired to thrust in the foreground of our constitutional system the dual role of the president as catalyst of public opinion and as legislative leader" (Corwin 1957, 220).

Beginning with Theodore Roosevelt, later adopted by Woodrow Wilson, and expressed boldly by Franklin Delano Roosevelt, the president's role in legislative affairs has grown more influential. The deeper involvement of the White House in the legislative drafting stage and the president's power to set the legislative agenda have created fertile territory for special interests seeking to influence the process.

The primary responsibility of the executive branch—to enforce the law—is also subject to the influence of special interests. As most students of American government eventually realize, enforcing a law is all the more complicated when interpreting the vaguely worded statutes emanating from Congress. One of the side effects of a system prone to compromise is a murky zone of implementation in which Congress gives bureaucrats broad discretion to interpret the laws. This leeway is no secret; interest groups have long understood the implications of Congress leaving such a task in the hands of presumably dispassionate government employees. Therefore, whether they win or lose in the legislative process, special interests seek to influence the next step in the political process—implementation—with the hope of maximizing their gains or minimizing their potential losses. These days, then, interest groups do not hesitate to lobby the executive, whether through the indirect means of campaign contributions or by more directly seeking a meeting with White House and administration staff members.

The relationship between interest groups and the executive branch can be viewed from many perspectives. The three chapters in this part describe "outside-in" studies of how interest groups influence the executive branch. Images of iron triangles, policy networks, and subgovernments come to mind as political scientists identify which groups exercise the most influence, evaluate their tactics, and attempt to determine their impact.[1]

It is equally important to recognize, however, that the presidency actively seeks support from pivotal interest groups. This *reverse lobbying*, a term coined by scholar Ronald G. Shaiko, requires substantial time and effort on behalf of the administration (Shaiko 1998).[2] During the latter half of the twentieth century, the White House not only expanded its efforts, but also established key White House offices dedicated to working with such groups. Whereas the chapters in this part provide important insights from the "outside-in" approach to lobbying, this introductory chapter draws attention to the "inside-out" approach by identifying those components of the White House Office that tend to special interests. The final section of this chapter looks at the effectiveness of these efforts by briefly examining the role of special interests in the legislative battle over President George W. Bush's faith-based initiative. This case study illustrates the limitations of "inside-out" lobbying.

Institutionalized Outreach

To gain a sense of the magnitude of the presidential role in lobbying, one need look no further than the expansion of the White House Office over the past thirty-five years. The addition of a series of office units and staff titles reveals the attention lavished on organized interests. These entities include the Office of Public Liaison, Office of Intergovernmental Affairs, Office of Legislative Affairs, Office of Political Affairs, and various constituency-based units.[3] Although some offices have a mission broader than outreach, each is responsible for fostering relations with key interest groups in an effort to gain support for the president's programs and proposals.

Office of Public Liaison

Of these many entities, the Office of Public Liaison is the one that most clearly reflects the importance of organized interests in presidential policymaking. Even though this office was not formally established until the Gerald R. Ford administration, similar efforts occurred in the FDR and Harry S. Truman administrations, suggesting that recognition of outside interests may predate the formal creation of a White House office (Pika 1987). The function of this entity is quite clear; perhaps best stated by presidential scholar John Hart, its mission is to "lobby the lobbies" (Hart 1994, 127). The office often calls in key groups in the hope of building legislative coalitions, or simply to obtain feedback on a future legislative initiative. By bringing in likely supporters, the White House can create a pre-legislative partnership and request assistance in reaching out to the groups' membership bases. According to political scientist Mark Peterson (1992, 612), "This new approach [in the Carter White House] was designed to fuse presidential and congressional perspectives by transforming the goals and resources of like-minded interest groups into the political assets of the White House."

Similarly, reaching out to likely opponents will enable the White House to extend an olive branch, giving it an opportunity not only to persuade such groups, but also to establish communication and clarify the benefits of its preferred program or initiative. Strategically, this outreach to supporters and likely detractors seeks to defuse potential conflict while maximizing the president's base of support. Conversely, the Office of Public Liaison can reach out to groups in an effort to broaden the opposition to pending legislation.

An inadvertent by-product of this formalized outreach is the creation of a White House contact point for outside interests. Therefore, although the purpose of the Office of Public Liaison is to maximize interest group support on behalf of the administration, it has the unfortunate consequence (for overburdened White House staff members) of creating a "casework" office for organized interests.

Office of Intergovernmental Affairs

Another White House unit designed to curry favor with organized interests, albeit less directly than the Office of Public Liaison, is the Office of Intergovernmental Affairs, which seeks support from state and local elected officials for administration efforts. The office deals primarily with six interest groups: Council of State Governments, National Association of Counties, National Conference of State Legislatures, National Governors Association, National League of Cities, and the U.S. Conference of Mayors (Patterson 2000, 449). In an effort to develop a rapport with these groups and officials, White House staff members attend national conferences and serve as contact points for mayors, governors, and other state officials.

Office of Legislative Affairs

Although the Office of Legislative Affairs works most directly with members of Congress, it often must build coalitions with key interests in an orchestrated attempt to build support (Andres 1997). According to Peterson (1992, 624), "White House liaison with interest groups writ large has become a central factor in the overall presentation of the president within the legislative process." In addition, this unit often works in tandem with other White House units, such as the Office of Public Liaison, as well as the national party organization. Because the party organization (Democratic National Committee, Republican National Committee) is essentially a White House annex staffed by presidential loyalists, presidents often enlist the party organization to campaign for or against a particular legislative initiative (Tenpas 1996).

Office of Political Affairs

Less directly engaged in nurturing relations with interest groups per se, the Office of Political Affairs is an outreach office that seeks to maintain and expand the president's electoral coalition. The office is primarily devoted to key constituents and state and local party organizations, but it also works to generate grassroots support for presidential programs. In doing so, it may find that key interest groups will facilitate White House efforts by calling on their members to endorse and actively support a particular program or presidential nomination.

After the midterm elections, this office turns its attention to the president's reelection campaign, coordinating with the campaign organization and seeking electoral support among various interest groups. With its finger on the political pulse, the Office of Political Affairs tends to the care and feeding of loyal interest groups, while reaching out to new interest groups in the hope of expanding electoral support.

Specialized Offices

The specialized offices for women's issues, Hispanic affairs, and AIDS policy predictably work with the interest groups that represent such issues. Other policy-based offices such as the Office of Environmental Initiatives (during the Clinton administration) or the Office of Faith-Based and Community Initiatives (OFBCI, during the George W. Bush administration) possess a roster of interest groups with whom they work to build a web of national support, ultimately broadening the president's base of support. These offices play varying roles across administrations, and some constituency-based offices exist only within certain administrations. Because presidents have the prerogative of organizing their own office, they choose different entities often reflective of their programmatic priorities (Patterson 2000).

Evaluating Presidential Outreach

Even though the presidency has an impressive capacity to reach out to organized interests, no noticeable trend of increased public support has resulted from these efforts. For example, although it is clear that the George W. Bush presidency possessed the capability to reach out to interest groups, its record of success was mixed. One illustrative example is the Office of Faith-Based and Community Initiatives (Tenpas 2002). The primary role of this office was to facilitate private-public partnerships with faith-based organizations in order to provide social services (for example, alcohol and drug rehabilitation, child care) to the public. According to Executive Order 13199 creating the office, "There is established a White House Office of Faith-Based and Community Initiatives within the Executive Office of the President that will have lead responsibility in the executive branch to establish policies, priorities, and objectives for the Federal Government's comprehensive effort to enlist, equip, enable, empower, and expand the work of faith-based and other community organizations to the extent permitted by law."

OFBCI was a key component of President Bush's "compassionate conservative" electoral campaign and then presidential agenda. Shortly after Bush's inauguration, the legislative battle over the central piece of faith-based legislation, the Community Solutions Act of 2001, revealed the difficulties inherent in maintaining support across a diverse constituency. Religious groups initially applauded the president's establishment of the OFBCI and his commitment to the issue, but the legislation drafted by House Republicans riled predictable sources of support and mobilized opponents of all stripes. OFBCI Director John J. DiIulio Jr. worked desperately to maintain the fragile coalition by arranging presidential engagements with important groups or speaking to them himself. Despite such efforts, the fundamental source of failure was the lack of a natural coalition for the initiative. Perhaps the White House team should have anticipated such a difficulty: "Outsiders seldom appreciate the degree of religious diversity among the large and heterogeneous populations suggested by the 'evangelical' label. . . . The groups are not simply different but may in some cases be antagonistic toward one another" (Wald 1997, 241, 251).

Such a state of affairs was boldly illustrated by the barrage of criticism from religious groups on the left and the right. Indeed, the opposition was so broad that it defies generalization. For example, those who favored the separation of church and state declared the initiative unconstitutional; conservative Christians feared that government involvement in providing such services would cause waste and corruption; and civil rights groups thought the initiative would lead to employment discrimination. Meanwhile, various religious organizations believed that government intrusion could potentially hinder their efforts and alter their practices.

Fortunately for the Bush administration, support for the issue also came from a broad spectrum of citizens. Some inner-city black churches perceived the initiative as a way to procure additional funding for their impoverished parishioners. Various Protestant churches seemed open to the idea of "charitable choice" as an additional means of assisting the needy, while Christian conservatives seeking a restoration of moral values praised the initiative.

In its substantial efforts to obtain support from key interest groups, the OFBCI found that the presidential connection alone was not sufficient. In addition, the Bush legislative agenda included competing items (for example, tax cuts, education reform) that consumed valuable resources and limited the effectiveness of OFBCI's efforts. Furthermore, the key provisions of the bill creating OFBCI did not, unlike tax cuts, represent an "easy" issue for guaranteed Republican support, let alone the bipartisan support ultimately necessary for the bill to become law. Throughout the legislative battle, predictable sources of support turned out to be critical bystanders, while the opposition remained vocal and expanded its ranks. The bill ultimately passed in the House, but the Senate completely rewrote it. In fact, the Senate version (the CARE Act) consisted primarily of financial incentives for charitable giving, effectively "gutting" the faith provisions favored by the House Republican sponsors. When the CARE Act finally passed in the next session of Congress, it was devoid of any "faith," thereby rendering the legislative quest for expanding charitable choice a failure.

What does the case of OFBCI say about presidential outreach to interest groups? Perhaps it is a none-too-subtle reminder of the complexities of the U.S. system, which consists of three separate but equal branches of government. The autonomy of these three branches explains why a president's quest to pass legislation can be so difficult (Jones 1994). The divisiveness and unpredictability of lawmaking will undercut or complicate any president's best efforts to curry favor within the special-interest community. It may well be that the best an administration can hope for is a "good fight"—one that communicates to its constituents that it is representing their interests, while occasionally garnering the support of an erstwhile opponent. Some efforts meet with success, but most meet with continued opposition or outright rejection.

Much like the "outside-in" lobbying world in which groups, try as they might, fail to persuade the various executive departments and agencies, presidential outreach suffers a similar fate. The three chapters in this part provide much insight into this aspect of interest group interaction. In Chapter 14, Suzanne J. Piotrowski and David Rosenbloom reveal the origins, development, and consequences of interest group participation in federal policymaking. Their analysis indicates that much policymaking, along with the values and trade-offs underlying it, moves beyond the direct reach of the electorate. In Chapter 15, Scott R. Furlong studies the lobbying behavior of five types of interest groups and examines their interaction with the executive branch. His analyses uncover the dominant role of economic interest groups such as businesses and trade associations, but the broader study finds that a relatively small proportion of interest groups participate in executive branch lobbying. Given the extent of legislative delegation to administrative agencies, this kind of lobbying remains fertile territory for special interests, and lobbyists best not ignore this opportunity to influence policy development. Finally, in Chapter 16 Paul J. Quirk and Bruce F. Nesmith consider whether the presidency is more likely than its legislative counterpart to advocate general interests by examining five policy areas strongly affected by organized interests. In so doing, they address the degree to which institutional structures affect interest group participation and conclude that the president is indeed the more reliable defender of general interests.

And so, just as James Madison predicted, the vigorous competition among groups has ameliorated the mischiefs of faction. Pluralism enables groups to compete, and a republican system does its best to create a level playing field that prevents any particular group from dominating the process. Clearly, presidents have no guarantee that their vigorous outreach efforts will produce successes, nor can interest groups count on their connections and campaign contributions to assist their cause. Perhaps the collapse of Enron provides the boldest illustration: a powerful corporation failed despite both its generous campaign contributions and its close ties to the administration. According to *New Yorker* columnist Nicholas Lehman, "When Enron got to the point of really needing some influence, it discovered that it hadn't bought any after all" (Lehman 2002, 31).

Despite the collapse of Enron (and many other corporations left in its wake), business interests and special-interest groups will continue to make campaign contributions and lobby the executive. Meanwhile, the president's advisers will continue to seek tactical support from within the special-interest community to promote the president's initiatives. The mere prospect of winning provides a powerful incentive to both elected officials and special interests. Though seemingly futile at times, the symbiotic nature of the relationship between presidents and interest groups (presidents need interest groups as much as interest groups need presidents) demands unremitting attention, reflecting the reality and complexity of governing in a separated system.

Notes

1. These terms refer to various extraconstitutional arrangements and relationships that emerge when interest groups interact with the executive branch.
2. See Shaiko (1998) for an examination of reverse lobbying during the Clinton administration, more specifically the COPS Program, a key component of the Violent Crime Control and Law Enforcement Act introduced in 1993 (pp. 259–267). For an interesting account of political outreach emanating from President Clinton's National Security Council, see Wilson (1997).
3. During the Clinton administration, the White House was also home to the Office of Environmental Initiatives, Office of the Initiative for One America, and Office of Women's Initiatives and Outreach. That said, an examination of interest group outreach should by no means be limited to the entities within the White House Office. These offices do, however, tend to be the primary vehicles for administration outreach. Other White House entities that seek interest group support, to name a few, are the Office of Policy Development (also known as the Domestic Policy Staff), the Office of the White House Counsel, and the Office of Presidential Personnel.

References

Andres, Gary J. 1997. "Lobbying for the President: Influencing Congress from the White House." In *The Interest Group Connection,* edited by Paul S. Herrnson, Ronald G. Shaiko, and Clyde Wilcox. Chatham, NJ: Chatham House Publishers.
Corwin, Edwin. 1957. *The President: Office and Powers, 1787–1957.* New York: New York University Press. Excerpted in Harry A. Bailey Jr. "The President as Legislative Leader." In *Classics of the American Presidency.* Oak Park, IL: Moore Publishing Company, 1980.
Hart, John. 1994. *The Presidential Branch: From Washington to Clinton.* 2d ed. Chatham, NJ: Chatham House Press.
Jones, Charles O. 1994. *The Presidency in a Separated System.* Washington, DC: Brookings.
Lehman, Nicholas. 2002. "Soft Money, Hard Lesson." *New Yorker,* January 28.
Patterson, Bradley. 2000. *The West Wing and Beyond.* Washington, DC: Brookings.
Peterson, Mark A. 1992. "The Presidency and Organized Interests: White House Patterns of Interest Group Liaison." *American Political Science Review* 86:612, 624.
Pika, Joseph. 1987. "Interest Groups and the White House under Roosevelt and Truman." *Political Science Quarterly* 102:647–668.

Shaiko, Ronald G. 1998. "Reverse Lobbying: Interest Group Mobilization from the White House and the Hill." In *Interest Group Politics,* 5th ed., edited by Allan J. Cigler and Burdett A. Loomis. Washington, DC: CQ Press, 1998.

Tenpas, Kathryn Dunn. 1996. "Promoting President Clinton's Policy Agenda: DNC as Presidential Lobbyist." *American Review of Politics* 17:283–298.

————— 2002. "Can an Office Change a Country? The White House Office of Faith-Based and Community Initiatives, A Year in Review." A preliminary report prepared for the Pew Forum on Religion and Public Life, February 20.

Wald, Kenneth. 1997. *Religion and Politics in the United States.* New York: St. Martin's Press.

Wilson, Ernest J., III. 1997. "Interest Groups and Foreign Policymaking: A View from the White House." In *The Interest Group Connection,* edited by Paul S. Herrnson, Ronald G. Shaiko, and Clyde Wilcox. Chatham, NJ: Chatham House.

14. The Legal-Institutional Framework for Interest Group Participation in Federal Administrative Policymaking

Suzanne J. Piotrowski and David H. Rosenbloom

The contemporary legal-institutional framework for interest group participation in federal administrative policymaking has its origins in a variety of decisions made by Congress in 1946 (Rosenbloom 2000). The framework not only guarantees interest groups access to administrative decision making, but often allows them to become direct participants in policy agenda setting and formation. Its overall purpose is to harmonize the rise of large-scale federal administration with the values of U.S. constitutional democracy, especially political accountability, participation, representation, responsiveness, and open government. However, it can also work to enhance the influence of interest groups and further remove policymaking from public view and direct electoral control. In this chapter, we explain the origins, development, and consequences of the main constitutional arrangements and administrative law provisions facilitating interest group involvement in policymaking by federal agencies.

The Rise of Administrative Policymaking

The New Deal and World War II thoroughly transformed the federal government's structure, operation, and locus of policymaking. Federal agencies emerged for the first time as a major power center—one that rivaled Congress in some respects. They thrived on the vast and often vague delegations of legislative authority bestowed on them by Congress. Their staff and budgets grew rapidly in response to the nation's efforts to achieve economic recovery and, then, military victory. For the most part, members of Congress reluctantly concluded that the growing complexity of public policy made an increase in the size and power of federal agencies inevitable (U.S. Congress 1946, 383, 5661; Rosenbloom 2000, 8). Between 1933 and 1935 alone, some sixty new agencies were created (Van Riper 1958, 320). The number of full-time federal civilian personnel mushroomed from about 600,000 in 1931 to over 4 million in 1945.[1] In some respects, the bureaucracy was "becoming greater as a lawmaking institution than the Congress of the United States itself" (U.S. Congress 1940, 4672), leading some members to ask, "Is Congress necessary?" (Kefauver and Levin 1947).

Federal administration was not only powerful, but also haphazardly regulated at best. Before 1946 there were no uniform procedures for rulemaking, adjudication, public and interest group participation in administrative policymaking, or openness. Nor were congressional standing committees charged with exercising systematic oversight of the agencies under their jurisdictions. Agencies seemed to function according to their own dictates, and sometimes abusively. Part of the congressional response was a steady stream of criticism of "bureaucrats gone mad with power," who "usurp power belonging to the Congress" and "promote a dangerous centralization of governmental power in the administrative branch." Some members feared administrators were transforming the United States into a "totalitarian state" (Rosenbloom 2000, 7). Others, such as Rep. John Jennings, R-TN, agreed that the threat to liberty was real, but viewed it as more subtle: "The Federal Government now touches almost every activity that arises in the lives of millions of people who make up the population of this country. The chief indoor sport of the federal bureaucrat is to evolve out of his own inner consciousness, like a spider spins his web, countless confusing rules and regulations which may deprive a man of his property, his liberty, and bedevil the very life out of him" (U.S. Congress 1946, 5662).

The potential for abuse was compounded by chaotic organization, inadequate transparency, and the absence of standardized procedures. As the President's Committee on Administrative Management noted in 1937, "the work of the Executive Branch is badly organized," "managerial agencies are weak and out of date," and the whole structure had "grown up without plan or design like the barns, shacks, silos, tool sheds, and garages of an old farm" (President's Committee on Administrative Management 1937, 32). The lack of consistent transparency was perhaps an even more substantial problem. In 1941 Dean Acheson, then assistant secretary of state, explained that "in many cases— . . . perhaps in the majority of them—the agency is one great obscure organization with which the citizen has to deal. It is absolutely amorphous. . . . There is someone called the commission, the authority; a metaphysical omniscient brooding thing which sort of floats around in the air and is not a human being. . . . The citizen . . . says, 'How can I talk to the commission?' But he can't talk to the commission. That is the thing that is baffling" (U.S. Congress, Senate 1941, 807).

Moreover, individuals and firms might be entirely unaware of the administrative rules that ostensibly regulated their behavior—at least until they were cited for violations. In 1934 the American Bar Association's Special Committee on Administrative Law reported a condition that persisted to some extent until 1946:

> Practically every agency to which legislative power has been delegated (or sub delegated) has exercised it, and has published its enactments, sometimes in the form of official printed pamphlets, bound or loose-leaf, sometimes in mimeograph form, sometimes in privately owned publications, and sometimes in press releases. Sometimes they exist only in sort of an unwritten law. Rules and regulations, upon compliance with which important privileges and freedom from heavy penalties may depend, are amended and interpreted as formally or informally as they were originally adopted. (American Bar Association, Special Committee on Administrative Law 1934, 228)

Adjudication had much the same quality. Speaking in 1940, Sen. William H. King, D-UT, noted that many agency rulings were made "in the form of letters, and nothing in the way of an even informal hearing is required. If the citizen gets a hearing, it is at the grace of the administrator or bureau chief" (U.S. Congress 1940, 13668).

Congress sought to deal with many of these problems through the Walter-Logan Act of 1940, which was successfully vetoed by President Franklin D. Roosevelt. The act would have significantly expanded judicial review of federal administration and placed a variety of time and procedural restrictions on agency rulemaking and adjudication. Among its provisions was a requirement that the agencies hold public hearings on any rule at the request of anyone substantially interested in its application. This provision would have greatly strengthened interest groups' ability to block rules and tie up rulemaking in procedural knots. The act would have applied to procedural and interpretative rules, as well as legislative (substantive) ones (Rosenbloom 2000, 30).[2]

Although it never became law, the Walter-Logan Act was a watershed in the evolution of American government, because its underlying premise was that politics, in the sense of policymaking, could not be completely separated from administration. Consequently, public administration should be informed by political values, such as transparency and due process, as well as by the standard managerial ones of efficiency, economy, and organizational effectiveness.

Congress returned concerted attention to federal administration in 1946. In a year of remarkable legislative output, it enacted the Administrative Procedure Act; the Legislative Reorganization Act, which includes the Federal Tort Claims Act as one of its titles; and the Employment Act. It also began a process of institutionalization (Polsby 1968), which included much better staffing (Fox and Hammond 1977). These actions fit together to define a lasting congressional response to the rise of the federal administrative state (Rosenbloom 2000). Henceforth, Congress would treat the agencies as its extensions for performing legislative functions, rely on its own standing committees and committee staffs to oversee or supervise the agencies, and develop the wherewithal to intercede in administrative decision making to promote members' constituency and district interests. In many respects, 1946 marked the beginning of the "career Congress" (Hibbing 1991), as well as the set of legal-institutional arrangements for interest group participation in federal administrative policymaking, which are the focus of the remainder of this chapter (see Rosenbloom 2003 for a more extended treatment of federal administrative law).

Substantive Rulemaking under the Administrative Procedure Act of 1946

The Administrative Procedure Act of 1946 (APA) imposed uniform procedures for rulemaking, adjudication, and transparency on federal agencies for the first time. It was premised on legislators' belief that Congress would increasingly delegate its legislative authority to the agencies, and, consequently, substantive rulemaking procedures should incorporate the same values that inform the legislative process itself. As Rep. Francis E. Walter, D-PA, put it, "Day by day Congress takes account of the interests and desires of the people in framing legislation; there is no reason why administrative agencies should not do so when they exercise legislative functions which the Congress has delegated to them" (U.S. Congress 1946, 5756). Senators and representatives hear from "the people" through elections, opinion polls, and mail, but when working on legislation in standing committees and subcommittees they are likely to hear more from interest groups. Under the APA, participation in rulemaking is predominantly (or largely) by trade and professional associations, public interest groups, and corporations. Few citizens have the time, inclination, or knowledge to track agency rulemaking from start to finish.

The APA provides for two main types of substantive rulemaking: informal and formal. Although both had parallels or precursors, neither was standard operating procedure (Kerwin 1999, 160). Both open rulemaking broadly to interest group participation. Informal rulemaking, also known as "notice and comment" rulemaking, requires agencies to publish notices of proposed rulemaking in the *Federal Register*, along with information about the relevant legal authority, terms, substance, or subjects of the rule, and the procedures for submitting comments on it. Informal rulemaking does not require hearings or open meetings. However, if an agency decides to hold them, it must place a notice in the *Federal Register* about their time, place, and nature. Anyone may submit written comments for agency consideration, including via e-mail. Over the years, it has become standard practice for agencies to enter comments onto a docket and to record responses to them. Maintaining such a record strengthens the agency's position if a rule is challenged in court. Rules are legally infirm if they are arbitrary, capricious, an abuse of discretion, or not in accordance with law. Informal rulemaking does not require that the rules be justified on the basis of the comments as a whole. Once a final rule is published in the *Federal Register*, affected parties are allowed at least thirty days to come into compliance, though often significantly more time is allotted.

Agencies can avoid informal rulemaking when it is "impracticable, unnecessary, or contrary to the public interest" (APA 1946, section 4[a]). Military, foreign affairs, internal personnel arrangements, and a variety of matters dealing with public property, contracts, benefits, loans, and grants are exempt from the APA's rulemaking provisions. Variants on informal rulemaking include "direct final" and "interim final" rulemaking. Direct final rules are published in the *Federal Register* and go into effect at a specified future date unless adverse comments are filed. Interim final rules, also published in the *Federal Register*, are effective immediately, but they are subject to post-publication comments and withdrawal or revision.

Formal rulemaking, the second main APA rulemaking process, is also known as "rulemaking on the record." It is far more elaborate, but agencies need not engage in it unless required by a specific statute. Hearings, a cornerstone of lawmaking in Congress, are mandatory. When a hearing is held, it may be presided over by the agency's commission or board or an administrative law judge or other hearing examiner of some kind. The proceeding itself is quasi-judicial, and, like a legislative hearing, is usually open to as many interested parties as is practicable. In the end, the agency's decision must be supported by substantial evidence from the record as a whole (a transcript is kept of the hearing). The burden of persuasion is on whoever proposes the rule, which may be the agency or an interest group or another outside party. As it is in informal rulemaking, the final rule must be published in the *Federal Register*.

These rulemaking requirements have a dual impact on interest groups. On the one hand, the requirements enable groups to protect their members from arbitrary administrative rulemaking. On the other, the requirements may forestall the ability of groups to obtain favored rules from the agencies.

A good illustration of how such rulemaking requirements can be used to block agency policy initiatives occurred in 1999 when the Occupational Safety and Health Administration (OSHA) sought to implement its Cooperative Compliance Program (CCP). Like several federal regulatory agencies, OSHA faces a daunting task: it is responsible for worker safety and health at over five million work sites throughout the nation. Because each of its inspectors is responsible for more than a thousand sites, a comprehensive inspection of each site more than once every several years is impossible (Kagan 1994, 404). In the late 1990s, as part of the Clinton-Gore administration's effort to use partnership arrangements in regulatory enforcement, OSHA identified 12,500 relatively dangerous workplaces and offered a deal to the firms involved: OSHA would reduce the probability of inspections at such sites by 70–90 percent if the employer would participate in the CCP. Among other requirements, the CCP mandated attention to "ergonomics, materials handling, bloodborne pathogens, confined space, hazard communication, . . . [and] compliance with applicable 'voluntary standards,' 'industry practices,' and even 'suppliers' safety recommendations'" (*Chamber of Commerce of the United States v. OSHA*, No. 98-1036 [D.C. Cir. 1999], 2).

These requirements appeared eminently reasonable to OSHA. It had implemented a prototype program in Maine, with excellent results. The firms involved identified and fixed "14 times more hazards than OSHA's inspectors ever could have found," and injury rates dropped 35 percent over a two-year period (Gore 1995, 25–26).

The U.S. Chamber of Commerce, National Association of Manufacturers, and other business groups took a dimmer view, however. To them, the CCP was "more like coercion than cooperation." Firms that failed to "voluntarily" sign on would face a heavier burden of inspections. The program also relied on "ambush rulemaking," because OSHA had not arrived at the CCP's substantive requirements through notice and comment rulemaking, which would have given the affected employers and employee groups an opportunity to voice concerns and offer suggestions for making the standards less burdensome and more workable. A federal circuit court of appeals agreed with the industry interest groups, nullified the program, and told OSHA that such a program could only be established pursuant to the APA's regulations for notice and comment rulemaking (Harris 1999; *Chamber of Commerce of the United States v. OSHA* 1999).

A different result had occurred in the early 1980s, when the National Cattleman's Association tried to convince the U.S. Department of Agriculture (USDA) to change the standards for grading beef. The cattlemen have had a long and generally harmonious relationship with the USDA. Therefore, they fully expected the department to back their proposal, which was developed in response to their sense that the public would buy more beef if it were leaner. The new standards would have required less fat in the form of "marbling" in the "prime" and "choice" categories. The USDA solicited public comments on the proposed change and held several public hearings across the country. The Cattleman's Association was no doubt surprised when 80 percent of the four thousand comments received opposed the change. According to a USDA spokesperson, "The strong common denominator was, rightly or wrongly, the perception that the new regulations would cause consumer confusion and destroy consumer confidence." Consequently, the department declined to change the standards (Sheraton 1982).

In late 2003 and early 2004, USDA rulemaking and the beef industry were back in the news after a single case of mad cow disease was discovered in Washington State. Like the CCP and beef standards episodes, the effort to address the mad cow threat illustrates how APA rulemaking requirements can both serve and potentially frustrate the impact of interest groups on public policymaking by administrative agencies. For the most part, the beef industry strongly supported the new safety regulations adopted by the USDA, including a prohibition against allowing individual animals unable to stand on their own ("downer cattle") from entering the food supply. These safeguards clearly served the industry by bolstering public confidence in their products. However, industry opposition quickly developed to an expensive and burdensome USDA proposal for exponentially increasing the number of cattle subject to mandatory testing for mad cow disease. Although the issue is currently in flux, USDA rulemaking about such tests will have to take the industry's comments into account and may be challenged in court if the final rule is procedurally defective or arbitrary in the sense that it is not based on sound analysis.

Judicial Review

Substantive rulemaking is often followed by litigation. For example, roughly 30–40 percent of the Environmental Protection Agency's rules are challenged in federal court (Coglianese 1997, 1286–1309). An interest group or other party's decision to litigate is affected by several factors. The more expensive compliance will be, the more likely affected parties will litigate. Litigation rates are also affected by statutes and judicial decisions that determine how difficult it is to initiate suits and to prevail in court. Greater ease in bringing legal challenges to agency rules tends to work to the advantage of interest groups even though these may not be "repeat players" (Golden 1998, 7). Agencies generally prefer to avoid the cost of and potential loss from lawsuits. Although the evidence is incomplete, there is little doubt that agencies sometimes modify their proposed and final rules in an effort to ward off legal action (O'Leary 1993; Melnick 1994).

The APA's provisions for judicial review were designed to check arbitrary administrative action while protecting agencies' flexibility. For the most part, standing to sue has not been a significant barrier to parties adversely and directly affected by agency rules. However, the thresholds for sustaining rules upon judicial review are modest at best. Informal rules will be overturned only if they are unconstitutional, arbitrary, capricious, abusive of discretion, or not in accordance with law. Formal rules must be constitutional and supported by substantial evidence on the record as a whole. In practice, substantial evidence is merely that which "a reasonable mind might accept as adequate to support a conclusion" (Black 1979, 1281). Nevertheless, the federal courts often take a hard look at the scientific and economic analysis and substantive logic behind agency rules. A court is likely to overturn rules if it cannot proceed rationally from the agency's premise to its conclusion. In addition, under the APA, rules may be overturned on the basis of procedural defects or excess of statutory authority. By contrast, the judiciary takes a "soft look" at agencies' interpretation of imprecise statutory language and almost "no look" at their routine decisions not to enforce rules or statutes in specific cases.[3]

The APA hardly tips the balance in favor of interest groups when they challenge agencies in court, but it is far from the last word. The APA requirements can be augmented by a wide variety of measures. Congressional delegations of legislative authority can include specific substantive and procedural requirements. To a lesser extent, presidential executive orders can impose similar tests, though these may be trumped by legislation and often cannot be made to apply to independent regulatory commissions such as the Federal Trade Commission (Moreno 1994). For example, agencies have been required to solicit the views of small businesses and local governments on proposed rules. They also have been required to issue rules within a specific time frame, to engage in cost-benefit analysis, and to protect concerns such as federalism, environmental justice, and strong American families. Interest groups devote much effort to establishing such extra-APA requirements — and litigating when they appear to have been breached.

Requirements that agencies develop impact statements when proposing rules or engaging in other actions also facilitate interest group legal challenges and judicial review. The National Environmental Policy Act of 1969 is probably the best-known example. It requires agencies to produce environmental impact statements when their activities will have a major effect on natural environments and ecologies. These statements must consider adverse environmental effects, alternatives to the proposed action, the relationship between short-run uses and long-term productivity, and any irreversible and irretrievable commitments of resources. Other agencies and private parties are encouraged to comment on the impact statements, which are public documents. They are of great importance to advocacy groups seeking to challenge agency actions that may damage the environment. Almost from the outset, the claims, findings, and conclusions of environmental impact statements became the basis of lawsuits.[4]

Congressional Review

Congress has always had the power to override agencies' substantive rules through legislation. It also can use its control of agency budgets to limit or prevent the enforcement of rules to which it is opposed. Since 1946, its standing committees have exercised oversight of the executive branch, which affords them considerable leverage in steering agency actions, including rulemaking. In 1996 Congress augmented its power to nullify agency rules by establishing a formal process of legislative review that provides organized interests with another forum in which to challenge or defend agency rules.

Title II of the Small Business Regulatory Enforcement Fairness Act of 1996 is known as the Congressional Review Act. It provides for two levels of review, depending on whether a rule is "major" or "ordinary." Major rules are those expected to affect the economy annually by at least $100 million or have a substantial effect on costs, prices, employment, competition, productivity, or other key aspects of the national economy. With some exceptions, major rules are subject to a sixty-day review period in Congress during which the legislature can pass a joint resolution of disapproval. The resolution is subject to presidential veto and congressional override. If Congress does not disapprove of a rule, it goes into effect as per publication in the *Federal Register* (Cohen and Strauss 1997). Ordinary rules are also subject to disapproval, but not to the sixty-day review period.

Any rule that is disapproved cannot be reissued in identical or similar form unless the agency receives specific statutory authorization to do so. The first rule to be voted down by Congress was the OSHA's "ergonomics rule" in 2001. It was favored by organized labor and opposed by business interests. The rule took a decade or so to write and was aimed largely at reducing repetitive stress injuries from work activities such as keyboarding (Dewar 2001). Disapproval came in the early days of the George W. Bush administration when regulatory actions taken toward the end of President Bill Clinton's term were being scrutinized.

Legislative review may give organized interests the upper hand when opposing agency rules, which ostensibly are supposed to promote the broad public interest. The Congressional Review Act encourages precisely what Sen. Forrest C. Donnell, R-MO, feared in 1946: "It would be unfortunate if the public should get the idea that they could go to various committees of the Congress and undertake to reverse that action of the specific departments" (U.S. Congress 1946, 6445). Formal joint resolutions of disapproval are cumbersome, but they should not be necessary to achieve the greater congressional purpose of steering the exercise of delegated legislative authority. Knowing that Congress can nullify rules should make agencies more sensitive to signals and directions from the committees that oversee them. Sensible administrators do not want to expend scarce resources on futile efforts. Now that congressional review has been used and is a credible threat, interest groups can lobby against proposed rules in Congress while voicing opposition to the agencies under informal and formal rulemaking procedures.

Executive Review

Since the administration of Richard Nixon (1969–1974), presidents have used executive orders and other measures to gain greater control of agency rulemaking (Kerwin 1999, 220–232). Their primary objective is to make rulemaking comport with the administration's overall policy directions and to prevent rules from conflicting with one another. It is now standard practice for the Office of Management and Budget (OMB) to review agencies' proposals for significant new rules or rule changes before these are published in the *Federal Register* as part of the public rulemaking process. OMB also may review final rules prior to their enactment. When OMB is dissatisfied with a rule proposal, an agency's rulemaking agenda, or the final form of a rule, it may return the proposal, agenda, or rule to the agency involved for reconsideration. Constitutionally, OMB's actions must comply fully with statutory requirements, which may fix deadlines, allow the agencies flexibility in the use of cost-benefit analysis, and contain a broad range of substantive objectives. For the most part, the independent regulatory commissions are constitutionally outside OMB's ambit, though they may voluntarily submit their rulemaking to OMB review (Moreno 1994).

Executive review of agency rulemaking is controversial, because when agencies make rules they are usually exercising legislative authority delegated to them, not to the president or OMB. Some see executive review as "little more than backdoors for politically powerful interests intent on frustrating normal and statutorily authorized regulatory processes" (Kerwin 1999, 230). It also delays the already lengthy rulemaking processes. Even though OMB has faced considerable criticism from Congress and individual agencies for its regulation of rulemaking, "presidential oversight is a permanent fixture in the rulemaking process" and is well recognized by interest groups as such (Kerwin 1999, 231). Like congressional review, executive review gives conventional and public interest groups another forum in which to voice their support or opposition to the substance of agencies' rulemaking efforts.

This opportunity was at no time clearer than in the early days of President George W. Bush's administration. Upon moving into his White House office, Bush's chief of staff, Andrew Card, issued the "Card memo," which permitted executive agencies to delay the effective date of final rules issued during the closing days of the Clinton administration. These rules included some high-profile ones dealing with arsenic levels in drinking water, medical privacy, and development in the national forests, as well as more than thirty others that had been considered final. Bush defended the Card memo on the grounds that he wanted rules to be based on science, realism, and common sense. However, few observers doubted that the new president was responding to a set of political interests different from those favored by the Clinton administration. In the words of one critic, "How about arsenic, how about ergonomics, hard-rock mining? Every one of these, there were clear corporate interests that were expressed to the Bush administration" (Goldstein 2001, A7). Meanwhile, the legality of the Card memo was hotly disputed. But the last word may have gone to an OMB spokesperson who defended the memo on grounds that seem sure to serve as a precedent for future presidential transitions: "We feel it's appropriate and lawful to take time to review last-minute regulations issued by the previous administration" (Skrzycki 2001).

Interest Groups as Partners in Agency Policymaking

The APA's procedures for informal rulemaking allow interest groups and others to participate by offering data and perspectives to the agencies. However, they do not enable those outside the agency to initiate rulemaking. The agency sets the agenda, frames the proposed rules, evaluates outsiders' views, and responds as it sees fit. Formal rulemaking allows more proactive participation—outsiders may propose new rules as well as the modification or rescission of older ones. But it is a cumbersome quasi-judicial process with the trappings of adversary procedure rather than a cooperative problem-solving exercise. Three major statutes have been adopted since 1946 that enhance the potential of interest groups to play more of a partnership role in administrative policymaking.

The Federal Advisory Committee Act of 1972

Federal advisory committees, which are established and funded by the federal government, have quasi-governmental status and are sometimes considered a "fifth branch" of government. Advisory committees have access to agency policymakers and political influence. The Federal Advisory Committee Act of 1972 (FACA) was intended to bring order, greater representativeness, better accountability, and more transparency to the committees' operations.

Advisory committees are considered a valuable source of information, data, and perspective for administrative agencies. Some are concerned with broad matters, but most have a relatively narrow focus. They frequently deal with specific geographic places or regions, crops and foods (such as peanuts and raisins), diseases, technologies, minerals, and chemicals. Before enactment of FACA, however, there was no general requirement that the membership of committees represent a variety of perspectives or interests. The committees may well have been dominated by the economically more powerful interests in any given field, such as large tobacco or cotton growers. Many seemed to operate as "a convenient and effective source of support for established programs or policies or those contemplated by the Government administrators" (U.S. Senate 1978, 48). The committees were not required to operate openly. Even their total number was unknown; during the legislative debates on FACA, estimates varied all the way from 1,800 to 5,400 (see U.S. Senate 1978, 46, 281).

FACA seeks to force legislative values into the advisory committee system. It requires that a committee's membership be "fairly balanced in terms of the points of view represented" and that a committee "not be inappropriately influenced by the appointing authority or by any special interest" (section 5). It promotes transparency through its public notice, open meeting, and reporting requirements. Closed meetings are to be the exception and only for specific causes (these parallel the exemptions in the Freedom of Information Act, which is discussed later in this chapter).

Committees can be established by Congress as well as by the agencies.[5] In 1998 fifty-five federal departments and agencies supported 892 advisory committees, totaling 41,259 members. The committees held 5,852 meetings and issued 973 reports (U.S. General Services Administration 1999). The net effect of all this activity is uncertain. Writing in 1984, Henry Steck concluded that "advisory committees become a technique for reducing political uncertainty vis-à-vis clientele groups, stabilizing existing political relations, deflecting group opposition, securing group cooperation, and mobilizing political support" (Steck 1984, 161). However, it is unlikely that the system is wholly co-optative. Many of the 41,000 people who serve on advisory committees are probably more motivated by the potential to influence agency policymaking than the desire to engage in public service or collect a modest per diem. Moreover, as discussed later in this chapter, there is reason to believe that the advisory committees' perspectives have become less homogeneous over time.

From time to time, FACA becomes a political lightening rod. The act does not apply to meetings comprised entirely of federal employees. During the Clinton administration's health policy initiative in the early 1990s, a question arose about whether First Lady Hillary Rodham Clinton was a federal employee within the meaning of FACA. Litigation determined that she was, but, otherwise, the meetings she spearheaded should have been governed by FACA's transparency requirements (*Association of American Physicians and Surgeons, Inc. v. Hillary Rodham Clinton*, 997 F.2d 898 [1993]). A similar question arose in 2001 about Vice President Richard B. Cheney's meetings on energy policy. Cheney maintained that FACA does not apply to the vice president, whereas the comptroller general of the United States, David Walker, several Democrats in Congress, and some environmental advocacy groups contended that it does. (The courts have yet to resolve this matter definitively.)

The Negotiated Rulemaking Act of 1990

The Negotiated Rulemaking Act of 1990 (NRMA) is another formal mechanism through which organized interests can influence administrative policymaking. It supplements the APA's provisions for informal rulemaking and can be used when only a limited number of identifiable interests will be significantly affected by a rule. The act authorizes agencies to make rules through face-to-face negotiation with interested parties. The general procedure is that agencies establish rulemaking committees after notice and comment in the *Federal Register*. Typically, these committees will include not more than twenty-five members drawn from the agency, regulated entities, trade unions, associations, and the public. The committee should adequately represent the range of affected interests. Facilitators or mediators can be used to help bring the parties to agreement on a proposed rule. Like meetings held under FACA, negotiating sessions should generally be open to public observation. After it is negotiated, a rule is subject to the same notice and comment requirements that apply to informal rulemaking. In other words, the agency could rewrite a negotiated rule after receiving outside comments. However, major changes could seriously undermine the agency's credibility with those involved in the negotiations. Similarly, if the committee fails to reach unanimous agreement, the agency is free to pursue its own preferences through notice and comment rulemaking.

Negotiated rulemaking, also called "reg-neg" (for regulatory negotiation), enables interest groups to participate fully in administrative policymaking. During negotiations, the agency has no special status—that is, it is on a par with the other parties. As noted earlier, however, it has ultimate control over the fate of the rule involved. Reg-neg offers organized interests a seat at the table in the fullest sense. It allows them to put forward their favored solutions to public policy problems and to urge others to adopt them.

The expectation behind the NRMA is that interest group participation in reg-neg will result in better rules, faster rulemaking, and less litigation.[6] However, the process also can encourage seemingly endless talk and delay. For example, the Environmental Protection Agency's effort to negotiate a farmworker pesticide rule took nearly seven years—and ultimately failed (Coglianese 1997, 1279).

The Government Performance and Results Act of 1993 (GPRA)

The Government Performance and Results Act of 1993 (GPRA, also known as the Results Act) further enhances the ability of interest groups to participate as partners in agency policymaking. The act requires federal agencies to engage in strategic planning, which is defined statutorily to include a mission statement, identification of general goals for the agency's major functions and operations, implementation strategies, the denotation of external factors that can undercut the achievement of goals, and an evaluation plan. A strategic plan must cover at least five years, with updates and revisions required in the third year. The act specifically provides that "when developing a strategic plan, the agency shall consult with the Congress, and shall solicit and consider the views and suggestions of those entities potentially affected or interested in such a plan" (section 3 [d]).

The GPRA was phased in over a seven-year period with considerable fan-fare and press attention. However, its full potential impact on interest group influence in administrative policymaking remains uncertain. The solicit-and-consider provision appears to give interest groups a legally enforceable right to be consulted whenever agency strategic planning would obviously affect their members' interests. As with informal rulemaking, the agency does not have to accept an interested party's suggestions, but agencies may try to accommodate the views of those organized interests that wield significant influence with congressional committees. After all, these committees also must be consulted as part of the strategic planning exercise, and they are well positioned to compel the agencies to rewrite their plans. Eventually, GPRA may strongly facilitate interest group participation in the definition of agency goals.

Interest Group Partnering with Individual Administrators

The formal institutional-legal arrangements for interest group participation in federal administrative policymaking are augmented by two personnel practices that can significantly strengthen groups' influence within agencies. One is the tendency of high-level officials to move back and forth between the interest groups and influential agency posts. These "in-and-outers" are engaging in a process known as the "revolving door." The second practice is for interest groups to gain a voice in—and sometimes a veto of—the appointment of high-level political executives to the agencies.

The Revolving Door

The revolving door is a long-standing issue. Interest groups, on the one side, and agencies, on the other, working in the same policy areas may value the expertise of one another's personnel. Each side can offer inducements to bring men and women with the knowledge they seek into their organizations. Interest groups can generally offer better pay, more flexible jobs, and less hierarchical control. Agencies offer an opportunity to affect public policy directly. The movement of personnel in and out of the groups and agencies can be beneficial to all concerned. However, it also raises the potential for the appearance of impropriety and conflicts of interest.

In 1946 Congress addressed the revolving door in relation to its own committee staff by banning staffers from taking positions in the executive branch within one year of leaving their legislative positions. But more than three decades elapsed before Congress took comprehensive action on the revolving door between interest groups and agencies.

In the early 1970s, the revolving door became the target of regulatory reformers (Roberts and Doss 1997, 65). The 1976 Democratic Party platform endorsed limits on revolving door careerism, defined broadly as "the shuttling back and forth of officials between jobs in regulatory or procurement agencies and in regulated industries and government contractors." After successfully winning the presidency, the Democrats made good on their pledge in the form of the Ethics in Government Act of 1978, which was modified by the Ethics Reform Act of 1989 and subsequent amendments. Among other features, these statutes place post-termination restrictions on the lobbying *activities* of many political appointees and career personnel. Depending on the specific circumstances, these personnel may be banned from representing private parties before the departments or agencies in which they worked for one to two years or even the lifetime of the administrative activity once under their responsibility. However, *postemployment* restrictions are few, and government employees are generally free to work for interest groups regardless of their prior administrative activity. Consequently, the revolving door may have slowed down, but it is definitely still swinging.

Political Appointments

Interest groups frequently lobby the White House and Senate committees to push for the appointment of political appointees they believe are sympathetic to their causes and the defeat of those who are not (Hrebenar 1997, 260; Gerhardt 2000, 217). They understand that political appointees in federal agencies can do much to steer, speed up, or delay the adoption and enforcement of regulations. The 2001 Bush administration transition and the political appointment process illustrate well the efforts of interest groups to gain influence at the top of the agencies. A U.S. Chamber of Commerce representative's statement that the Chamber looks for appointees "who could moderate the impact of rules and how they are enforced" rings true for many special interests (Skrzycki 2000). Congress is also acutely aware of the pressures interest groups place on political appointees. For example, Sen. Harry M. Reid of Nevada, the senior Democrat on the Environment and Public Works Committee, bluntly stated: "I'm looking for an EPA director whose number one concern is the environment, not satisfying any particular special interest group" (Pianin 2001).

Interest groups' objectives sometimes go beyond the confirmation or defeat of specific candidates to include "influencing the quality of the discourse or debate in the process; controlling the media's or public's perceptions of the issue(s) at stake in a given confirmation contest; and educating legislators, presidents (or their staffs or key advisers in their administrations), nominees, or members of the general public about the groups' primary areas of concern" (Gerhardt 2000, 217–218). An excellent illustration of how such diverse objectives might be advanced developed in 2001 when President George W. Bush nominated Thomas C. Dorr as USDA undersecretary for rural development. The appointment was opposed by a coalition of Farm Aid, United Farm Workers of America, National Campaign for Sustainable Agriculture, National Farmers Organization, National Catholic Rural Life Conference, and National People's Action. These groups were joined by some 160 other farm groups, as well as substantial elements in environmental, civil rights, labor, and consumer organizations. Their main objection was that Dorr disparaged family farms and favored large corporate agribusinesses. One independent hog farmer associated with the Missouri Rural Crisis Center charged, "We all thought feudalism ended in the Middle Ages, but Dorr wants to bring it back." Another critic contended that "the only role for farmers in Tom Dorr's vision is as serfs on their own land." Sen. Thomas R. Harkin, D-IA, chair of the Senate Agriculture Committee, which had jurisdiction over the appointment, indicated that he would take his time with the nomination and "go over everything carefully" (Claiborne 2001, A31). Dorr was not confirmed. Nevertheless, in a significant defeat for the groups who opposed his appointment, he took office as undersecretary for rural development in August 2002 after receiving a "recess appointment" by Bush. Constitutionally, the president can make such appointments to vacancies when the Senate is not in session. Recess appointees can remain in office until the end of the Senate's next session.

Transparency

Information is a prerequisite for effective participation in administrative policymaking. One of the chief complaints about federal administration has been that it is secretive and obscure. As noted earlier, prior to the APA there was no general requirement that agency rules be published or publicized. Nor was there a generic federal administrative disclosure law. Even those deeply affected by administrative policies might have no way of knowing when the agency adopted them or what they required. The APA's rulemaking provisions were a major step toward transparency. The act also required, for the first time, that agencies publish information about their locations, organization, methods of operation, and procedural and interpretative rules. It further required them to make information available about obtaining documents. Although these provisions seem minimalist in retrospect, at the time they were a major step toward more open federal administration. By the 1960s and 1970s, however, in the wake of the Vietnam War and the Watergate scandal, they appeared badly in need of upgrading.

Freedom of Information

The Freedom of Information Act of 1966 (FOIA) is a landmark statute of constitutional dimensions. Congressional debate on it was infused with concern about the future of American constitutional democracy. The Senate *Report* on the freedom of information bill approvingly quotes James Madison's view that "knowledge will forever govern ignorance, and a people who mean to be their own governors, must arm themselves with the power knowledge gives. A popular government without popular information or the means of acquiring it, is but a prologue to a farce or a tragedy, or perhaps both" (U.S. Senate 1974, 37–38).[7] One of the act's objectives was to eliminate any "standing" requirement for seeking information from federal agencies. The act permits *anyone* to request information, whereas the APA required requestors to show that they were "properly and directly concerned" with the information sought.

The Freedom of Information Act is a disclosure statute, but it includes broad exemptions for trade secrets, intra- and interagency predecisional memos, personnel and medical files, banking records, investigatory and national security information, geological and geophysical data on mineral wealth, anything that would constitute an unwarranted invasion of privacy, and material specifically exempted by other statutes. As amended, it calls on agencies to act fairly, reasonably, and promptly when releasing or deciding to release information. It also facilitates judicial review of agency failure to comply with its terms.

The act is useful to a wide variety of interests, as is suggested by the 1986 amendments dealing with the fees agencies may charge for producing requested information. Commercial requestors can be charged for searches, duplication, and possibly an expensive document review process to ensure that the material is not properly exempted from release. Educational, scientific, or news media groups are charged only for duplication. Nonprofits, public interest groups, and individuals may be charged for search and duplication, but not review. Fees may be waived for some groups when the agency determines that their request serves the public interest (Feinberg 1997).

Not surprisingly, "critics . . . have emphasized the acquisition of much information for commercial or business purposes . . . while proponents have noted the amount of health and safety information provided to consumers by information provisions" (Vaughn 1994, 471). Clearly, a number of nonprofits have made effective use of the FOIA for public service purposes, including the National Security Archive, Ralph Nader's Public Citizen Foundation, the American Civil Liberties Union, and People for the American Way (Foerstel 1999, 139–154). Nevertheless, available evidence suggests that use is heavily weighted toward business interests. For example, in 1993 the Food and Drug Administration received 48,000 FOIA requests. Only 1 percent came from public interest groups, whereas 9 percent came from journalists and 82 percent from industry, freedom of information service companies, and lawyers (Strauss et al. 1995, 910). Such numbers do not speak directly to the usefulness of released information to interest groups or the public, but the volume does suggest that the FOIA works largely as a tool for those seeking economic gain.

The Sunshine in Government Act of 1976

The Sunshine in Government Act of 1976 is an open meetings law. It applies to federal multiheaded commissions and boards when a majority of their members are appointed by the president with the advice and consent of the Senate. Agencies covered by the act are required to give at least one week's notice of meetings, and, in principle, all their meetings should be open to the public in their entirety. However, meetings or portions thereof can be closed by majority vote of the commission or board for reasons that parallel the FOIA exemptions.

An important exception is that meetings cannot be closed to protect predecisional discussions from public scrutiny. Depending on the reason for closure, the
agency must keep a transcript, recording, or set of minutes of the meeting, which
may later be obtained through civil suit if the closure was improper. The act was
a belated answer to congressional concerns, expressed as early as the 1930s, that
federal agencies were exercising delegated legislative authority behind closed
doors and possibly in ways that unreasonably favored some interests over others.
As one member of the House noted in 1976, "access to the decisionmaking
processes within the departments and agencies" is a way of ensuring "that the
intent of Congress, as expressed in the legislation we enact, is carried out" (U.S.
Congress 1976, 378).

That said, the Sunshine Act may be less effective than its chief sponsors in
Congress had hoped. Agencies have found ways to circumvent the act's intent. For
example, if the commission or board has more than three members, the chair may
discuss matters individually with each one. Agency staff may also take on a greater
role in decision making. The available data indicate that a large proportion of
meetings are closed (40 percent) or partially closed (20 percent). Litigation has
been limited, which suggests that either these closures are proper or interested
parties do not view bringing civil suits as a cost-effective way of enforcing the act
(Strauss et al. 1995, 948–949). Despite a variety of criticisms of the impact of the
Sunshine Act on agencies' collegiality and ability to have free-flowing discussions,
the law enables public interest groups, trade associations, and other interested parties to monitor decision making by the covered agencies.

The Politics of Interest Group
Participation in Administrative Policymaking

The legal-institutional framework for participation in federal administrative policymaking has a variety of consequences. First and foremost, it removes
much policymaking from Congress, an elective component of government, and
vests it in political appointees and career civil servants in administrative agencies.
It also calls on unelected federal judges to resolve a wide range of disputes about
what the framework requires. Delegations of legislative authority to the agencies
are constitutional under the fiction that they always contain an "intelligible principle" to guide or control administrative action (*J. W. Hampton, Jr. & Co. v. United States*, 276 U.S. 394 [1928]). The truth, however, is often otherwise. Consequently, much policymaking, along with the values and trade-offs underlying it,
moves beyond the direct reach of the electorate.

Administrators make decisions that go a long way toward defining how life
is lived in the United States. The economy, health, education, housing, food, air,
water, energy, transportation, broadcasting, ecology, employment, law enforcement, product safety, and much, much more are subjects of administrative policymaking. During the legislative debates on the Walter-Logan Act in 1940, a
member of the House charged that the United States was "fast becoming a gov-

ernment by the government and not by the people"—a condition that undoubt-edly has been exacerbated by the vast growth in administrative policymaking since then (U.S. Congress 1940, 4648; also see Lowi 1969). Although individuals as well as organized interests can use the participato-ry and transparency tools afforded by the legal-institutional framework, only a tiny number do so. Individual citizens can be expected to follow the political activities and votes of their representatives and senators. They also can expect these politicians to compete for their ballots. But, realistically, they cannot rou-tinely read the *Federal Register,* track agency regulations through the federal gov-ernment's rulemaking Web site (http://www.regulations.gov), comment on pro-posed rules, attend open meetings, make FOIA requests, join reg-neg and FACA committees, or lobby agencies. Public interest groups can try to represent broad swaths of the public effectively, as environmental groups sometimes do (Shaiko 1999). Administrators themselves may even be representative of the public at large (Krislov and Rosenbloom 1981). However, there is no reason to believe that administrators' *responsiveness* to the general electorate is anything but attenuated.[8] The question of how much better organized interests fare com-pared with individual citizens and why remains. The answer has two dimen-sions: first, the extent of these interests' ability to affect policy agenda setting and, second, what model or models best portray interest group influence in administrative policymaking.

Agenda Setting

Interest groups' influence on administrative policymaking can be proactive as well as reactive. In a somewhat extreme manifestation, private parties will use formal rulemaking to propose rules. More commonly, interest groups play an important role in agenda setting—that is, they help to make an issue or policy area highly salient in the agency or political system as a whole. In doing so, they may directly lobby those administrative agencies that have a good deal of legal and policy autonomy, such as the independent regulatory commissions, to adopt specific policies or policy directions. They may also apply indirect pressure on administrators who can influence a congressional committee's agenda or think-ing by highlighting policy alternatives (Kingdon 1995; Hrebenar 1997, 260). Although political appointees often take the lead in agency agenda setting and policymaking, career administrators typically have much longer job tenure, greater technical expertise, and, possibly, stronger connections to interest groups and others concerned about the agencies' missions. These resources can be fash-ioned into powerful tools in the overall policymaking process (Kingdon 1995).

Implementation, rather than policy formulation, may also be a target of interest group activity. As Kingdon (1995, 31) notes, "Implementation is one major preoccupation of career bureaucrats. Most of them are administering exist-ing programs, not concentrating on new agenda items. The power of bureaucrats often is manifested in the implementation activity." For some groups, setting or changing the agenda for implementation can be of great importance. For example, will an agency such as the Equal Employment Opportunity Commission or OSHA make a fundamental decision to pursue a strict and punitive enforcement policy or one that is more accommodative (Kagan 1994)? Will it rely on inspections, favor self-regulation, or impose duties on regulated entities (Sparrow 2000)? For some industries and firms, the answers to such questions make the difference between long-term viability and slow demise.

Models of Interest Group Influence in Administrative Policymaking

The two main models of administrative policymaking used to explain agencies' responsiveness to interest groups are the subsystems model (Lowi 1969) and the issue (or policy) networks model (Heclo 1978). Each is present in federal administrative policymaking to a substantial extent. However, researchers debate the precise scope of each model's application and the extent to which and reasons why issue networks are currently displacing subsystems.

The subsystem model posits harmonious relationships among three players: (1) an agency (or its subunits, such as bureaus), (2) the interest groups in its policy domain, and (3) the congressional (sub)committees with which it deals. Sometimes referred to as "iron" or "cozy" triangles, such subsystems have been powerful in setting public policy in specific areas such as broadcasting, water resources, agriculture, and transportation. Sometimes agencies are said to be "captured" by the dominant interests involved (Bernstein 1955). But each participant is assumed to be promoting its own interests and to benefit from the relationship (Fox and Miller 2000, 66). The agency may obtain more authority, budget, staff, slack, and protection from adversary oversight; the organized interests obtain the policies and subsidies they seek; and, in return, they help the congressional participants win reelection. A notable feature of the model is that it is relatively impervious to presidential intervention. This is especially true when the interest groups and congressional committees gain a de facto veto over political appointments to the agency.

Issue networks are more amorphous and permeable than subsystems. They are open systems composed of groups and individuals who share a body of specialized technical knowledge, but who advance competing policy perspectives. The number of participants is relatively large and fluid. In short, issue networks "are comprised of a large number of participants with varying levels of commitment to the group project and varying degrees of dependence on others in the network. . . . [P]articipation is not necessarily based on narrow economic interests" (Fox and Miller 2000, 66–67). Compared with subsystems, networks allow greater presidential impact and agency independence in decision making.

Based on a limited number of empirical studies, it appears that, to the extent subsystems were once characteristic of federal administrative policymaking, they will probably fade away or be replaced by networks. For example, a review of rulemaking at the Environmental Protection Agency, National Highway Traffic

Safety Administration, and Department of Housing and Urban Development conducted by Marissa Martino Golden (1998, 12) unequivocally revealed networks, not triangles. In her words:

> The patterns of participation documented in this article have all the hallmarks of issue networks. Groups moved in and out of the policy process, depending on the issue. Different groups participated in each rule making, even within the same agency. Most of the rules pitted groups against each other and featured identifiable winners and losers. Yet there was a fair amount of communication among groups; indeed, information was the currency of the networks. An examination of interest group participation in agency rule making provides concrete and tangible evidence of issue networks. . . . Moreover, our focus on agency rule making adds to the issue network model by developing the concept of agency rule makers as arbiters. In the rule-making process, agency personnel give shape to the heretofore formless issue networks.

Golden's failure to find significant traces of the subsystem model is supported by additional research (Furlong 1997; Kerwin 1999, 188–189).

But in either model, or both operating simultaneously in separate administrative units, just how much influence do interest groups have? This question is at the center of a continuing debate in large part because of the difficulties in measuring political influence in the administrative context. In 1995 Scott R. Furlong conducted a survey to examine, in part, "the bureaucratic agent's perception of influence from five other institutions in our system: Congress, the president, courts, interest groups, and the general public" (Furlong 1998, 40). He found that within executive agencies (as opposed to independent regulatory commissions), "Congress and the president have a greater perceived impact on agenda policy than do interest groups." But interest groups were perceived to have greater influence than the courts and the general public. Furlong concluded that "in general, the respondents of the survey perceived that Congress and the president have the greatest influence on agency policy," but that "interest group participation and influence can and do have relevance in agency policy making and should not be overlooked" (Furlong 1998, 61).

Furlong also surveyed officials in the independent regulatory commissions. He found that only the perceived influence of the courts exceeded that of interest groups; the public, Congress, and the president were perceived as less influential than interest groups (in that order). This finding, though only measuring perception, suggests that the ties between interest groups and independent regulatory commissions are stronger than between the groups and other agencies, even though the prospect of an agency being captured seems to be waning.

A final question is whether the legal-institutional framework for interest group participation favors some interests more than others. It remains unanswered. Golden (1998) concludes that business interests have an advantage. However, based on additional research and analysis of a variety of studies, Cornelius M. Kerwin (1999, 188–189) concludes that our knowledge is inconclusive:

> Businesses, and the trade associations that represent businesses, are involved in rulemaking more often than are other groups, and they devote to it greater slices of their probably larger budgets and staffs. A strong case can be made that their superior resources and experience lead to a degree of influence in rulemaking that others cannot match. But the data from my survey are not sufficient to establish such a case. The reason that fewer citizen organizations, a category that includes environmental and consumer groups, are involved in rulemaking could be because these types of groups specialize more than business groups. Perhaps business and trade associations are so frequently threatened by rulemaking that comparatively few can afford to devote their attention elsewhere. Other data from my survey do indicate that businesses and trade associations are more likely than citizens' groups to rank rulemaking ahead of other forms of political action. Still, is this evidence of their "defensive" posture or simply greater sophistication? Unfortunately, we just do not know.

What we do know is that the legal-institutional framework for participation in federal administrative policymaking works much better for organized interests and businesses than for individual citizens and the electorate at large (Lowi 1969). From this perspective, the 1946 framework has accomplished a great deal, but it will need further development if the modern administrative state is to be more fully integrated into American democratic constitutionalism.

Notes

1. This figure includes 3.8 million civilian federal employees and some 330,000 "without compensation" and "dollar a year" employees (Van Riper 1958, 373).
2. *Procedural rules* establish agency procedures for implementing their missions. *Interpretative rules* are policy statements and explanations of how agencies understand those missions. (Interpretative rules as the Administrative Procedure Act of 1946 [APA] defines them are more widely termed interpretive rules.) *Substantive (legislative) rules* are generically like statutes in establishing regulations, eligibility, subsidies, and so forth. The APA requires publication of all three types of rules in the *Federal Register* (with some exceptions for national security, impracticability, and other good causes). However, its rulemaking procedures apply only to substantive rulemaking.
3. The key cases are *Motor Vehicles Manufacturers Association v. State Farm* (463 U.S. 29 [1983]), *Chevron v. Natural Resources Defense Council* (467 U.S. 837 [1984]), and *Heckler v. Chaney* (470 U.S. 821 [1985]).
4. See *Wilderness Society v. Morton* (495 F. 2d 1026, 1029 [1973]).
5. Executive Order 12838 (February 1993) required agencies to reduce the number of discretionary, but not congressionally mandated, committees by one-third. See U.S. General Accounting Office (1998).
6. Whether rules are better is a value judgment, but so far speed and litigation do not seem to have been dramatically affected. Systematic data from all agencies are not

available, but, based on studies to date, "it is impossible to conclude that it [reg-neg] has successfully increased the speed of the regulatory process," and, in all likelihood, it has actually added hours to the process (Coglianese 1997, 1286; also see Langbein and Kerwin 2000, 619–620). Nor does the availability of reg-neg seem to have reduced litigation over rulemaking (Coglianese 1997, 1309).

7. The Senate version is at odds with another version of Madison's words: "A popular Government, without popular information, or the means of acquiring it, is but a Prologue to a Farce or a Tragedy; or, perhaps, both. Knowledge will forever govern ignorance: And a people who mean to be their own Governors must arm themselves with the power which knowledge gives" (Madison [1822] 1999, 790).

8. Some studies indicate that federal agency enforcement is responsive to state and local governmental officials (see Scholz 1991).

References

American Bar Association, Special Committee on Administrative Law. 1934. "Report of the Special Committee on Administrative Law." In U.S. Congress, Senate, Committee on the Judiciary, Subcommittee on Separation of Powers, *Separation of Powers and the Independent Agencies: Cases and Selected Readings.* 91st Cong., 1st sess., Document 91-49, 214–239. Washington, DC: Government Printing Office, 1970.

Bernstein, Marver H. 1955. *Regulating Business by Independent Commission.* Princeton, NJ: Princeton University Press.

Black, Henry. 1979. *Black's Law Dictionary.* 5th ed. St. Paul, MN: West Publishing.

Claiborne, William. 2001. "Farm Groups Assail USDA Choice." *Washington Post,* June 15, A31.

Coglianese, Cary. 1997. "Assessing Consensus: The Promise and Performance of Negotiated Rulemaking." *Duke Law Journal* 46:1255–1349.

Cohen, Daniel, and Peter Strauss. 1997. "Congressional Review of Agency Regulations." *Administrative Law Review* 49:95–110.

Dewar, Helen. 2001. "Ergonomics Repeal Prompts Look Back." *Washington Post,* March 9, A16.

Feinberg, Lotte. 1997. "Open Government and Freedom of Information." *Handbook of Public Law and Administration,* edited by Phillip Cooper and Chester Newland. San Francisco: Jossey-Bass.

Foerstel, Herbert. 1999. *Freedom of Information and the Right to Know.* Westport, CT: Greenwood Press.

Fox, Charles, and Hugh Miller. 2000. "Policy Network." In *Defining Public Administration,* edited by Jay Shafritz. Boulder, CO: Westview Press.

Fox, Harrison, and Susan Hammond. 1977. *Congressional Staffs: The Invisible Force in American Lawmaking.* New York: Free Press.

Furlong, Scott. 1997. "Interest Group Influence on Rulemaking." *Administration and Society* 29:325–347.

———. 1998. "Political Influence on the Bureaucracy: The Bureaucracy Speaks." *Journal of Public Administration Research and Theory* 8:39–65.

Gerhardt, Michael. 2000. *The Federal Appointments Process.* Durham, NC: Duke University Press.

Golden, Marissa Martino. 1998. "Interest Groups in the Rulemaking Process: Who Participates, Whose Voices Get Heard?" *Journal of Public Administration Research and Theory* 8:245–270.

Goldstein, Amy. 2001. " 'Last-Minute' Spin on Regulatory Rite." *Washington Post,* June 9, A1ff.

Gore, Al. 1995. *Common Sense Government Works Better and Costs Less.* Washington, DC: Government Printing Office.

Harris, Christy. 1999. "Lack of Procedure Kills OSHA Reinvention Program." *Federal Times,* April 26, 3, 18.

Heclo, Hugh. 1978. "Issue Networks and the Executive Establishment." In *The New American Political System,* edited by Anthony King. Washington, DC: American Enterprise Institute.

Hibbing, John R. 1991. *Congressional Careers: Contours of Life in the U.S. House of Representatives.* Chapel Hill: University of North Carolina Press.

Hrebenar, Ronald. 1997. *Interest Group Politics in America.* 3d ed. Armonk, NY: M. E. Sharpe.

Kagan, Robert. 1994. "Regulatory Enforcement." In *Handbook of Regulation and Administrative Law,* edited by David H. Rosenbloom and Richard D. Schwartz. New York: Marcel Dekker.

Kefauver, Estes, and Jack Levin. 1947. *A Twentieth-Century Congress.* New York: Essential Books.

Kerwin, Cornelius M. 1999. *Rulemaking: How Government Agencies Write Law and Make Policy.* 2d ed. Washington, DC: CQ Press.

Kingdon, John. 1995. *Agendas, Alternatives, and Public Policies.* 2d ed. New York: Longman.

Krislov, Samuel, and David H. Rosenbloom. 1981. *Representative Bureaucracy and the American Political System.* New York: Praeger.

Langbein, Laura, and Cornelius M. Kerwin. 2000. "Regulatory Negotiation versus Conventional Rule Making: Claims, Counterclaims, and Empirical Evidence." *Journal of Public Administration Research and Theory* 10:599–632.

Lowi, Theodore J. 1969. *The End of Liberalism.* New York: Norton.

Madison, James. [1822] 1999. Letter to William T. Barry, August 4, 1822. In *James Madison: Writings.* New York: Literary Classics of the United States.

Melnick, Shep. 1994. *Between the Lines.* Washington, DC: Brookings.

Moreno, Angel. 1994. "Presidential Coordination of the Independent Regulatory Process." *Administrative Law Journal* 8:461–516.

O'Leary, Rosemary. 1993. *Environmental Change: Federal Courts and the EPA.* Philadelphia: Temple University Press.

Pianin, Eric. 2001. "Whitman Faces Tough Task, Many Obstacles at EPA." *Washington Post,* January 16, A19.

Polsby, Nelson. 1968. "The Institutionalization of the U.S. House of Representatives." *American Political Science Review* 62:144–168.

President's Committee on Administrative Management. 1937. *Report of the Committee.* Washington, DC: Government Printing Office.

Roberts, Robert, and Marion Doss. 1997. *From Watergate to Whitewater: The Public Integrity War.* Westport, CT: Praeger.

Rosenbloom, David H. 2000. *Building a Legislative-Centered Public Administration: Congress and the Administrative State, 1946–1999.* Tuscaloosa: University of Alabama Press.

———. 2003. *Administrative Law for Public Managers.* Boulder, CO: Westview Press.

Scholz, John. 1991. "Cooperative Regulatory Enforcement and the Politics of Administrative Effectiveness." *American Political Science Review* 85:115–136.

Shaiko, Ronald G. 1999. *Voices and Echoes for the Environment: Public Interest Representation in the 1990s and Beyond.* New York: Columbia University Press.

Sheraton, Mimi. 1982. "Department of Agriculture Withdraws Proposed Changes in Grading of Beef." *New York Times,* September 21.

Skrzycki, Cindy. 2000. "The Regulators: System Overhaul? Business Groups Hope for a New Era." *Washington Post,* December 19, E1.

———. 2001. "The Regulators: Critics Assail Review of 'Final' Rules." *Washington Post,*

April 3, E1, 6.

Sparrow, Malcolm. 2000. *The Regulatory Craft*. Washington, DC: Brookings.

Steck, Henry. 1984. "Politics and Administration: Private Advice for Public Purpose in a Corporatist Setting." In *Politics and Administration*, edited by Jack Rabin and James Bowman. New York: Marcel Dekker.

Strauss, Peter, Todd Rakoff, Roy Schotland, and Cynthia Farina. 1995. *Gellhorn and Byse's Administrative Law: Cases and Commentary*. 9th ed. Westbury, NY: Foundation Press.

U.S. Congress. 1940. *Congressional Record*. 76th Cong., 3d sess., Vol. 86. Washington, DC: Government Printing Office.

———. 1946. *Congressional Record*. 79th Cong., 2d sess., Vol. 92. Washington, DC: Government Printing Office.

———. 1976. *Government in the Sunshine Act—S.5 (PL94-409): Source Book: Legislative History, Texts, and Other Documents*. Senate Committee on Government Operations and House Committee on Government Operations (Joint Committee Report), 94th Cong., 2d sess. Washington, DC: Government Printing Office.

U.S. Congress. Senate. Subcommittee of the Committee on the Judiciary. 1941. Hearings on S. 674, S. 675, S. 918. 77th Cong., 1st sess. (April 2 –29). Washington, DC: Government Printing Office. (No document number shown.)

U.S. General Accounting Office. 1998. *Federal Advisory Committee Act*. Washington, DC: General Accounting Office.

U.S. General Services Administration. 1999. *Twenty-seventh Annual Report of the President on Federal Advisory Committees, Fiscal Year 1998*. Washington, DC: General Services Administration (March).

U.S. Senate. 1974. *Freedom of Information Act Source Book: Legislative Materials, Cases, Articles*. Committee on the Judiciary, Subcommittee on Administrative Practice and Procedure, 93d Cong., 2d sess. Washington, DC: Government Printing Office.

———. 1978. *Federal Advisory Committee Act (Public Law 92-463): Source Book: Legislative History, Texts, and Other Documents*. Committee on Governmental Affairs, Subcommittee on Energy, Nuclear Proliferation, and Federal Services, 95th Cong., 2d sess. Washington, DC: Government Printing Office.

Van Riper, Paul. 1958. *History of the United States Civil Service*. Evanston, IL: Row, Peterson.

Vaughn, Robert. 1994. "Federal Information Policy and Administrative Law." *Handbook of Regulation and Administrative Law*, edited by David H. Rosenbloom and Richard D. Schwartz. New York: Marcel Dekker.

15. Exploring Interest Group Participation in Executive Policymaking

Scott R. Furlong

Popular perceptions of lobbying usually evoke images of well-dressed men and women prowling the halls of Congress in an effort to influence members to vote in a particular way. Indeed, some of the most popular U.S. government textbooks define lobbying as something that transpires primarily in the legislative arena. Yet lobbying is far broader in scope: "Lobbying can be directed at any institution of government—legislative, judicial, and executive" (Berry 1984, 6). Unfortunately, much of the academic research on lobbying concentrates on the legislative branch, and so much less is known about the ways and means of lobbying the executive branch. Although some studies tangentially examine executive branch lobbying (Schlozman and Tierney 1986) or discuss it in terms of the policy subsystems (Chubb 1983; Fritschler 1989), few studies have focused on this important area of interest group research (for exceptions, see Furlong 1997; Golden 1998; Kerwin 2003).

This chapter examines some of the issues of executive branch lobbying in the context of the larger lobbying behavior of organized interests. Even though the overall goals of interest groups remain the same when they lobby different institutions—that is, they want to influence policy for their group's benefit—the techniques will change, depending on the institution being lobbied. When lobbying Congress, organizations use tools for exerting electoral pressures (such as grassroots mobilization, donations to political action committee), but these tools are not as relevant when lobbying the executive branch. There, interest groups must rely more on their access to specialized information and the relationships they have developed with bureaucratic personnel as a way to influence administrative policymaking in its various forms.

In many important ways, the executive branch of the federal government is quite different from the legislative branch. Congress operates on two-year cycles, with one session of Congress held each year. The membership of the entire House and one-third of the Senate are up for reelection at the end of each Congress. By contrast, the executive branch is a more permanent government. Granted, the president is elected every four years, but the vast majority of the inhabitants of the executive branch are civil service employees who implement public policies regardless of which political party occupies the White House. This is not to say that presidents do not have an important role to play in the execution of laws. To the contrary, they may clearly register their policy preferences in the interpretation and execution of laws passed by Congress and signed by them or by past presidents. For this reason, it is important that organized interests not ignore the White House when designing and implementing an executive branch

Table 15-1 Examples of Executive Branch Lobbying Registrations, 2002

Interest group	Lobbying firm	Issue
Flight International	Greenberg Traurig	Department of Defense air safety policy
Microsoft Corporation	Harris Wiltshire and Grannis	Use and allocation of unlicensed spectrum
The Endocrine Society	Arent Fox Kintner Plotkin & Kahn	Medicare/Medicaid treatment of obesity-related health conditions
Vanguard Medical Concepts	Olsson, Frank and Weeda	Food and Drug Administration's guidance documents for reprocessing of medical devices
International Consultants	Pillsbury Winthrop	Government approval of airport on Targeted Security security systems
V. I. Technologies	Mindbeam	Medicare reimbursement for pathogen-inactivated blood
ABS School Services	Van Scoyoc Associates	Charter school issues; implementation of No Child Left Behind initiative

Source: Lobbying Disclosure Act Lobbying Registration Forms filed with the secretary of the Senate and the clerk of the House of Representatives, U.S. Congress, 2002.

lobbying strategy. However, much of what constitutes executive branch lobbying takes place at bureaucratic levels far below the White House.

Table 15-1 provides some illustrative examples of executive branch lobbying registrations filed by interest groups in 2002. These filings are representative of the types of organized interests attentive to executive branch policymaking, as well as the types of issues at the heart of attempts by interest groups and their lobbyists to influence executive decisions. Most often the issues that attract interest groups to the executive branch are highly technical in nature and involve some form of regulation of society, in particular the economic sector. As a result, those attentive to the permanent government and its decisions in implementing public policies tend to be skewed toward those economic interests directly affected by such decisions.

As for the interests represented, each corporation or association has an economic stake in the actions of the U.S. government. And in virtually all cases Congress has already acted to provide the broad legislative framework within which government action takes place. Thus it is more than likely that these interests have been and continue to be attentive to any actions taken by Congress to alter the "rules of the game" for executive branch implementation of federal policies and programs. As a result, organized interests with ample resources are not choosing between lobbying Congress and lobbying the executive branch; they are lobbying both institutions. The key phrase here is "with ample resources." Keeping a watchful eye on executive branch activities is time-consuming and costly. Now that the *Federal Register* is online, life has become a bit more manageable for interests seeking to monitor the actions of the entire executive branch systematically and regularly.

To take one example, the Endocrine Society, one of the interest groups listed in Table 15-1, contracted with the lobbying firm Arent Fox Kintner Plotkin & Kahn (now known simply as Arent Fox PLLC) to monitor how government health programs are treating obesity-related issues. This issue falls within the jurisdiction of the Department of Health and Human Services (HHS), but HHS has multiple subagencies and bureaus that could develop policy in this arena. Before the computerization and availability of online computer searches of government documents such as the *Federal Register* (in which all the actions or proposed actions of federal government departments and agencies are published), lobbying staffs had to pore over government documents page by page. Yet even with the improvements in computer technology, executive branch lobbying remains a highly technical and expensive proposition. Consequently, organized interests attentive to executive branch decision making are likely to be drawn from the ranks of those with long-term economic interests in the actions of the permanent government.

Efforts to discern systematically the extent to which this pattern of lobbying occurs within the executive branch have been problematic mainly because of lack of centralized sources of data. Scholars have had to rely on interviews and surveys of the relevant individuals and close looks at comments in the *Federal Register*. But even then, the picture of interest group involvement in administrative policymaking has been incomplete. Passage of the Lobbying Disclosure Act of 1995 has helped somewhat, however, because it provides for the systematic collection of data on lobbying contacts within the legislative and executive branches. The current data set (as opposed to the data set produced through the Lobbying Disclosure Act) covers the informal lobbying[1] that occurs within the two branches.

Interest Group Lobbying of the Executive Branch

Quantitative research on interest group participation in the regulatory processes of the executive branch is the most recent addition to interest groups literature (Furlong 1997; Golden 1998; Kerwin 2003). Groups may attempt to lobby the executive branch in the regulatory arena in at least four major ways (Gormley 1998). Two of these approaches—lobbying by providing specific comments on rules and policies and trying to influence the appointment of an agency head who supports policies advocated by the organized interest—tend to focus on organizational activities within the agency itself. The other two approaches— trying to convince members of Congress to influence the bureaucracy and organizing a grassroots campaign that may pressure an agency or Congress to change a policy—are geared more toward the political aspects of lobbying often associated with legislative lobbying.

Buying access to executive branch agencies has not been an issue, but many scholars have written about and warned against the problem of agency capture by interest groups (Bernstein 1955; Stigler 1971). According to agency capture theory, agencies act as servants of the organized interests they regulate rather than of the general public, or policies are made by the very groups that are affected by them (Lowi 1979). Generally, capture theory is associated with economic or business interests. Although capture theory has raised concerns about the impact of interest groups on administrative policymaking, most political scientists have dismissed the theory as inappropriate for the current, more complex policymaking systems because it is highly unlikely that an agency would be so beholden to one set of interest groups (Heclo 1978). Most, if not all, policies are associated with multiple issues, and an agency must work to balance these competing interests when developing policy.

Direct lobbying of the executive branch and the access associated with it can differ greatly from lobbying and access to the legislature. Often there are legal requirements, such as the Administrative Procedures Act and the Federal Advisory Committee Act, for open access to decision making within the executive branch. Access also varies in terms of how interest groups obtain it. Empirical evidence does link political contributions to access to members of Congress (Langbein 1986), but contributions to agency officials to buy access to the agency policymaking table are illegal. Perhaps more so in the executive branch than in the legislature, access is gained through interest group knowledge of public policies, alternatives, solutions, impacts, and processes. Because the bureaucracy is now intimately involved in the development of public policy in the United States, interest groups have recognized the importance of continuing their lobbying efforts within the executive branch (Schlozman and Tierney 1986; Gais and Walker 1991; Kerwin 2003). In fact, a large majority of interest groups rate their lobbying efforts with administrative agencies as "on a par with or of greater importance than lobbying Congress" (Kerwin 2003, 181).

Interest groups have many ways in which to lobby the bureaucracy. For example, in trying to influence agency rulemaking groups can provide written comments on proposed rules, attend and participate in public hearings, informally contact agency officials prior to or after the notice of the proposal, serve on advisory committees, or petition for a rulemaking (Kerwin 2003; also see Furlong 1997). In recent years, groups have been able to use a variety of electronic formats, such as bulletin boards, electronic policy dialogues, and e-mail, in contacting the bureaucracy. In addition, the federal government is promoting e-rulemaking and its regulations.gov Web site.

The most common form of executive branch participation is through the notice-and-comment process, which is dictated by the Administrative Procedures Act. Under this law, agencies that are developing informal regulations must

give interested parties an opportunity to submit comments, with certain exceptions, on proposed actions. Agencies publish their proposals in the *Federal Register*, and, as part of the discussion of the proposed policy, solicit comments from
the general public. In theory, the comments that agencies receive are incorporated into formulation of the final regulation that will become the binding policy.
Because administrative actions such as rulemaking tend to deal with relatively
specific areas of policy, the types of organizations likely to participate will have
some specialized knowledge of the policy arena. In addition, because the process
of rulemaking is not as well known as that of lawmaking, potential participants
must have a sound background in U.S. government policymaking and awareness
of which agencies have primary responsibility for which issues. Organizations
that have the substantive and procedural resources needed to understand agency
rulemaking therefore have some advantages. Such organized interests are likely
to have a more permanent economic stake in the outcome of the regulatory
processes conducted by federal agencies and departments and also have the
resources necessary to commit to a longer-term presence in the process.

Recent research in this area identified two trends that have emerged in the
composition of the interests participating regularly in rulemaking (Golden
1998). First, the composition of interests varies by agency. For example, citizen
advocacy or public interest group participation in the rulemaking process in two
of the regulatory agencies studied, the Environmental Protection Agency (EPA)
and the National Highway Traffic Safety Administration (NHTSA), was limited compared with the large amount of lobbying by these types of organizations
in a third, the Department of Housing and Urban Development (HUD). In
fact, over 75 percent of the comments on EPA and NHTSA regulations came
from business organizations.[2] Second, and perhaps more generally, is the
"absence of citizen representation," even to some extent with the HUD rules
(Golden 1998, 255).

Agencies often solicit comments and participation in other ways in the rulemaking process. For example, some agencies conduct public hearings in which
organizations and people can offer oral comments on proposed policies. Serving
on an advisory committee is another, more extensive form of participation; organizations might be asked to evaluate policies before they are made "public." In
some cases, interest group participation in executive branch policymaking has
become more direct and substantive through mechanisms such as regulatory
negotiation ("reg-neg"). The reg-neg process gives an interest group a seat at the
table, along with agency representatives and other organizations interested in a
particular policy, where it can help to generate a mutually agreeable policy (Harter 1982). Other regulatory reform efforts have also attempted to include interested organizations in policy development. The Environmental Protection
Agency, for example, implemented its Project XL (eXcellence in Leadership) as
a way to openly solicit organizational input from major stakeholders.

These methods of interest group participation are much more resource-
intensive and require a large commitment from the interest groups that want to

be involved. Regulatory negotiations, for example, typically occur within short periods of time and require attendance at intensive, multiple-day meetings devoted to discussions of information, alternatives, and ultimately proposals. On the one hand, organizations that do not have the necessary resources may be reluctant to participate in such intensive exercises that focus only on one small policy area when they have to worry about many issues. On the other hand, business and trade associations that derive specific benefits from being involved in the development of a rule may be more inclined to expend the resources with the hope of recouping them through their influence of policy outcomes.

The other major access point in executive branch lobbying is the Executive Office of the President. As presidents have established the agencies they need to manage the regulatory process more closely, interest groups have tried to influence these agencies as well. Over the past thirty years, presidents have used the Office of Management and Budget (OMB) and created ad hoc organizations to monitor regulatory policymaking. Since President Ronald Reagan's Executive Order 12291, OMB (specifically the Office of Information and Regulatory Affairs) has served as an extension of the presidency to review agency regulations and policies to ensure they conform to the administration's agenda. And presidents since Reagan have used OMB as a resource to manage agency policymaking. Reagan's successor in office, George Bush, continued to use the authority of Reagan's executive order, but President Bill Clinton issued his own regulatory review Executive Order 12866. Although in many ways it was similar to Executive Order 12291, the Clinton order opened up the process of regulatory review to allow groups outside OMB to monitor the agency's review of regulations. In addition, it limited the number of regulations subject to review. Once in office, President George W. Bush continued to use Executive Order 12866 as the primary mechanism for OMB review.

During the Reagan and Bush administrations, the secrecy in which OMB made some of its decisions raised some issues about the influence of outside groups. The Clinton order, by opening up the process of regulatory review, shed some sunshine on interest group influence. President George W. Bush's selection to head the Office of Information and Regulatory Affairs of OMB, John Graham, continued the idea of openness in the review process established by the Clinton administration.

A primary example of an ad hoc organization was the Council on Competitiveness, established by President George Bush in 1991. In those days, the organization served as a "super OMB," reviewing agency policies of particular importance. Interest groups may attempt to influence policy direction in those offices that are particularly close to the president, and evidence of just such contacts surfaced in connection with the Council on Competitiveness. It appeared that certain organizations and individuals friendly to the Bush administration were granted access to some of the key decisions in these reviews (Triano and Watzman 1991). Another noteworthy example was the energy task force set up by Vice President Richard B. Cheney at the outset of the George W. Bush administration.

Some observers claimed that the members of the task force, mainly industry types, were having an undue influence over the administration's energy policy and that other, more environmentally friendly organizations were shut out of this process. In the end, though, any interest group with access to the president and the president's immediate staff can be particularly effective in lobbying.

Executive Branch Lobbying Behavior

This section examines interest group lobbying of the executive branch using two data sources. One way to study interest group lobbying of the executive branch is to examine who is actually participating in notice-and-comment rulemaking. Participants in notice-and-comment are available through examination of the docket and represent a formal and direct lobbying contact with an executive agency. Another way is to use information from the data made available through the Lobbying Disclosure Act, as discussed earlier. These contacts tend to be less formal in that organizations may not be contacting agencies on specific issues or through the typical Administrative Procedure Act policies.

Notice-and-Comment Rulemaking

As mentioned earlier, one of the most popular ways in which interest groups can directly lobby administrative agencies is by providing comments to a proposed rule. Agencies must keep records in their docket of who provides these comments. In 1998, under the Freedom of Information Act (FOIA), I contacted seven executive departments and agencies to request a list of commenters to any proposed regulation published from January 1 to June 30, 1996.[3] Because regulations were limited to those that appeared in the *Unified Regulatory Agenda*, the request was limited to significant agency regulations, which numbered 103. The agencies provided usable information for fifty-one regulations.[4] Table 15-2 shows the extent of lobbying that occurred during notice-and-comment rulemaking by various interest group types.

Economic interest groups, such as businesses and trade associations, have certain advantages when it comes to lobbying in general and lobbying the executive branch in particular. For one thing, their greater budgetary and personnel resources allow them to participate through a variety of avenues. And their access to information, especially in areas that affect their economic interests directly, make them more likely to join in agency rulemaking proceedings that require the type of technical expertise needed for effective participation. Indeed, to make informed comments about a policy, organizations commenting on proposed regulations must understand the substantive policies and language in the proposal. Given the resources available to economic interest groups, one would expect businesses and trade associations to participate more in informal rulemaking proceedings. The evidence in Table 15-2 appears to confirm this predominance of economic groups participating in notice-and-comment rulemaking activities.

Table 15-2   Interest Group Participation in the Notice-and-Comment Rule-making Process, by Interest Group Type

	Mean number of comments[a]	Mean percentage[b]
Business groups	20.96	30.23
Trade associations	8.14	19.35
Unions	0.31	0.45
Public interest groups	1.84	4.88
Government groups	6.35	22.72
Other	25.29	22.47

[a] Average number of comments provided by each interest group type.

[b] Average percentage of total comments received for each regulation.

For the sample of proposed regulations, over 30 percent of the comments came from business and nearly 20 percent from trade associations, while less than 5 percent came from public interest groups.

Earlier work on participation in rulemaking confirms the idea of businesses participating in rulemaking, but also begins the process of examining the effectiveness of that participation. Golden (1998, 261) has observed that "when there is conflict rather than consensus among the commenters, the agency tends to hear most clearly the voices that support the agency's position." Is this evidence of effective lobbying or simple confirmation of an agency's policy direction? The answer is unclear at this point. When interest groups have gauged their own effectiveness at lobbying, a large percentage of them have found that they are able to successfully influence agency rulemaking at least "half of the time" that they participated in informal rulemaking (Kerwin 2003). Yet the perspectives of rulemaking agencies suggest that changes to the rule occur less then 50 percent of the time (Furlong 1992). Unfortunately, organizations may overstate their influence abilities. The question of how much influence interest groups actually have on rulemaking is still very much open to debate.

Informal Lobbying

As noted earlier, with passage of the Lobbying Disclosure Act it is now possible to examine interest group lobbying of the executive and legislative branches. Although the consistency of the information collected does present some problems,[5] it is a source of data that until now has not been available. It provides information on informal contacts that occur between interest groups and government, an important aspect of lobbying activity within the executive branch (Kerwin 2003).

To assess the role of informal lobbying, I drew a random sample of 100 interest groups from a population of 3,349 interest groups that registered within

the designated time period, January 1–June 30, 1996. Because the distribution of
these groups in terms of organizational type is similar to the distributions used
in other interest group studies, there is reason to believe the sample is representative of the group population. Information on legislative lobbying is provided for
comparative purposes.

Table 15-3 summarizes the legislative and executive issues lobbied by
these interest groups as well as the agencies lobbied and the policy areas they
may lobby. Two distinct aspects of lobbying are shown in this table: executive
branch lobbying in and of itself and a comparison of executive branch lobbying and legislative lobbying. Columns (2)–(4) of the table are a snapshot of
executive branch lobbying. Column (2), which shows the mean number of
executive issues lobbied, reveals once again (based on the lobbying data provided by the Lobbying Disclosure Act) that economic organizations have lobbied informally on more issues than public interest groups. Columns (3)–(4),
however, show some interesting results about public interest groups. The actual number of agencies lobbied is much more in alignment with the number
lobbied by other interest group types. Column (4) represents policy areas that
organizations said they *may* lobby during the reporting time period (there is
no distinction between executive lobbying and legislative lobbying). In other
words, groups had to select areas that might be of concern to them. Again,
public interest groups appear to want to lobby on a wide range of policy issues,
much like businesses and trade associations, but the actual follow-through on
these activities, shown in column (2), is less, or they are focusing on legislative lobbying.

Table 15-3   Issues and Agencies Lobbied by Interest Group Type, as Reported
in the Lobbying Disclosure Act Data

	N	Mean number of legislative issues lobbied (1)	Mean number of executive issues lobbied (2)	Mean number of agencies lobbied (3)	Mean number of policy areas lobbied[a] (4)
Businesses	42	11.05	1.21	3.81	8.50
Trade associations	37	9.73	1.68	2.81	5.92
Unions	4	11.75	2.00	5.50	16.25
Public interest groups	15	14.33	0.87	3.40	6.47
Total	98[b]	11.08	1.37	3.44	7.53

[a]Mean represents the number of policy areas organizations stated that they may lobby during the time
period (within both legislative and executive branches) and not necessarily the number of areas they
did lobby.

[b]Two of the groups in the sample are not classified under any of these group types and are not included for analysis.

A comparison of executive branch lobbying and legislative lobbying reveals that, in general, interest groups are lobbying more legislative issues than executive issues. But perhaps a more interesting point is that public interest groups are actually lobbying a greater number of legislative issues than any other interest group type. Given resource advantages, it would not have been surprising to see economic groups lobbying more legislative issues as well as executive issues, but these data show otherwise. Public interest groups appear to make a concerted effort to lobby the legislative branch.

An examination of the data from the Lobbying Disclosure Act from a different angle confirms the previous results. Each of the one hundred interest groups selected for the sample identified between one and thirty-four general policy areas that it intended to lobby. For these data, the unit of analysis is the interest group/issue area dyad. For example, if a group listed three different areas—environment, telecommunications, and welfare—the group would have three records of data. The data set contained 725 potential interest group/issue area dyads, of which 333 were available for analysis.[6]

Table 15-4 examines lobbying contacts by those organizations that made at least one contact with either the legislative or executive branch. It shows pronounced differences in lobbying behavior among interest group types. It is clear that businesses and trade associations are more active in lobbying in general. But it is equally clear that the difference between these economic organizations and public interest groups is much greater in the area of executive branch lobbying. Public interest group lobbying of the executive branch appears to have dropped off by about half compared with these groups' legislative lobbying efforts.

Table 15-4   Interest Group/Policy Dyads Making at Least One Contact with Legislative and Executive Branches

Group type[b]	N	Legislative lobbying[a]		Executive lobbying	
		No. of contacts	Percentage	No. of contacts	Percentage
Businesses	153	142	46	29	42
Trade associations	114	100	32	30	43
Unions	14	14	5	4	6
Public interest groups	52	52	17	6	9
Total	333	308	100	69	100

[a]Three hundred and eight separate dyads were making legislative contacts. Of those, 46 percent were business groups, 32 percent were trade associations, and so forth. The interpretation is similar for executive lobbying; 42 percent of those making contact (twenty-nine of sixty-nine) were businesses.

[b]Because of the small number of organizations classified as government or other, they are excluded from this analysis.

Table 15-5   Legislative and Executive Contacts Made by Interest Group/
Policy Dyads

Group type	N	Legislative lobbying		Executive lobbying	
		No. of contacts	Percentage	No. of contacts	Percentage
Businesses	153	142	93	29	19
Trade associations	114	100	88	30	26
Unions	14	14	100	4	29
Public interest groups	52	52	100	6	11
Total	333	308	93	69	21

Tables 15-5 and 15-6 provide additional confirmation of the differences in lobbying activity among group types. Table 15-5 again shows that all organizational types tend to focus on legislative lobbying. Not surprisingly, 93 percent of the dyads are engaged in legislative lobbying, but only 21 percent of them lobby the executive. Lobbying Congress, at least informally, still appears to be the target of most lobbying efforts. Of the dyads examined, almost all made contact with the legislative branch, but that was not the case with executive lobbying. For example, only 19 percent of the businesses (29 out of 153) made executive contacts. An even smaller percentage (11 percent) of public interest group dyads made executive branch contacts. Table 15-6 shows the total and mean number of legislative and executive issues lobbied by these organizational types, and it further confirms their lobbying behavior. Every group type lobbied the legislative branch and the issues of concern. In fact, the public interest groups actually lobbied more issues than the other organizational types. Once again, though, public interest groups lobbied the executive branch quite a bit less than the economic groups.

On the one hand, because public interest groups are typically membership groups, one would expect these groups to lobby the legislative branch more than the executive branch.[7] Indeed, interest groups that rely on individual memberships for support are more likely to lobby the legislative branch than executive branch agencies (Wright 1996). As noted earlier, a large and diverse membership has certain advantages when groups lobby the legislative branch, and these types of groups are more likely to use grassroots efforts in their lobbying techniques because of their ability to influence legislators who are responsive to electoral pressures. By contrast, the sheer number of direct contacts will have less of an effect on executive branch agencies that do not rely on this type of political support. Therefore, one would expect public interest groups to be more involved in legislative lobbying than executive lobbying.

On the other hand, businesses and trade associations have the relevant expertise to perhaps be more active in executive lobbying than public interest groups (Wright 1996; Golden 1998). It appears, then, that groups not depen-

Table 15-6 Legislative and Executive Branch Issues Lobbied, by Group Type

Group type	N	Legislative issues		Executive issues	
		Total[a]	Mean	Total[a]	Mean
Business	153	464	3.03	51	0.33
Trade associations	114	369	3.24	65	0.58[b]
Unions	14	47	3.36	8	0.57
Public interest groups	52	229	4.40[c]	10	0.19
Total	333	1,109	3.33	134	0.40

[a]These columns represents the total number of legislative or executive issues lobbied by the dyads.

[b]Trade associations lobbied executive issues significantly more than public interest groups (0.05, one-tail test).

[c]Public interest groups lobbied legislative issues significantly more than businesses (0.05, one-tail test).

dent on large memberships and more likely to have legal and administrative expertise lobby the executive branch more than the public interest groups. Businesses do not lobby the executive branch as much as trade associations, perhaps because they rely on the greater expertise of the trade associations in executive branch lobbying. Yet businesses rank higher in legislative lobbying than trade associations, perhaps demonstrating that businesses represent actual jobs in congressional districts and so possess a potentially powerful lobbying tool.

Conclusion

This chapter has examined how interest groups interact with the executive branch of government. A few studies have attempted to explore the actual contacts between interest groups and the executive branch, whereas most of the literature has focused more on the theoretical issues surrounding this relationship, such as agency capture by interest groups or the relationships within issue networks or policy subsystems. Although these theories of interest group relationships with the bureaucracy are important, a better understanding of what actually occurs in this relationship will help to reveal the potential impact that organizations can have if they can access and later influence agency policymaking. Through congressional delegation of authority, federal administrative agencies are able to develop a wide range of public policy, and they often are given a fair amount of discretion in which to operate. Interest groups that are aware of this arrangement have an added opportunity to serve their members' interests and try to influence these agencies. It is probably safe to say that the general population has even less knowledge of interest group lobbying of the executive branch than of the legislature.

Executive branch lobbying is alive and well. Agencies receive thousands of written comments from interest groups and the general public on rulemaking activities, and many more oral comments at public meetings held across the country. For example, the recent ergonomic rule issued by the Occupational Safety and Health Administration at the end of the Clinton administration generated over 11,000 public comments (U.S. Occupational Safety and Health Administration 2000). In addition, interest groups and the public can engage in more in-depth activities as agencies reach out for the best information possible. Yet interest groups—especially public interest ones—continue to concentrate their lobbying efforts on the legislative branch. Public interest groups appear to recognize that they can use grassroots efforts or their membership base to try to influence members of Congress. In the study described in this chapter, public interest group participation represented a greater percentage of lobbying activities within the legislature than those associated with notice-and-comment rulemaking. This trend was also evident when examining informal lobbying behavior using the Lobbying Disclosure Act data. By contrast, economic groups appear more active in lobbying the executive branch, perhaps taking advantage of their legal and administrative expertise within the policy arena. Even though these groups still focus most of their attention on the legislature, they are more active in lobbying the executive branch than public interest groups. These findings confirm previous theories on and studies of interest group participation within the executive branch. Rulemaking participation continues to be dominated by economic organizations.

Despite the amount of authority that Congress delegates to the bureaucracy and the important role that agencies play in policymaking, groups still see Congress as their primary target for lobbying efforts for several reasons. First, groups may be continuing historically effective practices because they perceive better access to Congress and legislators, whereas they may not perceive much benefit in lobbying a bureaucracy that is supposedly just carrying out congressional will. Second, Congress has an actual process for how lobbying should be conducted—and, in essence it has blessed the activity—whereas ex parte contacts with bureaucratic officials are more regulated. Third, although Congress may delegate authority to the agencies, it still has influence and oversight over them. Groups recognize the oversight authority and lobby the political principals of the agencies accordingly (McCubbins, Noll, and Weingast 1989).

To succeed, interest groups must conduct several interrelated lobbying activities (Schlozman and Tierney 1986; Heinz et al. 1993; Browne 1998). Yet not all groups can do all forms of lobbying because of various resource constraints. Similarly, any one group must make some choices in determining which tactics will provide the greatest payoffs. Both observations may be particularly true for public interest groups. If public interest groups do not participate in the administrative process to the same extent, they are perhaps hampered in their ability to influence policy within the bureaucracy. And when public interest groups do not participate in this arena, limited perspectives, biased toward economic groups, are put forth by the interest group community. Is this evidence of agency capture? Do agencies provide de facto representation of the public interest group (for example, the EPA representing the environmental groups)? Or do public interest groups get their point across to agencies through indirect lobbying of the legislature? The responses to these questions will go a long way toward explaining executive branch lobbying and the issues that could be associated with it.

Another possibility is that executive branch lobbying differs according to the policy arena in question. Current research suggests such a possibility, and much of the literature on policy types and the role of subsystems does as well (Ripley and Franklin 1984; Golden 1998). Although this question was beyond the scope of the data used in this study, more data are becoming available that will allow quantitative study of specific policy arenas (Baumgartner and Leech 2001). Such studies would further some of the research predicting a distinction in lobbying strategies based on the policy areas of interest (Heinz et al. 1993).[8]

Executive branch lobbying and its impact on policy development will continue to be an important issue well into the future. Even though most studies of lobbying have focused on the legislative branch, many recognize the issues and potential of lobbying the executive branch as well. The results of the study described in this chapter suggest that a relatively small proportion of interest groups participate in executive branch lobbying. In essence, if an interest group fails to influence policy in Congress, it will try to find a more sympathetic ear in the executive branch when it implements the policy—a form of executive "appeals court" (Berry 1984, 206–208). But if only a small number of interest groups take advantage of this appeals process, then relatively few groups are involved in influencing decisions coming out of the executive branch and ultimately the policy itself. In a practical sense, interest groups not lobbying the executive branch should expand their efforts, or they will find themselves left out of a significant part of the policy loop and may go unheard during critical times of policy development.

Notes

1. Here the term *informal lobbying* means those interest group lobbying activities that are not somehow identified or noted in other sources. For example, Congress keeps records of who testifies in front of a committee, and executive agencies track who provides written comments on a proposed rule. But contacts outside of the more formal policy-making structures are often much more difficult to track.
2. Golden classifies business organizations to include corporations, trade associations, and coalitions. Professional associations and unions are not included, but they participated very little in her sample of rules.
3. The seven departments and agencies were the Departments of Energy, Health and Human Services, Interior, Labor, and Transportation; the Environmental Protection Agency; and the Nuclear Regulatory Commission.
4. The Department of Transportation (DOT) did not respond to the FOIA request. Each agency that did not respond within a month received a follow-up letter, but again there was no response from DOT. This is unfortunate, because DOT had the largest number of regulations listed.
5. For example, individuals and groups that spend less than 20 percent of their time lobbying are exempt from the filing requirement. In addition, any information solicited by

government policymakers is exempt, which would include solicitation of comments for a proposed rule. For a full accounting of the potential problems of the act, see Furlong (1999).
6. The actual number for analysis is less because it is based on the actual lobbying that occurred during the study period. The 725 figure is based on the lobbying registration form, which lists what issue areas a group may lobby during that period.
7. Although trade associations are also membership groups in that their members are corporations, they differ from citizens groups in that members of the latter can exert electoral pressures on members of Congress.
8. Heinz et al. (1993) provide some evidence to support this theory. In their study of the lobbying of different policy domains, more targets within the executive branch were listed for those areas associated with bureaucratic or regulatory policy (agriculture and energy) than for other domains (labor and health).

References

Baumgartner, Frank R., and Beth L. Leech. 2001. "Interest Niches and Policy Bandwagons." *Journal of Politics* 63:1191–1213.

Bernstein, Marver H. 1955. *Regulating Business by Independent Commission.* Princeton, NJ: Princeton University Press.

Berry, Jeffrey M. 1984. *The Interest Group Society.* Boston: Little, Brown.

Browne, William P. 1998. *Groups, Interests, and U.S. Public Policy.* Washington, DC: Georgetown University Press.

Chubb, John. 1983. *Interest Groups and the Bureaucracy: The Politics of Energy.* Stanford, CA: Stanford University Press.

Fritschler, A. Lee. 1989. *Smoking and Politics.* 4th ed. Englewood Cliffs, NJ: Prentice-Hall.

Furlong, Scott. 1992. "Interest Group Influence on Regulatory Policy." Ph.D. diss., American University, Washington, DC.

———. 1997. "Interest Group Influence on Rulemaking." *Administration and Society* 29:325–347.

———. 1999. "The Lobbying Disclosure Act and Interest Group Lobbying Data: Two Steps Forward and One Step Back." *VOX POP* (winter).

Gais, Thomas L., and Jack L. Walker Jr. 1991. "Pathways to Influence in American Government." In *Mobilizing Interest Groups in America,* edited by Jack L. Walker. Ann Arbor: University of Michigan Press.

Golden, Marissa Martino. 1998. "Interest Groups in the Rulemaking Process: Who Participates, Whose Voices Get Heard?" *Journal of Public Administration Research and Theory* 8:245–270.

Gormley, William T., Jr. 1998. "Interest Group Interventions in the Administrative Process: Conspirators and Co-Conspirators." In *The Interest Group Connection: Electioneering, Lobbying, and Policymaking in Washington,* edited by Paul S. Herrnson, Ronald G. Shaiko, and Clyde Wilcox. Chatham, NJ: Chatham House.

Harter, Phillip. 1982. "Regulatory Negotiation: A Cure for the Malaise." *Georgetown Law Review* 71:1–113.

Heclo, Hugh. 1978. "Issue Networks and the Executive Establishment." In *The New American Political System,* edited by Anthony King. Washington, DC: American Enterprise Institute.

Heinz, John P., Edward O. Laumann, Robert L. Nelson, and Robert H. Salisbury. 1993. *The Hollow Core: Private Interests in National Policymaking.* Cambridge, MA: Harvard University Press.

Kerwin, Cornelius M. 2003. *Rulemaking: How Government Agencies Write Law and Make Policy.* 3d ed. Washington, DC: CQ Press.

Langbein, Laura. 1986. "Money and Access." *Journal of Politics* 48:1052–1062.

Lowi, Theodore J. 1979. *The End of Liberalism.* 2d ed. New York: Norton.

McCubbins, Matthew D., Roger G. Noll, and Barry R. Weingast. 1989. "Structure and Process as Solutions to the Politicians' Principal-Agency Problem." *Virginia Law Review* 74:431–482.

Ripley, Randall, and Grace Franklin. 1984. *Congress, the Bureaucracy, and Public Policy.* 3d ed. Chicago: Dorsey.

Schlozman, Kay Lehman, and John T. Tierney. 1986. *Organized Interests and American Democracy.* New York: Harper and Row.

Stigler, George. 1971. "The Theory of Economic Regulation." *Bell Journal of Economics and Management Science* 2:3–21.

Triano, Christine, and Nancy Watzman. 1991. *All the Vice President's Men: How the Quayle Council on Competitiveness Secretly Undermines Health, Safety and Environmental Programs.* Washington, DC: OMB Watch/Public Citizen.

U.S. Occupational Safety and Health Administration. 2000. *Ergonomics Program; Final Rule. 65 FR 68261.* Washington, DC: Government Printing Office.

Wright, John R. 1996. *Interest Groups and Congress: Lobbying, Contributions and Influence.* Boston: Allyn and Bacon.

16. Who Serves Special Interests?
The President, Congress, and Interest Groups

Paul J. Quirk and Bruce F. Nesmith

Rightly or wrongly, most Americans believe that the federal government is dominated by special interests. In national polls since the 1970s, almost two-thirds of respondents have said that the government is "pretty much run by a few big interests looking out for themselves" ("Is the Government Run" 1998). Although most scholars find such beliefs exaggerated, they acknowledge a systemic problem of excessive response to organized groups (Peterson 1990–1991; Mucciaroni 1994; Wright 1996). Indeed, the capture of government by interest groups is undoubtedly the source of policy failure most discussed in the academic literature and most often lamented in popular lore about American politics (Griffith 1939; Cater 1964; Freeman 1965).

An important question about interest group capture is what, if anything, institutional structures have to do with it. This chapter looks at a central issue about interest groups and American political institutions: how the influence of interest groups over public policy depends on the incentives and responses of the presidency and Congress and on the relations between the two institutions. Does the president tend to resist narrow interest group demands and act on behalf of broader, more general interests, as many commentators have suggested (Neustadt 1960; Burns 1965; Mezey 1989; Hardin 1974; Moe 2000)? Does Congress eagerly bestow favors on narrow interest groups and block general-interest reforms (Mayhew 1974; Fiorina 1977; Shepsle and Weingast 1987; Lohmann and O'Halloran 1994)? If so, how important are any such differences? Finally, from a practical standpoint, would institutional changes that enhance the president's power in relation to Congress help to control interest group influence (Wayne 1978; Edwards 1980; Kingdon 1984; Light 1991)?

Generations of analysts and participants in American politics have advanced this *presidential superiority thesis*. Some scholars, modifying this view, have granted that presidents sometimes support favorite special interests, but suggested that they do so substantially less than Congress (McCarty 2000). Other scholars, however, have largely rejected such claims (de Grazia 1965; Maass 1983; Cooper 1986; Arnold 1990; Gregg 1997), and held that the president and Congress do not differ consistently in this respect, a view we call the *congressional parity thesis*. Definitive evidence has been lacking.

In this chapter, we first review the theoretical debate about presidential and congressional responses to interest group demands. As Weaver and Rockman (1993) demonstrated, the effects of political institutions on governmental performance can be very difficult to sort out. And the theoretical debate about presidential general-interest superiority turns out to be inconclusive. We then turn to the evidence of presidential and congressional behavior in several areas of policy that are strongly affected by narrow interest groups—economic regulation, federal lands policy, tax expenditures, farm subsidies, and environmental regulation. We consider all the presidents from John F. Kennedy to George W. Bush. Our findings support a qualified version of the presidential superiority thesis. In the conclusion, we weigh the implications of our findings for reforming or managing the relations between the president and Congress.

The Theoretical Debate

Several arguments have been advanced in support of presidential general-interest superiority. But they all turn in some way on two fundamental structural features: first, the president is a single elected official, and, second, Congress is an assembly composed of a large number of separately elected members, 535 in the modern era. Both presidents and political scientists have argued that presidential superiority in dealing with narrow groups stems simply from the president's structural advantage as the only official elected by the entire nation (Neustadt 1960). Because the whole nation is their district, so to speak, presidents are attentive to the interests and well-being of the whole.

A political scientist before he became president, Woodrow Wilson found Congress and its committees riddled with special-interest influence: "The Committee on Commerce consents to listen to prominent railroad officials upon the subject of the regulation of freight charges and fares, and scores of interested persons telegraph inquiries to the chairman of the Committee of Ways and Means [seeking to testify on] the revision of the tariff. . . . They are as a rule the pleas of special pleaders, the arguments of advocates" (Wilson 1892, 84). Only the nationally elected president, Wilson argued, had the responsibility and sense of duty to lead in the public interest. A later president, Jimmy Carter, expressed similar views in his farewell address: "The president is the only elected official charged with the primary responsibility of representing all the people. In the moments of decision, after the different and conflicting views have been aired, it is the president who then must speak to the nation and for the nation" (Carter 1981).

Linking institutional structures to how citizens reward and punish elected officials, political scientist Morris Fiorina (1980) has argued that citizens recognize that the president and a single member of Congress differ in their ability to shape policy, and thus hold them accountable for different outcomes. Citizens hold the president accountable for major policies and national conditions, simply because the president alone has a large say in national policy; they evaluate individual members of Congress, who are far less able to reshape national policy, largely on other, nonpolicy grounds.

To some extent, survey research supports this logically compelling distinction. A comparative study of voter attitudes found that presidential approval was driven by an assessment of the nation's economy, as well as international relations and the threat of war, whereas members of the House of Representatives were judged on district service, empathy for constituents, and personal trustworthiness (Parker and Davidson 1979; Wayne 1982; Jacobson 1997, 108–116).[1] These contrasting citizen evaluations give presidents a strong incentive to produce policies that serve broad national interests — and to resist interest group demands if necessary to do so — because such policies will improve their performance evaluations and electoral prospects. But if members of Congress defer to interest groups on a major policy and thereby do harm to the general public, they do not expect to be held accountable for the policy.

That the president is a single official, instead of an assembly, may also matter in another, related way. Citizens may be able to hold the president to a higher standard of representation because they are more aware of the president's actions. As Wilson also wrote, the president's responses are shaped by "a consciousness of being in an official station so conspicuous that no faithful discharge of duty can go unacknowledged and unrewarded, and no breach of trust undiscovered and unpunished" (Wilson 1892, 284). Certainly, the national news media devote far more time to covering the president than they do Congress (Hess 1981). For example, even in the early months of Rep. Newt Gingrich's Speakership in 1995, when the Republican leadership claimed the right to define the national agenda, President Bill Clinton was mentioned in media coverage more often than Congress (Graber 1997, 270–272). In short, the president is more constrained to work in behalf of broad national interests, even if special interests demand otherwise, simply because the people are watching. Members of Congress find it easier to do favors for special interests, because their individual decisions are less likely to be observed. Even if voters would otherwise hold them accountable, they lack the information to do so.

Finally, the president's advantage in defending general interests is arguably enhanced by the way Congress chooses to organize itself — in particular, by its reliance on the committee system. Some observers believe that the very purpose of the committee system is to help individual members of Congress obtain benefits for their favored interest group and geographic constituencies (Mayhew 1974; Shepsle and Weingast 1987). Members join committees whose jurisdictions provide opportunities to seek such benefits, and the full chambers largely defer to the committees' wishes. With their gatekeeping role, the committees are also powerfully positioned to block general-interest proposals that challenge those special-interest benefits. Presidents, by contrast, can take general-interest positions when they wish to do so — if necessary, without the approval of the specialized agencies of the executive branch (Moe 2000, 451–454).

These considerations suggest, then, that overcoming the special-interest inclinations of Congress often depends on effective presidential leadership. Unfortunately, in this view such leadership is not generally possible. As James L. Sundquist wrote in the mid-1980s, "A president is expected to lead the Congress, but its two houses are independent institutions and, most of the time of late, one or both are controlled by his political opposition. And when a president fails as leader—whether because the Congress chooses not to follow or because of any of the many possible forms of personal inadequacy—the system has no safeguard" (Sundquist 1986, 7–8). Former secretary of Treasury C. Douglas Dillon stated the problem very simply: "Only the president has a national constituency, but he has no authority to put his policies in place or to see that they are carried out. All he can do is to exhort and hope that this will bring pressure on the Congress to act" (Dillon 1985, 25–26).

A few commentators have had the temerity to call for sweeping changes in the American constitutional system, amounting to substantial modification or even abandonment of the separation of powers (Robinson 1985). But advocates of the presidential superiority thesis mainly favor less dramatic, feasible measures to enhance the president's power in dealing with Congress. These might range from narrow procedural provisions, such as presidential fast-track authority on trade bills, to judicial policies favoring administrative discretion, to changes in election laws or campaign finance regulations designed to strengthen political parties, to a constitutional amendment providing for a line-item veto. For advocates of presidential superiority, whatever institutional practices strengthen the presidency are bound to benefit general interests.

Considering how frequently the presumption of presidential general-interest superiority appears in the literature, it is perhaps surprising that another view is even possible. But some observers have contested this presidential advantage, or at least questioned its magnitude—that is, they deny that there is a dramatic or consistent difference between the president and Congress in the ability to resist special-interest demands (de Grazia 1965; Cooper 1986; Arnold 1990). They advance a congressional parity thesis, suggesting that Congress's capability in this respect is roughly on a par with the president's. Of course, they also reject the implication that reforms designed to increase presidential power would improve the performance of government.

The congressional parity view argues both that Congress has virtues for dealing with narrow interests and that the president is far from pure. For one thing, these scholars argue, the claim of presidents to a uniquely national perspective is dubious. Congress, too, has a national perspective and is capable of vindicating general interests (Maass 1983). The reason is straightforward. Even if individual members of Congress are parochial and committees favor particular groups, Congress acts by aggregating majority opinion (Cooper 1986, 35). District-based special interests have to win approval of their measures from a majority of members. And committees need the same support. The president may be the only single elected official with a national constituency, but the 535 members of Congress, taken together, have the same national constituency.

Those who hold this view also point out that presidents have plenty of incentives to do favors for interest groups. Like members of Congress, they must be elected, and they may be inclined to reward whichever groups support them electorally (Levitt and Snyder 1995; McCarty 2000, 118). Because local support adds up to national support, presidents are attentive to local interests. Indeed,

according to one clever study, they are more likely to sign bills supported by senators from states whose votes they need in the electoral college (Grier, McDonald, and Tollison 1995). Robert J. Spitzer's study of presidential policy proposals
during the period 1954–1974 found a high proportion of pork barrel items, particularly during election years (Spitzer 1983, 98–100). And the evolution of
tightly defined iron triangles into more loosely bounded issue networks has
increased the routine contacts between presidents and interest groups (Gais,
Peterson, and Walker 1984, 178–182). In short, the president has all the same
constituencies as members of Congress and is likely to respond in a comparable
manner. In the most vivid statement of this view, de Grazia (1965, 72) described
the president as "a Congress with a skin thrown over him"—that is, the president
embodies all the same motives and interests as the entire Congress.

The assumption that the president is effectively more accountable for
national policy than Congress also comes in for questioning. Public evaluation of
the president is based largely on national conditions, especially the state of the
economy (Hibbs 1987; Brody 1991; Brace and Hinckley 1992). Such an evaluation does not imply close scrutiny of policy choices that affect interest groups or
other special interests. Rather, it implies only that presidents have a strong incentive to avoid special-interest policies that will hurt the economy significantly
before the next election. Short of such unusual effects, the president's accountability for national conditions is not relevant to these policies. Moreover,
notwithstanding the minuscule shares of decision-making power exercised by
members of Congress, research on congressional elections has shown that the
public does hold them accountable for their issue stances (Mann 1978; Jacobson
1997). And a member can be effectively attacked as "beholden to special interests." Broadly speaking, then, the president and members of Congress are electorally in the same boat: they do not know in advance which of their policy positions will receive public scrutiny. They therefore face both benefits and risks in
supporting special-interest measures.

Finally, the effects of Congress's organizational complexity and fragmentation, too, are not entirely clear. That the committees are designed to serve special
interests—the so-called distributive theory of congressional organization—is
controversial. According to one alternative view, they are mainly designed to
gather, evaluate, and disseminate information about the effects of policies (Krehbiel 1991). Committee members do not differ greatly from the full chambers in
their policy preferences, and their bills are adopted largely because the committees anticipate what the full chambers want. In addition, because Congress is
decentralized, no narrow interest group is able to decide policy; the opponents of
such groups have multiple points of access in Congress, and electorally safe
incumbents are able to resist interest group pressure (Salisbury 1990, 213–214).
Finally, R. Douglas Arnold has argued that the congressional leadership can
manage the legislative process—by referring bills to committees, structuring
floor action, and lobbying members—to favor the kinds of policies the leaders
prefer (Arnold 1990, chap. 5; also see Sinclair 1992).[2] By such means, they can

set up decisions in ways that favor general interests. To the extent that leaders have and use such power, Congress will act on a broad view of national interests in the same way that is attributed to the president.

Defenders of the congressional parity thesis naturally take a dim view of efforts to make Congress more responsive to the president. In Joseph Cooper's view, such a change in Congress's role would merely shift "the arenas of special-interest politics"; special-interest pleading would move to the executive branch. At the same time, the change would "severely impair [Congress's] ability to fine-tune consent, enforce accountability on behalf of the electorate, and provide the breadth of access required for divergent views and interests to check and balance one another" (Cooper 1986, 34).

In short, then, there are several important theoretical arguments for the view that the president is the main champion for general interests in the American political system and Congress is the main agent for interest groups and other narrow interests. But all of these arguments are subject to cogent rebuttals or at least significant qualifications. On theoretical grounds, it is impossible to evaluate the rival views. In particular, it is impossible to judge the magnitude of any difference in institutional tendencies: is the president consistently and massively more responsive to general interests, or just marginally so? Like the effects of institutions generally (Weaver and Rockman 1993), these differences can be judged only by observing performance.

The Record of Policymaking

To help resolve this dispute, we undertook a comparative survey of presidential and congressional representation of general versus narrowly based organized interests in several policy areas from 1961 to 2003. We looked in detail at two areas of policy—procompetitive deregulation (withdrawal of regulatory barriers to competition) and public lands policies—and more briefly at three areas we have examined elsewhere (Quirk and Nesmith 1999)—tax expenditures, agricultural commodity subsidies, and pollution control. In each area, there have been recurring, fairly well-defined, and widely recognized conflicts between general or broadly based interests and special or narrowly based ones. To minimize the confounding effect of political party, we selected policy areas that reflect differing and generally subdued partisan tendencies.[3]

Our method of analysis was conceptually simple (although labor-intensive and more complicated in practice than we will describe here).[4] For each area, we identified the entire set of relevant legislative proposals mentioned in academic histories or studies of policymaking over the period, including those that ultimately failed. Using a wide range of sources, we then classified each proposal according to its overall tendency to advance general or special interests—that is, to reduce or eliminate existing special-interest benefits or to defend those benefits or create new ones. Does a bill mainly protect firms from price competition, or open up more competition? Does it give grazing interests more or cheaper access to public lands, or the opposite? And so on. Finally, we determined whether the president or members of Congress initiated the proposal and what actions were taken by each institution. We asked in effect *who* (the president or Congress) *did what* (offered support or tendered opposition) *to whom* (special or general interests)? The results, although summarized briefly, amount to a large body of evidence on presidential and congressional tendencies in these policy conflicts.

What we found is perhaps not surprising in view of the theoretical considerations we have discussed. The president has a definite and substantial overall advantage in representing general interests. But there are also important variations. In one area, the environment, Congress has been the leading advocate for general interests. And even in other areas, Congress has played a major role in the initiation of general-interest reforms.

Procompetitive Deregulation

For most of the twentieth century, several federal regulatory programs, originally intended to nurture fledgling industries, functioned primarily to suppress competition, reduce services, and raise prices for consumers. Especially in transportation and communications, such programs literally decided whether new firms could enter an industry; whether existing firms could offer new services or expand into new markets; and whether firms serving a market could raise or lower prices from approved levels. The protected firms enjoyed reliable profits and a peaceful existence—for example, not a single major airline went bankrupt in the forty years of federal airline regulation. Bankers were said to have a 6-4-2 policy: lend at 6 percent, borrow at 4 percent, play golf at 2 o'clock.

The general-interest case for reducing or eliminating such regulation was clear from the standpoint of economic analysis. By midcentury, a consensus had developed among economists that programs that regulated competition in some industries had been badly conceived (Bernstein 1955; Stigler 1971; Brown 1987; Ayres and Braithwaite 1992; Eisner 1993; Vietor 1994). For at least two decades, however, this advice was ignored, because industries and labor organizations benefiting from regulatory protection were able to block repeal efforts. Finally, in the mid-1970s and early 1980s policymakers undertook a series of general-interest deregulation measures aimed at opening markets in airlines, trucking, railroads, intercity bus transportation, electric utilities, financial services, telecommunications, and maritime commerce. These general-interest reform efforts produced intense battles between deregulation advocates and interest groups, and even some special-interest bills intended to maintain or strengthen the regulatory regime.

We looked at eleven bills in the realm of procompetitive deregulation from the years 1977 to 2003.[5] Some members of Congress have been out in front of the executive branch in proposing general-interest deregulation measures, but other members have vigorously defended the regulatory regimes. Once general-interest bills aimed at deregulating protected industries have been initiated, presidents of both parties have supported them more consistently than the House or Senate has been willing to pass them. The pattern of congressional initiation and presidential support for procompetitive bills was found for airline, trucking, maritime, and intercity bus deregulation. The president was the main initiator of only two important procompetitive measures, both concerning production of electricity— the Public Utility Regulatory Policies Act of 1978 and the Energy Act of 1992.

The Bus Deregulation Act of 1982 illustrates the pattern of congressional initiation and presidential support. California Democrat Glenn M. Anderson, chair of the House Subcommittee on Surface Transportation, introduced a bill in 1981 to relax regulation of intercity bus rates and routes and limit the antitrust exemption that allowed bus companies to coordinate rate setting. "What we've been working under is a 1930s law, which is not bad, except it's 1981," commented Anderson. The bill emerged from negotiations among the subcommittee, bus companies, and unions. Small bus companies and labor unions expressed the most concern, fearing the companies would be swallowed up by larger lines and jobs would be lost. American Bus Association president Arthur D. Lewis expressed ambivalence about the bill, describing it only as "something the industry can live with" ("Bus Deregulation" 1981, 581).

Transportation Secretary Drew Lewis told the House subcommittee that President Ronald Reagan supported an even stronger procompetitive approach. In fact, Reagan withheld a formal endorsement of the Anderson bill in the hope of bringing pressure to strengthen it. The administration worried that the bill would maintain restrictions on Canadian and Mexican bus companies' entry into the American market. The Senate responded by softening the protectionist provisions in its version. The House accepted these changes, and President Reagan signed the bill ("Bus Deregulation" 1981, 581; "Bill Easing" 1982, 336–338).

General-interest procompetitive measures have sometimes failed either because advocates of competition failed to agree on specific provisions, or because their proposals have been overtaken by events. In a case of disagreement on specific provisions, President Clinton and key members of Congress agreed in 2000 to take further steps to deregulate markets in electricity, but could not reach a consensus on how to restructure the industry. Electric utility deregulation was supported by the natural gas industry and by independent power producers, but was strongly opposed by the utilities (Trumbull 1991; "Energy Bill Surges" 1992, 233).[6] In 1999 Texas Republican Joe L. Barton, chair of the House Energy and Power Subcommittee, sponsored a bill to break up local electric power monopolies by allowing consumers to buy their power from any utility, and his subcommittee passed the measure in the fall of that year. President Clinton joined in calling for opening up electricity markets.

Despite broad political support for that objective, however, the bill was blocked in both chambers in the summer of 2000 as deregulation advocates disagreed among themselves on several issues. Clinton and many congressional Democrats wanted to ensure equitable access to power transmission lines; in the absence of such provisions, charged Massachusetts Democrat Edward J. Markey, the Barton bill "gives [the utility companies] a green light to engage in a wide array of unfair, predatory and manipulative practices" (Pope 1999b, 2599). Clinton also wanted the bill to promote the growth of renewable energy sources, an objective opposed by congressional Republicans. Meanwhile, the House Commerce Committee was unable to agree on the roles of the state and federal governments in implementing the law or on a policy toward power firms that had suffered financial losses from investments in generating plants (Benton 2000, 1739). Thereafter, electricity deregulation was incorporated into the omnibus energy legislation that failed to pass Congress in 2002 and again in 2003.

In a case of policymaking being overtaken by events, both Presidents Carter and Reagan, along with the U.S. Senate, supported general-interest measures dealing with long-distance telephone services. But developments in a related antitrust suit delayed legislation until it was moot. In 1980 a procompetitive telephone deregulation bill was blocked in the House by Judiciary Committee chair Peter Rodino, D-NJ, who insisted on waiting for resolution of the Justice Department's antitrust suit against AT&T (Olufs 1999, 53). In the end, the settlement of the suit wound up governing long-distance competition without new legislation (Derthick and Quirk 1985).

Whereas presidents consistently supported procompetitive measures during the study period, Congress initiated and supported special-interest, anticompetitive measures much more often than the president. Congress passed two such measures during this period, and a third had strong support in both houses. In the first two cases, anticompetitive maritime bills were initiated by Congress and signed by the president despite reservations. The Maritime Anti-Rebating Act of 1979 restricted efforts by steamship companies to offer discounts from regulated prices. It passed both houses with massive bipartisan majorities, and President Carter signed it in exchange for a provision giving him flexibility in enforcement for national defense or foreign policy considerations ("Maritime Rebating" 1979, 349). The Shipping Act of 1984 expanded the antitrust exemption for ocean liner cartels. After years of White House opposition beginning in the Carter administration, President Reagan signed the bill as a way of helping a sagging industry ("Ocean Shippers' " 1984, 277).

Members of Congress allied with AT&T fell short of passing the anticompetitive Consumer Communications Reform Act in 1976 and again in 1977. Popularly known as the "Bell Bill" after its corporate sponsor, the measure would have restricted competition in long-distance service and telephone equipment, undoing decisions of the Federal Communications Commission that challenged AT&T's control of the industry. The bill was pushed in a massive lobbying campaign by AT&T, and it attracted nearly two hundred congressional cosponsors. But deregulation advocates blocked the bill in the House and Senate Communications Subcommittees (Horwitz 1989, 238; Olufs 1999, 51). Avoiding the controversy, Presidents Gerald R. Ford and Jimmy Carter both refrained from taking clear positions on telecommunications (Derthick and Quirk 1985, 112).

Public Lands

Beginning in 1964, federal policymakers debated a series of general-interest measures aimed at encouraging "multiple use" of public lands. In other words, traditional uses such as grazing, mining, and timber cutting had to make way for additional purposes such as recreation and environmental protection. Low fees and prices dating from the post–Civil War period had encouraged overuse—leading to polluted water, scarred landscapes, and loss of revenue to the federal Treasury (Pope 1999c). Policymakers also debated special-interest proposals intended to benefit lumber companies, miners, ranchers, and water users by preserving low-cost access to federal lands.

As they did with procompetitive deregulation, members of Congress did most of the initiating in this area, for both general- and special-interest measures. Regardless of party, presidents have more consistently than Congress supported general-interest legislation and, with one exception, opposed bills to protect interest groups' access.

We looked at thirteen bills in this area.[7] Congressional initiation and presidential support is the standard pattern for general-interest public lands bills. This pattern applied to federal lands containing natural resources, national forest management, and water project reform. One exception was the Classification and Multiple Use Act of 1964, which was introduced by the Department of the Interior and intended to promote multiple-use approaches to public lands.

The general-interest Natural Resource Lands Management Act of 1976 illustrates the usual case. In 1970 Washington Democrat Henry M. Jackson, chair of the Senate Interior and Insular Affairs Committee, began efforts to revise the statutory authority for the Bureau of Land Management (BLM). He argued that the BLM's steps toward multiple-use approaches on natural resource lands had been "impeded by its dependence on a vast number of outmoded public land laws which were enacted in earlier periods in American history when disposal and largely uncontrolled development of the public domain were the dominant themes" ("Land Management" 1974, 804).

Narrow interest groups associated with grazing, mining, timber, and other interests were able to block reform for six years in the House Interior and Insular Affairs Committee. They prevented House consideration of Senate-passed reform in both 1970 and 1974. President Richard Nixon expressed support for the reform effort in his February 1973 environmental message ("Land Management" 1974, 804). But when the House Interior Committee finally reported resource lands legislation in May 1976, it contained two major special-interest provisions opposed by the Department of the Interior: rolling back grazing fees and opening federal lands that had been closed to mining. Democratic amendments to repeal these special-interest provisions lost narrowly on the House floor, with 60 percent of Democrats in support ("Public Land Management" 1976, 185–186). Nevertheless, the House-Senate conference committee was able to weaken the special-interest grazing and mining provisions. The largely general-interest conference bill then passed both houses on voice votes, and it was signed by President Ford in October 1976.

Resistance in Congress has sometimes doomed reform proposals. Although congressional sponsors made several attempts to raise mining patent fees with the support of President Clinton, their efforts failed. Nick J. Rahall, a West Virginia Democrat and chair of the House Mining and Natural Resources Subcommittee, began efforts in 1987 to overhaul the 1872 Mining Law. His bill called for the elimination of mining patents, which amount to low-cost sales of federal lands, and would have required miners to rent land from the federal government and pay royalties on the materials they extracted. It also would have required the BLM and other agencies to balance mining claims with multiple-use criteria and environmental impact considerations ("Mining Law" 1992, 283–284). The mining industry argued that a system of rents and royalties would cut profits, forcing mines to close and jobs to move overseas ("Overhaul of Mining Law" 1993, 262). Speaking up for the mining companies, Rep. James V. Hansen, R-UT, charged Rahall's efforts would bring "an end to jobs and destroy a viable U.S. industry" ("Overhaul of Mining Law" 1993, 264).

Interest groups associated with the mining industry were able to block congressional consideration of the bill during the George H. W. Bush administration. Western lawmakers prevented action in Rahall's subcommittee until he was able to move the bill to the full House Interior Committee with a discharge petition. The committee narrowly approved the legislation in June 1992. But mining industry allies such as Barbara F. Vucanovich, R-NV, prevented floor consideration through delaying tactics, including a long series of amendments ("Overhaul of Mining Law" 1993, 262). In the Senate, a companion bill to Rahall's introduced by Dale Bumpers, D-AR, was blocked in the Environment and Natural Resources Committee ("Mining Law" 1992, 283).

Interest group lobbying in Congress stymied mining reform once again during President Clinton's first term. Clinton's 1993 deficit reduction package included a 12.5 percent royalty on minerals extracted from public lands. Although the House approved the provision, western senators, led by Max Baucus, D-MT, persuaded Clinton to drop it in the Senate ("Overhaul of Mining Law" 1993, 262; Clarke and McCool 1996, 174). The House, with mostly Democratic support, later passed a strong mining reform bill—including an 8 percent royalty, environmental regulations, and a system of rent and claims fees to replace patents ("Overhaul of Mining Law" 1993, 263–264). The Senate, more responsive to mining interests, then approved a weak, industry-backed bill that Energy and Natural Resources chair J. Bennett Johnston, D-LA, called a "ticket to conference," implying that he hoped to strengthen it there ("Overhaul of Mining" 1993, 261). But the industry refused to make significant concessions during the conference committee negotiations, and Johnston's efforts to fashion a compromise collapsed ("Rewrite of 1872" 1994, 236–237). Congressional allies of the mining industry from both parties consistently thwarted Clinton's mining reform efforts during the remainder of his administration (Pope 1999c, 2112).

Members of Congress were successful in pushing through Congress two of four proposed special-interest measures on public lands issues. In both of the successful cases, the president reluctantly signed special-interest bills to provide beleaguered industries with economic relief. In 1984 President Reagan signed the Timber Supply Relief Act, which required the U.S. Forest Service to renegotiate contracts with timber companies so that they would pay lower prices for trees on federal lands. Sen. Mark Hatfield, R-OR, and others had initiated the proposal two years earlier in an effort to bail out the troubled industry and maintain timber sales on those lands ("Timber Relief" 1982, 458; Clarke and McCool 1996, 62). Hatfield argued that, without the relief, "the government cannot collect its damages from bankrupt companies, workers will lose their jobs, and communities already in precarious situations will be thrust into chaos—all to prove an abstract legal principle that 'a contract is a contract.' " The Reagan administration resisted a full-scale bailout well into the fall. Budget Director David Stockman wrote to House minority leader Robert Michel of Illinois in October 1984, "I strongly urge you to help defeat this effort to force taxpayers to provide a small number of corporations with $400 million worth of special relief." The House agreed to the Senate bill by voice vote, however, and Reagan swallowed his objections and signed the bill ("Timber Contract Relief" 1984, 344). Similarly, President Carter in 1978 signed a bill, introduced by congressional allies of the livestock industry, that blocked increases in grazing prices sought by the Forest Service and BLM (Culhane 1981, 96).

Two other special-interest efforts begun in Congress also died there: a bill to aid the timber industry by facilitating the logging of national forests was defeated on the House floor in 1970, and provisions to weaken Interior Department mining regulations were dropped in a 1999 conference committee to avoid a veto by President Clinton ("Conservation Lobby" 1970, 334; Pope 1999a, 2783). The only special-interest public lands policies pushed by a presidential administration during this period were changes in BLM appropriations promoted in 1981 by President Reagan. In response to the "Sagebrush Rebellion" of public lands users, Reagan convinced Congress to increase funding for grazing lease programs and cut funds for planning, data collection, and environmental protection (Clarke and McCool 1996, 170).

The only instance of presidential initiation of special-interest public lands legislation came in 2003 with President George W. Bush's Healthy Forests bill. Built around the consensus objective of thinning dead trees that created fire hazards in national forests, Bush's proposal nonetheless catered to timber interests by weakening environmental review procedures and applying the measure to all national forests instead of just those near human populations (Jalonick 2003a). The special-interest features were removed in Congress, however, where a bipartisan compromise restricted the bill's coverage to forests within 1.5 miles of an inhabited area (Jalonick 2003b).

Tax Expenditures, Farm Subsidies, and Pollution Control

A similar pattern of presidential general-interest superiority appears in two of three other areas that we have discussed at length elsewhere (Quirk and Nesmith 1999)—tax expenditures and farm subsidies—but a quite different pattern emerges in the third—pollution control. In the three areas, we examined sixty measures from the years 1961–1997.

Tax expenditures are credits, deductions, or preferential rates that lower personal or corporate income tax obligations under specified circumstances. Even though these policies are always defended on the basis of some public purpose, economists rarely find that the general benefits of the policies are worth the complexities they create in the tax code and the distortions they produce in economic incentives (Hansen 1983; Witte 1985). They are sought by and mainly benefit the narrow groups that pay the reduced tax.

During the study period, presidents were almost always at the forefront of general-interest tax reform efforts: John F. Kennedy in 1963 and Jimmy Carter in 1978 initiated reform proposals, and Richard Nixon in 1969 and Ronald Reagan in 1986 collaborated with congressional efforts. Presidents also supported the two reform bills that originated in Congress. By contrast, Congress was generally a reluctant partner in reform initiatives. It defeated the 1963 and 1978 proposals outright (Witte 1985, 155–163, 204–211; Verdier 1988). In 1969 and 1986, tax reform passed Congress only after harrowing near-death experiences in the Senate (Witte 1985, 169–171; Birnbaum and Murray 1987).

Not surprisingly, Congress also was the source of virtually all proposals for new tax expenditures, with members on and off the tax-writing committees producing twenty-six of the twenty-eight separate special-interest measures we identified. Although many of these proposals were blocked in committee, presidents opposed congressional tax expenditure proposals much more consistently than the committees did. For example, Ford administration Treasury officials opposed a 1975 tax break proposed for shipbuilders (*Tax Notes* 1975a, 1975b). Carter administration Treasury officials criticized the "piecemeal" approach of a 1978 expansion of the investment tax credit to include chicken coops, greenhouses, and pig pens (*Tax Notes* 1978; "Congress Approves" 1978, 239). And Reagan in 1982 opposed four different tax incentives for oil refiners, arguing that the goal of increasing production would be better served by deregulating prices (*Tax Notes* 1982).

The federal government has subsidized production of various farm commodities since the Agricultural Adjustment Act of 1933. Inspired by depression conditions, the act sought to preserve small farms by guaranteeing specific crop prices. Because market prices usually fell below the specified levels, the government in most years made cash payments to farmers to make up the deficiency. The results have been higher food prices and generous cash payments that, in practice, go mainly to large agribusinesses (Wilson 1977; Paarlberg 1980).

Here again, presidents have outperformed Congress in reining in special-interest benefits. The executive branch initiated five of eight agricultural reform bills during the study period. President Nixon suggested replacing fixed price levels with discretionary targets, a provision that ultimately became a key element of the reform-oriented Agriculture and Consumer Protection Act of 1973. And Ronald Reagan supported a reform bill that originated in Congress in 1986.

In the most dramatic deviation from the pattern, Clinton, faced with a measure passed by the Gingrich-led Republican Congress in 1995 that called for the complete abolition of farm subsidies, vetoed agricultural reform. He objected to the structure of the transition plan, and his agriculture secretary said it would be "just plain stupid . . . to unilaterally disarm" while European countries were still subsidizing their crops ("Plan To Cut" 1995, 50). But Clinton later reconsidered his position and signed a new version of the bill in April 1996. Neither Congress nor the president stuck with this strict position, however, and subsidies quickly returned to previous levels through annual "emergency" appropriations culminating in a new special-interest farm law in 2002 (" '02 Farm Bill" 2002).

In summary, whereas presidential opposition to agricultural reform measures was rare, Congress blocked almost as many such measures as it passed. Meanwhile, members of Congress initiated all but one proposal to expand commodity supports.

Among the five areas we have examined, pollution control is the sole exception to the rule of presidential general-interest superiority. Environmental pollution had become a national issue by the 1960s because state controls, with federal financial assistance, had proven inadequate. By the late 1960s and early 1970s, the issue was propelled by a massive wave of environmental activism and supportive public sentiment that has made the environment a potent campaign issue even to this day. Although policy analysts as well as conservatives call for balancing environmental goals against other ones, especially economic goals, the most potent opposition to environmental regulation is largely generated by the narrow interest groups that represent the regulated industries.[8]

Members of Congress, especially Democrats, eagerly rode the environmentalism wave. They initiated eight bills to assert federal control over various forms of pollution, including motor vehicle emissions (Maine Democrat Edmund Muskie, chair of the Senate Public Works Subcommittee on Air and Water Pollution, in 1965), water quality (Muskie in 1971), and toxic substances (three junior members of the Senate Commerce Committee in 1976). Presidents were in the vanguard only three times. Congress, even though internally divided, also sided more consistently with the general interest in pollution control than presidents did.

Presidents reflected their party's positions on this issue, with Democrats Lyndon B. Johnson, Jimmy Carter, and Bill Clinton supporting expanded environmental controls, while Republicans' records were more mixed. Richard Nixon tried to top Muskie's water quality proposal in 1971 and introduced pesticides legislation that same year. But Ronald Reagan, mainly on ideological grounds, usually sided with regulated industries and opposed environmental controls. Reagan's fellow Republican, Sen. Robert Stafford of Vermont, criticized the president's 1981 proposal to weaken air pollution regulations on factories and cars: "Practically every important provision in the Clean Air Act would be repealed if H.R. 525 were to become law" ("Congress Fails" 1982, 426). Ultimately, the Senate Environment Committee, which Stafford chaired, blocked the proposal.

Although the strong ideological division over environmental policy complicates interpretation of institutional patterns, it is clear that, unlike general-interest positions in our other areas, the environmental cause has elicited a highly enthusiastic congressional response—one that is, if anything, stronger than presidents'. We attribute this response to the massive public support for pollution control (Page and Shapiro 1992)—and infer that the congressional disadvantage in representing general interests does not apply to such interests that are intensely popular.

More generally, we think that Congress's stronger response, when compared with that of presidents, to the general interest in environmental protection reflects the distinctive complexity of environmental issues. In many cases, environmental protection has gone so far, and imposed such costly requirements, that many commentators completely independent of regulated industries are highly critical (Kneese and Schultze 1975; Lave 1977; Lave and Omenn 1981; Crandall 1983; Meier 1985, 168–172; Portney 1990, 13–21). In a sense, environmental policy is subject to three kinds of interests instead of just two: the well-organized interest of affected industries opposed to regulation; the highly salient general interest in environmental quality; and the competing, but often less salient, general interest in economic efficiency and growth. The president's apparent general-interest inferiority in the environmental area may be, in truth, a more balanced response to the opposing general interests at stake.

Conclusion

By and large, then, the president is indeed the principal champion of general interests in American politics. Our survey of five policy areas, including most of the areas notorious for interest group influence in federal policymaking, largely supports the presidential superiority thesis. The president is, by a substantial margin, the main institutional advocate of general interests, and provides the most reliable resistance to the demands of organized interest groups and other narrow constituencies. In our survey, presidents provided clear and fairly consistent general-interest leadership in four of the five areas studied. Compared with Congress, they initiated fewer special-interest proposals, supported such measures at a much lower rate, and supported general-interest measures at a much higher rate. In the areas of tax expenditures and agriculture, they also initiated general-interest proposals more often than Congress. The superior presidential general-interest performance was consistent across Republican and Democratic administrations. From the standpoint of institutional theory, our findings confirm that an institution with a single focus of media attention and electoral accountability holds the advantage in representing general interests.

Nevertheless, the differences between the president and Congress were not always clear-cut. On the one hand, Congress sometimes responded to general interests. Paradoxically, it led in the initiation of general-interest proposals in three of the five policy areas. But because it led in initiation even more decisively on special-interest proposals, this finding shows only that Congress is the most frequent initiator, regardless of the direction of policy. An institution with numerous independently elected officials and standing committees for each major area of policy generates more proposals than a centralized institution like the presidency. Beyond initiation, Congress also demonstrated considerable ability to pass general-interest reforms and to block special-interest measures. Broadly speaking, policy moved in a general-interest direction in every area of policy during the forty-year study period. This movement could not have occurred if Congress had stood firm with special interests.

On the other hand, presidents occasionally caved in to interest group demands. Although often under pressure from Congress, presidents signed every special-interest bill that became law; none was passed over a presidential veto. And they even initiated a handful of them. Interestingly, the George W. Bush administration has provided ample evidence that presidents will sometimes attend to special interests. From 2001 to 2004, Bush produced a variety of special-interest initiatives: the national energy strategy developed by Vice President Richard B. Cheney in consultation with producer groups ("House Passes" 2001); an effort, blocked in Congress, to eliminate the corporate alternative minimum tax ("Modest Stimulus Bill" 2002); the "Clear Skies" bill, blocked twice in Congress, weakening regulation of air pollution and greenhouse gas emissions (Jalonick 2003c); the Healthy Forests bill discussed earlier; the imposition of tariffs on imported steel in 2002, reversed in December 2003 after an adverse decision by the World Trade Organization (Norton 2003); a provision sought by pharmaceutical companies in the 2003 Medicare reform bill that prohibits Medicare from negotiating with drug makers over prices (Pear 2003); and the April 2003 granting of contracts for rebuilding Iraq to a subsidiary of the Halliburton Corporation without a competitive bidding process (Fessenden and Riehl 2003). Some of these initiatives, though not all, have reflected the administration's conservative ideology and exceptionally strong ties to corporations and business groups. In any case, they have yielded widespread criticism of an alleged special-interest presidency.

We come finally to the practical question that we highlighted at the outset: would the American government do a better job of avoiding interest group capture, and acting in behalf of general interests, if institutional reforms somehow gave the president more leverage over Congress? Some caution is in order: if presidents did not have Congress to take the initiative on special-interest proposals, they might do so more often themselves. Nevertheless, judging from our systematic survey of five major areas of interest group influence, the president is indeed the more reliable defender of general interests. The implication is fairly clear. In the permanent struggle to prevent or overcome interest-group capture of public policy, it would help to have a stronger presidency.

Notes

1. The Senate seems to fall in between the two extremes. Kuklinski and West (1981) found in a study of the 1978 elections that senators were held responsible in their reelection campaigns for economic performance and presidential approval. However, data since then suggest that senators have moved to insulate themselves from national trends by doing more casework (Baker 1995, chap. 4).
2. Cox and McCubbins (1993) argue that Congress can act collectively, but frequently is limited by conflicting preferences among members.
3. It could be misleading if, say, the interest group constituencies in each area were allied with the same political party and the same party controlled the presidency or Congress for most of the study period. In that event, what looks like a presidential tendency could be a Democratic or a Republican one. Fortunately, for our analytic purposes most of the issues selected were not highly partisan, and the partisan direction of general-interest policy, in any case, varied. Also, during the study period there was considerable variation in partisan control of the presidency and Congress.
4. Details of case selection and coding are available from the authors.
5. The bills are the 1977 Consumer Communications Reform Act, 1978 Airline Deregulation Act, 1978 Public Utility Regulatory Policies Act, 1979 Maritime Anti-Rebating Act, 1980 Motor Carrier Act, 1982 Bus Deregulation Act, 1982 Communications Act rewrites, 1984 Shipping Act, 1992 Energy Act (provisions dealing with electricity), 1998 Ocean Shipping Reform Act, and 2000–2003 electric utility deregulation.
6. It was also opposed by some consumer and environmental groups, which feared that the absence of regulation would affect access, prices, and the environment.
7. The bills are the 1964 Classification and Multiple Use Act, 1970 National Timber Supply Act, 1976 Natural Resource Lands Management Act, 1976 Forest Management Act, 1978 Public Rangeland Improvement Act, 1981 Bureau of Land Management appropriation, 1984 Timber Supply Relief Act, 1987–1994 Mining Law reform, 1990–1993 grazing reforms, 1992 Central Valley Project reform, 1992 irrigation subsidies reform, 1995–1999 mining regulations, and 2003 Healthy Forests Act.
8. As explained in Quirk and Nesmith (1999), we limited our survey to bills that proposed expansion of federal control to new forms of pollution or that created exemptions for particular groups of polluters.

References

Arnold, R. Douglas. 1990. *The Logic of Congressional Action*. New Haven, CT: Yale University Press.

Ayres, Ian, and John Braithwaite. 1992. *Responsive Regulation: Transcending the Deregulation Debate*. New York: Oxford University Press.

Baker, Ross K. 1995. *House and Senate*. 2d ed. New York: Norton.

Benton, James C. 2000. "Electricity Bill Short-Circuits." *CQ Weekly*, June 17, 1739–1740.

Bernstein, Marver. 1955. *Regulating Business by Independent Commission*. Princeton, NJ: Princeton University Press.

"Bill Easing Intercity Bus Regulation Cleared." 1982. *CQ Almanac*. Washington, DC: Congressional Quarterly.

Birnbaum, Jeffrey H., and Alan S. Murray. 1987. *Showdown at Gucci Gulch: Lawmakers, Lobbyists, and the Unlikely Triumph of Tax Reform*. New York: Random House.

Brace, Paul, and Barbara Hinckley. 1992. *Follow the Leader: Opinion Polls and the Modern Presidents*. New York: Basic Books.

Brody, Richard A. 1991. *Assessing the President: The Media, Elite Opinion, and Public Support*. Stanford, CA: Stanford University Press.

Brown, Anthony E. 1987. *The Politics of Airline Deregulation*. Knoxville: University of Tennessee Press.

Burns, James MacGregor. 1965. *Presidential Government*. Boston: Houghton Mifflin.

"Bus Deregulation." 1981. *CQ Almanac*. Washington, DC: Congressional Quarterly.

Carter, Jimmy. 1981. "President Carter's Farewell Address: January 14." Jimmy Carter Library, Atlanta. http://carterlibrary.galileo.peachnet.edu/farewell.htm.

Cater, Douglass. 1964. *Power in Washington*. New York: Vintage Books.

Clarke, Jeanne Nienaber, and Daniel C. McCool. 1996. *Staking Out the Terrain: Power and Performance among Natural Resource Agencies*. 2d ed. Albany: SUNY Press.

"Congress Approves $18.7 Billion Tax Cut." 1978. *CQ Almanac*. Washington, DC: Congressional Quarterly.

"Congress Fails to Act on Clean Air Rewrite." 1982. *CQ Almanac*. Washington, DC: Congressional Quarterly.

"Conservation Lobby Instrumental in Timber Bill Defeat." 1970. *CQ Almanac*. Washington, DC: Congressional Quarterly.

Cooper, Joseph. 1986. "Assessing Legislative Performance: A Reply to the Critics of Congress." *Congress and the Presidency* 13 (spring): 21–40.

Cox, Gary W., and Mathew D. McCubbins. 1993. *Legislative Leviathan: Party Government in the House*. Berkeley: University of California Press.

Crandall, Robert W. 1983. *Controlling Industrial Pollution: The Economics and Politics of Dirty Air*. Washington, DC: Brookings.

Culhane, Paul J. 1981. *Public Lands Politics: Interest Group Influence on the Forest Service and the Bureau of Land Management*. Baltimore: Johns Hopkins University Press.

de Grazia, Alfred. 1965. *Republic in Crisis: Congress against the Executive Force*. New York: Federal Legal Publications.

Derthick, Martha, and Paul J. Quirk. 1985. *The Politics of Deregulation*. Washington, DC: Brookings.

Dillon, C. Douglas. 1985. "The Challenge of Modern Governance." In *Reforming American Government: The Bicentennial Papers of the Committee on the Constitutional System*, edited by Donald L. Robinson. Boulder, CO: Westview Press.

Edwards, George C., III. 1980. *Presidential Influence in Congress*. San Francisco: W. E. Freeman.

Eisner, Marc Allen. 1993. *Regulatory Politics in Transition*. Baltimore: Johns Hopkins University Press.

"Energy Bill Surges toward Enactment." 1992. *CQ Almanac*. Washington, DC: Congressional Quarterly.

Fessenden, Helen, and Jonathan Riehl. 2003. "White House Wins Flexibility in Planning for Postwar Iraq." *CQ Weekly*, April 12, 890.

Fiorina, Morris P. 1977. *Congress: Keystone of the Washington Establishment*. New Haven, CT: Yale University Press.

———. 1980. "The Decline of Collective Responsibility in American Politics." *Daedalus* 109:25–45.

Freeman, John Lieper. 1965. *The Political Process: Executive Bureau–Legislative Committee Relations*. Rev. ed. New York: Random House.

Gais, Thomas L., Mark A. Peterson, and Jack L. Walker. 1984. "Interest Groups, Iron Triangles, and Representative Institutions in American National Government." *British Journal of Political Science* 14:161–185.

Graber, Doris A. 1997. *Mass Media and American Politics*. 5th ed. Washington, DC: CQ Press.

Gregg, Gary L., II. 1997. *The Presidential Republic: Executive Representation and Deliberative Democracy*. Lanham, MD: Rowman and Littlefield.

Grier, Kevin, Michael McDonald, and Robert Tollison. 1995. "Electoral Politics and the Executive Veto—A Predictive Theory." *Economic Inquiry* 33:427–440.

Griffith, Ernest. 1939. *The Impasse of Democracy.* New York: Harrison-Hilton Books.

Hansen, Susan B. 1983. *The Politics of Taxation: Revenue without Representation.* New York: Praeger.

Hardin, Charles M. 1974. *Presidential Power and Accountability: Toward a New Constitution.* Chicago: University of Chicago Press.

Hess, Stephen. 1981. *The Washington Reporters.* Washington, DC: Brookings.

Hibbs, Douglas A., Jr. 1987. *The American Political Economy: Macroeconomics and Electoral Politics in the United States.* Cambridge, MA: Harvard University Press.

Horwitz, Robert Britt. 1989. *The Irony of Regulatory Reform: The Deregulation of American Telecommunications.* New York: Oxford University Press.

"House Passes Bush Energy Plan." 2001. *CQ Almanac.* Washington, DC: CQ Press.

"Is the Government Run for the Benefit of All?" 1998. *NES Guide to Public Opinion and Electoral Behavior.* National Election Studies, Center for Political Studies. Ann Arbor: University of Michigan. http://www.umich.edu/~nes/nesguide/nesguide.htm.

Jacobson, Gary C. 1997. *The Politics of Congressional Elections.* 4th ed. New York: Longman.

Jalonick, Mary Clare. 2003a. "Democrats, Environmental Groups Say White House Wildfire Plan Would Sacrifice Forests for the Trees." *CQ Weekly,* May 3, 1048.

———. 2003b. "Forest-Thinning Bill Is Cleared after Negotiators Resolve Issues Outside of Blocked Conference." *CQ Weekly,* November 22, 2901.

———. 2003c. "Prospects Dim for 'Clear Skies' as Industry Joins List of Foes." *CQ Weekly,* June 7, 1381.

Kingdon, John. 1984. *Agendas, Alternatives, and Public Policy.* Boston: Little, Brown.

Kneese, Allen V., and Charles L. Schultze. 1975. *Pollution, Prices and Public Policy.* Washington, DC: Brookings.

Krehbiel, Keith. 1991. *Information and Legislative Organization.* Ann Arbor: University of Michigan Press.

Kuklinski, James H., and Darrell M. West. 1981. "Economic Expectations and Voting Behavior in United States House and Senate Elections." *American Political Science Review* 75:436–447.

"Land Management." 1974. *CQ Almanac.* Washington, DC: Congressional Quarterly.

Lave, Lester B. 1977. "Clean Air Sense." *Brookings Review* 15 (3): 41–47.

Lave, Lester B., and Gilbert S. Omenn. 1981. *Clearing the Air: Reforming the Clean Air Act.* Washington, DC: Brookings.

Levitt, Steven D., and James M. Snyder Jr. 1995. "Political Parties and the Distribution of Federal Outlays." *American Journal of Political Science* 39:958–980.

Light, Paul. 1991. *The President's Agenda: Domestic Policy Choice from Kennedy to Reagan (With Notes on George Bush).* Rev. ed. Baltimore: Johns Hopkins University Press.

Lohmann, Susanne, and Sharyn O'Halloran. 1994. "Divided Government and U.S. Trade Policy: Theory and Evidence." *International Organization* 48:595–632.

Maass, Arthur. 1983. *Congress and the Common Good.* New York: Basic Books.

Mann, Thomas. 1978. *Unsafe at Any Margin: Interpreting Congressional Elections.* Washington, DC: American Enterprise Institute.

"Maritime Rebating." 1979. *CQ Almanac.* Washington, DC: Congressional Quarterly.

Mayhew, David. 1974. *Congress: The Electoral Connection.* New Haven, CT: Yale University Press.

McCarty, Nolan M. 2000. "Presidential Pork: Executive Veto Power and Distributive Politics." *American Political Science Review* 94:117–131.

Meier, Kenneth J. 1985. *Regulation: Politics, Bureaucracy, and Economics.* New York: St. Martin's Press.

Mezey, Michael L. 1989. *Congress, the President, and Public Policy.* Boulder, CO: Westview Press.

"Mining Law Overhaul Is Stymied Again." 1992. *CQ Almanac.* Washington, DC: Congressional Quarterly.

"Modest Stimulus Bill Enacted." 2002. *CQ Almanac.* Washington, DC: CQ Press.

Moe, Terry M. 2000. "The Presidency and the Bureaucracy: The Presidential Advantage." In *The Presidency and the Political System,* edited by Michael Nelson. 6th ed. Washington, DC: CQ Press.

Mucciaroni, Gary. 1994. *Reversals of Fortune: Public Policy and Private Interests.* Washington, DC: Brookings.

Neustadt, Richard E. 1960. *Presidential Power.* New York: Wiley.

Norton, Stephen J. 2003. "Net Political Gain for Bush in Dropping Steel Tariffs?" *CQ Weekly,* December 6, 2998.

"Ocean Shippers' Antitrust Measure Clears." 1984. *CQ Almanac.* Washington, DC: Congressional Quarterly.

Olufs, Dick W., III. 1999. *The Making of Telecommunications Policy.* Boulder, CO: Lynne Rienner.

"Overhaul of Mining Law Advances." 1993. *CQ Almanac.* Washington, DC: Congressional Quarterly.

Paarlberg, Don. 1980. *Farm and Food Policy: Issues of the 1980s.* Lincoln: University of Nebraska Press.

Page, Benjamin I., and Robert Y. Shapiro. 1992. *The Rational Public: Fifty Years of Trends in Americans' Policy Preferences.* Chicago: University of Chicago Press.

Parker, Glenn R., and Roger H. Davidson. 1979. "Why Do Americans Love Their Congressmen So Much More Than Their Congress?" *Legislative Studies Quarterly* 4:52–61.

Pear, Robert. 2003. "Medicare Law's Costs and Benefits Are Elusive." *New York Times,* December 9, A1, 18.

Peterson, Paul. 1990–1991. "The Rise and Fall of Special Interest Politics." *Political Science Quarterly* 105 (winter): 539–556.

"Plan to Cut Farm Programs Stalls." 1995. *CQ Almanac.* Washington, DC: Congressional Quarterly.

Pope, Charles. 1999a. "Conferees Agree on Interior Bill after Knocking Off Policy Riders Opposed by the White House." *CQ Weekly,* November 20, 2783.

———. 1999b. "House Subcommittee Moves Electricity Deregulation Bill with Big Issues Unresolved." *CQ Weekly,* October 30, 2599.

———. 1999c. "Political Ground May Be Shifting under Mine Operators." *CQ Weekly,* September 11, 2111–2114.

Portney, Paul R. 1990. "Air Pollution Policy." In *Public Policies for Environmental Protection,* edited by Paul R. Portney. Washington, DC: Resources for the Future.

"Public Land Management." 1976. *CQ Almanac.* Washington, DC: Congressional Quarterly.

Quirk, Paul J., and Bruce Nesmith. 1999. "Domestic Policy: The General Interest Presidency?" In *Presidential Policymaking: An End-of-Century Assessment,* edited by Steven A. Shull, 185–203. Armonk, NY: M. E. Sharpe.

"Rewrite of 1872 Mining Law Fails." 1994. *CQ Almanac.* Washington, DC: Congressional Quarterly.

Robinson, Donald L., ed. 1985. *Reforming American Government: The Bicentennial Papers of the Committee on the Constitutional System.* Boulder, CO: Westview Press.

Salisbury, Robert H. 1990. "The Paradox of Interest Groups in Washington—More Groups, Less Clout." In *The New American Political System,* edited by Anthony King. Washington, DC: American Enterprise Institute.

Shepsle, Kenneth A., and Barry R. Weingast. 1987. "The Institutional Foundations of Committee Power." *American Political Science Review* 81:85–104.

Sinclair, Barbara. 1992. "House Majority Party Leadership in an Era of Legislative Constraint." In *The Postreform Congress,* edited by Roger H. Davidson. New York: St. Martin's Press.

Spitzer, Robert J. 1983. *The President and Public Policy.* University: University of Alabama Press.

Stigler, George. 1971. "The Theory of Economic Regulation." *Bell Journal of Economics and Management Science* 2:3–21.

Sundquist, James L. 1986. *Constitutional Reform and Effective Government.* Washington, DC: Brookings.

Tax Notes. 1975a. July 15.

———. 1975b. December 20.

———. 1978. October 9.

———. 1982. April 6.

"Timber Contract Relief." 1984. *CQ Almanac.* Washington, DC: Congressional Quarterly.

"Timber Relief Bill Fails." 1982. *CQ Almanac.* Washington, DC: Congressional Quarterly.

Trumbull, Mark. 1991. "Power Deregulation Draws Critics." *Christian Science Monitor,* June 18, 8.

Verdier, James M. 1988. "The President, Congress, and Tax Reform: Patterns over Three Decades." *Annals of the American Academy of Political and Social Sciences* 499:114–123.

Vietor, Richard H. K. 1994. *Contrived Competition: Regulation and Deregulation in America.* Cambridge, MA: Belknap/Harvard.

Wayne, Stephen J. 1978. *The Legislative Presidency.* New York: Harper and Row.

———. 1982. "Great Expectations: What People Want from Presidents." In *Rethinking the Presidency,* edited by Thomas E. Cronin. Boston: Little Brown.

Weaver, R. Kent, and Bert A. Rockman. 1993. "Institutional Reform and Constitutional Design." In *Do Institutions Matter? Government Capabilities in the United States and Abroad,* edited by R. Kent Weaver and Bert A. Rockman. Washington, DC: Brookings.

Wilson, Graham K. 1977. *Special Interests and Policymaking: Agricultural Policies and Politics in Britain and the United States of America, 1956–70.* London: Wiley.

Wilson, Woodrow. 1892. *Congressional Government: A Study in American Politics.* 9th ed. Boston: Houghton Mifflin.

Witte, John F. 1985. *The Politics and Development of the Federal Income Tax.* Madison: University of Wisconsin Press.

Wright, John R. 1996. *Interest Groups and Congress: Lobbying, Contributions and Influence.* Boston: Allyn and Bacon.

" '02 Farm Bill Revives Subsidies." 2002. *CQ Almanac.* Washington, DC: CQ Press.

Part IV
Judicial Connection

17. Lobbying the Justices or Lobbying for Justice?
The Role of Organized Interests in the Judicial Process

Karen O'Connor

"[Justice Hugo] Black was huddled comfortably over his law books . . . when an old friend came through his doorway. 'Tommy,' Black called out, greeting Thomas G. 'Tommy the Cork' Corcoran, a Roosevelt brain-truster from the old days, now a lawyer in private practice in Washington"—and one whose firm was well known for its lobbying efforts on behalf of its corporate clients as well as its "backstairs deals." [1] Black had not been in touch with Corcoran for several years. But Corcoran's daughter, Margaret, a former Black clerk, was experiencing a series of severe family and personal problems. Black assumed that was why his old friend had come to visit.

Black thus was shocked when Corcoran began to complain about a Court ruling during the previous term. "No one came to the Supreme Court to lobby, even to 'put in a good word' for a petitioner. The mere mention of a pending case at a cocktail party was forbidden. Out-of-court contacts with Justices about cases were unethical." Now, here was Corcoran talking about a case that had a petition for rehearing pending. Aghast, Black got Corcoran out of his office as quickly as he could, cutting off his pleadings for his client.

A tenacious lobbyist, Corcoran did not give up. He quickly made an appointment with Justice William Brennan. Once in Brennan's office, he did not waste time. "A grave injustice" had been done to his client by the Court, said Corcoran. Brennan, like Black, was astonished. What should he do? Remove himself from the case? After discussing the issue with his clerks and the rest of the justices, that is exactly what he did. Thus, although Brennan was originally inclined to accept the case that so interested Corcoran for rehearing, the case failed by one vote and was never heard of again.

Incidents like this are everyday occurrences in the Congress, the White House, and the executive branch of government, but they are nearly unheard of in the halls of the Supreme Court. In the rarified atmosphere of the Court, justices are considered to be immune from the mundane sorts of lobbying so common to the other branches of government. Overt lobbying of the Corcoran genre, for example, can actually be counterproductive. But that is not to say that the Court is immune from political pressures or the affects of organized pressure group lobbying.

Noted interest group theorist Arthur F. Bentley (1908) was among the first to recognize that interest groups and organized interests viewed the judicial branch of government as a possible point of influence. According to Bentley, interest groups could exert their might in the nomination process as well as through actual participation in litigation. Few political scientists, however, were quick to pick up on Bentley's recognition of the role of interest groups in the third branch of government. Conventional wisdom at the time, and indeed until the late 1960s and early 1970s, held that the courts were nonpolitical and above the fray of interest group politics — an idea that still informs the treatment of the judiciary rendered by many high school civics courses. As the work of Wayne V. McIntosh and Cynthia L. Cates in Chapter 18 and Hans J. Hacker in Chapter 19 underscores, organized interests — be they liberal or conservative interest groups, big business, or law firms — not only view access to the courts and litigation as important to the achievement of their goals or the goals of their clients, but also use various forms of pressure, often not recognized as such in the interest group literature, to advance their goals.

This chapter explores the range of activities pursued by organized interests when they attempt to lobby the judiciary and the American legal system (see Table 17-1). When the framers crafted Article III of the U.S. Constitution creating the Supreme Court, they envisioned the Court as the "least dangerous branch" of government. To set it above the day-to-day machinations of politics, the framers called for life appointment of all federal judges. True to separation of powers principles, however, the framers left the selection of judges to an elected president and gave the U.S. Senate, whose members initially were chosen by state legislatures (before passage of the Seventeenth Amendment, which provided for the direct election of senators), the power to approve or disapprove of the chief executive's recommendation. Thus even though the Court, as well as all federal courts, was to be somewhat removed from politics, Supreme Court justices, and more recently, lower federal court judges have to survive a very political appointment process. Presidents, elected officials themselves, usually try to appoint jurists who share their political philosophy, and senators often have the wishes and desires of those they represent in mind when they cast their votes for prospective federal judges and Supreme Court justices (Segal, Cameron, and Cover 1992).

Appointees to the Supreme Court survive the political selection process only to become the targets of varied forms of overt and not so overt political pressures once on the Court. Whether protest marches on the streets of Washington, test cases, or media blitzes, it is impossible for the justices to remain entirely above the fray of politics. Separation of church and state, affirmative action, abortion, gay rights, gun control, campaign finance reform, and even the outcome of the 2000 presidential election are among the many hot-button issues that are at the center of interest group conflict, but often find their ultimate resolution in the

Table 17-1 Range of Activities Available to Organized Interests to Affect the Judicial Nominating Process

	Tactics
Internal group activities	• Testifying before the Senate Judiciary Committee
	• Submitting statements to the Senate Judiciary Committee
	• Lobbying individual senators
	• Conducting strategy sessions with members of Senate or their staff
	• Preparing witnesses
	• Alerting group members about nomination and issues involved
	• Organizing letter-writing, phone, fax, or e-mail campaigns[a]
Coalitional, intergroup activities	• Coordinating activities with other groups, including lobbying and media
	• Participating in joint group strategy sessions
	• Supplying staff or financial support to other groups
External group activities	• Getting the word out through op-ed pieces, television and radio appearances, and so forth
	• Conducting polls or other research aimed at building public awareness of nominee

Source: This framework draws from Christine DeGregorio and Jack E. Rossotti, "Resources, Attitudes and Strategies: Interest Group Participation in the Bork Confirmation Process," *American Review of Politics* 15 (1994): 1–19.

[a]This may also be an external activity.

halls of the Marble Palace, as the Supreme Court is often called. Interest groups frequently believe it is their duty to get their side of the issue before the Court, whether it be in the form of paid newspaper or television advertising, test cases, amicus curiae briefs, demonstrations, or letter-writing campaigns.

This chapter explores the range of interest group activities in the judicial system and seeks to explain the points of access for groups in that system— including the selection of federal court judges, the initiation of cases, judicial decision making, and even how cases are interpreted by the media and public Each of these activities often stems from, or is the object of, organized pressure group activity. The chapter opens by discussing the role of interest groups in the judicial appointment process. The following sections also detail the strategies and tactics used by most organized interests to lobby the courts—among them, directly sponsoring cases and filing amicus curiae briefs. Sections look specifically at the litigation strategies of several interest groups and the interest group activity that has surrounded the abortion issue and its treatment in the courts. The chapter concludes with an examination of "spin doctoring"—an underexplored and underrecognized tactic adopted by organized pressure groups to influence policymaking and to maintain their organizations. Spinning is used by a variety of organized interests, including the corporations and conservative religious groups discussed in Chapters 18 and 19. This mobilization of the law for policy and maintenance purposes has been used with particular success by organized interests on both sides of the abortion debate in an array of arenas from the nomination process to reaction to judicial opinions (Craig and O'Brien 1993; O'Connor 1996).

The Judicial Appointment Process

The extraordinarily controversial nominations of Robert H. Bork in 1987 and Clarence Thomas in 1991 to the U.S. Supreme Court highlighted the role and potential impact of organized interests on the Court's appointment process (Simon 1992). Both nominations triggered intense pressure group interest. Similarly, the recent lower-court nominations of Miguel Estrada, Charles Pickering, and Priscilla Owen, among others, have spurred interest groups to a full frenzy as they have tried to derail these nominations on ideological grounds.

Several political scientists have analyzed Supreme Court nominations in an effort to understand more about how and why interest groups participate in the judicial nominating process. In the first systematic study of the Bork nomination process, DeGregorio and Rossotti (1994) examined 147 groups that other studies found to be active participants in one or more phases of the process (Pertschuk and Schaetzel 1989; McGuigan and Weyrich 1990). DeGregorio and Rossotti found that some groups adopt an "inside the Beltway strategy," in which their own members make direct appeals to their elected representatives. Others adopt an "outside the Beltway strategy," seeking the support of the public through targeted media campaigns. Still other organized interests use some combination of the two strategies. DeGregorio and Rossotti (1994, 1995) and others (Lichtman 1990; Calderia, Hojnacki, and Wright 1996) have found that interest groups are a valuable source of information about judicial nominees for both senators and the public. After looking at the informational role of interest groups and group alliances in the nomination process, one study concluded that "senators on most nominations will have a full range of information from various quarters" (Caldeira, Hojnacki, and Wright 1996, 23). Most groups that participate in the process intend that like-minded men and women reach the Supreme Court, because any one of them may play a central role in shaping policies of great importance to a group. For that reason, many groups enter the judicial process at an early stage.

In addition to attempting to manipulate the press, media, and therefore public opinion during the judicial nominating process (DeGregorio and Rossotti
1994, 1995; Caldeira, Hojnacki, and Wright 1996), organized interests also participate extensively in the formal confirmation process. The Bork nomination, in
particular, was taken as a call to arms for many liberal groups who believed the
Bork appointment would tip the Court in a conservative direction and bring with
it a retreat from earlier liberal decisions on race, affirmative action, gender, and
abortion. Bork, moreover, was an easy target for liberals. Not only had he played
a pivotal role in the Watergate affair by firing the special prosecutor at President
Richard Nixon's request (the so-called Saturday Night Massacre), but he also had
served in that administration as U.S. solicitor general and therefore defended
many conservative positions before the Supreme Court. In addition, Bork had a
significant paper trail; as a law professor he had written extensively on controversial issues and had concluded that the right to privacy — the legal doctrine that the
Court had used to justify its decision in *Roe v. Wade* (1973)— could not be justified from his reading of the Constitution.

Similarly, the nomination of Clarence Thomas in 1991 triggered severe con-
sternation among liberal interest groups. Thomas, like Bork, had a long record of
conservatism, but during the Thomas hearings, the traditional coalition of liberal African American groups such as the National Association for the Advancement of Colored People (NAACP) parted ways with its usual liberal allies to
support the nomination of only the second African American to the Court.
Women's rights groups, however, turned out in full force against the Thomas
nomination, especially after the public learned that law professor and former
Thomas colleague Anita Hill had charged Thomas with sexual harassment. But
their efforts, along with those of other traditionally liberal groups were not
enough to derail the Thomas nomination.

Several studies of these two nominations have focused on the 147 groups
that *claim* to have participated to one degree or another in the Bork and Thomas
confirmation battles (DeGregorio and Rossotti 1994, 1995; Caldeira, Hojnacki,
and Wright 1996). In the study described here, only *actual* formal participation
in the Senate confirmation hearings of the nine justices sitting on the Supreme
Court in 2004 and the unsuccessful Bork nomination are considered to be measures of interest group activity in the confirmation process.[2] Over the years, a
variety of liberal and conservative groups, as well as the American Bar Association, law professors, and attorneys from prestigious law firms, have evaluated as
well as testified for or against Supreme Court nominees. Since Justice John Paul
Stevens was appointed to the Court by President Gerald R. Ford in 1975, 170
pressure groups have testified for, against, or about the ten Supreme Court nominations that have resulted in Senate confirmation hearings.[3] The Bork nomination attracted the most formal and the most public interest group involvement;
eighty-six groups testified or submitted formal statements to the Senate Judiciary Committee (see Table 17-2). The Thomas nomination was the next most
controversial — at least in terms of the numbers of groups testifying for or against

Table 17-2 Interest Groups and Law Professors Appearing in Selected Senate Judiciary Committee Hearings

Nominee	Year	Interest groups Liberal	Interest groups Con-servative	Law professors Pro	Law professors Con	Law firms Pro	Law firms Con	ABA rating	Senate vote
John Paul Stevens	1976	2	3	—	—	0	0	Well Qualified	98–0
Sandra Day O'Connor	1981	8	7	—	—	0	0	Well Qualified	99–0
Antonin Scalia	1986	5	7	2	—	2	1	Well Qualified	98–0
William H. Rehnquist	1986	6	13	1	1	4	0	Well Qualified	65–33
Robert H. Bork	1987	18	68	20	26	15	8	Well Qualified[a]	42–58
Anthony M. Kennedy	1987	12	14	4	—	4	0	Well Qualified	97–0
David H. Souter	1990	13	18	0	1	3	0	Well Qualified	90–9
Clarence Thomas	1991	30	46	8	9	3	0	Qualified[b]	52–48
Ruth Bader Ginsburg	1993	6	5	1	—	0	0	Well Qualified	96–3
Stephen G. Breyer	1994	8	3	5	4	0	1	Well Qualified	87–9

Source: Data collected by author from Senate Judiciary Committee hearing reports.

[a]Four members of the ABA's Standing Committee on Federal Judiciary found him "Not Qualified."

[b]Two members of the ABA's Standing Committee on Federal Judiciary found him "Not Qualified."

his nomination; forty-six groups testified or filed written statements against Thomas. Table 17-2 graphically reveals how idiosyncratic those two nominations were. Most nominations have generated far less pressure group interest or public action.

Fifteen groups publicly participated in four or more hearings by testifying or filing a prepared statement with the committee.[4] Many of the interest groups that testified against Robert Bork or Anthony Kennedy did so because they feared that the appointment of a conservative, pro-life justice could alter the delicate balance that existed on the Court and trigger a reversal or severe limitation of the Court's expansive abortion rights ruling in *Roe.* Judge Bork, in particular, drew vociferous opposition because of his earlier articulated beliefs that the privacy doctrine, on which the Court had based its decision in *Roe,* was seriously flawed. Indeed, most major pro-choice national organizations, including the National Abortion and Reproductive Rights Action League (NARAL), Planned Parenthood, and National Organization for Women (NOW), testified against Bork and Kennedy. Later, Justice Kennedy was in the majority voting in support of several Missouri abortion restrictions in *Webster v. Reproductive Health Services* (1989), and so it appears that their fears were well founded. Meanwhile, these three groups continue to raise the threat of the effect that a conservative justice could have on the Court. Just before the Court convened on the first Monday of October 2001, NARAL issued a press release entitled "First Monday: Will This Be the Last Court to Uphold *Roe v. Wade?*" (NARAL 2001).

Only one group has appeared to give testimony at all ten Supreme Court confirmation hearings, the American Bar Association. Until the election of George W. Bush, it enjoyed a unique role in the process; its recommendations were actually considered and weighed as a part of the formal confirmation process.

The American Bar Association and the Legal Profession

The American Bar Association (ABA) was founded in 1878, but it did not begin to play a formal role in the selection of Supreme Court justices and other judges for the federal bench until the creation of its Committee on the Federal Judiciary in 1946 (Grossman 1965). From then until 2001, the ABA's Standing Committee on Federal Judiciary evaluated candidates for the federal judiciary and then graded their qualifications. The ABA committee often screened nominees before they were formally nominated to avoid potentially embarrassing situations, but many presidents bristled at giving the ABA this much power. President Ford, however, forwarded fifteen names to the committee for screening before he nominated John Paul Stevens.

Despite criticism, George W. Bush became the first president not to consult the ABA about his prospective nominees (Means 2001). In fact, judicial insiders claim that Bush is drawing his list of nominees from the conservative Federalist Society in an unabashed effort to place conservatives on the federal bench. When Sen. James Jeffords of Vermont ended his affiliation with the Republican Party in 2001, thereby giving Democrats control of the Senate, Senate Democrats again brought the ABA into the process. Later, the ABA evaluated nominees after President Bush made formal nominations (Associated Press 2001).

The ABA continues to rate all federal judicial nominees as "Well Qualified," "Not Opposed (or Qualified)," or "Not Qualified." Votes of "Not Opposed" or "Not Qualified" are very rare, and generally are a harbinger of trouble in the U.S. Senate as was the case with the Bork nomination. In 1982, when Ronald Reagan nominated Robert Bork to the U.S. Court of Appeals, Bork received the ABA committee's highest rating. In 1987, however, although ten members of the committee found him "Well Qualified," four members rated him "Not Qualified" based on their concerns about the conservative votes he might cast (Carter 1994, 163). Clarence Thomas was rated as "Qualified" for the U.S. Court of Appeals in

1989, and he received the same rating in 1991, except that two members of the ABA committee rated him "Not Qualified."[5]

Conservatives and Republicans have not been alone in their criticism of the special role that the ABA plays in the nominations and confirmation process. Several interest groups, including the liberal Public Citizen and the conservative Washington Legal Foundation, filed suit in the 1980s challenging the ABA committee's closed meetings, arguing that under the federal Advisory Committee Act, it was obligated to hold open meetings. Opposing this interpretation of the act were the Department of Justice, the ABA, and the liberal Alliance for Justice, a coalition of more than a hundred liberal public interest groups. Ultimately, the Supreme Court ruled that the ABA was not covered by the act, thereby allowing the committee to continue its deliberations in private (*Public Citizen v. United States Department of Justice*, 1989).

George W. Bush's decision to try to minimize the impact of the ABA on judicial nominations did not mean that interest groups have been shut out of the process. In fact, as noted, the Federalist Society, founded in 1982, emerged as a major player in the Bush administration's judicial selection process. "Twelve to twenty of the first set of candidates interviewed for judgeships" by the Bush administration were Federalist Society recommendations, and over half of Bush's first nominees to the Court of Appeals were members (People for the American Way 2001). Robert Bork and Orrin Hatch, former chair of the Senate Judiciary Committee, are chairs of the Federalist Society's Board of Visitors (Carter 2001). Law professors and scholars, too, have tried to influence federal judicial appointments, although their participation is much less formal than the roles played by the ABA or Federalist Society. In 1932, for example, President Herbert Hoover nominated the widely respected Benjamin Cardozo for the Supreme Court at the urging of legal scholars. Conversely, legal scholar Louis Pollack apparently had some influence on the Senate Judiciary Committee considering Richard Nixon's nomination of G. Harrold Carswell to the Court. Pollack commented that Carswell presented "more slender legal credentials than any nominee for the Supreme Court put forth in this century" (Baum 1981, 30).

Legal scholars are frequent witnesses in Senate Judiciary Committee hearings on prospective Supreme Court justices, although only one law professor, Gerard Casper of Stanford University, appeared before the Senate Judiciary Committee more than twice in any of the ten nominations analyzed here. For example, in the Bork hearings forty-six law professors testified—twenty in favor of the Bork nomination and twenty-six against (see Table 17-2). Many of these liberal appearances against Bork were carefully orchestrated by the liberal Alliance for Justice and the Leadership Council on Civil Rights, an umbrella organization representing about 180 underprivileged interests ranging from racial minorities to the elderly to religious minorities (Phelps and Winternitz 1992, 73–74). The Alliance's Judicial Selection Project was, in fact, created to monitor the federal judicial selection and confirmation process, and it routinely shares its findings with the ABA. The White House ultimately did organize legal experts in behalf of Bork, but it did so only at the last minute, because it was caught off guard by the intense negative reaction to Bork's nomination.

Similarly, seventeen law professors spoke during Clarence Thomas's hearings—eight for and nine against. As noted, however, the Bork and Thomas hearings were somewhat of an anomaly. At the hearings on nominee Ruth Bader Ginsburg, once a law professor herself, only one law professor testified in her behalf; Herma Hill Kay was one of Ginsburg's coauthors on her seminal women and the law textbook (Davidson, Ginsburg, and Kay 1974).[6] Thus, although in general law professors are not routine actors in Senate confirmation hearings, their collective efforts, especially when coordinated by conservative or liberal groups, are noteworthy. In the Bork and Thomas hearings, the appearances and testimony of law professors—pro and con—were well orchestrated and clearly part of conservative or liberal pressure group attempts to influence judicial doctrine by influencing the outcome of the confirmation hearings.

Law firms, too, are often participants in the Senate confirmation process. The political science literature abounds with stories about Washington-based law firms ("insiders") that also lobby Congress and the executive branch agencies for their clients. Many of the so-called Gucci Gulch lobbyists are lawyers as well and often associated with some of the city's biggest and most prestigious law firms (Birnbaum and Murray 1987). Law firms are not, however, especially active in the public side of the Supreme Court judicial confirmation process (see Table 17-2). Of the last ten formal nominees, only seven had representatives of law firms testify for or against them. Indeed, only three nominees—Scalia, Bork, and Stephen G. Breyer—had any opposition from law firms, and by any measure that opposition was minimal (a total of ten firms). Far more law firms felt compelled to testify in behalf of a nominee. Indeed, it is perhaps surprising that more firms do not see the need to go on the public record in favor of a justice before whom their firm will probably soon be arguing.[7]

The Litigation Process

As noted at the beginning of the chapter, it is simply not true that members of the federal bench are above the fray of politics. Those who select judges are political and often select judges for political reasons. For example, once President Ronald Reagan's advisers realized that he was having trouble appealing to women voters in the 1980 presidential campaign, Reagan publicly pledged to appoint a woman to the first vacancy that occurred on the U.S. Supreme Court. Before him, Richard Nixon pledged to appoint "strict constructionist" judges to the federal courts in an effort to appeal to southern voters in his 1972 reelection bid. And most recently, George W. Bush echoed Nixon in vowing to appoint only "strict constructionists" to the federal bench.

Senators, too, may cast their votes for or against prospective nominees based on reelection considerations and pressure from organized pressure groups (Segal, Cameron, and Cover 1992). Even though the overtly political process often results in the selection of political people to the federal courts, the framers clearly intended for unelected judges appointed for life to be above the day-to-day rough and tumble of politics. And in many ways they are. Lobbyists (Tommy the Cork Corcoran being a notable exception) do not lurk around the Great Hall of the Supreme Court waiting to talk to justices. Nor do they shower Supreme Court justices with gifts in an effort to sway votes or to increase access, although a wide array of conservative groups have long hosted judicial seminars for federal judges in warm climates during the winter months (Mikva 2000). In fact, between 1992 and 1998 over two hundred federal judges took at least one trip to some desirable resort to attend "legal" seminars as the guests of conservative foundations and corporations litigating costly environmental issues in the federal courts (Mikva 2000; Kendall 2000). But organized interests do try to affect the Supreme Court's pronouncements on major issues, as well as set the Court's agenda. One study of D.C.-based interest groups, for example, found that 72 percent of the groups surveyed "fil[ed] suit or otherwise engaged in litigation" (Schlozman and Tierney 1988, 355).

The two most common forms of interest group lobbying of the Supreme Court—direct sponsorship and the filing of amicus curiae (friend of the Court) briefs—are similar to many of the other activities of organized interests discussed elsewhere in this volume. Moreover, the very nature of the rules of the Supreme Court itself encourages interest groups to participate in the litigation process. For example, the Court selects and decides "[o]nly those cases which present questions whose resolution will have immediate importance far beyond the particular facts and parties involved." In 1949 Chief Justice Frederick M. Vinson, speaking to lawyers at a meeting of the American Bar Association about their role in the judicial process, noted that they represent their "clients, but [more crucially] tremendously important principles, upon which are based the plans, hopes and aspirations of a great many people throughout the country."

Test Cases and Direct Sponsorship

Legal scholar Richard C. Cortner (1975, iv) once remarked that "cases do not arrive at the doorsteps of the Supreme Court like orphans in the night," and he was right. In fact, the majority of important constitutional cases decided by the Court are brought by organized interests in the form of test cases (O'Connor and Epstein 1984, 72). In the early 1900s, the National Consumers' League (NCL), a group of well-to-do women concerned about the long hours worked and low wages earned by poor women, convinced Louis Brandeis, later the first Jewish justice on the Supreme Court, to take over the defense of Oregon's maximum hour law for women. At the urging of the Oregon Consumers' League, the Oregon state legislature had passed a law prohibiting women from working more than ten hours a day (Vose 1957, 1959; O'Connor 1980). The NCL's sponsorship of the litigation, however, was limited to defense of the statute at the Supreme Court level. Later, *Muller v. Oregon* (1908) became famous, because its

members collected all sorts of sociological and medical evidence to bolster the
NCL's claims to the Court that long hours of work were injurious to women's
health. This "Brandeis brief"—that is, one composed of nonlegal data to convince the Court to find for a particular party—is now commonly used by all sorts
of interest groups that are attempting to convince the Court of the negative (or
positive) implications of the case at hand.

More common is the kind of sponsorship once pioneered by the NAACP.
As early as 1939, the NAACP created a separate, tax-exempt litigating arm and
decided to launch a full-blown attack on racial discrimination in housing and
public schools from the trial court level (Kluger 1976; Wasby 1995). First, it
began litigation that culminated in *Shelley v. Kraemer* (1948). In *Shelley*, the
NAACP successfully convinced the Supreme Court that state enforcement of
racially restrictive covenants was unconstitutional state action in violation of the
Fourteenth Amendment (Vose 1959). Later, a series of test cases commenced,
designed to whittle away at the separate but equal doctrine enunciated by the
Court in *Plessy v. Ferguson* (1896). *Plessy*, which had been used as the legal basis
for allowing the continuation of state-sanctioned segregation in education and
public accommodations, culminated in *Brown v. Board of Education of Topeka,
Kansas* (1954). In *Brown*, in which Justice Thurgood Marshall convinced the
Court that race-based classifications should be suspect, the NAACP's Legal
Defense and Educational Fund showed how important a carefully orchestrated
case could be in a group's ability to bring about a desired change in national policy. For politically disadvantaged groups like the NAACP, litigation was certainly a more feasible and realistic way of obtaining its goals than the more traditional
forms of lobbying.[8]

Since that time, the role of interest groups in sponsoring litigation has been
studied frequently (Greenberg 1974; Olson 1984; McIntosh 1985; Epstein and
Kobylka 1992; Wasby 1995). This tradition has continued (see Chapters 18 and
19). In Chapter 18 McIntosh and Cates are unusual in that they treat large corporations as organized interests and properly point out the potential for "haves"
in the legal system. Similarly, in Chapter 19 Hacker highlights how conservatives
and the development of a conservative bar affected not only the organizational
environment of abortion law and litigation, but also the legal strategies and tactics of many groups.

Sponsorship of cases, while costly, is the preferred tactic of many interest
groups—if they have the financial resources and personnel to carry out such a
strategy. When groups lack funds, or a case comes before the Court that may
affect a group's overall litigation strategy or it deals with an issue of interest to
the group, groups often file amicus curiae briefs.

Friends of the Court

By filing amicus curiae briefs, interest groups are able to inform the
Court of their views on the possible implications of its decision and urge

Table 17-3   Interest Group Participation in *Webster v. Reproductive Health Services*

FOR **MISSOURI:**
COUNSEL: William L. Webster, Attorney General of Missouri
SUPPORTED BY AMICUS CURIAE FROM:

1. National Association of Pro-Life Nurses
2. Alabama Lawyers for Unborn Children Inc.
3. American Association of Prolife Obstetricians and Gynecologists
4. American Family Association Inc.
5. American Life League Inc.
6. Catholic Health Association of the United States
7. Catholic Lawyers Guild of the Archdiocese of Boston Inc.
8. Center for Judicial Studies et al.
9. Covenant House et al.
10. Focus on the Family et al.
11. Holy Orthodox Church
12. Knights of Columbus
13. Lutheran Church-Missouri Synod et al.
14. Missouri Catholic Conference
15. National Legal Foundation
16. Right to Life Advocates Inc.
17. Rutherford Institute et al.
18. Southern Center for Law and Ethics
19. Southwest Life and Law Center Inc.
20. United States Catholic Conference
21. Agudath Israel of America
22. American Academy of Medical Ethics
23. American Collegians for Life
24. Association for Public Justice
25. Catholics United for Life et al.
26. Christian Advocates Serving Evangelism
27. Doctors for Life et al.
28. Feminists for Life et al.
29. Free Speech Advocates
30. Human Life International
31. International Right to Life Federation
32. National Right to Life Committee Inc.
33. New England Christian Action Council Inc.
34. Right to Life League of Southern California Inc.
35. Birthright Inc.
36. Crusade for Life

FOR **REPRODUCTIVE HEALTH SERVICES:**
COUNSEL: Frank Susman
SUPPORTED BY AMICUS CURIAE FROM:

1. American Civil Liberties Union et al.
2. American Jewish Congress et al.
3. American Medical Association et al.
4. American Psychological Association

5. American Public Health Association et al.
6. Americans for Democratic Action et al.
7. Americans United for Separation of Church and State
8. Association of Reproductive Health Professionals et al.
9. Bioethicists for Privacy
10. Catholics for a Free Choice et al.
11. Center for Population Options et al.
12. Committee on Civil Rights of the Bar of the City of New York et al.
13. 22 international women's health organizations
14. American Nurses' Association et al.
15. National Coalition Against Domestic Violence
16. National Family Planning and Reproductive Health Association
17. National Association of Public Hospitals
18. Population-Environment Balance et al.
19. 281 American historians
20. 2,887 women who have had abortions
21. California National Organization for Women et al.
22. Canadian Abortion Rights Action League
23. National Association of Women Lawyers et al.
24. National Council of Negro Women Inc. et al.
25. National Organization for Women
26. 77 organizations committed to women's equality
27. American Library Association
28. 167 distinguished scientists and physicians
29. 885 law professors

---

adoption of the resolution they favor of the legal dispute. Although they were originally envisioned as a "friend of the Court" and neutral toward the parties, amici are now more appropriately viewed as friends of the participants to the litigation. As political scientist Samuel Krislov puts it, amicus briefs are no longer "a neutral amorphous embodiment of justice, but important participant[s] in the interest group struggle" (Krislov 1963, 703). They are one way in which groups, such as lobbyists on Capitol Hill, can provide decision makers with information.

Amicus briefs are filed by interest groups and other interested parties for a variety of reasons. They may be unhappy with the type or quality of argument being made by the parties, or they may have been asked to do so by one of the parties. Often like-minded groups use amicus briefs as a way of presenting arguments that cannot be made by the party to the lawsuit. Others believe it is imperative to show the Court, the public, and their members that they are strongly committed to certain positions (O'Connor 1980).

Nowhere is the range of interest groups and organized interests participating in litigation as amici more clearly visible than in the abortion arena (see Chapter 19 and Behuniak-Long 1991). In 1989, for example, a new record was set for the number of amicus filings in a single case (see Table 17-3). *Webster v. Reproductive Health Services* challenged a series of restrictions passed by the Missouri state legislature severely limiting and regulating abortion rights as enunciated earlier by the Court in *Roe v. Wade* (1973).[9] As revealed in Table 17-3, thirty-six groups (plus the U.S. government) filed amicus curiae briefs for themselves or on behalf of some other group or groups in support of the restrictive legislation. Twenty-nine groups filed amicus briefs, actually representing several hundred groups,[10] urging the Court to find the abortion restrictions unconstitutional. Both sides also drew amicus briefs from several members of Congress, state legislators, and states.[11] The U.S. government filed an amicus brief supporting the Missouri law.

To further illustrate the role that interest groups play in the litigation process and to underscore the connection between the appointment and the argument/decision stages of the judicial process, the litigation activities of fifteen groups that testified in four or more Supreme Court confirmation hearings were examined in greater detail.[12] All fifteen interest groups participated in litigation either as a sponsor or as an amicus from 1979 to 2001 (see Table 17-4). Only two groups—the United States Justice Foundation and the Leadership Conference on Civil Rights—participated in fewer than twenty-five cases. Several groups sponsored cases and participated as amici. Eleven of the fifteen groups filed amicus briefs in one or more cases involving abortion rights.[13] Of those eleven, only the conservative Concerned Women for America submitted an amicus brief urging the Court to uphold abortion restrictions. Thus it appears that organized groups that could be termed "repeat players" in the Senate confirmation process were groups that were also repeat players before the Supreme Court, especially when abortion rights were at stake (Galanter 1974; also see Chapter 18).

Setting the Agenda

Few studies of interest groups and the courts have considered the role of organized interests in setting the legal agenda *outside* of the formal litigation process. This agenda setting largely takes two forms: (1) attempts to manipulate the press, media, and therefore public opinion in the judicial nominating process beyond the formal hearings; and (2) efforts to cultivate the press in order to sway the way legal issues are framed, discussed, and reported both before and after opinions are rendered.[14]

The Nominations Process

Liberal groups, among others, carefully orchestrated a media campaign against both the Robert Bork and Clarence Thomas nominations to the Supreme Court (Garment 1988; Simon 1992). In the Bork case, many national groups, including NARAL, the NAACP, and the American Federation of Labor–Congress of Industrial Organizations (AFL-CIO), urged their members to contact their senators to ask them to vote against the nomination. NARAL members, sporting "Borkbuster" buttons, planned "a series of demonstrations and letter-

Table 17-4   Litigation and Media Activities of Selected Organized Interests, 1979–2001

| | Litigation activities | | Spin control activities | | |
| | | | | Press conferences/releases | |
	Sponsor	Amicus	Briefings on upcoming cases	After oral argument	After decisions
American Bar Association		X	X		X
Americans for Democratic Action		X			X
Alliance for Justice		X	X		
AFL-CIO	X	X			X
Council on Civil Rights	X	X		X	X
Concerned Women for America		X	X	X	X
Leadership Conference on Civil Rights		X		X	X
International Association of Chiefs of Police		X			X
Mexican American Legal Defense and Education Fund	X	X		X	X
National Abortion and Reproductive Rights Action League[a]		X		X	X
National Association of Criminal Defense Lawyers		X		X	X
National Organization for Women/Legal[b] Defense Fund	X	X	X	X	X
National Women's Political Caucus		X	X[c]	X	X[d]
Women's Legal Defense Fund[e]		X	X	X	X
United States Justice Foundation		X		X	X

[a]Now called NARAL Pro-Choice America.

[b]Now called Legal Momentum.

[c]But not lately.

[d]In conjunction with other organizations.

[e]Now called the National Alliance for Women and Families.

writing and telephone campaigns during the August congressional recess in the home states of senators seen as important to the effort" (Bork 1990, 285).

The range of activities open to interest groups in the judicial nominating process is vast (Table 17-1), and different groups often utilize one or more strategies based on a variety of internal and external factors (Caldeira, Hojnacki, and Wright 1996). People for the American Way, for example, a group that has played an important role in the Court's treatment of First Amendment cases (see Chapter 19), mailed memoranda to editorial writers at nearly 1,700 newspapers across the nation in 1989 in an effort to drum up grassroots opposition to Bork. Indeed, "the hot steamy days of July and August were filled with frantic activity—but only on the part of Bork's opponents" in the form of radio ads, print ads, and letter-writing campaigns carefully orchestrated to block his elevation to the Supreme Court (Bork 1990, 285).

Liberal groups admit to spending about $2 million on paid advertising to defeat Bork; pro-Bork forces estimate that their opponents spent closer to $10–$15 million to defeat his nomination (Garment 1988). Nearly as much was spent in the Thomas proceedings. Interest groups clearly view the Court as a high-stakes game (Bork 1990, 285).

The American public is not particularly well versed in legal matters. Until recently, several public opinion polls found that few could identify Supreme Court justices, whereas judges meting out television justice enjoyed far more recognition. During the 2000 presidential campaign, several groups tried to make the composition of the Court and the kinds of appointees who would be offered by each candidate an issue. Pro-choice groups, in particular, spent millions of dollars to educate the public that the fate of *Roe* could depend on the outcome of the November 2000 presidential election. The power of the Supreme Court was given added credibility when the decision of a slim majority of the Court effectively decided the outcome of the presidential contest (*Bush v. Gore*, 2000).

More recently, liberal groups such as the Alliance for Justice, a national association of civil rights, environmental, women's, and consumer advocacy groups, have stepped up to the forefront to publicize their views of President George W. Bush's conservative appointees to the federal bench. Its Judicial Selection Project has compiled detailed analyses of nominees' records on issues of interest to Alliance members. The Alliance for Justice also has opposed several of Bush's nominees to the federal courts of appeals on the grounds that they are too ideologically extreme.

Spinning the Issues and More

Another tactic employed by organized pressure groups is "spin." Spin control generally takes one of two forms: interest groups try to either affect media reporting of legal issues or pending cases or put a positive or negative spin on a judicial decision immediately after it is handed down, much in the way campaign aides try to spin reporters after major presidential debates (Omicinksi

1992; Hagstrom 1993). Of the fifteen groups that participated in more than four Senate confirmation hearings, several routinely conduct press briefings about upcoming cases. The ABA publishes what it considers to be a neutral *Supreme Court Preview*, whereas NOW's Legal Defense Fund (now Legal Momentum) holds an annual press briefing in August to let reporters know its own views about upcoming Supreme Court cases.

Most groups also hold press conferences or issue statements immediately after oral arguments before the Court. Often their lawyers emerge from the Court and head straight for a microphone to put their spin on the arguments and the justices' reactions to them to shape how the news is reported.

NARAL is one of the best and most well-financed spinners. In addition to calling press conferences and issuing statements, since the 1980s it has been at the forefront of the efforts by pro-choice groups to spin the abortion issue. In 1989, for example, after *Webster v. Reproductive Health Services* was docketed for Supreme Court review, it launched a major national campaign to let women know that *Roe* was in jeopardy and that access to safe, legal abortions was in peril. Working closely with other organizations, including Planned Parenthood and NOW, NARAL designed a two-part strategy. The first part called for letting women know about *Webster*. The second part of the strategy was to educate the public to understand that even if *Roe* was not overturned, *Webster* could be a major setback, depending on the kinds of state restrictions the Court was willing to allow. NARAL's overall scheme was to convince Americans to ask "Who decides?" (O'Connor 1996).

To that end, NARAL launched a massive print and television ad campaign using a series of well-crafted ads aimed at the general populace as well as decision makers. One included photos of a young girl growing up. As the photos stopped abruptly in the girl's late teen years, an announcer intoned, "She grew up in the '50s and died in the '60s, a victim of illegal abortion" (Tribe 1992, 174). By stressing the possibility that abortion might soon be recriminalized, NARAL and pro-choice forces sought to shape the way abortion was being debated.

Pro-choice groups brought their "Who decides?" campaign to the Court by launching an unconventional letter-writing campaign. The justices' chambers were inundated with mail from irate women. Although the Court normally receives about a thousand pieces of mail a day, the volume soon reached forty thousand a day, effectively stalling the Court's communications systems. Toni House, the Court's public information officer, reacted to the onslaught by saying, "I hope they [the letter-writers] understand this is not a popularity contest. We are not keeping score of who favors abortion and who does not. While people have a right to write to the Court, I hope that they do not expect that the enunciation of their opinion will have any effect on the Justices" (quoted in Craig and O'Brien 1993, 65).

At the same time, pro-choice groups sponsored a march on Washington, D.C. The over 300,000 participants were bent on convincing the Supreme Court and the nation that women did not want to see the Court place abortion rights in jeopardy. On April 26, 1989, the day *Webster* was argued before the Court, both pro-choice and pro-life demonstrators (who had also filed amicus briefs) were out in full force in front of the Court: "Passions ran high as competing protestors squared off at the courthouse steps, chanting, singing, and screaming at each other" (Simon 1992, 128). Thus the range of activities pursued by groups to lobby the Court is clearly not limited to the ones most frequently studied by scholars. And many of these activities have yet another purpose: highly visible marches and other protest activities help to build group solidarity and support organizational maintenance.

Organizational Maintenance

Even while influencing the course of public opinion and judicial decision making, most groups often have another more immediately selfish goal: institutional maintenance. Liberals and conservatives alike send mass mailings to their members or potential members, asking them for funds to "fight a nomination" or "wage a judicial war or litigation battle." People for the American Way, for example, sent out over four million letters soliciting funds to help it stop the Bork nomination, and it reportedly raised nearly $2 million. Similarly, NARAL raised millions in its campaign against the Bork nomination as well as with its "Who decides?" campaign, ostensibly launched to help it litigate in *Webster*. In addition to its direct-mail effort, NARAL ran full-page advertisements in local newspapers headlined "What women have to fear from Robert Bork." The ad also included a form to accompany donations to help NARAL's lobbying activities (O'Connor 1996). NARAL and other pro-choice groups have continued this practice, using a Republican president and a Republican House as targets to help raise much-needed funds. Thus court-focused pressure group activities often present opportunities for groups to raise revenue and build member solidarity and support.

Conclusion

As this chapter and the two that follow it underscore, interest group involvement in the activities of the third branch of government are extensive and in many ways quite similar to those used to lobby the other branches of government. Interest groups try to get "their" supporters—or at minimum, their sympathizers—on the federal bench. And they often spend just as much money, if not more, than special interests do to get friendly legislators elected to Congress or the White House.

But interest group involvement in the judicial process does not stop there. Organized pressure groups, either individually or in coalitions, bring issues to the Court for its resolution in ways not all that different from how special interests convince sympathetic lawmakers to propose legislation. Groups often seek out plaintiffs to bring test cases and then ask like-minded groups for their support—

be it financial, technical, or in the form of individual or coordinated amicus curiae briefs. Thus at the litigation stage, parallels can be drawn with the activities of groups that seek out lawmakers to sponsor legislation. Groups often seek out an issue and then find plaintiffs who would allow the groups to make their case as it winds its way through the judicial system. That system contains just as many roadblocks as those hampering the passage of legislation in the lawmaking process.

Groups involved in litigation as a mechanism to achieve their policy goals are perhaps most like other groups in their external activities. They frequently go beyond the courts to reach out to their members and the public through mass mailings and television and print advertisements. Thus it is time to reintegrate the study of interest groups that participate in the judicial process into the broader study of interest group politics.

Notes

1. All quotes here and the entire vignette are drawn from Woodward and Armstrong (1979, 88–96).
2. This measure is used because it is one that forces groups to go on the public record where potential justices can easily see which groups, law firms, or individuals are for or against them.
3. A list of these groups is available from the author. Some groups testified or filed statements about candidates without taking sides. These appearances are not included in this analysis.
4. Those fifteen groups are the Alliance for Justice, American Bar Association, Americans for Democratic Action, American Federation of Labor–Congress of Industrial Organizations, Center for Constitutional Rights, Concerned Women for America,* International Association of Police Chiefs,* National Abortion and Reproductive Rights Action League, National Association of Criminal Defense Lawyers, Leadership Conference on Civil Rights, Mexican American Legal Defense Fund, National Organization for Women and NOW Legal Defense Fund, National Women's Political Caucus, United States Justice Foundation, and the Women's Legal Defense Fund (* indicates a generally conservative group).
5. The number voting "Qualified" was not released. It is known that at least one member did not vote.
6. Ginsburg did have the help of her friends, many of them law professors, before her nomination. In fact, her husband orchestrated a concerted letter-writing campaign to the president on her behalf (Randolph 1993).
7. What is not revealed in Table 17-2 is the somewhat surprising fact that of the twenty-five firms that publicly became involved in the confirmation process, only ten were DC firms. Thus, at least in this stage of the legal process, law firms, especially DC-based ones, did not attempt to intervene publicly in the process. Yet they may have participated in other ways, including preparing prospective nominees for their confirmation hearings, helping other testifiers produce their statements, or prepping other testifiers for their testimony in behalf of or against a nominee.
8. This is not to imply that only disadvantaged groups resort to litigation to obtain their goals. As McIntosh (1985) and others (such as Epstein 1985) point out, all sorts of organized interests may see resorting to litigation conducive to attaining their objectives.

9. This record was shattered by the number of amicus filings in the University of Michigan affirmative action case, *Grutter v. Bollinger* (2003).
10. The "et al." in Table 17-3 can often indicate numerous other groups signing on to the brief to indicate their support.
11. Although political scientists have found that the number of amicus curiae briefs filed in support of certiorari positively affects the Court's decision to accept a case for full review and oral argument (Caldeira and Wright 1987, 1990), it does not appear that the side with the most briefs, or with briefs from the most influential groups, will win.
12. The name of each group was run in the briefs file of LEXIS to determine how many times they participated.
13. Only the ABA, International Association of Chiefs of Police, National Association of Criminal Defense Lawyers, and the United States Justice Foundation did not become involved in the abortion issue before the Supreme Court.
14. Vose (1959) and others have also noted the tendency of some groups to flood the law reviews with articles urging particular judicial interpretation of the Constitution or statutes as a form of pressure group activity.

References

Associated Press. 2001. "ABA Keeps Its Role in Judge Selections." *Desert News*, August 5, A13.

Baum, Lawrence. 1981. *The Supreme Court*. Washington, DC: CQ Press.

Behuniak-Long, Susan. 1991. "Friendly Fire: Amici and *Webster v. Reproductive Health Services*." *Judicature* 74:261–270.

Bentley, Arthur F. 1908. *The Process of Government*. Chicago: University of Chicago Press.

Birnbaum, Jeffrey H., and Alan S. Murray. 1987. *Showdown at Gucci Gulch: Lawmakers, Lobbyists, and the Unlikely Triumph of Tax Reform*. New York: Random House.

Bork, Robert H. 1990. *The Tempting of America*. New York: Free Press.

Caldeira, Gregory A., and John R. Wright. 1988. "Organized Interests and Agenda Setting in the U.S. Supreme Court." *American Political Science Review* 82:1109–1126.

———. 1990. "The Discuss List: Agenda Building in the U.S. Supreme Court." *Law and Society Review* 24:807–835.

Caldeira, Gregory A., Marie Hojnacki, and John R. Wright. 1996. "The Informational Roles of Organized Interests in the Politics of Federal Judicial Nominations." Paper prepared for delivery at the 1996 annual meeting of the Midwest Political Science Association.

Carter, Stephen L. 1994. *The Confirmation Mess: Cleaning Up the Federal Appointments Process*. New York: Basic Books.

Carter, Terry. 2001. "The In Crowd: Conservatives Who Sought Refuge in the Federalist Society Gain Clout." *ABA Journal* (September): 46–49.

Cortner, Richard C. 1975. *The Supreme Court and Civil Liberties Policy*. Palo Alto, CA: Mayfield Publishing.

Craig, Barbara Hinkson, and David M. O'Brien. 1993. *Abortion and American Politics*. Chatham, NJ: Chatham House Publishers.

Davidson, Kenneth, Ruth Bader Ginsburg, and Herma Hill Kay. 1974. *Sex-Based Discrimination*. St. Paul, MN: West.

DeGregorio, Christine, and Jack E. Rossotti. 1994. "Resources, Attitudes and Strategies: Interest Group Participation in the Bork Confirmation Process." *American Review of Politics* 15:1–19.

———. 1995. "Campaigning for the Court: Interest Group Participation in the Bork and Thomas Nomination Processes." In *Interest Group Politics*, 4th ed., edited by Allan J. Cigler and Burdett A. Loomis. Washington, DC: CQ Press.

Epstein, Lee. 1985. *Conservatives in Court.* Knoxville: University of Tennessee Press.

Epstein, Lee, and Joseph F. Kobylka. 1992. *The Supreme Court and Legal Change: Abortion and the Death Penalty.* Chapel Hill: University of North Carolina Press.

Galanter, Marc. 1974. "Why the 'Haves' Come Out Ahead: Speculations on the Limits of Legal Change." *Law and Society Review* 9:95–106.

Garment, Suzanne. 1988. "The War against Robert H. Bork." *Commentary* (January).

Greenberg, Jack. 1974. "Litigation for Social Change: Methods, Limits, and Role in Democracy." *Records of the New York City Bar Association* 29:9–63.

Grossman, Joel B. 1965. *Lawyers and Judges: The ABA and the Politics of Judicial Selection.* New York: Wiley.

Hagstrom, Jerry. 1993. "So Now It Can Be Told." *National Journal,* March 20, 703.

Kendall, Doug. 2000. *Nothing for Free: How Private Judicial Seminars Are Undermining Environmental Protections and Breaking the Public's Trust.* Washington, DC: Community Rights Counsel.

Kluger, Richard. 1976. *Simple Justice: The History of* Brown v. Board of Education *and Black Americans' Struggle for Equality.* New York: Knopf.

Krislov, Samuel. 1963. "The Amicus Curiae Brief: From Friendship to Advocacy." *Yale Law Journal* 72:694–721.

Lichtman, Judith. 1990. "Public Interest Groups and the Bork Nomination." *Northwestern University Law Review* 84:978.

McGuigan, Patrick, and Dawn H. Weyrich. 1990. *Ninth Justice: The Fight for Bork.* Lanham, MD: University Press of America.

McIntosh, Wayne V. 1985. "Litigating Scientific Creationism, or Scopes I, II, III ." *Law and Policy* 7:375–385.

Means, Marianne. 2001. "ABA's Ouster Opens Courts to Right-Wing Idealists." *Houston Chronicle,* April 1, 3.

Mikva, Abner. 2000. "The Wooing of Our Judges." *New York Times,* August 28, A17.

NARAL. 2001. "First Monday: Will This Be the Last Court to Uphold *Roe v. Wade?*" Statement by Kate Michelman, September 27. http://www.naral.org/mediasources/press/2001.

O'Connor, Karen. 1980. *Women's Organizations' Use of the Courts.* Lexington, MA: Lexington Books.

———. 1996. *No Neutral Ground: Abortion Politics in an Age of Absolutes.* Boulder, CO: Westview Press.

O'Connor, Karen, and Lee Epstein. 1984. "The Role of Interest Groups in Supreme Court Policymaking." In *Public Policy Formation,* edited by Robert Eyestone. Greenwich, CT: JAI Press.

Olson, Susan M. 1984. *Clients and Lawyers: Securing the Rights of Disabled Persons.* Westport, CT: Greenwood Press.

Omicinski, John. 1992. "De Tocqueville Would Be Shocked by 'Spin Doctors.' " Gannett News Service, October 22.

People for the American Way. 2001. "The Federalist Society: From Obscurity to Power." August.

Pertschuk, Michael, and Wendy Schaetzel. 1989. *The People Rising: The Campaign against the Bork Nomination.* New York: Thunder's Mouth Press.

Phelps, Timothy M., and Helen Winternitz. 1992. *Capitol Games.* New York: Hyperion.

Randolph, Eleanor. 1993. "Ginsburg's Spouse Says He Arranged Letter Campaign." *Washington Post,* June 17, A17.

Schlozman, Kay Lehman, and John T. Tierney. 1988. "More of the Same: Washington Pressure Group Activity in a Decade of Change." *Journal of Politics* 45:351–375.

Segal, Jeffrey A., Charles M. Cameron, and Albert D. Cover. 1992. "A Spatial Model of Roll Call Voting: Senators, Constituents, Presidents, and Interest Groups in Supreme Court Confirmations." *American Journal of Political Science* 36:96–121.

Simon, Paul. 1992. *Advice and Consent: Clarence Thomas, Robert Bork, and the Intriguing History of the Supreme Court's Nomination Battles.* Washington, DC: National Press Books.

Tribe, Lawrence H. 1992. *Abortion: The Clash of Absolutes.* New York: Norton.

Vose, Clement E. 1957. "The National Consumer's League and the Brandeis Brief." *Midwest Journal of Political Science* 1:178–190.

———. 1959. *Caucasians Only: The NAACP and the Restrictive Covenant Cases.* Berkeley: University of California Press.

Wasby, Stephen L. 1995. *Race Relations Litigation in an Age of Complexity.* Charlottesville: University of Virginia Press.

Woodward, Bob, and Scott Armstrong. 1979. *The Brethren: Inside the Supreme Court.* New York: Avon Books.

Court Cases Cited

Brown v. Board of Education of Topeka, Kansas, 347 U.S. 483 (1954).

Bush v. Gore, 531 U.S. 98 (2000).

Grutter v. Bollinger, 539 U.S. 306 (2003).

Muller v. Oregon, 208 U.S. 412 (1908).

Plessy v. Ferguson, 163 U.S. 537 (1896).

Public Citizen v. United States Department of Justice, 491 U.S. 440 (1989).

Roe v. Wade, 410 U.S. 113 (1973).

Shelley v. Kraemer, 34 U.S. 1 (1948).

Webster v. Reproductive Health Services, 492 U.S. 490 (1989).

18. Cigarettes, Firearms, and the New Litigation Wars: Smoking Guns behind the Headlines

Wayne V. McIntosh and Cynthia L. Cates

Over the past several years, the headlines have become almost familiar, heralding, in dramatic tones, the downfall of the once invincible. They may, for example, scream: "$10 Billion Smoke Signal; Philip Morris Loses 'Light' Cigarettes Suit" (*Newsday*, March 22, 2003); "Big Tobacco Headed for Another Round of Trouble" (*Financial Times of London*, May 7, 2003); "Big Tobacco Suffers Big Loss" (Fox News, July 17, 2000); "Tobacco Loses Big" (*International Herald Tribune*, July 17, 2000); or "Tobacco's Invulnerability . . . Goes Up in Smoke" (CNN, July 8, 1999). They also might shout: "Jury Blames Gunmaker, Awards Alameda County Teen $50 Million" (*San Francisco Chronicle*, May 8, 2003); "Gun Manufacturers under Fire" (*Post Magazine*, January 7, 1999); "Gun Lobby in the Cross Hairs" (*Legal Times*, January 11, 1999); or "U.S. Gun Lobby Suffers Setback" (*Guardian*, April 23, 1999). Whatever the parlance, the once mighty—classic college textbook examples of insuperable interest group domination—are finally being vanquished. The "iron triangles" of the tobacco and gun lobbies are apparently crumbling.

Apparent, too, is the fact that the once comfy iron triangle arrangement among lobbies, congressional committees, and administrative bureaus is being breached by legal action, with attorneys, judges, and jurors in central positions. If tobacco's "invulnerability" has indeed gone "up in smoke," litigation has sparked the funeral pyre. Similarly, the gun lobby is increasingly "under fire" in the courts. But this, too, would seem to belie a certain wisdom—the wisdom that the powerful tend to predominate not only in legislative and administrative dealings, but in judicial transactions as well. As Marc Galanter (1974) put it in a classic treatise, the "haves" inevitably "come out ahead" in the nation's courts.

What, then, can be made of tobacco's recent courtroom losses and of pending litigation against gun manufacturers? Are the interest group "haves" finally breaking under the weight of lawsuits? Or are they merely bending, flexible in the face of the legal-political structure but still, relatively speaking, coming out ahead? We shall suggest the latter.

The first part of this chapter traces the already huge losses and potential losses of the tobacco and gun industries from litigation. If the front-page stories written over the past five years are taken as the benchmark of interest group strength, those stories would clearly suggest the eventual demise of the two Goliaths. Next, we depart from the news of the day to take a theoretical look at large-scale interests in the nation's legal system. Finally, we return to the news of the day, though not necessarily the news that garners big type above the newspaper fold. It is here, we submit, in the arcana of settlement tactics, procedural delays, reductions in damages, appellate reversals, and legislative maneuvers that the "haves" still come out ahead.

Big Tobacco Suffering: 'Tobacco Loses Big'

In April 2003, an Illinois judge, deciding that smokers had been misled about the dangers of light cigarettes as compared with the regular brands, awarded $10 billion in damages against the giant tobacco firm Philip Morris. When the cigarette company announced its plans to appeal, the judge ordered it to post a $12 billion bond, an amount Philip Morris said would force it into bankruptcy (*Price v. Philip Morris*, 2003; *Tobacco Industry Litigation Reporter* 2003a).

Significantly, that pending industry disaster came only three years after a Florida jury awarded sick smokers a stunning $145 billion in punitive damages to be paid by the nation's five largest cigarette companies. That assessment, in the first ever smokers' class action case to go to trial, was heaped atop an additional $12.7 billion in compensatory damages. It was, by far, the largest damage award ever handed down by any jury against any defendant. In fact, so huge was the award that, before the verdict came down and anticipating a lesser amount, a Phillip Morris attorney warned it would be a " 'death warrant' for the industry" (Wilson 2000).

And that "death warrant" followed by less than a year another headline-grabbing plunge into the deep pockets of big tobacco. In 1999, as part of a litigation settlement with forty-six state attorneys general—known as the Master Settlement Agreement (MSA)—major cigarette companies agreed to fatten state treasuries to the tune of roughly $240 billion over the next twenty years (MSA, accessed at National Association of Attorneys General, http://www.naag.org/issues/issue-tobacco.php).

Moreover, in September 1999 U.S. Attorney General Janet Reno filed a civil suit on behalf of the United States claiming that the five major tobacco companies had engaged in unlawful conduct, actionable under several federal statutes.[1] Elsewhere, states not party to the MSA, as well as some private parties, have either recently completed, or are in the midst of, trials against big tobacco. In one such case, a jury awarded damages of $50 million (*Henley v. Philip Morris, Inc.*, 1999); in another, $80 million (*Williams-Branch ex rel. Estate of Williams v. Philip Morris, Inc.*, 1999). In another, a Los Angeles jury awarded a single plaintiff a record-breaking $28 billion in punitive damages (*Bullock v. Philip Morris*, 2002). All in all, by the spring of 2003 Philip Morris alone was facing "approximately 1,100 individual claims, along with several class action suits (Esfahani 2003)—and this was in addition to suits brought by the Justice Department and the governments of Bolivia, Israel, and France (Haddad 2000). On top of this, the U.S. Food and Drug Administration (FDA) concluded that nicotine is a drug and that cigarettes are drug delivery devices, which gives it the authority to regulate cigarettes as drugs—an authority sanctioned by a U.S. District Court in North Carolina (*Coyne Beahm v. FDA*, 1997). When all is said and done, the superficial record suggests very tough times indeed for big tobacco.

'Gun Manufacturers under Fire'

While the cigarette industry finds itself in the eye of a litigation hurricane, the gun industry is clearly facing a heavy storm warning. The legal woes of gun manufacturers began in 1994 with the case of *Hamilton v. Accu-tek*. In this case, the relatives of six people killed by handguns and one survivor filed suit against twenty-five handgun makers, claiming they were collectively liable for "negligent marketing." After a four-week trial in 1999, a jury found fifteen of the defendants negligent; "nine were found to have proximately caused injury to one or more plaintiffs." The jury subsequently awarded damages of $520,000 to the injured plaintiff, holding three manufacturers "thirteen percent responsible" for his injuries.

The *Accu-tek* case, however, was only the beginning and small potatoes at that. Inspired by the tobacco litigation, in October 1998 the city of New Orleans filed a product liability suit against major gun manufacturers, distributors, and promoters, claiming that "guns are . . . inherently and unreasonably dangerous," lacking "adequate warnings and instructions as to their risks" (*New Orleans v. Smith & Wesson Corp.*, 1998). Within a mere two years, New Orleans's trail-blazing effort was being emulated by thirty-one other local governments, including Atlanta, Boston, Chicago, Cincinnati, Cleveland, Detroit, District of Columbia, Gary, Newark, Philadelphia, and St. Louis (Sills 2000).[2]

New York City, whose June 2000 complaint was the latest local suit to be filed, is illustrative of the approach taken. The New York complaint encompasses twenty-eight named defendants, including twenty-five manufacturers and three trade associations. In addition, the suit includes three "John Doe" defendant categories, designed to take in all manufacturers, dealers, and distributors doing direct or indirect gun business in the city. Going well beyond New Orleans, New York charges the gun industry with, among many things, causing a public nuisance, negligent marketing and distribution, defective design, inadequate warnings, deceptive trade practices, and false advertising. In judgment, New York seeks an injunction against these activities, compensatory damages for city expenditures related to treating gun victims and dealing with gun violence, and punitive damages aimed at forcing the industry to change its practices (*New York v. Arms Technology, Inc.*, 2000).

The nation's cities are not alone in the assault on guns. On October 5, 1999, the National Association for the Advancement of Colored People (NAACP) and the National Spinal Cord Injury Association (NSCIA) filed suit on behalf of their members against a number of gun manufacturers, distributors, importers, and sellers. Among other allegations, the suit, which seeks injunctive and equitable relief, charges defendants with intentionally targeting sales of unsafe handguns to children (*NAACP v. AA Arms, Inc.*, 1999).

On top of all this, in December 1999 the U.S. Department of Housing and Urban Development (HUD), with explicit White House backing, threatened to file suit against the gun industry on behalf of over three thousand public housing authorities with a history of gun violence. HUD estimates that it spends over $1 billion annually to provide security to housing projects. The administration is attempting to pressure the industry into changing its "irresponsible marketing practices" and into adding safety features to its products (Walsh 1999).

Such actions already have had some impact. Notably, Smith and Wesson, the nation's largest gun manufacturer, agreed in March 2000 to some government requests. Hoping to insulate itself against the onslaught of litigation, Smith and Wesson acceded to demands to place hidden, difficult-to-remove serial numbers and trigger locks on all its weapons. The company also agreed to implement so-called smart gun technology, which permits operation of guns only by authorized users, within the next three years. The agreement settled disputes between Smith and Wesson, fifteen cities, and the states of New York and Connecticut.

The Smith and Wesson pact itself has spawned further legal activity against the gun industry. Because they suspect other firearms companies of conspiring against Smith and Wesson for capitulating to government demands, the attorneys general of six states (California, Connecticut, Florida, Maryland, Massachusetts, and New York) have joined in an antitrust investigation of the industry (Butterfield 2000). One can only conclude, then, that the mighty are falling— and falling heavily, to say the least.

Why the 'Haves' Come Out Ahead?

Indeed, such an outcome seems quite astounding, for the "mighty" in this case have traditionally been two of the nation's most powerful interest groups. And interest group maneuvering for power has always been central to American government and politics. Special interests have long pressed the *political* establishment in attempting to get what they want. Indeed, since the founding of the nation, interest groups have lobbied the legislative and executive branches (the term *lobby* actually comes from the tendency of early congressional supplicants to hang around hotel lobbies in attempts to buttonhole members) and have financed the electoral campaigns of those seeking office.

In fact, big tobacco and guns, as mentioned earlier, have often been cited as prototypical examples of so-called iron triangles—models of powerful interests able to commandeer public policy through cozy arrangements with the relevant congressional committees and executive agencies (see, for example, Freeman 1965; McCool 1987; Ripley and Franklin 1987). Traditionally, tobacco interests have found willing allies on the congressional agriculture committees and within the Department of Agriculture. As E. E. Schattschneider pointed out in his critique of pluralism some four decades ago, "The flaw in the pluralist heaven is that the heavenly chorus sings with a strong upper-class accent" (Schattschneider 1960). Thus, part of the damning commentary of the so-called pressure system is characterized by the old saw that "money talks."

Such a classic means of political influence peddling, however, is considered unethical—even illegal—when applied to the judiciary. If interest groups want to influence the outcomes of legal disputes, they have to find alternative routes of lobbying—routes that correspond to the norms of the judiciary. Presumably, though, these routes are much more difficult ones—at least, the rules are far more rigid.

Common wisdom also would suggest that these routes are especially difficult for the most powerful of interests. Those with enormous influence over the political branches of government, political mythology would have it, lose some of their advantages in the courts of law. After all, the midcentury litigation successes of African American interests and Warren Court era decisions favoring defendants and other disadvantaged groups have fed the notion that courts are particularly amenable to minority interests and unpopular groups. Moreover, the media, which devote few resources to covering appellate decision making, tend to focus on the occasional high-profile *constitutional* case. Such cases frequently involve noneconomic issues such as race, censorship, and abortion. Alternatively, the media would suggest that, groups aside, the courts are where the little guy can win—and win big—in government. Perhaps that is why the "McDonald's Coffee Lady," the winner of a supposedly huge amount of money from the burger giant, is today known to many American households.[3]

Court statistics, however, tell a very different story. A look overall at groups that sponsor litigation—excluding government—reveals that commercial interests dominate pressure group activity, at least in the Supreme Court. In fact, commercial interests sponsor more litigation than all other interests combined, and statistical examinations of amicus participants—again, excluding government—similarly suggest commercial domination (Epstein 1991, 354). Thus the same interests that dominate the pressure system in the legislative and executive branches dominate the system in the judicial branch.

Quite aside from litigation sponsorship and amicus participation, one might argue that the powerful tend to come out ahead not only in such overtly political forums as the legislature and executive, but also in the supposedly apolitical judiciary. This is precisely what Marc Galanter has argued in his classic treatise "Why the 'Haves' Come out Ahead."

Galanter begins by roughly dividing the litigant world into those who are a one-shotter (OS) and those who are a repeat player (RP). One-shotters are those who only occasionally employ the judicial process—perhaps in a divorce proceeding, an argument with a neighbor, or an automobile accident. Repeat players are involved "in many similar litigations over time" (Galanter 1974, 97). One-shotters tend to be individuals; they tend to have few resources; and they tend to litigate for immediate outcomes (that is, they need compensation for medical expenses right away, or they want that divorce without delay). Repeat players, generally speaking, bear the opposite characteristics. They tend to be institutions (that is, corporations, governments); they tend to be relatively wealthy; and they tend, because of size and resources, to be able "to pursue . . . long-run interests" (Galanter 1974, 98). Thus, according to Galanter, "a repeat player could be expected to play the litigation game differently from a one-shotter."

This ability to play differently affords the repeat player some very substantial benefits (Galanter 1974, 98–100):

- Repeat players, having been through many similar litigations, "have
  advance intelligence." They are the process pros, "able to structure the
  next transaction and build a record. It is the RP who writes the form contract, requires the security deposit, and the like."
- The repeat player, because of its long-term position, becomes proficient
  in the process, helped along, in no small part, by its ability to access specialists. Moreover, it enjoys "economies of scale and . . . low start-up costs
  for any case."
- Because the repeat player frequently employs the system, it is able to
  develop helpful informal relationships with institutional insiders. Indeed,
  the very frequency of the repeat player's judicial transactions and the relationships it develops as a result make it something of an insider itself.
- The repeat player, because of its frequent use of the system, develops a
  "bargaining reputation" within the system, which is to its advantage.
  Because "the OS has no bargaining reputation to maintain, the OS has
  more difficulty in convincingly committing [itself] in bargaining."
- Like seasoned and wealthy gamblers, "RPs can play the odds." Given their
  size and resources, the stakes for repeat players in any given litigation are
  likely to be relatively small. They can thus "adopt strategies calculated to
  maximize gain over a long series of cases, even where this involves the risk
  of maximum loss in some cases." Conversely, any given case—particularly one involving large sums of money or life-altering issues—is likely to
  be extremely important to the one-shotter.
- Repeat players are well positioned to play not just for immediate gains but
  also for the rules: "It pays an RP to expend resources in influencing the making of the relevant rules by such methods as lobbying." And not only are
  repeat players in a position to change the rules through legislative channels,
  they "can also play for rules in litigation itself." The one-shotter inevitably is
  interested only in the tangible outcome of his particular case, not in legal
  precedent set down for future cases: "Because his stakes in the immediate
  outcome are high and because by definition OS is unconcerned with the outcome of similar litigation in the future, OS will have little interest in that element of the outcome which might influence the disposition of the decision-
  maker next time around. For the RP, on the other hand, anything that will
  favorably influence the outcomes of future cases—[that is, bench rulings or
  expensive appeals]—is a worthwhile result." Moreover, the repeat player, by
  virtue of its experience and expertise, is likely to know which rules are important—that is, which are worth maintaining and fighting for.

The repeat player is likely to have one other thing on its side: lawyers. But,
outside of small claims court, so does the one-shotter. Lawyers thus may appear

to be equalizing agents, but that tends not to be the case. Lawyers or law firms who service repeat players tend to develop long-term relationships with their clients and engage in specialized services for them if need be. Lawyers who cater to the one-shotters of the world serve dozens or hundreds of clients only once, or, if more frequently, still only sporadically. The episodic nature of the relationship the OS attorney has with any given client means it is to her or his financial advantage to process all clients quickly—and going often for the early settlement (Galanter 1974, 116–117). Moreover, OS lawyers tend, in Galanter's words, "to make up the 'lower echelon' of the legal profession; RP lawyers, the higher echelons" (also see also Heinz and Laumann 1978).

In short, the repeat player, unlike the one-shotter, is in an excellent position not only to manipulate, but also to make rules. Equally important, the repeat player can withstand long-run engagements in the judicial process, trading present legal costs—even losses—for future gains. The repeat player is, then, in a powerful bargaining position vis-à-vis the one-shotter, who generally cannot sustain lengthy delays or early losses. The repeat player brings to the judicial process these and other exceptional advantages—advantages Galanter maintains, that give it a powerful edge in the legal arena.

Big Tobacco and Gun Lobby Suffering: Behind The Headline Stories

Leaving aside theory for the moment, we now return to the original assessment we made about the fate of big tobacco and guns based on the bold headlines of the recent past: *the mighty are falling—and falling heavily.* Or are they? Although headlines shout about massive jury awards and novel legal strategies, rarely do they scream of settlement tactics, procedural delays, reductions in damages, appellate reversals, or legislative maneuvers. Yet all are characteristic of the tobacco and gun wars.

'Tobacco Loses Big'—Or Maybe Not

The Tobacco Wars, Phase I: OS v. RP. Although the tobacco litigation wars seem to be a wholly latter-day phenomenon, they actually go back some fifty years. Indeed, the first tort action against a tobacco company was filed in 1954, ten years before the first surgeon general's report causally relating smoking to lung cancer (U.S. Department of Health and Human Services 1964). More notable, however, is the fact that of the 813 private claims filed against cigarette companies between 1954 and 1994, only twice did trial courts find for the plaintiffs, and both times the trial court's decisions were reversed on appeal (LaFrance 2000, 190–191; Payne 2000). That is quite a winning record for big tobacco haves.

In many ways, the most successful of those early suits, *Cipollone v. Liggett Group, Inc.* (1988), is also the best example of the ability of repeat players to trump one-shotters. Rose Cipollone was fifty-eight years old in 1983 when she filed suit in federal court in New Jersey seeking compensation from the Liggett Group. At the time, Mrs. Cipollone had been smoking for over forty years and had lost a lung to prove it. Indeed, she died during the trial, leaving her husband, Antonio, to carry forth on behalf of the estate (*Cipollone v. Liggett Group, Inc.,* 1988).

In 1988 it appeared that the Cipollones were vindicated, when a jury awarded Antonio $400,000 in damages on the grounds that the Liggett Group had failed to warn of the risks of their products prior to 1966, the year that labels began appearing on cigarette packages (see the Federal Cigarette Labeling and Advertising Act of 1965), and that it had breached "an express warranty that the cigarettes were safe" (Jacobson 1989, 1023). Naturally, the tobacco company was not about to take the decision lying down: $400,000 was a pittance; the precedent, however, was far from trivial.

The company argued that the Cipollones' claims, mostly based in state tort doctrines, were largely preempted by federal law. And, in what seemed an early body blow to the industry, no less than the U.S. Supreme Court ruled that much of the Cipollone case was *not* superceded (*Cipollone v. Liggett Group,* 1992). The Court, however, remanded the case for a new trial. But that new trial never happened. Instead, after a bruising nine-year battle, the Cipollone family (now the couple's son, since Antonio, too, had passed away) quietly settled the case when its law firm, citing losses of about $5 million, pulled the plug. Meanwhile, Wall Street insiders theorized that the firm's other clients—mostly major corporations—were tiring of its assault on one of their own (Schroth 1992).

Whatever the reason, *Cipollone* is a clear illustration of the power of the repeat player. The tobacco company was in the game for the long haul, far better able to withstand delays and appeals than the Cipollones, whose deaths during the process stood as a sad metaphor for the inability of the one-shotter to play for long-run interests. This situation ultimately placed the cigarette group in the driver's seat, steering the surviving son and his weary lawyers almost inevitably toward the outcome favored by Liggett all along—a quiet settlement. Indeed, compared with the other 813 litigants, the Cipollones came out quite well—their estate at least got something.

The Tobacco Wars, Phase II: RP v. RP. Clearly, the repeat player—the "have" of the litigation world—would be most advantaged in squaring off against a one-shotter. Sometimes, however, Goliath is made to face Goliath in the judicial process. And there is no greater Goliath (repeat player) than the government. It is party to hundreds upon hundreds of civil suits every year, and it prosecutes all crimes.

Over the past several years, one of the hallmarks of the tobacco wars has been the active involvement of state and federal governments. A combination of increasing health care costs, the uncovering of damning internal cigarette company documents, and growing public aversion to tobacco products has forced government—or at least a portion of it—into the fray against big tobacco. On the headline face of it, government has been the winner, but a closer look might well reveal otherwise.

One of the earliest government efforts was the attempt by the Food and Drug Administration (FDA) to regulate nicotine as a drug and cigarettes as drug delivery devices—an attempt upheld by a trial judge in North Carolina, the very cradle of American tobacco. No doubt, U.S. District Judge William L. Osteen Sr.'s holding that the FDA did possess authority to regulate nicotine as a drug came as something of an unhappy surprise to the industry. As for the cigarette companies' decision to file the complaint in North Carolina, it was hardly serendipitous—one might reasonably surmise that a tobacco country judge would be a bit more sympathetic to tobacco interests than, say, some northern urban or western jurist.

But trial decisions can be appealed, particularly by litigants with deep pockets, and the industry's appeal to the Fourth Circuit had a far more satisfactory outcome: the appellate court reversed the district court's ruling (*Brown and Williamson v. FDA*, 1998). Even more satisfactory, however, was the outcome when the FDA appealed the circuit decision to the Supreme Court: tobacco scored a huge victory. Justice Sandra Day O'Connor, writing for a narrow majority, concurred with the appeals court, ruling that "Congress has clearly precluded the FDA from asserting jurisdiction to regulate tobacco products" (*FDA v. Brown and Williamson*, 2000). According to the Court, if the FDA wants specific authority to regulate cigarettes as drugs, it must gain the power explicitly via the legislative process, which traditionally has been a process pretty darned favorable to tobacco.

Still, one might argue that the FDA's loss was but a hollow victory for tobacco in light of other recent government developments—notably, the more than $240 billion and additional concessions extracted by the states in the Master Settlement Agreement. Here a bit of history is in order.

In the mid-1990s, tobacco interests were shaken when Mississippi attorney general Mike Moore filed suit against the cigarette industry (*Moore v. American Tobacco Company*, 1994). Moore claimed that the industry had knowingly manufactured and marketed a harmful, addictive product that caused major health damage to the citizens of the state. He asked the court to assess economic damages sufficient to reimburse Mississippi for past and future expenses related to treating sick smokers, and he requested punitive damages "in such amount as will sufficiently punish the defendants for their conduct and as will serve as an example to prevent a repetition of such conduct in the future." In addition, he asked the court to enjoin the industry from promoting or selling its product to minors. In what seemed to be a virtual steamroller bearing down on the beleaguered industry, similar suits were filed by nearly every other state attorney general by June 1997 (Kelder and Davidson 1999). Because repeat players generally prefer settlements to trials and because of the unwieldy nature of the multijurisdictional actions, the industry pushed for a general settlement proposal in order to conclude all state and class action claims against it. And because the proposed settlement

would have to bind all fifty states, it had to be in the form of a congressional enactment. Thus by mid-1997 the tobacco wars had moved to Washington, where a
bipartisan settlement of $368.5 billion was initially proffered. By all accounts, the
industry was agreeable to this amount.

Once it was referred to the Senate Commerce Committee in 1998, however, the bill permuted into a different—and considerably larger—animal. The
committee bill upped the ante by about $148 billion. The industry was not nec-
essarily averse to the higher price tag, but it was miffed by provisions that would
raise federal cigarette taxes by $1.10 a pack, give the FDA regulatory authority,
and drastically reduce cigarette marketing and advertising. Steven Goldstone,
chairman of RJR Nabisco, in rather imperious tones, informed Congress that
"the bill . . . requires my signature and there is no chance in the world it's going
to get my signature" (Rosenbaum 1998). The congressional effort thus died in
committee, sending the action back to the states.

The ultimate result was the consolidated agreement (MSA), finalized on
November 23, 1998, among industry participants and forty-six states. In what
was hailed by the attorneys general as a major tobacco capitulation, the industry
acceded to paying the states $206 billion over a seventeen-year period; to fund-
ing a $1.5 billion antismoking campaign; to opening previously secret industry
documents; to curbing significantly their advertising and marketing campaigns,
including banning cartoon characters such as Joe Camel and paraphernalia aimed
at youth; and to disbanding certain industry trade groups (National Association
of Attorneys General 1998). The attorneys general, significant system repeat
players, appeared to have come out ahead.

Well, maybe—and then maybe not. After all, the industry was powerful
enough to tell Congress to take a hike, and to go hiking itself for a better deal.
By most assessments, it got a better deal—in spades. Several facets of the agreement are particularly noteworthy.

To begin, there was the problem of the schedule of payments. Naturally, the
tobacco companies were loath to shell out a huge lump sum to the states. Thus to
seal the bargain, the attorneys general agreed to a very long, drawn-out system of
compensation. The $206 billion will be paid out in installments over a twenty-
five-year period. Significantly, these payments are directly tied to the tobacco
companies' continued fiscal well-being. This arrangement sets up what amounts
to a partnership situation between the states and the large cigarette manufacturers. State governments, salivating over millions of extra dollars flowing into their
treasuries, actually have an enormous incentive to guarantee the financial health
of their new partners. For example, Colorado is scheduled to receive the relatively small amount of about $2.9 billion over the time span. Flush with its tax-free[4]
windfall, the state legislature is set to fund some popular new programs, including
a third-grade reading program; children's health care plans; a tobacco and substance abuse research fund; and prescription drug subsidies for the elderly. Good
stuff, but, according to two members of that legislature, "Colorado's General
Assembly now finds itself in a dilemma: By depending upon annual payments to

fund new programs, the Legislature must expect—even hope—that domestic tobacco sales remain relatively strong. If it chooses not to condone smoking and improve public health by promoting smoking cessation, the Legislature may watch the tobacco money disappear and find itself committed to new programs that it can no longer financially support" (Dean and Feeley 2000).

The states therefore have a huge stake in the continued financial viability of tobacco. Just how huge was demonstrated recently in the light cigarette case *Price v. Philip Morris*. As described earlier, in April 2003 an Illinois court awarded $10 billion in damages against Philip Morris for misleading consumers about the safety of light cigarettes. Pending appeal, the judge ordered the tobacco giant to post a $12 billion bond, an amount Philip Morris said would force it into bankruptcy. True or not, the company's distress call was heard loud and clear by recession-wracked state governments. Should Philip Morris go under, the states' one sure source of income would go with it. Thus in an amicus curiae brief filed by the National Association of Attorneys General, Illinois circuit court judge Nicholas Byron was asked to "set the bond in an amount that would avoid any adverse effect on payments to the states (*BCD News and Comment* 2003). The judge did just that, allowing the company to put "$6 billion in escrow and pay an additional $800 million in quarterly installments." That decision was upheld by the Illinois Supreme Court, which, in a further victory for Philip Morris, allowed the company to proceed on expedited appeal (*Tobacco Industry Litigation Reporter* 2003b). As an attorney who took part in the negotiations noted: "Each State now has an incentive to *increase* tobacco sales. This dampens any likelihood of a taxing or regulatory strategy to reduce the sales of tobacco and reverses the position that States should advance, putting them in partnership with the tobacco companies" (LaFrance 2000, 197–198, emphasis added).

If other provisions of the MSA are any indication, the states are not the senior partners. For example, the MSA virtually guarantees that there will be no federal tax increases on tobacco products. "If within the next four years Congress increases the federal tax on cigarettes and shares the proceeds with the states, the companies will enjoy a dollar-for-dollar setoff against the payments to the states" (Galanter 1999). In other words, if Congress did try to raise the federal cigarette tax, forty-six states would "lose a corresponding amount from their tobacco payments" (Nemitz 1998). Moreover, the MSA grants the large participating companies near oligopoly status in the market. In effect, under the terms of MSA the major cigarette manufacturers can raise prices in order to fund the settlement without losing market share to smaller discount companies that were not part of the agreement. Arguably, the big companies' preferred place in the market is guaranteed in two ways. First, the MSA strongly encourages the enactment of "Qualifying Statutes," whereby states "effectively and fully neutralize . . . the cost disadvantages that the Participating Manufacturers experience vis-à-vis Non-Participating Manufacturers within such Settling State as a result of the provisions of this Agreement." Second, the MSA establishes a price cap on "Subsequent Participating Manufacturers" (SPM)—legal terminology for all of the small companies who were not part of the original agreement. According to small wholesalers and retailers, this clause means that, "as a practical matter, if an SPM lowers its prices to expand its market share, its sales will quickly reach the market share cap and it will be forced to either pay a share of the MSA settlement payments or restrict its output. The actual penalty for any sales by an SPM in excess of its quota is about $.19 per pack ($1.90 per carton) of cigarettes or about one-third of the $5 wholesale price of a carton of discount cigarettes" (*Antitrust Litigation Reporter* 1999).

Since implementation of the MSA, some small firms have launched antitrust actions against the large manufacturers. Thus far, they have been unsuccessful (see *A. D. Bedell v. Philip Morris, Inc.*, 2000) or quietly settled (*DeLoach v. Philip Morris*, 2003).

Thus among other benefits, the MSA shields the tobacco industry from major litigation, from increased federal taxes, and from competition, and it draws forty-six state governments into a mutually beneficial alliance—all for the relatively cheap price of $206 billion, easily passed on to its addicted clientele (see, for example, Galanter 1999 and Haddad 2000). But what of the pending federal litigation launched late in 1999 and as yet unsettled? Round one at least goes to tobacco. On September 28, 2000, U.S. District Judge Gladys Kessler sided with the industry, ruling that much of the government's case was based on a misapplication of two laws: the Medical Care Recovery Act and the Medicare provision of the Social Security Act. Although the judge has allowed the case to proceed on the racketeering counts, the ruling seriously weakened the government's case, now lumbering along to an anticipated fall 2004 trial date (Miller 2000; U.S. Department of Justice 2004). Moreover, as noted earlier, the industry had not been particularly averse to the $520 billion in long-term payments proposed in the failed 1998 congressional effort. Indeed, it had been ready to accept the arrangement. Thus, when it was able to settle with the states for a little over $200 billion, according to one analyst, "this left a balance . . . the industry would have been willing to pay. . . . In a sense, there is a $300 billion contingency fund, an 'account payable,' already contemplated by the industry for as yet unliquidated obligations which might be imposed by the federal government" (LaFrance 2000, 199). Experts anticipate a settlement of roughly that amount.

The Tobacco Wars, Phase III: RP v. OS, Round 2. Although big tobacco has traditionally fared well against small, individual claimants and in negotiations with government, in recent years it has had to face renewed battles with individual smokers and groups of smokers. Much of this new litigation has been spurred on by the discovery of internal documents revealing industry deception and misrepresentation. Whereas tobacco had prevailed for nearly four decades by blaming smokers for their ills, by the mid-1990s sufficient documentation of industry duplicity had been uncovered to embolden a new round of litigants. And, on the face of things, these litigants appear to be winning.

Four major cases are generally cited as indications of tobacco's new vulnerability. In 1999 a San Francisco jury awarded a smoker $50 million (*Henley v.*

Philip Morris, Inc., 1999). In Oregon, a jury returned a judgment of $80 million (*Williams-Branch ex rel. Estate of Williams v. Philip Morris, Inc.*, 1999). In 2000 another California jury found in favor of plaintiff Leslie Whiteley, awarding her $21.7 million (*Whiteley v. Raybestos-Manhattan Inc.*, 2000). In 2002 a Los Angeles jury awarded a single plaintiff a record-breaking $28 billion in punitive damages (*Bullock v. Philip Morris*, 2002). And, then, in the unkindest cut of all, came the record-shattering $158 billion awarded to the Florida class of sick smokers (*Engle v. R. J. Reynolds Tobacco Co.*, 2000).

Yet, despite these apparent antitobacco victories, the record of the cigarette giants remains quite impressive—even in the face of those damning internal documents. Big tobacco continues to win most of its cases at trial. Indeed, discounting the Florida class action, the industry seems to be back on a winning streak.

On July 6, 2000, in a very closely watched case, a Brooklyn jury decided that thirty years' worth of smoking was not related to the plaintiff's lung cancer (*Anderson v. Fortune Brands*, 2000). Only two weeks later, in Mississippi, home to crusading attorney general Mike Moore, a jury refused to hold cigarette companies responsible for the lung cancer death of a thirty-seven-year-old man, a smoker since childhood (*Nunnally v. R. J. Reynolds*, 2000). Rather, the jury agreed with the industry that Joseph Nunnally had known the risks of smoking and willingly assumed those risks. Moreover, and significantly, "the jury did not find that the cigarettes manufactured by the company were 'defective and unreasonably dangerous.' Nor did it find evidence that R. J. Reynolds could have produced a safer product" (*Mealey's Litigation Report* 2000).

In 2003 a Philadelphia jury found Brown and Williamson not liable for the lung cancer death of a man who smoked Carlton cigarettes, thinking they were safer than other brands (*Eiser v. Brown and Williamson*, 2003). And juries in Sacramento and Miami issued verdicts for Philip Morris and R. J. Reynolds, respectively (*Lucier v. Philip Morris*, 2003; *Allen v. R. J. Reynolds*, 2003). Later the same year, flight attendants lost yet another round of second-hand smoke litigation (see, for example, *Routh v. Philip Morris USA Inc. et al.*, 2003).

Just as important, although the industry has clearly sustained some trial losses—in San Francisco, Oregon, and, very notably, Florida—these all are just trial losses. Not surprisingly, the tobacco companies are in the process of appealing them all. And, although some appeals are pending nationwide (and the authors are not equipped with a crystal ball), it is crucial to note that so far tobacco has not lost a single appeal. And those who watch the industry with particular interest—major Wall Street analysts—believe that tobacco will come out on top. For example, Martin Feldman of Salomon Smith Barney notes: "The industry is having to fight harder, but in the long run it will prevail. It's a mistake to believe that this industry won't come up with new effective defenses." Marc Cohen of Goldman Sachs agrees, pointing to the industry's "compelling batting average" (quoted in Haddad 2000). Moreover, even if tobacco has to settle up for really big bucks, "it is the smokers who will bear the cost of litigation." Cohen thus estimates that even if the industry were to lose a hundred cases a year (and it would certainly settle if the legal tide appeared to be turning against it), "cigarette makers could— and would—recoup the cost of judgments through raising prices about 15 cents a pack" (paraphrased in Haddad 2000). As a headline in *Business Week* put it in May 2003, "The Smoke around Big Tobacco Clears" (Choe 2003).

And clear it did. In the most stunning appellate reversal to date, Florida's Third District Court of Appeal not only tossed out the $145 billion punitive damages verdict, but also decertified the plaintiff class of smokers, thereby presumably ending the watershed event of antismoking litigation (*Liggett Group v. Engle*, 2003; Haggman 2003). Moreover, in October 2003 the U.S. Supreme Court threw out an $80 million verdict against Philip Morris, ordering Oregon courts to review the award in light of *State Farm Mutual Automobile Insurance Company v. Campbell* (*Philip Morris USA Inc. v. Williams*, 2003).[5]

What accounts for tobacco's continued ability to come out ahead—or at least to hold the line? The early victories against sporadic individual plaintiffs might have been expected, but certainly less expected has been the cigarette companies' ability to hold the line in the wake of the virtual onslaught of individual and class claims over the past half-decade—claims well armed with all kinds of compelling evidence. Even more surprising, perhaps, the industry has come out of litigations and negotiations with the government (clearly another repeat player) smelling more like a rose than like stale tobacco. There are, in other words, RPs and RPs. And the public, possessing fewer resources and torn by multiple, often conflicting political claims and constituencies, has simply been overwhelmed by the private (see, for example, Galanter 1999).

'U.S. Gun Lobby Suffers Setback'—But How Much?

Like the tobacco industry, gun makers and distributors had long managed to lead charmed lives. Indeed, in some respects the firearms industry has out-charmed even the cigarette makers—people have been suing gun makers for injuries and death since the early twentieth century (Lytton 2000, 1255). And, with the exception of a few cases where guns literally malfunctioned, weapons makers managed, until very recently, to avoid any liability.

Still, all good things presumably come to an end. And, on the face of things, several contemporary events appear to have crashed the gun lobby's party. First, over the past several years some individual shooting victims or next of kin have launched litigations against manufacturers. Second, the threat of a lawsuit by the Department of Housing and Urban Development (HUD) eventually forced Smith and Wesson to bow to demands for reform. And, third, and most widely noted, a series of institutional lawsuits has been launched since 1998—most significantly, by cities and states. Unquestionably, bad times have found big guns. How bad remains to be seen.

Individual Lawsuits. The gun market, like the tobacco industry, began facing serious challenges during the mid- to late 1990s, when several sets of people filed suit. One of those suits, discussed earlier, was initiated in New York in 1994 by relatives of the victims and one survivor of handgun violence (*Hamilton v. Accu-tek,* 1994). In the same year in California, relatives of people killed in a San Francisco office building by a deranged person toting military assault pistols sued the weapons' manufacturer. A year later, the parents of Kenzo Dix sued Beretta after Kenzo was unintentionally killed by a fourteen-year-old friend playing with his parents' semiautomatic handgun. Similarly, in Massachusetts the parents of twelve-year-old Ross Mathieu sued Beretta after his best friend fatally wounded him with a 950BS pistol. In 1997 in New Mexico, another unintentional shooting prompted parents to sue manufacturers of "Saturday Night Specials." In 2000 families of the victims of the 1999 three-day shooting rampage by white supremacist Benjamin Nathaniel Smith began litigation against manufacturer Bryco Arms. And in 2003 victims and the families of victims of the D.C. area snipers filed suit against the gun shop Bull's Eye Shooter Supply and rifle manufacturer Bushmaster Firearms Inc.[6]

As the sniper lawsuit suggests, litigation has not been confined solely to the makers of guns. Distributors and dealers, too, have been under fire. A dealer in Michigan has been sued for selling a pistol to a man despite being warned by his sister that he was mentally ill. The man later shot several people in his psychologist's office. Similarly, a Texas pawn shop has been sued for selling a gun to a known mentally ill man, who later killed several persons. Also in Texas, the family of Alek Ambrosio sued a Houston dealer over Ambrosio's murder by a gun stolen from the store. In Kentucky, Jennifer Hicks sued T&M Jewelry for knowingly selling a gun to an underage person who later shot her in the face. And in 1998 the parents of the late Sherry Lee White sued Wal-Mart for selling a shotgun to her estranged husband, then under a domestic violence restraining order.[7]

It all sounds pretty bad for the industry, but the outcomes to date suggest a far more ambiguous situation. So far, that ambiguity has favored the defendant gun market. Of the five cases cited earlier that have actually gone to trial (*Accu-tek, Merrill, Dix, Smith* and *Ambrosio*), the defendant gun manufacturer or dealer has won four—a very impressive record. Moreover, and notably, the jury that delivered the industry's first ever loss in *Hamilton v. Accu-tek* awarded the relatively paltry sum of $520,000. It awarded that sum only to the single surviving gun victim, and it assessed manufacturer liability at only 13 percent. According to an attorney representing the gun manufacturers, "I just walked out of [Judge] Jack Weinstein's courtroom, and a Brooklyn jury had cut my people loose out of six wrongful-death cases. And I said, 'That's great'" (quoted in Van Voris 1999). The case is currently on appeal. The remaining cases are in various stages of discovery, motions, or settlement. But here is one indication of how long defendants' tactics can delay action: *Dix* was finally scheduled for trial in late 2003, nine years after the family of Kenzo Dix initially filed suit (http://bradycenter.org/).

The HUD Threat and Smith and Wesson Agreement. However successful the gun industry has been to date in its dealings with individual litigants, these battles are not the only legal troubles it is facing. As noted earlier, in December 1999 the Department of Housing and Urban Development, with explicit White House backing, threatened to file suit against the gun industry on behalf of over three thousand public housing authorities with a history of gun violence. Three months later, that threat apparently paid off for the government when manufacturing giant Smith and Wesson acceded to numerous demands, settling not only with the federal government, but also with fifteen cities and two states.

One could assume tough times for a beleaguered Smith and Wesson—that is, until reading the company's "Clarification" of the agreement. A few major examples will make the point. Smith and Wesson agreed to add hidden serial numbers to its weapons, something it "is already doing . . . on many of its firearms" (Smith and Wesson 2000). The company also agreed to manufacture guns with external locking devices, but it "has been including trigger locks in all of its handguns for several years." In addition, Smith and Wesson consented to install internal locking devices, several types of which are already available to the company and can be easily "incorporated in . . . designs over the next 24 months." Moreover, the company currently meets standards "acceded to" in much ballyhooed portions of the agreement such as child safety mechanisms, minimum barrel lengths, performance and drop testing. In other words, Smith and Wesson has shielded itself from major litigation pretty much by agreeing to do what it has already been doing. Such a deal!

Institutional Lawsuits. Remaining, however, is what would seem to be the biggest problem for big guns—the still active large institutional suits aimed at manufacturers, distributors, and dealers. By 2003 twenty-three local governments, the State of New York, and the NAACP and the NSCIA had launched litigation accusing major gun industry participants of, among other things, public nuisance, negligence, deceptive advertising, and defective design.

Although the large tobacco companies—several with far-flung, diversified holdings in food, beverages, and other commodities—tend to dwarf gun companies from a financial standpoint,[8] the firearms industry has been blessed by its connection with, and backing by, one of the nation's most effective independent lobbying organizations, the National Rifle Association (NRA), as well as several other well-funded sports-oriented organizations (Wilcox 1998, 99). The NRA alone boasts an annual budget of $168 million and an impressive voluntary membership of 3.7 million politically active gun owners (Powell 2000). Not surprisingly, the group has not taken the assault on guns lying down; it has waged a counterattack on several fronts.

Most effective has been the gun lobby's effort, since 1999, to have state legislatures pass "Firearm Industry Relief Acts," aimed at severely limiting the ability of local governments to bring lawsuits. As of 2003, the NRA had introduced such legislation in forty-six states, successfully passing acts in thirty-one (Legal Community Against Violence 2004). Such laws, while varying in their restrictiveness, generally prevent localities from suing gun companies without the express permission of the state's attorney general and limit grounds to matters such as manufacturing defects, breach of contract, or breach of warranty. In addition, the NRA is behind efforts to pass federal legislation in this area, and, to date, it has been very successful. The U.S. House of Representatives has already passed the Protection of Lawful Commerce in Arms Act, designed "to prohibit civil liability actions from being brought or continued against manufacturers, distributors, dealers, or importers of firearms or ammunition for damages resulting from the misuse of their products by others." Although the bill died over procedural wrangling, it had broad bipartisan support and fifty-five cosponsors, including Democratic minority leader Tom Daschle of South Dakota (Eilperin 2003).

The gun lobby has not confined its efforts to the legislative forums—traditionally, its most fertile ground. To begin with, the industry has had to fight back against jurisdictional lawsuits. As noted earlier, it has been greatly abetted by the NRA's legislative efforts, presumably nullifying the possibility of such suits in well over a third of the states. Still, a significant number of suits remain, although, to date, none has resulted in a full trial and several have been dismissed, marking clear victories for the industry and lobby. For example, in 1999 a court in Connecticut dismissed a suit brought by the City of Bridgeport (*Ganin v. Smith and Wesson*, 1999), and a court in Florida dismissed a suit brought by Dade County (*Penelas v. Arms Technology*, 1999). In 2000 a judge in Illinois dismissed Chicago's suit against the industry, chiding Mayor Richard M. Daley that he "might do better to combat city crime through law enforcement methods and legislation" (paraphrased in *AP News* 2000). Also in 2000 an Ohio appeals court upheld the dismissal of Cincinnati's lawsuit, holding that the city had "failed to state *any* claims against defendants that would allow it to recover for its municipal expenditures" (*Cincinnati v. Beretta USA Corp.*, 2000, emphasis added). The Cincinnati case was the first of the municipal suits to go to the appellate level. Although some other cities have survived attempts to dismiss, all of the cases have been delayed on motions or changes of venue.[9]

In 2000 the National Shooting Sports Foundation (NSSF), an 1,800-member pro-gun lobby, and seven gun manufacturers, including Beretta and Colt, filed suit in federal district court in Georgia against HUD Secretary Andrew Cuomo, the attorneys general of New York and Connecticut, and sixteen local governments (*NSSF v. Cuomo*, 2000). The suit, brought in reaction to the Smith and Wesson agreement, charges defendants with conspiracy in restraint of trade and violation of the Constitution's commerce clause primarily for instituting gun purchasing policies that favor particular firearms designs and market distribution schemes.

Earlier, in 1999, the gun lobby won a stunning legal decision when U.S. District Judge Sam R. Cummings declared unconstitutional a federal law banning individuals under court restraining orders from possessing firearms. Cummings based his decision on his determination that the Second Amendment guarantees an *individual's* right to own a gun, marking the first ever such finding by a federal judge (*U.S. v. Emerson*, 1999). Judge Cummings's decision was reversed by the Fifth Circuit in 2001 (*U.S. v. Emerson*, 2001). Interestingly, however, in 2003, in briefs asking it not to review *Emerson* or a companion case

(*Haney v. United States,* 2002) U.S. Solicitor General Ted Olson signaled to the Supreme Court that the George W. Bush administration views the Second Amendment as an individual, not a militia, right (Mauro 2003).

Finally, in the wake of the institutional lawsuits and the widely publicized school shootings of the late 1990s, the gun lobby has spent considerable resources on public relations efforts. Notably, during the 2000 Republican and Democratic National Conventions, the Hunting and Shooting Sports Heritage Foundation (HSSHF), an offshoot of NSSF, supported primarily by the gun industry and specifically instituted to "provide . . . funding for a professional, aggressive response to politically motivated lawsuits filed against the [gun] industry" (http://www.hsshf.org), ran a series of ads referring to "big-city mayors, whose greedy lawyers are using your tax dollars to sue us for criminals they won't prosecute" (transcript quoted in Sills 2000). Purportedly costing $10 million,[10] the ads featured the desecration of the American flag as a metaphor for loss of liberty, and they featured the voice of actor Joe Estevez. Estevez is the brother of, and sounds nearly identical to, actor Martin Sheen, who plays the president on TV's popular *West Wing* and is a longtime antigun activist.

Conclusion: Still Coming Out Ahead

It is certainly true that "the relative advantages between and among litigants is more nuanced and dynamic than the terms one-shotter and repeat player suggests" (Grossman, Kritzer, and Macauly 1999, 810). And nuance aplenty is provided with the rise of the class action and other aggregated claimants in both tobacco and gun suits. Such massing of plaintiffs can make one-shotters more like repeat players in two ways: like repeat players, the aggregated one-shotters now have size, and they are likely to have more proficient (in terms of expertise, resources, and status) lawyers. This would seem particularly true in the case of tobacco litigation. The 500,000 or so plaintiffs in Florida's *Engle* case obviously have mass, and their chief attorneys, Stanley and Susan Rosenblatt, now devote practically all their time to fighting big tobacco. But whether this situation puts the newly muscled one-shotters ahead is far from clear.

Indeed, in general, mass tort actions tend to favor settlements, which, in turn, tend to favor defendants. As Coffee (1995, 1349–1350) explains:

> Originally, the class action was viewed by both sides as the plaintiffs' weapon, a technique for extorting settlements even in non-meritorious cases. Throughout the 1980s, corporate defendants vigorously resisted the use of the mass tort class action, preferring even the alternative of a bankruptcy reorganization. But with the 1990s, their perception of the class action has changed dramatically. Defendants have not only adopted the class action as their preferred means of resolving their mass tort liabilities, but have also begun to solicit plaintiffs' attorneys to bring such class actions (as a condition of settling other pending litigation between them).

Behind this transition lies defendants' discovery of a variety of procedures for minimizing their tort liabilities.

Why is this happening? For one thing, the "courts themselves are 'conflict-ed' because of the threat of docket inundation from individual mass tort cases, and thus they may be more willing to countenance doubtful settlements that they probably would not otherwise accept." Moreover, and very significantly, "even when individual class members hold legally meritorious claims for significant damages, client passivity may remain the norm because many (and sometimes virtually all) class members are 'future claimants'—that is, persons who have not yet experienced any symptomatic illness or disease, but rather share only a statis-tically enhanced risk of future illness . . . because of their exposure to a toxic product. . . . To the extent that future claimants will remain rationally apathetic . . . defendants have a strong interest in resolving such an action at an early stage. . . ." Thus "unsuspecting future claimants suffer the extinction of their claims even before they learn of their injury" (Coffee 1995, 1350, 1351).

If aggregated one-shotters are not sufficient to thwart big guns and tobac-co, government certainly seems up to the task. "Far more than was the case in 1974, *government matters*" (Grossman, Kritzer, and Macauley 1999, 810, empha-sis in original). As Farole (1999, 1055) points out in his study of litigation before five state supreme courts, "State and local governments were significantly more successful than non-governmental litigants." After all, government, taken in the aggregate, is the repeat player to end all repeat players—it has experience, it has insider status, it has size, it has resources, and does it ever have lawyers!

Most earlier studies of interest group litigation focused on and stressed lit-igation by population-based groups and coalitions *against* governments. Such lit-igation—whether put forth by liberal or conservative groups—tended to have a constitutional basis or the goal of promoting some kind of social change. Although some such efforts were directed against corporations (civil rights and sexual harassment issues, for example), this litigation or counterlitigation also tended to involve constitutional questions with statutory support.

Currently, however, the major litigation against tobacco and guns is being brought by governments against corporations and market coalitions with the pur-pose of promoting social change, but with little or no constitutional content. Does this situation reflect a shift in the relative power of government and the corporate sector? We suggest that the answer is no. The problem is that "government" can-not be easily aggregated—clearly, it is not monolithic. The United States is blessed (or cursed, depending on one's perspective) with thousands of governments, and judicial expertise and knowledge vary widely among and within jurisdictions.

Government writ large could be expected to trump in criminal prosecu-tions—nobody else does that—but civil litigation involving tobacco and guns is a different matter entirely. Government is a very recent entrant into these wars— really not penetrating them until the mid-1990s. The tobacco industry, by contrast, has been building expertise for some fifty years, and the gun industry has been fighting liability claims of one sort or another for about century. Generalists like attorneys general and local corporation counsels, saddled with limited and politically hot-button budgets, can hardly be expected, in five years' time, to master the game in the same way as their opponents. Here again, politically expedient settlements would be (and have been) preferable to long, drawn-out court battles.

Certainly, no one would suggest that the tobacco and firearms industries are happy with the current situation. Big tobacco, we are sure, much prefers the good old days when cigarettes were touted as benignant tools of relaxation and glamour, when most of the adult population smoked, when only the intrepid few dared question their benefits, and when maintaining contingency funds in the hundreds of billions of dollars was unimaginable. The gun industry, for its part, would no doubt favor the halcyon days before the rise of public concern over violence and counterlobbies seeking to rival the policy hegemony of the NRA. In any comparison of the legal-political landscape of even ten years ago with that of today, it is difficult to call the tobacco and gun industries "winners."

But neither has either industry been vanquished on the battlefield of litigation—far from it. Tobacco remains a multibillion-dollar business worldwide.[11] It continues to have a very impressive "win-loss" record in the courts, and, as a result of settlements, it has been shielded from major litigation; it has been safeguarded against increased federal taxes; it has been secured from competition; and it has drawn forty-six state governments into a mutually beneficial alliance. The gun industry, too, is still more than economically viable, and it, too, maintains a winning trial record and an enviable finesse in settlement. Moreover, the gun lobby's legislative strength has allowed it, in the span of only one year, to thwart future damaging litigation in nineteen states. If, comparatively, all this is not winning, it sure is not losing.

Over time, power relationships can be expected to vary—at least somewhat—and even the mightiest lose sometimes. In the end, though, it is probably not about any given win or loss (or any of several wins or losses), but rather, as Galanter (1974) puts it, who "comes out ahead." As for tobacco and guns, previously unimagined losses may well have occurred, and industry executives, investors, and supporters may well not find the world nearly as rosy as it once was, but, overall, these "haves" continue to come out ahead.

Notes

1. The civil suit was *U.S. v. Phillip Morris et al.* (1999). The federal statutes were the Medical Care Recovery Act, the Medicare Secondary Payer provisions of the Social Security Act, and provisions of the Racketeer Influenced and Corrupt Organizations Act (RICO).

2. *City of Atlanta v. Smith and Wesson* (1999); *Boston v. Smith and Wesson* (2000); *City of Chicago v. Beretta* (1999); *Cincinnati v. Beretta USA Corp.* (2000); *White (Mayor of Cleveland) v. Hi-Point Firearms* (1999); *Archer (Mayor of Detroit) v. Arms Technology, Inc.* (1999); *District of Columbia v. Beretta* (2000); *City of Gary v. Smith and Wesson*

(1999); *James (Mayor of Newark) v. Arcadia Machine and Tools* (1999); *City of Philadelphia v. Beretta* (2000); *City of St. Louis v. Cernicek* (1999).

3. The real story of Stella Liebeck, a.k.a. "The McDonald's Coffee Lady," is quite different, however, than the popular myth would have it. The facts are that Ms. Liebach was very seriously burned and had tried to settle modestly with McDonald's before taking it to court; McDonald's had already received many complaints about the temperature of its coffee before Ms. Liebach's mishap; and the multimillion dollars awarded Ms. Liebach by the jury was reduced to a few hundred thousand by the judge (Marder 2003, 911).

4. Actually, the whole deal amounts to an extra tax on smokers. As Galanter (1999) put it, "The main difference from a tax is that legislators and governors are spared the dishonor of enacting it."

5. In *Campbell*, the Court found a jury's award in a Utah court trial of $145 million in punitive damages against an automobile insurer to be excessive, in violation of the Fourteenth Amendment's due process clause, where full compensatory damages had been found to be only $1 million.

6. See *Merrill v. Navegar Inc.* (2000); *Dix v. Beretta U.S.A. Corp.* (1998, 2000); *Mathieu v. Fabrica D'Armi Pietro Beretta SPA and Beretta U.S.A* (2000); *Smith v. Bryco Arms* (2001); and *Anderson v. Bryco Arms Corp.* (2000).

7. See *Rissman v. Target Sports, Inc.* (2000); *Estate of Raymond Lamb Payne v. EZ Pawn* (2000); *Ambrosio v. Carter's Shooting Center* (2000); *Hicks v. T&M Jewelry, Inc.* (1999); and *Hopper v. Wal-Mart Stores, Inc.* (2000).

8. Philip Morris Inc., for example, includes not only Philip Morris cigarettes, but also Kraft Foods, the Miller Brewing Company, and Philip Morris Capital Corporation. The company boasted 1999 revenues of over $78 billion (http://www.philipmorris.com/corporate/index.html). By contrast, Tomkins Ltd., the British conglomerate of which Smith and Wesson is only a small part, reported 1999 profits of about $780 million (http://www.tomkins.co.uk/investors/ar00/6.html).

9. See, especially, *Pro hac vice* applications of Allen Rostron for Plaintiffs and Terry F. Moritz and Roger Lewis for Defendant, JCCP 4095 FIREARM CASE (Sup. Ct. of Calif., San Diego Co., September 15, 2000), and *Boston v. Smith and Wesson* (2000).

10. See U.S. Department of Housing and Urban Development (2000).

11. As of September 2000, the Clinton administration was actually backing an export subsidy bill that would give American tobacco companies yearly tax breaks of about $100 million for products sold abroad (Kaufman 2000).

References

Antitrust Litigation Reporter. 1999. "Tobacco Cases Master Settlement Agreement: A. D. Bedell Wholesale Co. v. Philip Morris Inc." 7:2.

AP News. 2000. "Landmark $433M Gun Suit Dismissed," September 15. http://news.findlaw.com/ap/o/1110/92000/20000915224831540.html.

BCD News and Comment. 2003. May 1.

Butterfield, Fox. 2000. "3 More States Join an Investigation of Gun Industry." *New York Times* , 6 April.

Choe, Howard. 2003. "Smoke around Big Tobacco Clears." *Business Week Online,* May 22.

Coffee, John C., Jr. 1995. "Class Wars: The Dilemma of the Mass Tort Class Action." *Columbia Law Review* 95:1343.

Dean, Doug, and Mike Feeley. 2000. "One-Step Program Works." *Denver Post,* April 3.

Eilperin, Juliet. 2003. "Daschle Joins Move to Shoot Down Some Liability of Gun Merchants." *Washington Post,* October 20, A21.

Epstein, Lee. 1991. "Courts and Interest Groups." In *The American Courts: A Critical Assessment,* edited by John B. Gates and Charles A. Johnson. Washington, DC: CQ Press.

Esfahani. Elizabeth. 2003. "TV Ads: Maneuver or Candid Endeavor?" *Richmond Times Dispatch,* July 20, D1.

Farole, Donald J., Jr. 1999. "Reexamining Litigant Success in State Supreme Courts." *Law and Society Review* 33:795, 1043.

Freeman, John Lieper. 1965. *The Political Process: Executive Bureau-Legislative Committee Relations.* Rev. ed. New York: Random House.

Galanter, Marc. 1974. "Why the 'Haves' Come Out Ahead: Speculations on the Limits of Legal Change." *Law and Society Review* 9:95.

———. 1999. "Big Tobacco: Winning By Losing." *American Lawyer* (January/February).

Grossman, Joel B., Herbert M. Kritzer, and Stewart Macauly. 1999. "Do the 'Haves' Still Come Out Ahead?" *Law and Society Review* 33:795, 803.

Haddad, Charles. 2000. "Why Big Tobacco Can't Be Killed." *Business Week,* April 24.

Haggman, Matthew. 2003. "Decertification of Florida Smokers Raises Questions." *Legal Intelligencer,* June 20.

Heinz, John P., and Edward O. Laumann. 1978. "The Legal Profession: Client Interests, Professional Roles, and Social Hierarchies." *Michigan Law Review* 76:1111–1142.

Jacobson, Douglas N. 1989. "Note: After Cipollone v. Liggett Group, Inc.: How Wide Will the Floodgates of Cigarette Litigation Open?" *American University Law Review* 38:1021.

Kaufman, Marc. 2000. "Tobacco Exports Get Aid in Bill Set for House." *Washington Post,* September 12, A20.

Kelder, Graham, and Patricia Davidson. 1999. "The Multistate Master Settlement Agreement and the Future of State and Local Tobacco Control: An Analysis of Selected Topics and Provisions of the MultiState Master Settlement Agreement of November 23, 1998." Tobacco Control Resource Center, Inc., at Northeastern University School of Law, March 24. http://www.tobacco.neu.edu/msa/index.html#P160_16518.

LaFrance, Arthur B. 2000. "Tobacco Litigation: Smoke, Mirrors and Public Policy." *American Journal of Law and Medicine* 26:187–203.

Legal Community Against Violence. 2004. http://www.lcav.org/.

Lytton, Timothy D. 2000 "Lawsuits against the Gun Industry: A Comparative Institutional Analysis." *Connecticut Law Review* 32:1247.

Marder, Nancy S. 2003. "Introduction to the Jury at a Crossroad: The American Experience." *Chicago-Kent Law Review* 78:909–933.

Mauro, Tony. 2003. "Despite Personal Tragedy, Solicitor General Triumphs." *Texas Lawyer,* July 8.

McCool, Daniel. 1987. *Command of the Waters: Iron Triangles, Federal Water Development, and Indian Water.* Berkeley: University of California Press.

Mealey's Litigation Report. 2000. "Tobacco Company Wins Individual Case in Mississippi." July 20.

Miller, Bill. 2000. "Judge Undercuts Government's Tobacco Case." *Washington Post,* September 28. http://www.washingtonpost.com/wpdyn/articles/A364622000Sep28.html.

National Association of Attorneys General. 1998. "Tobacco Settlement Announcement." http://www.naag.org/tobac/npr.htm.

Nemitz, Bill. 1998. "Tobacco Deal Just Smoke and Mirrors." *Portland Press Herald,* November 22.

Payne, Tommy J. 2000. "States' Actions Make Sense." *USA Today,* March 27, 30A.

Powell, Michael. 2000. "Call to Arms." *Washington Post Sunday Magazine,* August 6.

Ripley, Randall B., and Grace A. Franklin. 1987. *Congress, the Bureaucracy and Public Policy.* 4th ed. Chicago: Dorsey.

Rosenbaum, David E. 1998. "Cigarette Makers Quit Negotiations on Tobacco Bill." *New York Times*, April 9.

Schattschneider, E. E. 1960. *The Semi-Sovereign People: A Realist's View of Democracy in America*. New York: Holt, Rinehart, and Winston.

Schroth, Tracy. 1992. "Poking the Ashes of Tobacco Liability: Why Five Suits against the Industry Were Dropped in a Single Week." *New Jersey Law Journal*, November 16.

Sills, James H. (Mayor, Wilmington, DE). 2000. "Press Conference with Andrew Cuomo, Secretary of Housing and Urban Development, and Members of the Mayors Coalition for Safe Guns." Federal News Service, August 22.

Smith and Wesson. 2000. "Clarification Settlement Document," March 17. http://www.smithwesson.com/misc/agreement1.html.

Tobacco Industry Litigation Reporter. 2003a. April 18.

Tobacco Industry Litigation Reporter. 2003b. September 19.

U.S. Department of Health and Human Services. 1964. "Smoking and Health: Report of the Advisory Committee to the Surgeon General of the Public Health Service." Washington, DC.

U.S. Department of Housing and Urban Development. 2000. "Cuomo, Mayors and Sheen Condemn Deceptive and Unfair Ad Campaign by Gun Makers." HUD Press Release No. 00225, August 22, 2000. http://www.hud.gov/pressrel/pr00225.html.

U.S. Department of Justice, Civil Division. 2004. "Litigation against Tobacco Companies." http://www.usdoj.gov/civil/cases/tobacco2/index.htm.

Van Voris, Bob. 1999. "Lawyers Debate Who Won Gun Suit." *National Law Journal*, March 1.

Walsh. Sharon. 1999. "Gunmakers Up in Arms over HUD Plan to Sue Them." *Washington Post*, December 9.

Wilcox, Clyde. 1998. "The Dynamics of Lobbying the Hill." In *The Interest Group Connection: Electioneering, Lobbying, and Policymaking in Washington*, edited by Paul S. Herrnson, Ronald G. Shaiko, and Clyde Wilcox. Chatham, NJ: Chatham House Publishers.

Wilson, Catherine. 2000. "Florida Jury Awards $145 Billion in Punitives to Smokers." *Legal Intelligencer*, July 17.

Court Cases Cited

A. D. Bedell v. Philip Morris, Inc., 104 F. Supp. 2d 501 (2000).

Allen v. R. J. Reynolds, reported at http://tobacco.neu.edu/ (2003).

Ambrosio v. Carter's Shooting Center, Inc., 20 S.W.3d 262, 265 (Tex. App. 2000).

Anderson v. Bryco Arms Corp., No. 00L 007476, complaint filed (Ill. Cir. Ct., Cook Co., June 29, 2000).

Anderson v. Fortune Brands, No. 4281/97 (N.Y. Sup. Ct., Kings Co. 2000).

Archer (Mayor of Detroit) v. Arms Technology, Inc. (Wayne Co. Cir. Ct. 1999).

Boston v. Smith and Wesson, No. 1999-02590 (Sup. Ct., Suffolk, July 13, 2000).

Brown and Williamson v. FDA, 153 F. 3d 155 (1998).

Bullock v. Philip Morris, No. BC 249171, Superior Court of State of California for the County of Los Angeles (2002).

Cipollone v. Liggett Group, Inc., 693 F. Supp. 208 (1988).

Cipollone v. Liggett Group, 505 U.S. 504, 524–531 (1992).

Cincinnati v. Beretta USA Corp., Nos. C-990729, C-990814, C-990815, 2000 (Ohio App. LEXIS 3601, Ct. App. of Ohio, First Appellate District, Hamilton Co. 2000).

City of Atlanta v. Smith and Wesson, No. 9VSO149217J (Ga. St. Ct., Fulton Co. 1999).

City of Chicago v. Beretta, No. 98 CH 015596 (Cook Co. Cir. Ct. 1999).

City of Gary v. Smith and Wesson (Lake Co. Sup. Ct. 1999).

City of Philadelphia v. Beretta (Phila. Co. Ct. of Common Pleas 2000).

City of St. Louis v. Cernicek, No. 992-01209 (St. Louis Cir. Ct. 1999).

Coyne Beahm v. FDA, 966 F. Supp. 1374 (M.D.N.C. 1997).

DeLoach v. Philip Morris, No. 00-CV-294 (D.N.C. 2003).

District of Columbia v. Beretta, No. 00-0000428 (Sup. Ct. D.C. 2000).

Dix v. Beretta U.S.A. Corp., No. 750681-9 (Alameda Co. Sup. Ct., 1998), No. A086018 (Calif. Ct. App., 1st Dist., Div. 1, 2000).

Eiser v. Brown and Williamson, No. 4367 (Pa. C.P., Phila. Co., August 15, 2003).

Engle v. R. J. Reynolds Tobacco Co., No. 94-08273 CA-22 (Fla. Cir. Ct., 11th Cir. 2000).

Estate of Raymond Lamb Payne v. EZ Pawn, No. D-155,500 (Dis. Ct. of Jefferson Co., Tex. 2000).

FDA v. Brown and Williamson, 120 S. Ct. 1291 (2000).

Ganin v. Smith and Wesson (Sup. Ct., Fairfield, Conn., December 13, 1999).

Hamilton v. Accu-tek, CV-95-0049 (E.D.N.Y. 1994).

Haney v. United States, 264 F. 3d 1161; *cert denied* (10th Cir. 2002).

Henley v. Philip Morris, Inc., No. 995172 (Calif. Sup. Ct., San Francisco County 1999).

Hicks v. T&M Jewelry, Inc., No. 97-Ci 2617 (Fayette Co. Cir. Ct., Lexington, Ky. 1999).

Hopper v. Wal-Mart Stores, Inc., Civ.-98-C-1496-NE (N.D. Al. 2000).

James (Mayor of Newark) v. Arcadia Machine and Tools (Essex Co. Sup. Ct. 1999).

Liggett Group v. Engle, 853 So. 2d 434 (Fla. Dist. Ct. App., 3d Dist. 2003).

Lucier v. Philip Morris, No. 02AS01909, Superior Court of State of California, County of Sacramento (2003).

Mathieu v. Fabrica D'Armi Pietro Beretta SPA and Beretta U.S.A. (D. Mass. No. 97-CV-12818-NG, 2000).

Merrill v. Navegar Inc., 89 Cal. Rptr. 2d 146 (Cal. Ct. App. 1999); review granted, 92 Cal. Rptr. 2d 256 (Cal. 2000).

Moore v. American Tobacco Company, No. 94-1429 (Ch. Ct. Jackson Co., Miss. 1994).

NAACP v. AA Arms, Inc., No. 99CV3999 (E.D.N.Y. 1999).

New Orleans v. Smith and Wesson Corp., No. 98-18578 (Civ. D. Ct. Parish of Orleans, filed October 30, 1998).

New York v. Arms Technology, Inc. (E.D.N.Y. June 2000).

NSSF v. Cuomo, No. 1 00-CV-1063 (N.D. Ga., Atlanta Div., filed April 26, 2000).

Nunnally v. R. J. Reynolds, No. 92-270-CD (MS Cir. Ct., Desoto Co., 2000).

Penelas v. Arms Technology, No. 99-01941 (Cir. Ct., Dade Co., 12/13/99).

Philip Morris USA Inc. v. Williams, 2003 U.S. LEXIS 5437 (2003).

Price v. Philip Morris, 793 N.E. 2d 942 (App. Ct. Ill., 5th Dist. 2003).

Rissman v. Target Sports, Inc. (Circuit Court for the County of Oakland, Mich. 2000).

Routh v. Philip Morris USA Inc. et al., No. 00-03030 CS 11 (Fla. Cir. Ct., 11th Cir., Miami-Dade Co. 2003).

Smith v. Bryco Arms, No. CV-94-09455 (N.M. 2d Dist. Ct.); on appeal, No. 20389 (N.M. Ct. of Appeal).

State Farm Mutual Automobile Insurance Company v. Campbell, 538 U.S. 408 (2003).

U.S. v. Emerson, No. 6:98-CR-103-C (N.D. Tex., San Angelo Div., April 7, 1999).

U.S. v. Emerson, 270 F. 3d 203; *cert. denied* (5th Cir. 2001).

U.S. v. Phillip Morris et al., complaint, D.C., filed September 22, 1999.

White (Mayor of Cleveland) v. Hi-Point Firearms (Cuyahoga Co. Ct. of Common Pleas, 1999).

Whiteley v. Raybestos-Manhattan Inc., No. 303184 (Cal. Sp. Ct., San Francisco Co., 2000).

Williams-Branch ex rel. Estate of Williams v. Philip Morris, Inc., No. 9705-03957 (Oregon Cir. Ct., Multnomah Co., 1999).

19. Defending the Faithful: Conservative Christian Litigation in American Politics

Hans J. Hacker

March 6, 1987, marked the beginning of a new era in conservative Christian litigation.[1] On that day, the U.S. Supreme Court heard oral arguments in *Board of Airport Commissioners of Los Angeles v. Jews for Jesus, Inc.* (1987). Several years earlier, the board had approved an ordinance aimed at stopping religious groups from handing out tracts or looking for converts in the Los Angeles airport. Then using the ordinance, the airport commissioners forced the removal of Jews for Jesus evangelists from the airport, after threatening legal action against them if they continued to distribute literature.

The evangelists hired a relatively inexperienced attorney, Jay Sekulow, to represent them. Sekulow convinced a federal district court to declare the ordinance unconstitutional. Eventually, the U.S. Supreme Court granted the airport's request to review the dispute. According to Sekulow, the airport's intolerance toward religious expression contributed to the ferocity of his onslaught during oral arguments before the Court.[2] Although Sekulow was extremely nervous and interrupted the chief justice several times, the Supreme Court ruled unanimously that the resolution was unconstitutional and had a "chilling effect" on protected speech.

This case marked a turning point in the tactics of the conservative Christian movement (commonly referred to as the New Christian Right or the NCR). Over the almost two decades after the Court's decision, the movement retooled its approach to the courts, changed the primary focus of its legal rationale, and spun off various new litigating firms. A new generation of litigators are now using sophisticated litigation strategies pioneered decades earlier by liberal interest groups to achieve extraordinary results. Among the most active and best-funded public interest law firms in the nation, they have developed highly responsive organizations capable of shifting emphases in response to political changes. Their participation in court is an essential component of the NCR's overall political strategy.

The First Amendment to the U.S. Constitution states that "Congress shall make no law respecting an establishment of religion, or prohibiting the free exercise thereof." The first half of this phrase is commonly known as the establishment clause, and it has been interpreted by the U.S. Supreme Court to bar excessive government entanglement with religion (see *Lemon v. Kurtzman*, 1971). The second phrase is called the free exercise clause, and it protects individuals' rights to worship and practice their religion. Many of the cases litigated by NCR groups involve the intersection of these two clauses — for example, the rights of students to use school property for a religious club. By framing these cases as free exercise cases instead of establishment cases, the NCR has had far greater success than in the past.

In this chapter, I use data drawn from the public record, legal databases, and extensive personal interviews to characterize NCR litigating interest groups. I begin by tracing the rise of litigation as a strategy of the Christian Right, and then describe the leading Christian conservative legal organizations and their preferred legal tools. A discussion of the evolving legal strategies of the Christian Right follows. It reveals that NCR litigators have shifted logic away from casting Christian claims as part of majoritarian politics; rather, they have provided courts with arguments presenting Christians as a protected minority rather than a majority asserting its will. They have also increased the sophistication of the legal arguments they present to courts. Finally, the movement is now characterized by an increased responsiveness to emerging issues such as gay rights.

To facilitate the analysis of conservative Christian litigators, I present case studies of three NCR groups. All three have particular influence within the movement as litigators and leaders. For example, they are affiliated with three powerful figures within the larger movement—Rev. Pat Robertson, Rev. Jerry Falwell, and Rev. Donald Wildmon. Each group can be distinguished from the others in its litigation emphases, but all use a similar approach to the courts. While characterizing these three organizations, I use them to make broad comparisons with other organizations within the litigating arm of the NCR.

Conservative Christian Politics and Litigation in the 1970s and 1980s

The influence of religion-based litigation on court-crafted policy has been a centerpiece of interest group scholarship for many years. Political scientists' early research efforts centered on liberal interest groups that were attempting to expand minority rights through litigation. For example, David Manwaring (1962) studied the American Civil Liberties Union (ACLU) and its support for the challenge by Jehovah's Witnesses of state-compelled flag salutes as a violation of religious liberty.[3] In part, this emphasis can be explained by conservative groups' concentration on lobbying legislative bodies. Until the 1970s, conservative groups rarely coordinated litigation on social issues. When they did so, their efforts were legally unsophisticated, uncoordinated, and focused on short-term policy gains (Epstein 1985).

After the Supreme Court's *Roe v. Wade* (1973) decision legalizing abortion, the conservative Christian movement began to develop a more comprehensive political strategy for influencing policy. Local antiabortion groups organized and participated in a series of March for Life rallies in Washington. The national Religious Right leadership struggled to establish a Washington presence and develop strategies for influencing public policy. The movement generated a set of groups with a national presence: National Christian Action Coalition, Religious

Roundtable, Christian Voice, Concerned Women for America, and Moral Majority (perhaps the most influential of the set during the early 1980s). New leaders emerged to direct the movement's political efforts. These policy entrepreneurs, who realized the need for politically astute organizations, felt confident they could play politics with some success for their followers. They represented the first attempt by conservatives to master the kind of political sophistication characteristic of other lobbyists and movements. As such, they continued to demonstrate the need for a highly flexible and sophisticated conservative political apparatus. The movement pointedly concentrated on abortion restrictions, with the ultimate goal of overturning *Roe v. Wade* in its entirety. Although litigation became a key element of that strategy, the conservative Christian Right continued to focus primarily on legislative politics (Wilcox 1996).

Led by Jerry Falwell, the Moral Majority pressured Congress to hold hearings on overturning *Roe v. Wade* and forced several unsuccessful floor votes on constitutional amendments banning abortion. Furthermore, it lobbied successfully for major legislative packages limiting or halting federally funded abortions.[4] Yet, ultimately, Falwell generated unrealistic expectations with promises for complete victory without compromise. The Christian Right of the 1980s was unwilling to moderate its message in pursuit of its political goals.

During this period, conservative Christian attorneys worked in tandem with states and the federal government to pass and then defend abortion legislation. For example, *Harris v. McRae* (1980) involved a challenged to the Hyde Amendment, a federal regulation severely limiting federally funded abortions. The movement lobbied the Carter administration to actively defend the legislation. Pro-life groups, including Americans United for Life, Catholics for Life, and Feminists for Life, filed amicus curiae briefs supporting state regulations in *Akron v. Akron Center for Reproductive Health* (1983), *Planned Parenthood Association of Kansas City v. Ashcroft* (1983), and *Simopoulos v. Virginia* (1986). In many other cases, the Christian Right supported state efforts to pass "model legislation" imposing comprehensive limitations on abortion rights and services. These took the form of consent provisions, parental or spousal notification, doctor limitations, funding provisions, and record-keeping requirements.[5]

Pro-life efforts at coordinating litigation were often chaotic, however. This was particularly true in *Akron v. Akron Center for Reproductive Health* (Craig and O'Brien 1993). In this case, the U.S. Supreme Court considered a model city ordinance that included all of the provisions just noted, plus an expansive definition of the state's interest in preserving human life. Elsewhere, pro-life leaders urged the Reagan administration to argue for directly overturning *Roe*. But the administration was reluctant to do so, which drew public criticism from pro-life groups. Thus, while the federal government was arguing that the courts should end judicial supervision of states' abortion regulations on grounds of federalism, pro-life groups were submitting amicus curiae briefs urging the Court to overturn *Roe*. The lack of a clear and coordinated argument hampered the pro-life position in court.

Three years later, responding to pro-life pressure, the Reagan administration attacked *Roe* directly. In *Thornburgh v. American College of Obstetricians and Gynecologists* (1986), Solicitor General Charles Fried urged the Supreme Court to abandon *Roe*. However, the arguments of government and pro-life attorneys were not well received. Until the decision in *Webster v. Reproductive Health Services* (1989), the movement largely failed in its efforts to substantially limit the decision in *Roe*.

At a 1984 conference in Chicago hosted by Americans United for Life, pro-life groups and their attorneys indicated that they were willing to develop new strategies in response to the mixed results they were receiving in the appellate courts. The conference, attended by pro-life lawyers, physicians, and clergy was an important step toward coordinated litigation efforts. Out of this meeting emerged a more refined strategy for litigating. Along the way, Christian attorneys had learned that they must change their arguments to influence the courts. Instead of focusing their efforts and resources on overturning *Roe v. Wade*, conservative Christian litigators began to execute a long-term strategy to chip away at the precedent. The results of this lesson were revealed in the arguments made by Christian Right attorneys. Regardless of the still strident nature of pro-life rhetoric, they learned to respect court norms such as compromise, incremental changes in court-crafted policy, and the evolving nature of law.

The Conservative Christian Bar

Abortion rights litigation continued into the 1990s,[6] but other trends in conservative Christian litigation gradually emerged. As the abortion issue became less salient in electoral and legislative politics, conservative Christian litigators took stock of the political changes afoot and began to develop competencies in other policy arenas. With the support of NCR leaders, conservative Christian litigating firms proliferated during the late 1980s. Many of the lawyers populating these firms came from the graduating classes of Regent Law School, a private institution founded by Pat Robertson.

Around 1990, after years of expressing concern about the influence of the ACLU in court, Robertson began to implement plans for a high-powered Christian litigating firm. The American Center for Law and Justice (ACLJ) would become the crown jewel of conservative Christian litigation. After hearing about his performance in *Board of Airport Commissioners of Los Angeles v. Jews for Jesus, Inc.* (1987), Robertson selected Jay Sekulow to guide the ACLJ as its general counsel. During the 1990s, the organization had an annual budget of over $12 million, its own endowment, and more than fifty attorneys, some thirty of whom were graduates of Regent Law School (Jay Sekulow, interview by author, Atlanta, August 20, 1998).

After the 2000 national election, the ACLJ shifted its goals toward national policy issues. Sekulow, who continues to argue cases at the appellate level, and the ACLJ remain influential within the New Christian Right, because together they have shaped the central logic of its legal arguments and provided some of its greatest victories in court. Yet today the ACLJ is far from the only member of the conservative Christian bar. Of the other Christian litigating firms founded in the late 1980s and early 1990s (see Table 19-1), a few, such as Liberty Counsel, the Becket Fund for Religious Liberty, and the Thomas More Law Center, have become contenders for movement leadership as a result of broader efforts to develop a stable funding base for new litigation firms.

Much like the public interest law firms on the left, NCR law firms are both interest groups and legal firms. Indeed, they are often closely tied to the more traditional interest groups that lobby legislatures and mobilize voters, and they raise most of their money using similar methods. For example, even though the ACLJ was established using Pat Robertson's influence among the NCR donor base, the organization immediately declared itself financially independent and developed its own fundraising model. Currently, it manages all of its fundraising drives. Other NCR firms manage their own fundraising activities using traditional techniques such as newsletters, regular issue updates, and pledge drives. However, NCR litigators are also licensed attorneys and members of legally recognized firms that conduct litigation in the area of public law. They can charge fees for their services (although many do not) and seek compensation for legal fees from their opponents in court. Thus public interest law firms blend the tasks of representing the political interests of their supporters with the role of lawyers in the legal system. In this chapter, I discuss NCR litigating organizations as both legal firms and interest groups that seek to represent their movement and fund their

Table 19-1 Leading Conservative Christian Law Firms during the 1990s, by Year Founded

Group	Founded
Rutherford Institute	1982
Christian Legal Aid Society	1985
Liberty Counsel	1989
AFA-CLP	1990
ACLJ	1991
Alliance Defense Fund	1994
Becket Fund for Religious Liberty	1994
Northstar Foundation	1998
Thomas More Law Center	1999

Source: Steven P. Brown, *Trumping Religion: The New Christian Right, the Free Speech Clause and the Courts* (Tuscaloosa: University of Alabama Press, 2002).

Note: AFA-CLP = American Family Association–Center for Law and Policy; ACLJ = American Center for Law and Justice.

activities. In fact, stabilizing funding sources for NCR litigators became an important issue as NCR law firms proliferated during the 1990s.

In the late 1990s and early 2000s, conservative Christian litigators began to develop an organization called the Alliance Defense Fund (ADF) to coordinate funding and stabilize resources for Christian litigation specialists. For a time, the ADF acted as a "peak" group—an organization whose membership is made up of other organizations (Green 2001). It trained Christian attorneys in the practice of religious liberties trial litigation, and it worked as a foundation for funding high-profile appellate litigation. For example, the ADF coordinated conservative Christian litigation efforts in the important case of *Board of Regents of University of Wisconsin System v. Southworth* (2000), which revolved around the use of student fees by universities to fund student groups to which other students objected. Although no ADF attorney participated in that case, the funding for the protracted litigation effort came directly from the ADF and was distributed to a new law firm, the Northstar Foundation. The ADF's decisions for funding litigation were guided by the most prominent conservative Christian litigators. However, tension over the policies of the organization and its director, Alan Sears, has led to the departure of many of its founding members. In 2003 both Donald Wildmon and Jerry Falwell withdrew their considerable monetary support, making the ADF simply one among many litigating firms.

The failure of the ADF to fulfill its role as strategy coordinator led to new efforts to stabilize the movement around educational centers such as Regent University and Liberty University. Educational centers have long been an important resource for the NCR. Now, however, litigation specialists are beginning to use centers of higher education to train the next generation of NCR attorneys, to develop relationships with more established NCR organizations that can provide a stable stream of funding and other resources, and to extend the reach of their influence. For example, Liberty University recently established a law school in consultation with Mathew D. Staver, chief litigator of Liberty Counsel. Staver now sits on Liberty University's board of directors, and he hand-picked the first dean of the new law school. He maintains a Liberty Counsel office at the law school and uses its internship program as a pipeline for resources and assistants.

Like other organizations, conservative Christian firms generally litigate for the purpose of influencing court-crafted policy. Pursuing "policy-oriented" goals allows groups to influence policy by building up precedent favorable to their preferred position (O'Connor 1980). The goal of influencing policy is certainly not an innovation of NCR law firms. Liberal groups, such as the National Association for the Advancement of Colored People (NAACP) and the ACLU, pioneered a policy-oriented approach and developed goals to effect policy nationally rather than pursue court cases in jurisdictions that had lesser impact.

Similarly, NCR litigating firms select cases that are likely to advance policy supporting the expression of religious faith in social, political, and cultural contexts. Therefore, most firms take only cases that incorporate some aspect of religious liberty and could clarify the courts' pronouncements in that area. Many conservative Christian firms seek out such "test cases" for exactly that purpose.[7] The importance that conservative Christian law firms attach to policy influence has been well documented in numerous media articles (Moore 1994; McCord 1995; Neibuhr 1995a, 1995b; Fisher 1997; Wolfe 2000). Most of these articles examine the efforts of firms in particular policy sectors and do not conduct broader analyses. Nevertheless, these articles reveal that firms seek out cases with good facts for distinguishing precedent in an effort to shape policymaking among appellate courts. Opponents of Christian litigators have noted the importance of policy influence to the movement, and especially the ACLJ. Arch foe and ACLU leader Bob Peck notes that Jay Sekulow has achieved success "because he thinks about long-term strategy. He does build on cases" (Roman 1993).

Sekulow himself is quite blunt about the role of courts as protectors of minority rights. He has acknowledged that "it is ultimately the courts which decide the scope of religious liberties in America" (as quoted by *NBC Nightly News*, October 22, 1997). Stephen McFarland, former general counsel of the Christian Legal Society, has also noted the centrality of the Supreme Court to policymaking and its place as the protector of minority rights. He goes so far as to claim a preference for the court-based civil rights protections of a liberal justice such as William Brennan over a conservative justice such as Antonin Scalia, who places primary reliance on majoritarian institutions as the first bulwark for civil rights protections. "But that is contrary to the oath he took," says McFarland. "As long as the Bill of Rights is still enforced, he [Scalia] doesn't have the luxury to minimize the role of the courts" (quoted in Moore 1994). Clearly, Christian litigators have departed from the old movement mantra that claimed deference to majoritarian interests when it came to religion in public life.

Even among those organizations most clearly committed to policy influence, differences exist in goal setting. In particular, a primary goal of Liberty Counsel is education. Mat Staver of Liberty Counsel says that its mission is to educate both its membership and public officials about the role of religion in public life. Only when efforts to mediate conflicts through education have failed will he resort to litigation to achieve policy aims. Thus Liberty Counsel is significantly slower than the ACLJ or other Christian litigating groups to "pull the trigger" on litigation. Liberty Counsel even views litigation as an extension of its mission to provide education about the state of religious expressive freedoms. It also seeks to resolve tensions associated with those policies by providing informational resources where those resources might mean the difference between tolerance and suppression of public expressions of faith.

Strategies and Tactics

NCR law firms use a variety of strategies to achieve their goals in court. They may sponsor test cases that move through an appellate process or participate in one-shot litigation. Sometimes, their role takes the form of counsel on brief. In this slightly more limited form of participation, groups may bear some of the costs of litigation or help prepare a party's brief for oral argument. Amicus curiae briefs are inexpensive forms of participation when compared with case sponsorship. In this limited form of participation, a group submits a "friend of the court" brief to the court and urges the court to rule in favor of one party and adopt a particular logic justifying the decision. The group does not argue the case or bear any of the costs of litigation.

Table 19-2 reveals that sponsorship is the preferred strategy of the three firms listed, but differences in emphases exist within this preference. For both the ACLJ and Liberty Counsel, sponsorship of cases through the appellate process is the preferred method for approaching the courts. The American Family Association–Center for Law and Policy (AFA-CLP) appears to shun appellate litigation and the test case strategy. It strives to influence policy in a more limited fashion, concentrating on sponsoring trial-level litigation. These cases often involve conflicts over separation of church and state or abortion policy. For example, the AFA-CLP defended abortion street counselors in a case brought jointly by the U.S. Department of Justice and the State of Connecticut under the Freedom of Access to Clinic Entrances Act (FACE). In this highly publicized case, the AFA-CLP did not mount a constitutional challenge to the act. It simply defended those individuals accused of violating it. Later, however, the AFA-CLP became one of only two organizations to mount a constitutional challenge to FACE (described later in this chapter).

Thus, even though policy influence dominates the goals of conservative Christian litigators, the preferred methods for achieving influence may vary sig-

Table 19-2   Preferred Litigation Strategies of New Christian Right Litigating Firms

	Case sponsorship					
Firm	Test cases	One-shot sponsorship	On brief	Amicus	Other	Total
ACLJ	33	27	10	26	2	98
	(34)	(28)	(10)	(26)	(2)	(100)
AFA-CLP	2	22	0	14	4	42
	(5)	(52)	(0)	(33)	(10)	(100)
Liberty Counsel	22	19	3	2	0	46
	(48)	(41)	(7)	(4)	(0)	(100)

Source: Searches conducted on the Lexis/Nexis legal database.

Note: Table shows the number of cases in which the firm actually participated. In parentheses is the corresponding percentage of overall participation. ACLJ = American Center for Law and Justice; AFA-CLP = American Family Association–Center for Law and Policy.

nificantly across groups. Defending the interests of the average Christian in the courts appears to be as important a goal to the movement as broad policy influence in appellate courts. Furthermore, it leads to a diversity of strategies for using the courts at all levels.

Litigation Agendas: Cases, Policies, and Issues

Conservative Christian litigation mainly occurs in four broad policy areas: abortion, church-state relations, "family values," and sexual orientation. These areas can, in turn, be broken down into policy subcategories. For example, although litigation over abortion rights dominated that policy sector throughout much of the 1980s and early 1990s, most of the abortion litigation over the last ten years has revolved around abortion protests—that is, the use of government force in limiting abortion protestation. The ACLJ, AFA-CLP, and Liberty Counsel have litigated abortion protest matters (see Table 19-3). Both the ACLJ and AFA-CLP mounted challenges to the FACE Act, which was signed into law by President Bill Clinton.[8] The AFA-CLP at one time maintained close ties to Operation Rescue, the lead organizer of abortion clinic protests. Liberty Counsel has also represented abortion protesters throughout the country.

The two subcategories in the church-state relations policy area are religion and religious expression in public schools. Rather than pursue a one-dimensional strategy of simply challenging established doctrines against state-sponsored religious exercises in public schools, NCR litigators have moved to support public school students who attempt to form student-led Christian clubs, who pray

Table 19-3   New Christian Right Litigation, by Issue Area

	Church-state: public schools	Church-state: public places	Abortion: Protesta-tion	Abortion: rights	Sexual orientation	Bankruptcy	Family policy	Other	Totals
ACLJ	16	29	31	5	1	3	9	4	98
	(16)	(30)	(32)	(5)	(1)	(3)	(9)	(4)	(100)
AFA-CLP	5	6	10	3	2	0	15	1	42
	(12)	(14)	(24)	(7)	(5)	(0)	(36)	(2)	(100)
Liberty	16	13	11	4	0	0	0	2	46
Counsel	(35)	(28)	(24)	(9)	(0)	(0)	(0)	(0)	(100)
Total	37	48	52	12	3	3	24	7	186
	(20)	(26)	(28)	(5)	(2)	(2)	(13)	(4)	(100)

Source: Searches conducted on the Lexis/Nexis legal database.

Note: Table shows the number of cases in which the firm actually participated. In parentheses is the corresponding percentage of overall participation. ACLJ = American Center for Law and Justice; AFA-CLP = American Family Association–Center for Law and Policy.

in school, or who have seen their expressive freedoms limited. Similarly, conservative Christian litigators have generally not challenged established doctrines guiding religion in the public square. Instead, they have attempted to represent Christians who are excluded from public life in various ways because of religious faith. From challenging zoning laws restricting church-administered soup kitchens to litigating against cities that restrict the activities of street evangelists, conservative Christian groups have championed the principle of equal access for religion in public life. At the same time, they have developed legal precedent supporting forms of expression that are more commonly used by those in the lower income and social strata.

Litigation in the area of family values does not have the same broad policy content as that in the abortion and church-state policy areas—it does not have any particular coherent line of cases to boost. Those groups litigating in the interests of the American family generally pursue actions against practices said to undermine the traditional family unit. The AFA-CLP has litigated cases involving pornography, portrayal of violence in the media, and textbook content. Of the three groups listed in Table 19-3, the AFA-CLP is the most active in this area. The majority of its work on family values issues is conducted outside of court, or with the threat of litigation. However, it has participated in several significant cases, including a series of zoning cases and television programming disputes (Hacker 2000).

The sexual orientation issue includes policy concerns about the legal status of gay couples such as same-sex partner and health benefits ordinances, same-sex adoption laws, civil unions, and laws criminalizing homosexual conduct. Although each firm was involved in various conflicts over gay rights as far back as 1990, these conflicts centered largely on challenges to city ordinances requiring business to provide same-sex partner health benefits, or punishing those who discriminate on the basis of sexual orientation, and laws allowing gay couples to adopt children. For example, Liberty Counsel participated as amicus curiae in *Lofton v. Kearney* (2001), a challenge to the Florida same-sex adoption ban. Since the Supreme Court's decision in *Boy Scouts of America v. Dale* (2000), gay rights have assumed an increasingly important position on the NCR litigation agenda. Currently, each group spends between one-fourth and one-third of its time on gay rights, and all have been involved in litigation on a national level. The issue, framed by NCR litigators as an attack on marriage, has become so central that Liberty Counsel and the AFA-CLP recently teamed up to coordinate litigation strategy and confront gay rights issues on both coasts—especially gay marriage (Staver 2004).

Although each law firm is active across all issues, the three firms maintain different issue emphases in their litigation agendas. Historically, the ACLJ has been most actively engaged in litigation on church-state (public places) and abortion (protestation). The AFA-CLP emphasizes litigation on family policy and abortion (protestation). Liberty Counsel is most active in both church-state issue areas. However, the firms do have common interests. For example, all have participated in litigation on abortion protestation, reflecting their ties to abortion protest groups and their concern about preserving the expressive rights of those opposed to abortion. And, as noted earlier, all three state that gay rights is currently a central concern.

The Conservative Christian Bar and the Equal Access Argument

Conventional wisdom suggests that conservative Christian litigators are having a negative impact on fundamental freedoms in the United States. Naturally, the attitudes of the critics of the Religious Right do much to bolster this view. According to Arthur J. Kropp of People for the American Way, "[the Religious Right's] agenda is having a corrosive impact on public education, on civil liberties and on the fundamental principles of tolerance and pluralism." "Ultimately their agenda is about limiting freedoms, not expanding them," says another critic (Moore 1994). Some scholars have suggested that at the heart of social conservative litigation is a desire to return to the majoritarian values and practices of the past (Ivers 1998).

During the 1990s, however, conservative Christian litigators maintained much more complex motives than these statements suggest. Not all of the changes occurring in NCR law firms' approach to litigation have been conservative or majoritarian in origin. Statements made by leading conservative Christian lawyers suggest that they have fused tolerant attitudes toward expression with the professional norms of the practice of law. This fusion has led to several developments among conservative litigators reflecting both a liberalization of and increased sophistication in conservative Christian thought. I use the term *liberalization* to describe the endorsement of attitudes more tolerant of diverse ideas by NCR litigators. Sophistication applies to the legal arguments presented by conservative Christian litigators in court. As a result of these developments, in some instances conservative litigators take a decidedly more liberal position on free expression than their liberal foes, particularly when it comes to the expressive rights of public school students. For example, in *Board of Education of Westside Community Schools v. Mergens* (1990) conservative Christian litigators took a particularly open stance to the expressive freedoms of public school students advocating religious beliefs. Even though the case centered on access to school facilities, conservatives managed to turn the central issue toward expressive rights and protection of minority views. Even traditional opponents have endorsed the position taken by NCR attorneys in these cases. For example, Kent Willis, director of the Virginia chapter of the ACLU, has publicly endorsed the free expression argument made by Sekulow in *Mergens* and other cases (Sinha 2001).

Liberalization and Tolerance: Concern for First Amendment Freedoms

The views of conservative Christian litigators on religion in public life have developed over time. Leaders of the dominant litigating firms see the voice of the church as one among many in a pluralist society. Groups such as the ACLJ, Liberty Counsel, and Becket Fund approach litigation with the idea that religious convictions are appropriate for social discourse — that is, society should welcome religion as one valid perspective. Thus their recent efforts in the courts center on themes of equal access, free expression, and securing a "place at the table" for the church in public life and civic discourse (Hacker 2000).

These litigators' change in rhetoric is perhaps the best indicator of this development. Whereas previous generations of conservative Christian leaders approached politics as an all‑out war on godlessness, many of the present generation do not see things quite this way. When queried about traditional conservative themes such as a breakdown in the moral fabric of the nation, one lawyer employed by a leading firm said, "We don't live in a Christian nation. We are not a Christian nation, and never have been one. It is not what was intended for us. I don't think God is too upset about that, and I differ with other Christians on this" (interview by author, 1998).

Jay Sekulow has noted the change in emphasis, stating that he "defend[s] the integrity of the church in the public square." He believes that those who make majoritarian arguments in his own movement lack faith in the efficacy of the Gospel message. Their thinking, he says, ignores basic freedoms and suggests that God needs a little help in foisting the Gospel on society to make it more palatable (Sekulow, interview by author, 1998). On the topic of majoritarianism, Sekulow also notes that he and many of his compatriots reject the image of Christians excluding the ideas of others. In fact, his position is quite the opposite — Christianity, as with any other religion, must be given the same protection afforded any other minority view. "I'm not concerned about competing worldviews," he says. "The danger is in keeping any of them out of the forum" (Roman 1993).

Staver of Liberty Counsel is also committed to finding a role for the church in a pluralist society. Through his early litigation experiences, he came to the personal realization that government endorsement of religious beliefs was not really at issue. What characterized the debate was a lack of tolerance for free speech on all sides.

Sophisticated Use of the Courts: Pioneering the Free Expression Claim

Acting on their views, Staver, Sekulow, and other NCR litigators collaborated in the early 1990s to develop a legal strategy for approaching the courts.[9] At the heart of this strategy was a logic for recasting religious establishment cases in free expression terms. NCR attorneys consistently employed this strategy in court during the 1990s, demanding heightened tolerance of faith‑based expression. Furthermore, many of them applied the liberal philosophy of tolerance across the board. For example, Staver has defended the rights of gay students to advocate a homosexual lifestyle in public schools. And while litigating several cases involving student‑initiated prayer in Florida schools, Staver publicly opposed Florida's 1995 state school prayer bill on the grounds that state-sponsored prayer runs contrary to the interests of a free and tolerant society. This position provoked harsh criticism from the American Family Association (Pinsky 1995).

The primary vehicle for carrying the NCR's goals into the courts has been the free expression argument. Indeed, NCR attorneys have had tremendous success in making a free speech defense in cases involving establishment clause claims.[10] They have exploited a tension between the free exercise and establishment clauses and offered the courts a rationale for resolving disputes arising under them. The central logic of the argument is that the free exercise of religion often involves an expression of faith, and that the Constitution protects religious expression as free speech. NCR attorneys have applied this logic in cases ranging from public expressions of faith (*United States v. Kokinda*, 1990) to equal access to public property *(Lamb's Chapel v. Center Moriches School District*, 1993) to abortion protests (*NOW v. Scheidler*, 1994).

Some other groups, however, still see things in much the same way as Religious Right leaders of the past. Some are certain that they are fighting a war to thwart social bias against Christians. For these groups, a corrupt and perverse society poses a secular humanist threat to the faithful. There remains a strong belief that the nation has rejected the values on which it was founded—ethics of Judeo-Christian origin. But the pronounced change in philosophy among conservative Christian litigators cannot be ignored. They have liberalized their ideas about religion in public life, and they have changed their rhetoric and adopted more sophisticated legal arguments that appellate judges find more acceptable.

Recent Trends in Litigation

In recent years, NCR attorneys have brought many high-profile cases to the Supreme Court. These cases (and their results) tend to confirm the notion that the New Christian Right fares better before appellate courts when it casts its claims in "minoritarian" terms (as a minority seeking protection). When conservative Christian litigators severely test the limits of the Court's current willingness to accommodate religion in public square and school, they either fail in their bid to expand the role of religion in public life or undermine the legitimacy of their free expression argument. Seven cases from recent Court terms reflect this notion: *Hill v. Colorado* (2000), *Santa Fe Independent School District v. Doe* (2000), *Board of Regents of University of Wisconsin System v. Southworth* (2000), *Boy Scouts of America v. Dale* (2000), *Good News Bible Club v. Milford Central School District* (2001), *Lawrence v. Texas* (2003), and *Locke v. Davey* (2004).

In only three of these cases (*Hill v. Colorado, Good News Bible Club,* and *Locke v. Davey*) did NCR attorneys follow their long-standing policy of depicting religion as the expression of a minority seeking constitutional protection. In *Hill v. Colorado*, Jay Sekulow argued against the use of legislatively mandated speech-free zones ("bubble zones") during public protests at abortion clinics. Although unsuccessful, Sekulow contended in both his brief and oral argument that courts were best suited to institute and monitor government regulation during protests, and that the rights of protesters to be heard outweighed government's power to regulate speech. In *Good News Bible Club*, NCR attorneys argued successfully that schools must provide access to religious clubs supervised by community religious leaders, and that granting such access did not excessively entangle government with religion. In *Locke v. Davey*, Sekulow argued unsuccessfully that denial of tuition money for a graduate degree in theology under a state-funded, inclusive scholarship program singled out religion for unfavorable treatment in violation of free exercise. The Court held that such support was permitted under the religious establishment clause of the Constitution, but not required by the free exercise clause. The decision, while certainly a defeat, does not undermine previous decisions of the Court more favorable to the free exercise of religion and to religious expression in the public square.

In each of the other cases, NCR attorneys appeared to abandon their previous template for litigation, or to select cases with facts that did not support their claims. In *Boys Scouts of America v. Dale*, NCR attorneys participated as amicus curiae in support of the Boys Scouts' position that it could use sexual orientation as a criterion for membership and leadership positions. Although the Boy Scouts were successful in the effort, participation by NCR attorneys effectively undermined their position relative to other minority views. Likewise, in *Board of Regents of University of Wisconsin System v. Southworth*, the effort to allow Christians (or those of other faiths) to opt out of a required university fee used for minority student–led groups suggested a conflicted view within the movement over the proper relationship between government and minorities in a society that encourages diversity.

Finally, in *Santa Fe Independent School District v. Doe*, Sekulow argued for a football prayer policy that, although placing control of selection procedures in the hands of students, amounted to state supervision of a religious practice. Sekulow agreed to take the case only after the Supreme Court accepted it for review (he had refused to participate at the trial and intermediate appellate levels). Unfortunately for Sekulow and the NCR, the case tested the bounds of the Court's willingness to accommodate religion in public schools. The facts behind this case emphasized the entanglement of government with religion, not the expressive element of the practice. Ultimately, the Court definitively clarified its position on state involvement in public religious observances. The result reduces the potential that the Court will accept other cases more incremental in their approach to adjusting policy in the area.

These cases and their results present a cloudy picture for the future of NCR litigation. The 1990s were a period of relative success in the courts for the conservative Christian movement, but more recent decisions have demonstrated that the Supreme Court can and will reject the movement's claims. The NCR's attorneys and its leadership are unlikely to undermine their long-term strategy before the courts, or to limit their influence on policy because of strict adherence to religious principle, but they do face several barriers to influence in the courts, not the least of which is the increasing conflict surrounding gay rights.

The gay rights issue has achieved extraordinary national attention since the U.S. Supreme Court issued its ruling in *Lawrence v. Texas*, a case in which both the ACLJ and Liberty Counsel submitted amicus curiae briefs. In that case, the Court struck down a Texas statute criminalizing certain homosexual conduct as "deviant sexual intercourse." In finding that the statute attempted to control a personal relationship and thus violated the personal liberty and privacy contained in the due process clause of the Fourteenth Amendment, the Court overturned its earlier decision in *Bowers v. Hardwick* (1986).

The decision in *Lawrence* was the impetus for a series of clashes at the state and local level over gay rights and gay marriage. On November 18, 2003, the Massachusetts Supreme Judicial Court ruled in *Goodridge v. Department of Public Health* (2003) that the state violated the Massachusetts constitution when it denied "the protections, benefits, and obligations conferred by civil marriage to two individuals of the same sex who wish to marry." Then in February 2004, the Massachusetts court ruled that proposed state legislation formalizing the legal status of gay couples by creating civil unions violated its earlier decision. The court insisted that the state could not create a special class for gay couples. It said: "Because the proposed law by its express terms forbids same-sex couples entry into civil marriage, it continues to relegate same-sex couples to a different status (Opinions of the Justices to the Senate 2004). At about the same time, city officials around the country began to force the issue of gay marriage. On February 12, 2004, the mayor of San Francisco, Gavin Newsom, ordered the county to begin issuing marriage licenses to gay couples. The mayor of New Paltz, New York, then initiated the same practice, as did officials in Ashbury Park, New Jersey, and Seattle, Washington (Curran 2004; Johnson 2004). The AFA-CLP, Liberty Counsel, and Alliance Defense Fund have filed suit to halt these efforts in San Francisco, and they are participating in the cross-complaint filed by the city against the State of California. Liberty Counsel filed suit against the mayor of New Paltz. Although Liberty Counsel was unsuccessful in its efforts to restrain Newsom, it did achieve some measure of victory when a judged halted issuance of marriage licenses to gay couples in the New Paltz case (Staver 2004).

Both the *Lawrence* and *Goodridge* cases prompted a flurry of activity because neither resolved the issues of gay marriage and the national legal status of gay couples. In fact, the *Lawrence* decision came under immediate attack in the Kansas Court of Appeals (*Kansas v. Limon*, 2004), revealing that considerable conflict exists within the courts over how to resolve the issue legally. Currently, no resolution is in sight, and the political battle lines have been drawn over a U.S. constitutional amendment, proposed by President George W. Bush, that would ban gay marriage, but would allow states to recognize the legal status of gays through the creation of civil unions and partnerships (Von Drehle 2004).

To remain consistent with their previous stance on minority rights, the NCR would have to at least tolerate efforts to expand gay rights. But that stance is unlikely given the nature of the conflict—a conflict as intense as that over abortion rights. If recent history gives any indication, the conservative Christian movement will likely reevaluate its most recent strategies and adopt practices more consistent with court norms and with rights doctrines. However, portraying those who support heterosexual marriage as a minority to be protected presents a logical problem that conservative Christian litigators must overcome if they are to succeed in court.

Conclusion: Conservative Christian Litigators and the Courts

With the changes in the legal arguments and philosophy of NCR attorneys has come a corresponding change in their use of the courts. Conservative litigators have combined their new-found tolerance with a concern for the institutional norms of court—respect for precedent, argument couched in legal terms, and an incremental approach to changing law and policy. They are now willing to tolerate losses, chip away at unfavorable precedent, and pursue change in policy with patience and deliberation. Furthermore, NCR litigators define victory in the courts by a measure different than complete validation of their core religious and ideological beliefs.

For NCR attorneys to succeed in court, judges do not have to adopt their particular views about the importance of Judeo-Christian ethics for making judicial determinations. Rather, they must simply endorse an interpretation of civil rights that tolerates religious expression in public forums—that is, allow the church to pursue its goals of evangelism, protest, and social criticism. This twist on religion in public life supports the role of the courts as protectors of civil freedoms and as policy developers. By striking down policies that the NCR brands as viewpoint discriminatory, the courts endorse the doctrines of liberty, individuality, and democratic participation—that is, they fulfill their role as instruments for preserving an atmosphere of expressive freedom. Thus conservative Christian litigators have taken a page from the playbook of those attorneys who represented Jehovah's Witnesses during the 1930s and 1940s (Manwaring 1962)

In pursuing their goals, conservative Christian litigators use the courts in much the same way other public interest litigators do; they develop a legal logic, use the test case strategy as a means for influencing policy, and respect the preferences of courts for slow and incremental policy changes. Although conservative Christians offer arguments that reflect their perspective on American law, they attempt to influence court outcomes in the same ways that other ideologically motivated public interest law firms do. In short, they behave in very much the way they could be expected to behave, given the legal adversarial context of the courts and the political context of interest group politics.

In using the courts, some conservative Christian groups have had to overcome religious and ideological barriers and change their legal strategies so that they enter the courts as actors offering policy alternatives that judges will consider. The cases brought to the courts, and the arguments made by NCR litigating firms, are those of Christians claiming recognition for religious practices associated with a conservative Christian tradition. However, these litigators are putting forth arguments that are significantly different from those of previous decades. They frame the interests they represent as minorities to be protected, not majorities imposing a set of preferred practices on the populace.

This research suggests that conservative Christian groups have adopted attitudes and practices that conform to the norms of courts such as compromise, incremental changes in court-crafted policy, and the evolving nature of law. These attitudes and practices are associated with a liberal tradition of tolerance for diverse perspectives and respect for rights doctrine. Where interest groups are incapable of framing their legal claims in terms that courts find understandable and recognizable under law, their capacity to influence outcomes is significantly reduced. Furthermore, the process of litigating discourages these groups from articulating perspectives that they know will be discounted by judges. Conservative Christian law firms have responded to this norm of "weeding out" particular perspectives by adopting perspectives that resonate with judges' preferences for developing legal principles.

Notes

1. The author thanks Lawrence Baum, Gregory Caldeira, Elliot Slotnick, Donald Gregory, and Hellmut Lotz for their assistance. Personal interviews with Jay Sekulow of the American Center for Law and Justice and Mat Staver of the Liberty Counsel were conducted at the law offices of those organizations during 1998. Interviews with Bruce Green, Stephen Crampton, and Brian Fahling took place at the offices of the American Family Association–Center for Law and Policy in 1998 and again in December 2003. In addition, Brian Fahling, Bruce Green (now dean of the Liberty University School of Law), and Jordan Lorance of the Northstar Foundation (now with the Alliance Defense Fund) kindly participated in phone interviews or mailed responses during 1998, 2001, and 2004. Data collection was supported by a grant from the Graduate School of The Ohio State University and by an internal grant from Stephen F. Austin State University Office of Research and Sponsored Programs.
2. *American Lawyer* called Sekulow's performance "rude, aggressive and obnoxious." See Deniston (1987, 119).
3. Also see Peters (1999), *Minersville School District v. Gobitis* (1940), and *West Virginia Board of Education v. Barnette* (1943).
4. For details of the debate over the Hyde Amendment, see Craig and O'Brien (1993, 110–137).
5. For example, *Planned Parenthood of Central Missouri v. Danforth* (1975), *Belloti v. Baird* (1976), *Beal v. Doe* (1977), *Maher v. Roe* (1977), and *Poelker v. Doe* (1977).
6. *Hodgson v. Minnesota* (1990), *Ohio v. Akron Center for Reproductive Health* (1990), *Rust v. Sullivan* (1991), *Planned Parenthood of Southeastern Pennsylvania v. Casey* (1992), *Lambert v. Wicklund* (1997), and *Mazurek v. Armstrong* (1997).
7. A "test case" strategy is defined as case sponsorship, or bearing the costs of litigating a case, through an extended appeals process. Groups that employ a test case strategy also prefer to sponsor cases. But sponsorship does not imply that a group is pursuing a test case strategy, as the discussion of Table 19-2 reveals.

8. The FACE Act was intended to address the potential for violence and intimidation of clinic patients during protests around abortion clinics. The law was passed after the Supreme Court's decision in *Bray v. Alexandria Women's Health Clinic* (1993).
9. Much of this collaboration took place at a meeting of all the major NCR litigation firms held in Washington, DC, in November 1992.
10. See *Board of Education of Westside Community Schools v. Mergens* (1990), *Lamb's Chapel v. Center Moriches School District* (1993), *Rosenberger v. University of Virginia* (1995), and *United States v. Kokinda* (1990). The core logic of this strategy has transferred well over to abortion protestation cases such as *Madsen v. Women's Health Center Inc.* (1994) and *Schenck v. Pro-Choice Women's Network* (1997).

References

Brown, Steven P. 2002. *Trumping Religion: The New Christian Right, the Free Speech Clause and the Courts.* Tuscaloosa: University of Alabama Press.

Craig, Barbara Hinkson, and David M. O'Brien. 1993. *Abortion and American Politics.* Chatham, NJ: Chatham House.

Curran, John. 2004. "N.J. Couples Seek Marriage Licenses." Associated Press, March 9.

Deniston, Lyle. 1987. "Airport Speech Ban: Foiled by the Facts?" *American Lawyer* 9 (May): 119.

Epstein, Lee. 1985. *Conservatives in Court.* Knoxville: University of Tennessee Press.

Fisher, Marc. 1997. "Unlikely Crusaders; Jay Sekulow, 'Messianic Jew' of the Christian Right." *Washington Post,* October 21.

Green, John C. 2001. "Elections and Amateurs: The Christian Right in the 1998 Congressional Campaigns." In *Congressional Primaries and the Politics of Representation,* edited by Peter F. Galderisi, Marni Ezra, and Michael Lyons. Lanham, MD: Rowman and Littlefield.

Hacker, Hans J. 2000. "Contesting the Constitution: Conservative Christian Litigating Interests and Their Impact." Ph.D. diss., Ohio State University.

Ivers, Gregg. 1998. "Please, God, Save this Honorable Court: The Emergence of the Conservative Religious Bar." In *The Interest Group Connection: Electioneering, Lobbying and Policymaking in Washington,* edited by Paul S. Herrnson, Ronald G. Shaiko, and Clyde Wilcox. Chatham, NJ: Chatham House.

Johnson, Gene. 2004. "Seattle Mayor Recognizes Employees' Gay Marriages." *Washington Post,* March 9, A03.

Manwaring, David. 1962. *Render unto Caesar: The Flag Salute Controversy.* Chicago: University of Chicago Press.

Massachusetts Supreme Judicial Court. 2004. *Opinions of the Justices to the Senate.* February 3. http://www.mass.gov/courts/opinionstothesenate.pdf.

McCord, Julia. 1995. "Defending Religious Rights Non-profit Christian Law Organizations Gain Ground." *Omaha World-Herald,* April 29, 57SF.

Moore, John W. 1994. "The Lord's Litigators." *National Journal,* July 2.

Niebuhr, Gustav. 1995a. "Conservatives' New Frontier: Religious Liberty Law Firms." *New York Times,* July 8, 1.

———. 1995b. "Victory on Religion Rulings Was Limited, Groups Say." *New York Times,* July 5.

O'Connor, Karen. 1980. *Womens' Organizations' Use of the Courts.* Lexington, MA: Lexington Books.

Peters, Shawn F. 1999. *Judging Jehovah's Witnesses: Religious Persecution and the Dawn of the Rights Revolution.* Lawrence: University Press of Kansas.

Pinsky, Mark I. 1995. "Fight for Religious Liberty Brings Lawyer Few 'Amens.'" *Orlando Sentinel*, September 9.

Roman, Nancy. 1993. "Center Uses Free Speech to Defend Religious Rights." *Washington Times*, July 18.

Sinha, Sonejuhi. 2001. "ACLU Discusses Civil Liberties." *Flat Hat: Student Newspaper of the College of William and Mary*, November 2001, 1.

Staver, Mat. 2004. "Liberty Counsel Files Two Suits against New Paltz Mayor." Press release, March 3. http://www.lc.org.

Von Drehle, David. 2004. "Legal Confusion over Gay Marriage." *Washington Post*, February 27, A08.

Wilcox, Clyde. 1996. *Onward Christian Soldiers: The Christian Right in Politics.* Boulder: Westview Press.

Wolfe, Alan. 2000. "The Opening of the Evangelical Mind." *Atlantic Monthly* 286, no. 4: 55–76.

Court Cases Cited

Akron v. Akron Center for Reproductive Health, 462 U.S. 416 (1983).

Beal v. Doe, 432 U.S. 438 (1977).

Belloti v. Baird, 443 U.S. 622 (1976).

Board of Airport Commissioners of Los Angeles v. Jews for Jesus, Inc., 482 U.S. 569 (1987).

Board of Education of Westside Community Schools v. Mergens, 496 U.S. 226 (1990).

Board of Regents of University of Wisconsin System v. Southworth, 529 U.S. 217 (2000).

Bowers v. Hardwick, 478 U.S. 186 (1986).

Boy Scouts of America v. Dale, 530 U.S. 640 (2000).

Bray v. Alexandria Women's Health Clinic, 506 U.S. 263 (1993).

Good News Bible Club v. Milford Central School District, 533 U.S. 98 (2001).

Goodridge v. Department of Public Health, 440 Mass. 309 (2003).

Harris v. McRae, 448 U.S. 297 (1980).

Hill v. Colorado, 530 U.S. 703 (2000).

Hodgson v. Minnesota, 497 U.S. 417 (1990).

Kansas v. Limon, 83 P. 3d 229 (2004).

Lamb's Chapel v. Center Moriches School District, 508 U.S. 384 (1993).

Lambert v. Wicklund, 520 U.S. 292 (1997).

Lawrence v. Texas, 123 S. Ct. 2472 (2003).

Lemon v. Kurtzman, 403 U.S. 602 (1971).

Locke v. Davey, 2004 U.S. LEXIS 1626 (2004).

Lofton v. Kearney, 157 F. Supp. 2d 1372 (2001).

Madsen v. Women's Health Center Inc., 512 U.S. 753 (1994).

Maher v. Roe, 432 U.S. 464 (1977).

Mazurek v. Armstrong, 520 U.S. 968 (1997).

Minersville School District v. Gobitis, 310 U.S. 586 (1940).

NOW v. Scheidler, 510 U.S. 249 (1994).

Ohio v. Akron Center for Reproductive Health, 497 U.S. 502 (1990).

Opinions of the Justices to the Senate, 440 Mass. 1201 (2004).

Planned Parenthood Association of Kansas City v. Ashcroft, 462 U.S. 476 (1983).

Planned Parenthood of Central Missouri v. Danforth, 428 U.S. 52 (1976).

Planned Parenthood of Southeastern Pennsylvania v. Casey, 505 U.S. 833 (1992).

Poelker v. Doe, 432 U.S. 519 (1977).

Roe v. Wade, 410 U.S. 113 (1973).

Rosenberger v. University of Virginia, 515 U.S. 819 (1995).

Rust v. Sullivan, 500 U.S. 173 (1991).

Santa Fe Independent School District v. Doe, 530 U.S. 290 (2000).

Schenck v. Pro-Choice Women's Network, 519 U.S. 357 (1997).

Simopoulos v. Virginia, 462 U.S. 506 (1986).

Thornburgh v. American College of Obstetricians and Gynecologists, 476 U.S. 747 (1986).

United States v. Kokinda, 497 U.S. 720 (1990).

Webster v. Reproductive Health Services, 492 U.S. 490 (1989).

West Virginia Board of Education v. Barnette, 319 U.S. 624 (1943).

Part V
Conclusion

20. 'Only Permanent Interests'? Creating and Sustaining Interest Group Connections in Changing Political Environments

Paul S. Herrnson, Ronald G. Shaiko, and Clyde Wilcox

The chapters in this volume have demonstrated that many connections exist between interest groups and government, between interest groups and political parties, and among interest groups. These connections, which are myriad and complex, are influenced by the rules and norms of the political process, including those applying to both lobbying and electoral politics. In carrying out their goals, interest groups have adopted a broad array of organizational arrangements, relationships, and activities. Indeed, some of the leading members of the interest group universe are quite sophisticated. They are able to change strategies and tactics in response to political reform, partisan shifts in political power, economic trends, developments in foreign policy, and other important events.

Interest Group Connections

Some lessons about interest group politics have emerged from the research described here. First, interests participate in virtually every arena of American politics. Groups are active in many aspects of the electoral process, and they seek to influence the executive, legislative, and judicial branches of government. Second, the institutional and political environments in which interests operate influence how they organize and the activities they carry out. When groups move from the legislative arena to try to influence the bureaucracy, for example, they must rely on different resources and use different tactics. And groups that specialize in judicial politics are organized in ways that are quite different from those that specialize in legislative politics. Third, most groups—whether they are organized as PACs, 501(c)s, 527s, corporate public relations offices, grassroots organizations, or other forms—use multifaceted strategies, adapting their tactics to suit new objectives and political circumstances. Groups forge, strengthen, and dissolve connections with various public officials, political institutions, and constituencies in order to pursue their

goals most effectively. Combined, these conclusions suggest considerable flu-
idity in the interest group universe.

The Electoral Connection

In the electoral arena, groups forge connections with policymakers by helping with their campaigns for office. The U.S. system of candidate-centered elections creates considerable uncertainty for candidates, who must assemble their
own coalitions, raise their own money, and reach out to diverse groups of voters.
The chapters in Part I on the electoral connection describe how groups assist
candidates' primary and general election campaigns by providing contributions,
fundraising assistance, and volunteers. They directly influence voters by endorsing candidates, making personal contact with voters, and conducting television,
radio, mail, and e-mail campaigns. By helping candidates, these groups gain
access to key members of Congress, including party leaders, committee chairs
and ranking members, and influential policy entrepreneurs. Even though groups'
access to presidents and presidential candidates is more limited, they do have
ready access to the party officials out of government, who tend to be grateful for
the support they give party committees and candidates.

Corporations, trade associations, and labor unions are highly skilled at
adapting their lobbying strategies to the changing political conditions they
encounter. During the 1980s, many business groups decided that Republicans,
with whom they agreed on most taxation and regulatory issues, would probably
remain the minority party in the House for the foreseeable future. Most corporate and trade association political action committees (PACs) therefore switched
from a pro-Republican pattern of contributions, designed to elect a free market–oriented Congress, to an incumbent-oriented pattern intended to give them
access to powerful House Democrats. The lobbyists associated with these PACs
had learned that they could accomplish some of their goals by working with
House Democratic leaders and the officials in a GOP-led executive branch.

Once the 1992 election led to the installation of a Democratic president, some
business leaders found themselves shut out of the White House, and more than a
few doubled their congressional lobbying efforts. The 1994 GOP takeover of Congress created new incentives for business-oriented PACs to switch their contributions to favor leaders of the newly installed Republican-led Congress. Even some
labor groups, which traditionally have given the vast majority of their contributions
to Democratic candidates, redirected some of their PAC money toward Republicans. Nevertheless, PACs did not completely abandon House Democrats, because
they recognized the possibility that Democratic leadership could return to Congress
and wanted to continue to curry favor with the Democratic-led administration.

The 2000 election brought in its wake Republican occupancy of the White
House, and the 2002 elections solidified GOP control over both houses of Congress. This turn of events further strengthened business leaders' inclinations to
support Republicans.

The Congressional Connection

Part II of this volume, devoted to the congressional connection, reveals that the relationship between members of Congress and lobbyists relies on an exchange: lobbyists provide members with valuable technical and political information on specific issues, and members may fulfill interest groups' objectives by enacting their preferred policies.

From the 1980s through the early 1990s, most liberal organizations enjoyed easy access to powerful congressional leaders, but they were shut out of the decision making that took place in the higher echelons of the Republican-dominated executive branch. Most conservative groups had to contend with the opposite situation: they were warmly received by the Ronald Reagan and George Bush White Houses, but had only limited clout with congressional Democrats. After the 1994 midterm elections, the situation was reversed. Conservative groups became the new congressional insiders, and liberal groups found that they were more likely to get a warm reception from the chief executive (then Democrat Bill Clinton), members of the cabinet, and other executive branch officials. The first two elections of the new millennium introduced a new set of realities for both parties. Conservative groups saw their power substantially enhanced after the establishment of Republican control over the both the executive and legislative branches of the federal government. Liberal groups, by contrast, saw their influence in the nation's capital plummet.

To approach Congress more effectively, groups form connections with other groups. These coalitions are even extremely important in the Republican-controlled Congress, because the GOP has centralized power, limited the access of interest groups, and even sought to limit the resources and actions of lobbyists for certain groups. Coalitions are now more important and more difficult to assemble because of the constraints of policymaking in the context of zero-sum budgetary politics. Under the Republican regime, groups that once could "logroll" to win support for additional spending must now work with allies to protect some sectors of the budget while also competing with these same allies for their slice of the budgetary pie.

Some of the interest groups' strategic responses to the current political circumstances are apparent through their campaign contributions to committee chairs, their participation in the appropriations process, and the decisions they make about coalition partners in Washington and their use of grassroots lobbying. The approaches used by the religious right, labor unions, and even physicians and scientists stand in stark contrast to one another, reflecting the types of receptions they anticipate and receive in the Republican-controlled Congress and the White House.

Regardless of the recent changing partisan tides, the leaders of most of the largest interest groups combine the electoral connection and the legislative connection to influence Congress. For example, many of the same lobbyists who routinely try to influence the policymaking activities of members of Congress use their position to influence the flow of their group's PAC contributions and to help candidates raise money from individuals and other PACs. And members of Congress are no less active in tying together the two connections for their own political gain—that is, they are not shy about soliciting lobbyists who seek policy favors for individual and PAC contributions and assistance with fund-raising.

The Executive Connection

The strategies that help groups form connections in the Congress are less effective in the executive branch. Technical information is a valuable resource in lobbying Congress, but it is far less useful in approaching the executive, which can draw on the expertise of the bureaucracy. The bureaucracy interacts with interest groups, but it does not accept campaign contributions. Many groups care deeply about the rules that are created by administrative agencies, but lack the ability to influence the decision directly. In the GOP Congress, these groups have appealed to the legislature to overturn the rules or limit the ability of the bureaucracy to enforce them.

Presidents are not subjected to the narrow, particularistic lobbying that occurs in Congress, but they do need interest group support to get reelected and to enact their policies. Presidents seeking reelection rely on groups to mobilize voters in their behalf. Before the 2004 elections, they also relied on the soft money generated by interest groups to help finance party efforts to bolster their campaigns. Since 1996 presidential elections have continued to be influenced by group-sponsored issue advocacy advertisements.

Finally, any president seeking to pass key legislation needs groups to mobilize their members and lobbyists behind the administration's proposals in order to help win the support of key legislators. In the absence of lobbyists' direct ties to key White House operatives, the White House Office of Public Liaison is an important generic nexus for presidents and the interest group community (Seligman and Covington 1996).

The Judicial Connection

Interest group connections with the judiciary are very different from those with the legislative and executive branches. Lobbyists are not allowed to communicate directly with Supreme Court justices; they must instead resort to test cases and amicus curiae briefs to influence judicial opinions. As such, many of the key resources of groups—especially membership and lobbying skills—are useless when approaching the courts. But money is useful, because judicial politics are quite expensive. Repeat players, such as corporations and groups that specialize in legal action, are advantaged, for they are able to litigate to affect the rules in areas such as standing. Yet judicial reforms and developments in recent decades, such as fee shifting and class action suits, have served to level the judicial playing field and lessen the advantages of repeat players. Public interest law firms representing interests across the ideological spectrum have also opened up the judicial arena to those interests previously underrepresented in the courts. As the federal court system continues to play an important role in public policy-making, organized interests will remain focused on this branch of government.

Interest Groups and Political Reform

Political reform has had a major impact on interest group politics. Long gone are the days when industrialists and other interest group leaders handed members of Congress bags full of cash in return for casting congressional votes to turn over mining rights on huge tracts of mineral-rich land, grant corporate tax breaks and subsidies, or support some other form of legislation from which a business, labor, or some other group would gain significant benefit. Even legendary icons such as Daniel Webster wrote on Senate stationery to the president of the Second Bank of the United States asking for his "usual retainers" to ensure his support (Sachs 1996). Mark Twain, in his fictional account of members of Congress, typified the conventional wisdom when he wrote: "A Congressional appropriation costs money. . . . A majority of the House committee, say $10,000 apiece—$40,000. A majority of the Senate committee, the same each, say $40,000; a little extra to one or two chairmen of one or two such committees, say $10,000 each. There's $100,000 gone to begin with" (Twain 1899, 192).

By contrast, the scandals of the 1990s involved smaller sums, and in many cases did not even involve violations of law. The "book deal" that led to the resignation of House Speaker James C. Wright Jr., D-TX, in 1989 and the check bouncing scandal at the House bank that resulted in the early retirements and defeats of numerous congressmen in 1992 are cases in point. The Webster example contrasts even more sharply with allegations that PAC contributions of $5,000 or less are used to "buy" members' votes. Political reforms have reduced the level of corruption in American politics, including the level of bribery, quid pro quos, and special payoffs that involve special interests.

Nevertheless, reforms have not, probably cannot, and definitely should not eliminate the influence of organized interests. Reform must be an ongoing process if it is to keep corruption at a minimum, limit the avenues that organized interests can use to influence the political process, and weaken the nexus between campaign contributions and policymaking. Individuals, politicians, and organized interests have time and time again proven themselves capable of adapting to institutional reform and structural changes in government. Problems arise when a small number of groups are able to dominate the political system.

The Federal Election Campaign Act of 1974 (FECA), the gift ban, lobby reform, and the movement toward centralization of power in Congress all demonstrated that interest groups are adept at altering the methods they use to participate in the political process. The FECA, for example, prohibited corporations, trade associations, unions, and other groups from contributing treasury monies to federal candidates, but it laid the groundwork for the skyrocketing number of

PACs that were formed in the late 1970s and 1980s. Moreover, the law was eviscerated in 1996 by court rulings that allow groups to use their treasury funds to carry out issue advocacy campaigns. As a result, a small sector of society that represents a limited number of viewpoints is the source of a disproportionate amount of the money spent in election campaigns. The enactment of the Bipartisan Campaign Reform Act of 2002 (BCRA) has done little to reduce the influence of political elites. Indeed, the rise of the multimillion-dollar contributions to 527 groups with close ties to each of the two major parties promises to undermine one of the major goals of the reformers: the reduction of the influence of wealthy individuals and groups on election outcomes.

Similarly, the Lobbying Disclosure Act of 1995 introduced major improvements in the disclosure and reporting of interest group lobbying activities, and the gift ban, also passed in 1995, curbed the practice of using expensive meals, vacations, and gifts to gain access to federal lawmakers. Yet less than one year after their passage, these reforms were already being legally sidestepped by some lobbyists and lawmakers. Interest group representatives learned to work around the gift ban's prohibitions against lobbyists wining and dining members by reporting their epicurean encounters as campaign contributions.

Apparently, then, the creativity and pragmatism of politicians and lobbyists limit the possibilities for major political reform. When old routes of political influence are shut down, they often blaze new ones. Sometimes, they benefit from assistance from the courts. The connections between government officials and group representatives thus seem impossible to sever. Political reforms typically reroute streams of influence rather than dry them up. Journalists, scholars, reformers, and ordinary citizens must continually be vigilant to prevent a small portion of society from amassing too much political clout.

As demonstrated by the lengthy battles over the BCRA, various dynamics make it difficult for Congress to reform the laws that govern campaign finance. Philosophical disagreements over federal funding, contribution limits, and campaign expenditure ceilings reflect broader tensions over the roles that money and the government should play in politics and society and are a major stumbling block. Partisan concerns, some based on disagreements in philosophy and some based on considerations of electoral expedience, make it difficult for Democrats and Republicans to agree on the kinds of reforms that should be enacted. Differences in the financing of House and Senate campaigns typically lead to disagreements between the chambers (Magleby and Nelson 1990). These are frequently exacerbated by the threat of a presidential veto or more subtle forms of White House involvement. The efforts of Common Cause and other so-called public interest groups that whip up popular opposition to incremental change in favor of "all or nothing" reforms make it difficult for members of Congress to back modest improvements and give them excuses for opposing most any kind of campaign finance legislation.

Perhaps the biggest obstacle to campaign finance reform is that those who enact the reforms know they will have to live under them. With the exception of the few legislators who are appointed to fill out a predecessor's term, every member of Congress has some claim of expertise on campaign finance. Members arrive in the House or Senate by way of elections, and fund-raising was a major component of virtually all their campaigns. In the face of their own expertise, experiences, and obvious self-interest, legislators find it extremely difficult to agree on a reform program. Even though many would like to improve the campaign finance system, their notions of what constitutes improvement incorporates both their political experiences and their calculations about how change will influence their future campaigns. Yet ultimately Congress did pass the BCRA, and interest groups immediately began to adapt. In the 2004 presidential campaign, labor unions, environmental and feminist groups, and other liberals formed 527 committees to run issue ads that helped John Kerry match President George W. Bush's phenomenal fund-raising. Some Republican-leaning groups responded by forming their own 527s to support Bush. These new committees were formalized variants on earlier coalitions, but they were able to raise money in large contributions from committed donors.

Similar calculations influence lawmakers' and lobbyists' thinking about other areas of political reform. Proposals to change the way interest groups and politicians approach one another, exchange information, and mobilize legislative and public support for their preferred projects and career aspirations always seem to benefit some participants to the detriment of others. Whatever the case, these proposals almost always result in some unanticipated outcomes that influence both the relationships between those in power and ways of doing things. Successful politicians—that is, those who are in power—and successful lobbyists—that is, those who have risen high enough in the ranks of their firms to form ties with successful politicians—have strong motivations to resist the efforts of reformers.

The result is that political reforms are enacted infrequently and usually in response to widespread public outrage. In the early twentieth century, campaign finance reforms prohibiting banks and corporations from making contributions to federal candidates and imposing ceilings and disclosure requirements on other contributions were passed in response to progressive era protests against the power of big business (see, for example, Alexander 1992, chap.3). In 1974 the FECA was passed after Watergate investigations revealed many improprieties in the financing of President Richard Nixon's 1972 reelection campaign. The 1995 Lobbying Disclosure Act and the gift ban were passed in the wake of the "Keating Five" scandal in the Senate, the post office and banking scandals in the House, and record levels of public hostility and anger at Congress (Bowman and Ladd 1994). In 2002 the BCRA was enacted after Sen. John McCain, R-AZ, raised the issue's profile during his unsuccessful 2000 presidential nomination campaign and after the Enron scandal, which encouraged citizens to perceive a link between soft money contributions and corporate corruption. It is unlikely that a legislative coalition in favor of reform can be built in the absence of a major showing of public displeasure. Without public sentiment threatening the electoral security of those who fail to support reform, politicians are unlikely to

approve fundamental changes in the campaign finance system. The gulf that sep-
arates legislators on reform issues is too wide, because their sense of self-interest
is too strong.

Moreover, should Congress and the president succeed in enacting further
political reform, interest groups seeking to influence elections and the policymaking process and politicians in need of campaign contributions and technical
or political information will undoubtedly find ways to work around the reform's
intent without violating the law. As long as interest group representatives wish to
influence the regulations, budgetary appropriations, courtroom decisions, public
decrees, and other outputs of Congress, the president, the executive branch, and
the courts, they will search for ways to present their cases to the government. As
long as politicians rely on interest groups for technical expertise and assistance
with building legislative coalitions and developing electoral support, they will
find more or less convenient ways for lobbyists to state their views. As regulatory regimes mature, those who operate under them test them, overturning some
statutes in the courts and unearthing loopholes that enable them to work around
the intent of others. What at first appear to be small leaks in a regulatory structure can turn into a flood of activity that may eventually call into question the
legitimacy of the framework itself.

Interest Groups, Reform, and American Democracy

The general unwillingness and practical inability of reformers to construct
regulatory regimes that shut out organized interests from the political process
were anticipated by the framers of the Constitution. When they created a decentralized government that featured many points of access and embraced the property values associated with capitalism, they laid the foundation for a political system that rewards the individuals and groups able to mobilize people and money.
The framers recognized that because groups would vary in their numbers and
financial resources, they would likewise vary in the representation of their views.
But the only way to completely prevent this outcome would be to deprive individuals of the freedom to use their talents to advance their interests and express
their views—an approach that was repugnant to the framers' notions of liberty.

So, rather than attempt to constrain individual liberty, the framers constructed a political system that utilized a series of checks and balances to prevent
any one group from tyrannizing others. The chartering of a national bank, the
Louisiana Purchase, and the other early decisions that put the nation on the road
toward a large commercial republic also encouraged the development of a diverse
population made up of individuals who had overlapping interests. The framers
believed that overlapping interests and group memberships would force individuals and organized groups to cooperate with each other in pursuit of their common goals, to respect each others' rights and liberties, and to understand that
mutual cooperation and respect were needed to maintain the political system that
defended those rights and liberties. The current interest group system is far from

perfect—favoring the well-off and the well organized over the less privileged. But, by connecting individuals to government and by allowing a diversity of views to be expressed in the public arena, it helps to protect some of Americans' most fundamental values—the rights of individuals to liberty, equality, and the pursuit of happiness. Interest group connections to the federal government fall short of the high standards set by reformers, but by facilitating representation and participation, the interest group connection makes an important contribution to contemporary American democracy.

References

Alexander, Herbert E. 1992. *Financing Politics: Money, Elections, and Political Reform.* Washington, DC: CQ Press.

Bowman, Karlyn, and Everett Carll Ladd. 1994. "Public Opinion toward Congress: A Historical Look." In *Congress, the Press, and the Public,* edited by Thomas E. Mann and Norman J. Ornstein. Washington, DC: Brookings.

Magleby, David B., and Candice J. Nelson. 1990. *The Money Chase: Congressional Campaign Finance Reform.* Washington, DC: Brookings.

Sachs, Richard C. 1996. "The Lobby Disclosure Act of 1995: A Brief Description." *CRS Report for Congress.* 96-29, January 4.

Seligman, Lester G., and Cary R. Covington. 1996. "Presidential Leadership with Congress: Change, Coalitions, and Crisis." In *Rivals for Power: Presidential Congressional Relations,* edited by James A. Thurber. Washington, DC: CQ Press.

Twain, Mark. 1899. *The Gilded Age: A Tale of To-Day.* Hartford, CT: American Publishing Company.

Index

✧ ✧ ✧